S0-BBW-880

MARKETING CHALLENGES

CASES AND EXERCISES

McGraw-Hill Series in Marketing

MARKETING CHALLENGES

CASES AND EXERCISES

Christopher H. Lovelock

Formerly
Associate Professor of Business Administration
Harvard University

Charles B. Weinberg

Alumni Professor of Marketing
University of British Columbia

McGRAW-HILL BOOK COMPANY

New York   St. Louis   San Francisco   Auckland   Bogotá
Hamburg   Johannesburg   London   Madrid   Mexico   Montreal   New Delhi
Panama   Paris   São Paulo   Singapore   Sydney   Tokyo   Toronto

This book was set in Optima by Better Graphics.
The editors were Cheryl L. Mehalik, Sheila H. Gillams, and Linda A. Mittiga;
the cover was designed by John Hite;
the production supervisor was Charles Hess.
The drawings were done by Volt Information Sciences, Inc.
R. R. Donnelley & Sons Company was printer and binder.

MARKETING CHALLENGES
Cases and Exercises

Copyright © 1985 by McGraw-Hill, Inc. All rights reserved. Printed in the United States of America. Except as permitted under the United States Copyright Act of 1976, no part of this publication may be reproduced or distributed in any form or by any means, or stored in a data base or retrieval system, without the prior written permission of the publisher.

2 3 4 5 6 7 8 9 0 DOCDOC 8 9 8 7 6 5

ISBN 0-07-038786-9

All rights reserved. No part of this book may be reproduced, stored in a retrieval system, or transmitted, in any form or by any means, electronic, mechanical, photocopying, recording, or otherwise, without the prior written permission of the copyright holder. The copyright on each case in this book is indicated on the bottom of the first page of each case and they are published herein by express permission. Permissions requests to use individual Harvard copyrighted cases should be directed to the Harvard Business School, Boston, MA 02163.

Case material is made possible by the cooperation of business firms and other organizations which may wish to remain anonymous by having names, quantities, and other identifying details disguised while maintaining basic relationships. Cases are prepared as the basis for class discussion rather than to illustrate either effective or ineffective handling of an administrative situation.

Library of Congress Cataloging in Publication Data
Main entry under title:

Marketing challenges.

    Includes bibliographical references.
    1. Marketing—Case studies. 2. Marketing—Problems, exercises, etc. I. Lovelock, Christopher H. II. Weinberg, Charles B.
HF5415.M29747 1985   658   84-28950
ISBN 0-07-038786-9

To Our Children
Timothy and Elizabeth Lovelock

and

Beth and Amy Weinberg

CONTENTS

LIST OF CONTRIBUTORS

M. Edgar Barrett is Professor of Management, Southern Methodist University.

Alan R. Beckenstein is Associate Professor, University of Virginia.

Terrie Bloom is an M.B.A. graduate of Harvard University.

Linda Carlson is an M.B.A. graduate of Harvard University.

Richard M. Cardozo is Professor of Marketing, University of Minnesota.

John D. Claxton is Associate Professor of Marketing, University of British Columbia.

George S. Day is Professor of Marketing, University of Toronto.

L. Frank Demmler was formerly a research assistant at the Harvard Business School.

Robert G. Dykes was formerly a research assistant at the University of Virginia.

Gerald J. Eskin is Professor, University of Iowa.

H. Landis Gabel is Assistant Professor, University of Virginia.

Peter Gilmour is Professor of Management, Macquarie University.

Gregrey W. Gorden is an M.B.A. graduate of Harvard University.

Caroline M. Henderson is Assistant Professor of Marketing, Amos Tuck School of Business Administration, Dartmouth College.

Peter T. Hutchison is an M.S. graduate of Stanford University.

Jean-Pierre Jeannet is Associate Professor of Marketing, Babson College.

Rick Jenkner is an M.B.A. graduate of the University of British Columbia.

C. B. Johnston is Dean, School of Business Administration, University of Western Ontario.

Kamran Kashani is Professor, IMEDE Management Development Institute.

Jay E. Klompmaker is Professor of Business Administration, University of North Carolina.

Robert J. Kopp is Assistant Professor, Babson College.

Charles M. Kummel was formerly a Research Assistant at the University of North Carolina.

Frederick C. Livingston is Vice President, Continental Cablevision, Inc.

Christopher H. Lovelock was formerly Associate Professor of Business Administration, Harvard University.

Molly Lovelock is Treasurer and Director of Administration, Massachusetts Government Land Bank.

William F. Massy is Vice-President of Business and Finance and Professor of Business Administration, Stanford University.

Shiv Mathur is Midland Bank Research Fellow at City University Business School, London.

Penny Pittman Merliss was formerly a research associate at the Harvard Business School.

David B. Montgomery is Robert A. Magowan Professor of Marketing, Stanford University.

Robert E. M. Nouse was formerly Professor of Business Administration, University of Western Ontario.

Don E. Parkinson is an M.S. graduate of Stanford University.

Richard W. Pollay is Associate Professor of Marketing, University of British Columbia.

Stuart U. Rich is Professor of Marketing and Director, Forest Industries Management Center, University of Oregon.

Adrian B. Ryans is Professor of Marketing, University of Western Ontario.

Arthur Segel is an M.B.A. graduate of Stanford University.

Kenneth Shachmut is an M.B.A. graduate of Stanford University.

Charles T. Sharpless was formerly a research assistant at Southern Methodist University.

Kenneth Simmonds is Professor of Marketing and International Business, London Business School.

Charles B. Weinberg is Alumni Professor of Marketing, University of British Columbia.

PREFACE

As in other fields of management, the study and practice of marketing are constantly evolving. Marketing texts and casebooks must reflect this evolution if they are to provide relevant training for future managers—or useful upgrading of skills for existing managers currently enrolled in business courses.

One of the most significant developments to take place during the 1980s has been the extension of marketing theory and practice to the service sector of the economy. Historically, the study of marketing focussed almost exclusively on manufacturing firms, with particular emphasis on those companies that marketed consumer goods. During the 1960s more attention was directed to the marketing problems of industrial manufacturing firms, and in the mid-70s both professional and academic marketers came to recognize that a marketing perspective could offer important insights to managers of public and nonprofit organizations. Even so, these extensions still ignored almost fifty percent of the economy, namely the marketing tasks and challenges facing managers of for-profit service businesses—a weakness in marketing curricula that this casebook helps to rectify by offering a balanced coverage of both the manufacturing and service sectors.

As the title *Marketing Challenges* suggests, marketing is both a demanding and exciting field. In this book, we've tried to select a mix of cases that would capture the breadth and depth of marketing management in the modern world. The materials embrace a broad cross-section of industries and types of organizations, both large and small, for-profit and nonprofit; the cases are set in a number of different countries and involve selling to both individual consumers and to industrial or institutional purchasers. The book is divided into nine parts, each focussing on a different aspect of marketing management, although there is, of course, some overlap between these parts. Each part comprises a brief textual introduction followed by four to six cases or other exercises. Complementing the textual notes is a glossary of selected marketing and management terms in Appendix 1. To help students understand some of the basic financial analyses required in marketing, we've included in Appendix 2 a short note on economic analysis of alternatives.

Another evolutionary change that affects both marketing practice and pedagogy is the use of computers for analytical and planning purposes. Although many marketing managers, especially in large- and medium-sized firms, have long had access to computers, a growing number of managers now have their own personal computers. The same situation holds true at many business schools. This casebook breaks new ground by making available to instructors an optional package that enables students to undertake computer-assisted analysis of many of the materials. Details are provided in Appendixes 3 and 4. However, we do want to emphasize that with one exception—The Diffusion Game—all the cases and exercises in this book can also be prepared simply with the aid of a pocket calculator.

Over fifty percent of the cases in this book are drawn from the collections of the Harvard and Stanford Business Schools. The balance were prepared by authors at a wide variety of other institutions, including the University of British Columbia, the University of Western Ontario, IMEDE, and the London Business School. All the cases have been carefully classroom tested. Our thanks are due to the individual authors, who are acknowledged in the list of contributors as well as on the title page of each case. We thank the copyright holders, too, for giving us permission to reproduce their materials. In addition, we are grateful to the managements of the many organizations—sometimes disguised—that form the subjects of these cases, since it is only their willingness to share experience and data that made case development possible in the first place.

A great many people have assisted in the preparation and publication of *Marketing Challenges*. We're particularly grateful to our secretaries, Beverly Outram in Boston and Patricia Morison and Nancy Schell in Vancouver, and to the staffs of the word processing centers at both Harvard University and the University of British Columbia. Gerald J. Gorn provided excellent guidance, often under tight time constraints, Michael Ball ably did the programming for the optional computer disc that accompanies the book, and Karen Lindsey gave much valued editorial assistance. Reviewers Noel Capon, Columbia University; O. C. Ferrell, Texas A & M University; David J. Reibstein, University of Pennsylvania; and Ronald Stiff, University of Baltimore provided valuable feedback. We're also very appreciative of the important role played by the editorial and production staffs at the McGraw-Hill Book Company, especially for the assistance given by Cheryl Mehalik and Sheila Gillams.

Finally, we want to thank our many students. Over the years their critical and enthusiastic classroom discussions have helped us to sharpen and refine many of the cases, serving to remind us that much of the challenge and satisfaction of case teaching comes from the interaction between students and instructors.

Christopher H. Lovelock
Charles B. Weinberg

ANALYZING AND LEARNING FROM CASES

Unlike methods of instruction which use lectures and textbooks, the case method of instruction does not present students with a body of tried and true knowledge about how to be a successful manager. Instead, it provides an opportunity for students to learn by doing.

For you, the student, dealing with cases will be very much like working with the actual problems that men and women encounter in their jobs as managers. In most instances, you will find yourself identifying and clarifying problems facing the management of a company or nonbusiness organization, analyzing qualitative information and quantitative data, evaluating alternative courses of action, and then making decisions about what strategy to pursue for the future. You will enjoy the process more—and probably learn more—if you accept the role of an involved participant rather than that of a disinterested observer who has no stake, or interest, in the resolution of the problems in question.

The goal in analyzing cases is not to develop a set of "correct" facts, but to learn to reason well with available data. Cases mirror the uncertainty of the real-world managerial environment, in that the information they present is often imprecise and ambiguous. You will find—and perhaps be frustrated by the fact—that there is no one right answer or correct solution to a case. Instead, you will see that there may be a number of feasible strategies management might adopt, each with somewhat different implications for the future of the organization, and each involving different trade-offs.

If you are using this book in a course or seminar, you will be exposed to a wide range of different management situations within a relatively short span of time. As a result, the cases presented in *Marketing Challenges* collectively will provide a much broader exposure to marketing problems than most managers experience in many years on the job. Recognizing that the problems with which managers must deal are not unique to a particular institution (or even to a specific industry) forms the basis for developing a professional sense of management.

CASES AND THE REAL WORLD

It is important to recognize that even though case writers try to build realism into their cases, their cases differ from "real-world" management situations in several important respects. First, the information is prepackaged in written form. By contrast, practicing managers accumulate their information through such means as memoranda, meetings, chance conversations, research studies, observations, news media reports, and other externally published materials—and, of course, by rumor.

Second, cases tend to be selective in their reporting because most of them are designed with specific teaching objectives in mind. Each must fit a relatively short class period and focus attention on a defined category of management problem within a given subject area. To provide such a focus—and to keep the length and complexity of the case within reasonable bounds—the writers may find it necessary to omit information on problems, data, or personnel that are peripheral to the central issue or issues in the case.

In the real world, management problems are usually dynamic in nature. They call for some immediate action, with further analysis and major decisions being delayed until some later time. Managers are rarely able to wrap up their problems, put them away, and go on to the next "case." In contrast, discussing a case in class or writing an analysis of a case is more like examining a snapshot taken at a particular point in time. However, sometimes a sequel case provides a sense of continuity and the need for future decisions within the same organization.

A third, and final, contrast between case analyses and the realities of real-world management is that participants in case discussions and authors of written case reports are not responsible for implementing their decisions, nor do they have to live with the consequences. This does not mean, however, that you can be frivolous when making recommendations. Your instructor and classmates are likely to be critical if your contributions are not based upon a careful analysis and interpretation of the facts.

PREPARING A CASE

Just as there is no one right solution to a case, there is also no single correct way of preparing a case. However, the following broad guidelines may help familiarize you with the job of case preparation. With practice, you should be able to establish a working style with which you feel comfortable. The guidelines on initial analysis and on developing recommendations should also serve you well for preparing written case reports or case-based exams.

Initial Analysis

First, it is important to gain a feel for the overall situation by skimming quickly through the case. Ask yourself:

- What sort of organization is the case about?
- What is the nature of the industry (broadly defined)?
- What is going on in the external environment?
- What problems does management appear to be facing?

An initial fast reading, without your attempting to make notes or to underline, should provide you with some sense for what is going on and what information is being presented for analysis. Then you will be ready to make a very careful second reading of the case. This time, seek to identify key facts so that you can develop a situation analysis and clarify the nature of the problem or problems facing management. As you go along, make some notes in response to such questions as:

- What decisions need to be made and who will be responsible for making them?
- What are the objectives of the organization itself and of each of the key players in the case? Are the objectives mutually compatible? If not, can the problems be reconciled or will it be necessary to redefine the objectives?
- What resources and constraints are present which may help or hinder attempts by the organization to meet its objectives?

You should make a particular effort to establish the significance of any quantitative data presented in the text of the case, or, more often, in the exhibits. See if new insights may be gained by combining and manipulating data presented in different parts of the case. But do not accept the data blindly. In the cases, as in real life, not all information is equally reliable or equally relevant. On the other hand, case writers do not deliberately misrepresent data or facts to try to trick you.

Developing Recommendations

At this point in the analysis, you should be in a position to summarize your evaluation of the situation and to develop some recommendations for management. First, identify the alternative courses of action that the organization might take. Next, consider the implications of each alternative, including possible undesirable outcomes, such as provoking responses from stronger competitors. Ask yourself how short-term tactics fit with longer-term strategies. Relate each alternative to the objectives of the organization (as defined or implied in the case, or as redefined by you). Then, develop a set of recommendations for future action, making sure that these recommendations are supported by your analysis of the case data.

Your recommendations will not be complete unless you give some thought to how the proposed strategy should be implemented:

- What resources—human, financial, and other—will be required?
- Who should be responsible for implementation?
- What time frame should be established for the various actions proposed?
- How should subsequent performance be measured?

Small-Group Discussions

The best results in the early stages of case preparation are generally achieved by working alone. But a useful step, prior to class discussion, is to discuss the case with a small group of classmates. (In some instances, you may find yourself assigned to a small discussion group as an integral part of the program experience, or you may be required to work with others to develop a written report for possible group presentation.)

These small groups facilitate initial "testing" of ideas and help to focus the discussion on the main considerations. Within such a discussion group, present your arguments and listen to those of other participants. Except in the case of group projects, the aim of such a meeting is not to reach a consensus, but to broaden, clarify, and redefine your own thinking—and to help others do likewise.

Effective management of the marketing side of a business or other institution involves adjusting the organization's resources to the changing character of the marketplace; this is different from just applying knowledge about what works and what doesn't work in marketing. Accordingly, the focus of small-group discussions should be on analysis and decision making: What are the facts? What do they mean? What alternatives are available? What specifically should management do? How and when?

CLASS DISCUSSIONS

Courses taught by the case method emphasize inductive learning, with conceptual frameworks and strategic guidelines being developed from the analysis of a variety of real-world situations. This approach contrasts sharply with the deductive approach to learning used in lectures where the concepts are presented first and must then be applied to actual situations.

Role of the Instructor

In class, you may find that the role played by an instructor teaching the case method differs significantly from that of a lecturer. The instructor's role in case discussions is often similar to that of a moderator—calling on students, guiding the discussion, asking questions, and periodically synthesizing previous comments. Teaching styles vary, of course, from one case instructor to another.

Many professors like to begin the class by asking a student to "lay out" the case, which may involve your being asked to identify key problems and opportunities, to present some preliminary data analysis, and perhaps to outline a possible plan of action.

Some instructors assign study questions in advance to help students with their case preparation, but others feel it is more realistic (albeit also more demanding) to let students define for themselves how they should approach each new case.

Responsibilities of Participants

Instead of being a passive notetaker, as in lecture classes, you will be expected to become an active participant in case discussions. Indeed, it is essential that you participate; for if nobody participates there would be no discussion! If *you* never join in the debate, you will be denying the other participants the insights that you may have to offer. Moreover, there is significant learning involved in presenting your own analysis and recommendations and debating them with your classmates—who may hold differing views or else seek to build on your presentation. But do not be so eager to participate that you ignore what others have to say. Learning to be a good listener is also an important element in developing managerial skills.

A few last words of general caution may be helpful. Avoid indiscriminate rehashing of the case facts in your presentations; the instructor and the other participants have already read the case, too. Work toward building a coherent class discussion rather than on repeating what others have said earlier or making random comments. Before jumping into the discussion, ask yourself if the points you plan to make are relevant to what has gone before, or if they will result in a significant redirection of the discussion.

Occasionally, it may happen that you are personally familiar with the organization depicted in a case. Perhaps you are privy to additional information not contained in the case, or perhaps you know what has happened since the time of the case decision point. If so, keep this information to yourself unless, and until, the instructor requests it. (This advice also holds true for written reports and case exams.) There are no prizes for 20/20 hindsight, and injecting extra information that nobody else has is more likely to spoil a class discussion than to enhance it.

Learning comes through discussion and controversy. In the case method of instruction, participants must assume responsibility not only for their own learning, but also for that of others in the class. Thus, it is important that you be well prepared, willing to commit yourself to a well-reasoned set of analyses and recommendations, and receptive to constructive criticism. If you do not accept this challenge, you are likely to find the case method aimless and confusing. On the other hand, if you do accept it, we are confident that you will experience in the classroom that sense of excitement, challenge, and even exasperation that comes with being a manager in real-world situations.

MARKETING CHALLENGES

CASES AND EXERCISES

PART ONE

THE NATURE OF MARKETING

Every reader of this book has been an active consumer for years, evaluating and purchasing a wide array of products from competing suppliers. But the cases in this book place the reader in a different role, that of the marketing manager in a diverse group of organizations, responsible for helping to develop, price, and distribute their products and encouraging customers to purchase them.

Purchases are transactions in which the customer offers something of value (typically money but also including time and personal effort) in exchange for the value represented by the product. Managing and facilitating these transactions lies at the heart of marketing management. Success in this endeavor requires an understanding of how individuals and organizations make decisions relating to purchase behavior and also of how this behavior may be influenced.

Historically, the study of marketing emphasized the purchase and sale of physical goods in the private sector of the economy. The greatest sophistication was achieved in consumer packaged goods, with attention later being directed to marketing consumer-durable and industrial goods. Today, the situation is different in that marketing expertise is now also highly valued by managers of service firms (whose output accounts for approximately half the gross national product). In the public and nonprofit sectors, too, there is widespread interest in developing a stronger marketing orientation among organizations as diverse as hospitals, transit authorities, museums, and performing-arts programs. Most nonbusiness organizations market services, but some sell goods through retail stores or mail order catalogs, and many promote social issues and behavior patterns—such as conserving scarce resources and voting in political campaigns. In this book, we will use the term *product* in its generic sense to include goods, services, and social behaviors.

MANAGEMENT AND CUSTOMER PERSPECTIVES

Success in developing a marketing program for any type of product requires the ability to understand both management and customer perspectives. The organization attempts to achieve profitability through the sale of its products (public and nonprofit organizations may seek to achieve *social* as opposed to *financial* profits and thus need to attract gifts or tax revenues to help cover their costs). Customers, by contrast, are interested in what the product will do for them.

At one level, the marketing process is used by the organization to develop an overall product-market strategy. Decisions must be made on which customers to serve with what products in order to meet organizational goals. Such decisions must be made in light of the company's resources and with regard to future as well as current market conditions. This perspective reflects the costs and benefits accruing to the marketer. At a second level, the marketing process is used to develop detailed marketing programs that reflect a good understanding of the needs of final customers and intermediary organizations. Managers should be asking: What specific combination of product features, delivery systems, pricing, and information dissemination will lead a specific customer (or group of customers) to purchase a specific product from us rather than from a competitor—or not at all?

The materials in this casebook are equally concerned with both levels of the marketing process. This dual focus requires, first, careful analysis and evaluation of each organization's product-market strategy. Is this strategy realistic and sound in the light of environmental trends, market characteristics, customer needs, and competitive activities? What modifications, if any, are required? Rarely is there one obvious strategy or plan. Widely varying solutions to a marketing problem may be appropriate, depending on the manager's knowledge and assessment of current and future conditions, creativity in generating plans of action, willingness to take risks, and judgment about the resources available and the goals to be met. Moreover, some strategies may be more difficult to implement than others. Although case analysis and discussion do not allow for actual implementation, likelihood of successful implementation is an important criterion in assessing a strategy. Different strategies are, of course, likely to have different consequences down the road.

Developing a specific marketing plan emphasizes the second level of the marketing process, since here the focus is on resolving a particular marketing problem or taking advantage of a specific opportunity. A critical part of most marketing plans is utilizing distinctive competences that will make the firm particularly effective in its chosen product market, relative to its competition. Developing a marketing plan usually proceeds in the following manner:

1 Identify and define the problem or opportunity.
2 Establish the marketing goals to be met.
3 Analyze relevant data on the market, customers, intermediaries, competitors, and other relevant environments.
4 Develop alternative approaches and plans of action.

5 Analyze the economic implications of alternative strategies as these relate to costs, revenues, and anticipated volumes. Consider other relevant criteria.

6 Use these analyses to select and justify a specific plan of action.

MARKETING TOOLS AND CONCEPTS

The cases in this introductory section of the book introduce various analytical tools and conceptual frameworks that are central to the development of marketing strategy. These include market analysis, market segmentation, buyer behavior, competitive analysis, and role of intermediaries. Many marketing decisions can be broken down into several elements that are collectively referred to as the marketing mix. These elements include product policy, pricing, distribution, and communication.

Market Analysis

Central to the development of any marketing program is information on market size, structure, and dynamics. From this information, managers can gain insights into the performance of existing products relative to the competition and into the prospects for existing or proposed products in the future.

Among the most significant questions that the manager should seek to answer are:

- How large is the market for the product in question?
- Is it growing, shrinking, or static?
- What are the major forces influencing the level of demand for this product?
- Can the market be broken down into segments? If so, what are the most useful bases for segmentation?
- At what stage in the product life cycle is this market? Are we dealing with a new-product category that is growing rapidly, a mature and well-established one, or an old-product category for which demand is falling?
- Is demand consistent over time or does it fluctuate sharply in response to random or cyclical factors?
- Who are the competitors serving this market? What is the basis of competition? Where is the competition vulnerable?

Market Segmentation

The concept of market segmentation is implicit in decisions on what customer groups to serve and on how to combine marketing variables to appeal to a particular group of potential customers.

Market segmentation is based upon the following propositions:

1 Not all customers are alike—many consumers (or institutional purchasers) differ from one another in marketing-relevant ways.

2 Segments of consumers can be identified and isolated within the overall market according to such factors as their personal characteristics, geographic location, life-styles, the needs they seek to satisfy, their buying behavior, and levels of usage of the product in question.

Most marketing organizations find themselves operating in "mass markets" of thousands or even millions of customers and prospective customers. Market segmentation represents a middle way between a strategy of *market aggregation*, in which all customers are treated similarly, and *market disaggregation*, in which each customer is treated uniquely. The goal is to combine the efficiencies of economies of scale with the attention to personal concerns that comes from focusing on the needs of individuals who share certain important characteristics. Effective marketing strategy requires an explicit choice of which segments to serve.

Buyer Behavior

How does a customer decide to buy a product and then go about purchasing it? Managers need to understand buyer behavior before they can move to strategy development. Some purchases are an impulsive act by a single individual, such as buying a magazine at a supermarket checkout counter. Other purchases entail more time and planning, whether they represent the decision of an individual or of a group. Large purchases in a family or institutional setting may involve several members who may act as a type of buying committee. Such a group is sometimes known as a *decision-making unit* (DMU), since its members arrive at the purchase decision collectively, even though a single individual may take responsibility for making the purchase or placing the order.

Individuals or DMUs are often influenced in their purchase decisions by advice or information received from other parties. Friends and relatives, for instance, may encourage or discourage a particular course of action, such as buying a new car. Large organizations may have a formal buying committee which is responsible for selecting a vendor or choosing which product to buy. Moreover, corporate executives outside the buying committee may influence the product "specs" in one way or another or impose requirements that specify which manufacturers and service suppliers represent approved vendors.

Although analysis of one's personal experiences in buying consumer goods and services may offer useful insights, it is unwise to generalize too broadly from these. Other people may approach similar purchases in different ways. The buying behavior of industrial firms and other institutions is frequently somewhat different from that of household purchasers, the former involving substantially larger volumes, unfamiliar product categories, and formalized procedures for decision making.

A general set of questions for understanding buyer behavior might include the following:

- Who initiates the buying process?
- What events or factors stimulate a need to purchase?

- Is this a one-time or repetitive purchase situation?
- What criteria are used to evaluate alternative products?
- How are these criteria set? Which criteria are most important and will they change over time?
- Whose opinions influence the evaluation of alternative purchases?
- Who makes the final buying decision, and does any one individual have effective veto power?
- Who implements the actual purchase transaction?
- Who uses the product once the purchase has been made?

Competitive Analysis

Actions taken by competitors play a major role in determining whether a particular marketing program will be successful. At the outset, analysis of the market should identify and evaluate the relative strength of current competitors:

- How long has each competitor been active in the market?
- What is its market share in both volume and financial terms? And has this share been rising or falling over time?
- Does each competitor appeal to a broad cross-section of customers, or does it pursue a "niche" strategy, targeting its product(s) and marketing programs at one or more market segments?
- What are key strengths and distinctive competences of each competitor?

Determining the current competitive situation, however, is not sufficient. Any manager who presumes, without good evidence, that competing organizations will continue their present strategies into the future is most unwise. Marketers need to know enough about each competitor—its financial situation, marketing strengths and weaknesses, people resources, short- and long-term objectives, potential for innovation, cost structure, and management values—to predict, with reasonable accuracy, how it is likely to respond to new initiatives.

Role of Intermediaries

Marketers of both consumer and industrial products may find it necessary, or simply advantageous, to delegate certain marketing functions to independent intermediaries. Thus, the design and execution of advertising campaigns are frequently contracted out to advertising agencies. Similarly, credit financing may be arranged through a financial institution such as a bank or credit card company. The most important use of intermediaries concerns the physical distribution of goods and the delivery of services (through franchising or the use of electronic channels for financial and information services). A major advantage of using intermediaries rather than doing the work oneself is that it substitutes variable costs for fixed overheads and semivariable costs.

Organizations that *choose* to market through intermediaries—such as wholesalers, retailers, distributors, brokers, or agencies—are looking for leverage. In return for a portion of the final selling price, the original marketer gets the intermediary to offer customer benefits like greater convenience, expert advice, added service features, and one-stop shopping for related products. Additionally, the intermediaries may take full or partial responsibility for selling, advertising and promotional efforts, credit, and display. In some instances, selected intermediaries may receive exclusive rights to distribute a specific product, as in franchising or exclusive dealerships. In other instances a qualified intermediary may be permitted to act as a distributor for the product in question.

Marketers should always remember that intermediaries are independent organizations which are free to enter into an agreement, or not, with primary suppliers of goods and services. The alternative for the marketer is to integrate vertically and operate its own distribution system—a strategy that is much commoner in the service sector than in manufacturing, particularly for consumer goods. Some distributor relationships are highly structured, as in franchising, and give the original marketer a significant degree of control. In other relationships, as with a small manufacturer selling through a well-established retail chain, the power lies more strongly with the retail chain.

In certain respects, analyzing current and prospective intermediaries is analogous to customer analysis. Intermediaries can be segmented according to a variety of factors (size, target market, geographic location, hours of operation, and so forth). Their involvement with competitors' products can be studied. An analysis can—and should—be made of how an intermediary makes decisions on whether or not to distribute particular goods and services, what criteria its management employs in making such decisions, and which individuals comprise its DMU. Finally, consideration should be given to what advantages might be gained over competitors by improving the margins provided to intermediaries, offering advertising and promotional assistance, providing market research data, and increasing contact with relevant managers.

The Marketing Mix

Putting together a marketing plan requires the manager to make strategic decisions in several important areas, collectively known as the marketing mix: (1) the *product,* (2) the *distribution and delivery system* through which products are made available to customers, (3) the *price* at which the product is sold, and (4) the *communications* by which prospective customers are informed about the product and encouraged to buy it.

Many people mistakenly equate marketing simply with communication activities—advertising, public relations, and personal selling. Viewed from the perspective of the marketing mix, we can see that the scope of the marketing function is considerably broader.

The marketing mix provides a very useful organizing framework for strategy development. First, product characteristics must be designed with reference to both customer needs and the requirement to differentiate the product from competing alternatives. Second, choices must be made on how to get the product delivered to the customer through physical or electronic channels. Third, a price must be set that will, at projected sales volumes, enable the marketer to cover costs and generate the level of profit desired. This price must also be set with reference to the prices of competing products and the ability and willingness of prospective customers to pay. Credit arrangements may be necessary to bring the product within reach of many would-be customers. Finally, the marketer must evaluate the most cost-effective ways of communicating with customers to tell them (or remind them) about the product and encourage them to buy it. This involves decisions on messages, advertising media, personal selling efforts, publicity and public relations, point-of-sale information, labeling, signing, and instructional materials. While this sequential approach may be a helpful first step, all marketing mix elements are ultimately interdependent and the marketing plan must recognize these interdependencies.

CONCLUSION

Marketing is the most externally directed of all the management functions, focusing on customers, intermediaries, competitors, and market dynamics. Successful marketers need to adopt multiple perspectives. They must understand the strengths and weaknesses of both their own organizations and their competitors', recognizing the goals that each seeks to achieve. They must also be able to see the world from the viewpoint of prospective customers and intermediaries, in terms of the needs that each seeks to satisfy and the criteria that they employ in evaluating alternative suppliers.

The first task of marketing is to establish an overall product-market strategy to meet organizational objectives. The second task is to develop a marketing plan including detailed substrategies for each element of the marketing mix. Decisions must be made on the features that the product should possess, how it is to be delivered to customers (should intermediaries be used?), how it is to be priced, and what information should be communicated through what media to potential customers. Each of these decisions must be oriented toward the needs and characteristics of the market segments at which the product is targeted. Managers should also take into account the strategies directed at each segment by competing organizations, to assess how much of a threat they represent. Sound plans should anticipate and counter or finesse competitive efforts. The third and final task—which is critical to the ultimate success of any plan—is to have the cooperation of all involved. The task is to persuade the organization to commit to the product the necessary resources and ensure that all managers, personnel, and intermediaries understand their role in helping to implement the plan.

HARRIS-JOHNSON ASSOCIATES

Linda Carlson
Christopher H. Lovelock

"So we thought you'd have some ideas for us, Beth," said architect Leslie Harris as he finished describing his firm's financial problems.

Beth Brigham, an MBA student whose brother Gary worked for Harris and his partner Leonard Johnson, mentally reviewed what the architect had just told her. The firm's expenses were increasing with inflation, clients were delaying payments and the bank had refused to increase the line of credit that was customarily used to meet payroll.

"We've always gotten by somehow," added Johnson. "We borrowed a little more or laid off employees. That's just the way architecture is if you're not hacks."

Harris said, "I think we've got to do something about marketing."

"What do you mean?" asked Brigham.

"Well, we're not invited to enough interviews for jobs," he replied.

Copyright © 1980 by the President and Fellows of Harvard College, Harvard Business School case 9–580–158.

"Yes, but when we do interview, we get jobs," said Johnson. "Look at last year—five interviews and three jobs. I'm not sure marketing is the answer. We don't know anything about it; we wouldn't know where to start. And who would do the work? I'm not sure we can afford to hire someone—if we could find someone qualified. And I don't think you or I can—or want to—take time out from architecture . . . "

Harris nodded. "That's a good point, Len. But why don't we have lunch, Beth, and we can tell you more about how we operate. Maybe then you can figure out what's wrong."

THE ARCHITECTURAL PROFESSION

Most architectural firms were small. In 1980, a management consultant to the profession estimated 71 percent of the firms had ten or fewer members; 26 percent had between 10 and 40, and only 3 percent had more than 40 employees.

The basic services an architectural firm offered included: schematic design, where the design concept was illustrated; design development, where the schematics were used to create more detailed drawings; and construction drawings, the final set of detailed working drawings and technical specifications from which the project was built.

Often the architect also helped the client negotiate a contract for the building's construction and supervised the construction. Some firms also did site analysis and selection; land-use studies; economic feasibility analysis; land-use and master planning; landscape, interior and graphic design. Two other services were programming, which involved studying how the building would be used and what provisions for foot traffic, offices, meetings, equipment, and the handicapped, etc. must be made; and second, construction management, where a member of the architect's staff managed the construction of the project.

Business Development

Few firms had formal marketing programs. Like other professionals, many architects had vague ideas that marketing was neither appropriate nor necessary. "Do good work and people will find you" was the traditional attitude. Many architects also perceived themselves as artists and expected to struggle financially; they resisted the idea of "selling" their creativity in the same manner in which packaged goods manufacturers sold soap and cake mixes.[1]

Although most firms were doing some promotion by 1980, such activities were often limited to entering awards programs. Winners in these programs received extensive publicity in the professional press (for example, in *Architectural Record*, *Progressive Architecture*, and the *AIA Journal*, the three leading architectural publications) but seldom much coverage in daily newspapers, the business press, or magazines serving related trades as construction.

Many observers of the profession were encouraging architects to do more marketing. In the January 1980 issue of *Progressive Architecture*, editor John Morris Dixon wrote:

> Marketing of professonal services has become not only respectable in recent years, but essential. Architects can no longer depend on previous work—or social connections—to get commissions. In the 1980's, marketing will do much to determine which firms flourish and how they work.

It was estimated that only about 10 percent of the country's architectural firms had marketing coordinators. These people might write proposals for jobs, maintain lists of leads on jobs, and prepare staff resumes and information on projects. Other responsibilities included organizing slide shows and photograph files, writing brochures and newsletters, and supervising general public relations. Such staff coordinators usually had little client contact.

Even fewer firms had marketing or "business development" directors. These people usually worked with a firm's principals to develop marketing strategies and plan integrated campaigns. In contrast to marketing coordinators, marketing directors often made presentations to prospective clients with or on behalf of principals. The firms that did not have full-time marketing coordinators often had someone—perhaps a secretary—who worked part-time on public relations.

Finding staff members experienced in marketing was difficult. Industry experts agreed that the demand for trained professionals far exceeded the supply. There were no formal academic curricula in marketing design services and only a few short programs for practitioners. As a result, most people hired to do marketing or even public

---

[1] However, some architects had always appreciated the importance of business development. In *Architectural Record*, this story was told about the well-known 19th century architect H.H. Richardson, designer of Trinity Church in Boston and Harvard University's Sever and Austin halls. A mother implored Richardson to advise her son, who wanted to be an architect. "What," she asked, "is the most important thing in architectural practice?" "Getting the first job!" Richardson replied. "Of course that is important," she agreed, "but after that what is important?" "Getting the next job!" was Richardson's gruff response.

relations for architectural firms had to train themselves. Some started with design training or architecture degrees; others had liberal arts degrees, writing skills and an interest in design. Some marketing directors had public relations or media experience; many marketing coordinators had started as secretaries in architectural offices.

A 1979 Society for Marketing Professional Services survey showed that the average salary for marketing coordinators in firms with fewer than 15 members was $15,000. Leslie Harris suspected a more accurate estimate for New York City was $18,000 to $20,000. Compensation for marketing directors was substantially higher. At a recent luncheon Harris had been seated next to a consultant who told him that marketing directors in larger firms might earn $60,000 plus profit-sharing and bonuses. "You have to pay for experience—and you have to give a marketing person your complete support," she told him. "Otherwise you're wasting time and money."

Few architectural firms advertised. Although the American Institute of Architects (AIA), the professional association to which many registered architects belonged, had lifted its ban on members' advertising in 1978, AIA members were still prohibited from using pictures of their work in advertisements.

Generally, architects obtained clients in one of three ways: by contacting potential clients themselves, by waiting for clients to contact them, or by using an intermediary like a friend, former client or consultant. Writing in *Architectural Record*, Bradford Perkins pointed out that virtually every successful firm used all three methods. "And there are neither ethical nor business reasons to favor one method over another," he added.

Architects usually were commissioned through direct selection, comparative selection, or a design competition. In the first instance, someone planning a construction project would hire an architect on the basis of the architect's reputation, personal acquaintance, or recommendations from the architect's former clients.

The selection process often involved only informal noncompetitive interviews and a slide presentation of the architect's work.

By 1980, the most common way of hiring an architect was comparative selection. A client would invite several firms to submit information about their experience, qualifications, special abilities and personnel. Government agencies required architects to use standard forms for submissions. A few firms, usually the three to six that appeared most qualified, would be invited to interview. Often these interviews involved elaborate presentations. Once the client firm had selected the architectural firm it preferred, the two firms negotiated a budget.

A third means of selecting an architect was the design competition, in which architects were asked to submit solutions to a particular problem. For example, in early 1980 the city of Portland, Oregon, was holding a competition for Pioneer Courthouse Square, part of its downtown renovation work. The winner of the competition would automatically be awarded the design contract for the project. Such competitions were infrequent and also expensive to enter, because of the need to prepare scale models in addition to the time cost of design development.

FIRM BACKGROUND

Harris-Johnson Associates (HJA) was established in 1974 when Leonard Johnson joined the architectural firm Leslie Harris had opened in 1964.

A New York City native, Harris had attended Rensselaer Polytechnic Institute and served in the military before moving to Cambridge, Massachusetts, where he worked for the prestigious firm, The Architects Collaborative.

After a few years, he returned to graduate school at Yale. As he was completing his studies, he began to design medical buildings commissioned by a family friend. After graduation, Harris returned to New York City to continue work on the projects, which were to be built on Long Island. Later he taught at the Pratt Institute and at the City College of New York while working part time for other architects. He opened his own office in his studio apartment when he received two commissions—his brother-in-law's dental office and a family friend's Fire Island vacation home. (The fee on the latter project, which Harris was still collecting in 1980, was use of the house one weekend every year.) In 1964, his first year of full-time practice, Harris hired a draftsman and billed about $20,000. He lived and worked in the studio until 1965, when he converted all the space to offices. In 1966, with a staff of four, he was forced to find larger office facilities.

In his first six years of practice, Harris received several state and national awards for his work from professional magazines and associations.[2] Features on many of his projects were published in leading journals. He did not order reprints of those stories because of the reprints' cost. As he admitted later to Beth Brigham:

> I didn't even think of marketing myself. I thought all I had to do was good work and someone would discover me.

In that period Harris also met Billy Brown, a brash young developer for whom he designed office buildings and 3,000 multifamily housing units in three Northeastern states. These jobs gave Harris the opportunity to move out of small projects like single-family houses and into site development. Remembering Brown, the architect said, "He wasn't too honest, but he had all the intuition of a builder; he knew how to get financing and he had the guts to build even without money."

This association, which ended when the developer failed to pay bills, was followed by commissions from the 40-year-old heir to a multinational conglomerate. Although trained in law, this man wanted to start a development company. Harris' work for this client, who de-

manded high quality, resulted in several design awards. However, most of the projects were never constructed. "He had the money to pay for studies and design but not the guts to build," the architect said.

The partnership with Johnson resulted when Harris realized he would have to offer equity in the firm to attract talented, responsible people. He was impressed with the way Johnson's technical skill complemented his emphasis on design. Both men believed the partnership had allowed them to grow, giving them experience on very different projects.

The partners had been invited to merge their organization into large, prestigious New York firms, but had always declined. They feared the loss of their autonomy. They also believed their skills—for example, their expertise in housing and in solar energy—would be exploited. Harris and Johnson had invited a landscape architect with whom they worked closely to join the firm, but he had declined because of the same desire for autonomy. The men had no plans to expand the firm by offering partnerships to current staff members.

Both Harris and Johnson were now in their forties, with children entering college. Both had been recognized by their colleagues. Harris, who still taught part-time at a New York architectural school, had been elected to the College of Fellows of the AIA in 1979. Johnson, who had worked in two nationally known architectural firms before joining Harris, had just concluded a lecture series at the Smithsonian Institution on the future of architecture. A graduate of the Pratt Institute, Johnson frequently testified on solar energy collection systems before members of state governmental agencies and spoke on energy to students and groups like the New York City Chamber of Commerce.

Both partners worked on every project which came into the office. Their general interests were the restoration and reuse of buildings and city areas, energy conservation and land use. Their work had included the conversion of a Brooklyn

---

[2] Such awards (not to be confused with those in design competitions) could be particularly helpful to young architects, since they conferred credibility, as well as publicity and introductions to editors of publications.

candy factory into studio apartments for artists, multifamily housing in rural areas and downtown revitalization projects like malls. Most of their work had been done in the Northeast, but both partners were certified by the National Council of Architectural Registration Boards, so they could be easily registered to practice in other states. The partners emphasized life-cycle costing[3] and they worked to relate their projects to the surroundings, whether rural or urban.

Staffing

Headquartered high in a New York City luxury hotel, the firm in early 1980 included the two partners, four design professionals and a secretary. An accountant and a bookkeeper worked part-time. The designers each made between $15,000 and $25,000. Harris, who was the senior partner, and Johnson, who was buying a third of the firm, would together draw $100,000 out of HJA in 1980.

The design staff included three associates: Oscar Weston, Jon Random and Anton Paulac. The title "associate" meant that employees were one step away from partnership, but as Harris pointed out, "it's a very large step." At HJA, employees were usually named associates after two years, once they were registered and ready to serve as project architects. Through the years, the firm had had about six other associates; most were practicing on their own by 1980. Gary Brigham, who had graduated from college in 1979, was the junior staff member.

Oscar Weston, 49, had joined the firm in 1974, shortly after the partnership was formed. He was a former colleague of Johnson's who had also worked for Skidmore, Owings, Merrill, one of the largest architectural firms in the U.S.

---

[3] Life-cycle costing, in contrast to initial or construction cost, considers all of the costs of operating a building during a fixed period, usually the length of the mortgage. Because life-cycle costing includes maintenance, interest and fuel costs, it became a popular theme in construction after the first energy shortage in the early 1970s.

Weston came to HJA because he was tired of large firms and internal politics. "I knew my design philosophy fit with Len's and Leslie's and I knew I'd have more responsibility and more direct involvement here," he said. Weston, who was not a registered architect, had no plans to open his own office. Harris and Johnson assumed Weston was one of the employees who would be interested in partnership if it were offered.

Although Weston had no experience in marketing, he believed the firm should be doing more promotion. Recently he had told Harris that the associates could handle more of the routine work to free the partners for marketing. The first marketing task the firm should tackle was a brochure, he suggested. "It's been at least a year in the works; we need something that tells the client what we're all about."

Weston also recommended the firm consider every way in which it presented itself. "For example, look at this conference room," he exclaimed. "I'd start by cleaning the carpet!" On the other hand, he emphasized, the firm should not have a luxurious office because clients might assume the staff could not work with limited budgets.

Anton Paulac, 45, recently had returned to the firm after two years in Paris with the French office of an international firm. Previously he had spent 14 years working in New York City, including two with HJA. Born in Hungary and educated there and in France, Paulac was a confirmed Manhattanite. "I won't even live in one of the other boroughs," he often said. Because of the expense of opening an office of his own in Manhattan, Paulac expected to stay with Harris and Johnson as their firm grew. Although he had no experience or training in marketing, he had been quick to respond to Beth Brigham's questions about business development, noting:

We need lots of contacts in every direction to help us. We're not dynamic enough about making contacts; we need to spend more time with former and potential clients.

Paulac believed the time spent to get projects featured in magazines was worthwhile, but he also felt that architects shouldn't concentrate on publications read only by their peers. "Getting a story in *Progressive Architecture* is excellent for our reputation with other architects," he remarked, "but it doesn't help us reach business people." Like Weston, Paulac believed that anyone hired to do public relations or marketing for the firm needed an architectural background. "That person has to understand the design process and has to be able to stimulate our clients' imaginations, too," he said.

The third associate, Jon Random, 27, had recently received his license. He had spent two years with the firm, and now frequently served as a project architect (the individual in charge of a project). Some staff members described him as "good with people"; others said he was sometimes less cooperative than desired.

Gary Brigham, 23, had spent the summer before college graduation as an unpaid intern in the office. He had selected the firm because he enjoyed the staff's concern with design. "It's not a bunch of hacks," he said. Hired upon graduation, he had received an unusual amount of responsibility for someone so inexperienced, because the office was so small. He had even served as the project architect on a very small job. Brigham hoped to begin graduate school in autumn, 1980. If he was not accepted at the school of his choice, he was considering staying with HJA for a few more years. Discussing the firm, he told his sister:

> This office is better than 95 percent of the others in the city . . . though I would like to see how the other 5 percent operate. But there's a lot to learn here. For example, sometimes the partners call everybody together and we discuss a problem with a project. It's almost like school . . . and when you have a problem, the partners take the time to teach you how to handle it. But the variety of opinions in the office—and the strength of each one—don't create an efficient system for getting work completed.

The office secretary, Evonne Rhodes, had joined the firm in 1978 after working for several years in government and publishing both in New York City and in Europe. She held a graduate degree in education. When Harris had mentioned hiring someone to handle marketing, she had expressed interest in the position.

The first part of the office to be seen by visitors was the entry, where Rhodes worked. The area was decorated with posters and a large calendar; several framed award certificates were hung on the wall, but they were difficult to see during regular business hours when the main door was open and against the wall.

The adjoining conference room overlooked Central Park. One wall was covered with a soft panel that could be used as a bulletin board, another was dominated by a large abstract photograph. The paint on the high ceiling was peeling. The space, which was leased until April 1984 on very reasonable terms, would accommodate as many as 20 professionals. Harris hoped the staff, which had never exceeded 15, could be increased to 25 or 30 within the next five years. "Then we'd have the skills to do almost anything. And we'd still be small enough that Len and I would be in touch with every project."

The partners' ideas about geographic expansion differed. Johnson wanted work outside New York City limited to very large jobs (for example, where construction costs exceeded $5 million) or to smaller projects done for very important clients who had other work in the immediate area. "Because we're a small firm, we have to use our time efficiently," he said. Harris, in contrast, was interested in international work and in a branch office in the growth areas of the Southwest.

THE FIRM'S SERVICES

Although HJA's promotional material listed site planning, interior and graphic design, programming and construction management among the services offered, the firm generally hired or associated itself with specialists (usually called consultants) in professions like structural engineering, lighting and interiors. Harris was trained in related fields like graphics, but he preferred to subcontract the work to specialists because he believed they usually did better work than he could. To handle the job site responsibilities of construction management commissions, the partners would have to hire another architect.

The firm was neither a "full service" office with staff people who could handle every step of the design and building process, nor a "specialist" firm that concentrated on medical buildings, banks, schools or other specific institutions. "We're really too general, considering our small staff," Harris explained, "but we're interested in several different kinds of projects and services." Because of this general approach, the firm had only done a few projects of each type. (See Exhibit 1 for representative jobs by HJA). Harris hoped that the firm's billings—which in the late 1970s had ranged from $200,000 to $400,000 per year—might reach $600,000 in 1980. Reflecting delayed payments from clients, the firm's receipts from fee income in 1979 had amounted to only $231,000 (Exhibit 2). Accounts and advances receivable amounted to over $200,000 at the end of 1979 (Exhibit 3).

Architects were usually compensated in one of three ways. A widely used method, percentage of construction cost, assumed a correlation between project size and the architect's effort. New York State paid architects by this method, so HJA was penalized for projects that came in under budget. Architects might also be paid by the hour; this method was designed to compensate them for every hour spent on the project plus overhead and a reasonable profit. By 1980, HJA was trying to do most of its work on this basis. A third payment method was lump sum or fixed fee; it was often used by government agencies. The receipt of revenues on a long job could be erratic. For instance, it might be established as 25 percent after delivery of the working drawings, 50 percent when construction was half done, and 25 percent on completion of the building.

One problem with government work was that both New York City and the State of New York were very slow to pay fees that were due. On one job for the state, it had taken two years for HJA to receive full payment because of funding problems.

To improve both their billings and their profits, both partners wanted to do more work for corporations. "That's the only time we make any money," Harris said. "But I don't know how to get corporate clients . . . I don't have any access to them." However, he had a friend who worked for a law firm representing many *Fortune 500* firms, and several of his former classmates worked for major corporations. Johnson, too, had contacts in government agencies that commissioned architecture.

Harris was ambivalent about some types of projects, especially housing. He and Johnson believed they should be interested in multifamily housing because they had designed award-winning projects that had been very successful financially. But working with developers could be difficult because the builders often paid poorly. "Single-family housing? We do it for fun," Harris said. "You can't possibly make money on it."

The partners were interested in institutional work like libraries and college campuses. Because Harris believed that buildings (what he called "the built environment") could help solve social problems, the firm was trying to obtain a jail commission. Such a job would be time-consuming because it would involve not only design but supervision, requiring monthly—even weekly—inspection visits as construction proceeded. However, he and Johnson did not want to restrict themselves to public sector clients.

Market Conditions

To give her an idea of HJA's best opportunities for work in the next few years, Harris showed Beth

EXHIBIT 1
REPRESENTATIVE HJA PROJECTS

Project	Client	Total contract amount	Contract signed	Status (1,000)	Architect's comments
Bronx hospital roof repair	New York State	$150,000	September, 1974	Under construction	Bread and butter job
Brooklyn school	New York City	$105,000	First contract signed in 1974; work interrupted by fiscal crisis; new contract in February, 1980	Final steps on working drawings to be started soon	Great project
Brooklyn mall, second phase	New York City	$131,500	To have been signed in September, 1979; now expected in Spring, 1980	Phase 1 under construction; Phase 2 to be designed	Another great project, but working with NYC is difficult.
Planned community, suburban New Jersey	Private	$ 50,000	Expected soon	No work started	Will be a feasibility study.
Corporate exhibit in New York City	Private	$ 80,000	1979	Just completed	Great job—and may result in several other jobs for same client.
Queens hospital restoration	New York State	$100,000	Phase 1, 1977 Phase 2, 1978 Phase 3, 1979	Phase 2 under construction Phase 3 (interiors) in design	Bread and butter; but allowed use of innovative system for completing working drawings.
Library and mall, suburban New York	City	$225,000	January, 1975	Just completed	LJ: not sure the aggravation was worth the rewards; LH: gave us a chance to work on so many areas of interest . . . but the political climate was the worst we've encountered.

Project	Client	Value	Date	Status	Notes
Pine Meadows multi-family housing	Private (project designed for one client and completed for another)	$170,000	1975	Under construction	Very good housing project. Client for whom job was finished took some short cuts. Model for project took months to build, is valued at $20K. Was rented to builder for marketing purpose for $2,500 for a year.
Microwave station, New Jersey	Private	$150,000	November, 1979	Design work cannot start until zoning commission approves	One of few corporate clients with whom we have good working relationship. A technically interesting project.
Nuclear plant emergency control center, suburban New York	Private utility	$ 50,000	On retainer	Design work starting	We're "no nuke" people, but the safety issue is challenging . . . and we want to keep client.
Bronx office building (30,000 square feet in existing building)	Same utility	$150,000	On retainer	Design work starting	Interior renovation.
White Plains office (5,000 square feet in storefront)	Same utility	$ 40,000	On retainer	Under construction	Another interiors job.
Planned community, Paterson, NJ	Private	$ 50,000	No contract yet; made proposal in early 1980	Would be a master plan for housing, church, shopping center.	

EXHIBIT 2
HARRIS-JOHNSON ASSOCIATES: INCOME STATEMENT FOR
YEAR ENDING DECEMBER 31, 1979

Income from fees		$231,664
Cost of services:		
Direct project salaries	$63,895	
Other direct costs	34,472	98,367
Gross profit		133,297
General expenses:		
Officers' compensation	61,360	
Office salaries	10,920	
Rent	15,417	
Taxes	9,639	
Interest	3,770	
Depreciation	802	
Subscriptions, dues, etc.	2,973	
Office supplies	3,635	
Telephone	3,144	
Insurance	9,847	
Employee hospitalization and major medical	4,680	
Auto and travel	8,796	
Cleaning	768	
Product brochures and proposals	3,391	
Postage	306	
Professional fees	500	
Reproduction and copying	2,062	142,010
Net profit (loss)		($8,713)

Source: HJA records.

Brigham a collection of recent newspaper and magazine articles.

A recent *Wall Street Journal* report had noted that many architectural firms had not been affected by the slump in construction. According to the article, major firms in San Francisco were expanding by 10 percent to 15 percent. In New York, business was described as "less brisk," but many firms were still growing through diversification. The managing partner of one firm with a staff of 100 told the *Journal*, "Only about half of our work is tied to new construction; the rest is related to renovation and interior design."

In "A View of the 1980s," *Progressive Architecture* said, "Energy considerations beyond any doubt, will have a greater impact on architectural design in the 1980s than any other factor. . . . Life-cycle cost will be the measure of building economy."

Architectural Record had discussed the changing market for institutional buildings. Because of demographics, which had caused a decline in educational building construction, and because of the dependence on public financing, the magazine's editors did not expect a strong institutional construction market. Rehabilitation of existing structures was the best potential market, they suggested.

Building Design & Construction also cited the market for reuse; a mortgage company official pointed out that the trend toward reviving choice inner-city residential areas had become a stam-

EXHIBIT 3
HARRIS-JOHNSON ASSOCIATES: BALANCE SHEET,
DECEMBER 31, 1979

Assets

Current Assets:

Cash	$ 1,720	
Accounts receivable*	186,685	
Advances receivable	27,254	
Due from officers (borrowed from HJA)	33,000	
Total Current Assets		$248,659

Fixed Assets:

Furniture, fixtures, and equipment (less accumulated depreciation of $6,606)		15,000
Total Assets		$263,659

Liabilities and Shareholder's Equity

Current Liabilities:

Accounts payable	$ 19,500	
Note payable (line of credit)	35,000	
Payroll taxes payable	9,394	
Total Current Liabilities		$ 63,894

Equity:

Capital stock	15,000	
Paid-in surplus	21,606	
Retained earnings	163,158	
Total Equity		199,764
Total Liabilities and Equity		$263,659

* Harris said most of the firm's receivables were at least 60 days old. Many were at least six months old. There was no provision for bad debts.
Source: HJA records.

pede. James W. Rouse, whose firm was involved in inner-city development in Baltimore, Philadelphia and Boston (where its work included Quincy Market) agreed that people and industry were moving back to cities because of young couples' changing life-styles, improved public transportation, and the financial difficulty in buying a single-family house in the suburbs.

Marketing at HJA

Harris knew HJA could not compete with full-service firms unless a prospective client had had unpleasant experiences with large firms where the client did not receive the partner's attention. He admitted:

> Our only real strength is that Len and I are working principals; we offer our abilities, our experience, our involvement in the jobs. What we have to sell is our personal work on every project. But our problem is getting interviews. We simply don't go after enough work.

In 1979 the partners had been invited to five interviews for specific jobs. They did not solicit any of the invitations. The firm received commissions for three of the five jobs for which the partners interviewed. At the third interview, it received the commercial job in question—and also was asked to renovate an apartment for the client. A fourth commission was lost because HJA would not cut its fee. The final job, a single-family house was rejected because Harris and Johnson did not like the prospective clients. "The couple would have been a nuisance to work with . . . and we wouldn't have made any money anyway."

The partners had made a sixth presentation to officials of the New York State Corrections Agency. Harris and Johnson had not been applying for a specific job; they wanted their firm considered when architects for each of several proposed new jails were selected. They did not expect to hear about the first of several jobs until spring.

The firm had not had a brochure since 1968, when Harris printed, but never distributed, an informational packet on his work. For the last year, the partners had been trying to collect photos for a new brochure and agree on text and design. At least two graphic artists had been commissioned to design brochures; neither one's work had satisfied the partners. Because no brochure existed, the partners did not respond to most inquiries about their work. For example, they had not even written to a group in Rochester, New York, that wanted information on mall design.

For HJA's few formal presentations, the secretary custom-bound existing photographs, prepared photocopies of newspaper stories about the firm's work and typed descriptions of the staff and their projects.

As a service to the consultants with whom they worked—these were specialists in engineering, landscape architecture, graphics and interior design—the partners distributed copies of their consultants' brochures to help them obtain work. If HJA had a brochure, Johnson said, he would ask the consultants to do the same for his firm. Harris agreed that consultants had been an unexpectedly valuable source of work:

We've gotten about 10 percent of our work because of introductions to potential clients by our landscape architects, through our graphic designers and through our engineers. But I've never expected them to promote us . . . although, of course, they're in a good position to give clients a fair assessment of how different architects work.

The firm frequently had its work featured in magazines, newspapers and professional journals. But these stories were seldom initiated by the partners or their staff. Two HJA projects were to be featured in architectural journals in spring 1980; both stories had resulted from the photographer's contact with the editors. (Architectural photographers usually owned all reproduction rights to their work, being paid every time a picture was published. For this reason, most photographers tried to interest editors in projects that had already been photographed.)

One project had been featured in the January issue of a magazine for developers because a consultant had sent in the story. The same project recently had been described in the *New York Times* because Harris had called an editor he knew. Johnson was also interested in having the firm's work mentioned in the business—not the design—pages of the *New York Daily News*. "An article there on an apartment we'd designed with solar energy brought lots of calls," he noted. Harris admitted the firm had done no followup on the inquiries.

Although HJA sometimes ordered reprints of magazine stories, it never used these as part of a mailing program. In fact, the firm had no mailing list. Even Christmas cards were addressed and mailed sporadically, as the partners thought of people who should receive cards. The firm did no advertising. Nor did it do any business entertaining, despite the attractive location of the office. "We could do some entertaining, though," said Harris. "People love to come to this hotel."

The partners belonged to no clubs for business and did not attempt to make clients of any former college classmates, neighbors or other social contacts. Neither partner believed social contacts were necessary in obtaining work. "Although I do know people who get work through their friends," added Harris.

All of HJA's work resulted from personal contacts—but these were strictly business associations. As Harris observed:

> Because of our contacts, our potential clients hear about us from many different sources . . . and we need that to get a job. For example, our presentation is one source of information, a reprint of a magazine article is another and a consultant's comment is a third.

A recent project in Brooklyn was typical of the way in which a variety of HJA's contacts could generate a commission. A member of the New York City mayor's staff had friends in Trenton, New Jersey, where Harris had designed a mall several years earlier. Having seen the Trenton work, the mayor's assistant called Harris and Johnson to suggest that they and an engineering firm submit a proposal. While preparing their presentation, the architects called an architect on the mayor's staff whom they knew slightly. They also called the staff members who would select an architect.

"You find excuses to call them," said Harris. "Often you can try out different combinations of consultants with them . . . you know, ask them what they think of a particular graphic artist or an engineer. . . ."

Before their interview with the mayor's staff, Harris and Johnson also called firms who had consulted with them on other projects and asked these firms' principals to call colleagues on the mayor's staff. Neither of the partners believed they had enough experience with such marketing "campaigns"; Harris believed they sometimes neglected to determine what was necessary for goodwill from the decision-makers. "For example," he said, "one of the most important groups in the state corrections agency is headed by a minority woman who likes to see firms that have minority staff members or consultants. We don't have any."

Sometimes, he added, corporate bureaucracies were so complex that determining the decision-makers was difficult. "We work with one corporation that has many different departments," he said. "Each department has its favorite architect. Our project overlaps at least two departments . . . so the selection of an architect becomes a power struggle between the groups."

Harris rarely had difficulty with those who initiated the contact ("they have a vested interest in seeing you get the job") or with those who influenced the selection decision. "I usually call people outside the client organization who might be able to help. . . . I don't feel awkward doing that. . . . I guess they just know I may be able to help them some day." He believed the real problem was the lack of a system for finding out about work and requesting interviews. "And we need someone to do the followup," he said.

HJA had once subscribed to *The Coxe Letter*, one of a few monthly bulletins describing forthcoming architectural jobs and marketing techniques. "But we never followed up on any of the leads, so I dropped the subscription," said Harris. "If I had a brochure I'd subscribe again because I could develop a systematic way to use the leads." (Exhibit 4 shows estimated costs for the newsletter, brochures, magazine reprints and other marketing-related activities.)

Johnson, however, questioned the value of such newsletters, noting, "By the time you've decided to follow up the lead, it's too late. Someone else's already got the job." To learn about possible work, Johnson said he would prefer to call the firm's consultants and the architects who worked in purchasing for large corporations like American Telephone & Telegraph Co., General Electric and IBM.

HJA's PROBLEMS

Back at her apartment, Beth Brigham cleaned out her briefcase and described her day at HJA to her roommate, Sue Adams, a fellow MBA student.

"Sue, I don't know what I'm going to tell them. They're both such nice guys and their work is terrific but they don't know anything about marketing. And I'm not sure they really want a

EXHIBIT 4
ESTIMATED COSTS FOR MARKETING-RELATED PROJECTS AT
HARRIS-JOHNSON ASSOCIATES

Brochure (500 copies)	$10,000*
Envelopes for mailing brochure, special order	Unknown
Photography of finished projects	$1,000–$3,000 per project**
Black and white prints for newspaper publicity and awards program entry books	$15 each
Mounted enlargements of photographs for office display	$300 each***
The Coxe Letter	$85 per year
Reprints of magazine features	$500–$700 per 1,000 copies
Awards program entry fees	$25–$100 per program

* This was a typical price paid by architectural firms for a brochure.

** Many magazine editors expected architects to pay for the photography of projects that were to be described in the publications. Although architectural photography was usually available for about $750 per day in 1980, HJA preferred to use one of the most expensive photographers in the New York area. Fees did not include film, processing, prints, or reprint rights.

*** HJA had its enlargements (usually about 20 inches square) mounted by the same craftsman who mounted photographs for museums.

marketing program, at least one where they have to do the work themselves."

"So why don't they hire someone?" asked Adams.

"First, they can't afford to. And secondly, people who are commissioning architecture want to work with the people who will do the design. That's one of the strengths of this firm: what you see is what you get," replied Brigham.

"But that doesn't solve my problem," she went on. "How do I—a student with no experience in architecture—tell these men that they don't seem to know what they want to sell? And that they don't really seem too interested in the selling task? And then what kind of recommendations do I make? Where should they start?"

GRENADIER CHOCOLATE COMPANY LIMITED: The Milk Mate Decision

Robert E. M. Nourse

"I've gotten into this for several reasons," explained Mr. Ronald Begg, president and founder of Grenadier Chocolate Company. "The potential of financial reward is one of them, although it will likely be some time before we begin to show a profit. I also wanted, however, to be in a position where I would make my own decisions. Procter & Gamble, where I spent seven years, provides great sales training. But as you develop you begin to want to flex your muscles. There are layers of managers up there above you, and they don't end in Canada. They go on and on. Finally, I have five children and, when they grow up, they're going to ask me where I was in the 1960s and 1970s when Canada was being sold out to the U.S. I don't want to have to say to them that I was there, helping the Americans take over."

Ronald Begg, 34, quietly explained his reasons for leaving a promising career with a large multinational food company. His background in sales, mass merchandising and promotion was

Copyright © 1975 by The University of Western Ontario.

extensive. For seven years, Mr. Begg had been a Proctor & Gamble brand manager for products such as Duncan Hines cake mix, Secret deodorant and Crisco shortening. Subsequently, he had become national sales manager of Frito-Lay, a division of PepsiCo Inc. In late 1973, Mr. Begg had left PepsiCo with the objective of forming his own company.

The first task had been to find a suitable product. Dozens of product categories were systematically examined and a "hundred-odd" product concepts were reviewed. Each was assessed against a set of criteria that attempted to recognize market opportunities while, at the same time, taking into account the limited financial resources at Mr. Begg's disposal. The criteria, for example, included market size, growth rate, competitors active in the category, their costs, degree of consumer satisfaction with existing products, feasibility of new product development, ease of product formulation and suitability for custom packaging by an outside source. Of the original product concepts three were selected for intensive study. Formulations were prepared, and small-scale consumer testing was undertaken. The eventual choice was a new, milk modifying, instant chocolate syrup for household use. Subsequently, the product was given the name Milk Mate.

By November 1974, the formulation of Milk Mate had been improved to a point where extensive consumer testing yielded highly satisfactory results. Arrangements with ingredient suppliers had been finalized. An outside blender had been contracted to manufacture the Milk Mate concentrate, and a similar contract with a custom packer was approved for the final addition of bulk ingredients and packaging. Several crucial marketing decisions, nonetheless, remained to be made. Selling prices and trade margins had to be decided upon. A program of advertising and promotion, if undertaken, would have to be preceded by establishing product availability through retail grocery outlets. Selling effort would be needed, and it would be necessary to decide whether to employ company salesmen or commissioned sales agents. A plan indicating rate of market penetration to national distribution would need to be formulated.

THE CANADIAN MILK MODIFIER MARKET

Milk modifiers were used by consumers to create a flavoured milk drink. The product was sold as a powder, with typical label instructions calling for two teaspoons of powder to be added to an 8-ounce glass of milk. Well-known brands included Nestlé's Quik, Hershey, and Cadbury's Choc-O. Chocolate was the dominant flavour, estimated to account for about 80 percent of total sales.

In 1974, total Canadian sales of milk modifiers were estimated at 23 million pounds. Market size had been relatively stable in recent years, growing roughly in proportion with population increase. Total sales were estimated to divide as follows:

British Columbia	10 percent
Prairies	14 percent
Ontario	38 percent
Quebec	30 percent
Atlantic Provinces	8 percent

Nestlé was thought to hold a 50 percent market share, Hershey 20 percent, Cadbury 10 percent, with the remaining 20 percent being accounted for by a number of small, regional brands. All major producers offered a one-pound package size, which accounted for one-third of total sales, and a two-pound size, which comprised virtually all of the remainder.

In November 1974, the major brands sold to retailers at a price of $10.00 per case of 12 one-pound packages. Typical retail price was $0.99 for a one-pound package. Throughout 1974, however, rapid escalations in sugar prices, which made up 85 percent of a manufacturer's ingredient cost, had drastically reduced or eliminated manufacturer profitability on milk modifiers.[1] Estimates prepared by Mr. Begg, shown in Exhibit 1, indicated that the market leaders were currently losing $1.00 to $1.25 per case relative to their full costs. On this basis, Mr. Begg was momentarily expecting a trade price increase to $11.50 per case.

MILK MATE

Milk Mate possessed several important qualities. Unlike existing products, it was a liquid that dissolved instantly and completely. By comparison, powdered milk modifiers had low solubility, were difficult to mix, and often left a residue in the glass after drinking. Standard 20-ounce and 36-ounce plastic containers could be used in packaging, thereby minimizing costs.[2] The Milk

---

[1] Sugar was priced at $60 per hundredweight in November 1974, compared to $20 per hundredweight at the start of 1974.

[2] The 20-ounce size of Milk Mate yielded roughly the same quantity of beverage as a one-pound container of powder.

EXHIBIT 1

ESTIMATED MANUFACTURER'S COSTS FOR NESTLÉ'S QUIK,
NOVEMBER 1974
(based on a case of 12 one-pound packages)

Ingredients	$ 7.25 ~~5.60~~
Packaging	0.75
Manufacturing	0.50
Distribution (warehouse, cartage, cash discount, etc.)	0.50
Selling expense	0.50
Total, exclusive of advertising and promotion	$ 9.50 7.85
Advertising and promotion expenses*	~~1.50~~
Total	$11.00 9.85

* Hershey costs were thought to be similar except for advertising and promotion expenses of $1.75 per case. No estimates were prepared for Cadbury.
Source: Estimates prepared by Mr. Begg.

Mate formulation required proportionately less sugar than competitors, resulting in lower ingredient costs. No specialized formulating or blending processes were needed. Refrigeration was unnecessary because the product contained a preservative.

Twelve generations of the Milk Mate formulation had been tested until an optimum blend was found. In the fall of 1974, the final blend was subjected to extensive consumer testing. Each of 100 families selected as heavy users of milk modifiers was given an unidentified sample of Milk Mate and a one pound package of the market leader, then asked to use both products in their home for two weeks. In a follow-up survey, just under 50 percent of the sample indicated an overall preference for Milk Mate. Mr. Begg viewed these results as encouraging, particularly since a new product form (a liquid) was being tested against an established one (a powder). Further, as shown in the reported results in Exhibit 2, Milk Mate was preferred on many specific dimensions such as taste, colour, ease of mixing, sweetness and convenience.

Throughout the past year, Mr. Begg had worked out of his home and had kept business and personal expenses to a minimum. Product

formulation and consumer testing, however, had been carried out by well-established professionals. To date, slightly under $25,000 had been invested in the project.

Mr. Begg hoped for a market launch by May 1975. In anticipation, he had recently hired a secretary and rented a second story, walk-up office in an older North Toronto building. He estimated that office expenses (secretary, rent, telephone, bookkeeping, legal, supplies and other general expenses) and his own salary would together total approximately $40–50,000. At current sugar prices, and exclusive of advertising and promotion costs, Grenadier's costs for ingredients, packaging, manufacturing, and distribution were expected to be about 10–20 percent lower than the comparable amounts shown for the market leader in Exhibit 1. These costs were almost fully variable since manufacturing and packaging were to be contracted to outside sources.

MARKETING PROGRAM

In considering a marketing program for Milk Mate, Mr. Begg was aware that the financial requirements of his plan would require almost

EXHIBIT 2
RESULTS OF CONSUMER BLIND PAIRED COMPARISON TEST CONDUCTED IN
FALL 1974

Methodology

Milk Mate was tested against the leading chocolate powder brand by an independent research company. The test sample was carefully selected to comprise approximately 100 heavy users of instant chocolate powders. Each family was given one pound of the market leader and a sample of Milk Mate and asked to use both products in their home for two weeks.

Results

	Percent of Consumers Liking Milk Mate Better than Market Leader	**Percent of Consumers Liking Milk Mate as Well as or Better than Market Leader**
Taste, flavour	39%	54%
Colour	49%	75%
Ease of Mixing	91%	93%
Sweetness	41%	64%
Convenience	90%	94%

Consumer Intention to Buy

After the consumers had tried both Milk Mate and the leading powder in their homes for two weeks, they were asked about their intention to buy Milk Mate.

• 52% of families said they would definitely or probably buy Milk Mate if it was the same price as the leading powder brand.
• 43% of families said they would definitely or probably buy Milk Mate if it was 5¢ per pound higher than the leading powder brand.

total bank financing. In turn, the bank's willingness to extend funds would depend on the amount required and the perceived viability of his program.

One important decision to be made was pricing. Milk Mate seemed superior, but could it support a premium price in the marketplace? Since the liquid product concept was new, it was important to get consumers to try Milk Mate, and this might prove easier at price parity with competition. On the other hand, a lower price might speed up market penetration, thereby establishing a consumer franchise before possible introduction of other imitative products.

A related question was that of trade margins.

Retailers, Mr. Begg felt, were unhappy with existing margins and would be far more receptive to a figure closer to 20 percent.

While Grenadier was small, Mr. Begg felt that big company advertising and promotion techniques would be needed to introduce and sustain Milk Mate. Television, magazine and newspaper advertising were all strong possibilities, but the objectives and budget for such a campaign would require close scrutiny. Mr. Begg also wondered if couponing would not be appropriate at the outset to induce trial. Selected advertising space cost statistics are shown in Exhibit 3. Advertising production costs, Mr. Begg estimated, would average 10 to 15 percent of space costs.

EXHIBIT 3

SELECTED MEDIA ADVERTISING COSTS, NOVEMBER 1974

(all rates are for one-time airing or insertion)

Television

Cost Per Minute (Bracketed figures are 30 second rates)

	Class AA Time (prime)		Class B Time (noon to 6:00 p.m. week days)	
CBC National Network (43 English Stations)	$4,775		$2,621	
CBC Mid-Eastern Region (16 Ontario and Quebec English Stations)	2,303		1,222	
CBLT, Toronto (spot)	700	(420)	270	(165)
CFTO, Toronto (spot)	850	(525)	325	(225)

Radio

Rates for Prime (Class AA) Time

	1 minute	30 seconds	15 seconds
CFCO Chatham	$ 23	$ 20	$ 18
CFPL, London	70	49	35
CFRB, Toronto	185	145	—
CHUM, Toronto	120	80	—

Newspaper Supplements and Magazines

	Circulation (in thousands)	B & W Rates (4-colour rates in brackets)	
		½ page	Full page
The Canadian Magazine*			
National Edition	1,903	$7,960 (11,300)	$14,490 (18,075)
Ontario Edition	1,243	7,895 (9,885)	11,790 (13,925)
Chatelaine (English)			
National Edition	984	4,860 (6,930)	8,450 (10,828)
Ontario Edition	444	2,820 (4,020)	4,900 (6,280)
Toronto Calendar†			
Magazine	172	2,005 (2,600)	3,195 (3,960)

Newspapers

	Circulation (in thousands)	Rate per Agate Line‡
Barrie Examiner	11	$0.18
Kingston Whig-Standard	33	0.30
Toronto Star	507	2.70
Windsor Star	86	0.58

* Inserted cents-off coupon, printed in 4 colours on heavy offset paper, available in national edition for $8,950. Also available regionally.

† Cents-off coupon may not be run in regular advertising space, but may be inserted at cost of $4,500 (commital to firm date basis) or $3,000 (first available date basis.)

‡ There are approximately 2,500 agate lines on a newspaper page.

A related question was the primary theme to be used in advertising. Milk Mate's principal consumer benefit was its ease of mixing. Mr. Begg felt, however, that taste was the ultimate choice criterion of consumers, and he wondered which feature to stress in his advertising.

If an introductory advertising campaign was scheduled, it would be necessary in advance to gain as widespread a retail distribution as possible. To obtain distribution in a chain, the first step would be to make a presentation to the chain's buyer. The actual decision, however, would be made by the chain's buying committee. Typically, sales representatives were never invited to buying committee meetings. Mr. Begg was concerned about Grenadier's credibility to the buying committees, since the company was new and unknown. For this reason, he felt that

highly professional sales presentation material would be necessary.

Some major chains might be willing to give a general order on which the product was sent to every store. More likely, however, the chain would give a "listing" by which individual store managers would make their own choice about stocking the product. Some chains might refuse even to give a listing.

Selected data on retail grocery outlets in Canada are shown in Exhibit 4.

If company salesmen were employed, Mr. Begg estimated that salary and expenses for each man would amount to about $25,000 per year. Alternately, trade sources indicated that the costs of commissioned sales agents could range from three to ten percent. A sales agent would be responsible for his own expenses.

EXHIBIT 4

MAJOR CANADIAN GROCERY CHAINS, VOLUNTARY AND COOPERATIVE GROUPS, 1974

Name	Total Canada	Estimated Number of Stores by Region				
		B.C.	Prairies	Ontario	Quebec	Maritimes
Chains						
A & P	174	—	—	142	32	—
Canada Safeway	269	89	169	11	—	—
Dominion Stores	394	—	14	228	109	43
Loblaws	188	—	32	156	—	—
Steinberg's	194	—	—	55	138	1
Becker Milk	411	—	—	411	—	—
Mac's Milk	432	41	71	320	—	—
Perrette Dairy	180	—	—	—	180	—
(29 other chains in Canada with a total of approximately 900 stores)						
Voluntary and Cooperative Groups						
Associated	255	255	—	—	—	—
Atlantic Wholesalers	189	—	—	—	—	189
IGA	730	50	172	271	201	36
Lucky Dollar	519	28	166	161	—	82
Maple Leaf	752	—	—	752	—	—
Much More	653	70	519	—	—	—
Provigo	2,049	—	—	—	2,049	—
Red & White	831	145	119	254	—	66
(70 other voluntary and cooperative groups with a total of approximately 4,400 stores)						

Source: *Blue Book of Food Store Operators and Wholesalers* 1974, pp. 119–122.

A final question was rate of market penetration. Mr. Begg hoped to achieve national distribution for Milk Mate within two years, but was unsure about how quickly he could move toward this goal. Rapid penetration seemed desirable, but financing and cash flow requirements could prove to be a limiting factor.

"There are two kinds of companies in the food industry," Mr. Begg concluded, "small Canadian firms and the dominant U.S. multinationals. Both have their drawbacks. The multinationals, with their huge overheads, are locked into economies of scale. They are their best with a $20 million brand, but not the $2 million one. Canadian companies can handle the $2 million product, but are reluctant to invest in marketing and promotion support programs. Somewhere in the middle, there's room for a company that combines a small scale product with multinational marketing techniques."

TIMELAPSE INCORPORATED

Adrian B. Ryans

"Much of what we do at Timelapse is in markets that are too small to interest a large company like Kodak or Braun. They could blow us out of the water if it were a big deal. But the markets are so small that it wouldn't be profitable for them; but for us it might be very profitable. We are aware we are very vulnerable to other people's decisions—many of our products are dependent on other manufacturers' products and we are vulnerable to their decisions to cancel products. What we are trying to do is to keep alive long enough and to make enough money to develop and bring to market some of our concepts, which we feel are much more useful than many products currently on the market." Greg Howell, vice president of Finance for Timelapse Incorporated, made these comments as he reviewed the situation Timelapse found itself in in October 1976.

The specific problem facing Timelapse was whether or not to proceed with the final develop-

Reprinted from *Stanford Business Cases 1976* with permission of the Publishers, Stanford University Graduate School of Business. Copyright © 1976 by the Board of Trustees of the Leland Stanford Junior University.

ment of a remote control unit for the Kodak Super 8 MFS8 movie projector that was much superior to the unit provided by Kodak with the projector. The market for the proposed unit appeared to be concentrated in high school football coaches, which was a considerable departure from the industrial users to which Timelapse sold its current product line. The basic remote control unit had just been developed for one of Timelapse's current product lines and the modifications required to tailor it to the needs of the athletic market were relatively minor. Mr. Howell, if he decided to proceed with the development and marketing of the athletic unit, realized he had some tough marketing decisions to make—in particular how to distribute the product.

TIMELAPSE PHOTOGRAPHY

Timelapse was located in Mountain View, California, a city near the southern end of San Francisco Bay. The area was well known for its heavy concentration of high technology companies, and, in particular, its electronics industry. Timelapse had been founded in 1967 by Mr. Parker, a professor in the Civil Engineering Department at Stanford University, and Mr. Johnston, a manager with a major construction company. Their interest in timelapse photography had been aroused because of its potential applications in the area of construction management.

To the layperson, construction did not appear to be very repetitive work, yet it was often quite repetitive, with the typical cycles involved being measured in hours rather than the seconds or minutes that were more common in industry. Timelapse photography, which involved taking a single frame of film with a movie camera at predetermined intervals (from one second to several hours), provided the construction manager with a new set of data to help in evaluating and planning construction projects. Often on reviewing the timelapse film (speeded up), the manager could see a complete cycle of work in a short interval of time and determine how the employees could have been more effectively used. Timelapse had films documenting a number of dramatic examples of this. Before joining Timelapse, Howell himself had been involved in using timelapse photography to study a quarry operation in New Jersey. After taking six rolls of film and studying them it became obvious to him how the quarry operations could be reorganized, allowing the quarry to produce the same amount of stone on a one-shift operation instead of the two-shift operation it was currently using. This had been successfully implemented.

From a technical viewpoint, the major problem in developing cameras for timelapse photography was to find a control system that would allow the user to select the desired interval between frames and which could then reliably take each frame at exactly the predetermined interval even under adverse weather conditions. In developing projectors and the hand-held remote control units for use with the timelapse system it was important to have a reliable control system that was easy to use, allowed the user a choice be-tween a variety of projection rates (including the capability to project a single frame at a time for careful analysis), and could easily be reversed to allow the user to go over a particular segment of the film again. The control systems for both the cameras and projectors made extensive use of electronic components.

Timelapse did not manufacture the basic camera or projector. It bought the Super 8 equipment from a manufacturer such as Kodak and adapted the equipment for timelapse photography. A basic timelapse system consisting of a camera, projector and remote control unit cost about $5,000 in 1976.

HISTORY OF THE COMPANY

After the company's founding in 1967, the company sold a number of systems but sales never really took off. This was probably due in part to the relative unreliability of the early products. This unreliability was generally not directly Timelapse's fault; rather it was a function of the state-of-the-art in electronics and the resulting unreliability of some of the electronic components Timelapse used in its system. By the mid-1970's this was no longer a problem.

In late 1973 Mr. Johnston sold his share of the business to Mr. Taylor, a prominent Bay Area venture capitalist, who had been previously involved with a number of successful high technology companies. Mr. Taylor proceeded to invest a large amount of his own money in the company and took an active interest in the management of the company. While Taylor was actively involved in the management of Timelapse it became clear that some users of the equipment desired to know the precise time a particular frame was taken. Timelapse decided that the most useful way to present this information would be directly on the frame, so the time would be visible on the projected pictures. This was a difficult technical problem to solve and Timelapse management hired a Mr. Lewis to help work it out. Lewis had had a long and distinguished technical career in electronics and optics with the Bay Area electronics industry and had been personally involved in several major innovations. At the same time Mr. Chandler, who had a similar extensive background as a photo-optics technology specialist and who had worked with Lewis, also joined the company. They eventually perfected the technology to place the time on each frame.

In spite of this technical progress sales declined in 1974 and for several months they were less than $5,000 per month. In early 1975 Taylor withdrew from the active management of the company, and transferred his equity in the company to Lewis, who became president. Taylor also lent the company an additional $20,000. Sales picked up briefly in 1975 mainly as the result of a major sale of equipment to Saudi Arabia.

In January 1976 Mr. Howell joined Timelapse. Howell was in his early 30's and had earned a Masters Degree in Civil Engineering at Stanford. He had experience in construction and construc-

tion management and for a period of time had operated as an independent consultant on the East Coast. While Lewis continued to concentrate on the technical side of Timelapse's activities, Howell assumed responsibility for the firm's marketing activities and the day-to-day business management of the company. Sales showed a steady improvement in 1976 and by the middle of the summer were averaging close to $15,000 a month, which was close to breakeven. An income statement for the fiscal year ending June 30, 1976, is shown in Exhibit 1. An income statement for the first two months of the 1977 fiscal year is also shown in Exhibit 1 and a balance sheet as of August 31, 1976, is shown in Exhibit 2.

Shortly after the end of the fiscal year a further restructuring of ownership occurred. After the restructuring Lewis, Chandler, Howell and a Mr. Burgess owned approximately equal shares in the company, with Mr. Parker, one of the original co-founders, owning a somewhat smaller share. Burgess, a successful industrialist who owned an electronics company in Southern California and

EXHIBIT 1

TIMELAPSE INCORPORATED INCOME STATEMENT FOR YEAR ENDING JUNE 30, 1976 AND TWO MONTH PERIOD ENDING AUGUST 31, 1976

	Year Ending June 30, 1976	Two Months Ending August 31, 1976
Net sales	$ 50,427	$ 27,693
Other income, net	11,894	1,657
	62,321	29,350
Cost of sales:		
Materials	17,149	9,546
Labour	7,072	4,692
Overhead	12,938	3,911
	37,159	18,149
Gross profit	25,162	11,201
Marketing expenses	15,028	2,510
Product development	2,833	964
General and administrative	43,937	10,628
	61,798	14,102
Net profit (loss)	$(36,636)	$(2,901)

who was a friend of Howell's, became Chairman of the Board. Lewis remained as president. An organization chart for the company in October 1976 is shown in Exhibit 3.

The Timelapse Marketing Program

One of the things Howell had done since joining the company was to do an analysis of the last 50 systems sold by Timelapse to determine exactly who had been buying the equipment. The customers fell into three major segments and a miscellaneous category. Fifty percent of the sales had been made to construction, with the sales being split evenly between construction companies and universities, who used the equipment in construction management programs. A second major user group accounting for 20 percent of the sales were traffic engineering firms who used the equipment to study traffic patterns on existing road networks. With the completion of most design work on the Interstate Highway System, increasing attention was being focused on improving existing road networks. Thus the traffic engineering market promised to be a continuing one. A third major user group accounting for an additional 20 percent of sales was companies who used timelapse photography to monitor emissions of pollutants from industrial plants. The cameras were purchased by the companies to provide a visual record that could be used to document the extent to which they had been emitting visible pollutants. Howell noted that none of the sales appeared to have been made directly to public agencies responsible for monitoring environmental pollution. The remaining 10 percent of the systems had been sold for a variety of miscellaneous uses including security purposes and athletics.

While conducting the sales analysis Howell had noticed that while 120 colleges and universities had major construction management programs, only about 60 percent of them had purchased timelapse equipment from Timelapse. Therefore, he wrote to the approximately 50

EXHIBIT 2
TIMELAPSE INCORPORATED BALANCE SHEET AS OF AUGUST 31, 1976

Assets

Current assets:	
Cash	$ 7,017
Accounts receivable	14,521
Inventories	39,498
Prepaid expenses	5,076
Total current assets	66,112

Depreciable assets:	
Office equipment	2,748
Lab & shop equipment	3,106
Rental equipment	8,605
Demonstration equipment	9,956
	24,415
Accumulated depreciation	17,925
Book value	6,490

Other assets:	
Unamortized patent expense	2,537
Total assets	$75,139

Liabilities and Shareholder's Equity

Liabilities:	
Accounts payable-trade	$ 1,468
Accounts payable-nontrade	7,980
Notes payable	22,500
Interest payable	2,167
Accrued taxes payable	1,426
Payroll payable	10,010
Accrued commission	513
Total liabilities	46,064
	513

Shareholder's equity:	
Common stock	34,800
Paid in capital	177,600
Retained earnings	(183,325)
Total capital	29,075
Total liabilities and shareholder's equity	$ 75,139

schools that did not use Timelapse equipment pointing out that most competitive schools used Timelapse equipment. The direct mail campaign was quite successful—25 percent of the colleges and universities he had contacted had bought some Timelapse equipment by October. Spurred on by the initial success of this program, Howell

EXHIBIT 3
TIMELAPSE INCORPORATED ORGANIZATION CHART

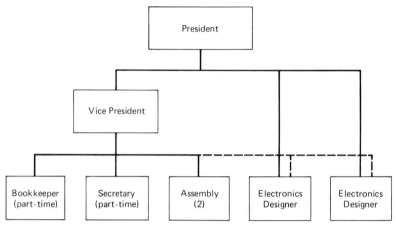

Note: Timelapse also employed a third designer on a temporary basis and a Stanford MBA on a part-time basis.

next wrote to 350 junior colleges which offered some type of construction management program. This second direct mail effort was much less successful, resulting in only 10 responses and 2 orders. He felt that the lack of success was partly attributable to the poor timing of the mailing which had been made during the summer. A follow-up mailing was being made in October.

Howell had also found out while he was delving into the files that a considerable amount of time often passed between the first contact with Timelapse and the actual purchase of the equipment. He therefore had initiated a program to follow up any leads he could find in the files. Although this was initiated late in the summer it had also resulted in some prospective customers phoning Timelapse for further information.

In its early years Timelapse had set up a network of manufacturers' representatives across the United States and Canada to handle the sales of the product line. These representatives were typically compensated with a 15 percent commission which was paid to them by Timelapse when Timelapse received payment from the customer. Since joining the company Howell had reviewed

the performance of each of the manufacturers' representatives and had found that only three of them had made one or more sales in the preceding six-month period. Based on this information he terminated Timelapse's relationship with all the other representatives.[1] Timelapse was left with only three manufacturers' representatives, located in Illinois, Texas and Western Canada. With customers in areas no longer covered by manufacturers' representatives, Howell handled marketing activities by direct mail and telephone. Howell realized that this was insufficient in the long run and he planned to make some selling trips in the Western United States later in 1976.

Timelapse had devoted only limited efforts to advertising and promotion. In 1976 the major advertising effort had been one $250 advertisement in the *Annual Directory of the Association of General Contractors*. The company had also recently committed itself to, and paid for, a booth at the Annual Convention of the Association of

[1] The agreement between a principal and a manufacturers' representative can generally be terminated by either party on thirty days notice.

General Contractors which was to be held in San Francisco in 1977.

As far as Howell knew there were only two competitors active in the timelapse field—Lafayette Electronics, a Midwestern company, and L & W in Southern California. While both were much larger than Timelapse, Howell believed that timelapse equipment only accounted for a small percentage of their sales. He believed they were active in two markets: professional photographers who needed an attachment that would allow them to take timelapse pictures, and in the military market where timelapse equipment was used to monitor missile launches. Their equipment tended to be higher priced than Timelapse's, was technically much inferior, and was probably less suitable for use in the types of markets to which Timelapse sold. Lafayette seemed to use its catalogue as its major selling tool in the United States and L & W had one active salesman. Both had representatives in Europe. In summing up the competitive picture Howell noted that he had never once had a customer refuse to buy Timelapse equipment because of being sold competitive equipment.

The New Product

In reviewing the company's operation in 1976 it became apparent to Howell and the others involved in the management of Timelapse that the company had probably suffered from a failure to be more focused in its marketing efforts. While its initial products had been developed with the construction market in mind, the marketing programs had generally not been focused on one or two target markets, thus dissipating Timelapse's limited marketing resources.

In attempting to come to grips with the targeting problem Howell had listed markets where timelapse photography had potential applications. In addition to the construction, traffic and environmental markets he had considered such potential markets as security, athletics and architectural analysis. The latter was concerned with the flows of people and materials in buildings, shopping centers, etc., to aid architects in the redesign of existing facilities or the design of new facilities. It occurred to Howell that a critical factor in the selection of target markets, especially given Timelapse's limited resources and desire to generate cash rapidly, was whether the potential customers in these markets were currently users of film. Viewed from this perspective athletics looked quite attractive, since film was widely used in football and to a lesser extent in other sports. Thus Timelapse's marketing problem would be a more limited one—convincing the customer to use the Timelapse equipment to slow the action so the coach could make more effective use of the film. This was in sharp contrast with the situation in their major current markets of construction, environmental pollution and traffic, where the users typically had to be educated on how they might use film and where there was often organizational resistance to the use of film.

His interest aroused, Howell called ten high school football coaches in the San Francisco Bay Area and learned more about how they used film in their coaching.[2] He also learned that six of them used the Kodak MFS-8 Super 8 projector. This was basically the same Super 8 projector that Timelapse used as the projector in their system. The MFS-8 projector could be operated as a still projector or at the slow-motion speed of six frames per second, the normal 18 frames per second, or an extra-fast 54 frames per second (for rapid searching). The projector also had a remote control unit that permitted the user to switch from forward to reverse and from movie to still projection. The user could not switch between the projector's slow-motion and normal speeds with the remote control box but had to use the controls on the projector itself. The projector's list price was $424.50, although a discount could usually be obtained by a school.

---

[2] Colleges and universities and professional teams generally used 16mm systems. Timelapse's equipment was all based on 8mm film.

Howell and the others in the company believed they could relatively easily modify a remote control unit they had recently developed for their industrial markets that would greatly increase the versatility of the projector for the coach and make it a much more useful tool for him. The proposed remote control unit would allow the coach to select any one frame or switch between any combination of single frames at a time, one frame/second, three frames/second, six frames/second and 18 frames/second. It would also allow him to back up at full speed so he could review a section of the game film.

After discussing the situation with the others in the company, Lewis and Howell decided to hire a Stanford MBA student on an hourly basis to do a more detailed analysis of the proposed product and its potential market. They were successful in hiring Mr. Harowitz, an MBA student between his first and second years in the Business School. Harowitz first familiarized himself with the time-lapse equipment and then had informal discussions with a couple of coaches. He then developed an interview guide and systematically interviewed a number of high school football coaches in different areas in and near the Bay Area, including San Francisco, the San Francisco Peninsula, and a town in a more rural and agri-

cultural area south of San Jose. Thus he covered as representative a group of coaches and school districts as he could find in the Bay Area, having touched an inner city, very affluent suburbs and a more rural area. All of the coaches made some use of film. While 50 percent of the schools on the Peninsula used the Kodak MFS-8 projector, which the proposed Timelapse unit would fit, only one of the eight San Francisco high schools he contacted did.

Harowitz was also able to obtain from a mailing list broker some information on the number of high schools in the United States with some breakdowns by enrollments and per-pupil expenditures on instructional materials. He was also able to get some similar information for selected states. This data is shown in Exhibits 4 and 5.

In his interview with the football coaches he tried to get some understanding of how they might buy a piece of equipment like the remote control unit. They identified five possible sources of funding: the school district budget, student body funds, booster clubs for football organized by groups of parents, candy and juice machine sales and the coach himself. Most football equipment was paid for out of the school district's athletic budget. The student body fund often paid for other football team needs which could not be

EXHIBIT 4

NUMBER OF U.S. HIGH SCHOOLS WITH GIVEN ENROLLMENTS AND PER PUPIL EXPENDITURE ON INSTRUCTIONAL MATERIALS

Type of High School	Enrollment	Number of Schools Spending More Than $20 per Pupil on Instructional Materials	Total Number of Schools
Public high schools with grades 7–12	300–499	447	2443
	500–999	806	3974
	1000 or more	516	5207
Public high schools with grades 9–12	300–499	365	
	500–999	760	
	1000 or more	2494	
Private high schools	300–499	Not available	546
	500–999	Not available	590
	1000 or more	Not available	261

EXHIBIT 5
NUMBER OF HIGH SCHOOLS WITH GIVEN ENROLLMENTS IN
SELECTED STATES

State	Type of High School	Enrollment		
		300–499	500–999	1000 or more
California	Public	62	97	584
	Private	61	43	16
Oregon	Public	38	49	57
	Private	3	0	0
Washington	Public	45	62	101
	Private	8	4	1
Illinois	Public	126	123	256
	Private	33	50	33
Total U.S.	Public	2,443	3,974	5,207
	Private	546	590	261

met out of the athletic budget. Booster clubs sometimes contributed money to purchase pieces of equipment or other items that might be difficult to fund out of the school district budget and which the student body fund would not, or could not, fund. They often paid for the filming of the football games which usually cost about $50–$80 per game. The juice machine and candy sales sometimes yielded some discretionary funds for football, but most coaches did not bother with them, citing the "hassle" involved and the relatively low revenue generated.

Timelapse also contacted Kodak to determine if they had any interest in marketing the product. They showed no real interest. Kodak was unwilling to provide Timelapse with any data on sales to date of the MFS-8 projector and did not have available even a partial listing of purchasers that Timelapse might buy. But Harowitz did get the feeling that the MFS-8 projector would remain the basic projector for the athletic market for a number of years.

Distribution of the Remote Control Unit

Harowitz also approached some possible distributors of the product. It seemed to him that two types of distributors might potentially be interested in the product: distributors of football equipment, such as protective gear and footballs, and distributors of audiovisual equipment who called on schools. From his discussions with the football coaches he found that the first group tended to be quite specialized, usually focusing on one equipment subgroup such as protective equipment. It seemed unlikely they would have the desire or the skills to sell the remote control unit. The distributors of audiovisual equipment seemed a more viable alternative and Harowitz approached two of the major companies operating in the San Francisco Bay Area in mid-September.

Audio-Visual West was a major distributor of all types of audiovisual equipment in the three Pacific Coast states. It had a separate sales force for educational institutions. In addition to its sales force, it used a catalogue and direct mail quite extensively. Harowitz discussed the Timelapse product with Audio-Visual West's sales manager in San Francisco. He indicated for that type of product his company would normally require a margin of 35 percent based on list price, although he did indicate that they would not normally realize the full margin since, if pressed, they would usually give an "education discount" to schools. However, the sales manager said, based on the information he currently had, he felt the market was too limited given the relatively low ticket price involved (Harowitz had been talking in terms of a $250 list price for the unit) for Audio-Visual West to be interested in carrying the product. At the conclusion of the interview he told Harowitz that he would like to see the finished product when it was ready.

The other distributor Harowitz approached was Bay Area Audio Visual Equipment, which carried a line similar to Audio-Visual West, but confined its marketing activities to the San Francisco Bay Area. The general manager of this company indicated that his company would expect to realize a margin of 20–35 percent for this type of product, but based on what Harowitz had told him he wouldn't be interested in carrying it.

Harowitz had obtained from Kodak a list of its approximately 600 major distributors in the United States (while Audio-Visual West was on the list, Bay Area Audio Visual Equipment was not), and a list of the approximately 600 film processors that could provide fast turnaround on film processing. These processors handled most high school game films. Some of these film processors also displayed and sold movie cameras and projectors. Harowitz thought they might also be a possible distribution channel.

Kodak had also provided Harowitz with a list of its audiovisual dealers. Again there were about 600 names on the list. Harowitz approached one of the dealers on the list, Black's, which was a major chain of camera stores in California. They showed some interest in the camera saying that, for a 20 percent markup, they might be interested in taking a couple of the units and "seeing how they move."

A final option Harowitz examined was direct mail. Direct mail brokers could provide him with a list of high schools in a given geographical area that met certain enrollment and expenditure per pupil on instructional materials criteria of the type shown in Exhibits 4 and 5. These brokers claimed that the expenditure per pupil on instructional materials was a good indicator of the general wealth of a school district.

The cost of a mailing would vary almost directly with the number of schools involved. Harowitz estimated the total cost to be 35 cents to 50 cents per school (including postage, pamphlet, and cost of using the mailing list).

The Situation in October 1976

In late September Howell and Harowitz met to finalize their cost estimates for the new product. They believed that Timelapse could manufacture a hundred units at an average cost of $95/unit. This cost was broken down as follows:

Parts	$60
Labor (2 to 4 hours at $5/hour)	15
Supervision & overhead	10
Shipping	10
Total cost	$95

Howell noted that he did not expect any significant reduction in parts costs even if the volume produced was substantially greater, since the parts were standard items and no production volume Timelapse could envisage would result in significant volume discounts.

They estimated that the total start-up costs would amount to between $3,000 and $3,500. The breakdown of this estimate is shown in Exhibit 6.

By late September a working model of the remote control unit had been completed. The "working model" was inferior to the final product Timelapse was considering building in that it did not have a fast reverse option and was too large to be operated with one hand. Harowitz took it to five of the football coaches on the Peninsula and in the rural area south of San Jose whom he had interviewed earlier to obtain their individual reactions. He found that initially they did not take full advantage of the potential of the unit. They continued to behave as before, using the six frames/second speed and going over particularly complex plays several times so they could concentrate on the moves of one player at a time and could critique his performance. Harowitz would usually then suggest that they try

EXHIBIT 6

STARTUP COSTS TO PRODUCE AND MARKET THE TIMELAPSE REMOTE CONTROL UNIT FOR THE ATHLETIC MARKET

Prototype design (3 units):	
Design labour	$ 520
Parts and equipment	350
Documentation—engineering drawings, etc.	500
Press release preparation	100
Brochure—design and printing*	500
Executive time	
Mr. Howell	300
Mr. Harowitz (100 hours)	600
Miscellaneous expenses—mail, phone, etc.	400
Total startup costs	$3,270

* Note that this brochure was for the use of distributors. If direct mail alone was used this cost would be avoided.

looking at complex plays using the three frames/second. The coaches found that this was generally slow enough that they could absorb the information even in fairly complex plays on one pass through the film. A couple of the coaches actually used the unit as they were going over a game film with their team, and they liked using the three frames/second speed for this purpose. One coach remarked that since he sometimes spent up to ten hours a week viewing game films the unit could probably save him a substantial amount of time. When asked if they would buy the unit if it were priced at $250, four emphatically said they would and the other was equally emphatic in saying he wouldn't. The latter simply didn't think it was worth the money.

It was with this information fresh in his mind that Howell sat down in early October to prepare his recommendations for Lewis and the Board of Directors, which was scheduled to meet on October 15. He wanted to present to them a concrete set of recommendations. He was particularly concerned about the distribution issue and to a lesser extent about pricing. As he sat there he was deeply conscious of the fact that he, Lewis, Chandler, and all the other shareholders had an important financial stake in the company. To all, the success of the company was critical. As he reviewed the information, one point kept recurring in his thoughts: ''Timelapse is a very small company and one bad mistake at this point will kill it.''

DE CORDOVA MUSEUM

L. Frank Demmler
Christopher H. Lovelock

Frederick P. Walkey, executive director of the De Cordova and Dana Museum and Park[1] in Lincoln, Massachusetts, sat back in his office and paused for reflection. He had been executive director when De Cordova opened its doors on September 30, 1950. In three months' time, De Cordova would be celebrating its 25th anniversary. At issue, said Walkey, was: "Where do we go from here?" As a first step, a market research study had been commissioned. The initial results had recently been received.

HISTORY OF THE MUSEUM

The Museum's original benefactor was Julian de Cordova. Born in New York in 1851, he had started in business at 16 with a New York tea broker. Discovering the universal key to success, he married Lizzie Dana, daughter of Thomas Dana, one of Boston's most prominent wholesale grocers, and entered his father-in-law's business.

Copyright © 1976 by the President and Fellows of Harvard College, Harvard Business School case 9–576–186.

[1] Hereafter referred to as "De Cordova" or "the museum."

Striving for social and financial prominence set the pattern for his entire life. De Cordova traveled extensively around the world, since this was "expected" of people of his "status." On these tours, he bought art objects—again, because it was expected of the upper class. However, while others were collecting masterpieces, Julian was attracted to "glittery knick-knacks" (as one art expert later described the collection). His purchases ranged from cuneiform inscriptions through Chinese screens to Italian paintings. While de Cordova believed his ultimate collection to be worth $2 million, it was appraised at only $20,000 after his death.

His home, which was later to house the museum, began as a simple wood frame structure in the middle of his scenic property in Lincoln, Massachusetts, near Boston. Subsequently, Mr. and Mrs. de Cordova

> . . . covered the wood frame with a layer of red brick gothic ornament to create what they felt was a true castellated mansion. Its turrets, aping the picturesque effects of a Norman chateau, clashed badly with the soft contours of the hilly landscape. The interior echoed this contrived elegance; a

grand double staircase looked out through a stained glass window onto a formal terrace. As in other wealthy contemporaries' homes, ornate fireplaces, inlaid furniture, and period decoration were the rule. But here, styles and periods were piled on top of one another with no semblance of harmony.[2]

As he grew older and his feeling of self-importance increased, de Cordova decided to leave a monument to his name and allow future generations to appreciate his collection. In 1930, he made the decision to leave his house and collection to the town of Lincoln and to provide a $1 million endowment. After some renovation, he opened his home as a museum in 1938. However, it was not until his death in 1945 at age 94 that the resultant De Cordova and Dana Museum and Park (named after both Mr. de Cordova and his wife's family) began to evolve.

Formation of the Museum and Park

Creation of the formal museum took five years. Operating control was vested in the museum's elected board of directors, comprised of Lincoln residents. The will was unclear, but a lawsuit brought by the Town of Lincoln determined that Mr. de Cordova had intended the museum to be opened to everyone, not just to residents of Lincoln. This lawsuit created ill will between the museum and some Lincoln residents, which occasionally still flared up. A particular source of irritation were activities that drew crowds exceeding the museum's parking facilities, so that visitors' cars lined the local streets, even though overflow parking for several thousand cars was available in a nearby field.

The first problem in developing the museum was the nature of Julian de Cordova's collection. On the advice of art experts, the board decided that the existing collection was not a suitable basis for a museum. The experts were instructed to select the most worthy and representative

[2] Herbert Levine, *The Life and Mind of Julian de Cordova* (Lincoln, Mass.: De Cordova Museum Press, 1973).

pieces, which would be displayed in Mr. de Cordova's honor, and to liquidate the remainder. However, while the $1 million endowment was considered sufficient to finance the operation of the museum, it was not adequate to acquire a new collection.

Recognizing these constraints, the board decided to view the museum and park as a center for the arts, involving as many people as possible. The thrust of De Cordova's activities would be threefold:

Exhibitions would be composed of borrowed works—since the museum could not afford to buy a collection—and built around particular themes, with an emphasis on contemporary American art.

The school was to emphasize active participation in art, through such things as drawing and painting classes, rather than "passive" classes in subjects such as art appreciation.

Special events would complement exhibitions through lectures and provide exposure to other art forms, like music, which were not available elsewhere in De Cordova's local environment.

In 1949, the board chose Frederick P. Walkey as executive director to implement these policies. Walkey, who was 27 at the time, had attended Duke University and later undertaken a joint degree program in education and fine arts at Tufts University and the Museum of Fine Arts School in Boston. Although an active artist himself, he had no previous experience in arts administration.

DE CORDOVA'S CURRENT SITUATION

The museum was situated in Lincoln, a low-density, upper income suburb of 4,900 residents, located 13 miles northwest of Boston (Exhibit 1). Although Lincoln had once been on the periphery of Greater Boston, in recent years new suburbs had grown up north and west of the town. De Cordova was about 40 minutes driving time from central Boston; however, the museum location was not served by public transportation.

EXHIBIT 1
MAP OF EASTERN MASSACHUSETTS

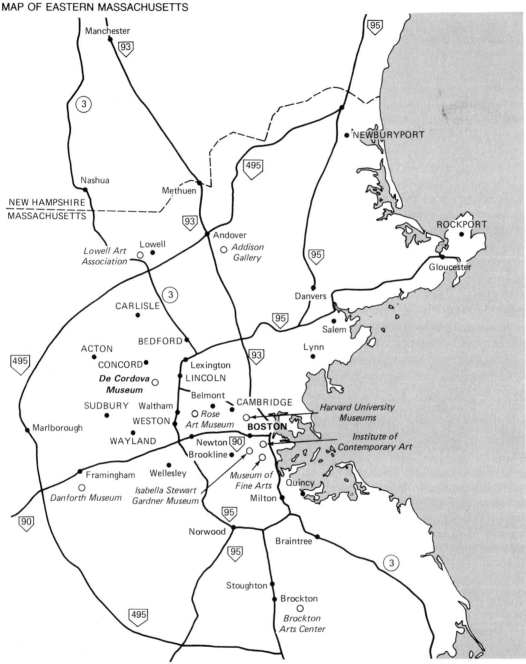

The original home had been renovated to house galleries and executive offices. With the aid of folding chairs, one of the galleries could also be used as a 200-seat makeshift "auditorium." The school operated out of separate buildings; in 1966, $250,000 had been raised to build four studios, and three more studios were later constructed in the caretaker's building. In 1974, an outdoor amphitheater was opened, which had allowed De Cordova to expand its activities for approximately two and a half months during the summer. Outdoor sculptures were located throughout the 30-acre park.

In addition to the remainder of Julian de Cordova's collection, the museum had accumulated its own permanent collection of 350 contemporary works by New England artists. Walkey hoped to expand this in the future to make it the best of its kind in the world. De Cordova also had a 1,450-volume library and a collection of 15,000 slides.

In its 25 years, the museum had established its reputation within the immediate geographic area and among informed art circles in Boston; however, Walkey believed that this reputation had not extended as much as was possible to the general public. In planning for the future, he hoped to be able to gear offerings more closely to patrons' needs, to swell membership lists, and to increase attendance at the exhibitions. He was concerned that membership had dropped slightly in recent years and that attendance at exhibitions had also slipped (Exhibit 2).

Over 50 museums were located in Greater Boston. Nonetheless, Walkey believed that only a handful could be realistically compared with De Cordova and that none were closely competitive in terms of offerings (Exhibit 3). On the other hand, he did recognize that there was strong competition from these and similar institutions for individual and corporate memberships, as well as for contributions. In his view, this provided an even greater incentive for upgrading De Cordova's public image.

De Cordova's Mission

Like many organizations that had grown under the leadership of one person, De Cordova reflected the beliefs and values of its executive director. Mr. Walkey's goal for De Cordova was "to make the arts an integral part of the lives of as many people as possible in the area it can serve." Elaborating on his philosophy, he said:

> I see De Cordova as an arts center, a social force in the community, not a museum in the conventional

EXHIBIT 2
DE CORDOVA MUSEUM STATISTICS 1950–1974

	Fall Term Enrollment		Total Classes Offered	Number of Associates (year end)*	Annual Sunday Attendance	Total Annual Income	Total Annual Expenses	Trust Income	Class Income	Associates Income
	Children	Adults								
1950	180	60	13	0	—	$ 34,000	$ 31,000	$ 33,000	$ 1,000	—
1955	215	332	42	619	10,210	85,000	86,000	50,000	19,800	5,400
1960	184	222	27	841	11,500	132,000	11,500	77,500	22,700	13,000
1965	175	300	35	2,055	13,500	203,000	196,000	80,100	33,800	33,500
1970	159	709	60	3,273	16,314	400,600	398,800	105,900	103,000	73,300
1971	220	724	73	3,014	16,789	399,000	395,100	109,700	122,600	71,600
1972	181	872	84	3,030	17,500	494,400	517,500	111,400	141,800	78,900
1973	176	924	95	2,657	30,500	495,000	503,000	110,900	152,600	87,100
1974	166	1,034	91	2,698	23,000	578,200	552,800	132,900	226,400	105,100

* Principal membership category.
Source: De Cordova Museum records.

ADDISON GALLERY OF AMERICAN ART, Phillips Academy, Andover. The Gallery, a department of Phillips Academy, displayed rotating exhibitions from its own permanent collection of contemporary American art. The primary goal of the Gallery was to serve the educational needs of the Academy and surrounding communities; it had participated with schools and institutions in the area to meet those needs. Admission free; 1974 attendance: 30,000; 1974 operation budget: $125,000.

BROCKTON ARTS CENTER, Brockton. The Brockton Arts Center displayed varied exhibitions of craft work, sculpture, etc. It offered Art Workshop classes plus lectures, concerts, films, and seminars. Admission: $1.00; 1974–75 attendance: 20,000; 1974–75 operating budget: $187,000.

BUSCH-REISINGER MUSEUM, Harvard University, Cambridge. The Busch-Reisinger housed Scandinavian, German, Austrian, and Swiss art from the Middle Ages to the present. In addition to temporary exhibitions, the Museum offered lectures, films, and concerts. Admission free; no data available on attendance or operating budget.

DANFORTH MUSEUM, Framingham. Co-founded by Framingham State College, this new museum was supported jointly by its membership and the College. It had a small permanent collection of prints, mostly of French and German origin. It was planned to mount exhibitions of 1½–4 months duration which would include displays of sculpture (both ancient and modern), craftwork, and paintings. Educational activities included plans for school groups, internships for students from local art schools and study grants for senior citizens. Admission free.

FOGG ART MUSEUM, Harvard University, Cambridge. The Fogg displayed permanent collections, which ranged from Egyptian antiquities through Cambodian sculpture to contemporary American art, as well as temporary exhibitions. In addition to formally organized educational programs for the Harvard community, the Museum offered lectures, guided tours, and gallery talks. Admission free; no data available on attendance or operating budget.

ISABELLA STEWART GARDNER MUSEUM, Boston. Fenway Court, built by Mrs. Gardner in the style of a 15th century Venetian palace, was incorporated as a museum in 1900. Her purpose was to create an atmosphere for the enjoyment of flowers, music and art. The collection of paintings, sculptures, tapestries, stained glass, furniture, and other objets d'art had remained unchanged since her death in 1924. The greatest strength of the collections was in Italian Renaissance and 17th century Dutch painting. Music recitals were held at the Museum on Tuesdays, Thursdays, and Sundays. Admission: $1.00 Sundays, free other days. 1974 attendance: 190,757; 1974 operating budget: $793,150.

INSTITUTE OF CONTEMPORARY ART, Boston. Maintaining collections of local artists, the Institute specialized in innovative temporary exhibitions of contemporary art, particularly in New England. A primary goal of the Institute was to give exposure to young artists through their own temporary shows. Admission $1.00; no data available on attendance or operating budget.

LOWELL ART ASSOCIATION, Lowell. Housed in the birthplace of James A. M. Whistler, the Association exhibited its Whistler and contemporary collections as well as presenting temporary exhibitions of contemporary American art. Other activities included lectures, films, concerts, and educational programs. Admission free; no data available on attendance or operating budget.

MUSEUM OF FINE ARTS, Boston. Largest of Boston's museums, the Museum of Fine Arts displayed its varied collections ranging from Egyptian, Greek, and Roman art, through French and Flemish tapestries and American and European furnishings, to contemporary American art. The standing display was supplemented by temporary exhibitions. Other activities included educational programs through the MFA school, lectures, films, concerts, and dance recitals. Fifty percent of the Museum's membership resided within a five-mile radius of the MFA. Admission: $2.50; 1974 attendance: 535,006; 1974 operating budget: $5,292,00.

ROSE ART MUSEUM, Brandeis University, Waltham. The Rose Museum was primarily an educational resource for Brandeis. Emphasizing modern and contemporary art, the Museum offered exhibitions of works from its own permanent collection and occasionally of those of New England artists. Admission free; 1974 attendance: 10,000; 1974 operating budget: $50,000.

sense of the term, where we squirrel art objects away.

The past decade had been spent expanding De Cordova's reputation further afield. Almost without exception, descriptions of the exhibitions presented by De Cordova could be prefaced by "the first of its kind presented in New England" (and occasionally, in the nation or worldwide). Innovative and unique exhibitions had given De Cordova an international reputation in knowledgeable art circles. Walkey remarked:

> I think we can say without contradiction that, exclusive of the [Boston] Museum of Fine Arts, the exhibitions being presented by the De Cordova Museum are more important artistically and more comprehensive than those presented by other museums in Greater Boston.

The executive director spoke enthusiastically of particular exhibitions, often using phrases such as "spectacularly beautiful," "dumbfounded visitors," "simply fantastic," and "first in the United States." He also emphasized their academic significance. However, attendance fluctuated widely and Walkey conceded that a glowing press review was no guarantee that an exhibition would prove popular with the public. Attendance at two recent exhibitions had been disappointing, although a third had been most successful.

Walkey found it difficult to accept the "no-growth" policy for De Cordova advocated by several board members, who exhorted: "Keep it a little jewel box, which we've proved we can manage successfully." He put the issue in terms of stagnation versus growth:

> I think that an institution either grows or it contracts. It's impossible to stay the same. There's a parallel with plants here. The process of growth is a regenerative activity. It helps an institution to renew itself.

Early expansion of physical facilities to provide new services to existing patrons was impossible because of the state of the economy. Thus the only short-term alternative was to expand the market served by De Cordova.

ORGANIZATION

The De Cordova organization (Exhibit 4) reflected its several activities. A seven-member board of directors oversaw the operation of the museum, with primary responsibilities in the financial area, including approval of annual budgets and determination of any capital expenditures.

The executive director was ultimately responsible for operation of all parts of De Cordova, and Walkey was directly involved in each to varying degrees. Exhibitions were under the curator, Eva Jacob; the assistant director, Miriam Jagger, was in charge of special events and financial management; while Katherine Steichen was director of the school. Ann Russell, development director, was responsible for soliciting individual and corporate memberships and for seeking grants.

Finances

In 1974, De Cordova achieved a surplus of income over expenses of $25,382 (Exhibit 5), the largest in its history. Revenues in that year totaled $578,217. The three largest sources of income were the school (39 percent), the trusts (23 percent), and individual memberships (15 percent). Other smaller income sources included contributions (7 percent) and exhibition admissions (7 percent).

Total expenses in 1974 were $552,835. Because the museum was on a cash budget, its expenditures did not include depreciation, and capital expenditures were included in the total. The school accounted for 34 percent of total expenditures, with three-fifths of school outlays being for the salaries of teachers and administrators. Salaries were also the largest item among administration and development expenses (22 percent of total); program expenses amounted to $106,563 (19 percent), but the salary component here was much smaller. Exhibition expenses, consisting primarily of insurance and transportation of exhibitions, totaled $33,307 (6 percent).

EXHIBIT 4
DE CORDOVA AND DANA MUSEUM AND PARK: ORGANIZATION

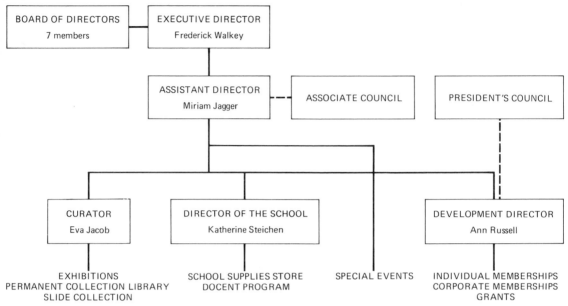

By comparison, the Boston Museum of Fine Arts and its school had operating expenses in 1972–73 of $5.7 million (of which the school accounted for $1.2 million) and an operating deficit of $139,000.

Development

Ann Russell, development director, had joined De Cordova in May 1974. A graduate of Radcliffe College (B.A.) and Brandeis University (M.A. and Ph.D.), Russell came to De Cordova from the Society for the Preservation of New England Antiquities where she had been membership and public affairs director.

Five levels of *individual membership* were available at varying annual dues: Associate ($30), comprising 95 percent of the total; Supporting ($50), Sustaining ($100), Contributing ($250), and Patron ($500). Individual membership revenues totaled $86,375 in 1974. The number of Associates that year was 2,698, significantly be-

low the high of 3,464 in 1968. Seventy percent of the members came from Lincoln and seven surrounding towns (Exhibit 6); the balance came from another 80 towns and cities. The benefits offered all members were:

- Free admission to exhibitions and summer concerts;

- Invitations to previews of exhibitions and receptions for artists;

- Fifteen percent discount on tuition for all classes (down from 20 percent in 1974);

- Priority for classes, concerts, lectures, films, etc.;

- Members' newsletters and announcements of all exhibitions and events;

- Use of the museum's lending library;

- Admission to "members only" events.

Members paying higher annual dues were en-

EXHIBIT 5
DE CORDOVA MUSEUM FINANCIAL REPORT, 1974
(With Comparable Figures for 1973)

	1973	1974
Income		
De Cordova Trusts	110,867	132,904.33
Corporate Membership	11,600	18,700.00
Individual Membership	75,526	86,375.25
Contributions	32,786	41,864.63
Grants	3,000	15,750.00
Sale of Publications	2,263	2,541.20
Admission, Exhibitions	32,528	37,368.60
Admission, Concerts & Lectures	10,516	8,786.44
Museum School & Store	177,563	226,430.24
Benefit Events	25,251	0
All other	13,055	7,496.50
Total Income	494,955	578,217.19
Expense		
Administration & Development	101,566	123,929.12
Program (exhibitions, events, library, collections)	72,303	106,562.74
Museum School & Art Supply Store	171,562	188,733.04
Buildings & Grounds (maintenance, repair)	57,504	58,248.50
Benefit Events	18,617	0
Capital Expense (furnishings, equipment, construction)	32,180	17,420.00
Printing & Publications	49,265	57,941.12
Total Expense	502,997	552,835.17
Excess of Income Over Expense (Expense over Income)	(−$8,042)	$25,382.02

titled to such extra benefits as complimentary copies of museum publications and invitations to events with attendance limitations. Lists of members and their levels of membership were included in the museum's annual reports.

During school registration, memberships were pushed strongly on the basis that membership tuition discounts, averaging $10 per class, could offset the annual dues. It was hoped that such new members would continue their memberships even when they were no longer taking courses. In 1974, over 800 of the students at the De Cordova School were members.

Another source of new members was the Associate Council, an organization of De Cordova members. Russell worked closely with the council to generate a list of potential members, then sent out informational brochures and membership applications and arranged for the council members to make personal follow-ups. In coordination with Miriam Jagger, she encouraged council members to invite prospective members to town events. However, the result of these efforts was that the same friends were being brought to these town events time and time again without any appreciable success in enrolling them as members.

A crucial task was to get new members to renew for a second year. Historically, the first renewal had been critical for continuing mem-

EXHIBIT 6
DE CORDOVA MEMBERSHIP BY CITY OF RESIDENCE, MID–1975

City or Town*	No. of Individual Memberships (all categories)**	Total Population
Acton	94	14,770
Bedford	117	13,513
Belmont	68	28,225
Boston	77	641,971
Cambridge	61	110,361
Carlisle	52	4,800
Concord	298	16,148
Lexington	388	31,886
Lincoln	433	4,900
Sudbury	203	13,506
Wayland	444	13,461
Wellesley	75	28,051
Weston	258	10,870
Other	682	
Total	3,250	

* Only cities and towns with 50 or more members are listed separately.
** Individual membership carried year-round family benefits.
Source: 1970 Census and De Cordova Records.

bership. The major effort in this area was an intensive direct-mail effort. There had been an overall renewal rate of 66 percent in 1974, with 847 new members. Typically, there was a 40 percent renewal rate at the end of the first year and 70–80 percent in succeeding years.

The *Corporate Memberships* program was in its fourth year when Russell assumed her post. At the end of 1974, there were 57 members, up from 37 in 1973, who contributed a total of $18,700. The goal for 1975 was 75 members and $24,000 in income. Corporations were offered a group of benefits including loans of works from the De Cordova permanent collection, in-plant programs (usually lunch-hour lectures at the place of business), company evenings at the museum, and complimentary passes for employees. In the history of the program, only the art-work loans and complimentary passes had been used with any regularity, although Russell hoped to encourage corporate members to take advantage of the other benefits as a way of ensuring continuing membership.

Foundations and *Government Grants*. Russell was also responsible for soliciting grants for specific programs or exhibitions. Formal requests were submitted at the earliest possible date, since approval generally took about nine months. Grants came from government agencies at various levels and from foundations. Grants accounted for $30,000 of income in 1974 and were made up as follows:

Source	Amount	Purpose
Codman Trust	$ 8,000	Summer concert series
National Endowment for the Arts	$ 5,000	Architecture show
Design Research	$ 1,000	Architecture show
Massachusetts Bicentennial Commission	$15,000	Amphitheater
Howard Johnson Fund	$ 1,000	Amphitheater

Russell believed that the intense competition in the area made grants unreliable as income sources. While the number of institutions applying for these funds was steadily increasing, the amounts available were decreasing because of poor stock market performance (which had cut into foundation funds) and stabilization or cutbacks in government budgets.

The Annual Appeal, directed by Russell in coordination with the assistant director, had historically consisted of a direct mailing to all members soliciting donations. In 1974 it was supplemented by a phone campaign. Over a 15-night period, more than 100 volunteers contacted every De Cordova member, referring to the mailing and emphasizing that contributions were necessary to produce the ambitious Bicentennial exhibitions. The Annual Appeal received $31,000 from 910 donors in 1974, as compared with $17,000 from 200 donors in 1973.

EXHIBITIONS

De Cordova used to present an average of six exhibitions each year. In 1974 there were five. Some 45,000 people had attended the exhibitions that year, down from 56,000 in 1973. It was thought that the gas shortage had hurt attendance in 1974, but the number of visitors had declined again during the first half of 1975.

Mr. Walkey believed that the exhibitions attracted three groups: families, "sophisticates," and "intellectuals." The families enjoyed the exhibitions and the park as family outings. The "sophisticates" were primarily interested in the social aspects of the museum. The "intellectuals" appreciated the educational value of the exhibitions and took advantage of the lectures and other educational opportunities. Informal surveys in the past had shown that proximity to De Cordova was a primary determinant of attendance at exhibitions. Generally, a majority of the patrons came from Lincoln and seven surrounding towns. A visitor looking briefly at each exhibit could tour most De Cordova exhibitions in half an hour or less. There were 90–120 items displayed at the typical exhibition.

Admission to an exhibition was $1.50 for non-members, but was free for members and all residents of Lincoln. Admission fees and statistics for other selected museums in Boston and Eastern Massachusetts are shown in Exhibit 3.

Eva Jacob, the curator, had primary responsibility for conceptualizing and executing the exhibitions presented by the Museum. Jacob was also responsible for De Cordova's permanent collection, library, and slide collection. The permanent collection reflected the museum's emphasis on contemporary American art in New England. Each year De Cordova added to this collection, primarily through solicitation of gifts. The library and the slide collection were used for internal research and were also available to members and students.

Prior to becoming curator in September 1974, Jacob had been a part-time lecturer and researcher at the Museum. Additionally, she had taught art and art theory at the Boston Architectural Center, Radcliffe Institute, and Tufts University. Discussing her job, she said:

> I think of the curator's work as broadly educative: helping the museum assemble significant exhibitions, and then making each of them count as much as possible to the viewer. I'm particularly interested in providing our visitors with the kind of background which will enable them to relate exhibitions to significant aspects of the past and present.

Development and Promotion of Exhibitions

Because of the financial constraints facing De Cordova, all exhibitions were based upon themes for which representative works could be found in or near New England. The major costs of exhibitions—the insurance and transportation of the works involved—increased rapidly with distance from the museum. Exhibitions took anywhere from six months to a year from inception to completion, with the first step the generation of a theme. The executive director noted:

> You don't succeed in this area by following, because people out there don't know what they want.

It's my job as an expert to provide the leadership of picking what the people should see and then selling them on the fact that if they want to be people of some cultural standing, then they have to get on our bandwagon.

Themes resulted from brainstorming sessions, at which Walkey, Jacob, and Jagger sought appropriate concepts or trends in the art world which had not received attention but which, in their opinion, deserved it. Themes had to be consistent with De Cordova's philosophy, finances, and facilities. While they emphasized contemporary American art, this was not an iron-clad constraint, and the exhibitions displayed considerable diversity in scope (Exhibit 7). The "Spirit of Independence," commemorating the United States Bicentennial, had been selected as an underlying theme for all shows in 1975 and 1976.

Following theme selection, the next task was to find a coherent group of works of art to illustrate the concept. Access to appropriate works had grown steadily easier because De Cordova had developed a reputation—particularly in New England—as an innovative and prestigious sponsor. Museums elsewhere often had reciprocal arrangements with De Cordova for displaying each other's works.

Exhibitors derived several benefits from displaying their works at De Cordova. Private galleries were able to expose their pieces to people whom they might not normally reach and thus generate sales (De Cordova's policy was to accept no commissions on works which were sold as a result of display at the museum). Additionally, participation in a De Cordova show might enhance a work's value. Private collectors received ego satisfaction from having audiences appreciate their possessions, while artists—especially the younger ones—enjoyed the exposure that De Cordova provided.

As the preparations for an exhibition progressed, the development director tried to raise the funds. Although each exhibition was funded from the annual budget approved by the board, contingency plans provided for enlargement based upon receipt of additional money from outside sources, such as government agencies and foundations.

In keeping with the educational spirit of De Cordova, Jacob supervised activities to supplement the exhibitions. These included a catalog to provide a historical background of the exhibition and describe the individual exhibits, a 12-minute audiovisual presentation, and a variety of lectures. Weekly evening lectures for members during the course of the exhibition were given by outside experts, and Museum staff members addressed guided tours which had been booked in advance.

Promotion took three forms. Members were sent brochures announcing and describing each exhibition; these included a tearoff coupon to make reservations for the scheduled weekly lectures. The media, through press releases and reviews by the critics, also served to promote exhibitions. According to the staff, the most important form of promotion was word-of-mouth among patrons. With this in mind, a series of activities was tied in with the opening of each exhibition. Previews were arranged for members on the weekend prior to the official opening. An informal opening on the afternoon of opening day attracted families, while the official opening took place in the evening. It was believed that success in these activities had a snowball effect which contributed to the overall success of the exhibition.

SPECIAL EVENTS

Although many of her previous responsibilities had been assumed by the curator and development director, Miriam Jagger had retained control of special events in addition to her responsibility for financial management at De Cordova. She had been assistant director since 1955.

Special events included all activities beyond the scope of standard exhibition operations—

EXHIBIT 7
RECENT EXHIBITIONS AT DE CORDOVA, 1973–1975

1973

"Refracted Images" surveyed the field of contemporary plastic and light sculpture. Containing work by 20 outstanding American and European artists, "Refracted Images" was the first comprehensive exhibition of its kind in New England.

"The Boston Printmakers' 25th Annual Exhibition" was presented under the joint sponsorship of De Cordova and The Boston Printmakers. More than 1500 prints were entered in the competition for the show, and 133 were selected for exhibition.

"Sculpture in the Park" was a display of large-scale outdoor sculpture during the summer months.

"New Talent" was an exhibition of paintings, prints, drawings and sculpture by 33 young New England artists.

"The Super-Realist Vision" was another survey of an important contemporary art movement (like "Refracted Images") and, again, the first major exhibition of its kind in this area.

"Primal Images" was devoted to recent work by four masters of 20th century art—Miro, Calder, Appel and Dubuffet.

1974

"Lytle-Offner-Zieman" was the first major exhibit in New England featuring the work of these artists.

"American Metalsmiths '74" containing over 200 objects (jewelry, silver, and hollow ware), by 50 distinguished metalsmiths, mirrored the diversity and vitality which characterized American metalworking. Emphasis throughout the exhibition was on form, rather than function.

"Drawings" was an open competition exhibition which demonstrated the activity of artists in the New England area and allowed viewers to expand their own ideas of drawing and the purpose of drawing for artists. The exhibition was described as "a feast of styles, techniques, and ideas."

"Corporations Collect" presented 75 works from the collections of 15 different firms. The exhibition was designed to hail the recent trend of corporations to develop their own collections and to salute the leaders of this movement.

"New Architecture in New England" presented architecture as art, to a museum public, through large mural photographs and multi-media slide projections which showed each building in relation to its surroundings. The exhibition's purpose was to recognize outstanding recent architectural design and to increase public understanding and appreciation of innovative architectural design.

1975 (First Half)

"New England Women" was a group show of recent work by women artists in New England.

"The British Are Coming" reviewed the British art scene in the last decade, including established masters, like Moore and Hepworth, as well as the new generation of artists of the 1970's.

"Bed and Board" was a craft exhibition which presented the skill and imaginativeness of contemporary woodworkers and quiltmakers. Contemporary furniture was complemented by a small collection of Shaker furniture and artifacts.

fund raising, exhibition supplements, and other art-form exposure. An important aspect of special events management was the coordination of the relevant Museum resources and people.

A key group used by Jagger in planning and execution of special events was the Associate Council, which consisted of eight officers and a representative from each of the 13 communities which had a sufficiently large and active De Cordova membership. Representatives were responsible for organizing their own town's membership and for arranging community events at the Museum. The Associate Council organized volunteers when necessary, aided in membership drives, and provided inputs during the planning of special events.

During the course of the year, Jagger attempted to have at least one special fund-raising event involving members. A "De Cordova Folk Festival" was scheduled for the summer of 1975. This would include arts and craft demonstrations, country dancing, folk songs, community singing, and a craft fair. In addition to raising funds, these events were designed to achieve greater member involvement in the Museum.

A second group of special events (174 in 1973) revolved around the exhibitions. These were usually gallery talks and tours provided for elementary schools, high schools, colleges, adult study groups, civic organizations, and membership groups. The development director worked closely with Jagger on these activities to maximize their impact on membership enrollments and renewals.

The third set of activities was intended to expand De Cordova's cultural offerings, primarily in the musical field. Following construction of the amphitheater, a series of 12 Sunday afternoon concerts was presented between June 23 and September 8, 1974. These concerts attracted an average crowd of 1,000 which represented the parking and seating capacity. The only promotion consisted of press releases and announcements mailed to members (Exhibit 8). Jagger planned to expand the series in 1975 to include

Saturday afternoon performances as well. Admission to the concerts and all museum facilities was $2.00 (up from $1.50 in 1974) for the public and free for all members.

During the remainder of the year, Jagger arranged an average of 25 lectures, films, and musical concerts. These were held in a museum gallery, which could be fitted with 200 seats for the purpose. However, this arrangement was not totally satisfactory since the acoustics were poor and the room tended to overheat when full.

The average admission fee was $3.00, since Jagger believed that members should have the opportunity of attending presentations at modest cost. With capacity fixed and performers' fees rising, Jagger had had increasing difficulty in paying high-quality performers. Always filled to capacity by members, these events required only the mailing of announcements by way of promotion.

Jagger expressed concern over the capacity of the "auditorium," since it limited the number of members who could take advantage of these opportunities. Like other De Cordova staff members, she also wondered if the events program might not be expanded to include more of the performing arts to help make De Cordova a center for all the arts, as opposed to its present emphasis on the visual arts. If such a transformation were to be made, auditorium facilities would be a critical factor.

THE SCHOOL

The school boasted some 3,000 class enrollments annually. Its director, Katherine Steichen, had joined De Cordova as a staff designer/photographer in 1969, upon receiving a Bachelor of Fine Arts in Painting degree from the University of Illinois. In 1971, Steichen became the first director of the school with studio experience; her predecessors had all been art historians.

The school year had three terms, two 15-week sessions in the fall and spring and an eight-week summer program. On average, 100 classes were

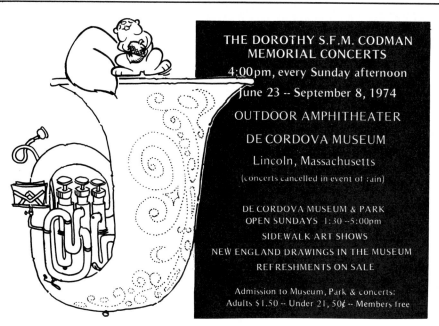

THE DOROTHY S.F.M. CODMAN
MEMORIAL CONCERTS
4:00pm, every Sunday afternoon
June 23 -- September 8, 1974

OUTDOOR AMPHITHEATER

DE CORDOVA MUSEUM

Lincoln, Massachusetts

(concerts cancelled in event of rain)

DE CORDOVA MUSEUM & PARK
OPEN SUNDAYS 1:30 --5:00pm
SIDEWALK ART SHOWS
NEW ENGLAND DRAWINGS IN THE MUSEUM
REFRESHMENTS ON SALE

Admission to Museum, Park & concerts:
Adults $1.50 -- Under 21, 50¢ -- Members free

DE CORDOVA SUMMER CONCERTS

JUNE 23
THE EMPIRE BRASS QUINTET
Five young "super-virtuosi" — two trumpets, horn, trombone, tuba — in a program of classical, jazz and avant-garde music.

JUNE 30
ARS CAMERALIS ENSEMBLE
A nationally acclaimed woodwind quintet performing music from the Baroque, Romantic, Classical and Contemporary periods.

JULY 7
CHORUS PRO MUSICA
Boston's distinguished choral group, under the direction of Alfred Nash Patterson, in an "all-American" program.

JULY 14
AMERICAN CHAMBER BALLET
Classical, modern and jazz ballet, performed by a dynamic young troupe hailed in appearances throughout the U.S.

JULY 21
NEWTON WAYLAND & FRIENDS
Versatile composer/conductor Newton Wayland directs an ensemble of voices and instruments in works by Ives, Jelly Roll Morton, Gershwin, Wayland and others.

JULY 28
COUNTRY GRANOLA & WHEATSTRAW
A tandem performance by two popular four-man groups, both masters of folk, blue grass and country rock.

AUGUST 4
NEW HUNGARIAN QUARTET
Chamber music by a string quartet that has won rave reviews in concerts throughout the U.S. and is currently in residence at Yale University.

AUGUST 11
NEW ENGLAND DINOSAUR
Boston's first repertory modern dance theater displays its own distinct blend of talent, wit and showmanship.

AUGUST 18
GARY BURTON QUARTET
Gary Burton, wizard of the vibraphone, leads his nationally famed group in the performance of sophisticated rock and improvisational jazz.

AUGUST 25
CAMBRIDGE BRASS QUINTET
A brilliant chamber ensemble plays music from the Renaissance, Baroque and Contemporary eras.

SEPTEMBER 1
MIKE SEEGER & BUCK N' WING
A gala Labor Day celebration featuring "people's music" by folk singer Mike Seeger and members of the Buck n' Wing Musicians Cooperative.

SEPTEMBER 8
BRANDEIS CHAMBER ORCHESTRA
Using instruments of the Baroque and Classical periods, the Brandeis Orchestra, directed by Robert Koff, recreates sounds and styles of the past.

offered each term, directed by some 50 teachers and attracting about 1,000 students. Maximum enrollment in each class was 12 for courses in jewelry, silver, ceramics, and metal sculpture and 18 for painting and drawing classes. Tuition ranged from $65 to $90, depending upon materials used and the need for models. Museum members received a 15 percent discount on tuition, as well as registration priority. With daytime, evening, and weekend scheduling of classes, the school optimized use of its facilities as well as offering flexibility for students.

The objective was to involve students in actual creation of art through studio courses. Although certain basic courses (painting, drawing, etc.) were offered every term, the majority were dependent on the interests and expertise of the teachers. Typically, artists in the Boston area, who often taught at other schools and universities, contacted Steichen with course proposals. One of De Cordova's advantages was that it could offer multiple teachers in a particular area, such as ceramics. Teachers were paid on an hourly basis. If a course did not attain an adequate enrollment, typically around two-thirds of its planned maximum, it was dropped from the curriculum.

The students were children, teenagers, and adults. Some were professional artists, but most were novices. Five-sixths of them were De Cordova members, attracted in part by the member benefits. The school enjoyed a high reputation in the Boston area, and classes were typically filled by repeat students and those who had heard about the school from present and former students.

The summer session was thematic in nature. In addition to regular studio classes, the curriculum included programs for both children and adults, held in tents on the museum grounds. Steichen tried to bring the selected themes to life by seeking artists who operated in the proper context; Indian and Japanese artists had demonstrated the themes of the past two summers. Children accounted for 25–30 percent of summer students,

but for less than 10 percent of fall and spring enrollments.

Steichen also developed a docent program to supplement the museum's educational offerings. Twelve volunteers, drawn from the membership and trained in art and communication skills, were available as museum lecturers, community speakers, and adjunct art teachers in schools. This program was made possible by a grant from the Massachusetts Council on the Arts and Humanities.

PLANNING FOR THE FUTURE

Over the years, the board of directors had repeatedly faced the issue of expanding De Cordova's offerings and facilities. Six years earlier, the board had commissioned plans for new buildings with an estimated cost at that time of over $1 million. These plans, which were never implemented, would have almost doubled the exhibition space and added a 400-seat auditorium as well as other improvements. Now, expansion was again being considered and information was needed to help decide what strategy would be most appropriate.

Among the shortcomings of the present facilities were the lack of storage or work space and the absence of any eating facilities. Additionally, the galleries were often crowded at weekends and enrollment at the school was constrained by the size of the present buildings. Mr. Walkey declared that the institution was "totally potbound" and that future growth was inhibited by the size of the facility. "We have the senior staff and skills to do 25–50 percent more," he said.

The only ways in which the board could evaluate the performance of the museum were through financial statements, personal observation, and discussions with Walkey and other staff members. Some board members believed that additional, more objective measures of how well De Cordova was meeting the needs of its patrons would be helpful. These issues prompted the board to undertake a market research study to aid membership solicitation, long-range program and facilities planning, fundraising, and such operational areas as prices.

Once the questionnaire had been designed, volunteers were organized to administer it. Over a three-month period, 434 visitors were interviewed as they entered the museum; interviewees were selected at the discretion of the volunteers. Similar questionnaires were administered over the phone to 96 De Cordova members and to 80 former members. The sample of current members was stratified by home location to provide a broad geographic base of respondents. The sample of former members was restricted to those who had terminated their subscriptions one to two years prior to the survey.

The initial results were in two parts (Exhibit 9). In the first, current members were compared with former members and nonmembers to see what differences were discernible. In the second part, residents of Lincoln and the surrounding communities of Sudbury, Wayland, Lexington, Weston, Acton, Bedford, and Concord (Exhibit 1) were contrasted with the remainder in an effort to determine the impact of distance from De Cordova on behavior patterns.

STRATEGIC OPTIONS

As he reflected on his years with the museum, Mr. Walkey's thoughts turned to the future. Several broad strategic options presented themselves. One was to follow the status quo philosophy espoused by some board members. A second was to transform De Cordova into a more complete cultural center for Lincoln and surrounding towns by diversifying the present offerings and placing more emphasis on music and the performing arts. Alternatively, he could maintain the existing thrust of the institution as a contemporary arts center, but seek to expand its coverage throughout the Greater Boston area. A final option would involve both diversification and geographic expansion.

Mulling these ideas over in his mind, Walkey went over the results of the market research study once more. He knew that De Cordova's performance in terms of exhibition attendance, membership levels, and fund-raising activities could be improved, while the whole issue of penetrating the Greater Boston market more deeply needed attention. In the light of present information, he wondered what action was called for and whether any further research or analysis should be undertaken.

EXHIBIT 9 RESULTS OF DE CORDOVA MARKET RESEARCH SURVEY BROKEN DOWN BY (1) MEMBERSHIP STATUS AND (2) RESIDENCE LOCATION*

Question	Membership status						Residence location[1]			
	Former Members[2] (N = 80) No.	%	Current Members[3] (N = 157) No.	%	Nonmembers[4] (N = 373) No.	%	Inside Local Area[5] (N = 185) No.	%	Outside Local Area (N = 365) No.	%
1 Are you currently a member of the De Cordova Museum?										
Yes—Current member	0	—	157	100.0	0	—	93	50.2	55	15.1
No—Former member	80	100.0	0	—	0	—	51	21.6	28	7.7
No—nonmember	0	—	0	—	373	100.0	40	27.6	282	77.3
2 If not a member, is this your first visit to De Cordova?										
Yes	N.A.		N.A.		210	56.3	18	9.7	157	43.0
No	N.A.		N.A.		161	43.2	154	83.2	194	53.2
3 Are you familiar with the De Cordova Museum School?										
Yes	66	82.5	134	85.4	118	31.6	143	77.3	160	43.8
No [if no, skip to question 6]	2	2.5	9	5.7	107	28.7	14	7.6	88	24.1
4 Have you enrolled in classes at the School?										
Yes	42	52.5	96	61.1	12	3.2	88	47.6	54	14.8
No	22	27.5	37	23.6	104	27.9	49	26.5	99	27.1
5 When were you last enrolled in a class?										
One year ago	6	7.5	33	21.0	1	0.3	26	14.1	11	3.0
2–5 years ago	33	41.3	38	24.2	9	2.4	42	22.7	35	9.6
6 or more years ago	5	6.3	9	5.7	2	0.5	12	6.5	3	0.8
6 What do you like most about De Cordova? (*Interviewer was instructed not to prompt answers.*)										
Classes	35	43.8	63	40.1	5	1.3	55	29.7	43	11.8
Lectures or gallery talks	6	7.5	11	7.0	3	0.8	13	7.0	6	1.6
Attractive exhibitions	25	31.3	68	43.3	90	24.1	68	36.8	100	27.4
Previews	—	—	26	16.6	21	5.6	16	8.6	26	7.1
Exhibition openings	8	10.0	17	10.8	2	0.5	16	8.6	6	1.6
Pleasant grounds	14	17.5	36	22.9	95	25.5	35	18.9	99	27.1
Films	3	3.8	4	2.5	5	1.3	3	1.6	6	1.6
Summer concerts	7	8.8	38	24.2	23	6.2	37	20.0	28	7.7
Other musical events	3	3.8	5	3.2	1	0.3	6	3.2	3	0.8
Art Expo	11	13.8	20	12.7	2	0.5	15	8.1	15	4.1
Special town events	4	5.0	7	4.5	1	0.3	7	3.8	5	1.4

	n	%	n	%	n	%	n	%	n	%
Location	1	1.3	4	2.5	12	3.2	6	3.2	11	3.0
Other	27	33.8	46	29.3	38	10.2	44	23.8	61	16.7

7 What do you like least about De Cordova? *(No prompting.)*

	n	%	n	%	n	%	n	%	n	%
Classes	5	6.3	8	5.1	—	—	8	4.3	5	1.4
Previews or exhibition openings	3	3.8	9	5.7	3	0.8	11	5.9	5	1.4
Admission fees	1	1.3	3	1.9	23	6.2	5	2.7	20	5.5
Courses too expensive	1	1.3	8	5.1	4	1.1	6	3.2	6	1.6
Too modern	7	8.8	1	0.6	1	0.3	5	2.7	4	1.1
Too much mail	1	1.3	5	3.2	—	—	5	2.7	—	—
Limited exhibits	2	2.5	6	3.8	3	0.8	5	2.7	5	1.4
Don't publicize enough	2	2.5	—	—	3	0.8	2	1.1	1	0.3
Location	6	7.5	5	3.2	9	2.4	1	0.5	19	5.2
Too small	1	1.3	2	1.3	8	2.1	2	1.1	8	2.2
Other	12	15.0	28	17.8	22	5.9	32	17.3	26	7.1
Don't dislike anything	43	53.8	61	38.9	90	24.1	58	31.4	107	29.3

8 Which, if any, of the following events have you attended at the Museum?

	n	%	n	%	n	%	n	%	n	%
Lectures or galley talks	23	2.8	44	28.0	16	4.3	49	26.5	28	7.7
Previews	9	11.3	52	33.1	117	31.4	52	28.1	120	32.9
Exhibition openings	35	43.8	66	42.0	19	5.1	68	36.8	46	12.6
Films	3	3.8	26	16.6	13	3.5	19	10.3	20	5.5
Summer musical events	17	21.3	53	33.8	46	1.2	59	31.9	55	15.1
Other concerts	7	8.8	41	26.1	13	3.5	30	16.2	31	8.5
Art Expo	34	42.5	54	34.4	20	5.4	62	33.5	44	12.1
Special town events	8	10.0	29	18.5	—	—	28	15.1	7	1.9
Other	9	11.3	10	6.4	2	0.5	15	8.1	5	1.4

9 Have you visited De Cordova within the past 12 months?

	n	%	n	%	n	%	n	%	n	%
Yes	37	46.3	132	84.1	109	29.2	126	68.1	141	38.6
No *[if no, skip to question 11]*	41	51.3	16	10.2	68	18.2	38	20.5	75	20.5

10 Approximately how many times within the past 12 months have you visited the De Cordova?

	n	%	n	%	n	%	n	%	n	%
1	16	20.0	8	5.1	34	9.1	19	10.3	36	9.9
2	10	12.5	16	10.2	29	7.8	20	10.8	34	9.3
3	6	7.5	13	8.3	10	2.7	15	8.1	14	3.8
4	2	2.5	26	16.6	18	4.8	18	9.7	25	6.8
5	—	—	16	10.2	4	1.1	13	7.0	6	1.6
6–10	3	3.8	22	14.0	10	2.7	21	11.4	12	3.3
over 10	—	—	19	12.1	3	0.8	12	6.5	8	2.2

EXHIBIT 9 *(continued)*

Question	Membership status						Residence location[1]			
	Former Members[2] (N = 80)		Current Members[3] (N = 157)		Nonmembers[4] (N = 373)		Inside Local Area[5] (N = 185)		Outside Local Area (N = 365)	
	No.	%	No.	%	No.	%	No.	%	No.	%
11 Did you make today's visit to the De Cordova primarily to see the Museum or is it only one part of a larger trip including other places to visit?†										
Primarily De Cordova	N.A.	N.A.	56	93.3	344	92.2	69	97.2	291	93.3
Part of larger trip			2	3.3	24	6.4	1	1.4	16	5.1
12 If part of a larger trip, what other events were included in your trip?†										
A stop for lunch or snack	N.A.	N.A.	2	3.3	11	2.9	—	—	10	3.2
A visit to other parks			—	—	2	0.5	—	—	2	0.6
Historical spots or public places			—	—	10	2.7	—	—	5	1.6
Out for ride			4	6.7	21	5.6	4	5.6	19	6.1
Other			2	3.3	20	5.4	2	2.8	11	3.5
13 What stimulated you to come to the Museum today?†										
Museum mailing	N.A.	N.A.	11	18.3	7	1.9	12	16.9	7	2.2
Poster			—	—	8	2.1	—	—	7	2.2
Newspaper article			4	6.7	78	20.9	10	14.1	64	20.5
Radio or TV announcement			—	—	22	5.9	1	1.4	18	5.8
Word of mouth			14	23.3	136	36.5	16	22.5	107	34.3
Other			31	51.7	144	38.6	33	46.5	126	40.4
14 In the last 12 months in the Boston area, have you visited or attended:										
Other museums	39	48.8	126	80.3	291	78.0	129	69.7	296	81.0
Art classes	14	17.5	27	17.2	80	21.4	24	13.0	88	24.1
Concerts	30	37.5	91	58.0	251	67.3	109	58.9	242	66.3
Professional theater	35	43.8	90	57.3	228	61.1	100	54.1	233	63.8
Dance or ballet performances	15	18.8	50	31.8	149	39.9	54	29.2	148	40.5
15 In what capacity is the head of your household employed? (*Interviewer was to put into one of the following categories.*)										
Educator	10	12.5	16	10.2	66	17.7	20	10.8	55	15.1
Professional	41	51.3	63	40.1	138	37.0	79	42.7	144	39.5
Managerial	18	22.5	44	28.0	45	12.1	47	25.4	53	14.5
White collar	5	6.3	8	5.1	35	9.4	11	5.9	32	8.8

Blue collar	—	—	3	1.9	21	5.6	3	1.6	20	5.5
Student	—	—	4	2.5	39	10.5	6	3.2	29	7.9
Retired	2	2.5	5	3.2	12	3.2	8	4.3	10	2.7
Unemployed	3	3.8	8	5.1	10	2.7	7	3.8	13	3.6
16 Approximately what is your age?										
17 or under	—	—	4	2.5	5	1.3	3	1.6	4	1.1
18–25	1	1.3	64	40.8	136	36.5	50	27.0	127	34.8
26–45	39	48.8	62	39.5	179	48.0	88	47.6	170	46.6
Over 45	38	47.5	23	14.6	52	13.9	41	22.2	60	16.4
17 [Members and Former Members Only] Why did you join De Cordova?[6]										
Wanted to be active	3	3.8	2	1.3	N.A.					
Interested in area/town	7	8.8	7	4.5						
Philanthropic reasons	8	10.0	11	7.0						
Classes	27	33.8	33	21.0						
Children's classes	10	12.5	6	3.8						
Discounts on classes	3	3.8	—	—						
Exhibits or events	17	21.3	23	14.6						
Family	3	3.8	8	5.1						
Other	10	12.5	25	15.9						
18 [Former Members Only] Why didn't you renew your membership?[6]										
Finances	18	22.5	N.A.		N.A.					
Other interests	23	28.8								
Distance	5	6.3								
Not using facilities	19	23.7								
Children grew up	6	7.5								
Oversight	4	5.0								
No longer taking classes	16	20.0								
Other	9	11.3								

* Non-responses and "Don't Knows" are not shown in tabulations, hence responses often add to less than 100%.
1 Not all respondents gave their home location, hence membership status totals exceed residence location totals.
2 Surveyed by telephone.
3 Surveyed by telephone and at Museum.
4 Surveyed at Museum only.
5 Denotes respondents resident in Lincoln and surrounding communities of Sudbury, Wayland, Lexington, Weston, Acton, Bedford, and Concord (see Exhibit 1).
6 Up to three reasons were coded for computer analysis.
† These questions were not asked of former members, nor of the 97 current members surveyed by telephone, consequently percentages are for those interviewed at Museum only.

PART TWO

MARKET SELECTION

Market selection, along with product policy, is one of the central elements of marketing management. Product-market choice—what products to offer to which markets—is at the core of every organization's strategy. In this section of the book, we shall focus primarily on the choice of which markets to serve; the following section emphasizes decisions on which products to offer. However, these two decisions are often closely interrelated, since different markets may have different needs, and not all products (or specific formulations of a particular product) will appeal to all markets.

Several companies in the same industry may make sharply different market selection decisions. To illustrate, one cosmetics firm may concentrate on developing highly advertised cosmetics sold in department stores at high prices to a style-conscious, upscale market, while another cosmetics firm devotes its efforts to women who prefer the convenience and advice obtained from a sales representative who brings product samples to the customer's own home. A third company may concentrate on budget-minded individuals who shop in discount stores. Each firm, by choosing a different market target, is simultaneously making a decision about the marketing skills and resources required to succeed, the nature of competition likely to be encountered, the potential for growth and profitability to be obtained, and the threats and opportunities to be met in the external environment.

It is critical that an organization's managers take an active role in selecting the markets in which their firm will compete. Failure to do so may result in the firm's efforts being scattered by their attempting to be all things to all people (which is rarely a successful strategy). It may also result in the firm's losing opportunities to enter newer markets or in their remaining committed to old markets which are declining, unprofitable, or crowded with other competitors. An organization's success is dependent on the opportunities available in the market or market segments it selects, as well as on how effectively it competes in the chosen markets.

OPPORTUNITY ANALYSIS

An early step in market selection is identification and analysis of the opportunities available to the enterprise. *Opportunity analysis* involves identifying markets of good size and growth potential. The competitive structure of the prospective market should allow for profitable entry into it, while the environmental threats and opportunities should be within the organization's capabilities. Opportunity analysis requires the organization to match its own strengths and weaknesses against the requirements for success in each market it is contemplating entering. When a company's own particular strengths—or "distinctive competences"— match the key success requirements of a particular market opportunity, then the company is likely to have a differential advantage which would allow it to become successful in that market if it can design and implement a sound strategy. Quite often, of course, a firm will be strong on some of the key success factors and weaker on others. At the same time the firm may also be uncertain as to what the likely current and future competitors are going to do. Proper balancing of risks and rewards is an important managerial function: excellent decision making is required to identify the best marketing opportunities available.

MARKET SEGMENTATION

Often an organization will find that the entire market is too broad to serv s a basis for analyzing opportunities. Therefore, managers should seek ways to sub-divide the overall market in order to determine where the best chances for success may lie. Most companies cannot analyze and develop a program for each cus-tomer individually, although this is sometimes done when firms are marketing to large or important organizations. On the other hand, there is generally too much variation in individual needs to treat everyone in the market uniformly. This is where the concept of *market segmentation* is of great value. Market segmentation calls for grouping existing or potential customers into segments, so that those in each segment share some marketing-relevant characteristics that distinguish them from those in other groups. Possible bases for segmentation include geographic location of prospective customers; demographic and socioeconomic charac-teristics—such as age, income, and education—that can be linked to purchase and consumption behavior; benefits sought from using the physical good or service offering; level of usage of the product; choice criteria, such as sensitivity to price or insistence on the attribute of a particular product; and lifestyle factors that relate to product needs and preferences.

The process of market segmentation consists of (1) dividing the market into meaningful groups for purposes of identification and analysis, (2) selecting the groups on which the organization should concentrate its efforts, and (3) developing specific marketing programs to appeal to each of the chosen market targets. A firm need not confine its efforts to just a single market segment but may choose to target several market segments, approaching each segment with a differentiated marketing strategy.

Since the objective of market selection is to compete in areas where the organization can expect to enjoy some competitive advantages, it is important for management to analyze the market in ways that will best reveal the opportunities available to the firm and the threats that may be faced. As was illustrated in the example of the cosmetics industry, firms may use different bases for segmenting a market and select their own unique segments on which to concentrate.

CONCLUSION

Market selection is a critical decision at all levels of an organization. It determines the types of customers that the firm will serve and often the specific geographic locations in which the firm will make its products available. These factors, in turn, serve to determine the nature of the competition that the organization will face as well as the types of marketing intermediaries (distributors, advertising agencies, retailers) with whom it may choose to work. Sound decisions on market selection should set the basis for the firm's success. Less carefully thought out decisions can expose the firm to competitive perils and environmental threats that endanger achievement of corporate objectives.

TRUS JOIST CORPORATION

Stuart U. Rich

Mike Kalish, salesman for the Micro = Lam® Division of Trus Joist Corporation, had just received another moderately sized order for the product Micro = Lam laminated veneer lumber; however, the order held particular interest for him. The unique feature of the order was the fact that the material Micro = Lam was to be used as a truck trailer bedding material. This represented the second-largest order ever processed for that function.

Earlier in the fall of 1978, Kalish had spent some time in contacting prospective customers for truck trailer flooring in the Northwest and Midwest; however, the response from manufacturers had been disappointing. Despite this reception, smaller local builders of truck trailers were interested and placed several small orders for Micro = Lam laminated veneer lumber. The order Kalish had just received was from one of the midwestern companies he had contacted earlier, thus renewing his belief that the trailer manufacturing industry held great potential for

Copyright © 1979 by Stuart U. Rich

Micro = Lam laminated veneer lumber as a flooring material.

COMPANY BACKGROUND

The Trus Joist Corporation, headquartered in Boise, Idaho, was a manufacturer of structural wood products with plants located in the Pacific Northwest, Midwest, Southeast, and Southwest. Annual sales, which totaled over $78 million in 1978, were broken down into three major product categories: the Micro = Lam Division, contributing 7 percent of sales (the majority of Micro = Lam sales were internal); the Commercial Divisions, with 82 percent of sales; and the Residential Sales Program, with 11 percent of sales.

In the late 1950s, Art Troutner and Harold Thomas developed a unique concept in joist design, implemented a manufacturing process for the design, and then founded the Trus Joist Corporation. By 1978, the company employed over 1,000 people, of whom about 180 were sales personnel. The majority of salesmen were as-

EXHIBIT
END VIEW OF AN ALL-WOOD I-BEAM (TJI)

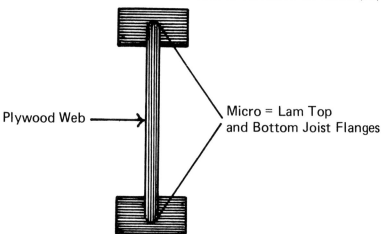

Plywood Web ⟶

Micro = Lam Top
and Bottom Joist Flanges

signed to the regional Commercial Division sales offices; four outside salesmen were assigned to the Micro = Lam Division. The functions of selling and manufacturing were performed at each of the five geographically organized Commercial Divisions; therefore, the salesmen concentrated on geographic selling. The Micro = Lam Division was more centralized in nature, conducting all nationwide sales and manufacturing activities from Eugene, Oregon.

In 1971, Trus Joist first introduced and patented Micro = Lam laminated veneer lumber. The product was made of thin ¹⁄₁₀″ or ⅛″ thick veneer sheets of Douglas fir glued together by a waterproof phenol formaldehyde adhesive. Under exact and specified conditions, the glued sheets were heated and pressed together. The Micro = Lam lumber, or billet,[1] was "extruded" from specially made equipment in 80′ lengths and 24″ widths. The billets could be cut to any customer-desired length or width within those limiting dimensions. The billets came in several

thicknesses ranging from ¾″ to 2½″; however, 1½″ and 1¾″ were the two sizes produced regularly in volume.

MARKETING MICRO = LAM

When Micro = Lam was first introduced, Trus Joist executives asked an independent research group to perform a study indicating possible industrial applications for the product. The first application for Micro = Lam was to replace the high-quality solid sawn lumber 2″ × 4″ trus chords[2] in its open web joist designs and the solid sawn lumber flanges[3] on its wooden I-beam joist (TJI). (See Exhibit 1.) Into the fall of 1978, this still represented the majority of Micro = Lam production. The findings of the research report suggested that Micro = Lam could be used as scaffold planking, mobile home trus chords, and housing components. These products accounted for about 25 percent of the Micro = Lam production. Kalish had also begun to develop new mar-

---

[1] Micro = Lam is manufactured in units called billets, and the basic unit is one billet foot. The actual dimensions of a billet foot are 1′ × 2′ x 1½″, and one billet is 80′ × 24″ × 1½″.

[2] Trus chords are the top and bottom components in an open web trus incorporating wood chords and tubular steel webs.

[3] Flanges are the top and bottom components in an all-wood I-beam. Refer to Exhibit 1.

EXHIBIT 2
MECHANICAL PROPERTIES OF WOOD USED FOR TRAILER DECKING

Common name of species	Specific gravity (percent moisture content)	Modulus of elasticity (million psi)	Compression parallel to grain and fiber strength maximum crush strength (psi)
Apitong	0.59	2.35	8,540
Douglas fir	0.48	1.95	7,240
Alaska yellow cedar	0.42	1.59	6,640
White oak	0.68	1.78	7,440
Northern red oak	0.63	1.82	6,760
Micro = Lam*	0.55	2.20	8,200

* Micro = Lam using Douglas fir as the veneer faces of the lumber.
Source: Wood Handbook: Wood as an Engineering Material, USDA Handbook no. 72, rev. ed., 1974; U.S. Forest Products Laboratory.

kets for Micro = Lam, including ladder rails and framing material for office partitions.

When marketing Micro = Lam to potential customers, Trus Joist emphasized the superior structural qualities of the product over conventional lumber. Micro = Lam did not possess the undesirable characteristics of warping, checking, and twisting; yet it did show greater bending strength and more structural stability. (One ad claimed, "Testing proves Micro = Lam to be approximately 30 percent stiffer than #1 dense select structural Douglas fir.") In some applications, Micro = Lam offered distinct price advantages over its competing wood alternatives and this factor always proved to be a good selling point. Manufacturers were often concerned about the lead/delivery time involved in ordering Micro = Lam. Trus Joist promised to deliver within one to three weeks of an order, which was often a full two weeks to two months ahead of other wood manufacturers.

The industrial application report had also suggested using Micro = Lam as a decking material for truck trailers. This use became a reality when Sherman Brothers Trucking, a local trucking firm that frequently transported Micro = Lam, made a request for Micro = Lam to redeck some of its worn-out trailers. To increase the durability of the flooring surface, the manufacturing department of Trus Joist replaced the top two veneer sheets of Douglas fir with apitong. Apitong is a Southeast Asian wood known for its strength, durability, and high specific gravity. This foreign hardwood had been used in the United States for several years because of the diminishing supplies of domestic hardwoods. (See Exhibit 2.)

The pioneer advertisement for Micro = Lam as a trailer deck material had consisted of one ad in a national trade journal and had depicted the Micro = Lam cut so that the edges were used as the top surface. (See Exhibit 3.) The response from this ad had been dismal and had resulted in only one or two orders. The latest advertisement depicting Micro = Lam as it was currently being used (with apitong as the top veneer layers) had better results. This ad, sent to every major truck or trailer manufacturing journal as a news release on a new product, resulted in 30 to 50 inquiries which turned into 10 to 15 orders. Approximately 15 decks were sold as a result of the promotion.

Everyone at Trus Joist believed that the current price on Micro = Lam was the absolute rock bottom price possible. In fact, most people believed that Micro = Lam was underpriced. The current

EXHIBIT 3
END VIEW OF REMANUFACTURED MICRO=LAM

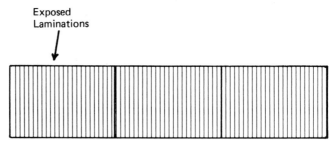

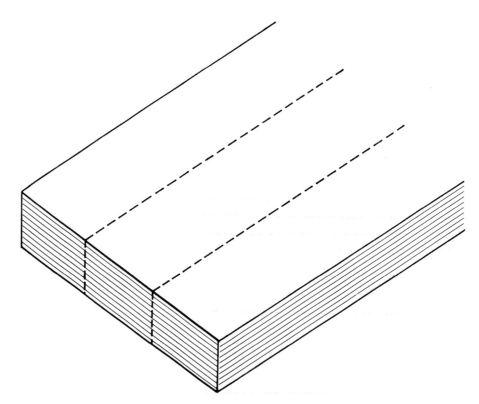

Original Micro = Lam billet depicting the cutting path (— — — — —) during the remanufacturing process.

EXHIBIT 4
TRUCK TRAILER SHIPMENTS AND DOLLAR VALUE
(By Calendar Year)

	1975	1974	1973	1972	1971
Complete trailers and chassis	67,888	191,262	167,201	141,143	103,784
Value	$613,702,000	$1,198,520,000	$ 956,708,000	$795,500,000	$585,264,000
Containers	4,183*	10,108*	18,626	18,166	8,734
Value	$ 18,071,000	$ 27,343,000	$ 60,159,000	$ 51,527,000	$ 26,514,000
Container chassis	2,936	12,883	12,790	15,498	9,775
Value	$ 14,898,000	$ 42,076,000	$ 33,143,000	$ 39,028,000	$ 24,999,000
Total units	75,007	214,253	198,617	174,807	122,293
Value	$646,671,000	$1,267,939,000	$1,050,010,000	$886,055,000	$636,777,000

Note: Data for 1975 preliminary and subject to slight possible change.
* Containers not reported June–October 1974 and January–March 1975.
Source: Truck Trailer Manufacturers Association, *Ward's Automotive Yearbook, 1978,* p. 91.

price of Micro = Lam included a gross margin of 20 percent. The price of 1¼″ thick and 1½″ thick Micro = Lam was based on the costs of a 1½″ billet. The total variable costs of 1½″ material were multiplied by ⅚ to estimate the same costs of 1¼″ material. There had recently been some discussion over the appropriateness of this ratio. Some of the marketing personnel believed that a more appropriate estimate of the variable costs for the 1¼″ Micro = Lam would be the ratio of the number of veneers in a 1¼″ billet to the number of veneers in a 1½″ billet, or ¹⁴⁄₁₆. At the present time, the costs of veneer represented 55 percent of the selling price. Glue cost was approximately 13 cents/square foot; fixed overhead represented 14 cents/square foot; and other variable costs amounted to approximately 12½ cents/square foot. The total variable costs were divided by 0.80 to cover all selling and administrative expenses and to secure a profit.[4]

In 1977, truck trailer manufacturers ordered and used 46 million square feet for installation in new truck trailer construction. This figure was understated because redecking or replacement of worn-out floors of trailers had not been incorporated, and there was little organized information to determine what this potential could be. As of 1975, 236 truck trailer manufacturers located

throughout the U.S. produced $646.7 million worth of trailers (Exhibit 4).

The problem Kalish saw with this aggregate data was that it was not broken down into the various segments of trailer builders. For example, not all of the 236 manufacturers produced trailers which used wooden floors. Among those not using wooden floors were tankers and logging trailers. Kalish believed that the real key to selling Micro = Lam in this industry would be to determine the segment of the trailer industry on which he should concentrate his selling efforts. Kalish also knew that he somehow had to determine trailer manufacturers' requirements for trailer decking. The Eugene-Portland, Oregon, area offered what he thought to be a good cross section of the type of trailer manufacturers that might be interested in Micro = Lam. He had already contacted some of those firms about buying Micro = Lam.

GENERAL TRAILER COMPANY

Jim Walline had been the purchasing agent for General Trailer Company of Springfield, Oregon, for the past 2½ years. He stated, "The engineering department makes the decisions on what materials to buy. I place the orders after the requisition has been placed on my desk."

General Trailer Company was a manufacturer

[4] All cost figures have been disguised.

of several different types of trailers: low-boys, chip trailers, log trailers, and flatbeds. In 1977, General manufactured five flatbeds and redecked five flatbeds. General did most of its business with the local timber industry; however, it sold three flatbeds in 1977 to local firms in the steel industry.

The flatbeds General Trailer manufactured were 40' to 45' long and approximately 7' wide. Log trailers were approximately 20' to 25' long.

General Trailer manufactured trailers primarily for the West Coast market, although it had sold a few trailers to users in Alaska. On the West Coast, General's major competitors were Peerless, Fruehauf, and Trailmobile, all large-scale manufacturers of truck trailers. Even though General was comparatively small in size, it did not feel threatened, because "we build a top-quality trailer which is not mass-produced," as Walline put it.

General had been using apitong as a trailer decking material until customers complained of its weight and its expansion/contraction characteristics when exposed to weather. At that time, Mr. Schmidt, the general manager and head of the engineering department, made the decision to switch from apitong to laminated fir.

Laminated fir (consisting of solid sawn lumber strips glued together) was currently being used as the material for decking flatbeds, and Pacific Laminated Company of Vancouver, Washington, supplied all of General's fir decking, so General would only order material when a customer bought a new trailer or needed to have a trailer redecked. Walline was disappointed with the two- to three-week delivery time, since it often meant that much more time before the customer's trailer was ready.

Laminated fir in 40' lengths, 11¾" widths, and 1¼" thickness was used by General. General paid approximately $2 to $3 per square foot for this decking.

Even though Pacific Laminated could provide customer-cut and edged pieces with no additional lead time, General preferred shiplapped fir in the previously noted dimensions, with the top two layers treated with a waterproof coating.

The different types of trailers General manufactured required different decking materials. Low-boys required material 2¼" thick and General used 3" × 12" rough-cut fir lumber. Chip trailers required ⅝"-thick MDO (medium density overlay) plywood with a slick surface.

Walline said General had used Micro=Lam on one trailer; however, the customer had not been expecting it and was very displeased with the job.[5] Therefore, the current policy was to use only laminated fir for the local market unless a customer specifically ordered a different decking material. Trailers headed for Alaska were decked with laminated oak, supplied by a vendor other than Pacific Laminated.

Walline said that if he wanted to make a recommendation to change decking materials, he would need to know price advantages, lead times, moisture content, availability, and industry experience with the material.

MAYFLOWER MOVING AND STORAGE CO.

"We already use Micro=Lam on our trailers," was the response of Mr. Sherman, president of Mayflower Moving and Storage Company, when asked about the trailer decking material his company used. He went on to say, "In fact, we had hauled several shipments for Trus Joist when we initiated a call to them asking if they could make a decking material for us."

Mayflower Moving and Storage owned 60 trailers (flatbeds) which it used to haul heavy

---

[5] After purchasing Micro=Lam, General Trailer modified the material by ripping the billets into 1½" widths and then relaminating these strips back into 12"- or 24"-wide pieces of lumber. This remanufacturing added substantial costs. Also, the laminations were now directly exposed to the weather. Moisture could more easily seep into cracks or voids, causing swells and buckling. (See Exhibit 3.)

equipment and machinery. It had been in a dilemma for eight years about the types of materials used to replace the original decks. Nothing seemed to be satisfactory. Solid apitong was tough, but it was too heavy and it did not weather very well. Plywood did not provide adequate weight distribution and had too many joints. Often the small wheels of the forklifts would break through the decking, or heavy equipment with steel legs would punch a hole through the decks. Laminated fir was too expensive.

Mayflower Moving and Storage was currently redecking a trailer per week. It usually patched the decks until the whole bed fell apart; then the trailer would sit in the yard waiting for a major overhaul. By that time the trailers needed to have the crossbeams repaired and new bearings as well as a new deck.

Sherman went on to say, "The shop mechanic just loves Micro = Lam. This is because it used to take the mechanic and one other employee two days to redeck a trailer, and now it just takes the shop mechanic one day to do the same job." Advantages (over plywood and apitong) of the 2' × 40' Micro = Lam pieces were ease of installation, excellent weight distribution due to the reduced number of seams, and reduced total weight of the bed.

Sherman explained that Mayflower Moving and Storage usually purchased four or five decks at a time and warehoused some of the materials until a trailer needed redecking.

Sherman thought the original decking on flatbeds was some type of hardwood, probably oak, which could last up to five years; however, a similar decking material had not been found for a reasonable price. The plywood and fir decks used in the past eight to ten years had lasted anywhere from one to two years, and some had worn out in as little as six months. After using Micro = Lam for six months, Mr. Sherman expected the decking to last up to three to five years.

When asked about the type of flooring used in the company's moving vans, Sherman emphasized the top care that those floors received. "We sand, buff, and wax them just like a household floor; in fact, we take such good care of these floors they will occasionally outlast the trailer." The original floors in moving vans were made out of a laminated oak and had to be kept extremely smooth, allowing freight to slide freely without the possibility of damaging items of freight with legs. The local company purchased all of its moving vans through Mayflower Moving Vans. The only problem with floors in moving vans was that the jointed floors would occasionally buckle because of swelling.

The fact that Micro = Lam protruded ⅛" above the metal lip which edged the flatbed trailers (see Exhibit 5) posed no problem for Mayflower. "All we had to do was plane the edge at 40 degrees. In fact, the best fit will have the decking protrude a hair above the metal edge," Sherman said. Just prior to this, he had recounted an experience which occurred with the first shipment of Micro = Lam. Because the deck was too thick, Mayflower Moving and Storage had about ⅛" planed from one side of the decking material. However, the company shaved off the apitong veneer, exposing the fir. Sherman said that he laughed about it now, but at the time he wasn't too pleased.

PEERLESS TRUCKING COMPANY

"Sure, I've heard of Micro = Lam. They [Trus Joist salesmen] have been in here . . . but we don't need that good a material." This was the response of Mel Rogers, head of Peerless' Purchasing Department, Tualatin, Oregon, when asked about the use of Micro = Lam as a truck decking material. Rogers, a 30-year veteran of the trailer manufacturing industry, seemed very skeptical of all laminated decking materials.

The primary products manufactured by Peerless (in Tualatin) required bedding materials

EXHIBIT 5
CROSS-SECTIONAL END VIEW OF TRAILER DECKING (TONGUE AND GROOVE)

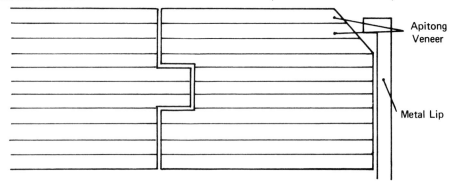

Apitong Veneer

Metal Lip

very different from Micro = Lam. Chip trailers and rail car dumpers required metal beds to facilitate unloading. Low-boys required a heavy decking material (usually 2″ × 12″ or 3″ × 12″ rough planking) as Caterpillar tractors were frequently driven on them. Logging trailers had no beds.

Approximately 60 decks per year were required by Peerless in the manufacture of flatbeds and in redecking jobs. Micro = Lam could have been used in these applications, but fir planking was used exclusively except for some special overseas jobs. Fir planking was available in full trailer lengths, requiring eight man-hours to install on new equipment. Usually, five or six decks were stocked at a time. The estimated life of a new deck was two to three years.

Fir planking was selected for decking applications on the basis of price and durability. Peerless purchased fir planking for $1,000 per MBF. Tradition supported fir planking in durability, as it was a well-known product.

Decking material thickness was critical, according to Mr. Rogers, as any deviation from the industry standard of 1⅜″ required extensive retooling.

Any new decking materials for use in original equipment manufacture had to be approved by the Peerless engineering department. Alternative decking materials could have been used locally if specified by the customer.

Rogers was certainly going to be a hard person to sell on the use of Micro = Lam, Kalish felt.

"Why use Micro = Lam when I can buy fir planking for less?" Rogers had said.

FRUEHAUF TRUCKING COMPANY

"I'd be very happy if someone would come up with a durable [trailer] deck at a reasonable price," was the response of Wayne Peterson when asked about Fruehauf's experience with decking materials. Peterson was service manager for Fruehauf's factory branch in Milwaukie, Oregon. Fruehauf Corporation, with its principal manufacturing facilities in Detroit, Michigan, was one of the nation's largest manufacturers of truck trailers.

The manufacturing facilities in Milwaukie produced 40-ton low-beds as well as assembled truck bodies manufactured in Detroit. The low-beds were subjected to heavy use, often with forklifts, which required a decking material of extreme strength and durability. Laminated decking materials then available were therefore excluded from this application.

The decking materials used in the truck bodies were specified by the sales department in Detroit, based on customer input. Generally, apitong or laminated oak was installed at the factory. Any new product to be used in original equipment manufacture had to be approved by Fruehauf's well-developed factory engineering department.

The Milwaukie operation also did about 15 redecking jobs per year. The decking material was specified by the customer on the basis of price and weathering characteristics. The materials used were laminated oak (11½" W × 40'), apitong (7" × ⅛"—random lengths), Alaska yellow cedar (2" × 6" T&G), fir planking (2" × 6" T&G), and laminated fir (24" W × 40'). Alaska yellow cedar was priced below all other decking materials, followed (in order) by fir planking, laminated fir, laminated oak, and apitong.

Fruehauf's suppliers of decking materials were as follows: laminated fir—Pacific Laminating, Vancouver, Washington; Alaska yellow cedar— Al Disdero Lumber Company, Portland, Oregon: and apitong—Builterials, Portland, Oregon. There were no specific suppliers for the other materials.

A minimum inventory of decking materials was kept on hand to allow for immediate repair needs only. Orders were placed for complete decks as needed.

A redecking job typically required 30 man-hours per 7' × 40' trailer, including the removal of the old deck and installation of the new one. Decking materials that were available in full trailer lengths were preferred, as they greatly reduced installation time, improved weight distribution, and had fewer joints along which failure could occur.

The use of alternative products, such as composition flooring of wood and aluminum, was not under consideration.

Alaska yellow cedar and fir planking had the best weathering characteristics, while apitong and laminated oak weathered poorly. Oak and apitong did, however, have a hard, nonscratching surface that was desirable in enclosed use. When asked about the weathering characteristics of laminated flooring in general, Peterson responded, "It's all right for the dry states, but not around here."

COMPETITION

There were a large number of materials with which Micro=Lam competed in the trailer flooring market, ranging from fir plywood to aluminum floors. Trus Joist felt that the greatest obstacles to Micro=Lam's success would be from the old standard products like laminated fir and oak, which had a great deal of industry respect. For years, oak had been the premier flooring material; recently, however, supplies had been short and delivery times long (two months in some cases), and prices were becoming prohibitive. (See Exhibit 6.)

Kalish had found that in the Northwest Pacific Laminated Company was one of the major flooring suppliers to local manufacturers. Pacific Laminated produced a Douglas fir laminated product that was highly popular; however, like oak, it was relatively high-priced. Despite the price, Pacific Laminated could cut the product to dimen-

EXHIBIT 6
DECKING MATERIAL PRICES, NOVEMBER 1978

Product	Price	Form
Alaska yellow cedar	$650/MBF	2" × 6" T&G 15' lengths
Apitong	$1.30–$2/lineal foot*	1⅜" × 7" random lengths
Fir planking	$1/bd. ft.	2" × 6" T&G random lengths
Fir, laminated	$2.50/sq. ft.	1¼" × 11¾" × 40'
Micro=Lam	$1.30/sq. ft.	1¼" × 24" × 40'
	$1.50/sq. ft.	1½" × 24" × 40'
Oak, laminated	$2.20/sq. ft.	1⅜" × 1½" × 40'

* Lineal foot = price per unit length of the product.
Sources: Al Disdero Lumber Company, Portland, Oregon; Builterials, Portland, Oregon

sions up to 2' wide and 40' long. Delivery time was excellent for its customers, even with special milling for shiplapped or tongue and groove edges and manufacturing to user thickness.

CONCLUSION

Although Kalish had had limited success marketing Micro = Lam to truck manufacturers, he was concerned with the marketing program for his product. Several trailer manufacturers had raised important questions concerning the price and durability of Micro = Lam compared to alternative decking materials. He knew Micro = Lam had some strong attributes, yet he was hesitant to expand beyond the local market. Kalish was also wondering about the action he should eventually take in order to determine the additional information he would need to successfully introduce Micro = Lam nationally as a trailer decking material. One thought that crossed his mind was to define the company's marketing strategy for this product. Meanwhile, small orders continued to trickle in.

BETH ISRAEL HOSPITAL, BOSTON

Terrie Bloom
Christopher H. Lovelock
Penny Pittman Merliss

In spring 1978, David Steinberg,[1] a trustee of Beth Israel Hospital, was reviewing the status of the hospital's maternity service. He was faced with a complex problem. On one hand, obstetrics was losing money. On the other, Beth Israel's maternity unit provided a major service to the Greater Boston community and constituted an important part of the teaching program of Harvard Medical School. Finally, obstetrics and gynecology were so closely related clinically that any major change in the status of obstetrics would have significant repercussions in gynecology.[2]

The finance committee of the board of trustees had requested that Steinberg, chairman of the special projects subcommittee, come up with specific recommendations for the future. He was considering various options. The hospital could replace all or some of its maternity beds with medical/surgical beds. Or it could try to reduce the deficit in obstetrics by attracting more obstetrical patients, by improving the income realized on each patient, or both. No matter which course he proposed, Steinberg would have to devise a strategic plan presenting his recommendations to the finance committee and ultimately to the board of trustees.

HOSPITAL BACKGROUND

The Beth Israel Hospital of Boston was a 432-bed major teaching hospital of Harvard Medical School. In addition to its role as a tertiary care center,[3] it served as the community hospital for the adjoining town of Brookline (Exhibit 1). Finally, as a constituent agency of the Combined Jewish Philanthropies, Beth Israel provided leadership in the planning and delivery of health care

Copyright © 1979 by the President and Fellows of Harvard College, Harvard Business School case 9–579–180.

[1] Disguised name.

[2] Obstetrics concerns the medical management of pregnancy, labor and delivery; gynecology is that branch of medicine dealing with the female genital tract.

[3] Tertiary care is the most sophisticated level of health care, delivered by specialists, usually located in academic medical centers, to patients with relatively serious or unusual medical problems. Primary care is the treatment of ambulatory ("walk-in") patients with more routine problems.

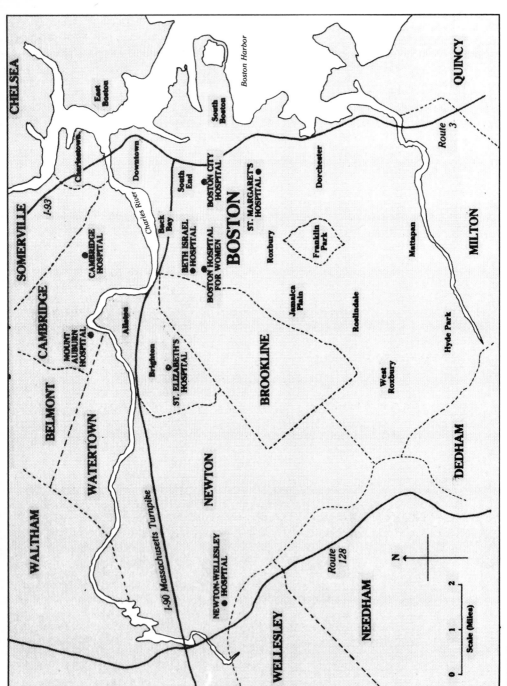

EXHIBIT 1

to the Jewish community, in addition to serving the needy of every faith, race, and nationality.

Institutional Philosophy

Since its opening in 1916, Beth Israel had developed a close relationship with Harvard Medical School as well as a growing reputation for excellence in medical teaching and research. The hospital participated in the training of about 1,200 physicians and other health care professionals each year, including medical students; new physicians (known as interns, residents, and fellows) who were doing postgraduate work; and various types of occupational and physical therapists.

At the same time, Beth Israel had become known as an institution that sought to address the emotional as well as the physical needs of patients. Its mission was stated as the delivery of "patient care of the highest quality, in both scientific and human terms"; Beth Israel had been the first hospital in the U.S. to issue a statement on the rights of patients. Both inpatient and outpatient services were focused on patient care, with teaching designed to strengthen the quality of that care as well as to educate physicians and nurses.

Organization

The hospital's board of trustees was its governing body. The board delegated certain powers and duties to a number of standing committees, including the medical conference committee, which reviewed patient care, and the finance committee. The finance committee, in turn, designated subcommittees to monitor the hospital's financial operations. Among these was the special projects subcommittee, chaired by David Steinberg, which reviewed clinical services. The board delegated responsibility for ongoing operations to the hospital's general director, Mitchell T. Rabkin, M.D.

Dr. Rabkin, who had been general director for eleven years, believed strongly in the importance

of good care throughout all phases of the hospital environment:

> Most patients judge the quality of their hospital experience not so much on the basis of clinical excellence as on the basis of the personalization of care and the caliber of the "hotel" services. We seek to maintain the highest standard in all areas. We also recognize that the institution is people, and that in order for the staff to sustain the level of warmth and personalization that we strive for, we have to maintain a working environment conducive to their happiness as well.

Facilities

In 1978, Beth Israel's facilities comprised 12 buildings. Eight of these were dedicated to patient care, and four were sites for research or administration. Within these buildings the hospital annually provided care to 18,000 in-patients, received 200,000 outpatient visits, and maintained about $5 million of research.

Beth Israel had experienced more growth during the early 1970s than in any other period. The construction of the $28 million Feldberg Building added 78 beds in 1976, bringing maximum capacity to 452 beds. Of the 432 beds available in spring 1978, 329 were medical/surgical, 89 were ob/gyn, and 14 were psychiatric. The hospital also maintained 52 bassinets for newborn babies.

Despite the increased number of beds, occupancy rates on the medical and surgical floors and in the psychiatric unit had remained uniformly high. Occupancy in obstetrics and gynecology, however, was lower. With rare exceptions, obstetrical beds could not legally be used to accommodate overflow demand from other services. Gynecology beds could be used for surgical patients, but this practice was avoided, since the two services were located on different floors of the hospital. The psychiatry inpatient unit had a long waiting list at all times; a policy of allowing short leaves of absence accounted for the less than 100% occupancy level. Exhibit 2 summarizes Beth Israel's projected oc-

EXHIBIT 2
BETH ISRAEL HOSPITAL: PROJECTED OCCUPANCY RATES
Average Daily Census and Payor Mix (Inpatients) for Fiscal Year Ending 9/30/78

	Number of Beds	Occupancy Rate	Census (Average No. of Patients per Day)	Payor Mix by Financial Class*				
				Blue Cross/ Blue Shield	Medicare	Medicaid	Private Insurance	Other
Medicine	150	97%	145.0	24%	50%	7%	9%	10%
Surgery	155	88%	136.8	34%	36%	6%	13%	11%
Gynecology	44	61%	26.8	43%	3%	28%	18%	8%
Psychiatry	14	94%	13.2	35%	13%	29%	11%	12%
Obstetrics	45	65%	29.2**	42%	0%	29%	18%	11%
Other adult units (intensive care; clinical research center)	24	70%	18.3	29%	44%	8%	10%	9%
	432	85%	369.3	32%	33%	12%	13%	10%

* Blue Cross/Blue Shield and Medicare reimbursed hospitals the reasonable cost of providing services to their beneficiary groups; Medicaid paid a "per diem" rate for inpatient care regardless of actual services rendered (which in the aggregate represented most, but not all, of the costs); and private insurance paid the hospitals' charges or a fixed dollar amount for covered services.

** Obstetrical census is made up of women who deliver as well as those who are in the hospital for obstetrical problems. As many as 20–25% of the patients on the obstetrical service may be in for reasons other than to deliver a baby.

Source: Beth Israel Hospital (disguised data).

cupancy rates, average daily patient census, and payor mix for 1977–78.

THE BOSTON HEALTH CARE ENVIRONMENT

The health care industry in Boston was large and complex. There was a general consensus that the city was "overbedded" (had more inpatient beds than were needed to accommodate demand) and suffered from costly duplication of services, although the extent of these phenomena was disputed. The net result was keen competition for patients.

The problem of duplication and high costs could be traced to three major causes. First, the health care delivery system was centered around Boston's three medical schools—those of Harvard University, Tufts University and Boston University—each of which maintained academic and clinical relationships with a number of teaching and community hospitals (Exhibit 3). Since each medical school required a full spectrum of teaching services in order to educate its students, there was considerable duplication of services in hospitals affiliated with these schools.

In addition to the expenses resulting from duplication of services, the cost-reimbursement system of financing much hospital care also contributed to rising costs. Most health insurers (so-called third-party payors) followed the practice of reimbursing hospitals for "reasonable costs" incurred in the process of delivering care. This system was claimed not to give hospitals any incentive to choose the most cost-effective way to provide care, since any costs under a certain limit would be reimbursed.

The third factor was the advent of the Medicare and Medicaid health insurance programs, developed in the mid-1960s to assure access to care for two previously underserved populations, the elderly and the poor. The demand for health care services generated by the introduction of Medicare and Medicaid had exceeded expectations and reinforced the trend toward increased

bed capacity and greater expense during the late sixties and early seventies.

Planning and Regulatory Efforts

Inflation in health care had been running at almost twice the overall rate. As the percentage of GNP devoted to health continued to climb through the late sixties and early seventies, the federal government adopted two tactics to control costs: planning and regulation. The goal was to consolidate duplicate services wherever possible and to discourage unnecessary capital expansion.

In 1972, the Certificate of Need (CON) program was initiated. This required that any major capital expenditure or major change in service proposed by a hospital be reviewed by a state agency to determine (1) the need for the project, and (2) whether the proposal represented the most cost-effective means of achieving the desired result. In Massachusetts, any capital expenditure in excess of $150,000 was considered major, as was a transfer of more than four beds from one service to another. Any hospital that made a major capital expenditure or change in service without CON approval risked loss of reimbursement.

Approval of new construction could be made contingent upon the elimination of some other, underutilized service currently provided by the hospital. One of the most common compromises made by a hospital seeking a CON was elimination of either its obstetrical or its pediatric unit.[4] These services had proliferated historically as a result of strong community preference for local care, but they became underutilized as the birth rate dropped. With the negotiating power afforded by CON, planners were able to eliminate some of the duplication and to work toward regionalization of obstetrical and pediatric services.

---

[4] Pediatrics is that branch of medicine concerned with the diseases of children and their treatment.

EXHIBIT 3
BOSTON, CAMBRIDGE AND NEWTON TEACHING HOSPITALS*

Hospital	Medical School Affiliations	Control	Total Number of Beds	Number of Maternity Beds	Occupancy Rate for Maternity Unit in 1975
Beth Israel	Harvard	Nonprofit	432	45	74.8%
Boston City	Boston University	City	500	72	57.6%
Boston Hospital for Women	Harvard	Nonprofit	222	116	80.4%
Boston State	Boston University, Tufts	State	230	—	—
Boston VA	Boston University, Tufts	Veteran's Administration	815	—	—
Carney	Boston University	Church	376	—	—
Children's	Harvard	Nonprofit	343	—	—
Faulkner	Tufts	Nonprofit	248	—	—
Kennedy Memorial	Boston University	Church	88	—	—
Lemuel Shattuck	Tufts	State	200	—	—
Massachusetts Eye & Ear	Harvard	Nonprofit	174	—	—
Massachusetts General	Harvard	Nonprofit	1084	—	—
Massachusetts Mental Health Center	Harvard	State	106	—	—
N.E. Deaconess	Harvard	Nonprofit	472	—	—
N.E. Medical Center	Tufts	Nonprofit	452	—	—
Peter Bent Brigham	Harvard	Nonprofit	332	—	—
Robert Breck Brigham	Harvard	Nonprofit	96	—	—
St. Elizabeth's	Tufts	Church	417	24	62.6%
St. Margaret's	Tufts	Church	117	68	65.6%
University	Boston University	Nonprofit	383	—	—
West Roxbury VA	Harvard	Veteran's Administration	279	—	—
Cambridge	Harvard	City	187	30	39.6%
Mount Auburn	Harvard	Nonprofit	300	20	48.1%
Newton-Wellesley	Tufts	Nonprofit	339	33	54.4%

* Excerpted largely from the *Directory of Accredited Residencies 1977–1978,* Liaison Committee on Graduate Medical Education (American Medical Association, Chicago, 1977, pp. 58–89. Maternity Unit data are taken from *The Health Systems Plan for Massachusetts,* Vol. 2A (HPCGB, Inc., September 1977), and from Massachusetts Department of Public Health Annual Hospital Statistical Report, Fiscal Year 1975.

The effectiveness of CON as a planning tool was somewhat limited, since it could only be applied reactively, in response to a hospital's request for approval of a major capital expenditure or change in service. Moreover, a hospital that was dissatisfied with a CON decision could file a bill with the state legislature requesting permission to proceed with its plans anyway.

Pressures on Maternity Units

The federal government continued to strive for a more systematic approach to health planning and published the National Health Planning Guidelines in 1978. These guidelines set minimum standards for obstetrical units of 75 percent occupancy and 1,500 births per year. A considerable number of maternity units in Massachusetts and throughout the country did not meet these standards; each was liable to lose its obstetrical service unless it succeeded in increasing its total. Additionally, the draft of the new Massachusetts State Health Plan recommended a 25 percent reduction in the number of maternity beds in Boston, from 325 to 244.

The state's move to reduce maternity beds was prompted by the recognition that underused obstetrical services were relatively expensive to maintain. Medical/surgical procedures were often elective rather than emergency, and therefore were scheduled as beds became available. In contrast, obstetrical admissions were predominantly random events (Exhibit 4). Thus, a maternity unit had to be staffed to accommodate an above-average census (occupancy rate) to ensure that this fluctuating demand could be met.

In addition to increased regulation, hospitals were also experiencing a variety of pressures from their patient population. The women's movement was having a major impact on women's attitudes toward birth. Not only were women tending to have fewer children (Exhibit 5), and spending less time in the hospital per delivery (in 1978 the average stay for a normal delivery was four days), but they collectively

EXHIBIT 4

DAILY NUMBER OF PATIENTS IN THE OBSTETRICS WARD: FREQUENCY DISTRIBUTION, NOVEMBER 1, 1977 TO MAY 1, 1978

Number of Patients	Frequency (Days)	Percent of Days
13	2	1.1
14	2	1.1
17	5	2.7
18	3	1.6
19	1	0.5
20	5	2.7
21	7	3.8
22	6	3.3
23	8	4.4
24	4	2.2
25	9	4.9
26	12	6.6
27	12	6.6
28	15	8.2
29	10	5.2
30	11	6.0
31	7	3.8
32	10	5.2
33	11	6.0
34	9	4.9
35	5	2.7
36	5	2.7
37	1	0.5
38	6	3.3
39	5	2.7
40	3	1.6
41	2	1.1
42	3	1.6
43	2	1.1
45	1	0.5
	179	100.0%

Note: Interpret this chart as reading: on two days during this six-month period (1.1% of the time) there were 13 patients in the Obstetrical Unit; on 11 days (6.0%) there were 30 patients.
Source: Beth Israel Hospital Daily Census

voiced the opinion that the bearing of children was a healthy process over which they should have some measure of control. As noted by *Boston* magazine:

There is a reevaluation of what used to be routine clinical practices for all women giving birth and a growing tendency among doctors now to apply

EXHIBIT 5
TOTAL BIRTHS IN BOSTON AND MASSACHUSETTS FISCAL YEARS 1970–1977

Hospitals	1970		1971		1972		1973		1974		1975		1976		1977	
Beth Israel	3,096	16.0%	2,859	16.2%	2,766	17.4%	2,517	16.8%	2,335	16.7%	2,152	15.5%	2,016	14.9%	2,010	14.5%
Boston Hospital for Women	7,023	36.3%	6,380	36.1%	5,924	37.2%	6,001	40.0%	5,946	42.6%	6,028	43.4%	6,168	45.4%	6,283	45.2%
Boston City	2,343	12.1%	2,085	11.8%	1,826	11.5%	1,665	11.1%	1,296	9.3%	1,598	11.5%	1,601	11.8%	1,679	12.1%
St. Elizabeth's	1,610	8.3%	1,534	8.7%	1,230	7.7%	1,141	7.6%	1,057	7.6%	1,121	8.1%		7.3%	1,024	7.4%
St. Margaret's	5,299	27.4%	4,819	27.3%	4,161	26.2%	3,697	24.6%	3,318	23.8%	3,007	21.6%	2,808	20.7%	2,900	20.0%
Total Boston Hospitals	19,371	100.0%	17,677	100.0%	15,907	100.0%	15,021	100.0%	13,952	100.0%	13,906	100.0%	13,577	100.0%	13,896	100.0%
Cambridge City	939		969		923		849		762		752		743		N/A	
Mt. Auburn	1,369		1,236		1,066		893		680		693		696		N/A	
Newton-Wellesley	1,220		1,162		1,114		1,021		1,039		1,036		1,158		N/A	
Total All Massachusetts Hospitals	96,290		83,337		79,063		74,110		71,777		69,574		67,555		N/A	

those practices only when needed. . . . More attention is being paid to the emotional needs of the entire family—mother, father, newborn and siblings.[5]

A growing number of women were also interested in out-of-hospital delivery. In the Boston area, groups such as Home Birth and Birth Day were encouraging births at home. A newspaper report estimated that between 1957 and 1977 the annual number of home births in Boston had risen from about 70 to some 500. Also becoming popular were "birthing centers," where women with normal pregnancies could be delivered by midwives and return home after a short stay, incurring costs far below those of most deliveries. Since home births and birthing centers provided little sophisticated, on-site, technological back-up, physicians disagreed as to their safety for mother and baby. Because Massachusetts law required that midwives work under a doctor's supervision, no birthing centers had opened in the Boston area.

IDENTIFYING TARGET MARKETS

A hospital attracted maternity patients principally through its obstetrician/gynecologists, particularly those in private practice. Most women, especially those from the suburbs, tended to place a higher priority on choice of obstetrician than choice of hospital; the physician's reputation and the convenience of his or her private office were the most compelling factors in choosing a doctor. Since obstetricians in private practice tended to restrict their practices to no more than one or two hospitals, in order to minimize their travel time, a woman's choice of hospital would be dictated by her obstetrician's affiliation. Hence, a key to a hospital's success in filling its beds was to attract private physicians to the active staff and maintain their loyalty.

[5] Gail Kelley, "Special Delivery: A Consumer Guide to Giving Birth in Boston," *Boston,* April 1978, p. 74.

The obstetrician/gynecologist's choice of hospital might stem from any of several considerations, ranging from academic to social. Some preferred a major academic hospital, with its many opportunities for teaching and continuing education. Graduates of obstetrical residency programs frequently became loyal staff members after their training was completed, if they could be set up in a practice. Others might be influenced by the quality and scope of services offered by a given hospital: for this reason, some might choose a general hospital with specialty backup in internal medicine and general surgery over a hospital that restricted its practice to obstetrics and gynecology. Likewise, a hospital that included an obstetrical service but lacked gynecology would have a lower appeal than one with both services. Finally, an obstetrician might join the staff of a hospital with a religious affiliation out of personal preference or to accommodate patients' wishes.

A second major target market consisted of women who placed their first priority on choosing the hospital. This group of women then had the option of selecting a private obstetrician on the hospital's staff or of using the hospital's outpatient obstetrical services (where available). In contrast to her suburban counterparts, the urban woman was more likely to choose a hospital directly, either because she perceived the hospital as offering more comprehensive services, or because financial circumstances virtually excluded her from the private physician's office. Boston women, who had a number of maternity services to choose from, might weigh a variety of factors, including recommendations of friends or relatives, cost of services, convenience, and a hospital's religious affiliation. However, there was no market research available to indicate the relative importance of these factors in a woman's decision.

A third market consisted of groups, such as health maintenance organizations (HMOs) and neighborhood health centers, that provided walk-in obstetrical care but turned to hospitals for inpatient services.[6] Groups selected hospitals for their members on the basis of price, quality, and practice arrangements (e.g., opportunities for neighborhood health center staff to follow their patients in the hospital).

Competitive Strategies

Facing a declining birth rate as well as constant pressure from government, hospitals began to develop strategies for attracting maternity patients. Virtually all Boston-area hospitals were aware of the importance of favorable publicity in generating demand for their obstetrical services. Most relied on publicity from stories in the local media; some used other communication strategies, too. St. Margaret's Hospital, for instance, had published an eight-page, full-sized, paid supplement in the *Boston Sunday Globe* on June 19, 1977, promoting its "Center for Life" concept in obstetrical care. Other hospitals developed newspaper advertisements or brochures for general distribution discussing their obstetrical services.

Since many health insurance policies did not provide comprehensive coverage for maternity services, pricing was often an important competitive strategy. Even such well-known third-party payors as Blue Cross/Blue Shield did not always provide maternity coverage as extensive as that which covered other medical and surgical costs. Because the extent of coverage depended on the policy negotiated within each insured organization, some women with Blue Cross insurance were covered for all prenatal visits, plus delivery; others found that only in-hospital labor and delivery charges would be paid. Most Blue

Cross plans also required that members be enrolled at least ten months before delivery in order for coverage to apply. Coverage offered by for-profit commercial insurers was even more variable. Some paid 100 percent of prenatal and delivery costs; others paid as little as $500 per pregnancy. Patients holding these policies, according to the hospital's financial office, were often "employees of smaller companies that can't afford good Blue Cross coverage." Indigent patients covered by Medicaid in Massachusetts enjoyed the highest state Medicaid benefits in the U.S. Medicaid generally paid 80–85 percent of their prenatal and delivery costs; the rest were absorbed by the hospital.

Some women would telephone each of the local obstetrical units to determine the cost of a delivery, and base their choice partly or wholly on this factor. Most of Boston's hospitals responded to this price-sensitive market by instituting a so-called "package price." This covered prenatal clinic visits in the hospital's outpatient department, delivery, and postpartum care. Women delivered by private obstetricians were not eligible for the package price; on the other hand, they tended to be better insured for maternity services. The package price ranged from $500–850 at different hospitals; individual charges for comparable services totalled from $1,200–1,600. Although the package fee did not cover the hospital's entire cost (including overhead) of providing the services, it did cover direct costs. Some patients who initially entered the hospital as self-pay patients turned out to be eligible for Medicaid, which was a better source of reimbursement.

Hospitals recognized that the physical appearance of their maternity units was important in attracting patients. Since the prevalent mode of delivery was to have the mother awake and the father (or another companion) present, the physical appearance of the labor and delivery area was now even more important than in the past; most hospitals provided tours for couples who

---

[6] A health maintenance organization (HMO) was a prepaid health plan through which, for one annual premium, a person became eligible for comprehensive medical care. HMOs provided ambulatory care on site, but arranged for inpatient care to be provided in one or two selected hospitals. HMOs generally reimbursed hospitals the "reasonable cost" of whatever inpatient services their patients used.

were "shopping around" for an obstetrical service. The Boston Hospital for Women (BHW), the Peter Bent Brigham, and the Robert Breck Brigham hospitals had recently merged and would be moving in 1980–81 to a new $118 million facility, in the same neighborhood as the present BHW buildings. Both physicians and hospital administrators felt that the new facility could offer BHW a competitive edge in attracting obstetrical patients.

One of the biggest sources of patients for any of the Boston hospitals was the Harvard Community Health Plan (HCHP), a fast-growing HMO with branches in Kenmore Square and in nearby Cambridge. Prior to January 1, 1975, the Kenmore branch of HCHP had divided its 400 deliveries between BHW and Beth Israel, but it proved infeasible for one obstetrician to cover two separate units during evenings and nights. Observers believed that the decision to consolidate the entire operation at BHW rather than Beth Israel was probably based on the allegiance of HCHP obstetricians toward the hospital at which most of them had trained. As a result of the transfer of these 200 deliveries, Beth Israel experienced a slight drop in market share (from 16–15 percent of all deliveries in Boston hospitals). But in the spring of 1978, the Cambridge branch of HCHP was considering a transfer of its now more than 700 annual deliveries away from the Boston Hospital for Women, and possibly back to Beth Israel. HCHP's decision would have a major impact on the balance of obstetrical services in Boston.

Beyond these considerations lay the problem of planning the management of maternity services so as to conform, as far as practicable, to the expectations of the women who were giving birth. The philosophies of the obstetrical staffs of each Boston hospital were considerably different, as were their interpretations of current trends and their willingness to innovate in an effort to cultivate new markets.

St. Elizabeth's, Boston City, and Beth Israel exemplified three different approaches to obstetrical care, as summarized by local media:

St. Elizabeth's: "We're traditionalists." That's how Dr. James Whelton, director of ob/gyn services at St. Elizabeth's Hospital in Brighton, characterizes his hospital. "A number of hospitals have alternative birth centers. We don't. We've concentrated our efforts in renovating the postpartum area." Which is indeed festive, with its magenta, orange, green, and yellow color scheme.

The hospital hasn't had much incentive to explore alternatives; according to Whelton, only 7 or 8 percent of the women who gave birth there last year requested natural childbirth.[7]

Boston City: Boston City Hospital offers a contractual setup that allows patients of private physicians to use the hospital. The woman writes a list of requests that is signed by her doctor and evaluated by the staff. As long as the attending physician goes along with the woman's wishes and she has had extensive childbirth preparation, the requests are usually approved. At the time this story was being researched, one woman who was planning to have her baby at Boston City asked that her four-year-old daughter be allowed to witness the birth. A child and an adult psychiatrist were going to interview the family before any decision was reached. "But we're considering it," said staff pediatrician Jeffrey Gould, "which is more than we would have done a year ago."

Beth Israel: "Have It Your Way," the fast-food advertising pitch is serving a loftier purpose in the maternity ward at Boston's Beth Israel Hospital. A framed version of the slogan hangs on the wall to inform mothers—and fathers—that they have a choice in the way their child will be delivered.[8]

Exhibit 6 summarizes obstetrical procedures and other policies at four Boston hospitals, as reported in the *Boston Globe.*

Some obstetricians, even in the most patient-oriented maternity units, were reluctant to

[7] Kelly, "Special Delivery," pp. 135–7.
[8] Herbert Black, "The Revolution in Childbirth," *New England Magazine (Boston Sunday Globe)*, May 14, 1978, p. 22.

EXHIBIT 6
PROFILES OF OBSTETRICAL POLICIES AT FOUR MAJOR BOSTON HOSPITALS

Question	St. Elizabeth's (1,000 babies/year)	St. Margaret's (3,000 babies/year)	Beth Israel (2,061 babies/year)	Boston Hospital for Women* (6,000 babies/year)
1. How much can the father participate?	Through delivery, including nonemergency C-sections.	Through delivery. Still considering C-sections.	Through delivery, including nonemergency C-sections.	Through delivery, including nonemergency C-sections.
2. How much can the family's other children participate?	Visits Wed. & Sun. in family room; can only see baby through window.	Visits in family room and cafeteria, not allowed in mother's room. See baby through window.	Visits in mother's room if baby not there. Can see baby through window.	Special visiting hours if accompanied by other parent; every morning 7:30–8:00 in mother's room. See baby through window.
3. How much medical intervention is routine?	Episiotomies & fetal monitors almost always; drugs–doctor's option. Enemas optional.	Fetal monitors routine. All other up to doctor.	Fetal monitors almost always. Episiotomies, drugs, use of stirrups no longer routine, up to doctor.	Everything up to doctor; trying for fewer episiotomies.
4. What are minimum costs?	$550 package plan for outpatient. $1300 for private patients.	$105/day.	$850 package plan for outpatients, private patients $150/day for mother, $93 for baby, plus $321 delivery room.	$1600 approximately for average stay.

5. Are certified nurse-midwives available for delivery?	No.	No, but childbirth teachers can accompany mother through birth.	Yes.	Yes, but still working out rules and regulations for deliveries.
6. Can baby "room-in" with mother?	Yes, except when other children present.	Yes, at mother's choice, except when other children present.	Yes, baby also 'given' to parents at delivery. Not if children also in room.	Yes, except when other children present.
7. Are alternate methods of childbirth (Lamaze, Leboyer) accepted?	Yes, modified.	Yes, modified.	Yes, modified.	Yes, modified.
8. Are homelike "birth rooms" available?	No.	Soon. Room being built.	Soon. Establishing ABC (Alternate Birth Center) in fall.	Looking into it.
9. What emergency infant care is available?	Special care (level 2) nursery.	Intensive care (level 3).	Special care (level 2) but Joint Program in Neonatology with BHW and Children's Hospital provides intensive care for infants.	Same as Beth Israel.

* Formerly known as the Boston Lying in Hospital.
Source: The Boston Globe, July 21, 1977.

change their traditional modes of practice to accommodate what they perceived as transient fads. Others feared the potentially adverse financial consequences of patient-supported practices such as midwife delivery. Thus, even though all institutions were interested in determining patient preferences, the actual implementation of change in obstetrical practice—indeed the perception of a need to change—varied considerably from hospital to hospital and even from one practitioner to another.

THE BETH ISRAEL MATERNITY SERVICE

In 1978 the medical staff of Beth Israel's obstetrical service consisted of twelve full-time obstetrician/gynecologists, whose practices were located within the hospital, and thirty-eight "attending" physicians in private practice who admitted patients to the hospital. The service's chief of staff, Emanuel A. Friedman, M.D., was somewhat concerned about the fact that the attending obstetrician/gynecologists were getting older, for older practitioners tended to concentrate their practices in gynecology rather than obstetrics.

Newborn babies were cared for either by private pediatricians or by the Joint Program in Neonatology[9] (JPN)—a joint venture between Children's Hospital, the Boston Hospital for Women, and Beth Israel. The JPN began its operation in 1974, subsequent to Beth Israel's decision to give up its 14-bed pediatrics unit as a condition for getting a Certificate of Need to construct the Feldberg Building. Conceived as "one nursery in three locations," the JPN provided care at all three hospitals, yet the most sophisticated technologies were available in only one site. Thus, infants born at BHW or Beth Israel who required surgical treatment were transferred to Children's Hospital; and Beth Israel babies

requiring medical intensive care were transferred to BHW. Although the number of transfers was minimal (1–2 percent of babies born at Beth Israel and BHW), the system made it possible for each baby to receive the best possible care.

Beth Israel's obstetrical unit consisted of forty-five beds distributed over two floors. During the early 1970s, in response to the declining birth rate, the hospital had considered converting its maternity beds to medical/surgical beds. However, because the hospital would have lost some of its obstetrician/gynecologists as a result, it could have been forced to eliminate the gynecology service as well. The net result would have been a much narrower clinical and teaching program, and the idea was abandoned.

The unit had been built in 1952, and had not undergone any major renovations (with the exception of air conditioning) since. The majority of patient rooms were semi-private, containing two beds, although there were some private rooms as well as some triples. The physical appearance of the obstetrical unit was adequate, but it paled by comparison to the colorful, spacious Feldberg Building opened in 1976.

The hospital's administrators were considering the possibility of renovating the labor and delivery area. Changes in the character of obstetrical practice at Beth Israel had rendered the size and layout of the existing facility inadequate. The teaching program had increased in both quality and size since Dr. Friedman's appointment in 1969. Accordingly, as more high-risk obstetrical cases came into the hospital, there was a need for more space for resuscitation equipment for babies and for additional personnel in each delivery room. The inclusion of fathers in the labor and delivery process also required more space; and if the Cambridge branch of HCHP were to bring its deliveries to Beth Israel, one or more additional delivery rooms might also be needed.

Proposals ranged from renovating the existing labor and delivery area ($1.5 million), to renovating another, larger area within the hospital ($2.5

---

[9] Neonatology was a subspecialty of pediatrics concerned with the care of newborn babies.

million), to adding another floor to the Feldberg Building ($3 million or more).

The first option would improve the appearance of the labor and delivery suite, but would not provide any additional space. The second option, which included renovation and conversion of the old operating room suite, would provide additional delivery rooms, each larger than the current ones. On the other hand, the location of this space was not ideal; it was several floors away from the rest of the maternity unit and did not provide all of the support space considered desirable. The third option, the addition of a ninth floor to the Feldberg Building, would free the space in the old operating rooms for other needs. Given the constraints on the hospital's capital resources, and pressure from the state's Determination of Need office to keep capital expenditures as low as possible, the hospital administration felt it imperative to choose the proposal that fulfilled current and future requirements at least cost.

Complicating the issue was the problematic financial position of Beth Israel's obstetrical unit. Its loss for FY 1978 was projected to run close to $400,000 (Exhibit 7).[10] A major contributing factor was the inadequacy of third-party reimbursement (health insurance) for obstetrical services. Twenty-nine percent of the obstetrical patients at Beth Israel during FY 1977 were either holders of commercial insurance policies or self-pay patients (without coverage). Commercial insurance generally contributed a fixed dollar amount toward the cost of maternity stay, but the maximum rarely came close to the $1,600 average charge for a normal delivery. And even though self-pay patients were charged only the $850 package price, many could not pay even this amount. Thus, adjustments to revenue for bad debts and free care were high.

[10] The magnitude of the unit's total contribution, including related admissions of OB patients to other services (notably gynecology), could not be ascertained.

Service Changes

Historically, Beth Israel's obstetrical services had followed the same narrowly prescribed policies as many other academic maternity units. Indeed, as Carmel Brochu, R.N., clinical (nursing) director of obstetrics and gynecology, recalled:

> When I came to Beth Israel, it had very rigid rules and regulations. There were nurses that dealt with the babies, and nurses that dealt with the mothers, and there was little interaction between them. The mother was heavily sedated and the baby was given to her at set times in the same way she would be given a meal tray. The nurses had particular ways of wrapping the infant, and the mother was not allowed to undress the baby; consumers had not reached the point of making demands. My background as a nurse-midwife in England had taught me to view the family as a whole; it was difficult for me to adapt to practices I saw here.

Brochu felt that the turning point at Beth Israel had occurred with the introduction of family-centered maternity care, around 1970. From that point on, the father could attend the birth in the delivery room, and remain with mother and baby for as much time as the couple desired; the mother could keep the baby in her room as long as she wished; and family visits to the mother's room were encouraged.

As the women's movement gained momentum, Beth Israel attempted to respond to demands by women for medical services that met their needs in a sensitive manner. There were several female obstetrician/gynecologists on the staff, and half of the hospital's ob/gyn residents were women. Staff members stated that the hospital was committed to the idea that women should control the birth process to the greatest extent possible. Beth Israel made optional many of the medical interventions—including drugs, anesthesia, and surgical incisions—that had formerly been considered routine. In Dr. Friedman's view:

> Flexibility is the byword for obstetrics. Within the

EXHIBIT 7

BETH ISRAEL HOSPITAL: COST ANALYSIS OF OBSTETRIC SERVICE AND RELATED ACTIVITY FISCAL Year (FY) 1978
(Projected Actual)*
(All Figures in Thousands of Dollars)

	Obstetrics Floors	Delivery Room	Nursery	Fetal Monitoring	Outpatient (Prenatal & Postpartum)	Total
Gross revenue	$1,478	$ 815	$ 987	$126	$ 196	$3,602
Adjustments	(182)	(100)	(10)	(15)	(90)	(400)
Net revenue	1,295	714	976	111	105	3,201
Direct costs						
Salaries & wages						
Nursing service	447	393	320	—	—	1,151
OBS–GYN administrative office	44	179	—	55	—	280
Neonatology service	—	—	9	—	—	9
Outpatient clinics	—	—	—	—	92	92
Total salaries & wages	492	563	330	55	92	1,534
Fringe benefits	98	112	66	11	18	306
Total compensation	591	675	396	67	111	1,841
Supplies**	68	115	62	21	5	273
Total direct cost	659	791	458	88	116	2,114
Allocated costs	728	336	206	18	87	1,378
Total direct & indirect costs	1,388	1,128	6,665	107	204	3,493
Fixed depreciation & interest	48	29	13	—	5	97
Total cost	1,436	1,157	678	107	210	3,590
Margin—gain (loss)	$ (141)	$ (443)	$ 297	$ 3	$(104)	$ (388)

* Disguised Data.
** Approximately 30 percent of supplies costs were variable, the balance were treated as fixed costs.
Source: Beth Israel Hospital

bounds of safety for both mother and baby, we allow the patient virtually to formulate her own delivery process.

As an example of the unit's desire to provide services that accommodated the individual mother's needs, a staff member cited its dealings with neighborhood health centers. The nursing staff had "gone out of their way" to learn Chinese customs relating to the birth process, as well as Chinese dietary prescriptions, as part of the relationship the hospital maintained with the South Cover Community Health Center in Boston's Chinatown.

A major innovation in Beth Israel's maternity service occurred in July 1977 when the hospital responded to a change in Massachusetts law allowing nurse midwives to deliver babies. Previously, Massachusetts had prohibited this practice, and limited the activities of midwives to pre- and postdelivery care. Although Beth Israel had hired two nurse midwives some years earlier, their activities had been limited in accordance with law. Once the restrictions were lifted, however, Beth Israel became one of the first institutions to implement midwife delivery.

Patient satisfaction with the midwives was said to be high. Women felt that the midwives paid a great deal of attention to them during prenatal visits, and were sensitive to their concerns. The midwives expressed a desire to help women choose the type of birth experience that they would feel most comfortable with. In the words of one woman,

> The delivery was as close to a home birth as possible. I was awake and participating in everything and needed no drugs, but all the technical backup was ready in case anything went wrong.

A second major innovation was the construction of an Alternative Birth Center (ABC) early in 1978. The ABC was a further response to women who wanted to deliver their babies with a minimum of medical intervention, while knowing that help was close at hand should it be required. Accordingly, the ABC was made available to low-risk mothers who had a high probability of

normal delivery and who wished to deliver by "natural" childbirth (without anesthesia or surgical intervention).

The ABC differed from traditional labor and delivery suites in several ways. Each of the two "birthing rooms" within the ABC was furnished to look like a bedroom. The sophisticated instruments that were kept in the room for use in emergencies were hidden from view. The process of delivery differed markedly as well. In traditional suites, a woman was wheeled from labor room to delivery room and had to shift from a bed to a delivery table during the most active phase of labor. By contrast, a woman in the ABC labored and delivered in one room and one bed. In both instances, the mother returned after delivery to a standard hospital room for her postpartum care.

Due to the cost of anesthetic equipment and the fact that the long-term popularity of the ABC concept was not known, the ABC did not provide anesthesia; thus, some women who favored the concept might still choose to deliver in the labor and delivery suite, where anesthesia was available. If a major renovation of the main suite were undertaken, it was reasonable to assume that the concept of combined labor and delivery could be expanded to rooms where anesthesia could be administered.

Pricing, Communications, and Outreach

The hospital had instituted an $850 package price for obstetrical services, which included prenatal and postpartum care in the Beth Israel outpatient clinic in addition to a routine delivery. A deposit was required at the time of the initial prenatal visit, and the remaining balance was divided by the number of months remaining until the expected date of delivery. In total, about 10 percent of births at Beth Israel were paid for on this basis.

The hospital's direct cost for providing a delivery in the ABC was slightly less than the direct cost of a delivery in the traditional labor and delivery suite. However, Beth Israel offered only one package price lest some women be encouraged to deliver in the ABC (without anesthesia) not by choice but by financial necessity.

Beth Israel pursued several strategies in publicizing its patient and family-centered maternity services. Dr. Friedman stated that he favored the concept of advertising within ethical boundaries, but that the medical profession "is limited by custom to minimal advertising." There were specific professional guidelines as to what was and what was not appropriate. Although a few advertising programs had been initiated by Beth Israel, Dr. Friedman believed these to be less extensive than those carried out by obstetrical units at other hospitals.

J. Anthony Lloyd, who had been the hospital's director of public relations since November 1977, believed that publicity should emphasize the human side of care at Beth Israel:

> The care and attention that our patients receive go far beyond that required for competent delivery of services, and we try to convey that idea. For example, when I was working on a press release on the Alternative Birth Center, I applied this principle by focusing on one family's relationship with the Beth Israel from prenatal visits through postpartum care. The story unfolded from the family's point of view, and illustrated the warm, personalized care for which we strive.

Lloyd listed print, broadcast, direct mail, and professional staff as media through which the public relations office had informed the community about the hospital's maternity services.

Beth Israel also participated in educational programs, both within the hospital and outside in the community. These included a women's health series, headed by a group of Beth Israel obstetricians and nurses and advertised through local newspapers; parent education courses held at the hospital for expectant parents; and film festivals to which the general public was invited.

Finally, the hospital sought to facilitate patient access to its services. Through contracts with several health centers scattered throughout the city, Beth Israel staff provided prenatal care in a convenient, local setting to a variety of distinct patient groups. The easy availability of Beth Israel's prenatal care for these clinics greatly enhanced the appeal of the hospital's delivery services. Moreover, because the offices of Beth Israel obstetricians in private practice were widely dispersed (located up to 20 miles west of Boston), the hospital had succeeded in making its services available throughout a wide geographic area (Exhibit 8).

REVIEWING THE SITUATION

As he tried to evaluate Beth Israel's obstetrical service, Steinberg asked himself how it contributed to teaching and community service. Should the hospital continue to offer obstetrical care, or could a good argument be made for closing or shrinking the size of the OB unit? If so, should these beds be transferred to another service, or eliminated?

On the other hand, if the hospital's board decided to continue offering obstetrical services at Beth Israel, then it would have to find ways of improving the unit's financial performance. Steinberg believed that the obstetrical package price merited some study. The $850 fee had not been increased for several years, and he wondered if it might be possible to raise it—perhaps to $1,000—without sacrificing its value as a marketing tool or negating its philanthropic purpose.

Also, he needed to evaluate the possibility of promoting the obstetrical service to a patient population with better insurance coverage, and determine the strategies that might best achieve this goal. Although the hospital was committed to providing its services to all patients regardless of their ability to pay, a well-rounded payor mix was needed to keep the deficit in obstetrics at a minimum.

Lastly, Steinberg knew he must address the issue of renovating the labor and delivery area. Confronted with the prospect of the BHW's forthcoming move to new quarters, he was acutely aware that Beth Israel's obstetrical facilities had not had a facelift in more than 25 years.

EXHIBIT 8

DISTRIBUTION OF MATERNITY ADMISSIONS FOR BOSTON, CAMBRIDGE, AND NEWTON BY PATIENT'S HOME LOCATION, 1974–75

	Beth Israel Hospital		Boston City Hospital	Boston Hospital for Women	St. Margaret's (Boston)	St. Elizabeth's (Boston)	Mt. Auburn (Cambridge)	Newton-Wellesley (Newton)
	Medical-Surgical*	Maternity						
Boston								
Allston/Brighton	5.9%	2.9%	0.0%	3.2%	0.3%	18.0%	1.9%	1.3%
Charlestown/East Boston	0.3	0.3	4.8	2.2	0.9	4.3	—	—
Back Bay/South End/Downtown	6.4	6.0	8.1	6.5	0	3.3	0.5	—
South Boston	0.5	0.8	2.7	0.7	12.6	0.6	0.1	—
Dorchester	5.3	10.5	37.4	7.2	26.1	2.2	0.3	0.2
Roxbury	6.2	12.9	30.0	8.1	2.3	0.6	0.4	—
Mattapan/Hyde Park	4.3	6.9	5.7	3.5	6.7	3.0	1.0	0.7
Jamaica Plain/Roslindale/ W. Roxbury	7.8	7.9	5.5	7.5	10.1	9.3	—	1.7
Other Boston	1.4	1.4	1.3	0.2	0.3	0.1	0.1	0.2
Total Boston	38.1	49.5	95.7	39.0	59.3	41.3	4.3	4.1
Belmont	0.7	1.0	—	—	—	1.5	6.5	0.7
Brookline	15.1	4.9	—	2.5	—	2.6	0.3	0.6
Cambridge	2.4	4.2	0.2	4.5	0.2	3.1	18.5	0.2
Chelsea	2.4	0.9	0.1	1.3	—	4.2	—	—
Dedham	0.3	0.4	—	0.9	1.6	1.3	0.4	2.6
Milton	1.1	0.4	—	1.1	2.7	0.9	—	0.2
Needham	0.7	0.9	—	0.7	0.1	1.1	—	5.2
Newton	4.7	2.9	—	4.4	0.3	4.6	1.5	23.4
Quincy	1.2	1.3	—	1.5	7.7	1.0	0.5	0.3
Somerville	1.3	1.5	0.1	2.8	0.6	2.2	10.3	0.5
Waltham	0.7	1.4	—	1.1	0.2	3.0	3.5	9.0
Watertown	0.7	1.2	—	1.4	0.2	5.4	11.5	4.6
Wellesley	0.2	0.5	—	1.0	—	0.6	0.1	7.3
Other locations	30.6	29.1	2.5	37.7	27.0	27.1	42.6	42.2
Total	100.0%	100.0%	100.0%	100.0%	100.0%	100.0%	100.0%	100.0%

* Medical-surgical admissions at Beth Israel shown for comparison.
Source: Massachusetts Hospital Association

93

"BABY WALLY": Marketing A Broadway Show

Gregrey W. Gorden
Christopher H. Lovelock

Another business day was under way in New York's Broadway theatre district. Jim Hughes heard one of his assistants answer the phone, "The Baby Wally Company," as he turned to look out his window to Times Square and the construction below. Hughes was the producer of the successful musical comedy "Baby Wally" which by March 1982 was in its third season on Broadway. In the past two years Hughes had also produced two national companies of "Baby Wally," which were touring the major cities of the U.S., and was coproducer of a London company which had opened just two months ago. In any given week the four companies of "Baby Wally" grossed over a million dollars in ticket sales.

"Baby Wally" was a musical, based on a popular fictional comic book character, which had opened on Broadway in February 1979 following out-of-town tryouts in Boston and Washington, D.C. It had received generally favorable critical reviews and had clearly been a big hit with the

Copyright © 1982 by the President and Fellows of Harvard College, Harvard Business School case 9-582-137.

public. Hughes could remember the morning following "Baby Wally's" opening night. He had walked by the Mark Patrick Theatre on his way to his office. It was only 8:00 a.m. and the box office would not open for another two hours, yet there was a line of several hundred would-be ticket buyers spilling out of the lobby onto Broadway and stretching around the corner to 50th Street. Last night the *Times's* and *Post's* reviews had been great but this was it! He had produced a hit! A hit! This show was a producer's dream: he felt at the time that "Baby Wally" would run forever.

THE SITUATION IN MARCH 1982

As Mr. Hughes looked uptown toward the Mark Patrick Theatre, he was concerned about the box office health of his "Baby." In March 1982 there were a lot of pressures affecting the Broadway box offices, including inflation and rising production expenses which had pushed ticket prices to an all-time high. David Merrick, the producer of another popular musical, had recently raised the price of his best seats to $50, establishing a new top price. "Baby Wally's" top price was currently $40 for a Friday or Saturday evening performance and Hughes was worried about how long he would be able to hold the ticket at that price. He was also concerned about the current recession and the possibility of price resistance developing for a show that was no longer the hottest ticket in town.

Hughes remembered he had an appointment that afternoon with Terry Diefenbach, who had worked for Hughes before returning to the Yale School of Drama to get a graduate degree in arts management. Diefenbach had called him wanting to discuss the development of a new Broadway marketing idea that seemed to include merchandising and retail distribution. Although Diefenbach did not explain the complete proposal over the phone, Hughes had been intrigued. If there were one thing Broadway was not guilty of, in Hughes' opinion, it was innovative marketing techniques. Only in the past eight years had most box offices even agreed to accept credit cards and checks.

THE BROADWAY BUSINESS

Jim Hughes was but one of the hundreds of entrepreneurs who called themselves theatrical producers. They were an eclectic and unusual group of individuals. Although the skills required to make a great producer—taste, creativity, strong interpersonal skills, flair, flexibility, iron will, boundless energy, a penchant for risk taking, and an ability to raise large sums of money for high-risk ventures—were rarely found in an individual, people entered theatrical producing from a wide variety of backgrounds. Most of the season's newcomers were gone within a year or two, having either failed to finance their project or opened on Broadway and flopped, losing the entire investment. They quickly returned to careers with less anxiety and ambiguity, but steadier paychecks.

In a typical season (June 1 to May 31) over 200 projects would be announced for development and production; 50 to 70 of these new projects would be financed and eventually make their way to Broadway, which had 35 theatres. In an average season, 20 of those theatres would be filled with hit shows held over from previous seasons. Clearly not all new shows would have extended runs on Broadway. In fact, the odds of survival were not good. Most shows would close in the first four weeks of their run, sometimes closing on opening night if the reviews were poor or even mixed and the show had no major box office star. Ten of the 60 might live to see their 100th performance, but on average only five would settle into a long and profitable run. In March 1982 the longest running play on Broadway was the enormously successful musical, "A Chorus Line"; conservative estimates were that it had brought in over $70 million in its six and a half seasons on Broadway, plus hundreds of millions more from national and international companies.

The Risks and Returns

It was that kind of box office smash that attracted the theatrical entrepreneur to Broadway. But the risks were high. In 1970 the average play or comedy had cost about $100,000 to produce and the average musical, about $420,000. Ten years later *Variety* estimated that the average play cost $600,000 and average musical, $1,200,000. This investment could be lost overnight. One recent example of the instant flop phenomenon was a revival of the George M. Cohan musical "Little Johnny Jones," which opened and closed on March 21, 1982, losing its entire $1.2 million capitalization.

When a show hit, it was a different story. Among Broadway's most successful investments were returns of over $3,000 for each dollar invested by the original investors in "Hello Dolly," $6,000 for $1 for "Oklahoma!" and over $6,400 for $1 for "My Fair Lady." These earnings continued to be distributed by the production company to investors for 18 years following the closing of the Broadway or first-class national touring company of the play or musical.

Most Broadway theatrical productions like "Baby Wally" were financed through limited partnership agreements. Wealthy individuals and less frequently corporations invested in the project as limited partners. The producer was the general partner and was liable for expenses beyond the original capitalization. In exchange for his producing efforts the general partner usually received 50 percent of the profits after recoupment of the original investment. The limited partners also received 50 percent of the profits following the recoupment of their original investment. Profits were defined as the weekly gross box office less theatre rental, royalties, and all fixed operating costs, which included cost and crew salaries, marketing expenses, costumes and set repair contingencies and the like.

As the capital risks of a Broadway show had increased, so had the weekly operating costs. These could range from $50,000 to $100,000 for a play and from $75,000 to $200,000 for a musical. Thus capital and the ability to raise capital were the major entry barriers into the theatrical producing business. It was a fragmented industry with minimal other barriers except for the ability to negotiate a theatre for the production.

Broadway's Landlords

Thirty of the 35 theatres on Broadway were controlled by just three organizations. The theatre owners' power was broadly based in many aspects of production, including funding of workshop productions, promotional and marketing experience, and long-term personal relationships with creative artists. Major decisions which affected a producer's chances of success included the availability of an appropriate theatre for the production. Theatre selection was critical from several viewpoints, including artistic considerations, economic house size, and location within the Broadway theatre district. Other important

issues were the structure of the rental agreement and whether the theatre owners would invest in and/or coproduce a production.

Once owners agreed to provide a theatre, they usually became active partners in the production even if they had not made a capital investment. Most theatre rental agreements required a flat rental fee per week to cover operating expenses plus a percentage of the weekly gross box office revenues. This agreement not only protected the owner against downside risk but also provided an incentive for theatre owners to help make the production a hit. It was commonly believed that the laws of competition did not function in traditional fashion within the bounds of Broadway. Instead of drawing audiences from competing plays, it was thought that a new hit drew more attention to Broadway, creating larger audiences for many productions—not just the new hit.

The most difficult decision for a theatre owner occurred when a long-running show began to lose its audience or when a new show opened and faltered, doing only marginally profitable business. The theatre was earning rental revenues which covered most operating expenses, yet this revenue was substantially less than the potential to be earned from having a hit in the house. Almost all rental agreements included a "stop" clause, allowing the theatre owner to evict a production if the gross box office receipts fell below a specified amount for a period of (usually) two consecutive weeks. The risks of evicting a marginally profitable production included balancing the possibility of attracting a new production to the house with a greater appeal versus the possibility of having a "dark house" which generated no revenues but still incurred substantial property taxes and salary expenses. Theatre owners often believed that new plays, which opened to good or mixed notices but poor box office, could build and "find" their audiences. In such instances the owners might waive their percentages to give the producer time to get the show on its feet and improve ticket sales.

The Broadway theatre was a business which represented creativity, glamour, illusion, and excitement for those looking in from the outside. For those on the inside, it meant endless hours, anxiety, frustration, and ambiguity—plus enormous personal, professional, and financial risk. Yet despite the risks, Jim Hughes felt there was simply no other business like show business in terms of personal rewards and potential financial rewards. With "Baby Wally" he had struck a very rich vein. His immediate goal was to maximize the box office potential of his long-running Broadway hit.

Marketing on Broadway

Unlike film producers and distributors who would spend from 25 percent to 100 percent or more of a film's production cost for marketing, it was rare for a theatre production to set aside even 15 percent of the production budget for marketing. Because a producer was restricted by law from using the limited partnership's funds until the partnership was fully capitalized, often little advance market planning was done.

Once a project was completely capitalized, the production went into full swing and it would be only six to eight weeks before the curtain went up for the first preview. In that period the image of the product had to be created, a logo designed, T.V., radio, and print advertisements designed and approved, posters and window cards printed and distributed, among many other tasks. This was done in the midst of casting, securing a theatre, overseeing set and costume designers' work, and pampering stars, director, choreographer, and major investors. As important as the marketing plan was to the success of the production, it took a back seat to the creation of the play or musical. If a producer did not have a particular interest in, or flair for, marketing (and most did not), he or she would abdicate responsibility and turn it over to an advertising firm.

Advertising firms, although more skilled than most producers, rarely had the time, budget, or financial incentives to develop a carefully constructed, innovative marketing plan. Under pressures of time, tradition, and budget they fell back on marketing instruments which Hughes believed had limited impact on the theatre consumer of 1982. An example of one of these instruments was the window card, typically 10" × 16". Expensive to produce, the window card's primary function had been to occupy the windows of ticket agencies, shops and restaurants in the Broadway area. Although a few restaurants still used the theatrical motif, the cards' popularity had declined along Broadway. Less than 3 percent of the Broadway audience bought their tickets from ticket agents; some observers questioned whether window cards sold a single seat.

Once a show's visuals and copy had been created and the target market delineated, the next step was selection of appropriate media to reach that market. Television had become the number one medium for Broadway advertising, although its use was a relatively new phenomenon. In 1972, "Pippin," a musical comedy, opened to mixed reviews and unenthusiastic ticket sales. Its producers then decided to go to the public via an elaborately produced television commercial which featured the show's highly stylized dancing, magic, colorful sets, and costumes—as well as several upbeat tunes from the show's score. Overnight, ticket sales improved dramatically, quickly changing Broadway's passive attitude towards the power of television advertising.

Television's major disadvantage was its cost. To produce a one-minute commercial of a stage musical could cost as much as $150,000 by the time all expenses had been added in. Furthermore, the cost of broadcasting local TV spots tended to be quite expensive when compared to the cost per thousand of media such as radio, newspapers, magazines, subway posters, bus sideboards, posters, and window cards. Cable television seemed to offer a promising opportunity for marketing, but most of New York's boroughs were not yet wired and few producers had been willing to experiment.

Pricing Strategies on Broadway

Until 1970, theatre tickets were available only at the theatre box office and had to be purchased with cash. Since then, box offices had agreed to accept credit card and local bank checks. Distribution had improved as well. Theatre tickets could now be purchased at many Ticketron outlets around the city and country, and through Telecharge and Chargit.

In successful Broadway shows, the top price tickets were nearly always the first to go. Hughes felt that the consumer identified price with the quality of both the show and the seat. Most ticket buyers seemed willing, in fact determined, to have the best available seat, even if that meant spending an extra $5 to $10 for the best ticket. This had naturally led theatre owners and producers to price the vast majority of the seats in the house at the top prevailing price. In the Mark Patrick fewer than 25 percent of the seats sold below the top price of $40 and they were always the last to move. In the Mark Patrick balcony only seven rows marked the difference between a $40 seat and one in the third price group of $32.

Little experimentation or research had been done to demonstrate the effect of price on demand for individual shows. Virtually all musicals were priced at similar levels, as were most Broadway plays. The prevailing wisdom was that few consumers selected a Broadway entertainment on the basis of price. But price did seem to affect the frequency of theatre attendance (and thus overall demand for the Broadway product). A 1980 study found that 35 percent of respondents felt that ticket cost was a "major obstacle" to more frequent attendance; the figure was even higher among certain segments of the theatregoing audience (Exhibit 1).

It was clear, however, that hit shows had often been priced well below the price they could demand. When a hit show opened, ticket brokers swooped down on Ticketron outlets and theatre

EXHIBIT 1
TICKET COST AS FACTOR IN THEATRE ATTENDANCE

	Percentage of Respondents Rating Ticket Cost as a "Major Obstacle"
Segments above Average	
Traditionalists	52
Now attend few shows	44
Age 50 and over	40
Age 35–49	40
Women	40
Income under $15,000	40
Segments below Average	
Single people	30
Men	29
Now attend more shows	28
Age 18–24	27
Theatre enthusiasts	25
New patrons	25
All Theatregoers	35

Source: Survey of the New York theatre audience by the New York League of Theatre Owners and Producers, 1980.
See pages 101–104 for more details of specific segments.

box offices and attempted to purchase large blocks of prime tickets for resale. This was legal as long as brokers limited their resale markup to $2 per seat. However, the public was often willing to pay much more than this, so brokers quickly became scalpers. As the *New York Times* noted in a 1980 article:

> Many ticket brokers in New York frequently, even routinely, ignore the law that allows them to mark up a theatre ticket by only $2 and charge double or triple the box office price instead. "Evita" tickets that cost $25 or $30 at the box office, for example, are scalped for $50 to $85, while tickets to lesser hits are scalped for $50 to $60.

Producers had been extremely reluctant to use price increases or discounts to manage demand. Historically, the reason for this was that prices were set and tickets printed several months in advance. By 1982, however, box offices could change the printing of ticket prices at the touch of a finger or a computer keyboard. But producers were hesitant to boost prices sharply when they had a hit on their hands. They feared the adverse publicity and public outcry that could result from a price boost that followed close on the heels of favorable reviews. Of course, the biggest fear was the chance of the disastrous: a drop off in sales.

The first concerted strategy of discounting theatre tickets took place when TKTS opened its windows in 1973. TKTS was created by the Theatre Development Fund and the League of New York Theatre Owners and Producers to market unsold tickets on the day of the performance only. These seats were sold for one-half the normal box office price, plus a surcharge on each ticket sold. TKTS was an immediate hit with students and other low-income theatregoers who were willing to brave the elements, stand in line, and gamble that the show they desired would be available. TKTS imposed a modest service charge to pay for operation of its two outlets. It was completely up to producers whether they elected to have tickets for their shows available at TKTS. Since TKTS was independent of all productions it had no vested interest in pushing one show's tickets over another. In 1974, TKTS was responsible for 6 percent of all tickets sold for Broadway shows that year and for about 4 percent of total Broadway revenues. By 1980 TKTS accounted for 16.6 percent of the 9.62 million theatre tickets sold that year; it generated $14.2 million in revenue, representing 9.7 percent of the year's gross.

Generally the TKTS box offices in Times Square and on William Street in the Wall Street area opened at 12 noon to sell tickets for matinee performances and at 3 p.m. for evening performances. Each day a producer—or more likely the production's treasurer—would decide how many unsold seats to release to TKTS for sale at half price. These seats were usually the highest priced in the house but the least desirable in that price range, and thus were the least likely to be sold at full price at the box office (Exhibit 2).

If a show was "going clean" at the box office, that is, selling out every performance, the pro-

duction would elect not to utilize TKTS but to keep all tickets in-house for possible last minute full-price sales. Virtually no Broadway shows were playing consistently to sold-out houses in March 1982. Some musicals, like "Dreamgirls" and "42nd Street," would be depended upon to go clean on weekend evening performances, but even with TKTS sales would not reach capacity on most weekday performances. "Baby Wally" had been on TKTS for most weekday performances since the end of the Christmas and New Year holidays.

Sometimes during previews, before a show opened, the producer would paper the house. Papering was a method of building word-of-mouth advertising for a show. Papered seats were given away free, usually to members of the theatre community who knew someone involved in the production. Occasionally, papered seats would be sold at deeply discounted prices, 10–20 percent of face value, to nonprofit groups. Although useful as a marketing mechanism to get out the word about a show, papering was not a meaningful way of generating revenue once a show had opened.

When business at a theatre box office declined, producers occasionally elected to distribute free vouchers enabling customers to buy discounted tickets at the theatre box office or through the mail. These "twofers" (so-called because some vouchers entitled the purchaser to two tickets for the price of one) could be used for any performance. Producers who used twofers were usually attempting to generate advance sales as well as day of performance sales. Ticket buyers at the box office gave the image of popularity the producer wanted to maintain; further, box office personnel could control seat allocation for advance twofer sales by selling less desirable seats at the discount price and holding back prime seats for later full-price sale.

The discounts varied but usually ranged from 15 percent to 45 percent off the full price. In March 1982, 12 of 27 Broadway shows utilized twofers, which were being distributed in supermarkets, drugstores, hotels, and restaurants.

EXHIBIT 2
TICKET SALES FOR BROADWAY SHOWS THROUGH TKTS BY DAY OF THE WEEK, MARCH 1–7 AND 8–14, 1982

	Day and Time of Performance								
	Mon. Eve.	Tues. Eve.	Wed.		Thur. Eve.	Fri. Eve.	Sat.		Sun. Mat.
			Mat.	Eve.			Mat.	Eve.	
March 1–7									
Number of tickets sold	2,096	2,627	3,724	3,911	3,314	5,097	3,137	5,242	2,044
Percentage of all Broadway shows running that had tickets available for that performance	44%	47%	47%	53%	50%	47%	36%	36%	47%
March 8–14									
Number of tickets sold	1,837	2,216	5,163	5,583	3,589	5,939	3,213	6,224	1,864
Percentage of all Broadway shows running that had tickets available for that performance	44%	50%	47%	47%	50%	50%	38%	36%	47%

Eve. = Evening performance, typically starting at 8:00 p.m.
Mat. = Matinee performance, typically starting at 3:00 p.m.
Source: Variety magazine, March 1982.

Some producers distributed twofers themselves; others utilized a specialist company, typically paying $2,000 for distribution of 100,000 twofers. There was no dependable yield ratio but some producers reported up to 25 percent of their weekly gross was due to twofer sales. Although a useful marketing tool, many producers preferred to avoid twofers since they implied that a show was nearing the end of its run.

Seasonality

Broadway ticket sales typically varied by season as well as by day of the week. Like film attendance, peak demand was a weekend phenomenon; Friday and Saturday evening performances were the most popular. During the week, demand varied with the night of the week and the audience segment most attracted to the play. Traditionally, the performances ranked, in declining order, Thursday evening, Wednesday matinee, Wednesday evening, Tuesday evening, Monday evening, and finally Sunday matinee or evening performance. All productions, by contractual agreement with Actor's Equity Union, played no more than eight performances per week, performing on only six of the seven days. Thus a theatre was dark at least one day a week, usually a Monday or less frequently a Sunday. "Baby Wally's" performance schedule was typical of a major family Broadway attraction, with five evening performances, Tuesday through Saturday, and three matinees, Wednesday, Saturday, and Sunday.

In the past, most producers would not elect to bring new productions to Broadway in late spring since the summer months—July, August, and September—were considered a slow period. However, tourism had been on the rise in New York in recent years and visitors were increasingly attracted to Broadway theatre. In a 1979 poll, Broadway was the top attraction for tourists visiting New York, with 37 percent mentioning the theatre as their first stop. This affected demand and, of course, the seasonal composition of the audience. In a poll of theatregoers taken in August 1980, some 50 percent named a permanent residence outside the New York metropolitan area.

The traditional seasonal high points were the weeks preceding major holidays—Christmas, Thanksgiving, and New Year—as well as the spring months during school vacations. The off periods usually lay a week or two behind the peaks—for example the second and third weeks of January.

Theatre Parties and Group Sales

Some ticket brokers specialized in purchasing blocks of tickets for resale on a subscription basis. The block would be sold at 10 percent off face value with the subscription agent receiving 10 percent of face value from the producer as a commission. Theatre clubs could often exert substantial pressure on a producer to get the seats they wanted if they negotiated before the show became a hit. Once a show opened and was declared a hit, the power position was reversed and the producer controlled the tickets that all the theatre clubs now wanted to have. Theatre parties were usually organized as benefits for charity groups. The broker purchased the tickets at a discount, 10 percent, and the charity resold the tickets for a price significantly exceeding the face value, perhaps $100 to $150, with the proceeds of the sale going to the charity. The ticket broker usually received a commission on the sale but this was paid by the charity.

THE BROADWAY AUDIENCE

Although the number of Broadway theatres had declined (the Bijou, Helen Hayes and the Morosco theatres were in the process of being de-molished in March 1982) and the number of new productions undertaken for Broadway had declined each season since 1972, the number of tickets sold in 1980–81 had increased over 30 percent from the 1971–72 season. Admittedly slow in its growth, Broadway had defied critics who had proclaimed its demise. One indicator of Broadway's growth was the number of playing weeks. This was the sum of the number of weeks that all productions played Broadway in a given season. The 1980–81 season was up 40 percent over 1971–72. Reflecting inflation, total box office receipts in 1980–81 were up 280 percent from 1971–72.

On average, 85 percent of the Broadway audience during the 1980–81 season lived in New York City or in the suburban communities of New York, Connecticut and New Jersey. The remaining 15 percent of the audience were non-New York residents who came from literally all over the world.

The New York Audience

A study commissioned by the New York League of Theatre Owners and Producers (of which Jim Hughes was a member) and published in April 1980 found a large segment of the audience to be new to the theatre. Three of ten members of the audience had started going to Broadway theatre in the past five years. Young people dominated this group; almost half were under 25 and close to 90 percent were under 35. This trend was affecting the composition of the average Broadway audience (Exhibit 3). Other characteristics of the average theatregoer were unchanged. Not surprisingly, most theatregoers tended to be well educated, white, and in the higher income brackets. Exhibit 4 shows the demographic profiles of the New York theatregoing and non-theatregoing audience segments.

The study found four distinct segments of the New York theatregoing audience, labeling them: Traditionalists, Theatre Enthusiasts, Entertainment Seekers, and Dispassionate Theatregoers.

EXHIBIT 3
THE NEW GENERATION
OF THEATREGOERS

	Percentages	
Number of Years Attending		
1–5 Years	30%	
6–10 Years	19	
10 Years	51	
Age of New Patrons		
Under 25	46%	
25–29	25	(71)
30–34	16	(87)
35 and Over	13	(100)
Age of All Theatregoers		
Under 25	22%	
25–34	35	(57)
35–49	24	(81)
50 and Over	19	(100)

( ) = number of new patrons.
Source: Survey of the New York theatre audience by the New York League of Theatre Owners and Producers, 1980.

As outlined in Exhibit 5, each group attended with different degrees of frequency. Each segment had distinct attitudes, desires, and motivations with regard to the Broadway theatre.

Traditionalists could be considered the elitist segment. They tended to be the best educated and most affluent of the four segments. They were drawn to Broadway to see a specific play, primarily dramas and more serious theatre. An older and well-informed segment, they knew the names of major writers, directors, and actors and often followed critical reviews in the *New York Times, New Yorker,* and other print media. Although they had the highest incomes, they were also the most cost conscious segment and frequently bought their tickets at TKTS. This segment rarely planned theatre attendance more than a week in advance. The Traditionalists considered the Broadway theatre to be a cultural event rather than a social one, and it was but one of a number of cultural interests which often included Off-Broadway theatre, concerts, ballet, and the opera. Consequently they usually had very high critical expectations of Broadway theatre.

Theatre Enthusiasts were younger than the Traditionalists, had below-average education and incomes and included the highest proportion of nonwhites. This group loved Broadway. Musicals were their favorite, followed closely by comedies and dramas. Broadway was this segment's prime cultural interest and was considered the most enjoyable night out, although they were interested in other performing arts too. Enthusiasts liked to read about the theatre and were well informed about many shows. Unlike the Traditionalists, Enthusiasts wanted to see all the major shows and were far less critical in their expectations. This was the segment most likely to be satisfied with the product and to display the strongest desire to go to the theatre more often. The major obstacle to fulfilling that desire was the expense involved. Consequently this group exhibited above-average usage of TKTS. Like the Traditionalists, this segment did not plan far in advance; over 50 percent planned less than two weeks in advance.

Entertainment Seekers were the oldest of the four segments; most were married with several children. The segment was the least well educated yet had above-average income and had been attending the Broadway theatre for over 10 years. The Seekers considered an outing to the theatre to be an exciting social event and tended to go with friends, often on special occasions. They had a rather superficial knowledge of the Broadway theatre and tended to be highly influenced by advertising, usually television. Like the Enthusiasts they were not very critical and preferred lighter shows such as musicals and comedies. This group planned theatre occasions, most over four weeks in advance. Because theatre attendance was planned and Seekers were not well informed about the Broadway theatre, their use of TKTS was limited. They had above-average attendance on weekdays and matinees.

EXHIBIT 4

DEMOGRAPHIC PROFILE OF BROADWAY THEATREGOERS AND NON-THEATREGOERS

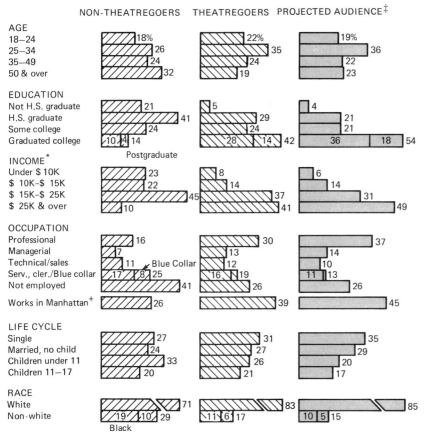

* Household income.

\+ Respondent or family member.

‡ Theatregoers weighted by frequency of attendance.

Source: Survey of the New York theatre audience by the New York League of Owners and Producers, 1980.

Dispassionate Theatregoers represented the youngest segment of the theatregoing audience, with two-thirds under 35. Most were married, well educated with average incomes and young children. This group was the least informed about the theatre, which was far from their prime entertainment activity, placing well behind dining out, rock concerts, sports events, discos, the movies, and drinking. Like the Entertainment Seekers, this group preferred light shows, either appealing to young adults or family entertainment suitable for young children. Dispassionate Theatregoers often planned three or more weeks in advance and responded to word-of-mouth recommendations and advertising. This group had the lowest level of TKTS usage.

EXHIBIT 5
MOTIVATIONAL AUDIENCE SEGMENTS

	% of Theatregoers	Average Frequency of Attendance per Year	% of Projected Audience*
Traditionalists	24%	4.5	33%
Theatre Enthusiasts	23	4.3	30
Entertainment Seekers	35	2.2	24
Dispassionate Theatregoers	18	2.1	13
	100%		100%

*Weighted average based on percent of theatregoers times average frequency of attendance.
Source: Survey of the New York theatre audience by the New York League of Theatre Owners and Producers, 1980.

The Non-New York Audience

Relatively little was known about the 15 percent of the Broadway audience which came from outside the New York metropolitan area. Almost by definition, most were tourists or business visitors. The business visitors segment probably did not have a significant seasonal variation; the tourists, however, did. A survey in August 1980 found that virtually 50 percent of the summer audience were from outside the New York metropolitan area. Twelve percent of the summer audience were, in fact, foreign visitors coming from (in decreasing order of percentages) Canada, the United Kingdom, Israel, Japan, Venezuela, Germany, the Caribbean, Mexico, and Switzerland.

Of the American non-New York audience, half came from the midAtlantic, Southeast and Great Lakes States and another quarter was from the New England area. The cities in the U.S. sending patrons to the Broadway theatre were (in decreasing order) Los Angeles, San Francisco, Boston, Miami, Chicago, Washington, D.C., Houston, Detroit, Philadelphia, and Dallas.

In recent years the New York League of Theatre Owners and Producers had cooperated with the State of New York to promote tourism through the "I Love New York" campaign. Their most popular television commercials, which were aired in major national and international markets, featured the productions and stars of Broadway. The campaign featured a brief segment of a colorful "Baby Wally" production number in one commercial as well as segments of several Broadway shows with international stars and reputations.

"BABY WALLY"—THE MUSICAL

In 1978, when Jim Hughes optioned the rights to produce a musical based on the comic strip character Baby Wally, the strip was syndicated in some 60 newspapers nationwide. Unlike another musical based on a comic strip character, Little Orphan Annie, Baby Wally had really only been before the public for five years. Baby Wally was the creation of a talented young cartoonist, Hal Rogers, whom Hughes had known since their freshman year in college. In his comic strip, Rogers had successfully created a delightful and whimsical fantasy world in which Baby Wally dwelled. Human-like, most of the characters in Baby Wally were allegories for contemporary popular social, political, and entertainment figures. The strip had captured the imagination of many young Americans and was read religiously on college campuses.

Hughes had taken the humorous characters and fantasy world of Baby Wally and produced a satirical but light-hearted and optimistic musical comedy which dealt in allegory with many of the principal figures and issues of the day. The musical was filled with contemporary popular music, magical and colorful sets and costumes, and a plot line that could be enjoyed on several levels by both children and adults.

"Baby Wally" was produced at a cost of $1.9 million which, in February 1979, made it one of the most expensive musicals to come to Broadway. The royalty structure of "Baby Wally" was typical for a major Broadway musical. The author, composer, lyricist, and director each received 2 percent of the weekly gross box office receipts. Hal Rogers, the creator of the characters and premise from which the show was developed, received 1 percent of the box office take and the choreographer received 0.5 percent. Although several of the production's actors had been highly acclaimed in their roles, none had been offered a percentage for their participation, being paid on a straight salary basis.

Weekly running expenses, which included $20,000 for media expenditures but excluded the contract rental, totalled $135,000. The contract rental for the Mark Patrick Theatre that Hughes had negotiated with the theatre owner called for $20,000 per week base, plus 9 percent of the gross to $150,000 and 10 percent of the gross over $150,000.

For "Baby Wally," the 1,513-seat Mark Patrick Theatre had been scaled for three price levels. Seats for Friday and Saturday evenings were available at $40, $35, and $32. The remaining six performances had tickets priced at $35, $30, and $26. The vast majority (1,100) of the seats in the house were in the top-price category. The second-price tier had 200 seats and the remaining 213 seats were in the lowest-price tier. This gave the theatre a weekly gross capacity of $415,860. For many weeks after the show had opened the theatre's weekly gross regularly exceeded this figure through the sale of forty standing room spaces in the rear of the orchestra. These tickets, sold at $10 each, were frequently purchased by young people who did not mind

standing if no other seats were available for the three-hour performance.

Jim Hughes had twice increased the ticket prices to "Baby Wally," with as little publicity as possible. He made the move only after several other hit musicals had raised their prices, blaming rising operations costs. The scalping of Baby Wally tickets annoyed him but he was unsure whether raising prices further for a section of the house would effectively reduce scalping or further segment the ticket buyers.

MEDIA PLAN

When "Baby Wally" opened, Jim Hughes had targeted his marketing toward a young audience for Broadway—men and women aged 18 to 34. He felt he had been successful in reaching that market by advertising in more youth-oriented media than any producer before him. His campaign had used papers like the *Village Voice*, *Interview*, and *After Dark* magazine, as well as the newspapers of a number of colleges and universities in the city. Baby Wally was also advertised in the *New York Times* and listed in the *New York* and *New Yorker* listings. About 30 percent of the advertising budget was spent on print and the remaining 70 percent went toward spot television purchases. Hughes chose youth-oriented programs like "Saturday Night Live" and "M*A*S*H," as well as spots on the "Today" show and "Good Morning America" for broader exposure.

Once "Baby Wally" opened, it became clear that it was going to be a broad-based hit appealing to both young and old. In recent months, Hughes had sensed a growing proportion of families and groups of older people in the audience. Given the 1980 League media surveys (Exhibit 6), he wondered if this shift in the audience should be met with a shift in his marketing focus.

TERRY DIEFENBACH'S PROPOSAL

While waiting for Terry Diefenbach to arrive, Hughes reviewed "Baby Wally's" box office re-

EXHIBIT 6
MEDIA AS SOURCES OF INFORMATION ABOUT THE THEATRE

	Percentages According to Audience Use		
	Newspapers	**Magazines**	**Television**
Total Sample, Projected Audience*			
Have used as source	76%	32%	24%
Use on regular basis	39	14	7
Segments			
Traditionalists	92	45	13
Theatre enthusiasts	72	42	24
Entertainment seekers	67	23	30
Dispassionate theatregoers	57	13	29
Geographical Areas			
Manhattan	81	40	15
Remaining boroughs	72	30	29
Suburbs	75	30	25

* See Exhibit 5 for definition of projected audience.
Source: Survey of the New York Theatre audience by the New York League of Theatre Owners and Producers, 1980.

ports for the month of February. The two national touring companies were going strong, playing to virtually capacity audiences in large theatres in Washington, D.C., and Los Angeles. The London company had built several months of advance sales. Unfortunately the Broadway company was continuing to experience the softening trend in sales that had begun in January. The first two weeks of March had been even less encouraging since the seasonal boost that Hughes was expecting had not materialized (Exhibit 7).

Hughes greeted Terry Diefenbach warmly and after exchanging news of the past several years, the latter began to explain his idea. He was interested, he told Hughes, in establishing a new distribution channel for theatre ticket sales. Because the Broadway theatre seemed to enjoy a unique position in the entertainment market as an activity suitable for special occasions, Diefenbach wanted to make the product more convenient, so that it could be given as a gift. The concept was to package theatre vouchers, which would be good for full-price orchestra seats for any performance of "Baby Wally," with a piece

of merchandise related to the production. The merchandise could be the Original Cast Album recording of "Baby Wally," a special color brochure illustrating the show and its stars, or a product such as a T-shirt, coffee mug, or book bag, with the "Baby Wally" logo imprinted on it. The vouchers and merchandise would be attractively packaged and sold in department and specialty stores in the New York metropolitan area.

Diefenbach felt that this type of packaging and distribution would allow the theatre experience to be considered as a gift purchase. The gift market had been a difficult one to tap for the theatre because of the planning required. He offered an example:

Suppose I have an Aunt Joan and Uncle Bob who live in Darien, Connecticut. They have an anniversary coming up. I have seen and loved "Baby Wally" and know that they would enjoy it, too; but because of Aunt Joan's business travels, I am uncertain when they would be free to come into the city to go to the theatre. This way I could send them the "Baby Wally" gift package with the prepaid vouchers and they could make their own arrangements to

EXHIBIT 7
"BABY WALLY" TICKET SALES BY DAY OF THE WEEK, MARCH 1–7 AND 8–14, 1982

	Tues. Eve.	Wed. Mat.	Wed. Eve.	Thur. Eve.	Fri. Eve.	Sat. Mat.	Sat. Eve.	Sun. Mat.
Week of March 1–7*								
$40.00 seats					1,048		1,023	
35.00 seats	922	987	977	960	149	1,006	163	946
32.00 seats					139		142	
TKTS seats	60	60	60	60	—	60	—	60
30.00 seats	86	112	126	118		181		102
26.00 seats	47	101	97	112		141		96
Standing positions**		7			23	21	27	10
Week of March 8–14*								
$40.00 seats					1,084		1,100	
35.00 seats	897	993	1,007	1,016	142	982	180	951
32.00 seats					114		126	
TKTS seats	100	60	60	60	—	60	—	100
30.00 seats	104	125	101	140		122		87
26.00 seats	57	93	8	68		93		46
Standing positions**		14			31	33	40	21

* "Baby Wally" had no Monday performances.
** Forty standings at the rear of the orchestra were available for each performance at a price of $10.00.

enjoy my gift at their convenience. The merchandise, the packaging, and the copy enhance the theatre experience by creating excitement and expectation, as well as offering a tangible product that is associated with the theatregoing experience.

The package would also contain a seating chart of the theatre so that recipients could select the seats they preferred from among those available, and know with confidence where they would be sitting; in the League's 1980 survey, some 63 percent mentioned that it was important to know where the seats were in the theatre (Exhibit 8). This service was not normally available through other channels, except when buying the ticket directly from the box office.

The voucher would act as a gift certificate. It would require the user to notify the theatre box office 48 hours in advance of attendance to guarantee seats for a given performance. These tickets would be held at the box office and exchanged for the vouchers up to thirty minutes before curtain. If users wished to make arrangements well

in advance of attendance, they could send the vouchers to the theatre box office and have tickets for the desired performance sent to them. Further, the voucher could be coded so that no physical transfer of the voucher would actually need to take place. The user would simply read the voucher code to the telephone ticket operator, the voucher number would be stored and confirmed as a legitimate number and then deleted from the list of outstanding vouchers. The tickets could be held at the box office or mailed.

Diefenbach believed the gift package could be sold on the retail level at a premium. He felt that two $40 vouchers and a cast album or souvenir book with a retail value of $10 could be sold for $100 to $105. It would offer buyers the opportunity to give a unique, specialized, and exciting gift which could be used by recipients at their convenience, enabling them to select from among available seats at a given performance. At the same time, said Diefenbach, distribution in a retail setting removed from Broadway would

EXHIBIT 8
SOME ATTITUDES TOWARD THE BROADWAY THEATRE

Statement	Total Sample	Percent of Projected Audience* by Segment Who Completely or Strongly Agree with Each Statement			
		Traditionalists	Enthusiasts	Entert. Seekers	Dispassionate
In my opinion, Broadway offers the best theatre anywhere.	62%	50%	69%	74%	57%
Going to see a Broadway show is a special event for me.	49	42	52	62	30
Seeing a Broadway show is the best evening out for me.	43	35	60	48	16
For me, the best way to celebrate an anniversary or special occasion is to see a Broadway show.	42	34	56	46	21
I like to dress up when going to a Broadway show.	42	33	35	61	45
Going to a Broadway show is a great way of getting together with relatives or friends.	32	31	30	45	15
When buying tickets, it is most important for me to know where the seats are.	63	57	65	70	63
I only go to a Broadway show if I can get good seats.	24	23	16	33	26

*See Exhibit 5 for definition of projected audience.
Source: Survey of the New York theatre audience by the New York League of Theatre Owners and Producers, 1980.

bring the product closer to the consumer and create a tangibility which was missing when a ticket was purchased through conventional channels.

Although his proposal was targeted as a gift purchase within the market segment familiar with the Broadway product, Diefenbach felt that there was potential for spillover into other market segments. He was convinced that nonusers or infrequent users did not understand how one went about securing tickets and going to the Broadway theatre, and there were some who found the Ticketron, Chargit, and Telecharge systems too confusing or risky. He hoped that this product would appeal to those people. The gift package would attempt to tie the unknown—and for some, mysterious—world of Broadway theatre to a well-known, respected, and stable retail institution like Bloomingdale's.

Economics

Diefenbach explained to Hughes that he had spoken with a number of buyers responsible for gift-type merchandise in major retail institutions in the New York area. He had been encouraged by their responses and had worked out the following structure for the product:

1 "Baby Wally" would receive 75 percent of the face value of the ticket; that is, all ticket vouchers would have a face value of $40 and Jim Hughes and company would receive $30 for each voucher sold when redeemed at the box office.

2 Diefenbach would manufacture the voucher, package it with a piece of "Baby Wally"-related merchandise for which the "Baby Wally" company would receive an appropriate licensing fee, and wholesale this package to the retailers for $79.

3 The retailers would place a retail value on the package of between $100 and $105.

Diefenbach felt that retailers would be attracted to the product because of its show business appeal. They would be able to use the product for theatre-oriented window displays, tying in with theatregoing fashions or related merchandise. Recognizing the unique qualities of the product as a prestige gift item, retailers might use it as a traffic builder. He envisioned retailers featuring the product in advertising and promotion, using a copy tag like the record industry's "Give the Gift of Music"—perhaps "Give the Gift of Theatre." It would also be an ideal product, he felt, to combine with in-store appearances of theatrical personalities, events that stores like Macy's and Bloomingdale's frequently scheduled to create excitement in the retail environment. Although buyers had not handled an item similar to this one, most indicated that 25 percent to 30 percent of the retail margin might be applied to advertising the product.

For a discount that ranged from 14 percent to 25 percent, depending upon which night the voucher was redeemed, the "Baby Wally" company would obtain a new marketing and distribution channel (Exhibit 9). Increased exposure through retail distribution and any subsequent advertising and promotion for the gift package by retailers could, Diefenbach believed, spur box office and charge sales by reminding consumers of the show's availability through conventional channels.

Mulling it Over

After Diefenbach had left, Hughes mulled over his friend's proposal. Down on Broadway he could see the demolition of the Helen Hayes Theatre continuing. He wondered if this package and retail distribution could effectively increase the longevity of "Baby Wally's" run. Would it cannibalize or increase full-price box office sales? Would it work if the voucher were restricted to ticket availability for certain days of the week only? Could the package be sold outside the New York market in other cities to presell New York-bound tourists? What retail stores should be targeted? How large could the market for this type of product be? Diefenbach's idea had raised a lot of questions for Jim Hughes, who recognized that the marketing decisions he made could have important implications for the length of run and profitability of his four "Baby Wally" companies.

EXHIBIT 9

METHOD AND PLACE OF TICKET PURCHASE FOR LAST BROADWAY
SHOW ATTENDED

	Percent of Projected Audience			
	Total Audience (1,891)	Manhattan (586)	Remaining New York City Boroughs (571)	Metro Area Suburbs (735)
Method of Purchase				
In person	73%	85%	70%	66%
By telephone*	22	13	25	27
By mail**	4	2	5	5
Do not know	1	—	—	2
Total	100%	100%	100%	100%
Place of Purchase				
Box Office				
In person	45	49	47	39
By telephone***	19	12	22	24
By mail	3	#	3	4
Tickets (TKTS)	16	29	7	12
Ticketron	12	7	17	13
Broker/Agent	3	1	2	5
All Others	2	2	2	3
Total	100%	100%	100%	100%

* Telephone includes Telecharge 12%, Chargit 7%, Broker 2%, and Others 1%; figures are for total sample.

** Mail includes Box Office 3%, and TDF and Others 1%; figures are for total sample.

*** Includes Telecharge and Chargit.

\# Less than .5%.

Source: Survey of the New York theatre audience by the New York League of Theatre Owners and Producers, 1980.

DEXION OVERSEAS LTD.

Shiv Mathur

In November 1975, John Foster, recently appointed Managing Director, and Keith Galpin, Marketing Manager, of Dexion Overseas Limited (DOS), were attempting to give new direction to Dexion's overseas activities. Dexion had, over the years, grown substantially but somewhat haphazardly in its export markets and it seemed to the two managers that it was time for a full review of the company's present position and future overseas activities. They were particularly concerned with DOS's operations in Africa and the Middle East, as these regions characterized the changing political and economic conditions in most of Dexion's overseas markets.

DEXION-COMINO INTERNATIONAL LTD.

Dexion-Comino International Ltd., was founded before the Second World War to manufacture slotted angles invented by Demetrius Comino as a solution to the recurring need for easily erect-

Copyright © 1976 London Business School. Revised 1981. (Financial support for the preparation of this case was provided by the British Overseas Trade Board.)

able and demountable industrial structures. What was initially jokingly referred to as "industrial meccano" soon acquired wide acceptance. Comino's initial investment of £14,000 in a 4,000-square foot factory in North London had by 1968 grown into a 200,000-square-foot site at Hemel Hempstead, producing well over 50 million feet of slotted angles. By 1973 Dexion was well established as a worldwide name with wholly owned subsidiaries in North America, Europe and Australia, with exports accounting for over 60 percent of the UK factory's total turnover.

Product Range

As the group's turnover and geographic coverage had increased, so had the company's range of products. What had started as ordinary slotted angles (known as DCP—Dexion Catalogue Products) that could be erected by almost anybody, had gradually grown in sophistication. By 1975 Dexion was a world leader in manufacturing and installing complete materials handling systems.

In the developed countries the continuing

search for more efficient techniques of storage and materials handling resulted in a rapid growth of the unit load concept (various small parts being containerized for efficient storage)—and in particular the use of pallets. Dexion systems like "Speedlock" adjustable pallet racking were developed to meet this need. The Speedlock range permitted vertical storage to a height limited only by the height of the building itself. When fitted with wheels the racks, then known as "Poweracks", could be mounted on steel rails permitting the closing down of an aisle and opening up of a new one at the touch of a switch.

By 1975 Dexion manufactured a whole family of products that served particular applications. "Apton" square tube framing had been designed for the smarter display of goods, "Clearspan" and "Impex" shelving for better storage of hand-loaded goods and "Maxi" for storing small items. The basic DCP range was also modified and extended to meet entirely new applications. For example, DCP products that were usually used for storage had been modified to facilitate the construction of prefabricated housing units in developing countries. The growth of new products in many instances had also produced growth for DCP products as they constituted basic ingredients of the more advanced designs.

Overseas Activities

Until 1970 overseas growth of Dexion's activities had been largely organic. As Dexion products had gained popularity, the company had set up subsidiaries in North America, Europe and Australia. In other countries of the world Dexion had appointed distributors to stock and retail the products. Where local demand was fairly substantial but import restrictions prevented direct export and circumstances did not justify a subsidiary, local manufacturers had been licensed to produce and sell some products in the Dexion range. By the early 1970s Dexion had licensing arrangements with manufacturers in various parts of the world (Exhibit 1), although few were in Africa and the Middle East.

The actual agreement varied from licensee to licensee and reflected the company's attitude at the time the agreement was actually signed. Agreements usually specified a royalty income based on a percentage of turnover, often with a minimum annual payment. Dexion had little control over the pricing and marketing policies of its licensees, though sometimes restrictions were placed on their export activities. As the majority of licensees were mainly concerned with building up strong positions in their home markets, pressure to export to third countries in competition with Dexion's own direct export activities was not a major factor. The problems as seen at Dexion headquarters were not so much of licensee exports to third country markets, but of ensuring that they developed their home markets and that licensee income due was in fact repatriated. Since many of the licensee markets had recurring balance of payment problems the actual collection of royalties was of continuing concern.

Competition with Dexion products both in the UK and overseas had multiplied. Dexion, however, had maintained its market leadership in the UK. Overseas, in addition to budding indigenous manufacturers, Dexion was facing growing competition from Italian and Continental exporters and lately the Japanese and Indians. But Dexion products were well established and the company prided itself on having a much more comprehensive product range and better design and other back-up services than the non-European competition. Cheaper British steel gave Dexion exports a very real advantage, but it seemed that the position was gradually changing. Mr. Foster was getting increasingly concerned about Japanese and subsidized Indian competition in the Middle East and the gradual erosion of the cost advantage of using steel made in Britain.

DEXION OVERSEAS LIMITED

In 1970 Dexion-Comino International Ltd had set up Dexion Overseas Limited (DOS) as a separate company within the organization to look after

EXHIBIT 1
LICENSED PRODUCT SALES, ROYALTY INCOME AND PRODUCTS LICENSED

Country (year of agreement)	Licensee 1974 Sales (£s)	Royalty Rates*	Products Licensed
Spain (1957)	650,000	£13,000 per annum (fixed sum)	DCP, pallet racking
Portugal (1957)	620,000	2%	DCP, Apton, Speedlock
New Zealand (1959)	210,000	2%	DCP
India (1960)	420,000	Profit participation agreement	DCP, Apton
El Salvador (1961)	50,000	4%	DCP
Canada (1964)	1,950,000	£25,000 per annum (fixed sum)	DCP and accessories
Mexico (1964)	1,170,000	2%	DCP, Apton, Speedlock
Brazil (1966)	490,000	4%	DCP, Apton, Speedlock
Argentina (1966)	160,000	4%	DCP, Speedlock
Peru (1967)	230,000	£4,000 per annum (fixed sum)	DCP
Jamaica (1968)	87,000	4%	DCP
Nigeria (1970)	490,000	4%	DCP and accessories
S. Africa (1971)	325,000	4%	DCP, Apton, Speedlock
Hungary (1971)	650,000	£65,000 (lump sum royalty)	DCP

*Expressed as percentage of turnover unless otherwise indicated.

and coordinate its entire overseas export and licensing activities. Markets where Dexion had established subsidiaries or associates were excluded. In order to supervise distribution closely, DOS had divided the overseas market into five regions and appointed regional sales managers (RSMs) located in London to oversee Dexion's interests in each of these areas. The five regions were: (1) the Middle East and North Africa, (2) Europe, (3) the Rest of Africa, (4) the Far East and Southeast Asia, (5) the Caribbean and South America. Exhibit 2 gives DOS results for 1973 to 1975 and Exhibit 3 gives a breakdown of 1975 results by region.

Direct exports and involvement in the Far East and Central and South Europe were comparatively small. Dexion's operations in Europe

were mature in nature and the increasing similarity between the UK and continental Europe in terms of competition, products and customers had gradually resulted in most of Western Europe being treated as an extension of the home market, at least so far as the existing product range was concerned. With UK entry into the EEC in 1973, this similarity between the home market and continental Europe was becoming even more obvious, although differences in channels of distribution remained.

Keith Galpin had carried out a detailed analysis of the various international markets that could provide it with substantial business in the future. This analysis had incorporated not only informed views within the company but also interpreted demographic and economic data. The attempt

EXHIBIT 2
DOS OPERATING RESULTS (£000s)

	1973	1974	1975
Invoiced sales	5,672	6,444	6,914
Gross profits*	1,076	1,770	2,088
Variable distribution costs	156	221	290
Gross profit (after distribution costs)	920	1,549	1,798
Home office and regional expenditure	565	560	703
Operating profit	355	989	1,095
Miscellaneous income (including royalties)	94	122	136
Interest	(13)	(75)	(75)
Profit before tax	436	1,036	1,156

* After deducting transfer prices payable to Dexion-Comino International Ltd.

was to highlight not only those markets which would continue to grow, but also select those which could become major profit generators in future. This exercise had brought to light some Southeast Asian and Middle Eastern countries which could be the target for more concentrated attacks.

DOS was of the opinion that during the next five years the company's business in the oil-rich countries of the Middle East and North Africa would expand much more rapidly than elsewhere. This called for a strategy that took into account the prominent position of the region. But the company felt that such a strategy would be applicable in principle to most overseas activities of the company, and Africa generally might follow the developments in the north.

DOS's International Policy

Markets and Organization Galpin divided the Dexion market in Africa and the Middle East roughly into three kinds of buyers. *Bazaar buyers* were customers who bought mostly DCP-type products to erect small and fairly crude storage and other structural units. Though DOS had no hard data on the buying behaviour of these customers, it was generally believed that they designed their requirements themselves or with some help from local Dexion dealers. Their main criteria for buying Dexion products in preference

EXHIBIT 3
ALLOCATION OF 1975 DOS Results by Region (£000s)

	Invoiced Sales	Gross Profit	Regional Expenses
Middle East and North Africa	3,016	1,006	96
Europe	1,829	378	33
Africa	1,090	408	42
Far East	257	61	26
Caribbean, and South America	426	142	49
Miscellaneous	296	93	13
Total	6,914	2,088	259
Variable distribution expenses		290	
Gross profit (after distribution)		1,798	
Less			
Regional expenses	259		
Central expenses	133		
Marketing and promotion	104		
Administration and rent	130		
Technical	77		
Total		703	
Operating profit		1,095	

to those of other suppliers were price and availability. The demand was more for the less sophisticated Dexion products and an important characteristic of the buyer was a lack of awareness and perhaps need for more sophisticated storage and material handling systems.

The second group were *installation buyers.* Installations could vary from small simple racking units (similar to those put up by the bazaar buyer) to complete warehouse units made up of products such as Speedlock pallet racking and Impex hand-loaded shelving. This type of business was invariably handled by local distributors, sometimes with the help of Dexion staff, and often required detailed designs and site construction. This design and construction service was increasingly being provided by the local distributor, although Dexion's UK-based units assisted with jobs which were outside the resources and capability of a particular distributor.

There was occasional demand for relatively large and sophisticated systems requiring special resources such as system analysis, structural design, subcontracting, contract negotiation, financing, project management, etc., outside the scope of any distributor. DOS referred to this third type of business as *project business* and it invariably involved sales and implementation resources not available locally from a distributor even when supported by a local Dexion sales representative. Support of the local distributor for this type of work was by the payment of a negotiated commission.

In order to serve the growth in both installation and project business, DOS had established in London a technical services cell (see Exhibit 4 for organization chart). The regional sales managers could refer their design problems to this unit and the cell itself undertook some marketing activities. It stayed in touch with UK-based architects, specifiers and designers to influence them to use Dexion equipment in projects they were associated with. The cell had developed over the years the expertise to quote for and supervise a wide variety of overseas projects. Its links with the regional sales managers were close.

As part of its central marketing function the DOS staff at headquarters attempted to coordinate the advertising and sales promotion campaign for Dexion products in national markets. Films, pamphlets and information material in various languages had been prepared. The marketing department together with regional staff undertook to arrange seminars in various overseas capitals aimed at specific audiences. The marketing department also looked after the promotion of individual products and retained staff product managers who coordinated the activities for a particular product in the regions.

Pricing DOS was supplied by the plant at Hemel Hempstead at a transfer price that reflected the direct costs of production and an allocation of works and general overheads. DOS, in turn, set prices for its distributors by adding a percentage markup to cover the cost of its own operations and provide a satisfactory profit.

In Mr. Foster's view, the essence of DOS's policy on distributor pricing was:

> A question of competitive activity—we should evaluate what price competitive products are selling at and adjust our margins to account for the comparative advantages and disadvantages of Dexion goods.

Distributors in national markets were quoted different prices to take into account expected local distributor mark-up, the prices of competitive products, and the local customers' ability to pay. For example, during 1974, when transfer prices charged to DOS rose by 15 percent (Exhibit 5a), there was no corresponding across-the-board increase in prices charged to customers. European customers were charged only an extra 5 percent, while Middle East prices went up the full 15 percent in sterling prices. When the devaluation of the pound sterling had been accounted for, however, the local prices ended up lower.

As a result of the policy of value pricing, the markups distributors charged on various Dexion products differed considerably. Exhibit 5b gives

EXHIBIT 4
DOS ORGANIZATION CHART

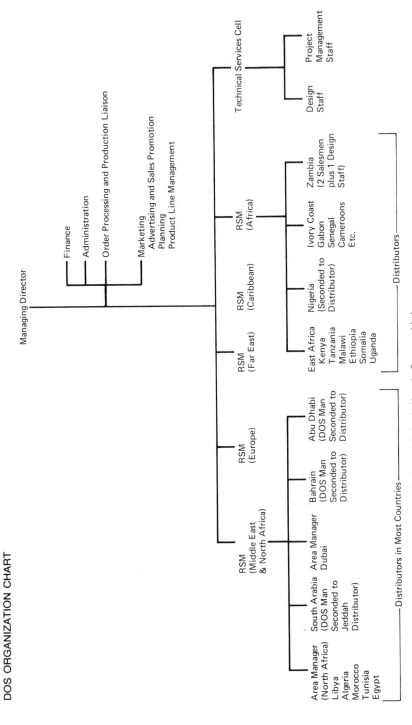

Managing Director

Finance
Administration
Order Processing and Production Liaison

Marketing
Advertising and Sales Promotion
Planning
Product Line Management

RSM (Middle East & North Africa)

Area Manager (North Africa)
Libya
Algeria
Morocco
Tunisia
Egypt

South Arabia (DOS Man Seconded to Jeddah Distributor)

Area Manager Dubai

Bahrain (DOS Man Seconded to Distributor)

Abu Dhabi (DOS Man Seconded to Distributor)

RSM (Europe)

RSM (Far East)

East Africa
Kenya
Tanzania
Malawi
Ethiopia
Somalia
Uganda

RSM (Caribbean)

Nigeria (Seconded to Distributor)

RSM (Africa)

Ivory Coast
Gabon
Senegal
Cameroons
Etc.

Zambia (2 Salesmen plus 1 Design Staff)

Technical Services Cell

Design Staff

Project Management Staff

——— Distributors in Most Countries ———

——— Distributors ———

Note: Full-time distributor staff looking after DOS sales and design in Kuwait, Oman and Lebanon.

EXHIBIT 5a
INCREASE IN TRANSFER PRICE TO DOS, 1974

	Cost Increase		Percentage Costs	Increase
Steel	− 5%	on	40%	− 2.0%
Auxiliary material	20	on	35	7.0
Accessories	10	on	10	1.0
Other costs	0	on	15	0
Volume down 30% on budget				9.0
Total increase in transfer price				15.0%

EXHIBIT 5b
DOS PRODUCT MARGINS
(excluding project sales, £000s)

	1973			1974		
	Sales	Gross Profits	Percent	Sales	Gross Profits	Percent
DCP	2,079	610	29.3	2,530	874	34.5
Apton	305	120	39.3	481	164	34.1
Speedlock	1,120	238	21.3	1,347	393	29.2
Others	590	108	18.3	570	107	18.8
Total	4,094	1,076	26.3	4,928	1,538	31.2

an indication of gross margins by product category. Though DOS informally indicated to its distributors in various national markets the price at which they should retail their products, it did not, and in management's view could not, lay down firm directives. This policy had both its advantages and disadvantages. The company did not retain any firm control on its prices and occasionally found distributors in well-protected or prosperous markets charging exorbitant markups. But with its flexible pricing policy, DOS had built for itself an extensive distributor network. Distributors, it was hoped would in turn set retail prices to maximise their own and consequently DOS's profits. That this did not always happen was seen as a largely unavoidable consequence of using independent companies as part of the distributor system.

Africa The regional sales manager (Africa) had for administrative convenience divided the countries south of the area of Arab influence into four areas: East Africa, Zambia, Nigeria, and the erstwhile French West Africa. The four areas were roughly equal in terms of market potential and four area managers were based in convenient local capitals. Though Dexion had a distributor in virtually every African capital, choice had been limited and determined more by the distributor's general business standing and connections with the local government than by previous experience of selling products related to storage and materials handling.

Apart from South Africa and Nigeria, the region was comprised largely of developing countries with foreign exchange problems and complicated systems of tariff and exchange controls. Often there was no dearth of demand for Dexion products but a noticeable lack of buying power for foreign products. (See Exhibit 6.) This was in the regional sales manager's view the single most important impediment in exporting to

EXHIBIT 6
AFRICA: ORDERS RECEIVED (£000s)

	1973			1974			1975		
	DCP	Other	Total	DCP	Other	Total	DCP	Other	Total
Ethiopia	32	—	32	25	2	27	16	—	16
Ivory Coast	12	—	12	5	3	8	38	7	45
Kenya	26	—	26	18	5	23	55	8	63
Nigeria	44	61	105	60	79	139	103	109	212
South Africa	3	8	11	11	9	20	16	56	72
Sudan	44*	—	44	—	—	—	—	—	—
Tanzania	—	—	—	5	—	5	18	—	18
Zambia	74*	35*	109	61*	71*	132	140*	279*	419
Zaire	5	13	18	1	2	3	—	—	—
Others†	85	26	111	72	29	101	49	8	57
Total	325	143	468	258	200	458	435	467	902

* Project activity.
† Cameroons, Gabon, Ghana, Gibraltar, Senegal, and Niger.

the African market. There were few areas where concentrated marketing effort could be justified. Not only was the entire region plagued by controls but it was also in a state of constant economic and political flux.

Many suppliers besides those in the developed countries had found it possible to meet the less sophisticated level of African demand. Continental, Japanese, and Indian exports abounded, but Dexion with its wide and well-established network of distribution had a firm grip and in some countries like Tanzania had almost wiped out the use of competitive products. In virtually all markets, small local manufacturers making a restricted range of generally low quality products were a continuing threat. In the regional sales manager's opinion, what Dexion had and the competition did not, were the local contacts and a name for quality and service that was well established.

It was not the overseas exporters who provided the major threat in African markets but the growing desire in most developing countries to set up their own production units. As the outlay for such a project would be about £500,000 it was well within the reach of most governments, if not individual entrepreneurs. It was possible that the small African markets would not support economic production units. But there was always the possibility of some countries getting together to come to tariff arrangements to form a quasi common market or to look actively for regional exports. Some countries in East Africa and French West Africa had shown just this sort of inclination and this was seen as the thin end of the wedge at DOS headquarters.

The richer countries of Africa—Nigeria, Zambia, and South Africa—were different in their purchasing behaviour. Areas of industrial concentration had resulted in a demand for a host of Dexion products and services. To South Africa and specially Nigeria, in spite of the presence of local licensees, Dexion directly exported the more modern systems, which were not manufactured locally. In Zambia, the company had obtained a large contract to design, supply, and erect a complete materials handling and storage system. The Zambian case characterized an obvious trend in buying behaviour. Developing country governments, keen to put up large indus-

EXHIBIT 7
MIDDLE EAST AND NORTH AFRICA—ORDERS RECEIVED (£000s)

Country	1973			1974			1975		
	DCP	Other	Total	DCP	Other	Total	DCP	Other	Total
Abu Dhabi	73	7	80	155	25	180	285	33	318
Dubai	32	11	43	78	3	81	85	27	112
Iraq	147*	—	147	478*	2	480	209*	4*	213
Libya	377*	21*	398	356*	17*	373	252*	60*	312
Oman	18	15	33	58	80	138	130	104*	234
Saudi Arabia	65	48	113	134	247	381	257	369†	626
Bahrain	18	9	27	35	34	69	25	21	46
Qatar	9	—	9	17	3	20	25	—	25
Algeria	—	1,235†	1,235		47*	47	—	—	—
Others‡	94	14	108	294	29	323	91	9	100
Total	833	1,360	2,193	1,605	487	2,092	1,359	627	1,986

* Project activity.
† Projects not broken up by product groups.
‡ Cyprus, Egypt, Iran, Jordan, Kuwait, Lebanon, Malta, Pakistan, Syria, Tunisia, and Yemen.

trial complexes, often with the help of overseas funds, increasingly contracted for the complete supply, design, and erection of turnkey projects.

Middle East and North Africa

The regional sales manager (Middle East) described his region:

> In spite of popular beliefs it is not all gold. For us there are three to four countries that contribute most of the sales. And it would be fair to say that in most countries the results are directly proportional to the effort we put in. When I say "we", I mean "we"—the local distributors have far too much on their plates and are often so badly organized that they need all the assistance we can give. The real selling force is frequent visits and resident expatriate staff—people who are willing to live in Arab countries and promote the Dexion name. And they are harder to find than you would imagine.

In spite of the massive oil revenues there was a growing inclination in some Arab countries to ban foreigners from setting up purely trading companies. The United Arab Emirates, Iraq, Iran, and Algeria had formulated, or were in the process of formulating, controls for limiting the activities of foreigners. Others like Libya, who were at that moment big customers of DCP products, had already outlined their intention to set up their own slotted angle plants to reduce the economy's dependence on imports.

Everywhere there was an explosive industrialization under way. All over the Middle East new plants were being constructed and the host countries, while embarrassingly rich financially, lacked human skills and infrastructure to cope with the growth. Even Iraq and Algeria, while attempting to lower their reliance on foreign companies, recognized the necessity to permit foreigners to bid for and undertake large projects. In fact, almost all Dexion's business in Iraq, Algeria, Iran, and a substantial portion of that in Saudi Arabia had been obtained by negotiating large contracts. (See Exhibit 7.)

Though the growth in project activity was generally welcomed by Dexion management, it had created some organizational problems. Contract negotiation took a comparatively long time and resulted more often than not in "next year's sales and this year's expenses." The regional sales managers were always under considerable pressure to maintain expenditure within agreed budgets and treated project activity with mixed emotions. However, when the organizational problems, both within DOS and with the local distributors, had been overcome, the profits were very welcome. Gross profits on successful tenders in the Middle East were broadly similar to those obtained on the sale of hardware alone.

Competition in the Middle East was strongest from the Japanese, Italians, and Indians in the supply of DCP-type hardware and from Japan and Germany in the project market. The Japanese and Germans often had a slight edge on Dexion as they had been able to quote for complete turnkey projects. In Libya, DOS's distributor had established very good links with the local government and Dexion products had reached a large market share, but only by pricing below DOS's normal markup to offset the price advantage of Italian products. In Saudi Arabia and the U.A.E., which still constituted the bulk of the hardware business, DOS's response to competition had been first to pare margins and second to promote slightly more advanced systems like Speedlock. In spite of overseas and local manufacturers crowding these markets, there was still ample opportunity for all. Saudi Arabia and the U.A.E. had five-year plans that budgeted a threefold increase in public expenditure—justification enough for the most forceful of selling efforts.

Alternative Possibilities

With its target of achieving a 15 percent annual increase in sales and profits, DOS management was aware that a series of long-term strategic decisions had to be made. These decisions would have to encompass almost all the activities of the company and would have to bear in mind that 100 percent owned subsidiaries would be difficult to establish overseas. They included:

1 Should the company continue to license overseas manufacturers to produce the DCP range in areas of high tariffs and foreign exchange problems, or should the licensing policy be extended to cover more products and markets? In particular, should DOS agree to permit the manufacture of the Speedlock and Apton range in Nigeria?

2 If licensing was not a viable option, in view of local government hostility to royalties, should DOS look to joint ventures?

3 Another possibility could be to discontinue all overseas manufacture and cancel where possible the existing licensing arrangements and manufacture and export from the U.K., or another suitable European base.

4 Which markets should be focused on and with what products?

5 Should the existing policy be changed?

6 Was there any need to restructure the distribution strategy?

The list of issues which needed to be questioned and sorted out seemed endless. DOS management was also aware of the fact that it would be impossible to put hard figures on many of these options, but John Foster felt that the data he had were reliable, in the sense that they were indicative of the situation. He was particularly aware that the issues were interrelated (e.g., the company could not have a production policy that required licensing arrangements and a marketing strategy that required distributors) and that the direction that DOS's total strategy took should at least be compatible within itself.

THREE

PRODUCT POLICY

An organization's choice of products influences all the other elements in the marketing program and also has significant implications for managers in such functional areas as finance, production, and personnel.

Product policy decisions center around what goods and services the organization should offer for sale and what characteristics these should have. They involve matching the resources and needs of the organization with market opportunities—hence the close link between market selection and product planning. Policy formulation, therefore, requires careful analysis of existing and potential products relative to the characteristics of both the market and the organization.

For many marketing managers, appraising the need for changes in the product line is a continuing process, reflecting the dynamic nature of the marketplace as well as changes in the nature and resources of the organization itself. One objective should be to eliminate or modify products which no longer satisfy consumer needs or fail to contribute significantly (either directly or indirectly) to the company's objectives. Another set of objectives relates to addition of new products or product features which will meet consumer needs better, enhance the organization's existing product line, and improve utilization of present resources. Complacency in product management in the face of a dynamic, competitive environment is a sure road to ruin for any organization.

PRODUCT DECISIONS

Virtually all manufacturing firms and service organizations produce a variety of different products. Policy decisions, therefore, may be approached from three possible levels:

- *Individual product items* which have a separate designation in the seller's list.
- *Product lines,* namely a group of products which are related in the sense of satisfying a particular class of need, being used together, possessing common physical or technical characteristics, being sold to the same customer groups through the same channels, or falling within given price ranges.
- *The product portfolio,* which comprises all products offered for sale by an organization. Although a particular product item—or even an entire product line—may not be profitable in itself, it may contribute to the well-being of the firm by enhancing the overall product mix. Some large corporations produce several thousand product lines, which together constitute the firm's product portfolio.

Product portfolio decisions should reflect not only market factors and corporate resources but also the underlying philosophy of company management. Most organizations are faced with several options over time. Some choose to pursue a policy of diversity; others prefer to concentrate their efforts on a narrow portfolio, offering a limited number of products in only a few sizes and varieties to a small set of targeted market segments.

The choice of product strategy should be determined by management's long-run objectives concerning profit levels, sales stability, and growth, as modified by personal values and attitudes toward risk taking. Market opportunities for the organization's products serve to determine the upper limits for potential corporate profitability, while the quality of the marketing program tends to determine the extent to which this potential is achieved.

While the "ideal" product portfolio is likely to vary from one organization to another, and may be hard to define, the following situations may indicate a *suboptimal* mix of products: chronic or seasonally recurring excess capacity in production, storage, or transportation facilities; a high proportion of profits coming from a small percentage of product items; competitors taking the initiative in markets; and steadily declining profits or sales.

Adjustments to the Product Portfolio

Changes in product policy designed to correct any of the above situations or otherwise enhance the firm's ability to meet established objectives can take one of three basic forms:

- *Product abandonment,* involving discontinuance of either individual items or an entire line;
- *Product modification,* involving changes in either tangible or intangible product attributes. It may be achieved by reformulation, redesign, change of unit sizes, and addition or removal of certain features;
- *New product introduction,* involving the development, test-marketing, and commercialization of new product items or product lines.

Product Positioning

The ability of an organization to compete effectively in any given market is determined in large measure by its ability to position its products appropriately relative to (1) the needs of specific market segments and (2) the nature of competitive entries.

Development of an effective product positioning strategy requires careful analysis of the ways in which the market is segmented and an evaluation of how well competing entries are meeting the needs of specific segments. Instead of competing head-on against a strong competitor, a firm may choose to finesse the competition by appealing to a different market segment.

Product positions often reflect not only intrinsic product characteristics but also the image created by promotional strategies, pricing decisions, and choice of distribution channels. For instance, the Cadillac name carries different connotations for car buyers than does Chevrolet, although both are products of General Motors. Similarly, hotel corporations such as Holiday Inns may sometimes use different names to differentiate their luxury hotels from their budget motor inns. These are examples of selective use of alternative brand names in multibrand companies to achieve a desired image. As an alternative to physical modification of an existing product, firms sometimes elect to *reposition* the product simply by revising such marketing mix elements as advertising and promotion, distribution strategy, pricing, or packaging. However, a revision of the entire mix, including product features, may also accompany a repositioning strategy.

Sometimes repositioning represents a deliberate attempt to attack another firm's product and take away its market share; in other instances the objective is to avoid head-to-head competition by moving into alternative market segments whose needs are not presently well served by existing products.

Analysis of competitive offerings involves not merely a review of product features and other marketing mix strategies but also an evaluation of competitive advertising *content*. The image generated by advertisements and the nature of the slogans employed may constitute a major positioning tool, especially for "commodity-type" products such as beer, cigarettes, or airline travel.

Product-Organization Fit

The fact that good opportunities exist in the marketplace for a new or repositioned product does not necessarily mean that the organization should proceed to offer such a product. Unless there is a good "fit" between the proposed product and the organization's needs and resources, the net result of a decision to proceed may be harmful or, at best, suboptimal.

Important preliminary considerations include how well the product matches the organizational mission and what its impact will be on the firm's financial situation. Questions should be asked concerning the product's fit with other resource inputs, such as labor availability, management skills, and physical facilities. An evaluation should also be made of the feasibility of using the existing sales force, advertising media, and distribution channels or service delivery systems and of the consequences of introducing new alternatives.

Other issues concern the proposed product's impact upon the market position of other goods and services marketed by the organization, as well as its consistency with the organization's existing image. Finally, attention should be paid to the cyclicity of demand patterns for existing products. Will the new product exaggerate existing fluctuations or will it counterbalance them?

Product-Market Fit

Managers should be concerned, too, with how well the product matches customer needs, interests, purchasing habits, and consumption patterns. Can prospective customers afford the money and time it takes to buy and use the product? (Consumption of services, in particular, is often time-dependent.) Will prospective customers patronize the locations in which the product will be made available? Even if the product appears to match customer needs quite well, do competing products fit those needs even better? Will introduction of the product result in competitive retaliation to which the firm cannot adequately respond?

The fact that a proposed product is not consistent with one or more organizational or market factors does not necessarily mean that management should drop the idea. Indeed, the major objective may be to diversify into new markets. However, the poorer the fit, the greater the financial resources needed to develop the requisite new skills, production and operations facilities, market contacts, and competitive superiority.

CONCLUSION

Product policy determination is an ongoing task, reflecting the changing nature of the marketplace. Because an organization's choice of products has such important implications for every facet of the business, it tends to be of great concern to top management.

Key considerations in the formulation of product policy are the resources of the firm, its existing product portfolio, the corporate objectives established by management, the characteristics of existing and potential markets, and the nature of the competition.

ARCTIC ENTERPRISES, INC.

Richard M. Cardozo

In the late summer of 1977, officials of Arctic Enterprises, Inc., were faced with the need to develop a marketing program for the Wetbike, a new product planned for commercial introduction in 1978.

THE WETBIKE

The Wetbike would be ridden like a motorcycle or snowmobile, but operated on top of the water riding on two in-line skis (Exhibit 1). After instruction in mounting the vehicle, an individual could typically learn to operate the Wetbike in less than an hour. Two people could ride, or a driver could tow a waterskier. Maximum speed was to be 30 miles per hour.

A 50 horsepower engine in the fiberglass body would drive a jet pump which propelled the Wetbike. This 50 horsepower jet pump would deliver a performance approximately equal to a 30 to 35 horsepower propeller-driven motor. Arctic officials considered the jet pump safer, because the operator would not be hurt by a propeller if he or she fell from the Wetbike. Power would shut off if the operator fell, and the Wetbike would promptly, but not abruptly, stop and settle down into the water. When stopped, the Wetbike would draw about 30 inches of water; when operated from 12 to 30 mph, it would plane atop the water, drawing only about four inches.

The noise level of the Wetbike was equal to a modern outboard motor to the bystander, although it might be a little louder to the operator. The Wetbike would be as reliable as an outboard motor. Six gallons of fuel would generally last one-half day with normal use of the vehicle, although this time might be cut to less than three hours if the Wetbike were driven continuously at full throttle. The Wetbike would have Coast Guard approval, and would have to be licensed as a boat in most states.

For $250,000, plus a royalty of 4 percent of the factory price on each unit sold, Arctic obtained from the product's inventors an exclusive, worldwide license to manufacture and market the Wetbike. The engine and pump would be

Reprinted with permission from *Product Policy* by Richard N. Cardozo. Copyright © 1979 by Addison-Wesley, Reading, Mass.

EXHIBIT 1
ARCTIC ENTERPRISES, INC.—THE WETBIKE®

Source: Company Records.

supplied by Suzuki Motor Co., Ltd., of Japan, with which the company held an exclusive worldwide license, and which supplied the engine for Arctic's snowmobiles and outboard motors. Arctic already had available production facilities, but an initial investment of approximately $200,000 would be needed to refine product engineering, prepare the vehicle for manufacturing, and purchase tooling sufficient to produce 10,000 units. Plant capacity to produce 50,000 to 80,000 units per year was presently available. Direct manufacturing costs for the Wetbike were expected to total $885 per unit for annual production of 3,000 or more units. In addition, Arctic had historically budgeted an amount equal to two-tenths of one percent of sales for the self-insured portion of its product liability insurance, and five- to six-tenths of one percent of sales for warranty fulfillment costs. Apart from expenses, investment in inventory and receivables for the Wetbike would come to $400 to $500 per unit, based on the company's experience with snowmobiles. Accounts payable were typically paid within 30 days. Company officials believed that, to duplicate the Wetbike, a competitor not in the business would need to invest more than a million dollars.

Three devices similar to the Wetbike had been introduced within the past three years, but had achieved only limited sales. Kawasaki introduced its "Jet-Ski" in 1974. Arctic personnel estimated that Kawasaki sold 1,000 units to dealers in 1974, 2,000 in 1975, and 7,000 in 1976 through an intensive "dealer loading" program. Sales in 1977 were not known. Dynafoil and PowerSki had each recently introduced propeller-driven machines. To date, however, only limited quantities had been manufactured. Exhibit 2 summarizes comparative data on the Kawasaki, Dynafoil, and PowerSki units and the Wetbike. Exhibit 3 contains sketches of the three devices. Arctic management believed that the Wetbike was superior to these competing products because of the Wetbike's front steering, high performance, second-passenger capability, ability to pull a water skier, and passenger comfort.

EXHIBIT 2
ARCTIC ENTERPRISES, INC.—COMPARATIVE DATA ON MOTORIZED WATERBIKES

	Arctic	**Kawasaki**	**Dynafoil**	**PowerSki**
Propulsion	jet	jet	propeller	propeller
Passengers				
Number	1 or 2	1	1 or 2	2 seated, or 1 standing
Position	seated	standing	seated	or seated
List price to consumers	not yet determined	$1,595	$2,400	$2,295
Maximum speed	30 mph	30 mph	up to 30 mph	30 mph
Engine	50 hp	27 hp	26 & 36 hp	35 hp
Carriage	trailer or van	station wagon or van	trailer	trailer
Distribution	not yet determined	motorcycle dealers	n.a.	n.a.

Source: Company Records.

Arctic officials became interested in the Wet-bike because it appeared to meet the criteria established for the company's diversification program, whose objective was to have, within five years, half of Arctic's sales and earnings coming from products not related to snowmobiles. The criteria laid down for new product lines included the following: (1) substantial long-term earnings potential; and (2) earnings dependent upon seasons, geographic areas, and customer groups different from those of snowmobiles. Financial criteria for the diversification program were summarized in the Company's 1977 annual report:

> We intend to retain cash in the business in order to take advantage of opportunities for diversification that will provide a return on investment of at least 10 percent after tax. We are also prepared to borrow capital to finance new ventures and thereby increase our debt-to-equity ratio. We believe this ratio should not exceed 1:3 since we intend to sustain profits even during downturns in the cyclical industries in which we participate.

Company executives believed that certain recreational products could meet these criteria and cited an article in the February 21, 1977, issue of *U.S. News & World Report,* which stated in part:

> The recession of the past two years put no visible dent in total spending for leisure. Outlays for everything from tennis balls and snowmobiles to speedboats and foreign vacations soared to 146 billion dollars in 1976. . . . Few people realize the sturdy prop that such spending provides for U.S. business. . . . The total far exceeds annual outlays for national defense, or for home building. If past trends are a guide, leisure-time expenditures can be expected to double every eight or nine years. . . .

Among recreational products, marine-type products appeared attractive for three reasons, according to John C. Penn, president of Arctic Enterprises:

> (1) The marine market is very large with more than $5.3 billion spent each year in boating, including sales of new and used craft, accessories, safety devices, club memberships, launching fees, and insurance; (2) we already have experience in the marine industry with Silverline (boats); and (3) our engineering, marketing, and distribution expertise is compatible with these products.

THE COMPANY

Arctic Enterprises, Inc., had been engaged in the manufacturing and marketing of outdoor recrea-

EXHIBIT 3
ARCTIC ENTERPRISES, INC.—ILLUSTRATIONS AND COPY HEADLINES FROM
BROCHURES FOR OTHER WATER VEHICLES

Kawasaki Jet-Ski®
"discover the most exciting sport
that ever hit the water."

Dynafoil®

"it's different and it's dynamite."

PowerSki® "water sports enters a
new era."

Source: Drawings based on published brochures.

tional products since 1962. Its principal products were "Arctic Cat" snowmobiles, snowmobile parts, and accessories; "Arcticwear" clothing; snowmobile trailers and "Heavy Hauler" boat trailers. Arctic also manufactured and marketed, under the "Silverline" name, a variety of out- board and inboard/outboard motor boats, rang- ing from 15 to 26 feet in length. The company marketed "Spirit" outboard motors, ranging from 2 to 65 horsepower, which were manufactured for it by Suzuki Motor Co., Ltd., Japan. All these products were marketed throughout the United

States and Canada, and in parts of Europe. In addition, the company had recently begun manufacturing and marketing in Canada a line of aluminum fishing boats, runabouts, and canoes. Although Arctic at one time manufactured lawnmowers and garden tractors, those lines had been discontinued. Because snowmobiles and related products constituted a major portion of Arctic sales, the company experienced losses in 1974 and 1975 when the snowmobile market declined sharply (see Exhibit 4). In 1977, however, Arctic earned more than $1.5 million on

EXHIBIT 4 ARCTIC ENTERPRISES, INC. FIVE-YEAR* SUMMARY OF OPERATIONS
(000 omitted except on per share amount)

	1977	1976	1975	1974	1973
Net sales	$98,911	$85,156	$79,625	$84,371	$107,185
Cost of sales	79,791	69,154	69,552	72,919	86,302
Gross profit	$19,120	$16,002	$10,073	$11,452	$ 20,883
Expenses					
Selling, administration, and others	$14,250	$11,988	$12,107	$14,515	$ 11,608
Interest	1,797	1,812	3,470	3,210	1,540
Total expenses	$16,047	$13,800	$15,577	$17,725	$ 13,148
Income (loss) before income taxes	3,073	2,202	(5,504)	(6,273)	7,735
(Provision for) benefit from income taxes	(1,550)	(1,186)	2,717	3,048	(3,982)
Income (loss) from continuing operations	1,523	1,016	(2,787)	(3,255)	3,753
Credit related to (loss on) discontinued operations	0	150	125	(5,024)	(1,615)
Net income (loss)	$ 1,523	$ 1,166	($ 2,662)	($ 8,249)	$ 2,138
Depreciation	$ 1,745	$ 1,558	$ 1,683	$ 3,484	$ 2,172
Sales by product line					
Snowmobiles	$66,003	$52,412	$47,872	$53,170	$ 75,595
Snowmobile parts, accessories, and Arcticwear clothing	19,036	19,715	17,254	17,379	18,543
Silverline boats and related lines	12,121	9,002	9,287	9,645	9,669
Other	1,751	4,027	5,212	4,177	3,378
General leisure division (Discontinued 1973)	0	0	0	0	12,916
Earning (loss) by product line					
Arctic (snowmobiles, related lines, and other)	$ 1,166	$ 834	($ 2,928)	($ 3,012)	$ 3,466
Silverline	357	182	141	(231)	287
Discontinued operations	0	150	125	(5,024)	(1,615)
Snowmobiles manufactured	56	54	37	61	99
Position at year end					
Working capital	$23,946	$23,007	$21,301	$22,226	$ 26,391
Current ratio	2.7	2.8	2.8	1.8	1.7
Property and equipment, net	$13,064	$12,237	$12,614	$14,722	$ 17,711
Goodwill, net	$ 602	$ 699	$ 780	$ 923	$ 2,692
Total assets	$52,664	$49,540	$47,347	$67,215	$ 85,185
Long-term debt	$ 7,781	$ 7,394	$ 7,625	$ 8,221	$ 9,138
Shareholders' investment	$30,003	$28,449	$27,277	$29,904	$ 38,151
Outstanding common shares	3,065	3,053	3,050	3,050	3,049
Shareholders' investment per share	$ 9.79	$ 9.32	$ 8.94	$ 9.80	$ 12.51
Share price, November 1	$ 6.25	$ 2.38	$ 3.75	$ 4.38	$ 5.38

* Years ended March 31.
Note: No cash dividends had been paid by Arctic during the five years ending March 31, 1977.
Source: Arctic Enterprises, Inc., 1977 Annual Report.

sales of almost $99 million. Capital expenditures were increased from $1.4 million in 1976 to $2.9 million in 1977. The company planned capital expenditures of $1.7 million in 1978 for existing lines of business. Income statements and balance sheets appear in Exhibits 4 and 5, respectively.

In 1977, Arctic sold just under 25 percent of the 192,000 snowmobiles sold by the industry as a whole. Company officials believed that Arctic Cat snowmobiles held the largest share of the United States snowmobile market. Arctic's sales had increased from 44,200 units in 1976 to 47,200 units in fiscal 1977 against a 20 percent industry decline (see Exhibit 6).

Arctic personnel expected their snowmobile sales to increase, along with those of the industry, about 5 percent annually for the next several years. Company officials expected profits to increase as a result of reductions in manufacturing costs; these reductions were not expected to require substantial additional capital investment. Arctic executives foresaw no new competitors entering the industry. The number of manufacturers had declined steadily over the past five years; currently six manufacturers produced 13 brands. (Some companies manufactured snowmobiles for others who marketed those snowmobiles under their own brand names. Arctic manufactured both its own brand of snowmobiles and a separate brand marketed by another company.)

EXHIBIT 5
ARCTIC ENTERPRISES, INC.—CONSOLIDATED BALANCE SHEET MARCH 31 (000)

	1977	1976
Assets		
Current assets		
Cash	$ 945	$ 2,735
Receivables	4,061	2,957
Inventories	31,481	29,222
Prepaid expenses	1,639	1,008
Total current assets	38,126	35,922
Property and equipment (Net of depreciation of $7,958)	13,064	12,237
Other assets	1,474	1,381
Total	$52,664	$49,540
Liabilities and Equity		
Current liabilities		
Current maturities of long-term debt	$ 1,131	$ 411
Accounts payable	9,112	9,107
Accrued expenses and income taxes	3,937	3,397
Total current liabilities	14,180	12,915
Long-term debt	7,781	7,394
Deferred income taxes	700	782
Shareholders' investment	30,003	28,449
Total	$52,664	$49,540

Note: The company must be free of all short-term debt for a period of 60 consecutive days during any calendar year; for the year ending March 31, 1977, the maximum short-term borrowing was $23 million, and the company had arranged total short-term bank lines of credit of $26 million for the year ending March 31,1978.
Source: Arctic Enterprises, Inc., 1977 Annual Report.

EXHIBIT 6
ARCTIC ENTERPRISES, INC.—
TOTAL INDUSTRY SNOWMOBILE
RETAIL SALES 1963–1977

Year	Units
1963	10,000
1964	18,000
1965	30,000
1966	45,000
1967	65,000
1968	85,000
1969	255,000
1970	425,000
1971	495,000
1972	460,000
1973	450,000
1974	435,000
1975	305,000
1976	242,643
1977	192,000

Source: 1963–1967 Company
Estimates, 1968–1977 Industry
Association Tabulations.

EXHIBIT 7
ARCTIC ENTERPRISES, INC.—PERCENTAGE
DISTRIBUTION OF ARCTIC SNOWMOBILE DEALERS
(by volume category)

Snowmobile retail sales volume	Percent of dealers
less than $25,000	18%
$ 25,000–$ 50,000	26
$ 50,000–$ 75,000	15
$ 75,000–$100,000	16
$100,000–$150,000	13
More than $150,000	12
	100%

Source: Sample Survey of Arctic Dealers.

Distribution

About 70 percent of Arctic's snowmobiles and related products were sold through eight company-owned distributorships to more than 1,400 retail dealers. This percentage had increased from 50 percent in 1975. These company-owned distributorships were located throughout Canada, and from Michigan west throughout the northern snowbelt. The remaining 30 percent of sales were made through three independent authorized distributors who served other regions of the United States. Limited sales were made through independent distributors in Norway and Sweden. Sales to all distributors were handled directly by a small staff at company headquarters. Approximately 40 percent of Arctic's snowmobile sales came from Michigan, Minnesota, Wisconsin, New York, and Pennsylvania. Arctic also used its company-owned distributors plus one independent distributor, who did not handle snowmobiles, to distribute Silverline boats to almost 300 retailers. Approximately 15 percent of the retailers who carried Arctic snowmobiles also handled Silverline boats.

A sample survey of Arctic's snowmobile dealers revealed that most of them sold between $25,000 and $100,000 worth of snowmobiles per year at retail (see Exhibits 7 and 8). Most Arctic dealers did more volume in snowmobiles than in any other product line. Twenty-nine percent of Arctic's dealers carried at least one competitor's snowmobile, and many handled product lines in addition to snowmobiles.

Exhibit 9 lists the total number of marine, motorcycle, and snowmobile retailers by state, along with the number of Arctic snowmobile dealers in each state. There was no consistent

EXHIBIT 8
ARCTIC ENTERPRISES, INC.—PERCENT OF ARCTIC
SNOWMOBILE DEALERS HANDLING OTHER
PRODUCT LINES

Product Line	Percent of Dealers
1. Marine	26.1%*
2. Lawn and garden equipment	25.6
3. Motorcycle sales and service	31.3
4. Farm equipment	9.3
5. Bicycle sales and service	9.3
6. Camper sales and service	10.9
7. Automobile sales and service	10.6

* Approximately 15 percent carry Silverline boats.
Source: Company Records.

EXHIBIT 9

ARCTIC ENTERPRISES, INC.—MARINE, MOTORCYCLE, AND SNOWMOBILE DEALERS BY STATE

State	Total marine dealers	Total motorcycle dealers	Total snowmobile dealers	Arctic snowmobile dealers
Alabama	181	159	0	0
Alaska	107	40	45	33
Arizona	91	96	10	3
Arkansas	155	99	0	0
California	815	777	77	10
Colorado	92	145	390	15
Connecticut	248	78	148	12
Delaware	32	20	7	2
Florida	688	326	0	0
Georgia	252	201	0	0
Hawaii	41	13	0	0
Idaho	63	88	172	25
Illinois	643	375	287	27
Indiana	393	264	94	13
Iowa	236	180	241	44
Kansas	128	150	10	0
Kentucky	225	121	0	0
Louisiana	182	138	0	0
Maine	183	73	123	38
Maryland	227	90	31	2
Massachusetts	362	130	197	19
Michigan	780	459	1,183	118
Minnesota	375	224	895	112
Mississippi	98	82	0	0
Missouri	223	186	5	0
Montana	65	110	154	23

relationship between Arctic's share of snowmobile dealers and the company's share of the market by state.

Approximately 44 percent of the dealers were located in towns of fewer than 10,000 persons; 12 percent, in towns of 10,000 or more. Almost 40 percent were located outside of towns, but within 50 miles of towns of at least 10,000 population. The remaining dealers were more than 50 miles away from a town of 10,000.

Advertising and Sales Support

Although they had not yet prepared an advertising plan for the Wetbike, Arctic officials knew that the company ordinarily budgeted 5 percent of the snowmobile sales for advertising and promotion of snowmobiles. Approximately two-thirds of that budget was spent on media advertising. (Illustrative media costs appear in Exhibit 10.) Somewhat more than half the media budget was devoted to television; radio and print advertisements split the remainder about equally. Dealers could claim up to 20 percent of the total budget for cooperative advertising (each dealer could claim an amount equal to 1 percent of his or her purchases). Arctic paid 50 percent of the cost of dealer cooperative ads. If the cooperative advertising allowance were not claimed by dealers, Arctic could use the funds for media advertising or other purposes.

Arctic provided its dealers with in-store dis-

EXHIBIT 9 (continued)

State	Total marine dealers	Total motorcycle dealers	Total snowmobile dealers	Arctic snowmobile dealers
Nebraska	70	93	43	9
Nevada	41	30	11	3
New Hampshire	93	71	110	24
New Jersey	311	136	129	7
New Mexico	51	61	158	2
New York	882	416	658	144
North Carolina	245	187	1	1
North Dakota	46	61	79	29
Ohio	413	416	168	19
Oklahoma	173	117	0	0
Oregon	163	149	78	10
Pennsylvania	297	452	521	100
Rhode Island	55	25	12	1
South Carolina	119	89	0	0
South Dakota	49	57	92	19
Tennessee	176	168	1	1
Texas	537	456	1	1
Utah	84	70	94	17
Vermont	74	39	84	15
Virginia	210	156	5	2
Washington	333	169	81	25
West Virginia	57	89	9	0
Wisconsin	479	237	1,199	105
Wyoming	46	50	166	18
D.C.		2		
Canadian dealers			3,428	396
Total	11,889	8,390	11,197	1,444

Source: Recreation Industry Mailing List (Totals) and Company Records (Arctic and Suzuki).

play materials and a variety of sales aids in dealer kits, which required 5 to 10 percent of the total budget. The remainder covered production costs and administration. Arctic's own advertising and sales promotion efforts were augmented somewhat by those of its independent distributors.

Because dealers were reluctant to carry large inventories of snowmobiles, Arctic held inventory at its own and independent distributors' warehouses. In addition, the company provided inventory loans to dealers through a "floor planning" program. Arctic was, however, liable to repurchase inventories financed under the program up to a specific dollar limitation. Because the production cycle for large quantities of snowmobiles exceeded six months (from ordering raw materials and components to delivering the finished product) and the selling season lasted only the winter months, Arctic had to forecast demand as accurately as possible to avoid losing sales during the peak selling season or carrying large stocks of a previous year's models over to the next selling season. Arctic officials knew that the production cycle for Wetbikes would be similar to that for snowmobiles, but thought that the length of the selling season might vary by geographic region.

Prices and Margins

In 1977, Arctic Cat snowmobiles carried list prices ranging from $995 to $1,995. The most

EXHIBIT 10
ARCTIC ENTERPRISES, INC.—ILLUSTRATIVE MEDIA RATES*

Television, 30-second announcement

	Network	Top 10 markets (34% of T.V. homes)	Markets 11–20 (12%)	Markets 21–30 (9%)	Top 30 markets (55%)
7:30–11:00 P.M.	$50,000	$10,000	$4,300	$2,700	$17,000
6:00–7:30 P.M. Mon.–Fri.	20,000	3,500	1,500	1,000	6,000
11:30–1:00 A.M. Mon.–Fri.	15,000	1,800	750	450	3,000
Daytime	10,000	1,200	500	300	2,000

Magazines, one-page

	Black-and-white	Four-color
Newsweek, Time, Playboy	$25,000	$40,000
Sports Illustrated	20,000	30,000
Field & Stream, Outdoor Life, or *Esquire*	10,000	15,000

Sunday supplements, one-page

	Black-and-white	Four-color
To reach 20 million families	$100,000	$135,000

Outdoor

To reach 89 percent of adult males 17 times, $430,000 per month for top 30 markets.

* These costs are rounded average estimates based on quoted media rates, and are considered useful for illustrative purposes, though not precisely reflecting actual individual media rates.
Note: Rates for half-page approximately 60 percent of full-page costs; rates for regional editions 15–20 percent higher per household.
Source: Estimates based on Standard Rate and Data Service, 1976.

popular model had a list price of $1,425. Arctic's list prices positioned the company in the middle to upper range of industry retail prices. In addition to the price of the snowmobile, the customer paid freight costs from the factory to the retailer. This practice prevailed throughout the snowmobile industry. (Although Arctic officials had not determined price for the Wetbike, they planned to have customers pay freight from the factory to the Wetbike dealer.)

Retail dealers earned margins of approximately 25 percent on sales of Arctic Cat snowmobiles at list prices. Distributors earned margins of 20 percent on their sales to retail dealers. The company's discount structure was similar to that of other snowmobile manufacturers.

Snowmobile Owners

A survey of snowmobile owners conducted in 1976 by an industry source showed that the average number of snowmobiles owned was 2.5 per household, up from 1.8 in 1972. Far more than half of the machines were less than five years old. When buying additional snowmobiles, two-thirds of the buyers sold or traded in an older machine; one-third kept it for the family. Almost three-fourths of all snowmobiles purchased were bought new. More than 70 percent of all snowmobile purchases (new and used combined) were made for $1,200 or less. In deciding whether to purchase a snowmobile in the future, personal financial situation was the single most important determinant. Two-thirds of all snow-

EXHIBIT 11

	Percent of respondents
Age 25–49	67
Married	85
Have children	76.3
Live in or near city of less than 25,000	80
Earn more than $10,000	90
Earn more than $15,000	65.5

mobilers rode at home, i.e., without transporting their snowmobile(s) to another site.

A separate survey of Arctic's snowmobile consumers revealed the characteristics shown in Exhibit 11. When Arctic owners were asked what types of recreational equipment they owned or were planning to buy within the next two years, they responded as shown in Exhibit 12.

THE BOAT INDUSTRY

Because Arctic officials expected the Wetbike to appeal to users of water-ski equipment and to motorcyclists, they reviewed information on both the boat and motorcycle industries.

EXHIBIT 12

	Percent who plan to buy within two years	Percent who currently own
Motorcycle	24.0	39.4
4-wheel drive vehicle	15.7	26.9
Pick-up truck	13.4	58.8
Chain saw	7.7	60.0
Inboard/outboard boat	7.0	15.5
Pick-up camper	6.6	16.1
Motorhome	6.1	4.7
Riding lawnmower	5.0	43.4
Cabin or second home	4.6	25.3
Garden tractor	4.6	37.5
Outboard motor	4.6	42.9
Live-in travel trailer	3.3	10.4
Hunting equipment or guns	2.0	86.1
Fishing equipment	1.8	84.6

Total United States marine equipment and service sales in 1976 were $5.3 billion, of which recreational boats (both motorized and non-motorized) and motors represented more than $1.9 billion. Sales by category of boats and motors appear in Exhibits 13 and 14. The major segments of the industry had been growing steadily since 1972. One forecast for the continuing growth of the industry placed volume at $8 billion and 1,550,000 units by 1990. A major industry source stated that the primary reason for the continuing growth over the last thirty years has been that manufacturers had designed and built equipment to suit every taste and budget. Competition in the industry was extremely intense, particularly in pricing and advertising. A large number of companies manufactured and marketed boats.

Marine sales and dealerships had traditionally been concentrated in the East, North Central, South Atlantic, West South Central, and Pacific regions (see Exhibit 15). Florida and Texas held top ranking as outboard equipment consumer states. In 1976, significant gains in consumer sales were recorded in California, but both Wisconsin and Minnesota dropped sharply.

More than 94 percent of boat dealers were one-establishment firms. Eighty-five percent had fewer than ten employees, and the average establishment had annual sales between $100,000 and $300,000. The typical marine dealer was thought to be quite conservative with respect to new products, particularly those that might either be inconsistent or competitive with present lines. Marine dealers ordinarily earned margins of 20 to 30 percent, and bought through distributors who maintained margins of 10 to 20 percent.

The majority of boat consumers were between 25 and 45 years old, with an average age of 43.5. Most buyers were part of a two-person family, although four-person families were the second largest group of purchasers. About two-thirds of the boat and motor purchases were made by skilled workers, managers, proprietors, and professionals. These consumers expected to use their purchases for a variety of activities. Approx-

EXHIBIT 13

ARCTIC ENTERPRISES, INC.—ESTIMATED ANNUAL RETAIL DOLLAR VOLUME, BOATS, MOTORS, AND TRAILERS 1972–1976

	1972	1973	1974	1975	1976
Motors					
Units (000)	535	585	545	435	468
$ volume (000)	432,300	501,300	463,300	411,100	514,800
Average cost ($)	808	857	850	945	1,100
Horsepower					
(% of total)					
0–7	21.5	21.6	24.0	24.6	21.0
7.1–19.9	18.0	16.7	17.0	17.8	18.0
20 and over	60.5	61.7	59.0	57.6	61.0
Outboard boats					
Units (000)	375	448	425	328	341
$ volume (000)	267,800	325,200	310,200	262,700	358,100
Average cost ($)	714	726	736	800	1,050
Inboard/outdrive boats					
Units (00)	63	78	70	70	80
$ volume (000)	307,800	410,400	386,700	420,000	576,000
Average cost ($)	4,885	5,261	5,524	6,000	7,200
Boat trailers					
Units (000)	265	330	325	255	285
$ volume (000)	72,100	94,400	98,100	87,700	121,100
Average cost ($)	272	286	302	343	425
Totals					
Units (000)	1,238	1,441	1,365	1,088	1,174
$ volume (000)	1,080,000	1,331,300	1,258,300	1,181,500	1,570,000

Source: Company Records.

imately one-half expected to fish, cruise, and water ski (see Exhibit 16).

THE MOTORCYCLE INDUSTRY

Industry sources estimated that some 20 million Americans used more than 8 million motorcycles in 1976, and spent $4.7 billion on motorcycling. Of that amount, $1.3 billion went to sales of new motorcycles. Used motorcycles, parts, and accessories amounted to $1.8 billion. The remaining $1.6 billion went to services, state taxes, and license fees.

Motorcycle registrations had increased four-fold since 1965, and two-thirds of the motorcy-cles in use were purchased new within the previous five years. Although unit sales of motorcycles had declined from a 1973 peak, sales in units and dollars had increased since 1975 (see Exhibit 17).

Japanese manufacturers dominated the American motorcycle industry. Of the new motorcycles registered in 1976, 87 percent were manufactured by four Japanese firms. Honda accounted for 38 percent of the new registrations; Yamaha, 20 percent; Kawasaki, 17 percent; and Suzuki, 12 percent. (Harley-Davidson had 7 percent of the new registrations in 1976; five other manufacturers divided the remaining 6 percent.) This pattern of market share had prevailed for several years.

EXHIBIT 14
ARCTIC ENTERPRISES, INC. ESTIMATED RETAIL
SALES OF NONMOTORIZED BOATS, 1976

Sailboats	
Units (000)	86
$ volume (000)	$241,000
Average unit price	2,802
Houseboats	
Units (000)	1.4
$ volume (000)	$ 34,300
Average unit price	$ 24,500
Pontoon and Deck Boats	
Units (000)	12.5
$ volume (000)	$ 32,500
Average unit price	$ 2,600
Canoes	
Units (000)	78
$ volume (000)	$ 22,600
Average unit price	$ 290
Rowboats, Fishing Boats, etc.	
Units (000)	86
$ volume (000)	$ 32,680
Average unit price	$ 380

Source: Company Records.

Within the United States, the motorcycle population was concentrated most heavily in the West, least heavily in the East (see Exhibit 18).

The number of franchised motorcycle dealerships in the United States had grown significantly over the last few years (see Exhibit 19). In addition to the 8,390 franchised dealers, in 1976 there were 1,912 other retail establishments that handled motorcycle replacement parts and accessories. A recent industry survey revealed that the typical motorcycle dealer had been in business seven years and employed six persons. Almost half of the dealers had total annual sales between $100,000 and $500,000 while about 19 percent had retail sales less than $50,000, and 5 percent had sales in excess of $1,000,000. Fifty-three percent of dealers' sales came from new and used motorcycles; 47 percent, from accessories. Financing for both dealer inventories and customer purchases came primarily from banks.

Ninety percent of all motorcycle owners were male, and 60 percent were married. The median

EXHIBIT 15
ARCTIC ENTERPRISES, INC.—BOAT INDUSTRY SALES BY REGION

	1972		1976	
	Retail sales ($000)	Number of dealers	Retail sales* ($000)	Number of dealers
Northeast	105,060	354	62,231	1,015
East N. Central	258,576	752	296,163	2,708
West N. Central	102,289	329	170,838	1,127
Middle Atlantic	175,785	542	163,803	1,490
South Atlantic	366,436	925	320,639	1,830
East S. Central	74,970	213	88,993	680
West S. Central	186,923	494	230,832	1,047
Mountain	46,420	109	96,356	533
Pacific	243,850	600	236,547	1,311
Total	$1,560,309	4,318	$1,665,402*	11,741†

* Sales figures include outboard motors, outboard boats, and inboard/outdrive boats, which together amount to 86.2 percent of total boat sales.
† Total differs from 11,889 in Exhibit 9 because of slight differences in definitions used and timing of counts.
Source: U.S. Census of Retailers, 1972, and Company Records.

EXHIBIT 16
ARCTIC ENTERPRISES, INC.—INTENDED USES OF BOATS BY
BUYERS, 1972–1976

Intended use by %*	1972	1973	1974	1975	1976
Fishing	36.1	36.4	33.0	42.3	32.2
Cruising	32.1	31.1	32.7	40.0	34.8
Skiing	49.2	49.3	41.7	40.2	37.8
Hunting	30.0	28.8	31.4	26.1	20.4
Other	6.8	6.8	7.6	11.6	13.7

* Percentages do not total 100 percent because of multiple mentions.
Source: Company Records.

EXHIBIT 17
ARCTIC ENTERPRISES, INC.—MOTORCYCLE SUPPLY AND DEMAND, 1969–1976

	U.S. motorcycle imports (units) (000)	Estimated U.S. production (units) (000)	Estimated retail sales (units) (000)	Estimated wholesale dollar volume (000)	Estimated retail dollar volume (000)
1969	640	40	670	n.a.	n.a.
1970	1,090	35	1,010	n.a.	n.a.
1971	1,540	25	1,240	n.a.	n.a.
1972	1,690	35	1,360	$ 782,910	$1,179,906
1973	1,210	45	1,520	984,684	1,305,994
1974	1,540*	40	1,200*	1,003,546*	1,320,200*
1975	950*	40	940*	912,654*	1,152,438*
1976	660*	80	1,050*	1,050,158*	1,300,000*

*Excludes estimated imports of mopeds: 1974—13,000 units; 1975—32,000 units; 1976—78,000 units.
Source: 1977 Motorcycle Statistical Annual.

age of the motorcycle owner was 27.6 years. Fifty-two percent of owners had a high school education and 38 percent had some college education. The largest group of owners were students (23 percent), while 20 percent of motorcycle owners worked in professional or technical positions. The annual cost of owning and operating a motorcycle was estimated at $313 in 1976.

If Arctic were to use motorcycle dealers for the Wetbike, the company would sell to those dealers through its existing distributors, or through comparable distributors that served retail motor-

EXHIBIT 18

	Total motorcycle population	Motorcycle population per 1,000 persons
West	1.9 million	5.1
East	1.1 million	2.3
Midwest	2.5 million	4.3
South	2.7 million	4.0

EXHIBIT 19
ARCTIC ENTERPRISES, INC.—MOTORCYCLE INDUSTRY SALES BY REGION, 1972 and 1976

	1972		1976	
	Retail sales new motor-cycles only (000)	Number of dealers	Retail sales new motor-cycles only (000)	Number of dealers
Northeast	$ 46,884	146	$ 59,500	416
East N. Central	260,965	667	283,500	1,751
West N. Central	110,277	326	137,400	951
Middle Atlantic	104,136	336	141,200	1,004
South Atlantic	184,282	481	167,000	1,160
East S. Central	55,622	194	78,600	530
West S. Central	105,985	345	122,300	780
Mountain	73,780	242	87,100	650
Pacific	237,975	679	223,400	1,148
Total	$1,179,906	3,416	$1,300,000	8,390

Source: 1972 U.S. Census of Retail Trade and 1977 Motorcycle Statistical Annual.

cycle dealers, if satisfactory arrangements could be made with the latter.

THE TASK

John C. Penn, President of Arctic, had asked the executives responsible for developing the market program for the Wetbike to prepare a five-year plan and budgets. (The year ending March 31, 1979, which Arctic termed "fiscal 1979," constituted the first year.) The plan was to include all major marketing activities envisioned for the Wetbike, supported by statements of objectives and brief descriptions of the market environment foreseen. Penn and the executives involved rec-ognized that the objectives and environment might change from time to time throughout the planning period, and that plans for the first few years could be more detailed than those for later years.

The budgets were to include, for each year, estimated income statements and assets committed to the Wetbike line. Penn reminded the executives responsible for preparing the budgets that investments for the project had to be consistent with the financial capabilities of the company.

"This is a difficult forecasting and planning task," Penn stated, "for we must pioneer a new sport with the Wetbike."

SIERRA CLUB PUBLISHING DIVISION

Arthur Segel
Charles B. Weinberg

The Sierra Club was the oldest and largest conservation organization in the world. To many, the Sierra Club was virtually synonymous with conservation and environmental activism. The Club's board of directors had included over the years a number of nationally prominent political leaders, business people, educators, and conservationists.

In 1974, nearly 150,000 members participated in its outings, subscribed to its publications, and joined forces on environmental issues arising in cities and towns, state legislatures, and Congress.

THE PROBLEM

Jon Beckmann came to the Sierra Club's publishing division in early January 1974 from a small, high quality publishing house in Boston. As Editor-in-Chief of the Club's publishing business

(over $500,000 in sales annually), he and a small staff were responsible for the day to day operations of the division as well as future planning. Mr. Beckmann had been hired by the Publishing Committee (PubCom), a group of Club members both in and outside the publishing industry who were appointed by the Club President to attend quarterly meetings to set policies. PubCom members included some of the most influential members at the Club.[1]

While the Committee was the final decision-making body for the Publishing Division, the Editor-in-Chief traditionally had a great deal of authority and his recommendations were seriously considered. Mr. Beckmann had a number of critical decisions to make for the next Committee meeting. The publishing industry traditionally sold its greatest volume during the Christmas season, and because more than a year was usually required for editorial work, printing, promotions,

Reprinted from *Stanford Business Cases 1975*, with permission of the Publishers, Stanford University Graduate School of Business. Copyright © 1975 by the Board of Trustees of the Leland Stanford Junior University.

[1] The PubCom Chairman in mid-1974, Kent Gill, was later elected as President of the Sierra Club. His primary opponent, the Treasurer of the Club, was also a member of the PubCom (see Exhibit 1).

EXHIBIT 1
PUBLISHING COMMITTEE MEMBERS*

Donald Bradburn	Doctor
Paul Brooks	Writer, former editor-in-chief, Houghton Mifflin Co.
Richard Cellarius	Professor
Michael Fox	Washington book store manager
Kent Gill	High school principal
Richard Grossman	Professor, former head Grossman Publishers
Dave Harris	Comptroller, Sierra Club
Holway Jones	Librarian
H. R. Kessel	Sales manager, University of California Press
Mort Levin	Vice President, Viking Press
Michael McCloskey	Executive Director, Sierra Club
Cliff Rudden	Comptroller for Publishing, Sierra Club
Paul Salisbury	Architect
Will Siri	Physicist
Paul Swatek (Treasurer of Club)	Massachusetts Audubon
William Webb	Publishers representative
Denny Wilcher	Fundraising, Sierra Club

* All members of the Committee, except for Mr. Holway Jones who was a recent appointee, had long been affiliated with the Club and most had served on the Publishing Committee for several years.

and distribution, the Committee had to select new titles it wished to print for the following year at its next meeting. A June print run allowed a short time for a Fall promotional campaign followed by distribution to the bookstores in early October for Christmas. Specifically, Mr. Beckmann had a number of already researched manuscripts or books from members, writers, and photographers from which he had to select the types of books the Club wanted, the specific titles, and their selling prices. The Publishing Division had already contracted its calendars, photographic portfolios, posters, and necessary reprints for the upcoming year. Although Mr. Beckmann was completely new to the organization, he was in a position to make decisions that would have an impact on the division's finances over several years. Obviously, he wanted to be as knowledgeable as possible for his appearance before the PubCom in three weeks.

CLUB BACKGROUND

The Sierra Club Bulletin of December 1967 pointed out that:

> John Muir, Scottish immigrant, farmer, inventor, sheep-herder, pre-med dropout, botanist, explorer, sawmill operator, historian, geologist, writer, wanderer and disciple of wilderness, might have difficulty today in recognizing the small, intimate Sierra Club he helped found seventy-five years ago.

The Club Bylaws, written in 1892 by Muir himself, were still relevant and stated the purposes of the Sierra Club as follows:

> To explore, enjoy and preserve the Sierra Nevada and other scenic resources of the United States and its forests, waters, wildlife and wilderness;

> To undertake and to publish scientific, literary and educational studies concerning them;

> To educate the people with regard to national and state forests, parks, monuments and other natural resources of special scenic beauty; and

> To enlist public interest and cooperation in protecting them.

The Club's first battle was a fight to save Yosemite Valley from being reduced by one-half and sold to developers. In 1912 Muir accompanied President Theodore Roosevelt on a pack trip through the region with the purpose of turning Yosemite into a National Park, which was accomplished later that year. Other early efforts included pressing for the establishment of National Forests and creating trails. In 1901 the Club began its Outing Program; by 1974 it was sending members on expeditions all over the world. Its conservation efforts in California—to preserve Hetch Hetchy Valley in Yosemite and to extend natural park status to Kings Canyon (1935) gained the Club national support and recognition. Vigorous efforts to save Dinosaur National Monument on the Colorado-Utah border from a huge reservoir and power plant in 1950 initiated the Club's surge in national membership. Since that time, the Club had used its money, time and efforts to push for the North Cascades National Park in Washington, Redwood National Park in California, and to support smaller campaigns for Point Reyes and Cape Cod National Seashores and for Canyonlands, Guadalupe, Oregon Dunes Seashore and Great Basin, Prairies, Channel Islands, and Kauai National Parks. The Club's legal confrontations over the Disney Corporation's proposed Mineral King development and its lobbying efforts against strip mining, the Alaskan pipeline and the supersonic transport (SST) in the late 1960's and early 1970's brought the Club national prestige at a time when environmental questions were first being raised by legislators and the public at large. In 1974, the Club had a reputation for political activism, expertise in hiking, camping, and quality publications.

Club policies had not, however, been without their internal strife. For example, many members debated whether the Club should actively commit itself against the use of nuclear reactors as an alternative energy source. Others, although a minority, felt that the Club should discontinue its political activity altogether and concentrate its time and efforts on outings for its membership, trail guides for hikers, and photographic essay type books for the general public. In 1973, Club membership reached 142,000 spread geographically in the following way:

California	77,000
West	18,000
Midwest	14,000
Northeast	19,000
South	12,000
Foreign	2,000

One of the Sierra's Club membership recruitment brochures stated:

> Wherever nature needs defense, the Sierra Club wants to be on the scene . . . to rescue these untrammelled places from those who see them only as wasted space. The environment of the cities now also needs to be made fit for man: we must be more effective in combatting air and water pollution and the prevalence of chemical contaminants, noise, congestion, and blight. . . . Technology must be challenged to do a better job in managing the part

of the planet it has already claimed. The Club offers programs as diverse as the environmental challenges that man faces. Each offers an opportunity to become involved.

The Sierra Club had almost 50 regional chapters and more than 200 local groups which organized and presented a variety of talks, films, exhibits and conferences. The Club offered a local and worldwide outing program which included wilderness outings, activity trips such as mountaineering and bicycling, local trips (walk, knapsack, or climb), and clean-up and trail maintenance trips. The Club also published a monthly magazine, *The Sierra Club Bulletin,* and a monthly chapter newsletter which were both distributed free to members, books available to members at a discount, and a calendar. And finally, the Club provided an opportunity to do conservation work.

The Sierra Club Bulletin

The *Bulletin* was published ten times a year and was distributed free to all members of the Sierra Club. It was lavishly illustrated with color photographs, reproduced to the highest standards. A typical issue of about forty pages would contain two stories about wilderness areas, two stories about battles to protect natural areas against encroachment by industrial or commercial developers, and a story about a person who had done battle for the environmental cause. In addition, a number of short articles appeared. Approximately ten of the pages in the center of the magazine were joined together in a section labeled "Commentary" which reported and commented upon news items thought to be of interest to club members. For example, the July–August 1972 issue included stories entitled "Club granted [legal] standing to sue in Mineral King case," "Coast initiative [to protect coastline] wins spot on California ballot," and "Canada rejects Village Lake Louise." The *Bulletin* usually contained a few pages of advertising from companies marketing to hikers and campers, and to readers of wilderness books; it also included a few pages of advertising about such Sierra Club offerings as foreign trips, calendars, and, of course, Sierra Club books.

PUBLISHING HISTORY

In 1964, the Club published a few expensive publications. Ten years later, some 80 publications were sold, ranging from expensive picture books to inexpensive trail guides. Membership growth seemed to have closely paralleled the Club's expanding publishing operations, and many attributed the Club's success and reputation to its quality books (see Exhibit 2).

1965–1969: Years of Boom and Bust

In 1965, Dave Brower, long associated with the Club in almost every position, became Editor-in-Chief. It was during his tenure that publications grew enormously and also developed serious problems. Brower left in 1969 to start Friends of the Earth (F.O.E.) in a belief that the Sierra Club's increasing involvement in political issues was detracting from its purpose; however, Brower still served as an honorary vice-president.

Under Brower's leadership, the Club developed a large market in photographic-essay type books ("exhibit format") that successfully transmitted information and catalyzed concern in conservation issues. According to members of Congress active in the conservation cause, such books (especially ones on the Northern Cascades, Point Reyes and the Redwoods), played an important role in the establishment of new national parks. They also served to promote what members referred to as "the Sierra Club philosophy."

Brower sought out quality publishing firms in New York and Europe. In efforts to maintain the highest quality product, it was not unusual to send a single photograph back and forth to London several times until the picture was acceptable. Many books and calendars were printed in a remote town in Italy.

But expansion and quality had their costs. In only three out of the last 12 years had publishing activities resulted in a surplus. While this may have been offset by the volume and dollar gains in membership, publishing had generated hundreds of thousands of dollars of losses to the Club. In 1969 alone, publishing lost in the area of $250,000 (see Exhibits 3, 4, and 5 for financial data).

EXHIBIT 3
HISTORICAL SUMMARY OF OPERATING
SURPLUSES AND DEFICITS
(thousands of dollars)

Fiscal Year Ended	Surplus (deficit)	Comment
1973	$ 90.0	Estimated year-end results
1972	99.5	Reflects $100,000 bequest of Katherine Squire
1971	(469.8)	
1970	84.8	
1969	(119.2)	Nine months due to change in fiscal year
1968	(158.9)	
1967	(65.6)	
1966	56.9	
1965	(28.2)	
1964	193.6	Reflects $200,000 bequest of Bertha Rennie
1963	(93.3)	
1962	43.9	
1961	(17.2)	
1960	(22.6)	

EXHIBIT 2
BOOKS SOLD AND NUMBER OF MEMBERS

Year	Number of Books Sold (000's)	Number of Members (000's)
1966	52	42
1967	118	58
1968	192	65
1969	151	81
1970	135	107
1971	144	135
1972	138	136

EXHIBIT 4
EXPENDITURES BY DEPARTMENT

	1972 Actual	1975 Budget
Outings	22.5%	22.2%
Conservation	21.1%	28.9%
Publications	19.9%	17.0%
Member services	7.8%	8.4%
Bulletin	7.3%	6.5%
General overhead	21.3%	16.9%
Total	$3,290,500	$4,310,800
Chapter subventions	313,000	349,100
	$3,603,500	$4,659,900

1970–1973

Brower's resignation eventually brought John Mitchell as Editor-in-Chief in 1970. Mitchell attempted to relieve Publishing's dollar burden on the Club and make his division "more business-like." Offices were moved from the head offices in San Francisco to New York. Scribners, who previously handled book distribution for the Club, enlarged its responsibilities and took over the accounts receivable—a problem which had begun to plague the Club to a serious degree. Scribners had a "big stick" with bookstores,

EXHIBIT 5
INCOME STATEMENT
(thousands of dollars)

	Fiscal Year 1974 Budget		Fiscal Year 1975 Budget	
	Amount	% of Sales	Amount	% of Sales
Revenue:				
Sales				
Trade	$304.6	53.4	$370.0	55.2
Chapter	40.4	7.1	50.0	7.5
Member	225.0	39.5	250.0	37.3
Net sales	$570.0	100.0	$670.0	100.0
Subsidiary income				
Subsidiary rights*	$120.0		$140.0	
Less costs and royalties	35.0		20.0	
Net subsidiary income	$ 85.0		$120.0	
Miscellaneous income	5.0		0	
Total revenue	$660.0		$790.0	
Expenses:				
Costs of sales				
Production costs	$264.0	46.3	$249.3	37.2
Inventory write down	15.0	2.6	15.0	2.2
Royalties	65.0	11.4	86.2	12.9
Total cost of sales	$344.0	60.3	$350.5	52.3
Editorial expenses	40.0	7.0	40.0	6.0
Selling expenses				
Sales and distribution	$ 77.0	13.5	$ 92.4	13.8
Shipping and warehouse	61.5	10.8	67.5	10.1
Total selling expenses	$138.5	24.3	$159.9	23.9
Promotion expenses				
Advertising	$ 31.5	5.5	$ 40.0	5.9
Direct mail	15.6	2.7	18.0	2.7
Catalogues	10.0	1.8	12.0	1.8
Review copies (gratis)	4.0	0.7	6.0	0.9
Exhibits	3.0	0.5	4.0	0.6
Total promotion expenses	$ 64.1	11.2	$ 80.0	11.9

EXHIBIT 5 *(continued)*

	Fiscal Year 1974 Budget		Fiscal Year 1975 Budget	
	Amount	**% of Sales**	**Amount**	**% of Sales**
Administrative expenses				
Salaries and related costs	$ 77.7	13.6	$93.2	13.9
Travel	18.0	3.2	21.0	3.4
Interest	9.8	1.7	10.0	1.5
Meetings	8.6	1.5	8.6	1.3
Outside services	2.6	0.5	4.0	0.6
Telephone	7.0	1.2	10.0	1.5
Rent—office	5.8	1.0	6.0	0.9
Duplicating and copier	4.0	0.7	4.0	0.6
Supplies	3.0	0.6	3.0	0.4
Legal fees	1.0	0.2	2.0	0.3
Rent—equipment	0.3	—	1.0	0.2
Equipment	0.5	0.1	1.0	0.2
Repairs and maintenance	0.2	—	0.2	—
Membership, dues, and subscriptions	0.4	—	0.5	0.4
Other	1.0	0.2	—	—
Total administrative expenses	$139.9	24.5	$164.5	24.6
Total expenses	$726.5	127.5	$794.9	118.7
Surplus (deficit)	($ 66.5)		($ 4.9)	
Subsidies†	$124.0		$ 64.0	
Surplus (deficit) after subsidies	$ 57.5		$ 59.1	

* Subsidiary Income is considered by publishers as the only profit making area in the publishing industry. Most publishers break even and rely on subsidiary income for profits. Subsidiary income includes income from calendars and non-calendar items such as paper/hardcover reprints, book clubs, serial sales and foreign sales. Needless to say, subsidiary income has grown dramatically as calendar sales have increased. Industry wide subsidiary rights usually accounted for 14% of sales.

† The Publishing division traditionally received large amounts of subsidies from the Sierra Club Foundation. The Foundation met yearly to allocate its funds to specific projects, i.e., specific books in Publishing's case, within the Club. The Foundation was created as a separate legal entity in 1969 after the Club was refused tax deduction status for its contributions because of its political lobbying. The Foundation was set up to receive tax deductible gifts and operates independently of the Club.

namely its size and predominance in the publishing field, whereas the Sierra Club had little or no clout to effectively pursue receivables. The Club's staff was reduced accordingly.

As the Club's financial worries temporarily lessened, tensions emerged on another front. Mitchell had started publishing books on specific environmental issues, or so-called "battle books." The battle books were successful in providing support for the Club's conservation efforts. On the other hand, they also became a source of conflict between the publishing staff and the conservation staff which directed the Club's political lobbying. Conservation people often became irritated with the technical quality of some of the books since books on oil spills or energy policy, for example, sometimes contained inaccurate information. Furthermore, coordination of efforts often floundered. For example, a book on clear-cutting of forests came out too late to generate any effective support for a Congressional bill. This resulted in a strong desire for the publishing division to move back to San Franciso for greater coordination and control.

A serious rift developed in this regard. Mitchell, with the support of some committee members, felt that a professional operation could not be run outside of New York. Others, headed by the conservation people, felt that it was important that the Club remain "small-time" and "*un-*

professional." There was a fear of a bureaucratic bigness and, concomitantly, of becoming dysfunctional. Just prior to Beckmann's arrival in January, an upheaval occurred, resulting in Mitchell's leaving and a major reshuffling of positions in the Committee.

Publishing, January 1974

Beckmann had his own ideas on what was wrong. He focused his initial efforts on seeking out a small but professional staff. Next, he wanted to steer the Publishing Division toward a break-even situation. He recognized that, while quality was important, too often the Club had suffered enormous financial consequences in its mission to preach the conservation movement—enough losses at times to impair the Club's very existence. Through luck, fund-raising drives and gifts from estates, the Club had always managed to survive. But Beckmann did not want the Club to be hurt any further by exorbitant publishing losses. He perceived that this was particularly critical in light of the energy crisis recently sparked by the Arab oil embargo. He questioned whether the whole environmental cause might become less popular because of the newly realized quest for energy sources. Furthermore, the economy as a whole was showing serious signs of weakness as rapid inflation raged and recessionary fears mounted. It was at such a time that the Club should have been in its most robust financial state to keep environmental issues alive among legislators and the public.

He followed a different vein in discussing the uniqueness of the Sierra Club in publishing its own books:

Publishing, by nature, is not terribly adaptable to short-run changes. The longer the time allowed for production of a book, the better the quality will be and a lower cost product will result. A book in a "normal" business takes about two years from start to finish. The Club has tried in the past to turn out books within a matter of nine or ten months in order to be responsive to conservation issues. This re-

sponsiveness, however, has its costs. As the span of time is reduced to churn out a book from a normal two-year cycle, there is an increased tendency to publish badly; that is, to lose control over the quality of the book or the costs or both. Furthermore, operating and selling expenses for the division are high compared to industry averages. A Club that is inherently short-sighted in a volatile short-sighted world of changing political constituencies is always in conflict with a sub-part of the organization that demands long-term planning for stability and growth.

This conflict is much more than psychological. Planning requires large dollar commitments long in advance of actual publication to explore new titles and pay for the development of new titles before the actual selling period. The percentage of funds going towards advances on future publishing projects is far below the industry average. If the Club wants to maintain the high quality of its publications and reduce the financial instability that publishing has encountered in the past, the Club must recognize this essential difference in Publishing's need for long-term funding and planning versus the Club's need to be continually responsive to member needs and conservation issues.

Beckmann did not feel that the Club in the past had made a commitment to its publishing program. The program expanded when the Club funds were plentiful and contracted when monies were lean. Beckmann continued:

A publishing program's health depends upon a combination of imprint identity, reliability, publishing activity, and the staff skills to support these characteristics. A program in which these characteristics are fragmented or maintained erratically cannot publish to maximum advantage—that is, cannot inform, persuade, inspire—reach those people whom the program (or individual titles) is designed to interest.

Beckmann also spoke of the shift in product line:

We have an image as a gift or "coffee-table" book. But I wonder if the time for our large photographic books has gone by. On the other hand, while our efforts increasingly seem to be to generate technical and informational books, they don't always sell.

We seem to be more and more dependent on our calendar market which might some day collapse. Maybe we need a few books like *On the Loose* and issue oriented lines. We need to strike a balance. People will be willing to read about some subjects in newspapers or magazines but wouldn't buy a book about them. Our goal is to remain a non-commercial publisher and produce books of quality with the environmental message. At the same time there would be no point in publishing books that did not really reach the public.

THE MARKET FOR SIERRA CLUB PUBLICATIONS

Members accounted for less than 40 percent of present sales. They received 20 percent off on the retail book prices, and Beckmann expressed concern that the Club was actually losing money on membership sales. In theory, member sales should be less expensive than commercial sales, but the figures seemed to indicate that selling costs to members were abnormally high. Traditionally, members of the Club were outdoor enthusiasts, although the Club's political action on environmental issues had widened its membership base. Wage-earning members were largely composed of business executives, professionals, and teachers (see Exhibit 6). About one-half of the membership had belonged to the Club for more than three years. Sixty percent of sales were to commercial outlets. The proportion of member sales to commercial sales had been diminishing over the past two to three years; before 1965, the Club had sold almost entirely to its members.

Commercial outlets not only included book sellers but camping and sporting stores. Approximately 45 percent of "Tote Book" sales (hiking guides, etc.) were sold through camping stores in 1974. Since Sierra Club book purchasers were often campers and hikers who were either students or young professionals, Sierra Club purchasers had long been regarded by the Club staff as being highly price conscious. Because of this and because the Club had no capital for over-

printings, a policy had been established to avoid remaindering books—particularly the high-priced "exhibit-format" (photographic essay-type) books. "Remaindering" involved selling left-over stock books that were not "moving" to booksellers at a reduced rate. Booksellers often used remaindered books for special sales. Thus far, remaindering had occurred only three or four times, and the Book of the Month Club had sometimes purchased remainders for their book dividends.

Forty-five percent of retail sales occurred between October 31 and December 31, or during the "Christmas rush." With this in mind, the Club had been severely hurt by timing problems in the past. If books ran late, if there were a dock strike or if stores failed to receive shipments in September and October, sales could be drastically affected for the year. The purchase of *new* books (or calendars) at Christmas also increased, perhaps because people were fearful of giving books that someone might already possess.

California, particularly the San Francisco Bay Area, had traditionally generated the greatest number of sales for the Club. As with the publishing industry as a whole, book sales were also strong up and down the Eastern urban corridor. Sales were very heavy for the Club in Massachusetts, New York and New Jersey. In states in which environmental issues were popular, such as in Alaska, Oregon, and Colorado, sales were also strong. Finally, the Club had witnessed surprising growth in book sales and in membership from the South, particularly the Southeast. Tennessee commercial book sellers, for example, sold as many volumes as Colorado book sellers for the first half of 1974 (see Exhibit 7).

Pricing

Pricing strategies in the publishing industry were complicated. Because the market was fickle, pricing was considered to be "more an art form than a science."

In the Sierra Club, a price was suggested to the

EXHIBIT 6

MEMBERSHIP DATA*

Length of Membership

	Percent of Members
Less than 1 year	27%
1 to 2 years	26%
3 to 4 years	19%
5 to 7 years	12%
8 to 12 years	8%
13 years or more	9%

Occupation	Occupations of Club Members	Occupations of Main Wage Earners of the Households from Which Members Come
Managers and executives	11%	17%
Lawyers, doctors, and dentists	8%	12%
Other professionals	7%	11%
College teachers	7%	9%
Other teachers	11%	0%
Clerical and blue collar workers	7%	9%
Engineers	3%	7%
Technicians	5%	7%
Students	19%	6%
Homemakers	12%	1%
Other	10%	12%

Percentages by Length of Membership

Reasons for Joining	Less than 1 yr.	1–2 yrs.	3–4 yrs.	5–7 yrs.	8–12 yrs.	13 yrs.	Average
A. To participate in outdoor activities	30%	30%	18%	30%	46%	61%	32%
B. To personally participate in conservation activities	24%	15%	10%	8%	6%	3%	14%
C. To show general support of Club's conservation activities	25%	43%	57%	55%	40%	17%	41%
D. A and B	5%	4%	4%	2%	3%	8%	5%
E. A and C	8%	4%	4%	4%	5%	3%	5%
F. Other	5%	3%	7%	2%	1%	7%	5%

* Based on a mail survey done in 1971 on a random sample of club membership. A total of 859 questionnaires were returned which represents a 56% response rate. Figures do not always add because of rounding error.

EXHIBIT 7
GEOGRAPHIC DISTRIBUTION OF COMMERCIAL SALES OF SIERRA BOOKS: 1974

Area	No. of States	Percent of Sales	Selected States	Percent of Sales
Far West	3	29	California	25
Mid Atlantic	8	17	Massachusetts	8
North Central	6	13	New York	5
South	10	11	Illinois	5
New England	6	10	New Jersey	4
Mountain	8	9	Tennessee	3
Southwest	3	5	Colorado	3
Great Plains	5	2	Texas	3
Other*	2	4	Alaska	3

*Includes Alaska, Hawaii, plus Canadian and European sales.
Source: Scribner State Sales Report Data on Sierra Club, May 31, 1974.

Publishing Committee by the Editor-in-Chief. New books were examined for their (1) effects on cash flow, (2) relevance to book lists, (3) price to the consumer, and (4) type of production. In the industry there were standard pricing guidelines. A common "rule of thumb" was that a book should sell for about five times production costs, except when royalties and promotional monies were not required or if a substantial market appeal existed; then this figure could be four to one. In the past, Sierra Club books had been underpriced with the intention of subsidizing customers to promote a concern for conservation issues.[2]

Suggested Offerings

Specifically, Mr. Beckmann had to make recommendations on the following titles in each of the following categories:

Exhibit Format
 1 *The Rockies* (color)
 2 *Thoreau's Country* (b&w)
Totes
 1 *Golden Gateway*
 2 *Nature Photography*

[2] For additional information on sales and costs of books, see Exhibits 8–11.

Battlebooks
 1 *Parks in Peril*
 2 *Impact of the Military on U.S. Lands*
Underground
 1 *Woodstoves*
 2 *Better Homes and Garbage*

Each of these categories and titles are explained in detail in the next few sections.

EXHIBIT 8
PUBLISHING INDUSTRY RULES OF THUMB*

	% of Retail Sales Price
Discount to bookstores	46
Cost of sales:	
Manufacturing	20
Royalties	8
Operating expenses:	
Editorial	3
Production	1
Marketing	9
Fulfillment	5
General and administrative	6

*See Exhibit 5, first footnote for a better understanding of "other publishing income" or what is known as "subsidiary rights." The above figures reflect that without "subsidiary rights" income, the publishing industry makes little or no profit.
Source: 1973 Industry Statistics of the Association of American Publishers.

EXHIBIT 9
NUMBER AND TYPE OF BOOKS SOLD
FOR TWO YEARS
(thousands of units)

Book Type	1970–1971	1972–1973
Exhibit format	42 (32%)	23 (17%)
Battle books	20 (14%)	13 (10%)
Totes and guides	42 (32%)	45 (33%)
Calendars	21 (16%)	49 (36%)
Other	8 (6%)	8 (4%)
Total	134 (100%)	138 (100%)

Exhibit Format

"Exhibit Format," or the large hard cover photographic-essay type books, had been the trademark of the Club to much of the public. The Club usually had a first printing of 7,500 copies and followed up with reprintings when necessary. In the middle 1960's, when the Club was the first producer of these kinds of books, the book sizes were often too large for normal presses or binding equipment. Machinery had to be specially adapted for printing; and binding was often done by hand. Quality was not sacrificed. One of the most successful of the prototype photographic conservation book series, *In Wildness*, sold 54,000 copies at $25 each, with a $7.00 cost of production. Although its success was attributed to its "name" photographer, its superior production and its uniqueness at the time, *In Wildness* sold 2,000 volumes in 1974. *On the Loose*, a similar idea but not quite an exhibit format book, due to its paper production and smaller size, exceeded all other book sales with its student-oriented nature photography and poetic text.

Others had been less successful. In fact, the great financial drag incurred by the Club during the late 1960's was caused by what the staff felt was an overemphasis on the Exhibit Format series. Furthermore, Exhibit Format books that didn't move were expensive to inventory. *Floor of the Sky*, published in 1972 at a production cost of $5.75 and a selling price of $19.75, sold only 4,000 volumes in three years. Beckmann felt that the book's failure was due to its subject matter—The Great Plains—which did not have wide appeal to Sierra Club book purchasers. Other staff members claimed that the topic was too broad and that there were insufficient people in the Great Plains States to constitute a market. *Slickrock* (1971) and *Everglades* (1970), both selling at $27.50 and costing about $7.50 to produce, had similarly mediocre sales of only 5,000 and 8,000 volumes respectively. Another problem, in addition to lagging sales for the Ex-

EXHIBIT 10
NEW VS. OLD BOOKS SOLD*

	1970–71	1971–72	1972–73	1973 (Sept.–Dec.)
Total number of items sold†	134,713	144,309	138,024	57,747
Number and (percent) of old items	76,170 (57)	82,257 (57)	82,021 (65)	39,186 (71)
Number and (percent) of new items	58,441 (43)	61,982 (43)	48,777 (35)	16,663 (29)

* A publisher is interested in how much of the new or old line of books is selling. If the old line is selling well, inventory is depleted and the firm may consider reprinting popular volumes. If the new line is selling well, the new volumes may have "caught the market" and old volumes may have lost their appeal.
† Items include books and calendars. Some items are not classified as new or old in the Club's records.
Source: Sierra Club Memorandum, Publication Sales through December, 1973.

EXHIBIT 11
SALES SUMMARY

	Pub. Date	Production Cost ($)	List Price ($)	Books in Inventory	1966 & Prior	1967	1968	1969	1970	1971	1972	1973	1974 to Aug.	Total
Exhibit Formats														
Floor of the Sky	9/72	6.18	19.75	2,973	—	—	—	—	—	—	1,484	2,409	166	4,059
In Wildness	10/62	7.00	25.00	152	31,241	5,234	4,826	2,160	3,491	2,618	1,821	2,023	1,131	54,625
On the Loose	5/67	1.12	7.95	5,865	—	18,978	37,029	14,167	12,060	8,498	4,426	3,391	1,815	100,346
Everglades	10/70	7.56	27.50	1,470	—	—	—	—	—	6,347	1,044	305	268	7,964
Slickrock	9/71	7.34	27.50	1,592	—	—	—	—	—	1,860	2,215	596	296	4,967
Glacier Bay	5/67	7.80	17.50	651	—	4,090	1,011	362	587	487	249	245	537	7,568
Galapagos (2 volumes)	10/68	15.60	55.00	—	—	—	5,996	238	690	384	262	25	—	7,595
Baja	10/67	8.07	17.50	40	—	5,032	2,203	685	919	1,140	698	488	247	11,412
Totes														
Climbers Guide Yosemite	4/71	1.44	6.95	555	—	—	—	—	—	3,944	1,774	1,519	1,343	8,580
Food for Knapsackers	5/71	.67	2.45	691	—	—	—	—	—	9,586	18,839	11,647	7,892	47,964
Hiking Tetons	11/73	1.87	4.95	1,017	—	—	—	—	—	—	—	—	4,197	4,197
Smokies Guide	7/73	2.75	7.95	3,373	—	—	—	—	—	—	—	3,999	4,426	8,425
Survival Songbook	4/71	1.47	4.95	4,002	—	—	—	—	—	13,009	6,804	974	346	21,133
Battle Books														
Energy	1/72	.60	2.75	3,638	—	—	—	—	—	—	6,720	5,923	5,241	17,884
Clearcut	1/72	1.25	2.75	224	—	—	—	—	—	—	6,911	1,520	19	8,450
Oilspill	1/72	.82	2.75	432	—	—	—	—	—	—	4,927	981	496	6,404
Mercury	5/71	.57	2.75	412	—	—	—	—	—	5,441	2,160	288	(29)	7,860
Stripping	4/72	.73	2.25	2,504	—	—	—	—	—	—	2,736	1,583	781	5,100

Sales per Year

hibit Format series overall, was that material and production costs for high quality paper and photography—particularly color—had soared in recent months.

Thoreau's Country was a black and white photographic study based on the work of Herbert Gleason (1855–1937) of the landscapes—meadows, woods, farms, Walden Pond, Cape Cod, the Maine Woods—which inspired the writings of Henry David Thoreau. Gleason, an excellent photographer although largely unrecognized until the early 1970's, had taken these photographs in the early 1900's. The production cost of the book would be at least $7.50. *The Rockies* was a magnificently photographed survey of the Rocky Mountains area in the United States and came within the traditional framework of Sierra Club exhibit format books. Its production cost would be substantially higher than that of either *Everglades* or *Slickrock*.

Totes

The "Tote book" series consisted of small, inexpensive paperbound books meant to be taken on hikes. List price for totes were $4.95, at a production cost of around $1.75. As production costs were increasing, more recent totes sold for $7.95. The Club usually had a first printing of 10,000 copies. The tote line actually began in 1971, although similar kinds of books had been printed earlier. Totes covered either specific trails—such as in the Tetons, Grand Canyon, Austrian Alps, Dolomite Alps, and the Smokies— or more general subjects such as cooking, hiking, and backpacking. The general subject totes were, on the whole, much more successful than the specific trail guides. For example, a High Sierra guide published back in 1959 sold 67,000 copies and was still popular in 1974. A *Food for Knapsackers* tote sold nearly 50,000 copies since its publication in 1970. On the other hand, the *Survival Songbook* tote was considered a failure after sales of 21,000 copies since reprintings of the book had never "moved" after the year of its introduction to the market.

Guides to specific trails or areas of the country usually sold on a different magnitude. A *Climber's Guide to Yosemite* or *In the Smokies* each sold around 9,000 volumes and were still selling well since their publication around 1972.

The Club's staff felt that totes enhanced the Club's reputation and provided a service. On the whole, Beckmann felt that "Totes do well over the long pull." Beckmann also noted that "The totes are taking a different direction, more toward appreciation of the area's natural characteristics than a trail guide." The *Golden Gateway* was a guide to the area set aside in and around San Francisco, from Point Reyes in the North through Golden Gate Park to San Gregorio beaches in the South. The Gateway was the largest urban area park of its kind. The purpose of *Nature Photography* was self-explanatory.

Battlebooks

The "Battlebooks" series were highly technical books on specific currently relevant subjects and usually had a 5,000 copy initial printing. They were published as paperbacks, with prices being kept low ($2.75) to encourage sales. Production costs were generally around $1.00 each. Books on *Clearcutting, Mercury, Energy, Stripping,* and *Oilspill* were attempts to respond quickly to important political issues and generally met with wide approval by Club members and the conservation community at large. It was this series, however, that had caused problems in 1973; a rush to publish had led to the subsequent discovery of technical errors, while some books appeared after Congressional action had already been taken.

Many volumes received wide acclaim for their substantive content. They provided an easy to read but informative format to the pressing issues of the day. *Energy* and *Ecotactics,* two of the most successful Battlebooks, sold around 19,000 copies each. Most sold from 5,000 to 8,000 copies. There was a strong feeling that the public expected an expert job to be done. While the Club wanted to continue the Battlebooks, sales (except to libraries) were generally poor and inventories increased. However, the Club felt a responsibility to continue investigative reporting and to use Battlebooks as weapons to generate political support.

Underground

The Sierra Club did not have an "Underground" series per se. However, Mr. Beckmann had received two manuscripts which he felt would start the Publishing Division on a different type of book. These essentially appealed to the "counter culture" and were in the nature of the *Whole Earth Catalogue,* which had met with considerable success over the past few years. Since the Club had not published anything like this before, Mr. Beckmann had no specific cost comparisons. He used his general knowledge about the industry and the Club's other experiences to make some calculations.

Specifically, the proposed book entitled *Woodstoves* consisted of hand-lettered descriptions, with handsome drawings and photographs of wood burning stoves found around the country. Beckmann felt the timing of such a book might fit perfectly if the energy crisis continued into the future. Furthermore, he felt that more and more people were appreciating rural life styles and antiques. He was met, however, with one objection by a staff member who claimed:

> I hope this book doesn't have the thrust that we should all go out and start burning wood. If any appreciable fraction of our 210 million population thinks that, the result would be horrendous.

Beckmann pondered over whether the book was consistent with the Club's philosophy.

The second possibility, *Better Homes and Garbage,* was a manuscript that had been prepared by several faculty members and students from Stanford University. Beckmann said:

> It's in the school of technical "how to" manuals that are being published more and more. Essentially *Better Homes . . .* is a reference book that is an attempt to summarize available information on a

low impact technology that is useful in developing alternative life styles. If we do it, I see it selling in paper for around $8.95. It would appeal to those who have already left the cities and need specific information on how to get the most heat out of glass panels or whatever. I think it might also appeal to the secondary armchair market which the *Whole Earth Catalogue* did. The text is lucid and practical.

While *Better Homes . . .* was appealing, Mr. Beckmann was concerned that the book might be too different from the other books in the Club's line and might somehow damage the Club's quality image.

CONCLUSION

Beckmann reviewed the list once more. He was concerned about the future economic health of the Club and the role that this decision would play vis-à-vis the Club as a whole. Immediately pressing was the problem of what books to sell at what prices. Which books would be consistent with the Club's philosophy but not jeopardize the Club's ability to continue? Which books might best enhance the Club's image and spread the conservation cause?

He felt that these immediate questions could not be answered without examining longer range questions. For example:

> How might publishing become less dependent on calendar sales?
> Should members continue to receive significant discounts?
> How could the division reduce its backlist titles in inventory?
> How might publishing best use its clientele and the momentum it has generated from past successes?
> What new directions, if any, should the Publishing division undertake?

Underlying these questions was still a basic decision that the Club would have to make regarding its commitment to the Publishing division. Beckmann foresaw the need for a large initial capitalization for planning and researching future manuscripts. Unless the Club would be willing to make that commitment, Beckmann saw two alternatives: either "an erratic program which is crippled every two or three years and does not publish effectively or efficiently; or a package operation in which the Club lends its name to books to be published by other pub-lishers, and in which case the Club ceases to be a publisher in the accepted sense of the word." Beckmann pondered these questions, and began to draft his thoughts for an agenda for the upcoming PubCom meeting.

ACE FRAMES

Peter Gilmour

John Howe, the building products group general manager of Bayswater Consolidated Industries was concerned about the future viability of the Ace Frames division in Melbourne, Australia.[1] With a population of over two million, Melbourne was the largest city in the State of Victoria. Ace manufactured timber windows, doors and flywire screens as well as doing a quantity of specialized work. New building starts in Australia had been declining steadily since 1974, and with the prices of Ace products averaging 15 per cent above the rest of the market Ace had dropped in market share from 10 per cent at the beginning of 1976 to 6 per cent two years later. The price of raw materials was escalating rapidly and Ace was near to losing money.

In January 1978, Howe had called in Geoff Miller, who had recently completed his Master of

Reprinted from *Australian Marketing Casebook* by David L. Rados and Peter Gilmour. Copyright © 1981 by University of Queensland Press, St. Lucia, Queensland.

[1]All names and certain data in this case have been disguised to protect the interests of the company.

Business Administration degree at a nearby university, and told him:

> Geoff, I am going to move you out of your head office job and into the Ace Frames operation. We have problems there and I will let you have six months as General Manager of Ace within which time I want you to come up with a plan to turn this division around—otherwise we will sell it.

THE AUSTRALIAN HOUSING INDUSTRY

The housing industry was an important part of the Australian economy. During 1976–77, 110,400 new houses were completed. The value of all dwellings built during that year was $4,013 million, which was equivalent to 4.9 per cent of the gross domestic product and 20.8 per cent of the gross fixed capital expenditure. At the end of June 1977 the industry employed 131,200 people, or just over 2 per cent of the total Australian civilian work force.

During the 1970s the Australian housing industry experienced a steady downturn as shown in Exhibit 1. The total number of loans made by

155

EXHIBIT 1
NUMBER OF DWELLINGS COMMENCED

Year	Private	Government	Total
1972–73	155,385	15,126	170,511
1973–74	150,134	14,288	164,422
1974–75	99,103	19,006	118,109
1975–76	123,766	13,192	136,958
1976–77	126,400	15,300	141,700
1977–78	105,500	13,200	118,700

Source: *Building Statistics*, Australian Bureau of Statistics, Canberra.

savings banks, trading banks and building societies for new dwellings also declined, but somewhat erratically, during the early- and mid-1970s (Exhibit 2).

PRODUCTION AT ACE FRAMES

Ace manufactured doors and windows either from kiln dried hardwood—locally supplied ash—or from imported western red cedar. Orders were taken daily by the sales representatives or telephoned directly by the customer. Once the order was received at Ace it was scheduled for production regardless of the final due date. Because of this system of order receipt, production occurred on a jobbing basis even though a substantial proportion of total output was standard products.

Rough sawn timber stock was converted into molded components (in the molding mill) and then stored. The supervisor in the machining section replenished these stocks of molded components by periodic visual inspection. Availability of these components was almost always adequate as the employees at the molding mill were paid according to mill throughput levels. From this point in the factory, work-in-process inventories, finished goods inventories and the production level in the factory were dependent upon the actual orders in process.

A timber window, as an example, would undergo these three major steps as it proceeded through the Ace factory:

EXHIBIT 2
LOANS FOR NEW DWELLINGS

	Number			
Year	Savings Banks	Permanent Building Societies	Trading Banks	Total
1972–73	36,371	32,551	24,035	92,957
1973–74	32,679	18,012	22,480	73,171
1974–75	31,932	11,592	13,501	57,025
1975–76	36,453	20,746	15,888	73,087

	Savings banks		Trading banks		Permanent building societies		Terminating building societies		Finance companies	
Year	No.	$'000	No.	$'000	No.	$'000	No.	$'000	No.	$'000
1976-77	33,717	634,152	14,912	225,386	19,207	487,970	4,706	97,874	4,634	162,207
1977-78	31,571	652,814	13,509	225,884	19,304	532,786	5,830	136,958	4,360	137,063

Source: *Housing Finance for Owner Occupied Houses*, Australian Bureau of Statistics, Canberra.

Molding of components—the head, sill, jambs, transome, chair rail and sash rails (see Exhibit 3) were molded to the required profile from rough sawn timber and docked to required lengths.

Machining of components—trenches, mortice and tenons, rebates and stops were machined into the molded components by up to three additional machining operations.

Assembling and glazing—the machined components were assembled, glued and nailed, and glass inserted using putty.

About sixty standard products—windows, door frames and sidelights—were being made in the latter part of 1977 and all these were made in local ash and in western red cedar. A typical hardwood window frame sold for around $110 and a western red cedar window frame for about $120.

THE MARKET FOR ACE PRODUCTS

In early 1978 the Australian market for windows and doors was split 68 percent for timber, 30

EXHIBIT 3
COMPONENTS OF A TYPICAL WINDOW

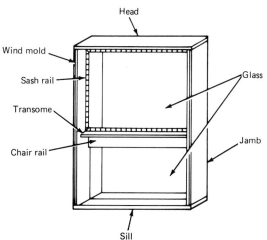

percent aluminum and 2 percent steel. Of the timber products 65 percent were made from the hardwoods meranti and kapur (imported mostly from Malaysia), 25 percent from western red cedar (imported from North America) and 10 percent from local ash. Regardless of the type of material used, Ace management estimated that, on average, a new dwelling used a total of twelve windows and door frames.

Three quarters of all home building in the state of Victoria was in the Melbourne metropolitan area (see Exhibit 4) and almost all builders of any size had their offices in Melbourne. Ace believed that potential buyers of their products came from three groups: registered home and flat (apartment) builders or architects, unregistered home and flat builders, or architects and owner builders and renovators (see Exhibit 5).

The six thousand registered builders in Victoria ranged from those who were well aware of quality and service considerations to those who considered only price. In the larger firms a purchasing manager, chief estimator or the construction manager made the purchasing decisions while in smaller firms they were made by the owner or partner or the site supervisor. (Exhibit 6 shows housing starts by size of builder.) But in all cases the site supervisor had an important influence on the decision.

Unregistered builders were a rather transient group of about eight thousand home renovators and sub-contractors. Mostly this group bought solely on the basis of price. Owner builders and home improvers were usually responsive to quality and service considerations and often willing to pay extra for perceived quality or superior service.

After specifying the potential market for Ace products, Geoff Miller prepared a listing by market share of all competitive firms in both the timber and aluminum sectors of the industry. Based on discussions with his management group at Ace he was able to evaluate each of these competitors in terms of their relative strengths

EXHIBIT 4
BUILDINGS APPROVALS IN VICTORIA 1976–77

Statistical Division	Number of New Dwellings			Value of Building $'000			Number of Local Government Areas in Division*
	Houses	Other Dwellings	Total	Houses	Other Dwellings	Total	
Melbourne	18,497	5,608	24,105	546,531	104,350	650,881	57
Barwon	2,385	371	2,756	62,602	6,030	68,632	14
South Western	561	184	745	14,864	2,741	17,605	17
Central Highlands	1,061	288	1,349	27,543	4,798	32,341	16
Wimmera	295	61	356	7,818	882	8,700	14
Northern Mallee	445	72	517	12,082	1,163	13,245	8
Loddon-Campaspe	1,552	209	1,761	43,103	3,133	46,236	27
Goulburn	1,095	130	1,225	29,572	2,118	31,690	21
North Eastern	752	150	902	21,775	2,468	24,243	13
East Gippsland	647	82	729	15,116	1,290	16,406	9
Central Gippsland	935	185	1,120	24,996	2,957	27,953	14
East Central	1,019	42	1,061	23,349	696	24,045	8
Total Victoria	29,244	7,382	36,626	829,351	132,626	961,977	218

*Details given in source document for individual local government areas.
Source: *Building Approvals by Local Government areas, 1976–77*, Australian Bureau of Statistics, Victorian Office, Melbourne, 1977.

EXHIBIT 5
PRIVATE HOUSES COMPLETED IN AUSTRALIA*

| | Class of Builder | | | | | |
| | Contract | | Spec | | Owner-Builder | |
Year	'000	%	'000	%	'000	%
1972–73	51.2	53.1	31.5	32.8	13.6	14.1
1973–74	52.2	53.4	30.9	31.4	14.9	15.2
1974–75	50.7	60.6	20.0	23.5	14.4	16.9
1975–76	46.5	54.8	22.2	26.1	16.2	19.1

* Information not collected by the Australian Bureau of Statistics in this form after 1975–76.
 Source: Australian Bureau of Statistics, Canberra, various years.

and weaknesses. While Miller recognized that some of these evaluative comments were rather subjective he felt the exercise was still a good starting point. The evaluation of the timber sector is shown as Exhibit 7 and the evaluation of the aluminum sector as Exhibit 8.

MARKETING ACE PRODUCTS

Ace's strategy of marketing a premium quality product at a premium price was running into difficulty in a market that was depressed and much more price sensitive; at least, this was the evaluation at Ace where it was considered that the 15 percent price premium was almost entirely the cause of the drop in market share among

timber products from 10 to 6 percent over the last two years. One way to reduce the price of the product was to use a less expensive raw material. Ace used local ash and imported western red cedar. These cost $55 and $70 per 100 super feet[2] respectively compared to $45 for imported Malaysian hardwood. As all Ace products were priced on the basis of cost plus a fixed percentage margin, the cost of raw materials was a very important factor. At the end of 1977 pricing at the cost of production (excluding administration costs) plus 35 percent was providing about a 6

[2] A super foot is 12 inches by 12 inches by 1 inch. (1 cubic metre of wood is equal to 423.78 super feet.) On average, a window used approximately 30 super feet of wood.

EXHIBIT 6
PRIVATE HOUSE STARTS BY SIZE OF BUILDER*

| | Small (1–9 employees) | | Medium (10–24 employees) | | Large (24 + employees) | |
Year	'000	%	'000	%	'000	%
1972–73	45.2	43.9	18.0	17.5	39.8	38.6
1973–74	45.2	47.0	16.2	16.9	34.7	36.1
1974–75	37.5	51.2	11.9	16.2	23.9	32.6
1975–76	46.2	51.5	14.1	15.7	29.5	32.8

* Information not collected by the Australian Bureau of Statistics in this form after 1975–76.
 Source: Australian Bureau of Statistics, Canberra, various years.

EXHIBIT 7
COMPETITORS IN TIMBER PRODUCTS

Company*	Market Share (%)	Strengths	Weaknesses
Remcraft	26	• High market share in the low priced Malaysian hardwood segment (40%) • Efficient production • Low overhead • First into low priced product segment • Recently taken over by a competitor (Dowell) in the aluminium segment • Dowell has considerable resources and know-how • Well known in the trade as the "cheapest" • Very successful in gaining market share by penetration pricing	• Reputation for low quality • Some industrial relations difficulties • Take over has caused some staff disruptions • Limited factory facilities • Assembly lines soon relocated to new site • No advertising • Produce to order only • Two weeks lead time • Product range in only one type of timber—meranti
Stegbar	25	• High market share in cedar segment (70%) • Heavy promotion has established a strong quality image • Backed by the ACMIL group • Extensive interstate and country distribution • Products frequently specified by architects • Products well known to both the trade and the final consumer	• Dependency on cedar with cedar segment contracting due to large price increases (70% in six months) • Image built on cedar—difficult to change timber • Service levels have dropped
Trend-Hicks	10	• Dual product range—cedar and meranti • Good promotion to owner builders and final consumers • Primary strength in New South Wales • Good production facilities • Efficient production methods • Attempting to gain market share with lower grade products	• Some quality problems • Service levels and lead times slipping • No clear strategy • Poor direct selling • No stock holding • Lead times 2–3 weeks

percent profit margin on sales. Material costs (timber, hardware such as nails, screws and hinges, and glass) were about 45 percent of sales and direct labor costs about 25 percent of sales.

Ace produced about sixty standard products in ash (timber awning windows, door frames and sidelights in a range of sizes) and sixty standard products in western red cedar. These made up about 60 percent of the firm's total volume with specialized "once-off" joinery providing the remainder.

During 1977 Ace had done no advertising of their products, the only promotion being the direct selling done by the sales force. Several years prior to 1977, Bayswater Consolidated Industries had set up a distribution division which performed the sales and distribution tasks for the entire company. Eighteen salesmen from the dis-

EXHIBIT 7 *(continued)*

Company*	Market Share (%)	Strengths	Weaknesses
Trimview	7	• Quality image • High price image • Quality custom joinery • Strong distribution channels	• No promotion • Long production lead times • Limited product development • High priced raw materials
Stolar	4	• Long experience in the industry • Good local following • Low overhead	• Only one range—hardwood • No promotion • No stock holding • Lead time 2 weeks • Keys on price and service
Windmill	4	• Backed by overseas group • Good timber supply source	• Quality problems with kapur—very hard which often results in poor finish • Poor service levels and lead times (2–3 weeks) • Reputation for low grade product • Labour intensive production • Little promotion
F.D.A.	3	• Own timber mills • Very price competitive	• Management poor • Quality poor • Service levels poor • No advertising
Settle Bros	2	• Very price competitive • Low overhead	• Limited production facilities • Quality poor • Service poor • No advertising • Undue concentration on price • Poor materials supply
Eagle	2	• High local loyalty • Low overheads	• Limited production facilities • Poor materials supply • Long lead times

* In addition to these companies, there were between ten and fifteen small operations typically with low overheads and local appeal.

tribution division sold Ace products. These salesmen also sold other timber products, framing material, flooring and hardware—timber windows in 1977 provided an average of 10 percent of the dollar volume for the sales force. Upon investigation Geoff Miller found that salesmen "sold windows as an afterthought." Remuneration for a salesman consisted of salary plus a commission on sales volume. The commission rate was not standard over all Bayswater Consolidated Industries products, but varied by division—Ace paid the lowest commissions (at 2 percent), averaging about half of the rate paid by other divisions.

With a premium pricing policy Ace was "trading on traditional customer loyalty and high service standards." But this policy was edging Ace out of the high volume section of the market

EXHIBIT 8
COMPETITORS IN ALUMINIUM PRODUCTS

Company*	Market Share (%)	Comments†
Dowell	36	• Backed by Overseas Corporation • Aggressive • Strong in country areas • Good promotion and image
KM Cyclone	13	• Backed by Boral • Losing market share • Increasing promotion • Production problems
Trimview	13	• Backed by Jennings Industries • Holding market share • Good quality image • Not price competitive • Good distribution network • Strong in replacement market
Comalco	7	• Major aluminium producer • Holding market share • Good quality image
Wunderlich	7	• Backed by CSR • Gaining market share • Strong promotion against timber
Stegbar	3	• Part of ACMIL group • Major strength in timber-aluminium complements range

* In addition to these companies are some twenty small fabricators offering low prices to a local trade.

† Aluminium producers are planning a major promotional campaign against timber products.

where price as well as performance was important.

THE JUNE 1978 DECISION

Geoff Miller spent much of May generating ideas from which he could develop a strategy to present to his boss, John Howe, in June.

One possibility was to move most of the product range from local ash and imported western red cedar to the less expensive imported Malaysian hardwood. While the timber cost differential was significant, the lower priced product would provide some production problems: it was furry and therefore not easy to paint or stain; it had a tendency to twist and warp; and it often had inactive borer tracks in it which had to be filled and sanded. Miller had discovered that other users of the Malaysian meranti timber were experiencing a 25 percent rejection rate. But many of these problems would be avoided if the Malaysian timber was first specially treated. Several of Ace's major competitors were evaluting the benefits of installing such treatment plants, which cost around $50,000. On current production volumes Ace could only utilize about half of the capacity of the smallest treatment plant even with a major swing to the Malaysian timber.

Miller also felt that the production process itself could run more efficiently. New silicone sealants and the use of air powered nail fixing would allow the use of simpler "butt" joints and a drastic reduction in the amount of secondary machining required. The use of air cramps, air nailing and the automatic coordination of cramps and nailing guns together with rollers to facilitate material flow would provide many of the benefits of mass production and the potential to increase the throughput of these sections of the factory by an estimated factor of three times. Timber glazing beads nailed to the frame instead of putty would also speed up this operation as well as provide a better quality finish. The preservative treatment plant, if installed, would remove the need to manually prime or seal the timber (a practice designed to temporarily protect timber on site prior to normal painting).

The amount of specialized joinery work done by Ace was another area which concerned Miller. A much higher degree of product standardization and even production to stock were options he would need to evaluate.

Data provided by the Australian Bureau of Statistics on Victorian housing starts showed no relief from the economic decline in the building industry. Information on the relative price of building materials (Exhibit 9) indicated that timber was feeling the full effect of price increases in the industry.

To help him evaluate the competition faced by Ace, Miller consolidated the information on competitive profiles (Exhibit 7) into a more quantitative format (shown in Exhibit 10) focusing on market share, price, quality and lead time.

Miller sat back at his desk and wondered if he would be able to sift and organize all this information into a meaningful form in time for his meeting with John Howe in three weeks time.

EXHIBIT 9
THE PRICE OF BUILDING MATERIALS

Building Material	Price index (base year 1966–67 = 100)			
	1972–73	1975–76	1976–77	1977–78
Concrete	127.0	193.0	215.6	235.3
Cement products	139.9	220.0	244.7	268.4
Bricks, stone	130.7	202.7	244.7	241.0
Timber, board and joinery	137.0	219.3	243.6	263.2
Steel and iron products	136.8	223.4	251.7	273.4
Aluminium products		193.6	213.7	230.8
Other metal products	124.9	173.3	195.0	198.1
Plumbing fixtures	129.6	232.1	251.2	263.7
Miscellaneous materials	124.9	186.8	204.2	221.9
Electrical installation materials	126.2	177.4	199.6	215.3
Mechanical services components		201.3	225.4	247.2
All groups		206.2	230.3	249.7

Source: Monthly Review of Business Statistics, Australian Bureau of Statistics, various years.

EXHIBIT 10
SUMMARY ANALYSIS OF COMPETITORS

Competitor	Market Share Ranking	Competitive differential with Ace (points)*										
		Ace better						Competitor better				
		−5	−4	−3	−2	−1	0	+1	+2	+3	+4	+5
Remcraft	1		Q			L						P
Stegbar	2				L				Q		P	
Trimview	3					Q	L	P				
Trend Hicks	4			Q	L				P			
Stolar	6				L	Q						P
Windmill	7	Q						L				P
FDA	8	Q		L								P
Sette	9	Q			L							P
Eagle	10				L	Q						P

*P = Product price; L = lead time to fill order; Q = product quality.

THE PARKER HOUSE, I

Robert J. Kopp
Penny Pittman Merliss
Christopher H. Lovelock

Yervant Chekijian, group director of operations for the Classic hotels division of Dunfey Hotels, didn't mince words. "Business at the Parker House has never been better—but our biggest challenge may be right around the corner."

Robert McIntosh, general manager of the Parker House, Boston's oldest hotel, watched as Chekijian picked up a newspaper clipping dated April 1979 and headlined, "Hotels Bring Jobs to Boston, Tax Money to State."

"This story in the *Globe*," he continued, "confirms what we've suspected for some time—that within five years, as many as five or six brand new hotels may open within three miles of the Parker House. Business travelers in this town are going to have more atriums, swimming pools, and king-size beds than they know what to do with. Our mission statement outlines the market position we want for the Parker House; now we need to establish how each department of the hotel will contribute to that position."

Copyright © 1980 by the President and Fellows of Harvard College, Harvard Business School case 9-580-150.

McIntosh nodded in agreement. "We'll need more than old-world charm to hold on to our market share," he observed. "What we're really talking about is competition-proofing the Parker House."

HISTORY OF THE PARKER HOUSE

The Parker House, the oldest continuously operating hotel in America, opened on October 8, 1855, and was immediately popular with Bostonians and visitors alike. Charles Dickens, the most popular English novelist of the nineteenth century, was a regular visitor to the Parker House during his American tours and in 1867 described it to his daughter as "an immense hotel, with all manner of white marble public rooms. I live in a corner high up and have a hot and cold bath in my bedroom." Dickens was unusually well qualified to judge the merits of his bath, having fallen into it fully dressed one night after enjoying the Parker House wines.

The founder of the hotel, Harvey Parker, was a former stableboy from Maine who began his career in the hospitality industry by operating a moderately priced lunchroom in Boston's Court-house Square. After opening his new hotel, Parker directed his energies toward food and beverage development and was the first hotelkeeper in the world to offer a formal American Plan: lodging plus three meals daily at a single price. His French chef, hired for $5,000 in a day when many hotel cooks earned about $500 annually, created lavish banquets that brought additional fame to the hotel; Boston cream pie was first served at the Parker House, and the soft, crustless Parker House rolls created by the hotel's German baker were shipped as far west as Chicago.

Refurbished and enlarged throughout the nineteenth century, the Parker House was almost totally rebuilt in 1927. Constructed from yellow-gray brick, the 14-story building stood on the corner of Tremont and School streets, both busy, narrow thoroughfares in the heart of Boston. The Boston Common, a large public park established as a cow pasture by the Puritans, was two blocks away.

Although the exterior of the Parker House resembled an office building more than a grand hotel, the wood-paneled lobby with its rich carpeting, framed 18th century engravings, and ornate brass elevator doors created an aura of elegance which was reflected in the handsome first floor dining room and the other public rooms on the second floor. In 1927 the newly built hotel contained a total of over 550 guest rooms and suites, and throughout the 1920s and 1930s continued to attract the rich and famous.

But the following decades were not kind to the hotel. During the 1950s and 1960s Boston's waterfront and many of the downtown streets which bordered it fell into decay, and new shopping and commercial areas grew up in the suburbs and the Back Bay. With its main entrance tucked away on a narrow side street and its facade growing darker with age, the Parker House failed to catch the eye of many tourists and corporate travelers. By 1969, occupancy was down to 35 percent, and the former grand old lady of Boston had fallen into bankruptcy.

The Parker House was brought back to life in 1969 by Dunfey Family Hotels, a privately owned, regional lodging chain which at that time operated 11 hotels and inns in the northeast U.S. The company was founded in 1954 by six Dunfey brothers and their mother. To finance further expansion following the purchase of the Parker House, the Dunfey family sold the company to Aetna Life Insurance in 1970. Five years later, Jon Canas, formerly head of international marketing for the Sheraton Corporation, joined the company as vice president of sales and marketing. In 1976, Aer Lingus, the national airline of Ireland, acquired Dunfey from Aetna and arranged to lease the hotel properties through a subsidiary. Throughout these changes of ownership, Jack Dunfey remained chief executive officer of Dunfey Hotels Corp.

Initial Renovations

In February 1973, as a major step in their effort to revive the Parker House, the Dunfeys hired Yervant Chekijian, who had managed the prestigious Mayflower Hotel in Washington, D.C., as general manager. Chekijian arrived in Boston to discover a city in renaissance. The huge Prudential Center, a network of apartments, shops, hotel, and plazas built on former railroad yards in the Back Bay area of Boston, had ignited redevelopment in 1959. Next came Government Center, a 60-acre project planned by I.M. Pei, which transformed shabby Scollay Square into an open plaza surrounded by two large government office towers, a sweeping curve of retailing and office space, and other government buildings. The focal point of the project was a dramatically modern City Hall, which one architectural critic considered "as fine a building for its time and place as Boston has ever produced." Nearby was Boston's financial district, where banks and other financial firms were building new 30- and 40-story office towers.

Dunfey management could see that the Parker House's location now offered the hotel a distinctive advantage over its major competitors. Built in a day when many business travelers in the city still preferred to walk to their destinations, the Parker House was closer to Boston's corporate, legal, and financial offices than any other hotel in town. Three rapid transit stations lay within a five-minute walk; Logan Airport was only 2½ miles away, and could be reached by taxi in half the time it took to travel there from any other downtown hotel. Although the Parker House did not have its own parking garage, guest parking was available within one block.

Impressed by the hotel's distinguished history, the Dunfeys saw a chance to rebuild its dominant position by catering to corporate and professional travelers and discriminating tourists rather than large groups of conventioneers. They knew that much individual business was booked locally, since travelers frequently relied on those whom they were visiting to make lodging arrangements. The key to rebuilding wide demand for the Parker House, they decided, was reestablishing the hotel's image within Boston itself.

The first public area of the Parker House to be renovated in 1973 was The Last Hurrah, an informal bar and restaurant in the basement, created from a former grillroom. The Last Hurrah offered moderately priced drinks and meals and, later, one of the only live swing bands in Boston. Decorated with photographs depicting figures from Boston's colorful political past, The Last Hurrah soon attracted a loyal lunch and after-work following from City Hall, the state legislature, and the financial district.

Total renovation of most of the Parker House guest rooms and corridors was the second stage of the repositioning of the hotel. During 1973–74 walls were stripped, repainted and repapered; new furniture and carpets purchased; new bathroom fixtures installed and bathtubs reglazed; and new lighting and mirrors added. Additionally, the entire hotel was rewired and individual heating and air-conditioning controls (costing approximately $2,500 per room) were installed in each bedroom. "Not one piece of old furniture was left in the renovated rooms," Chekijian recalled. "Our objective was to create a first-class facility that would not offend any top-of-the-line traveler; by adding a very high level of service to this new physical plant, we could then market the Parker House as a luxury hotel."

In 1975, Dunfey management renovated the hotel's once-elegant dining room, used as a meeting room since 1969. Reopened as Parker's Restaurant, it was furnished with overstuffed sofas and large wingback chairs, its brown and beige color scheme accented by spectacular floral arrangements. Its warm atmosphere and mixture of French and American cuisine soon made Parker's one of the most popular fine restaurants in town: readers polled by *Boston* magazine considered it one of the top ten in the city and felt that Parker's service was second only to that of the Ritz. Bostonians were particularly fond of Parker's Sunday brunch; diners were served from a buffet line as a harp played softly in the background. Adjoining Parker's Restaurant was Parker's Bar, which had been transformed into a quiet, luxurious piano lounge.

"This was the key to our repositioning effort," Chekijian commented. "It's important to sell a dining room to the local community, since local residents, not those who are visiting, usually make dining decisions. We saw the dining room as a window onto us for the community, and we wanted to create a room which would define the hotel."

The total cost of renovations through 1975 exceeded $5 million. The following year, the south wing of the hotel, which had been closed off since 1969, was completely renovated at a cost of $500,000, adding another 51 guest rooms and giving the Parker House a total of 546 rooms. Occupancy rose from 52 percent in 1973 to 83 percent in 1976, when Chekijian was promoted to a new position at Corporate Headquarters.

By 1979, the only restaurant to remain substantially unrenovated was the Revere Room, a 108-seat coffee shop serving breakfast and lunch. A holdover from Dunfey's early days at the hotel, when management had instituted a colonial theme, the Revere Room was prominently located near the Tremont Street entrance. It offered fast, reasonably inexpensive meals in what management conceded was a rather dull and conventional setting.

THE DUNFEY ORGANIZATION

The rising popularity of the Parker House mirrored the growing success of the Dunfey corporation as a whole. Revenues had doubled since 1977, when Jon Canas became executive vice president. Chainwide occupancy rates leaped from 56 percent in 1975, below industry average, to a projected 76 percent in 1979. By late 1979, the company, now known as Dunfey Hotels, owned or managed 23 hotels and inns. These properties were divided into six distinct groups, among which was the Classic hotels division, consisting of the Parker House, the Ambassador East in Chicago, and the Berkshire Place in New York City.

The Dunfey Management Process

The character of Dunfey inns and hotels varied widely; within the Boston area alone, Dunfey-managed facilities included a 275 room executive inn and a 120-room suburban motor inn in addition to the Parker House. Accordingly, the corporation made it a point to maintain clear distinctions in planning, pricing, and promotion between the Classic hotels and other Dunfey properties.

The foundation of the Dunfey management process, established by Jon Canas, was the annual mission statement developed for each hotel. Responsibility for this detailed planning document was shared between corporate marketing and operations executives and the Executive Operating Committee (EOC) of each individual property. The Parker House EOC included Robert McIntosh, general manager; the director of sales; the resident manager for food and beverage; the

resident manager for rooms; and the personnel director. Working closely with Yervant Chekijian, they attempted, through the mission statement, to specify what kind of customer, at what time of year, at what rate, was most desirable for the hotel. After this "ideal business mix" (IBM) had been determined, objectives could be set for the rooms division and the food and beverage division, capital needs established, and a marketing plan designed.

Through this marketing plan, based on the mission statement, detailed strategic blueprints covering four-month and twelve-month periods could be devised for each hotel. Essential to the plan in each case was a supply/demand analysis for each major revenue-producing area (rooms, banquets, a la carte operations, lounges). Such a study showed demand by market segment; it also analyzed the features of the competition and the hotel's competitive advantages and disadvantages vis-a-vis the needs of each market segment. The mission statement expressed the desired market position of the hotel; the supply/demand analysis provided data through which a plan designed to achieve that position could be constructed.

THE CLASSIC HOTELS

Each Dunfey Classic hotel was considered a unique facility with a character and tradition all its own. This individuality was reflected in the hotels' decorating schemes: Manhattan's Berkshire Place, acquired in 1978, was furnished in a sophisticated contemporary mixture of marble, plants, oriental rugs, and overstuffed furniture; the decor of Chicago's Ambassador East, acquired in 1977, blended 18th century antiques with contemporary accessories; and the Parker House evoked a wood-paneled comfortable club.

Like the Parker House, the Ambassador East and the Berkshire Place were restorations of old, centrally located hotels. Such restorations were advantageous to Dunfey for several reasons. It was faster and less expensive (on a per-room basis) to restore an old hotel than to construct a new one. In the long run this could produce a relative cost advantage for Dunfey Classic hotels challenged by newly constructed competitors. Moreover, the location of such hotels—in the heart of the downtown business district—was often difficult for a new property to duplicate.

The history and physical facilities of the Classics also created an atmosphere which many Dunfey executives felt was missing in more modern hotels. As the company's newsletter stated:

Our Classic hotels have a tangible quality and an intangible ambience . . . much like an older, cultured, grand lady whose very presence exudes charm, sophistication, and prestige. We believe that many travelers seek an escape, an oasis from the sterile sameness of some national hotel chains. Even in the newer, plush megastructures of modern hotels, there is the risk of being lost in a sea of conventioneers, of experiencing impersonal service. We know there is a growing market for hotels where guests are treated as individuals in distinctive settings.

On the other hand, hotels constructed during an era when guests frequently traveled with their servants generally had many bedrooms considerably smaller than those offered by more modern competitors; 50 rooms at the Parker House, for example, were too small to include a full bathtub and contained only showers. Even after renovation, the rooms of older hotels tended to vary widely in size and location, a potential source of annoyance to guests charged the same rates for "different" rooms. Repair and maintenance costs were higher than for new hotels.

Pricing Policy

As Jon Canas described it, "pricing is the exteriorization of your marketing position"; with this philosophy in mind, Classic hotel rates were customarily set to fall within the top 10 percent of local competition. Local rates could also be an inhibiting factor: although Parker House manage-

ment felt that the hotel's high average occupancy rate had given them substantial pricing leverage, Boston hotel rates in general were much lower than those in New York. Yervant Chekijian summarized the situation as follows:

Right now, at the Parker House, we're running $53–65 single and $63–75 double. Personally, I'd like to see these rates brought closer to parity with New York, where the Berkshire, for instance, is charging $85 single. But local custom heavily influences pricing. In Chicago, when a number of hotels began offering substantial discounts to their corporate customers, we had to lower rates at the Ambassador East to match competition.

On the other hand, continuing inflation in construction and furnishings costs meant that rates charged by new hotels generally had to be set higher than prevailing rates in the same area. The average rate for Massachusetts hotels in 1979 was projected to reach about $42. Discussing this figure, Chekijian noted:

The average rate, even for a luxury hotel, can appear surprisingly low. It's important to remember that heavy seasonal and day-of-the-week variations give a hotel much flexibility in discounting. The average room rate is thus the result of sales to many different market segments at significantly different rates.

According to Dunfey management, any hotel operating at 85 percent room sales efficiency or above needed a rate increase. Room sales efficiency (RSE) was a standard used throughout Dunfey Hotels to measure the occupancy-price performance of an operation in which substantial discounting was common; RSE was defined as the ratio of total room sales revenues achieved during a specific period divided by the sum of the maximum revenues that could have been obtained if all available rooms had been sold at full (or "rack") rates during the same period. For example, if occupancy was 90 percent and the average room rate obtained was 90 percent of the full rate, the RSE would be 81 percent.

Room sales accounted for close to three-fifths

EXHIBIT 1

THE PARKER HOUSE: OPERATING STATEMENTS

1979 Budget vs. 1978 Actual

	1978	**1979 (budgeted*)**
Dept. Revenues		
Rooms	$ 6,273,078	$ 6,865,270
Food	2,829,678	3,078,900
Beverage	1,454,066	1,560,600
Food & bev.—misc. income	53,852	59,100
Telephone	251,655	259,480
Valet & guest laundry	39,677	34,700
Other income	16,129	11,400
Check room	5,149	11,500
Operated dept. revenues	10,923,554	11,880,950
Profit (or Loss)		
Rooms	4,682,429	5,198,601
Food & beverage	824,007	962,096
Telephone	(153,007)	(122,730)
Valet & guest laundry	13,209	11,880
Check room	(9,952)	(5,070)
Operated dept. profit	5,356,686	6,044,777
Other income	16,129	11,400
Gross operating income	5,372,814	6,056,177
Deductions		
Administrative & general	701,310	657,214
Marketing	371,769	471,854
Energy costs	695,385	815,961
Property operation	531,079	892,617
Total deductions from inc.	2,299,543	2,837,646
House profit	3,073,750	3,218,531
Commercial rental**	190,479	173,580
Gross operating profit	3,263,750	3,392,111
Property tax & fire ins.	813,544	712,000
Operating rentals***	59,379	59,640
Operating profit	2,390,827	2,620,471
Depreciation and amortization	1,342,000	1,435,000
Hotel earnings	1,048,827	1,185,471

* "Budgeted" amounts were a low estimate for financial purposes and did not represent what was expected of management.

** Derived from shops approached through the Parker House lobby.

*** Cost of rented color television sets in rooms.

Source: Company records.

of the hotel's departmental revenues in 1978 (Exhibit 1); because the incremental costs of room rental were relatively low, the hotel's high occupancy meant a substantial profit margin in that department—72 percent in 1978. The margin for food and beverage, by contrast, could be as low as 18 percent. The Parker House's earnings, like the earnings of every Dunfey hotel, returned to the corporation for distribution.

Advertising and Sales Efforts

National and major regional advertising for each Classic hotel was supervised by Dunfey's director of advertising and public relations, who was based at the head office in Hampton, N.H. In addition to placing ads for individual Classic properties in such periodicals as *The New Yorker* and *Forbes* (Exhibit 2), the advertising department was developing an advertisement which would promote the Classic hotels as a group in such print media as *Business Week, Sports Illustrated,* and *Time.* Total national advertising for the Classics was budgeted at about $784,000 for 1979.

As well as creating demand for rooms at the three Classic properties, the promotional campaign was designed to meet two other objectives: first, to create awareness of Dunfey Classic hotels as a group in order to pave the way for expansion of the division in other key metropolitan areas; and second, to establish a favorable institutional image for the corporation as a whole. Obtaining management contracts for prime properties from third-party owners was a continuing part of Dunfey's plans for expansion.

Local advertising for the Parker House was supervised by Bob McIntosh, working with the hotel's director of sales, and was used primarily to promote Parker's Restaurant and The Last Hurrah (Exhibit 2). A Boston public relations firm also worked closely with McIntosh in achieving local visibility for the hotel. Sales department expenditures totalled $371,769 in 1978, of which 52 percent went to salaries and wages, 38 percent to advertising, and 10 percent to sales and promotions. Newspaper advertising, which totalled about $51,000 in 1978, was budgeted at almost $130,000 in 1979.

Although most hotels segmented their guests into two or three categories (tourists, corporate travelers, and groups), the Parker House identified eleven major segments. The three most important—individual professionals and executives, corporate groups, and professional or special-interest associations—were contacted regularly by the Parker House sales staff. The hotel did not have space to accept large conventions. "Customers contribute to the atmosphere or hotel experience," declared one Dunfey executive.

"You should choose your clientele selectively to match your mission."

Two Parker House salespeople represented the hotel's Executive Service Plan (ESP) sales effort, targeted toward individual business travelers; they had a weekly quota of 40 sales calls to Boston-based organizations. According to McIntosh, no other hotel in the city carried out an equivalent direct sales campaign. In a further effort to attract ESP guests, who were always charged rack rate, the hotel offered an unlisted telephone number for reservations, larger rooms, express check-out, complimentary newspapers, and free weekend accommodations for an ESP guest's spouse. Other Parker House sales representatives solicited business from associations and groups in or near Boston. Obtaining bookings from companies, associations, and tour groups outside the Boston area was the responsibility of Dunfey's corporate sales department.

The Parker House in 1979

In May 1979, the 546 Parker House guest rooms were divided into the following eight categories:

Room Type	Number	Daily Rate	
		Single	Double
Patriot	36	$ 35	(none)
Airline	117	47	(none)
Standard	151	53	$ 63
Deluxe	168	57	67
Top of the Line	23	65	75
Mini-Suites	33	75	85
Suites	17	110	
Deluxe Suite	1	210	

Rooms were classified according to size, location (i.e., whether the room had an outside view), and quality of furnishings and appointments. The hotel's 36 Patriot rooms were the smallest it offered, accommodating only single occupancy, and were located in the interior of the building, overlooking a central airshaft. These rooms were sold at a substantial discount

EXHIBIT 2
EXAMPLES OF PRINT ADVERTISING BY THE PARKER HOUSE, 1978–79

Advertising in National Print Media.

For People Who Appreciate the Classics.

Classic Accommodations   Classic Service

In Boston

PARKER HOUSE

A DUNFEY CLASSIC HOTEL

Tremont & School Sts., Boston, MA 02107   617/227-8600
Reservations: 800-228-2121

PH

Advertising in Boston-Area Print Media.

Local Advertising.

A lot of Boston restaurants are simply replicas of Boston's best.

There is only one great Boston night spot with authentic turn-of-the-century atmosphere, delicious traditional fare, moderate prices, free garage parking by valet, no cover charge and nightly dancing to the delightful sound of the Winiker Swing Orchestra.

The others can only try their best.

At The Parker House
Dining/Dancing/Sunday Brunch
Tremont & School Streets/
Boston/Reservations
227-8600

PARKER'S

Dine exquisitely on Boston's favorite dishes, American and continental cuisine. Serving lunch, dinner and Sunday Brunch.

PARKER'S BAR

Our cosmopolitan lounge adjoining Parker's restaurant. Perfect for light lunch at noon. Cocktails till closing.

THE LAST HURRAH

Come eat, drink, dance and be entertained in a plush turn-of-the-century place. Open at 11:30 a.m. to 2 a.m.

PARKER HOUSE
A DUNFEY CLASSIC HOTEL
School & Tremont Street
Boston

to government employees; similar, somewhat larger rooms were sold, by annual contract, to airline personnel. Standard and Deluxe rooms were larger than Patriot rooms, possessed an outside view, had better quality furniture, and contained such amenities as color television and an AM-FM clock radio. Top of the Line rooms were more spacious still and had king-sized beds. Suites consisted of one or more very large rooms—often constructed by combining two smaller rooms—with superior appointments; many suites had kitchen facilities such as a sink or wet bar.

In addition to its guest rooms, the Parker House contained a variety of facilities for meetings, including three small "board rooms" accommodating 8–15 people; ten meeting rooms accommodating 25–200; and one ballroom accommodating 350. Duplicating machines, blackboards, and audio-visual equipment were available to groups at a small fee. Opening off the main lobby were a gift shop, a bank, a small shop selling newspapers, magazines, and sundries, and an Aer Lingus ticket office. A barber shop was located on the basement level. Laundry/valet service, airport limousines, and rental cars could all be requested through the hotel's front desk.

Occupancy rates at the Parker House, in keeping with the upward trend enjoyed by the city's hotels at large, had risen sharply in recent years. However, Dunfey executives realized that these figures were averages, in which the high weekday occupancy balanced out significantly lower weekend levels. As the corporation's director of sales explained:

> The Parker House is favored with a very heavy demand on Monday, Tuesday, and Wednesday nights. Management still has to stretch the Sunday night arrivals that are staying through the week. On Thursday, Friday, and Saturday nights, the hotel is not favored with a tremendously high turnaway. The ideal, of course, would be to have people coming in Sunday, checking out Friday, and followed by a heavy weekend influx. That's still not true for the Parker House.

At the same time, the hotel had also shown an improvement in room sales efficiency. Published room rates at the Parker House had risen at least once each year; the most recent increases had been posted on December 1, 1977; September 1, 1978; and April 1, 1979. Exhibit 3 shows occupancy rates, room sales efficiency index, and room, food, and beverage sales figures at the Parker House for calendar 1978 and early 1979.

THE BOSTON HOTEL MARKET

The average occupancy rates for Boston hotels had been considerably higher than the national average for a number of years (Exhibit 4). The city offered many diverse attractions to visitors: in addition to its status as a financial and commercial center, the Boston area boasted the greatest concentration of colleges and universities in the world, including both Harvard University and the Massachusetts Institute of Technology. Known as the "Medical Mecca" of the United States, Boston was also home to the Massachusetts General Hospital and a host of other renowned medical centers and research institutions. The Museum of Fine Arts and the Boston Symphony Orchestra were world famous, and the area's many colonial historic sites also attracted a substantial number of tourists.

A major Atlantic seaport, Boston had a very accessible airport and one of the most extensive public transportation systems in the U.S. But driving in the city could be difficult; many downtown streets followed the meandering patterns of colonial cow paths, and parking was scarce and expensive. Driving was particularly a problem in winter, when heavy snow falls and illegally parked cars (Bostonian drivers, according to a *New York Times* article, were notorious scofflaws) rendered some streets almost impassable. The city's most pleasant season, many felt, was fall, when tourists flocked to the area on their way to view autumn foliage.

The city had not always been so popular; be-

EXHIBIT 3
SELECTED PERFORMANCE MEASURES AT THE PARKER HOUSE, 1978–79

Period	Room Nights	Occupancy Rate (%)	Room Sales Efficiency (%)	Room Sales ($)	Food Sales ($)	Beverage Sales ($)
Total 1978	160,062	80	68	6,273,077	2,829,678	1,454,066
January 1978	11,565	68	53	411,868	194,618	106,487
February	11,402	75	59	418,806	177,638	105,908
March	12,944	77	63	489,657	247,263	141,023
April	13,710	84	72	541,328	250,043	120,689
May	13,863	82	70	547,462	242,681	119,742
June	13,598	83	71	545,280	220,276	105,067
July	12,638	75	63	496,233	168,230	81,632
August	15,081	89	76	598,732	217,394	101,655
September	14,516	89	76	577,712	254,965	125,853
October	15,495	92	79	623,768	316,894	142,092
November	13,659	84	75	573,061	260,021	135,576
December	11,591	69	56	449,170	279,655	168,162
January 1979	13,244	78	61	522,829	234,525	132,179
February	11,741	77	60	463,630	208,382	118,915
March	14,809	87	73	624,512	275,125	154,401
April	14,527	89	80	661,863	280,206	139,566

Source: Company records.

tween 1930 and 1955, not a single new hotel room was built in Boston. Between 1930 and 1960, the city posted a net decrease of 4,938 hotel rooms. Although construction resumed during the 1960s, many hoteliers put aside plans for expansion following the recession of 1974–75.

With a restricted supply of hotel rooms, the city's economic revival pushed occupancy rates steadily higher (Exhibit 4). In 1978, average occupancy rates exceeded 80 percent during six months out of twelve, reaching a peak of 90 percent in September and October. Since weekend occupancy tended to drop sharply, this meant that many hotels were fully booked Monday through Thursday for several months of the year.

The supply/demand imbalance in Boston had reached what many city officials described as a crisis by early 1979, when two major national organizations called off plans to hold conventions in the city, citing lack of space. Hynes Auditorium, located in the Prudential Center, was Boston's only major convention center and contained only 150,000 feet of floor space; al-though Boston was the eighth largest population area in the nation, 30 other cities could accommodate larger conventions. It was estimated that the loss of major conventions, plus straight business and tourist turnaways, was costing the city and state $30 million annually.

Despite Boston's severely limited convention facilities, convention visitors composed 31 percent of local hotel guests in 1978. Tourists accounted for 20 percent, and business travelers, 49 percent. Business demand was expected to reach 5,683 rooms by 1985, a 67 percent increase over 1978.

According to a recent study conducted for the mayor of Boston by the Boston Redevelopment Authority (BRA), the city was noted for possessing an unusually large concentration of what the BRA defined as "luxury" hotels. More than half of the town's 6,925 rooms were classed as luxury by the BRA; one third were classed as moderately priced; and less than ten percent were categorized as inexpensive. Exhibit 5 presents the BRA's analysis of Boston's hotel stock by class and major use.

EXHIBIT 4
AVERAGE HOTEL OCCUPANCY RATES IN BOSTON BY MONTH, 1965–78

	1965	1966	1967	1968	1969	1970	1971	1972	1973	1974	1975	1976	1977	1978	Weighted Average 1965–77
January	61.9	59.3	69.8	68.7	62.6	58.6	53.3	53.8	59.7	53.9	49.8	51.4	56.6	59.3	57.8
February	65.0	63.7	73.0	75.0	70.8	60.8	57.8	58.3	57.0	58.1	51.6	54.8	57.2	64.1	61.1
March	67.9	66.4	75.5	78.9	73.1	66.7	62.6	68.0	63.3	68.0	55.1	62.9	65.7	73.5	70.2
April	69.6	71.3	82.3	79.6	80.5	80.1	66.7	78.3	71.1	72.6	68.5	69.8	74.8	80.3	73.9
May	66.0	79.6	78.9	84.2	79.5	71.9	69.4	68.5	73.0	76.1	75.6	74.9	76.1	83.6	74.7
June	68.6	80.7	83.4	82.4	83.1	77.4	72.2	78.3	78.5	80.8	74.7	81.7	81.8	87.6	78.7
July	56.7	67.5	75.0	73.1	74.6	63.5	66.9	67.3	67.4	69.9	61.7	72.3	67.8	76.8	68.0
August	65.3	76.0	82.0	80.2	77.8	77.6	75.3	71.6	72.6	78.1	68.3	76.9	78.3	87.1	75.3
September	73.1	82.0	88.0	80.9	80.6	74.2	77.2	75.6	76.5	73.9	74.2	80.4	84.8	90.1	78.4
October	77.4	91.0	85.5	90.1	85.4	81.6	83.9	87.7	84.8	82.3	83.7	84.1	88.6	89.9	85.1
November	65.5	71.5	72.2	72.3	67.1	62.5	63.0	69.1	64.2	62.4	62.0	59.6	67.6	75.1	65.8
December	50.0	53.6	56.6	52.4	58.3	51.3	47.3	51.9	50.3	43.9	43.4	55.1	52.8	58.7	51.1
Total	66.7	72.2	76.8	76.5	74.4	68.9	66.4	68.9	68.3	68.3	64.1	68.9	71.2	77.1	69.9
National averages	71.3	72.2	74.6	73.6	73.3	67.6	64.1	65.0	66.3	65.8	62.5	65.9	67.7	N.A.	

Source: Cited in *Hotel and Convention Center Demand and Supply in Boston,* Boston Redevelopment Authority, March 1979, p. IV-4.

EXHIBIT 5
CURRENT HOTEL STOCK AND PROJECTED DEMAND IN DOWNTOWN BOSTON BY CLASS AND MAJOR USE, SPRING 1979

	Class A Luxury hotel rooms			Class B Moderately priced hotel rooms			Class C Inexpensive hotel rooms			Totals		
	Current Stock	1985 Demand*	1985 Stock*	Current Stock	1985 Demand*	1985 Stock*	Current Stock	1985 Demand*	1985 Stock*	Current Stock	1985 Demand*	1985 Stock*
Business Visitor	2,169	3,845	4,019	1,003	1,536	1,487	211	302	221	3,393	5,683	5,727
Tourist	518	1,321	1,123	599	1,342	949	296	642	296	1,413	3,305	2,368
Convention	1,294	2,487	3,894	720	1,234	720	105	148	105	2,119	3,869	4,719
Total	3,981	7,653	9,036	2,322	4,112	3,156	622	1,092	622	6,925	12,857	12,814

* Projections.
Source: Boston Redevelopment Authority study, 1979.

Competition

Visitors to Boston could choose from approximately a dozen major hotels, as well as several lesser ones, located within a three-mile radius of the central city (Exhibit 6). The Boston hotel stock was positioned to absorb the cream of hotel demand, leaving the adjacent metropolitan region to accommodate the overflow of convention delegates and tourists (an additional 2,883 rooms were located outside the city in Cambridge and other suburbs).

McIntosh and Chekijian agreed that the Parker House's most significant competitors were the Ritz Carlton, the Copley Plaza, and the Hyatt Regency (the latter located across the river in Cambridge). Built in 1927 by a Harvard graduate who for decades admitted guests according to his evaluation of their social status, the Ritz never suffered the temporary decline that blighted the Parker House. Ninety percent of its guests were repeat visitors, and though its dining room was felt to have slipped somewhat in recent years, it was still considered one of the best restaurants in town. After its owner's death in 1961, the Ritz had been sold to a local real estate investor, and several senior employees resigned in the ensuing years, stating, it was reported, that the hotel's rigorous standards had declined. (One chef, for example, expressed indignation over the presence of frozen food in the kitchen.)

Nevertheless, the Ritz remained a formidable competitor. Its Back Bay location, between Newbury Street and Commonwealth Avenue, was some distance from Boston's congested financial center, but very convenient to the city's shops, theatres, and galleries; the public rooms and many guest rooms offered a fine view of the Boston Public Garden, situated across the street from the hotel's main entrance. Guest rooms were also equipped with working fireplaces, and the hotel's average ratio of 0.7 rooms per staff member was the lowest in town (Exhibit 7). Although one industry expert interviewed by *Boston* magazine in 1977 considered the Ritz somewhat "tired looking," he nevertheless de-

clared that "if there were a list of great hotels in the United States, and a hotel in Boston had to be on it, the Ritz is the only Boston hotel that would make it." A tower extension to the Ritz was presently under construction and scheduled to open in 1981. This addition would add 50 new rooms and a ballroom to the hotel; the remainder of the tower would be divided into condominiums.

Discussing the Hyatt Regency, opened in 1976, Yervant Chekijian commented:

> Although the Cambridge location is a bit isolated and thus somewhat of a disadvantage, this is our toughest competition. They have a unique physical plant, the freshest rooms, and a beautiful view of Boston across the Charles River. Food and beverage is very good, and there is a wide selection of room configurations in the hotel. They are well managed and have the highest rates in town, as well as a national identification. All in all, a customer who doesn't like the Parker House will probably go to the Hyatt Regency.

The Hyatt offered visitors a swimming pool, a revolving rooftop restaurant, and an exotic lobby described by one local journalist as

> . . . nothing short of spectacular, a soaring brick atrium built on the scale of a railroad station . . . the main attractions here are four glass-enclosed elevators that glide aloft to the revolving Spinnaker lounge and swoop swiftly down to a thrilling splashdown in the fountain.

The Hyatt also offered special "Regency Club" service, reserved for guests on the tenth floor of the hotel, who enjoyed the full-time attention of their own concierge in the private Regency Club lounge. Industry observers estimated that occupancy at both the Hyatt and the Ritz would reach 80–85 percent for 1979.

The Copley Plaza, located a few blocks from the Ritz in the Back Bay, had been built in 1912. According to Chekijian, "The Copley's physical plant is beautiful—as you approach from the outside, you know it's a luxury hotel." Like the Parker House, however, the Copley had suffered a long eclipse; during the 1940s it was bought by

EXHIBIT 6
LOCATION OF MAJOR EXISTING AND PROPOSED HOTELS IN THE BOSTON AREA, 1979

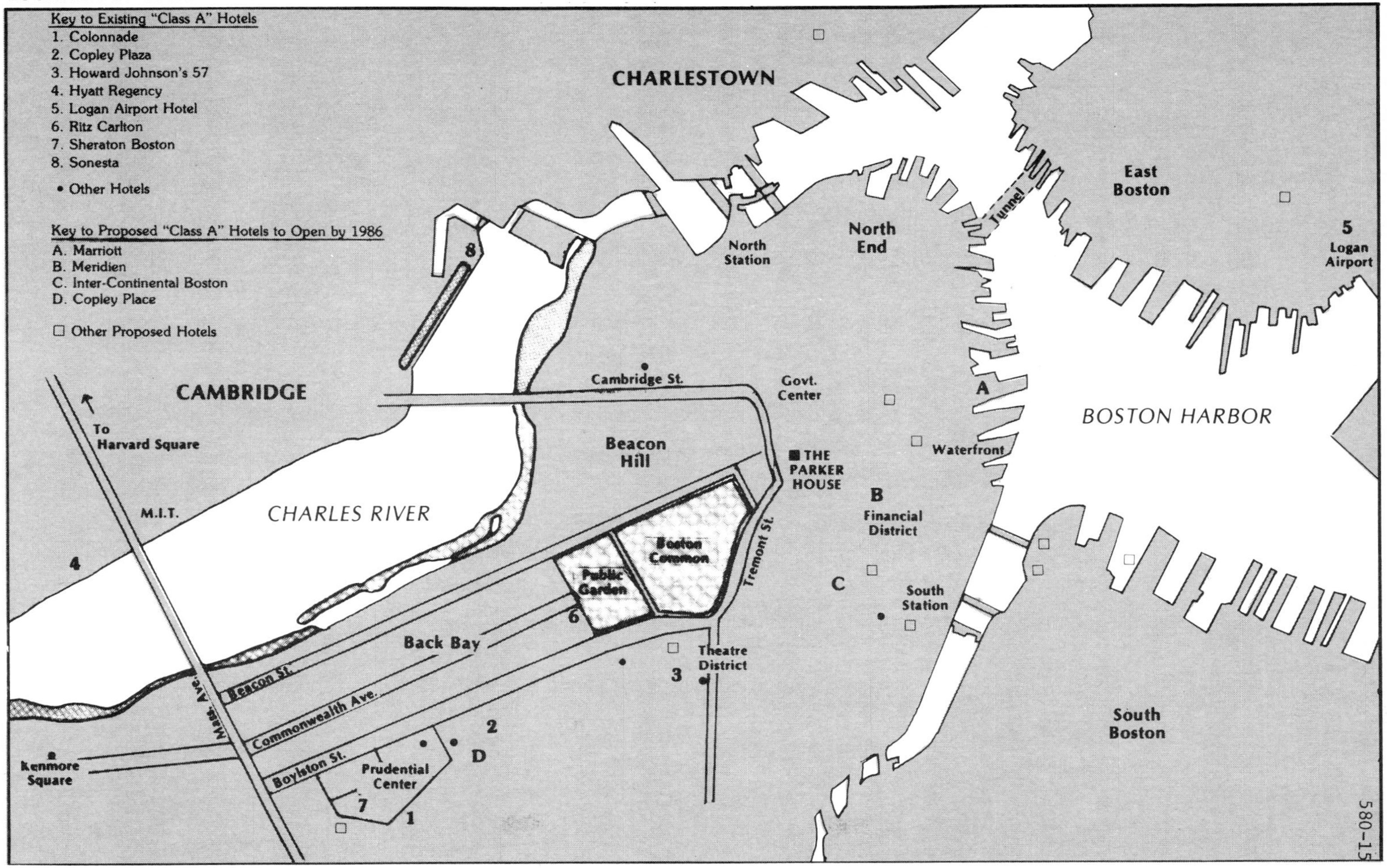

Key to Existing "Class A" Hotels
1. Colonnade
2. Copley Plaza
3. Howard Johnson's 57
4. Hyatt Regency
5. Logan Airport Hotel
6. Ritz Carlton
7. Sheraton Boston
8. Sonesta
• Other Hotels

Key to Proposed "Class A" Hotels to Open by 1986
A. Marriott
B. Meridien
C. Inter-Continental Boston
D. Copley Place
□ Other Proposed Hotels

580-15

EXHIBIT 7　CHARACTERISTICS OF HOTELS COMPETING IN THE CENTRAL BOSTON MARKET

Hotel	Opening Date	Number of Rooms	1979 Price range		Class*	Major Use**	Employees	Rooms Per Employee	Permanent Residents
			Single	Double					
Boston Park Plaza	1927	1100	$32–42	$38–50	B	C	375	2.1	0
Bradford Hotel	1927	322	24	29	C	T	70	4.6	7
Children's Inn	1968	82	31	33	B	B	75	1.1	0
Colonnade Hotel	1971	306	58–64	66–72	A	B	260	1.2	0
Copley Plaza Hotel	1912	450	41–58	49–66	A	B	420	1.1	4
Copley Square Hotel	1895	160	28–32	32–38	B	T	45	3.6	15
Essex Hotel	1900	300	21–27	27–32	C	B	45	6.7	60
Fenway Boylston	1956	94	29	37	B	B	50	1.9	0
Holiday Inn	1968	300	41	45	B	B	175	1.7	0
Howard Johnson's 57	1972	400	44	52	A	B	225	1.8	0
Howard Johnson's Kenmore Square	1963	178	30–32	38–42	B	B	130	1.4	0
Hyatt Regency (Cambridge)	1976	478	45–73	58–68	A	B	600	.8	0
Lenox Hotel	1900	220	34–46	40–54	B	C	140	1.6	0
Logan Airport Hilton	1975	600	42	52	A	B	270	2.2	0
Midtown Motor Inn	1961	161	42	49	B	T	90	1.8	0
Parker House	1927	546	53–65	63–75	A	B	432	1.3	0
Ramada Inn-Logan	1972	209	39	47	B	B	150	1.4	0
Ritz-Carlton Hotel	1927	250	60–75	65–75	A	B	350	.7	8
Sheraton Boston	1965	1428	35–58	59–70	A	C	1000	1.4	1
Sonesta Hotel (Cambridge)	1963	200	48–52	53–60	A	B	150	1.3	1

* Class: luxury (A), moderate (B), inexpensive (C).
** Major use: tourist (T), business visitor (B), and convention (C).
Source: Boston Redevelopment Authority study, 1979; Cambridge hotel data added separately.

the Sheraton Corp. and renamed the Sheraton Plaza. The neighboring John Hancock Life Insurance Company bought the Copley in 1972, and in 1974, when the hotel regained its former name, many rooms were lavishly redecorated with Chippendale chairs, bronze and marble chests, and ornate mirrors—what one local magazine called "the only truly rococo grand-hotel-style chambers in Boston." But the same writer went on to say that some of the rooms, particularly those on the "inside" overlooking the hotel's maintenance plant, were "cramped and dingy." Occupancy was estimated at 75–80 percent for 1979.

The remaining large hotels in the city, according to Chekijian, were less attractive than the Parker House and its three serious competitors:

> The Colonnade has an exceptional physical plant, built in 1971. It's not in a particularly convenient location, but President Ford stayed there when he visited Boston for the Bicentennial.
>
> The Park Plaza was formerly the Statler Hilton, which fell on hard times and closed in November 1976. The building was renovated and reopened in February 1977. Its location is fairly convenient, but the neighborhood is somewhat unattractive. They only compete with us for the discount segments, where they do an exceptional job.
>
> The Sheraton Boston is a typical large Sheraton. Everything about this hotel is middle-of-the-road: food and beverage, rooms, and its location on the far side of the Prudential Center. The Sheraton attracts conventioneers and tour groups.
>
> Howard Johnson's 57 has an excellent physical plant, built in 1972. The location is convenient but not very desirable—right on the edge of the adult entertainment district. Their restaurant is fairly good, and they have a movie house in the building. I think the Howard Johnson name and chain image negates the market position they're striving for.
>
> Finally, there's the Holiday Inn. They have the highest occupancy rate in town because of their proximity to Massachusetts General Hospital. They have relatively spacious rooms and average, predictable Holiday Inn standards. In addition to visitors to the hospital, they get federal, city, and state government travelers, plus the people who always stay in a Holiday Inn.

Exhibit 7 summarizes key statistics for 20 hotels and motor inns in Boston and immediately adjacent suburbs.

Plans for New Construction

According to the Boston Redevelopment Authority, future business expansion would generate the need for almost 6,000 new rooms in Boston by 1985 (Exhibit 5) plus more than 4,000 additional rooms between 1985–90. However, some observers viewed these forecasts as optimistic. They pointed out that much of the new demand was projected to result from projects not yet approved—the construction of a second convention center and the expansion of existing convention facilities. Others pointed to the likelihood of a slowdown in demand resulting from the recession which economists had forecast for late 1979 or early 1980.

Developers and hotel chains alike had nevertheless become very interested in new hotel construction in Boston. By 1979, no fewer than 17 new hotels were in various stages of planning, although informed observers doubted that all proposed would actually be built. (Exhibit 6 shows the location of selected current and proposed hotels.) A plan to convert the liner *United States* to a hotel (known as *S.S. Boston*) and moor it next to Commonwealth Pier appeared particularly unlikely to materialize.

In the view of Bob McIntosh and his associates, the greatest threats to the Parker House would come from the proposed Marriott Hotel, the Meridien, the Inter-Continental Boston, and the hotel planned for Copley Place. The first three would all be located within a ten-minute walk of the Parker House. Architects' sketches of Marriott's Long Wharf Hotel showed a dramatically modern, low-rise design on a wharf jutting into Boston Harbor. It was rumored that construction on the 400-room property in the city's attractive new Waterfront area would begin in early 1980, and that the hotel would open in late 1981 or early 1982.

The shell of the elegant old Federal Reserve Bank building in the heart of the financial district was being converted into a new luxury hotel by Meridien Hotels of Paris, a subsidiary of Air France. Preliminary work had already begun. The 330-room hotel, to be called the Hotel Meridien, would be joined via a glass atrium to a new 40-story office tower. Construction was scheduled to begin in late 1979, with the opening expected in mid-1981. Plans called for the hotel to appeal primarily to the executive and luxury markets. The architect's design included large suites and guest rooms (some on two levels), ornate board rooms, a ballroom for banquets and conferences, and specialty retail shops on the ground floor.

Inter-Continental Hotels, a worldwide chain and wholly owned subsidiary of Pan American-World Airways, planned to build a 21-story, 500-room hotel, scheduled to open in late 1982, as a major element of Lafayette Place. This proposed new complex in Boston's reviving downtown retail area would include retail stores, a large circular public mall, and a parking garage for 1,300 cars. The hotel would contain a swimming pool, sun terrace, and health club as well as a large outdoor terrace for open-air receptions. Convention facilities, equipped with four simultaneous translation booths, could accommodate 1,000 people.

The proposed Copley Place complex, to be built over the Massachusetts Turnpike next to the Prudential Center, would be located near the Copley Plaza hotel on the fringe of the Back Bay,

an area whose shops and art galleries already attracted many tourists and city residents. An 800-room luxury hotel was planned for Copley Place, in addition to enclosed parking for 1,500 cars; a two-level retail center; a five-story, mixed-income apartment building; and four connecting seven-story office buildings, each located on top of a two-level shopping mall. There was talk of the plans being revised to include a second hotel. The Copley Place project had generated considerable community opposition and had not yet been approved; the earliest completion date was seen as 1984.

The only other new hotel scheduled to open before 1985 was a 160-room tourist hotel near the waterfront; this was not considered major competition by Parker House management.

It was estimated that the average construction cost per room for each of the four new luxury hotels would range from $80,000 to $100,000. The pricing rule of thumb followed by the hotel industry in opening new properties was that the initial daily "rack rate" per room (i.e., the maximum published rate established by hotel management) should be set at one dollar for each thousand dollars of construction cost.

Contemplating the competitive challenge he would be facing in the next five years, Bob McIntosh summarized his position:

> Unless we get a significant amount of corporate capital invested in substantial renovations for the Parker House, we'll be offering our guests fairly well-worn rooms that haven't been significantly redecorated since 1974. Faced with this or the chance to try out a brand-new luxury property, which do you think they're going to choose?

PART FOUR

FOUR

DISTRIBUTION AND DELIVERY SYSTEMS

Distribution and delivery systems are concerned with making desired goods and services available to customers at locations and times that are convenient. Distribution decisions often involve long-term commitments of the firm's resources and directly affect its interaction with customers. Manufacturers of physical goods frequently use intermediaries such as wholesalers and retailers to distribute their goods, as an alternative to handling this task directly. Selecting, managing, and motivating such distributors becomes an important aspect of marketing strategy. What margins will motivate distributors to stock and promote our products? Can we expect exclusive distribution or will our goods be simply one of several competing brands stocked within that product category? How much promotional and advertising support will the distributor put behind our brands? How good is the distributor's image, geographic coverage, and level of customer service?

Manufactured goods flow through physical channels from a factory to a warehouse or retail outlet, but services are often produced and sold at local retail service units. Restaurants, hospitals, hotels, and universities, for example, all share this characteristic. Other services, such as broadcasting, information retrieval, and financial transactions, may flow through electronic channels. In both instances, certain tasks may be assigned to intermediaries. For instance, airlines and hotels frequently rely on travel agents to provide information and make reservations, doctors may select the hospital in which a patient will be treated, and bankers may delegate certain routine banking tasks to supermarkets or other retail stores.

For enterprises providing services, the design of the service delivery system becomes particularly important. In many instances, consumption takes place at the site of the service provider and is simultaneous with final production of the service. Thus the site itself and the manner of delivering a service can influence the way consumers view the product and determine whether or not they are satisfied. Given the difficulty that present and potential consumers have in judging the quality of an inherently intangible service, the physical attributes of a site may be used by the consumer to evaluate the quality of the service organization and its products. Site characteristics include a wide range of variables, such as geographic location, accessibility, manner of providing service, service personnel, physical appearance, and operating hours. The latter is of particular concern as service providers often must cope with the problem of matching capacity to time-varying demand. Because many services are perishable and cannot be stored (an empty seat on a midday flight cannot be saved for the evening peak), service marketers often face complex timing problems to which physical-goods companies need pay but limited attention.

Because convenience is frequently an important factor in the purchase decision, marketers of both physical goods and services must be concerned with how intensively their products are distributed. Is the firm offering a *convenience* product, such as detergent, banking services, or simple pain relievers, which the consumer expects to find readily available, or is it offering *shopping* or *specialty* products which customers are willing to spend time and effort on evaluating and purchasing? If the market becomes more convenience-oriented, then a company must either develop a more intensive distribution system or recognize that some parts of the market will be lost unless the firm can develop a strategy that gives prospective customers an incentive to make an extra effort to acquire its products.

PHYSICAL DISTRIBUTION TASKS

In physical-goods marketing, distribution management consists of two main areas: (1) logistics or physical distribution, which is concerned with the activities involved in physically moving and storing goods, and (2) channels, the set of perhaps independently owned and operated resellers that represent the path that a product takes in moving from manufacturer to buyer.

Physical distribution tasks include transportation, order processing, warehousing, and inventory management. Physical distribution needs to be managed on a *systems* basis, as opposed to focusing on each element individually. One company may find that a system that utilizes few warehouses and frequent use of air freight results in the lowest cost for them, while another may determine that using many warehouses served by inexpensive transportation modes yields the most efficient results. Beyond looking at costs, physical-distribution management must consider the impact of service-delivery performance (such as speed, protection from spoilage, and so forth) on consumer satisfaction, level of demand, and, ultimately, profits. Those involved with setting distribution goals need to be concerned not only with directly measurable financial costs but also with the cost of lost sales that result from being out of stock, having late deliveries, or generating customer ill will.

The most common distribution channel for physical goods sold to individuals and households is:

manufacturer→wholesaler→retailer→consumer

However, there are many variants, such as use of mail order and factory outlets. In the case of industrial goods, distribution channels tend to be shorter. There is greater likelihood of sales directly from manufacturer to customer, or use of a single intermediary. Beyond the basic functions of transporting, storing, and displaying the product, intermediaries may carry out many other functions. Advertising, selling, offering credit, providing customer service, developing combinations of products in a "package" to serve customer needs better, getting market information, and taking business risks are some of their services. Effective performance of each of these functions may be vital to the market success of a product.

EFFICIENCY VERSUS CONTROL IN CHANNEL SYSTEMS

Marketers use intermediaries because they increase the efficiency of a distribution system. Imagine the waste and inconvenience to customers if every item in a supermarket had to be sold in its own retail outlet with no competing brands present! Or if every airline had to sell all its seats through its own retail offices and telephone reservation system. In addition to having greater efficiency, distributors have specialized skills and knowledge—particularly of local market conditions—that a manufacturer would rarely possess. However, the use of independent intermediaries by a company reduces its control over a number of important functions. The retail price and terms of sale, while suggested by the marketer, are under control of the retailer, as is the nature and method of retail display and much of the local advertising and sales support. At times, channels may be marked by conflict over which members will have the most power—the producer, who develops, produces, and markets the product or the retailer, who controls the direct interaction with the ultimate consumer. No matter who has the greatest power in the channel, market success requires that all members be motivated to work jointly toward achieving goals of the system. Although occasional conflicts arise in almost all channel systems, a well-managed distribution system will have a means to limit the number of conflicts that do arise and to treat fairly the sometimes differing opinions, needs, and goals of its independent members. Independent distributors are service organizations that are in business to achieve their own goals; they will only cooperate with the original supplier to the extent that this arrangement advances their own enterprise. If the producer cannot obtain the degree of cooperation desired from channel intermediaries, then possible solutions include changing the financial terms of the agreement, switching distributors, or establishing a wholly-owned, vertically integrated channel.

The design of a channel system starts at the level of the ultimate users and is based on a careful analysis of these customers' needs relative to the acquisition and use of the product. On this basis, the organization determines the appropriate channel strategy at the primary level, which links the customers to the channel system (usually through the retailer). Once the retailer level is specified, then the same strategic process is repeated at each intermediate level until the producer level is reached. Of course, these plans are subject to the availability and capabilities of intermediaries. The economics of each possible distribution channel system must be assessed carefully; management must be wary of designing a system with too many levels between itself and the ultimate consumer. The key test of a distribution system is its ability to link an organization to its markets in ways that are economically efficient and also that allow it to leverage the marketing programs of the various channel participants. A well-managed company will regularly test the ability of its own distribution system to meet such a standard.

CONCLUSION

Providing the "right product at the right place at the right time" is the crucial goal of distribution management. Whether offering physical goods or services, marketers must effectively manage a complex set of distribution tasks often involving distant locations and autonomous intermediaries to ensure delivery of a product in a manner that meets customer needs. A well designed and excellently implemented distribution and service delivery strategy can provide an important competitive advantage; an inadequate distribution system can quickly lead to lost sales and customer ill will that dissipates the potential of an otherwise sound marketing program.

ROLM CORPORATION

Adrian B. Ryans

In October 1973, Kenneth Oshman, President of the ROLM Corporation, and other members of ROLM's top management team were finalizing a business plan to market a private branch exchange system (PBX), thereby entering the telecommunications industry. The plan was to be presented to ROLM's Board of Directors at their November meeting in order to obtain approval for market entry. The initial product was to be a computer-controlled electronic PBX with capacity to handle from 100 to 800 telephone extensions. This market entry would bring ROLM into direct competition with AT&T, ITT, Northern Electric, Philips, Nippon Electric and many others.

THE COMPANY

ROLM corporation had been founded in 1969 by four electrical engineers: Messrs. Richeson, Osh-

Reprinted from *Stanford Business Cases 1979* with permission of the publisher, Stanford Graduate School of Business.
Copyright © 1979 by the Board of Trustees of the Leland Stanford Junior University.

man, Loewenstern and Maxfield. In fact, the name of the corporation was an acronym based on the first letters of their names. All were in their late-twenties to early-thirties at the time of the founding and all were, or had been, employed by electronic or computer firms in the San Francisco Bay Area. As Bob Maxfield recalled: "The company was the result of four guys deciding they wanted to go into business for themselves and having a couple of ideas about the kinds of products they might offer." Their original ideas were basically commercial applications of systems developed originally for the military and included a system for police departments to keep track automatically of the location of every police vehicle. Another idea was a system that would allow toll bridges to monitor regular users of the bridge automatically by means of a transponder attached to each vehicle, thus permitting bills to be issued to each regular user at the end of the month. A business plan was developed around these ideas and was presented to venture capitalists, but it did not arouse much enthusiasm among potential suppliers of capital.

In the fall of 1968, Bob Maxfield and Gene Richeson attended the Fall Joint Computer Conference. This particular show in many respects heralded the coming minicomputer boom. Data General, subsequently to become a major factor in the minicomputer industry, and a dozen other new manufacturers announced their first products at this show. A few months later, while the four of them were sitting around "blue-skying" about potential businesses, Gene Richeson suggested that what the world really needed was a low-cost off-the-shelf military minicomputer.

No standard computer could withstand the severe environmental conditions encountered in military missions. At that time, the major manufacturer of militarized computers ('mil-spec') were IBM and Sperry Univac, who manufactured the computers on a custom basis resulting in long lead times and high cost—often $150,000 for a system. The Data General commercial NOVA minicomputer, on the other hand, cost about $10,000 and Gene Richeson, based on his knowledge of the requirements of the various military applications, felt that such a computer would have sufficient power for most of these applications. Bob Maxfield, who had the most experience with computers, felt that a militarized version of the Data General computer could be manufactured to sell for less than $30,000. As they discussed the possibilities further, they decided that it would be ideal from the customer's viewpoint if a militarized computer could be made software compatible and input-output compatible with an existing commercial minicomputer. This would allow the user to do the development work and system testing on the lower cost commercial machine in a laboratory environment, only using the 'mil-spec' computer when the system was actually deployed in the military equipment.

The next question they addressed was which commercial minicomputer they should choose. They selected the Data General NOVA computer for two reasons. First, Data General was a start-up company and thus might be interested in licensing the design and software to ROLM; and, given the company's small size, the decision would probably be made quickly. The second reason was the Data General machine used the latest technology which required a smaller number of components than competitive minicomputers. This was an important factor in designing a reliable machine for military applications. They phoned Edson de Castro, President of Data General, and told him they were thinking of starting up a company to manufacture 'mil-spec' computers and asked him if he would be interested in licensing hardware and software designs to them. Mr. de Castro was interested, so they flew to Data General's home office in Boston and negotiated an agreement with him.

On the basis of their idea, they developed a business plan and were successful in getting sufficient money to start the business. ROLM began operation on June 1, 1969, and a working model was displayed at the Fall Joint Computer Conference in 1969. The first production unit was shipped in March 1970. In the first quarter of fiscal year 1971, which began in July 1970, ROLM showed a profit and remained profitable thereafter. Subsequent computers were based on ROLM's own designs.

The ROLM 'mil-spec' computers typically were purchased by contractors of the U.S. Department of Defense, the Defense Department itself and certain industrial customers who required computers that could operate in severe environments. The computers were generally used in research, development and testing applications. Individual purchase orders were usually for small quantities. The company generally provided a central processing unit (CPU), a main memory, a chassis, a power supply and a variety of input-output equipment, peripheral equipment (terminals, printers, magnetic discs and tapes) and software. Customers could thus configure a system to meet their own needs. The company employed a direct sales organization which totalled about eight people in 1973. Kenneth Oshman, besides being President of ROLM, also acted as head of the marketing organization.

The Decision to Diversify

By fiscal 1973, sales had reached $3.6 million. An income statement and balance sheet for ROLM are included in Exhibit 1. Early in 1973, top management of ROLM became concerned about the potential size of the segment of the military computer market in which ROLM competed. There was a strong feeling among ROLM's top management that their market segment would be saturated by the time their annual sales reached $10 to $20 million. Given that they had an objective to build a major company, they began to look for areas of diversification that would allow ROLM to continue its growth. They felt that any diversification should build on their main technological expertise in computers, so they investigated other computer-related businesses that they might enter.

The PBX market was an obvious candidate. As Oshman pointed out, "The computer-based PBX is very much a computer system, and we already had 80 percent of the technology; we figured we could get the other 20 percent easier than the telephone companies could get the computer technology." The idea was initially abandoned when they realized that the cost of setting up a national sales and service organization would be beyond ROLM's resources. Nevertheless the proposal kept resurfacing during the following months. As Bob Maxfield recalled: "We all felt it would be fun to develop a computer-controlled telephone system, so we decided to look at it more carefully in March 1973." Once the decision had been made to look at the PBX business more closely, it was decided to set up a separate organization to do the product development and market analysis. They felt either the 'mil-spec' computer business or the proposed PBX business would receive second-class treatment, if person-

EXHIBIT 1
ROLM CORPORATION FINANCIAL DATA

Income statement for fiscal year ending June 29, 1973

Net sales	$3,637,000
Costs and expenses	
Cost of goods sold	1,572,000
Product development	455,000
Marketing, administrative & general	964,000
Interest	14,000
Total costs and expenses	3,005,000
Income before taxes	632,000
Provision for income taxes	311,000
Net income	$ 321,000

Balance sheet for quarter ending September 28, 1973

Assets

Current assets:	
Cash	$ 202,000
Receivables	442,000
Inventories	994,600
Other current assets	43,100
Total current assets	$1,681,700
Other assets:	
Capital equipment	$ 440,700
Accumulated depreciation	228,300
Net capital equipment	212,400
Other assets	24,100
Total other assets	$ 236,500
Total Assets	$1,918,200

Liabilities and stockholder's equity

Current liabilities:	
Accounts payable & accrued payroll	$ 306,700
Income tax payable	139,400
Other current liabilities	31,900
Notes payable	24,400
Total current liabilities	$ 502,400
Lease contracts payable—Long-term	$ 97,500
Stockholders' equity:	
Capital stock	$ 170,800
Paid in surplus, net	610,800
Retained earnings	536,700
Total equity	$1,318,300
Total Liabilities and Equity	$1,918,200

Source: Company records

nel attempted to work in both areas simultaneously.

To head the product development side of the project, Maxfield was successful in recruiting Jim Kasson from Hewlett-Packard. Kasson, whom Maxfield had known socially for a number of years, had a background in data acquisition and control systems and was very knowledgeable about computers. He also brought with him from Hewlett-Packard another very good engineer. Together with ROLM's top computer software specialist they became, in June 1973, the three-person ROLM PBX technical feasibility team. In August 1973, Dick Moley, a marketing manager in Hewlett-Packard's computer division, joined ROLM to do the market analysis for the PBX.

THE TELECOMMUNICATIONS INDUSTRY IN THE UNITED STATES

The telecommunications system in the United States was operated by American Telephone and Telegraph (AT&T) and some 1,760 independent telephone companies. AT&T was split into five major operations:

1 The General Department, which provided staff assistance in advertising, finance, engineering, legal and marketing to the rest of the corporation.

2 Western Electric, which manufactured telephone equipment for the Bell System operating companies. Under the terms of a 1956 consent decree with the Justice Department, Western Electric sold its products exclusively to the Bell System operating companies and to the U.S. Government. In 1972, Western Electric's total sales were greater than $7 billion.

3 The Bell Telephone Laboratories, which conducted basic research and designs equipment for manufacture by Western Electric.

4 The Long Lines Department, which installed and operated the interstate long distance network and handled all international calls. It received revenues from both the Bell System operating companies and the independent telephone companies for providing these services.

5 The twenty-four Bell System operating companies which provided and operated the telephone system at a local level. They covered about 85 percent of the telephones in the United States. Sixteen of the operating companies were wholly owned by AT&T, and it owned a majority interest in six of the others.

In 1972, AT&T had telephone operating revenues of $21.4 billion and had 109 million phones in service of which some 14 million were business phones connected to PBX, or functionally similar, systems.

The 1,760 independent telephone companies provided local telephone service in areas not served by AT&T. These companies, as well as the Bell System operating companies, were regulated by state public utility commissions. They varied greatly in size from very small rural telephone companies to major corporations such as General Telephone which had operating revenues in the United States of almost $2 billion. The ten largest independent telephone companies are shown in Exhibit 2.

The Emergence of the Telephone Interconnect Industry

Prior to 1968, all telephone company tariffs in the United States had contained a blanket prohibition against the attachment of customer-provided terminal equipment (such as telephones, answering machines and PBX's) to the telecommunications network. The historic 1968 Carterfone decision of the Federal Communications Commission (FCC) held that these blanket prohibitions were unreasonable, discriminatory and unlawful, and the FCC required that the telephone companies file new tariffs that did not contain such blanket prohibitions. This decision opened up the vast market for terminal equipment to a variety of new competitors.

The Carterfone decision did allow the tele-

EXHIBIT 2
TEN LARGEST INDEPENDENT TELEPHONE COMPANIES

Names and Addresses	Telephones	% of Total Independent Telephone Industry	Total Operating Revenues
1 General Telephone & Electric Corp. (U.S. only), New York, N.Y.	10,622,000	45.81	$1,881,000,000
2 United Telecommunications, Inc. Kansas City, Missouri	2,642,300	11.40	448,684,000
3 Continental Telephone Corporation (U.S. Only), Chantilly, Virginia	1,774,200	7.65	299,536,000
4 Central Telephone & Utilities Corporation, Lincoln, Nebraska	1,059,600	4.57	194,055,000
5 Mid-Continent Telephone Corporation Hudson, Ohio	593,500	2.56	82,842,000
6 Rochester Telephone Corporation Rochester, New York	535,100	2.31	89,502,000
7 Puerto Rico Telephone Company San Juan, Puerto Rico	357,400	1.54	64,277,000
8 Lincoln Telephone & Telegraph Company Lincoln, Nebraska	239,800	1.03	37,176,000
9 Commonwealth Telephone Company Dallas, Pennsylvania	154,900	.67	18,857,000
10 Florida Telephone Corporation Ocala, Florida	143,600	.62	29,068,000

phone companies to take reasonable steps to protect the telephone system from any harmful effects of interconnected equipment. New tariffs filed in early 1969 by the telephone companies required that protective connecting arrangements be installed on each line to protect and insulate the public network. In the next few years these connecting arrangements became a major bone of contention between the suppliers of customer interconnect equipment and the telephone companies. Interconnect equipment suppliers charged that the connection arrangements sometimes caused technical problems, that the telephone companies used delaying tactics in installing them, and they they unnecessarily raised costs (an average charge by the telephone companies of $7–10 per line per month) for the users of the interconnect equipment. The telephone companies responded to these charges by pointing out that they had rapidly developed a large number of protective connecting arrangements for different types of terminal equipment and had installed several hundred thousand of them by 1974.

PBX'S AND KEY SYSTEMS

Interconnect equipment was any equipment attached to where incoming telephone company lines terminated on a customer's premises. Although such equipment took a wide variety of forms, including answering and recording devices, in the business market most of the sales volume was in two product classes: private branch exchanges (PBX) and key telephone systems.

A PBX was a local telephone switching system within a company which handled incoming, outgoing and intraoffice calls.[1] As shown schematically in Exhibit 3, a PBX consisted of four major parts:

1 Switching equipment and control system. The switching system was the electromechanical or electronic equipment that connected the various internal (telephone extensions) and external lines in the system and provided ringing, busy signals, dial tone and intercom services. The control system was the system that actuated the switching functions.

2 Trunk circuits. These were lines connecting the PBX to the public switched network.

3 Attendant console. This was the equipment used by an inside operator to complete or transfer calls, to determine which lines were busy and to handle a variety of other tasks such as taking messages and paging.

4 Telephone station equipment. These were the individual telephones and key systems (a telephone that allowed a person access to several lines with a single illuminated pushbutton set) located throughout the building or organization.

While key systems were commonly part of the PBX telephone system in large companies, stand-alone key systems were commonly used in smaller organizations (typically those with 40 or fewer telephones) as the sole system. Here they connected the outside lines directly to the user's extension telephone. Usually one pushbutton on each telephone was connected to a common line providing an intercom capability.

The technology involved in automatic PBX's had evolved in recent years—from electromechanical step-by-step systems, to electromechanical crossbar systems, to electronic systems.[2]

Step-by-step systems were first offered at the beginning of the century and were the primary PBX product of the telephone companies for many years. These electromechanical systems could be expanded indefinitely as long as the customer had space for the very bulky equipment. If maintained well, they provided economical and reliable service, but offered only very limited features. They were also expensive in terms of installation labor and maintenance and generated a large amount of "noise," making them unsuitable for data communications.

Crossbar systems were the next step in PBX evolution. These were again electromechanical switches, and variations of them had been available for years. These systems were much more compact than the step-by-step systems, being housed in cabinets, and had lower labor and maintenance costs. Once they were set up and adjusted, they provided very reliable service but were costly to expand beyond the capacity of the original installation. Modern crossbar systems offered the user a number of features, such as:

- Selective toll restriction. The system could be set up so that only certain individuals could dial long distance calls.
- Station transfer. The user could transfer an incoming call from outside the company to another extension within the system without going to the switchboard operator.
- Consultation hold. An incoming call could be held while the person dialed another number to secure information for the caller. This procedure did not require the telephone to be a key telephone equipped with a hold button.
- Add-on conference. A third person could be dialed so that a three-way conference could be held. Again, a key telephone was not required.

Electronic telephone switching systems were

---

[1] Some companies distinguished between PBX, a manually switched private branch exchange, and PABX, an automatic PBX, where all switching was done without operator intervention. Here PBX will be used to cover both types of equipment.

[2] A brief description of the switching and control systems technology can be found in Appendix (see end of case).

EXHIBIT 3
PBX SYSTEM INCLUDING KEY SYSTEM

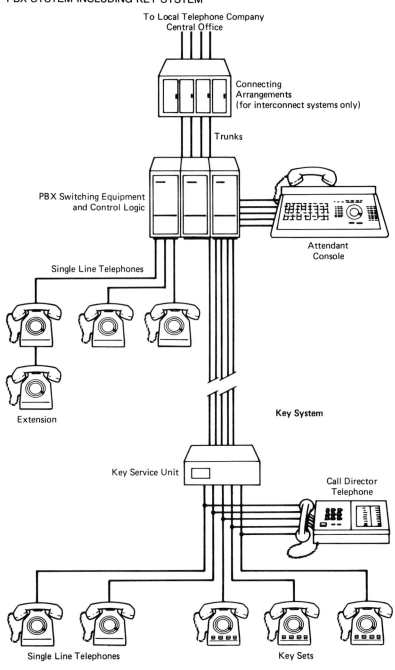

To Local Telephone Company
Central Office

Connecting
Arrangements
(for interconnect systems only)

Trunks

PBX Switching Equipment
and Control Logic

Attendant
Console

Single Line Telephones

Extension

Key System

Key Service Unit

Call Director
Telephone

Single Line Telephones

Key Sets

Source: SRI Long Range Planning Service

the most recent technological development. The original work on electronic switching systems had been done at Bell Laboratories in the mid-1950's and the first commercial electronic central office (i.e., a switching system within the Bell system) was opened in 1965. Electronic switching technology only began to be used in the PBX market in the early 1970's and by 1974 there were about 20 electronic PBX models on the market. Most of these electronic systems used space division multiplexing (SDM)[3]. Electronic systems with time division multiplexing (TDM), which allowed several signals and calls to go over one pair of wires, promised to significantly simplify and reduce the costs of cabling a building for the PBX system. Electronic systems contained both memory and logic capabilities. The control logic—that is, how the appropriate circuits were interconnected during use—was implemented in two basic ways. The method greatly affected the flexibility of the equipment. The two ways were:

1 Wired logic. Here the logic was stored on printed circuit cards and control actions were predetermined by the wiring connections on the cards. This limited the flexibility of the system and the ease with which it could be modified.

2 Stored program logic (computer controlled). Here all logic was stored either in exchangeable memory or by programming. Changes in the control logic could be readily made by changing the program.

Stored program logic gave a PBX great flexibility and the potential to meet future demands that wired logic systems could not match. Besides providing the normal control (connection) functions and a range of features to aid the telephone user, a computer-controlled electronic PBX could be used to record details of all toll calls (call detail recording), could monitor usage of the system, and could even perform self-diagnostic

functions if there were problems with the equipment. In addition, if a company placed Tie Lines and WATS (Wide Area Telephone Service) lines on direct access (i.e., no operator was needed) the electronic switch could be programmed to seek the least cost route for a long distance call. With additional memory a wide range of features could be made available on an electronic PBX, including all those available on a crossbar system. Thus, in an electronic PBX, the systems features were in the central switching unit rather than the particular telephone or key unit. The user could make use of a particular feature either by dialing a code or pressing a couple of buttons on the telephone. Some of the features that could be offered on electronic systems included:

• Classes of service. Each telephone station could be given access to only those services necessary for the person to perform his or her job. For example, some telephones could only be allowed to call certain long-distance area codes.

• Automatic dialing and speed calling. Each user could store frequently called numbers in the system. The switch dialed the number when the user dialed a code. The stored numbers could easily be changed by the user.

• Call forwarding. A code instructed the switch to forward any incoming call to a specified number.

• Station number changes. When the user was relocated and wished to retain his or her current number, this change could easily be entered into the system. No telephone moving charges would be incurred as long as a telephone existed at the user's new location.

• Automatic call distribution. A number could be set up for a particular department and any incoming calls to that number were distributed by the switch to any free department telephone.

Electronic systems could therefore provide a range of useful features to the user. While basic electronic systems were more costly than similar electromechanical systems, the marginal cost of adding features after installation was much

---

[3] Again see end-of-case Appendix for explanation of technology.

lower. They promised to be more reliable than electromechanical systems, although experience with electronic systems was not yet large enough to provide a convincing maintenance and reliability record. Electronic systems, particularly those based on the TDM technology, were also more suitable for tying into data communication terminals. This was expected to become an increasingly important consideration by the late 1970's when many more users were expected to be using their telecommunications system for both voice and data transmission.

Competition in the PBX and Key Systems Market

After 1968 a customer could purchase a PBX or key system from one of two basic types of suppliers: (1) the telephone company providing service in that area, or (2) an interconnect company. As Exhibit 4 suggests, the structure of the interconnect market was quite complex. In some cases companies manufactured the equipment and distributed it through one or more suppliers who installed and serviced the equipment. In other cases, the manufacturer might be a manufacturer-supplier selling directly to the end user or through a separate supplier subsidiary. These subsidiaries often would distribute the products of other manufacturers also.

Manufacturers of PBX and Key Systems

The manufacturers of PBX equipment were a pretty diverse group. Western Electric, the supplier of the Bell System; Northern Telecom, the U.S. subsidiary of Northern Electric; the Bell Canada manufacturing arm; and the major suppliers to the independent telephone companies, such as GTE-Automatic Electric, North Electric and Stromberg Carlson, were all well-established in the North American market—having supplied equipment to the various telephone companies since prior to the 1968 Carterfone decision. The PBX equipment manufactured by these suppliers

for the independent telephone companies was, in 1968, generally similar to Western Electric's and offered only traditional features.

The Carterfone decision provided an opportunity for another group of manufacturers to enter the U.S. market. These were largely European and Japanese manufacturers who had extensive experience with PBX's and key systems in other markets. With the encouragement of the interconnect suppliers (i.e., the companies selling to the end users), they modified their equipment and were able to offer end users features previously unavailable in the U.S. By the early 1970's the Japanese and European companies had captured about 75 percent of the U.S. PBX and key system interconnect market.[4] The major companies in this group were OKI, Nippon Electric, Hitachi and Nitsuko (all Japanese) and L. M. Ericsson (Swedish). International Telephone and Telegraph (ITT) also entered the U.S. market after the Carterfone decision and by 1973, some industry observers felt it had the best line of PBX equipment available in the U.S. A list of the major manufacturers ranked in terms of their estimated 1973 sales to U.S. interconnect suppliers is shown in Exhibit 5. As Exhibit 4 also suggests, some of these companies had also been quite successful in selling their products to some of the telephone operating companies. This resulted, in some cases, in end users being able to obtain identical equipment from either the telephone operating company or an interconnect supplier.

The opening of the interconnect market had also brought a number of new U.S. manufacturers into the market. Wescom, Tele/Resources and Philco Ford had all developed electronic PBX's and were supplying them to the independent telephone companies or to interconnect suppliers. Litton and RCA, which had entered the market as national interconnect companies, were buying PBX's from others and were both rumored to be developing electronic PBX's. Other large

---

[4] That is, 75 percent of PBX and key system market which was not serviced by the AT&T operating companies or the independent telephone companies.

EXHIBIT 4
STRUCTURE OF THE MARKET FOR PBX'S AND KEY SYSTEMS

TELEPHONE COMPANIES

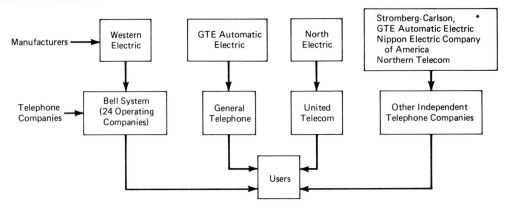

* Also occasionally sell to Bell, GTE, and United Telecom.

INTERCONNECT INDUSTRY

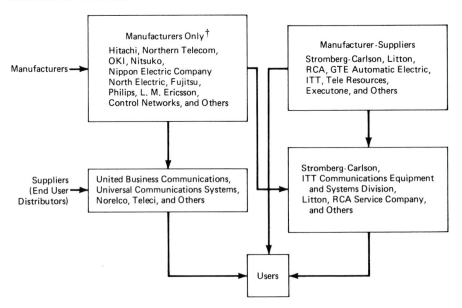

† Some sell exclusively to their own suppliers.

Source: SRI Long Range Planning Service

EXHIBIT 5

MAJOR MANUFACTURERS OF INTERCONNECT EQUIPMENT

Ranked in Order of Estimated 1973 Sales to U.S. Interconnect Companies

Company	Manufacturing Locations
OKI Electronics of America/OKI Electric of Japan	Japan and U.S.
Nippon Electric Company	Japan and U.S.
Hitachi	Japan and U.S.
Nitsuko*	Japan
International Telephone and Telegraph (ITT)	U.S. and Spain
L. M. Ericsson	Sweden
Northern Telecom (subsidiary of Northern Electric of Canada)	Canada and U.S.
Stromberg Carlson	U.S.
North Electric (subsidiary of United Telecommunications)	U.S.
Fujitsu	Japan
General Telephone and Electronics (GTE)-Automatic Electric	U.S.
North American Philips-Norelco	Netherlands and U.S.
CIT/TELIC	France and U.S.
Iwatsu*	Japan
Meisei	Japan
Siemens	Germany
Lynch	U.S.
Toshiba*	Japan

* Key systems only

Source: SRI Long Range Planning Service

manufacturers, active in foreign markets, were also believed to be ready to enter the market. IBM was also viewed as a possible entrant, since it had developed a very strong position in the European PBX market with two expensive electronic PBX's. The major manufacturers of electronic PBX's and a brief description of their equipment and market position is contained in Exhibit 6.

Notable in their absence from the list of manufacturers in Exhibit 6 were the Japanese and European manufacturers. The major Japanese manufacturers (Nippon, Hitachi, Fujitsu and Oki) and the leading European manufacturer, L. M. Ericsson, produced high-quality electromechanical PBX equipment. Until the devaluation of the dollar in 1973, the Japanese PBX equipment had been very competitively priced. Ericsson had always sold its equipment at premium prices in the U.S. Both the major Japanese manufacturers and

Ericsson were rumored to be developing electronic PBX's.

Interconnect Companies

The number of interconnect companies had grown rapidly since 1968 and by 1973, there were thought to be about 300 of them in the U.S. These interconnect companies analyzed customer needs for PBX's and key systems, designed and recommended a system, installed it and serviced it. Interconnect companies could be subdivided into two basic groups, national suppliers and small regional or local suppliers. Estimated sales for the major interconnect suppliers in 1973 are shown in Exhibit 7.

The four largest national companies—Litton, Stromberg-Carlson, ITT and United Business Communications—had offices throughout the U.S. and were divisions of much larger corpora-

EXHIBIT 6
ELECTRONIC PBX MANUFACTURERS AND THEIR PRODUCT OFFERINGS IN 1973

Manufacturer	Model	Technologies used[1]		Number of Lines PBX Can Handle	Comments
		Control	Switching		
Western Electric	801A	Electronic-wired logic	Space division (SDM)-reed relay [2]	46–270	Western Electric produced a very broad line of PBX's, most of which were still electromechanical. The 801A and 812A were both semi-electronic. In the 101 systems all switching was actually done in a Bell System central office, not on the customer's premises. An electronic central office was needed for the ESS. Only a small proportion of Bell central offices was electronic.
	812A	Electronic-wired logic	SDM-crossbar	400–2000	
	101 ESS (3A)	Electronic-computer	Time division (TDM)-electronic (PCM)[3]	400–800	
	101 ESS (4A)	Electronic-computer	TDM-electronic (PCM)	2000–4000	
ITT	TD-100	Electronic-wired logic	TDM-electronic (PAM)[4]	40–100	ITT's fully electronic PBX's covered all line sizes. Many observers felt it had the best line of PBX's on the market in 1973. Shipment of the TD-100 PBX was expected to begin in early 1974.
	TE-400A	Electronic-wired logic	SDM-electronic	100–400	
	TE-400G	Electronic-wired logic	SDM-electronic	400–800	
	TCS-2	Electronic-computer	SDM-electronic	600–6000	
Stromberg-Carlson	400A	Electronic-wired logic	SDM-reed relay	100–400	Both were semi-electronic PBX's.
	800A	Electronic-wired logic	SDM-reed relay	400–800	
Wescom	501	Electronic-wired logic	SDM-electronic	40–120	This PBX was being sold to independent telephone companies. Shipments were expected to begin in early 1974.

Company	Model	Logic	Switching	Range	Notes
Tele/Resources	TR-32	Electronic-wired logic	TDM-electronic (PAM)	40–164	This PBX required unique and expensive phones and was sold only to interconnect suppliers. There were large order backlogs in late 1973.
Philco Ford	PC-192	Electronic-computer	SDM-electronic	64–192	The PC-512 was introduced in 1972 and was marketed to independent telephone companies. It was very expensive relative to competitive offerings and was not believed to be selling well.
	PC-512	Electronic-computer	SDM-electronic	128–512	
IBM	2750	Electronic-computer	SDM-electronic	256–756	IBM had been successfully selling these very expensive PBX's in Europe. They were really only feasible for installations requiring more than 500 telephones.
	3750	Electronic-computer	SDM-electronic	256–2264	
Northern Telecom	SG-1	Electronic-wired logic	TDM-electronic (PAM)	40–80	The SG-1 was introduced in 1972 and had been selling very well in the U.S. and Canada. The SG-2 was not yet in production.
	SG-2	Electronic-wired logic	TDM-electronic (PAM)	80–120	
ROLM	Proposed	Electronic-computer	TDM-electronic (PCM)	100–800	

[1] See end of case appendix a for a brief discussion of the technological issues.
[2] Reed really was an evolutionary switching approach that bridged the gap between electromechanical crossbar and fully electronic switching.
[3] PCM—pulse code modulation. Here all signals that are transmitted are digital signals.
[4] PAM—pulse amplitude modulation. Here all signals that are transmitted are analogue signals.

EXHIBIT 7
ESTIMATED SALES BY INTERCONNECT COMPANIES IN 1973

Company	Sales (millions of dollars)
Litton Business Telephone Systems	25
Stromberg-Carlson Communications* (subsidiary of General Dynamics)	25
ITT-Communications Equipment and Systems Division	18
United Business Communications (subsidiary of United Telecommunications)	14
Universal Communications Systems (subsidiary of American Motor Inns)	9
RCA Service Company	8
Norelco Communications* (subsidiary of North American Philips)	5
GTE-Automatic Electric*	7
Teleci (subsidiary of Holiday Inns)	3
Tele/Resources	4
ITT-Terryphone**	4
Others (about 300, mostly local)	60
Total	182

* Excluding sales to local suppliers, figures for which are included under "Others."
** Key system sales only.
Source: SRI Long Range Planning Service.

tions. In 1973, ITT was the only one of the four that had a wholly-owned manufacturing subsidiary. Stromberg-Carlson Communications was the result of the acquisition by General Dynamics, in June 1973, of Arcata Communications, Inc. and Arcata Leasing from Arcata National. The two Arcata National units had offices in twenty major metropolitan areas across the United States, and had generated losses of close to $4 million after taxes on sales of $25 million in the final year before General Dynamics acquired them. Eventually, as the acquired interconnect supplier was integrated with the Stromberg-Carlson manufacturing unit, Stromberg-Carlson would, like ITT, have an integrated manufacturing and distribution organization.

There were also three other companies that were national in scope. Universal Communications Systems, a subsidiary of American Motor Inns, and Teleci, a subsidiary of Holiday Inn, both specialized in the hotel/motel segment of the market, and RCA Service Company specialized in hospitals and universities. Industry observers believed these companies were profit-

able. The hotel/motel segment of the market had some unique characteristics that made it a good candidate for specialization. It required only a voice communications system, phones were not moved, key sets were rarely used, most calls were ingoing or outgoing, and a record of all outgoing calls had to be made for billing purposes. Universal Communications Systems and Teleci chose to meet the needs of this segment by importing Japanese electromechanical PBX's that could meet these requirements at low costs.

The regional interconnect suppliers were generally small companies which typically served a geographical area within a 50- or 100-mile radius of their home office. Many had originally been in the sound and/or communications equipment business and had simply diversified into the interconnect market. Some of the major regional interconnect suppliers were Tele/Resources (New York), The Other Telephone Company (Minnesota), Fisk Electric (Texas) and Scott-Buttner Communications (California). Most of the interconnect companies were very small with telecommunications sales generally being less than

$2 million—Tele/Resources, believed to be the largest of these companies, had sales of about $4 million. Industry observers believed that these companies, unlike many of the national suppliers, were profitable. This was probably the result of lower overheads, knowledge of local requirements and the flexibility of small companies. Many of these companies were seriously undercapitalized.

Some industry observers felt that the interconnect suppliers had been unable to fully exploit what they believed to be the major weaknesses of the telephone companies, namely, their fairly obsolete product line and their inability to respond quickly to the changing market and technology. Much of the Japanese and other PBX equipment the interconnect suppliers were handling was only marginally superior in terms of features to the equipment manufactured by Western Electric. Thus they were forced to compete largely on the basis of lower price, more flexible pricing arrangements and greater installation flexibility. Even the Tele/Resources PBX, while fully electronic and easy to install, was not a great deal more flexible than conventional PBX equipment and, in addition, required expensive special phones. Also, it was said to be difficult to maintain. Nevertheless the first two years of production of this PBX was sold out within a few months of it being introduced.

Interconnect companies, both regional and national, stocked spare parts for their customers' PBX's so that they could rapidly get a customer's malfunctioning telephone system operating again. The faulty parts were then returned to the manufacturer for repair. Since this could take weeks—even months—the interconnect companies generally carried substantial inventories of spare parts.

Response of the Telephone Companies

The AT&T operating companies and the independent telephone companies were vigorously resisting the encroachment of the interconnect suppliers into the PBX and key systems market. In 1970, AT&T had established a huge task force with people from Bell Labs, Western Electric and AT&T marketing and engineering at a new facility in Denver, Colorado, to develop a new, more competitive PBX product line. This resulted in four new competitively priced electronic or semi-electronic PBX's being introduced between 1971 and 1973. But even this progress was not rapid enough for some of the AT&T operating companies and they began to buy PBX's from outside suppliers. General Telephone had also taken similar steps to remain competitive.

The telephone operating companies also modified their pricing structures to improve their competitive position. Traditionally, telephone companies only leased equipment to users; thus the user paid an installation charge and a monthly rental/service fee (which could, of course, be increased from time to time) that continued as long as the customer had the equipment. By 1973, some of the telephone companies were giving their customers the option of paying for the use of the equipment with a "two-tier" pricing arrangement. With a "two-tier" pricing scheme, the customer signed a lease for the equipment for a specified number of years (usually between 5 years and 10 years). Then the cost of the equipment was split into two portions—the "capital" cost of the equipment, which could be paid off immediately, and the maintenance/administrative charge, which was paid over the life of the lease and which could be increased during this period.

CURRENT STATUS OF THE INTERCONNECT MARKET AND FUTURE PROSPECTS

In a proprietory report published by the Long Range Planning Service (now the Business Intelligence Program) of SRI International, it was estimated that sales by interconnect suppliers had grown from virtually zero in 1968 to $182 million (at end-user prices) in 1973. Manufacturers' selling prices were approximately 50 percent of end-user prices, and given that there was a substantial amount of inventory at the supplier level, manufacturers' shipments were expected to total $120 million in 1973.

The $182 million sales estimate was broken into three categories:

1 $130 million in PBX sales. This included 3,300 PBX's with 248,000 telephones. This was estimated to be 12.4 percent of the dollar value of all new and replacement PBX installations in 1973.

2 $47 million in key systems sales. This included 6,000 key systems with 72,000 telephones. This was estimated to be 6.7 percent of the dollar value of all new and replacement key system installations in 1973.

3 $5 million in service and maintenance revenues which included charges for telephones added to the original system, moving telephones within an office, etc.

SRI also attempted to project the market growth through 1985. Given the uncertainties surrounding the interconnect market, both conservative and optimistic projections were made. These projections took into account probable shakeouts in the industry, stronger competition from the telephone companies, regulatory factors and a shortening life cycle (hence more frequent replacement) for this type of equipment.

On the basis of SRI's assumptions, total interconnect supplier sales were expected to be in the range of $1.1 to $1.7 billion by 1985; this was expected to give interconnect suppliers an installed base penetration of 21 percent to 30 percent for PBX's and 15 percent to 21 percent for key systems. During this period SRI expected rapid technological development to continue with computer-controlled or stored-logic electronic switching systems being standard in PBX and key systems by 1980.

PBX AND KEY SYSTEMS CUSTOMERS

One of the first things Dick Moley had done after joining ROLM in August 1973 was to talk to several large companies about their communication problems. Commenting on these interviews Moley said:

> What they came up with was very interesting—because what they said their problems were, were problems that were not being addressed by the interconnect equipment or the Bell System equipment at the time, and that is where we saw our opportunity.
>
> What they said was that the largest portion of their bill, frequently 70–80 percent, is toll expenses. If you are a large electronics company, for example, you have Foreign Exchange lines, Tie lines and WATS lines. Trying to get people to use these—to get them to go to the proper tables and look up how to call a number in a particular city, say Los Angeles—to dial 76 for Los Angeles, then dial 9 for an outside line, then dial the telephone number—is very difficult. Even if a person does all this the line frequently will be busy. Similarly, to gain access to a WATS line the caller may have to call a special operator and wait for a line to become available. So what happens in many companies, of course, is that many people make many long distance calls without bothering to use these expensive facilities.
>
> Furthermore, many companies wish to keep track of who was calling which numbers, both to control abuse and to bill departments for their real use of facilities, rather than simply making an arbitrary allocation. Many people also felt restrictions on toll calling on a telephone-by-telephone basis and automated queuing for WATS lines seemed to be needed features. The equipment available in 1973 simply did not address these needs and the Bell System obviously didn't have a great incentive to optimize the use of toll calling facilities, since it would negatively impact its revenues.

A second major area of concern that surfaced in these interviews was the cost of making, and the time required to make, changes in the telephone system when people were relocated. This was particularly true in firms that used a project type of organization or in organizations that were experiencing rapid growth, where the average times between moves of a phone could be as short as six months. Every time personnel changes were made and people were relocated, the telephone company had to be called in to change wires and relocate the phones and sometimes the companies had to wait quite a long time for these changes to be made. Furthermore, the Bell System and independent telephone company tariffs to make these changes varied across the country. In some areas it cost about $15 to move a phone, whereas in other areas, such as New York, it might cost $75 for the same service. ROLM estimated on average the real cost of performing this service was about $50. Many large companies operating in several parts of the country were aware of these differences and realized that under pressure from the Public Utility Commissions for the telephone companies to stop "subsidizing business," these charges would probably rise in areas where they were low. One very large firm of consultants operating in San Francisco, where the cost of moving a phone was only about $20, was already spending over $400,000 per year on these moves and changes.

"Another area that was an absolute nightmare was key phone systems," commented Dick Moley.

> We saw that in our own offices that year when Ken Oshman's office had to be relocated. Two men spent a whole day recabling 125-pair cables to the new location for the key phone system. The cost was nominal, but it clearly cost the telephone company a lot of money to make these changes.
>
> We then asked ourselves why are key systems so difficult to move? The reason is that each light on the call director's pushbutton set takes six wires to activate, so you may need a very thick (1 inch in diameter) 125-pair cable from the switching equipment to the call director telephone with 20 or so lines and you clearly can't afford to run such a cable all over the building. So essentially the wiring is customized for the key system. That seemed to us to be totally insane with the available electronics.
>
> So we said, we can do it differently. What we can do is use a key phone with a three-pair cable— one pair for voice, one pair to power the electronics and the third pair to digitally signal which button is depressed and to indicate which button to light.

> Thus, if we standardize the building wiring completely on three-pair cables which connect to wall sockets much like electrical wiring, the user will not have to rewire the building if some phone is moved. They might have to plug in a special box and make an arrangement back in the switching equipment to make sure it was connected to a switch to drive a key phone rather than a single line phone, but no rewiring will be necessary.

Large customers would be critical to ROLM's success in the marketplace, since the computer-controlled PBX system that they were developing was designed to handle 100 to 800 lines. This line range had been chosen because cost-effective computer controlled models that would provide the kind of benefits customers desired could not yet be cost competitive for installations of less than 100-line capacity. In 1973 only a very small number of Fortune 500 companies were buying from interconnect suppliers. Most of the sales by the interconnect companies had been made to smaller organizations; in fact about 75 percent of the interconnect equipment was sold to hotels and motels, wholesalers and retailers, stockbrokers, insurance agencies, hospitals and clinics, attorneys, banks, stockbrokers, manufacturers and service industries. Few of the installations made by the interconnect companies had more than 100 lines. For these reasons a final issue Dick Moley raised in his interviews with the large companies was why they had not bought equipment from interconnect suppliers.

A major reason the companies cited was that they saw few economic benefits from buying from interconnect suppliers. The main benefit was that they could purchase the equipment and hence freeze their equipment cost (since they would be unaffected by telephone company rental rate increases). But since equipment was usually only 20 to 30 percent of their costs, and when a discounted cash flow analysis of the purchase versus rental choice was made, the savings often turned out to be minor. Meanwhile if the equipment was purchased, the company was locked into equipment that might soon become obsolete. It seemed that smaller companies were much less likely to do a discounted cash flow analysis and seemed to be largely attracted to the interconnect PBX's by their marginally better features and the belief they would get better service from these companies than they would from the telephone operating companies. An additional factor that might help explain the failure of the interconnect companies to penetrate larger companies was that few of the interconnect suppliers appeared to have sales organizations that were capable of conducting a multilevel sales campaign at several levels of decision-making in prospective large companies.

From his discussions with the large companies Mr. Moley also gained a better appreciation of the decision-making process for PBX's and key systems. Voice communication decision-makers were generally low level office managers or communications managers. These decisions had historically been made at a low level because the decisions to be made with respect to telecommunications equipment were generally of a minor nature. Until 1968, the Bell System operating company or the independent telephone company was a monopoly supplier and hence there was no choice of vendor. The office or communications manager often relied greatly on the recommendations of the telephone company salesperson and, in fact, frequently the manager was a former Bell System employee. The main responsibilities of the manager were largely those of placing orders with the telephone company and coordinating installation and service activities. When alternative suppliers to the telephone companies became available, the managers were very cautious about recommending them, since the risks of poor service and the possibility of the interconnect supplier going out of business were not inconsequential. Furthermore since switching to an interconnect supplier typically required that the equipment be purchased rather than leased, they usually lacked the authority to make the decision themselves, and the capital expenditure had often to be ap-

proved at very high levels in the organization—sometimes even at the Board of Directors level. The communication manager was not usually accustomed to preparing these types of proposals and doing the necessary internal selling to get the proposals approved.

The results of the customer interviews made ROLM management very enthusiastic about their potential entry into the telecommunications market. As Mr. Moley remarked, "Out of our discussions I and the others in ROLM management became really enthusiastic, because clearly here is a vast market where we potentially have the capability to solve meaningful customer problems and save companies large amounts of money. Computer technology was the key to solving these problems—we could optimize call routings, handle toll restrictions, etc. If there are telephones in place, handling moves and changes becomes simply a matter of remotely reprogramming the switching equipment—nobody needs to visit physically the customer's office or plant."

THE ROLM PBX

By October 1973, Jim Kasson and his two associates had made considerable progress on the technical aspects of the ROLM product. The conventional wisdom in the telephone industry trade magazines at the time was that time division multiplexing (TDM) with pulse code modulation (PCM) switching technology and stored logic (computer control) control technology would not be viable, cost-effective technologies until the late 1970's or early 1980's. Jim Kasson was now convinced it was a viable technology in 1973. As a result of some clever circuit work and ROLM's knowledge of minicomputers, software and PCM technology, they were convinced their approach would work and would be cost-effective. They had already "bread-boarded" (i.e., laid out the electronic circuitry in a crude way) key technology elements that were new to ROLM and they even had a couple of telephones in the laboratory working with their switching circuitry. In effect, the technological advances they were taking advantage of promised to change the nature of PBX manufacture from a labor and capital intensive operation to a technology intensive electronic assembly operation which would require the manufacturer to have minicomputer, software and solid-state switching expertise. These were all technologies in which ROLM management felt their company had significant strengths.

The management of ROLM was convinced that the flexibility of a computer-controlled PBX built on a TDM technology would change the economics of a business communication system's installation, maintenance and operation, besides providing excellent user convenience. For example, with their PBX it would be possible to prewire a building with standard 3-pair cable connected to wall outlets. Then all that was necessary to install a complete system was to connect the cables to the PBX, plug the standard telephone sets into the sockets, and enter into the computer the locations and extension numbers of the telephones. In the case of a multiline key set, the information entered into the PBX would include information on all the extensions which are to be routed to the set. Moves and changes of extensions would be a straightforward matter of entering the new configuration information into the computer. No longer would it be necessary to have the wiring tailored to the specific configuration and have ancillary keyset switching equipment located remote from the PBX. The features, both standard and optional, that they proposed to offer on the ROLM PBX are listed in Exhibit 8.

Thus their proposed product was a minicomputer-controlled TDM system which could handle both voice and data communications. In essence it had all the capabilities of the successful IBM computer-controlled PBX's, plus the additional capability of handling key telephones without requiring large cables and key service units. Furthermore, unlike the IBM PBX's, which cost from two to three times as much as conventional systems, the ROLM PBX was expected to be price competitive in the range of 100 to 500 extensions, a range which, they estimated, accounted for 60 percent of the dollar value of all PBX systems.

DECISIONS FACING ROLM IN OCTOBER 1973

Although many of the technical uncertainties with respect to the product had been resolved, there were several dark clouds on the horizon. The Bell System was aggressively attempting to stop the competitive erosion by moves on both the regulatory front and by improving their equipment, developing new pricing schemes, etc. In June 1973, at the urging of the telephone companies, the North Carolina Utility Commission had proposed banning all interconnect equipment from the state. Although in January the Federal Communications Commission ruled that its own ruling preempted state regulation of interconnect equipment, the issue was still in the courts. ROLM management was also concerned about other regulatory actions the Bell System might take. On the pricing front, the Bell System and the independent telephone companies had made their pricing structures more competitive and had the potential to make further moves in that direction. Furthermore, the Bell System's intensified product development efforts were likely to result in products that were technically much more competitive with the proposed ROLM offering than was the current product line, although ROLM would probably have a year or so lead time. Other interconnect manufacturers would probably be into the market with more competitive offerings even earlier than the Bell System.

ROLM's Board of Directors, in preliminary discussions of the proposed entry, were not totally convinced of the wisdom of ROLM, a $4 million company, moving against such formidable competitors and openly questioned whether this was the best area in which to invest the company's limited resources. Investment bankers

EXHIBIT 8

FEATURES AND SERVICES TO BE OFFERED ON THE PROPOSED ROLM PBX

Standard	Optional
Station features	
Direct Outward Dialing	Alternate Routing (toll call optimization)
Station-to-Station Dialing	Automatic Redial
Non-consecutive Station Hunting	CCSA Access
Programmable Class of Service	Dictation Access and Control
Consultation Hold-All Calls	Direct Inward Dialing
Call Forwarding, Unlimited	Direct Inward System Access
Flexible Station Controlled Conference	Discriminating Ringing
Group Call	Plug-in Station (with Keyset Adapter)
Indication of Camp—On to Station	Secretarial Intercept
Individual Transfer—All Calls	Station DTMF to Rotary Dial Conversion
Lockout with Secrecy	Tenant Service
One-Way Splitting	Automatic Identification of Outward Dialing
Outgoing Trunk Camp-On	Redundancy
Processor-Controlled Changes—Type A	Off Premises Extension
Trunk Answer from Any Station	Private Lines
Tie Trunks	Music on Hold—Attendant
Toll Restriction	Music on Hold—System
Trunk-to-Trunk Connections—Station—Type B	Music on Camp-On
Trunk-to-Trunk Consultation	Reserve Power—Inverter
	Speed Calling
	Area Code Restriction
	Traffic Measurement
	Paging Interface
Attendant features	
Attendant Camp-on	Busy Lamp Field
Attendant Conference	Busy Verification of Stations
Attendant Console	
Attendant Transfer of Incoming Call	
Attendant Transfer—Outgoing	
Attendant Trunk Busy Lamp Field	
Switched Loop Trunk Selection	
Switched Loop Station Selection	
Flexible Intercept	
System Alarm Indications	
Multiple Trunk Groups—Unlimited	
Attendant Key Sending—Touch Tone	

also raised similar concerns. Even within the top ranks of ROLM management there were executives who were quite unsure about whether a move into the telecommunications market was in ROLM's best interest. The Treasurer and the Director of Manufacturing had both formerly worked for Arcata Communications and had seen at first hand the problems in the interconnect business. They were among those expressing concern.

From a manufacturing cost viewpoint, ROLM management was not concerned about the disparity in size between ROLM and its competitors, whose manufacturing experience base for the most part was built on electromechanical equipment (which was labor and capital intensive) whereas ROLM's equipment was largely electronic. In their view, this made it feasible for ROLM to compete with the likes of Western Electric.

Pricing the PBX

Kasson and his team had concluded that with a further investment of $500,000 in engineering and manufacturing they could get the product into production. If given the go-ahead, they expected to have a prototype working in the laboratory by mid-1974 and to begin shipping systems in early 1975.

Detailed estimates of manufacturing costs had been developed by Kasson and others on the PBX team. With a sales price based on two and one-half times manufacturing cost (direct materials, direct labor and overhead based on direct labor cost) the ROLM PBX promised to be cost competitive with the most closely competitive models available in the United States. They anticipated that volume discounts would be given to customers ordering multiple PBX's, if they decided to market the product through telephone companies or interconnect companies. Since the ROLM PBX made heavy use of electronic components (e.g., the minicomputer, the computer memory and integrated circuits), the cost of the PBX was expected to decline over time as the cost of electronic components continued their decline. Electromechanical PBX's, and even electronic PBX's based on analogue technologies, were expected to experience a much more static cost future.

Channels of Distribution for the PBX

In many respects ROLM's management felt the most crucial decision facing them in 1973 was the choice of channels of distribution for their PBX system. Dick Moley felt they had several alternatives open to them:

1 Sell to the Bell System. The operating companies of the Bell System had traditionally relied exclusively on Western Electric for all their equipment. However, the competitive pressures from the interconnect companies had resulted in several of the operating companies, including the largest one, Pacific Telephone, buying equipment from other suppliers. Pacific Telephone had bought electromechanical PBX systems from Japanese suppliers and more recently it had bought Northern Telecom's fully electronic PBX which handled up to 120 lines. The former move was not a very radical one since the Japanese designs were similar to Western Electric designs and could be installed and maintained by their field service force without any extensive retraining. The Northern Telecom purchase was more significant since this did require retraining the field service force. Since the Bell operating companies were still believed to control some 80 percent of the installed PBX base, even a small share of this market would represent a huge sales volume to ROLM.

2 Sell to the independent telephone companies, such as General Telephone. While the independent telephone companies covered about 15 percent of the phones in the U.S., they were more concentrated in rural areas and were growing about 50 percent more rapidly than AT&T. This reflected the movement of industry and population away from major metropolitan areas. Since larger companies still tended to concentrate in major metropolitan areas, the independent telephone companies' share of the large PBX (greater than 100 lines) market was much less than 15 percent. Their captive manufacturing subsidiaries were not as strong as Western Electric and the independent telephone companies had never relied on them as much. But even taking into account that the independent telephone companies were a much smaller factor in the market than the Bell System, they still represented, a large, burgeoning market—with companies like Stromberg-Carlson and several Japanese and European manufacturers—and were very active in it.

3 Sell to the interconnect companies. These were concentrated in the larger metropolitan areas. Here ROLM had two alternatives: (a) The national companies such as Litton Business Systems, ITT, RCA Service Company, United Business Communications and Stromberg-Carlson Communications or (b) The regional companies such as Tele/Resources, Fisk Telephone Systems and Scott-Buttner Communications. Many of the national suppliers were in trouble due to the lack of experienced managers, higher than anticipated investments, heavier than anticipated installation and maintenance expenses, too rapid geographic expansion resulting in loss of control, and the difficulty of providing quick and adequate service capability on a nationwide basis. These problems were exacerbated by the fiercely competitive nature of the markets, the heavy legal expenses, and the drain on management time necessary to challenge some of the telephone companies' new pricing schemes before the regulatory commissions. These chaotic market conditions had resulted in some companies getting into difficulties and being forced to merge with others. Some of the regional interconnect companies were doing quite well in their local markets. They bought their equipment from a variety of manufacturers including Nippon, Stromberg-Carlson and Tele/Resources. Generally the manufacturers required them to handle the equipment on a non-exclusive basis, so that two or more interconnect companies in the same

market area might carry the same PBX line. The regional companies typically were under-capitalized and sold small systems. It was very seldom that one handled a PBX with a capacity larger than 100 lines. Most of the equipment they were handling was still electromechanical. While marketing through regional interconnect companies had some advantages, particularly from a servicing perspective, there was a real question of whether large companies with multiple locations would want to deal with multiple interconnect companies. Some of the other manufacturers, including Northern Telecom, handled large sales directly, and simply subcontracted with the regional interconnect companies for installation and maintenance services.

4 Sell direct. ROLM had given little thought to this alternative, since they felt they were simply too small. But from a sales viewpoint it had some obvious advantages, especially when it came to dealing with large accounts with multiple locations around the country.

Dick Moley's Task

Dick Moley had to make decisions with respect to channels of distribution and pricing and also with respect to such closely related issues as the amount and nature of advertising and sales promotion to be directed at end users. By the November 1973 Board meeting he hoped to have selected and laid out in some detail the marketing plan for the ROLM PBX. He hoped he would be able to present a convincing case for ROLM's entry into the PBX market.

APPENDIX: PBX and Key Systems Technology

Much of the technological change in PBX systems was occurring in the switching and control systems. The technological alternatives in both the switching and control systems are shown in Exhibit 9. With respect to the switching system, two major alternatives were possible: space division multiplexing (SDM) and time division multiplexing (TDM). An SDM system was one in which separate individual transmission paths were set up for the

EXHIBIT 9
PBX TECHNOLOGICAL ALTERNATIVES

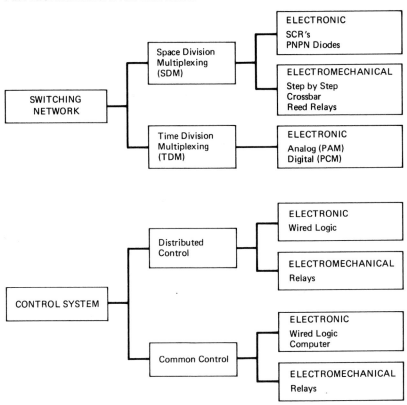

duration of the call. A TDM system was one in which the speech on each active line was sampled at a very high rate, so that no information was lost, and the samples were assigned to unique time slots on a common transmission line. The original signal could be reconstructed from these samples when needed. The ability to handle many calls on one line promised to lower costs. In a TDM system the samples could be transmitted as either an analogue [pulse amplitude modulation (PAM)] signal or a digital [pulse code modulation (PCM)] signal. If pulse code modulation was used, then all signals were digital—making such a system ideal for transmitting data as well as voice. This was expected to be an increasingly valuable feature by the late 1970's, as more and more companies wished to transmit both data and voice over the same telecommunications system. Furthermore, if a digital signal was sent over a reliable transmission line there was no cross-talk or distortion, which one could get if an analogue system were used. ROLM engineers believed that a PBX with a TDM analogue system could not (with the technology then available) be designed to handle more than 120 lines without excessive cross-talk. Partly for this reason, TDM with pulse code modulation was carrying an increasing share of the Bell System's long-distance traffic. Nevertheless many observers in the early 1970's did not expect that the pulse code modulation technology would be cost-effective in PBX's until the late 1970's.

The control system could be either distributed control or common control. A distributed control system was one in which the control logic was distributed throughout the PBX system (e.g., if key phones were used some of the control logic was in the key phone unit), whereas a common control system was one in which all the control functions were centralized in one set of logic. With a common control system the control equipment was only tied up during the time the connection was made and not during the conversation. A wired logic common control system basically did with electronic components what was otherwise done by electromechanical relays. On the other hand, a computer controlled common system added a new dimension to the PBX. New circuits had to be added to a wired logic system in order to alter its properties and capabilities, but a computer controlled system's functions could be altered by changing its program. This gave a computer controlled system great flexibility and the potential to meet future demands that wired logic systems could not match.

BUFFALO SAVINGS BANK

Penny Pittman Merliss
Christopher H. Lovelock

Robert W. Ramsey, chairman and chief executive officer of the Buffalo Savings Bank, was discussing marketing strategy with his four most senior officers. Glancing around the conference table on June 17, 1977, he began:

> Gentlemen, we're here to make a decision on whether or not to continue Buffalo Savings Bank's simultaneous participation in two point-of-sale terminal networks. As you know, the bank presently operates its own group of 16 POS terminals in the Buffalo area; we also participate in eleven outlets of the Metroteller POS system, developed by Erie Savings Bank. My understanding of the situation is that our own POS network is highly reliable and has become very popular with our customers, but Metroteller is giving everybody problems. Warren, can you elaborate?

Warren E. Emblidge, Jr., group vice president for marketing and banking services and the officer charged with overseeing the POS project, responded:

> Let me begin with some bad news. From the start,

Copyright © 1980 by the President and Fellows of Harvard College, Harvard Business School case 9-581-059.

through no fault of our own, we've had problems getting our customers' daily Metroteller transactions logged into our computer on time every night. Every delay in sending us data on Metroteller's end guarantees dissatisfied customers on ours. But what happened last night was much worse than a simple delay: I've just found out that Metroteller fed us the same magnetic tape two nights in a row, and we ran thousands of transactions twice.

Pausing as a murmur of surprise and displeasure ran around the room, Emblidge shook his head and continued:

> That kind of disaster can cast a blight over even the best reputation for customer service. We've got to reevaluate the entire rationale behind our decision to participate in Metroteller, from the customer's perspective as well as our own—and we've got to reestablish the credibility of our own POS banking before our customers begin to distrust any and all innovations in our delivery of financial services.

THE BANK

Chartered in 1846, Buffalo Savings Bank (BSB) was the tenth largest savings bank in New York

State, with total assets of some $1.9 billion in January 1977. Buffalo Savings Bank defined its trading area as the entire Niagara Frontier, a 1,587-square-mile area extending from the Canadian border at Niagara Falls, 20 miles north of the city, to Hamburg, N.Y., ten miles south. This region comprised approximately 1,750,000 people.

Five commercial banks and four other savings banks constituted BSB's primary competition. The most significant competitors were Marine Midland Bank and Manufacturers & Traders Bank (both commercial banks), and Erie County Savings Bank (Exhibit 1). In recent years, BSB's share of consumer accounts had been rising as Marine Midland's slipped. Use of banking services within the Buffalo market was extensive. Over 88 percent of all households used checking accounts; over 80 percent held savings accounts (Exhibit 2). BSB held approximately 26 percent of savings accounts in the Buffalo area, and 13 percent of personal checking accounts.

The bank's headquarters was an imposing granite building constructed in 1899, located on

EXHIBIT 1
HOUSEHOLD AND ACCOUNT COVERAGE BY MAJOR BANKS
IN THE BUFFALO AREA, 1972–79

Banks	Household coverage				
	1972–3	1975	1977	1978*	1979*
Commercial					
Marine Midland	51.3%	53.4%	55.2%	45.4%	44.7%
Mfrs. & Traders	34.0	35.2	32.8	38.0	33.3
Liberty National	15.5	16.8	15.0	14.0	14.5
Citibank	—	4.9	6.4	9.9	7.8
Bank of New York	7.9	9.6	12.3	8.2	6.7
Savings					
Buffalo Savings	22.9	28.0	33.9	35.9	37.5
Erie Savings	21.9	24.7	28.8	27.0	28.7
Western NY Savings	10.5	14.4	13.0	15.9	14.1
Permanent Savings	1.8	4.6	6.3	5.0	5.0
Niagara County Savings	1.7	2.0	3.0	5.0	4.7
	Share of accounts				
Commercial					
Marine Midland	30.8%	27.1%	24.0%	21.0%	21.9%
Mfrs. & Traders	21.4	17.9	15.2	15.2	14.9
Liberty National	8.9	7.3	6.8	5.3	5.9
Citibank	—	1.7	2.2	3.0	2.5
Bank of New York	4.2	4.1	4.5	3.1	2.6
Savings					
Buffalo Savings	9.6	11.1	14.9	16.7	17.6
Erie Savings	8.6	10.0	12.3	12.0	11.5
Western NY Savings	4.1	4.9	4.7	6.4	5.6
Permanent Savings	.8	1.4	2.3	2.0	1.8
Niagara County Savings	.7	.8	1.2	2.0	2.3

* Projected.
Source: Independent market research commissioned by Buffalo Savings Bank.

EXHIBIT 2
USE AND MARKET SHARE OF BANKING SERVICES IN THE BUFFALO MARKET, 1975–77

	Percentage of households using services		Accounts per household with service		Accounts per household in the market		Commercial bank account share			Savings bank account share		
	1975	1977	1975	1977	1975	1977	1975	1976	1977	1975	1976	1977
Total households	84.3%	88.3%					91.1%	88.6%	88.0%	57.7%	60.7%	62.9%
Total accounts					4.11	4.65	65.3	60.9	59.2	27.7	33.5	34.2
Total checking			1.11	1.19	.93	1.05	94.6	80.4	76.2	4.4	19.2	22.2
Savings account	82.2	86.6	1.45	1.60	1.19	1.39	40.4	37.4	36.8	51.4	55.3	55.1
Savings club	12.8	9.9	1.13	1.12	.15	.11	64.0	60.1	64.8	23.9	30.1	27.9
Savings certificate	14.6	18.4	1.35	1.45	.20	.27	25.9	20.6	21.0	62.1	67.5	64.4
Auto loan	15.9	16.8	1.04	1.06	.17	.18	88.6	95.6	94.3	5.2	2.2	3.6
Personal loan	14.7	12.7	1.06	1.05	.16	.13	72.0	78.8	74.5	23.1	19.1	21.7
Extra cash	7.4	12.9	1.06	1.08	.08	.14	99.7	79.4	77.0	.3	20.6	21.5
Credit card	48.1	54.4	1.25	1.25	.60	.68	99.8	100.0	98.2	.2	—	1.8
Mortgage	42.7	44.5	1.01	1.02	.43	.45	21.9	22.9	21.7	52.1	56.3	54.1

Source: Independent market research commissioned by Buffalo Savings Bank.

EXHIBIT 3
LOCATIONS OF BSB BRANCHES, BANK-AND-SHOP,
AND METROTELLER FACILITIES

	Location	Date Opened
BSB Conventional Offices (11):		
Headquarters	Buffalo, NY	1/46
Branch	Buffalo, NY	6/47
Branch	Buffalo, NY	4/48
Branch	Kenmore, NY	10/60
Branch	Cheektowaga, NY	6/67
Branch	Amherst, NY	6/68
Branch	Williamsville, NY	10/72
Branch	West Seneca, NY	6/73
Branch	Williamsville, NY	5/74
Branch	Orchard Park, NY	6/75
Branch	Amherst, NY	12/76
Bank-and-Shop:		
Supermarkets (6)		
Bells	Hamburg, NY	2/77
Bells	Hamburg, NY	2/77
Bells	East Aurora, NY	2/77
Bells	Buffalo, NY	2/77
Bells	Cheektowaga, NY	3/77
Bells	Buffalo, NY	6/77
Department Stores (5)		
Hengerers	Buffalo, NY	9/76
Hengerers	Amherst, NY	9/76
Hengerers	Amherst, NY	9/76
Hengerers	Kenmore, NY	9/76
Hengerers	West Seneca, NY	9/76
Drugstores (5)		
Rite Aid	Amherst, NY	1/77
Rite Aid	Amherst, NY	1/77
Rite Aid	West Seneca, NY	1/77
Rite Aid	Wheatfield, NY	1/77
Rite Aid	Tonawanda, NY	1/77
Metroteller Facilities Shared by BSB:		
Supermarkets (11)		
Bells	Williamsville, NY	8/76
Wehrle Super Duper	Amherst, NY	8/76
Bells	Cheektowaga, NY	8/76
Super Duper	Amherst, NY	8/76
Bells	Cheektowaga, NY	8/76
Bells	West Seneca, NY	8/76
Super Duper	Depew, NY	8/76
Bells	Amherst, NY	8/76
Bells	Tonawanda, NY	9/76
Bells	Tonawanda, NY	9/76
Bells	Buffalo, NY	9/76

Source: Company records.

the fringe of Buffalo's reviving downtown area. Its gilded dome, a local landmark, was 54 feet in diameter. In addition to its main office, the bank had ten branches located within a 58-square-mile area along the Niagara Frontier. BSB also either directed or participated in 27 point-of-sale facilities, located in supermarkets, drugstores, and department stores within a 30-mile radius of Buffalo (Exhibit 3). The bank had no automatic teller machines.

Branches ranged in size from the newest in Amherst, N.Y., open three weeks with 5,000 accounts and $2 million in deposits, to the main office, with over $500 million in deposits. Commercial banks, which had unlimited branching privileges in New York State, often established numerous small branches, some under 2,000 square feet. Savings bank branches, on the other hand, were much larger, at least 6,000 square feet, and held significantly more deposits. The locations and opening dates of all BSB branches and POS facilities are listed in Exhibit 3.

All savings banks in New York State were mutual institutions paying out their net earnings to depositors as interest and dividends. The banks took in the savings of individuals and families and invested them in low-risk home mortgages and government bonds. Commercial banks, by contrast, had been founded to serve the needs of trade and were in business to earn a profit.

Marketing

Marketing at the Buffalo Savings Bank was directed by Edward K. Duch, Jr., assistant vice president-marketing, who had joined the bank five years earlier after obtaining his MBA from SUNY Buffalo. Duch reported to Warren Emblidge, who held the position of group vice president, marketing and bank services. Emblidge had joined the bank in 1965 on graduation from college, left to pursue graduate studies at The Wharton School, but returned in 1969 after obtaining his MBA.

Appraising Buffalo Savings Bank's internal marketing environment, Duch stated:

> Marketing in the banking industry, especially savings banking, has traditionally been thought of as public relations. A lot of marketing decisions in the past have been made directly by a bank's president, working in conjunction with an ad agency. Buffalo Savings Bank is an exception, and I think the competitive environment in Buffalo has a lot to do with that. We have very aggressive, very innovative competition, and that has stimulated our own development. We view marketing within this bank not as a staff function but as a catalyst which can bring about change based on research and numbers.

But Duch noted that regulation placed strict restrictions on many areas of bank operations:

> If you look at the four p's of the marketing mix— price, place, product, promotion—we're limited on almost every one that we can offer. "Price"—our interest rate—is fixed by law. Our "place" or distribution is limited to the opening of only one new branch a year. Similarly, we can offer a major promotion like a giveaway only once a year, and thus we usually reserve it for the opening of a new branch. And, of course, almost every product or service we devise is subject to intense regulatory scrutiny, particularly if it has the potential to draw business away from commercial banks. It took years of lobbying, and extensive advertising, before savings banks were allowed to offer checking accounts in this state.
>
> We have to look hard for opportunities within the current law to offer new services, and basically, they all hinge on our interpretation of what's permissible. Recently we developed a depositor discount plan which allowed customers making a $2,000 or greater deposit to get a 20 percent discount on merchandise in one day of shopping at a major local department store. We also created an Instant Refund Savings plan which gave customers immediate interest on their expected federal income tax refund, even though the refunds wouldn't reach us for three months.

Creating new products could be difficult, but

the decision to offer them was usually not. According to one Buffalo Savings Bank executive:

> We offer every single product or service that we legally can. We're so regulated that we've never had the problem of choosing from a wide variety of potential products.

Duch also directed the bank's extensive market research program, which included regular shopping surveys of the competition to determine prices and services as well as "mystery shopper" inspections of Buffalo's own branches. Each branch was monitored quarterly by an independent market research firm to survey the quality and consistency of its customer service. Researchers measured the quickness of service at teller stations and customer service areas and checked to see how hard the customer service representatives tried to sell other bank services to new customers opening checking or savings accounts. The friendliness, courtesy, and even degree of eye contact exhibited by all bank personnel were monitored. "Too often banks have a paternal relationship with their customers," Emblidge explained. "We want to treat our customers as knowledgeable adults."

Research into demographics showed that 37 percent of Buffalo Savings Bank's customers were college graduates and 39 percent were high-level white collar workers. Respondents to an independent survey of consumer attitudes toward banking rated Buffalo Savings Bank first in the area (32 percent), followed by Erie Savings (24 percent) and Marine Midland (22 percent). Current customers of Buffalo Savings Bank were most impressed by its "good reputation" and "financial responsibility."

NEW APPROACHES TO RETAIL BANKING

Alternatives to human tellers had been gaining in popularity since the 1960s, when bank-by-mail systems achieved wide use. These plans allowed customers to mail in their deposits and receive a confirmation by return mail, thus avoiding long lines at tellers' windows. The first automatic teller machines (ATMs) were introduced in Britain in 1967 and reached the U.S. in 1969, with increasingly sophisticated models being introduced during the '70s. ATMs allowed customers to make limited withdrawals, deposits, and account transfers 24 hours a day, seven days a week, using a specially coded magnetic card. Some would print account balances on request. By mid-1977 over 6,000 ATMs were operating in the U.S., many functioning as "mini-branches" in high-traffic areas like shopping centers and airports.

About 11,000 point-of-sale (POS) electronic banking terminals were being used in retail stores, mostly to verify checks. POS systems ranged from rudimentary check verification devices, operated by punching an identification number into the machine, to sophisticated terminals using magnetic cards to contact a central computer for approval of deposits, withdrawals, and transfers. Few POS systems operated on "real time"; in most cases an account was not debited or credited until the next business day.

Telephone bill-paying had also been introduced. In 1973 a Seattle bank offered customers with touch telephones a package of services (record keeping, reminders, bill-paying) for $6.50 monthly—but was forced to withdraw the service after a few months when fewer than 1,000 customers subscribed. Subsequent systems in other cities enjoyed somewhat more success.

Remote Electronic Banking

Remote electronic banking facilities (as distinct from automatic teller machines located on bank premises) made their first appearance in the U.S. in January 1974, when First Federal Savings and Loan of Lincoln, Nebraska, set up electronic terminals in two Hinky Dinky supermarkets. The extension of banking hours made possible by the terminals attracted consumers immediately, and First Federal began opening more than 100 new accounts per week. Within three years, this net-work, now called TMS-Nebraska, was shared by seven savings and loan associations, a credit union, and a bank and operated at 92 merchant locations.

"Store" banking was most successful in areas like Iowa and Nebraska, where banks' relatively small size encouraged them to share the some-times heavy capital expenditures which a POS system required (a single terminal could cost up to $3,000; ATMs ran up to $50,000). However, the expansion of POS networks was inhibited by regulation in some states.

Although both branches and consumers were pleased by the extended hours of service which the terminals allowed, the new equipment was often difficult to cost-justify. One banking execu-tive observed:

> Every attempt to cost-justify electronic delivery sys-tems tends to be a function of the personality of the company. Aggressive marketers cost-justify based on new account acquisition and related values of market share and image. Cautious conservatives justify terminals as substitutes for the live teller and other direct and indirect labor expenses. Ag-gressive, geographic competitors justify on the basis of cost avoidance vis-à-vis conventional brick-and-mortar offices.[1]

Metroteller

Remote electronic banking reached Buffalo in January 1976, when the Erie Savings Bank opened a pilot facility in a local supermarket. This facility consisted of a single terminal adja-cent to the supermarket's service booth. In accordance with state banking regulations, the teller was an employee of the retailer rather than the bank. Four supermarket employees were trained for two days at the bank to operate the POS machine, which resembled a large, compli-cated typewriter.

[1] "Why Put a Teller Station Here?" *Savings & Loan News,* August 1976, p. 45.

A customer began a transaction by filling out a one-part deposit/withdrawal ticket, then pre-sented this ticket and plastic "EZ Banking" card at the customer service booth, where a clerk ran the card through a reader attached to the terminal (Exhibit 4). The customer then entered a four-digit Personal Identification Number (PIN), and the store operator next keyed in the dollar amount of the transaction, a function key, and a transmit key which sent all the data to the com-puter. The transaction was logged for subsequent processing in remote computers, and teller totals were updated. Finally, a message was sent back to the store to validate the deposit or withdrawal ticket. In addition to making deposits and with-drawals, customers could, with the teller's as-sistance, cash personal and payroll checks and make monthly mortgage payments. Withdrawals were limited to $300 daily.

According to an Erie marketing officer, public acceptance of this pilot facility was "immediate and enthusiastic." The service was available throughout daily supermarket hours, 8 a.m.-11 p.m., Monday-Saturday; it attracted 97 transac-tions during its first week of business and aver-aged 250 transactions weekly after six weeks. During this time $10,000 in new deposits was attracted and $25,000 in mortgage payments col-lected. Erie made no secret of its plans to expand the remote banking network, beginning in the latter part of summer 1976 with 15 more loca-tions in supermarkets across the Niagara Frontier. The name chosen for this POS was Metroteller.

Metroteller was administered by the Consum-R-Serv Systems Corporation, an entity established by Erie Savings Bank. Erie had no intention of restricting Metroteller to its own customers; on the contrary, it sought to enroll as many Niagara Frontier savings banks as possible under the Met-roteller umbrella. All banks sharing a specific Metroteller facility were listed by name on the large sign above the terminal. Consum-R-Serv obtained retail locations, provided computer sys-tems and equipment, and trained retail store em-

EXHIBIT 4
BUFFALO SAVINGS BANK: THE METROTELLER AND BANK-AND-SHOP TERMINALS

Metroteller Terminal

Bank-and-Shop Transaction Telephone

ployees to operate the terminals. By June 1976, the Niagara County Savings Banks of Niagara Falls had announced its intention to participate in Metroteller; savings banks in Rochester and Schenectady had also expressed interest; and Buffalo Savings Bank had agreed to share in the operation of eleven Metroteller facilities within Buffalo area supermarkets.

State regulation prohibited commercial banks from sharing a POS system with savings banks. As of mid-1977, no commercial bank in the Niagara Frontier had attempted to start its own POS system. However, the three largest commercial banks each operated ATMs built into their own premises. There was a total of about 40 ATMs in the Buffalo market.

In deciding to join Metroteller, Emblidge and his colleagues had been impressed by independently conducted marketing surveys which showed that 27 percent of western New York householders would make deposits and withdrawals to their checking and savings accounts at retail establishments where they shopped, if facilities existed to handle such transactions. Consumers listed supermarkets as a first choice for this activity, followed by department stores and drugstores. Furthermore, the more frequently someone shopped, the higher that person's perceived need for the store banking service. The main user segment consisted of women under 35 who wrote about 20 checks a month. Merchants, too, were interested in the new system as a potential traffic builder for their stores.

Bank-and-Shop

In June 1976, Buffalo Savings Bank signed an agreement with the Wm. Hengerer Co. to open "Bank-and-Shop" facilities in Buffalo's five Hengerer department stores. In addition to competitive pressure, Warren Emblidge saw four major reasons for Buffalo Savings Bank's own entry into what he called "store banking." It would permit the bank to expand its locations, to extend

banking hours, to reduce customer traffic at existing branches, and to increase its penetration of the customer and retail marketplace. The bank did not feel that ATMs could be economically justified at this point in time and had no plans to introduce these machines.

The need for extended service had been underscored by an analysis of the bank's current transactions. On average, checking account customers made three transactions per month, substantially more than savings account customers. BSB had opened 45,000 checking accounts since May 1976; these accounts added 1.6 million transactions annually. The conventional branches, with 475,000 savings accounts, processed about three million transactions annually already. Thus, when the number of checking accounts reached 80,000, the number of transactions would more than double to over 6 million, putting severe pressure on the distribution system's capability to service customers. Emblidge believed that store banking would be an economic way of diverting some of the projected traffic and transaction flow without costly branch expansion or a decline in service quality.

Having made the decision to go into store banking, Emblidge and his colleagues began the search for proper equipment. Since the system would be operated by retail clerks, simplicity was thought to be a key requirement. Emblidge recalled the bank's needs:

> We wanted a banking system that required minimum operator training, and was simple for the merchant to use. One recurring complaint about store banking is that bankers design their systems for other bankers, instead of for the merchant. Most important, we required a low upfront capital investment.

Emblidge's choice was AT&T's Transaction I Telephone, essentially a Touchtone telephone with a plastic-card reader on top (Exhibit 4). Installed and maintained by the New York Telephone Company, each Transaction Telephone could be leased for $40 per month, after a one-time $50 installation charge. It occupied about one square foot of space. Both the equipment and procedures were different from those used by Metroteller, and it was not feasible to add other banks to the same unit. A large sign above the service booth carried the BSB symbol and the words "Buffalo Savings Bank Service Center."[2]

Using the Transaction Telephone, a customer could make a deposit or cash a check in 30 seconds. As Emblidge described the process:

> The terminal operator (a retail clerk) "dials" the bank at the start of each business day by passing a magnetically encoded card through the reader slot in the Transaction Telephone. To process an individual transaction, the customer's own magnetic card is passed through. The operator then enters a two-digit transaction code, plus the amount of the transaction. Next, the customer enters a four-digit confidential PIN. A computer-generated voice response then provides the necessary account information, and the transaction is completed.

Retail employees could be trained to operate the Transaction Telephone in half a day. As time passed, Emblidge noted that store employees familiar with the terminal operation frequently trained new personnel themselves.

Bank-and-Shop locations within retail stores handled only deposits, withdrawals, check cashing, and provision of account balances. No mortgage or small loan payments were accepted and state regulation did not permit the opening of new accounts there. Withdrawals were limited to $300 daily, and the maximum number of daily transactions was three. Cash to operate the system was supplied by the individual merchants. Store accounts were struck daily by the bank, and a fee of $.20 per transaction was paid monthly to the merchants. One service representative was on call at the bank between 8 a.m. and 11 p.m. to handle questions and problems; other service reps visited each location at least once a week.

---

[2] The fully allocated costs to BSB of opening a new Bank-and-Shop outlet were estimated at $5,000.

Metroteller had a service rep on call, but visits were much less frequent.

CONTRASTING METROTELLER AND BANK-AND-SHOP

Both Consum-R-Serv and BSB employed sales representatives to market their respective systems to store owners. The task was to convince merchants that terminals in their stores would stimulate traffic and generate fee income without significantly increasing expenses.

Bank-and-Shop was sold on the basis that BSB had the largest number of customers in the area and that, by promoting its system, it could bring depositor/purchasers into participating retail stores. BSB representatives emphasized the compact size of the terminal, its ease of operation, and the simplicity of training new personnel. Metroteller, by contrast, was presented as a shared system, available to all savings banks in the area, which the stores could use to generate the maximum customer traffic. BSB's initial contract with a merchant was for one year, with several two-year options to extend—if initiated by the bank.

From the start, in Emblidge's opinion, Buffalo Savings Bank's proprietary system enjoyed two great advantages over Metroteller: it was on-line and real-time, and it clearly announced to customers that they were dealing with BSB. "Let me give you an example," he explained:

> A customer can go to a supermarket location identified by Buffalo Savings Bank signs and make a deposit, which is immediately credited to her account through our computer. Five minutes later, her husband can withdraw the money at another location. Half an hour later, she can stop at a neighborhood branch, get her new balance, make another deposit, and get her latest balance again. Both the customer and her husband were able to use Bank-and-Shop just as they'd use a neighborhood BSB branch, and they perceived that they were, in fact, dealing with Buffalo Savings Bank.

Under Erie's Metroteller system, in contrast,

the customer might also visit a supermarket POS location, but information on account balances would not be available, nor could users draw on their deposits until some time during the next business day. At the conclusion of each day's processing, transactions generated in the Metroteller network were sent via magnetic tape to member banks like BSB, which then updated their own account records. Member banks in turn sent Metroteller any updates generated through conventional branch or internal activity.

The Metroteller system thus required the maintenance of duplicate account data—one set at Metroteller, one set at the member bank. Because account activity was not entered into the computer until evening, no one could be certain during the day how much money was really in a Metroteller account; withdrawals were automatically screened according to a customer's credit record and any other standards which a member bank desired to establish. Nor could merchants be sure at the end of the day how much money they owed to (or were owed by) Metroteller.

Emblidge explained his bank's use of two separate POS systems. "Since the startup and incremental costs of our own system were so low," he remarked, "we thought we could afford to experiment with the higher fixed-cost Metroteller network—and gain valuable experience by participating in two dramatically different systems."

Introductory Promotions

Both Metroteller and Bank-and-Shop were heavily promoted by their sponsoring banks. To introduce its first 15 Metroteller locations, opening in August–September 1976, Erie mailed 100,000 magnetic cards to its checking, savings, and mortgage customers, followed by a second mass mailing of PIN codes. Erie also launched an ambitious regional marketing campaign that featured a nationally known television and radio star as sponsor for all the new "Easy Banking" services. Television, radio, and print advertising, in addition to billboards, bus cards, and point-of-

sale signs, promoted Metroteller's availability, services, and convenience. Letters and statement inserts repeated the message. After two weeks, the Metroteller was handling a weekly average of 1,800 transactions.

Buffalo began its campaign by promoting the introduction of POS banking to its customers and listing at its branches all the retail locations where POS service—either Bank-and-Shop or Metroteller—was available. Subsequently, in a specific promotion of Bank-and-Shop, BSB mailed 15,000 "Cashmate" cards to checking account customers, inviting them to visit the bank to select a PIN code. Approximately 50 percent of checking customers responded. The bank then turned to its savings account customers, of whom 5,500 expressed interest in POS service by completing and returning a postcard attached to a brochure which had been enclosed with the statement (Exhibit 5).

All BSB cards, store banking facilities, and advertisements were built on a red, white, and blue color scheme; Metroteller's cards, facilities, and promotion were predominantly orange and brown. Buffalo customers who wanted to use both systems required only one card.

Buffalo's marketing strategy also included hostesses at both branch and retail locations, who demonstrated how to use the new system, answered customers' questions and, at branches, opened new accounts. Hostesses and bank personnel stressed to these new customers the advantages of making transactions at a Bank-and-Shop location. Additionally, monthly statement stuffers encouraged existing customers to use Bank-and-Shop. Promotional incentives included inexpensive cooking spatulas and four-color prints of the Buffalo hockey team, both available free at all Bank-and-Shop locations. Unlike Erie, BSB made no effort to promote Bank-and-Shop to the general public. This concerned some of Bank-and-Shop's merchant sponsors, who thought more publicity would build more traffic for their stores.

Emblidge had heard that Erie spent approx-

EXHIBIT 5
BUFFALO SAVINGS BANK: DIRECT MAIL PROMOTIONAL BROCHURE

BANK AND SHOP IS EASY TO USE!

BANK WHERE YOU SHOP

DETAILS ON ALL SAVINGS ACCOUNTS AVAILABLE AT ANY OFFICE.

UP TO 15 HOURS A DAY, SEVEN DAYS A WEEK...

To cash a check, just:
1. Hand the check and your ID card to the clerk.
2. Key-in your private security code.
3. Your transaction is complete.

To make a deposit or withdrawal, just:
1. Fill out a deposit or withdrawal slip (they're located right at the Bank-and-Shop counters).
2. Hand the slip and your ID card to the clerk.
3. Key-in your private security code.
4. Your transaction is complete.

You need a card
Your identification card and private security code are necessary for all Bank-and-Shop transactions. Passbooks CANNOT BE USED at these locations.

Bank-and-Shop Locations
For a complete list of department stores, supermarkets and retail businesses where you can bank and shop, call 847-5800.

SERVICE CENTER

B BUFFALO SAVINGS BANK

YOU CAN BELIEVE IN BUFFALO

B BUFFALO SAVINGS BANK Member FDIC

Phone 84 - 5800

Reorder 0180 200M

Mail this card today!

Banking where I shop sounds good to me. Please send me the necessary forms to open the following account:

☐ Absolutely Free Checking
☐ Statement Savings
☐ Interest-on-Checking

Name _____

Address _____

City _____ State_____ Zip _____

Telephone _____

(Please use ball point pen)

imately $300,000 to launch and promote Metro-teller. Expenses for introductory promotion of Bank-and-Shop facilities during their first twelve months of operation totalled $75,000.

ASSESSING THE EXPERIMENT

Initial consumer reactions to the new POS services were favorable to both Metroteller and Bank-and-Shop. In August 1976, personal interviews with 50 households living within one mile of a selected Metroteller supermarket facility shared by Erie and BSB showed that 84 percent of respondents were aware of the service; 38 percent stated that they intended to use it. Both Buffalo and Erie were equally associated with the Metroteller service by respondents, 70 percent of whom identified it with one or both of the two banks. BSB transactions through Metroteller rose rapidly, reaching 6,535 by the end of 1976—more than double the number made through Bank-and-Shop.

By January of 1977, however, operational difficulties with Metroteller had begun to cast doubts on the value of a shared service network. In a memo to Emblidge, Buffalo's auditor noted several problems. Cash settlements from Metroteller were running up to a week late, and both Metroteller and Erie Savings Bank appeared relatively unconcerned about Buffalo's complaints. The auditor also noted the difficulties of attempting to operate a POS network through an intermediary, in this case the Consum-R-Serv Corporation (CRS). He commented:

> CRS managers seem to think that they act only as an intermediary that settles with us after they settle with the supermarkets. Transactions that are obviously wrong are not credited to us until the funds are straightened out with the supermarkets, most often after a great length of time. But we feel that we are doing business with CRS, and that it is our contract with them that should be honored.

Despite these concerns, Emblidge and his colleagues believed that the advantages of staying with Metroteller outweighed the risks. However, BSB did not significantly expand its participation in Metroteller as that network grew; its ties to Metroteller remained limited to eleven supermarkets, giving Metroteller time to improve its operational performance. Bank-and-Shop had suffered occasional operational problems, but never any continuous difficulties. During the first six months of 1977 Buffalo Savings Bank continued to expand its Bank-and-Shop network, adding five drugstores in January, five Bells supermarkets in February and March, and one Bells supermarket in early June (Exhibit 3).

By mid-June 1977, Emblidge thought the time had come for an exhaustive reassessment of Buffalo's experiment in simultaneous shared and proprietary POS operations. Operational difficulties with Metroteller had not abated. Robert D. Weiss, assistant vice president and manager of the POS network, observed to Emblidge:

> We've always known that our on-line, real-time capability offers better customer service by instantly updating accounts. But as POS banking becomes more familiar to consumers, I see another problem—a lot of customer confusion over the name Metroteller, which isn't directly associated with any bank. The fact is that customers have difficulty understanding why they get a higher level of service at Bank-and-Shop than they get at Metroteller, when they're making transactions with the same bank. Frankly, some of our Metroteller customers are having fits.

In using Metroteller, Weiss pointed out, BSB was forced to adopt the operational procedures set by Consum-R-Serv. In its proprietary system, on the other hand, BSB could clearly identify itself and its product and provide service consistent with that provided at its branches. Some bank officials believed that Metroteller's chief goal was to penetrate the market as rapidly as possible and enroll all types of financial institutions from throughout the state; removing operational flaws and maintaining a high level of customer service, they thought, were somewhat less important concerns for Metroteller. Bank-

and-Shop's primary objectives, in contrast, were to relieve the load of transactions on BSB branches and to provide good service to customers; expansion of the network to other institutions was secondary.

Transaction data prepared by BSB revealed that Buffalo's share of Metroteller transactions at shared locations had been steadily increasing (Exhibit 6), leading Weiss to comment, "I think Metroteller may need us more than we need them." By May 1977, Metroteller had expanded to 31 POS facilities, up from 21 in January. Several local banks now shared all or part of the Metroteller network. Metroteller transaction volume for April was 42,683, as compared to 21,692 in January.

Emblidge next looked at cost data. He noted the near impossibility of attributing the production of new, profitable accounts directly to Buffalo's proprietary POS system, simply because of the difficulty inherent in determining why a customer opened an account. In evaluating the cost-justification for POS, Emblidge used what he called "the cost-indifference point"—the point at which it would cost the same to service an account in a retail store as it cost at a bank office. He calculated that the cost of a POS transaction would approximate the cost of a conventional branch transaction by the end of 1978.

A key factor in Emblidge's analysis of the comparative costs of future participation in Metroteller and Bank-and-Shop was his estimate of Buffalo Savings Bank's checking account and transaction growth (Exhibit 7). He also assembled a list of the major costs that would accrue if the bank decided to drop Bank-and-Shop and expand its Metroteller participation from eleven outlets to 50 (Exhibit 8). He then assembled similar costs to accrue if BSB left Metroteller and expanded Bank-and-Shop (Exhibit 9). From these figures, Emblidge believed he could produce a comparison of the total projected costs associated with each strategy.

Emblidge was particularly pleased that Bank-and-Shop's deposit dollars outnumbered dollars withdrawn by a ratio of 9 to 1. He attributed this phenomenon to the bank's decision to emphasize the use of store banking services to checking rather than savings account customers. "Additionally," Emblidge noted, "we chose to limit distribution to a single terminal located at a store's courtesy booth, rather than placing one terminal at the end of each checkout line. The latter approach encourages customers to pay for their groceries but make few deposits."

DISCUSSION

Ramsey and the bank's other officers listened in silence as Emblidge presented his findings. When the floor was open for discussion, John Gilbert, group vice president, commented:

> Warren, a lot of your findings would seem to point toward a break with Metroteller. Bob Weiss may be right—they may need us more than we need them. But let me bring up a number of problems you haven't addressed. How real *is* customer dissatisfaction? What we've got is a lot of hearsay. If Metroteller is so inefficient, why was it used for over 12,000 BSB transactions last month—more than we processed through Bank-and-Shop? And assuming that we do withdraw from Metroteller, how can we take those 12,000 transactions with us? Have we figured out whether we can convince a shopper to change supermarkets so we can cash her checks?
>
> Another point. Are we prepared to collide head-on with Metroteller in a fight for the remaining potential POS outlets in this area? Right now our research shows that about 60 percent of the prime locations for POS on the Niagara Frontier have already been signed up. You'll have a hard time trying to convince Metroteller merchants to switch to a Bank-and-Shop facility. What kind of inducements are we prepared to offer an undecided merchant to make him choose us instead of them?
>
> And what about the future? You know we're in a fight with commercial banks for market share. Let's not hurt each other and let the commercial banks beat us both. A lot of experts think that merchant demands and economic pressure will make it im-

EXHIBIT 6
BUFFALO SAVINGS BANK: BANK-AND-SHOP AND METROTELLER TRANSACTION DATA, 1976–77

	BSB Transactions at Shared Metroteller Facilities	Erie Transactions at Shared Metroteller Facilities	Total BSB/Erie Metroteller Locations*	BSB Transactions at Bank-and-Shop	Total Bank-and-Shop Locations	Total BSB POS Transactions	Percent of Branch Activity
1976							
August	193	N/A	8	0	0	193	.1%
September	1,115	1,570	11	220	5	1,335	.3
October	3,233	6,269	11	1,171	5	4,404	1.7
November	4,686	7,458	12	2,314	5	7,000	2.0
December	6,535	8,427	12	3,132	5	9,667	3.8
1977							
January	6,352	7,552	12	2,568	10	8,920	3.7%
February	7,799	9,142	11	3,580	14	11,379	4.5
March	10,078	11,569	11	6,307	15	16,385	5.0
April	11,886	12,392	11	8,651	15	20,537	6.2
May	12,759	***	11	10,004	15	22,763	7.2
June**	14,418	***	11	12,037	16	26,455	7.9

* One of the stores containing a Metroteller outlet shared by BSB subsequently went out of business.
** Projection.
*** Metroteller stopped supplying competitive transaction data in April 1977.
Source: Company records.

EXHIBIT 7
BUFFALO SAVINGS BANK: ESTIMATED CHECKING ACCOUNT
AND TRANSACTION GROWTH

Year Ending	Number of Checking Accounts	Percent of Checking Accounts Active at POS	Monthly Transactions at POS	Estimated Number of POS Locations
12/31/77	55,000	12	2.5	30
12/31/78	70,000	18	2.7	50
12/31/79	83,000	23	2.9	70
12/31/80	93,000	27	3.1	90

Note: For every four checking account transactions at a POS, it was estimated that one statement savings account transaction would occur. In addition, for every five account transactions, it was expected that there would be one transaction where the customer would simply ask to cash a payroll (or other) check without actually making a deposit. Such a transaction at a POS incurred the same costs as any other.
Source: Company records.

EXHIBIT 8
REPRESENTATIVE COMPONENTS OF METROTELLER
PRICING SCHEDULE*

Type of Cost	Amount
Store Origination Charges**	
Year 1	$10,000. per store
Year 2	7,000. per store
Transaction Fee***	
less than 10,000 transactions/month	$1.15
10,001–20,000 transactions/month	1.05
20,001–30,000 transactions/month	.95
30,001–40,000 transactions/month	.85
40,001–50,000 transactions/month	.75
over 50,000 transactions/month	.65
Interchange Fee	
Per active account per year	$ .90
Data Processing Fee	
Per account per month	$ .01
New account set up	.10

* Data are disguised.
** These charges were paid to Consum-R-Serv by Buffalo Savings Bank for the first two years that it was associated with each Metroteller location.
*** This fee was paid to Consum-R-Serv by Buffalo Savings Bank for each Metroteller transaction made by a BSB customer. The sliding scale related to the total number of BSB transactions through all Metroteller outlets in a given month.
Source: Buffalo Savings Bank.

EXHIBIT 9
REPRESENTATIVE COMPONENTS OF BANK-AND-
SHOP COST ALLOCATION SYSTEM *

Type of Cost	Amount
Store Opening Charge	$5,000. per store
Retail Costs per Transaction	
Merchant fee	$.20
Telephone line	.09
Bank Departmental Costs per Transaction (Administration** and Computer Center)	
10,000–40,000 transactions/month	$.65
40,001–70,000 transactions/month	.45
70,001–100,000 transactions/ month	.35
Over 100,000 transactions/month	.25

* The data, which are disguised, refer to costs incurred by Buffalo Savings Bank.
** Includes depreciation, merchant account reconciliation, location servicing, and plastic card production. Marketing not included.
Source: Buffalo Savings Bank.

possible for any proprietary network to survive against a shared system. What makes you think Bank-and-Shop will be an exception?

Gilbert leaned back in his chair and pursed his lips. "I'm sorry," he concluded, "but right now I think we should be directing our efforts toward getting better service from Metroteller, not toward breaking away from it. We're accounting for over half their transactions now at the outlets we use; we must have some clout with their organization."

Before Emblidge could respond, Ramsey cut into the discussion. "Warren," he commented, "I share your misgivings about Metroteller, but John has brought up some good points. Why don't you give the whole situation some more thought over the weekend?" He continued:

On Monday, I'd like to see a memo reviewing all the relevant data and making concrete recommendations as to how we should proceed on this question. Assuming you decide that we should withdraw from Metroteller—and I'll admit I share some of your misgivings about that system—I want you to address John's objections specifically. In particular, I want a detailed comparison of the costs associated with participation in each system, and I want to see a strategy for taking those 12,000 Metroteller transactions with us in the event that we do decide to withdraw.

REDIPLANT

Kenneth Simmonds

Early in 1981 John Bryant, owner of an English timber products firm, was asked by his close friend Martin Nievelt whether he would consider becoming a commisar[1] of Rediplant NV—a company being formed to exploit the new Rediplant method for packaging bulbs. Martin also wanted John's opinion on the number of sealing machines that should be purchased in advance of the first full season of Rediplant sales. This was a particularly difficult decision for him, as there was little guide as to how much they would sell and most of the packaging would have to be carried out during the month of August.

Martin Nievelt and Walter Praag were owners and joint Managing Directors of Hans Praag & Co., an old established Dutch bulb exporter based in Hillegom, Holland. Before the Rediplant development, Praag had concentrated on bulb sales to France, the United Kingdom, Switzerland and Germany. They sold to nurserymen, wholesalers and large retailers as well as directly to the public through mail order catalogues. There were two seasons each year. The larger was for spring bulbs which were lifted from the bulb fields and distributed in the autumn for planting up to mid-winter. This season represented 70 percent of the bulb market and covered tulips, crocuses, narcissi and hyacinths.

Recent performance of firms in the bulb business had been poor and there had been numerous failures over the previous two years. The 600 exporting houses all belonged to an industry association and argued the need to hold price levels, but competition amongst them resulted in continual margin cutting. Praag had recorded losses both years, mainly because of low response to their mail order catalogues, attributed by Martin Nievelt to cold, wet weekends that discouraged customers from thinking about gardening. While substantial profits could still be made in a good mail order season, the response rates had been dropping at an average rate of 8 percent per year. The development of the Re-

Copyright © 1984 by Kenneth Simmonds (revised)

[1] Commissars of Dutch corporations are outside directors appointed by the shareholders to oversee the employee directors. They have a number of specific powers and their consent must be obtained for all borrowing by the company.

diplant system therefore came at a particularly opportune time and gave Praag an opportunity to differentiate its product and increase its margins. Praag decided to withdraw from the direct mail order side of the business and concentrate on building the broadest possible sales of Rediplant packed bulbs. Sales of the mail order list, moreover, would provide finance for the new effort and avoid surrender of ownership interest which was usually required in order to obtain long-term bank lending for small private companies.

The French, German and Swiss mailing lists were sold to Beinum & Co. late in 1980. Beinum was the largest Dutch bulb merchant with a turnover around 100 million guilders (Fl. 100m) and a mailing list of 5 million catalogues.[2] Praag's United Kingdom mail order list and the U.K. wholesale business were sold to Sutcliffe Seeds Ltd. of Norwich. Sutcliffe were moving into the bulb market as an extension to their traditional seed activities and the agreement provided for Praag to supply all Sutcliffe's requirements for Dutch bulbs, whilst retaining the right to go directly to a selected list of retail chains and large stores in the United Kingdom.

DEVELOPMENT OF THE REDIPLANT SYSTEM

The idea for Rediplant was first conceived in November 1979 by Walter Praag, who concentrated on the engineering and production side of the business, leaving the commercial side to Martin Nievelt. (See the appendix at the end of the case for a chronology of Rediplant development). Rediplant was basically a transparent plastic strip moulded to hold bulbs in equally-spaced blisters open at the top and bottom. It was designed as a usage container that could be planted directly in the soil without removing the bulbs, giving them protection from frost, birds, rodents and slugs,

[2] The standard abbreviation for a Dutcher guilder or florin is "Fl." Exchange rates were £1.00 (U.K.) = Fl. 4.30, $1.00 (U.S.) = Fl. 3.00.

and enabling the bulbs to be easily retrieved for planting in subsequent seasons.

Walter Praag explained the development in this way:

> I got the idea at the end of 1979 and aimed only to make our competitive position easier and to solve planting problems for the buyer. We ran trials and found that it made not only for easier planting but also gave protection and a better flower, though it was not invented for that purpose. We tested a great quantity with a sensitive control test and the packaged bulbs showed up better than bulbs planted by hand. We limited our tests to hyacinths, tulips, narcissi, crocuses and gladioli, because the others have extra difficulties for packaging and these are the main selling items. With gladioli we had some trouble and I had to redesign the pack as the sprouts came out of the side of the bulb rather than the top. When we told people the name of our new pack was Rediplant many remarked that it was not a very good name—but minutes later they would all use the name without any prompting. We decided it must be a very good name.

The bulbs were packed automatically into previously formed plastic strips which were then sealed and fitted into a cardboard sleeve printed with details of the bulbs and planting instructions. After considerable experimentation the new pack was ready for launching and in May 1980 a vacuum forming machine was purchased to make quantities of the strips. At this stage the pack was comparatively crude, with a single coloured cardboard sleeve which totally enclosed the plastic strip which was in turn stapled together to hold the bulbs.

Mr. Nievelt did his own market research by asking friends, acquaintances and the general public what they thought of the packs and if they would buy them. On his frequent sales trips to England, for example, he asked customers in garden centres and large stores he visited whether they would buy the packs and they all said they would. The packs contained six tulips with a suggested retail price of £1.30 as against a price of £1.00 for similar loose bulbs. Martin also asked retailers in England what they thought of the packaging. He recalled:

> Large retail chains, Woolworths, Boots, Debenhams and John Lewis liked it and after a while the larger garden centres would say that they would buy it. Small centres and garden stores, however, generally said they did not like Rediplant. They gave few reasons but they seemed worried that it would mean other types of stores would find it easier to sell bulbs.

Martin also persuaded three different outlets to test market the strips—a store on a U.S. air force base at Woodbridge, a seedshop in Ipswich and a garden centre at Ramsey, Essex. Each received one hundred strips, without charge, and each quickly sold the entire assignment at £1.30 each.

Rediplant packaging was next featured in Praag mail order catalogues for spring bulbs sent out in autumn 1980. These were mailed to some 300,000 customers in Britain, France and Germany at a cost including postage of £0.20 (or equivalent) each. Prices for a Rediplant package of six bulbs were set about 30 percent below the catalogue prices for a standard quantity of 10 loose bulbs, making the price for a Rediplant bulb 15 percent higher than an equivalent loose bulb. Rediplant packaging appeared on the cover, and the catalogue started with a two-page spread outlining the Rediplant system and offering a 200 percent guarantee to replace every non-flowering Rediplant bulb with two new bulbs. The spread also showed how Rediplant strips could be planted in evenly spaced rows or in cartwheel or zigzag patterns. Walter Praag commented that this sort of thing seemed to appeal particularly to the German market, which was also much more concerned with rodent and insect damage than other nationalities. He thought the British tended to be keener gardeners and more knowledgeable about bulbs, while many more potential customers in France and Germany would avoid buying loose bulbs that they did not understand, or else buy some and plant them upside down. With Rediplant pack-

ages these customers would find planting much easier. Praag's experience had been, too, that the British tended to be much more price conscious than the others, while the French tended to identify value with the price charged.

As orders began to come in during the early winter months, Praag was very encouraged by the high proportion of Rediplant sales. Final figures were as follows:

Country	Catalogues Posted	No. of Orders Received	Average Order Size
U.K.	150,000	8,056	£14.00
France	101,000	5,581	£20.80
W. Germany	50,000	2,091	£21.80

% of Total Bulbs Ordered in Rediplant Packs			
	Tulips	Hyacinths	Narcissi
U.K.	18	20	10
France	27	32	13
W. Germany	44	39	39

Examination of 160 U.K. orders at random showed the average order for Rediplant to be £8.00, representing on average 50 percent of the customer's total order.

Walter Praag continued work on the Rediplant design. The cardboard sleeve was redesigned with full colour pictures of the blooms and better instructions, and the strips were made narrower and extended to include seven bulbs rather than six in a new pack measuring 40 centimeters. Martin Nievelt thought this might discourage price comparison with loose bulbs sold in dozens. Exhibit 1 shows these new strips on the display stand.

For sales through retail outlets, special units were designed containing 180 strips with wire pegs for each six strips. These pegs could be fitted onto pegboards or specially designed Rediplant display stands for floor or counter displays. The mix of varieties for the units was based on a statistical analysis of the historical proportions of

EXHIBIT 1
REDIPLANT DISPLAY STAND

Assortment 180 s

REDIPLANT

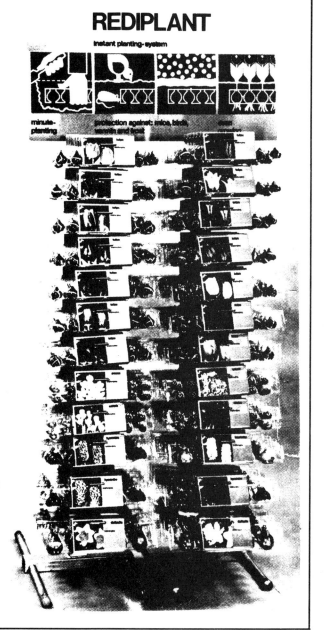

An exclusive new pre-assembled Assortment for You !

112 packs of tulips in 14 varieties 7 bulbs
      per pack

 24 packs of hyacinths in 4 varieties
      5 bulbs per pack

 12 packs of narcissi in 2 varieties
      5 bulbs per pack

 32 packs of crocus in 4 varieties
      14 bulbs per pack
____
180 packs in 24 well-chosen varieties

Floor space: 15" x 33"
Height display: 63"
Size display poster: 31½" x 18½"
Weight case: 59 lbs.

This display offers an easy and fast set-up
with a minimum of floor space

Advantages:
REDIPLANT is unique (patent pending)
Honest presentation in see-through packs
Optimal ventilation preserves the quality
of the bulbs
Packs are delivered on pegs, saving labour
in setting up display (except assortment 180
and 90)
REDIPLANT has been successfully tested
Over a century of successful bulb-growing
experience guarantees a high quality
product
Your Department as well as the Dutch Dept.
of Agriculture inspects all bulbs before
they are exported

bulb sales and would not be varied for individual orders. The unit contained 112 strips of tulips in 14 varieties, 24 strips of hyacinths in 4 varieties, 12 strips of narcissi in 2 varieties and 32 strips of crocuses in 4 varieties. Large display posters illustrating the planting of Rediplant strips were designed to accompany each unit, which would be boxed with or without a display stand as required.

Patents for the Rediplant system of packaging were applied for and obtained in the Benelux countries, the United Kingdom, France, Germany, Canada and the U.S.A. This patent was granted for a 'usage' package and competitors would find it difficult to break through simply by altering the design. Moreover, anyone wishing to compete would find it essential on a cost basis to package in Holland, rather than to ship, pack and then redirect the bulbs—and Praag was sure that they would be advised by the Dutch Customs if their patent was infringed.

Partnership with Van Diemen Bros.

In late 1980 Praag was approached by Van Diemen Bros., who had seen the packages and wanted to explore ways by which they, too, could use the new packaging method. Discussions led to the idea of a partnership for developing the system. Van Diemen had the largest sales force in the Dutch bulb industry, owned their own bulb fields and research laboratories, and were suppliers by appointment to the Netherlands Royal Family. "The idea went against the mentality of the industry that it is not right to work together," said Martin Nievelt. "We had the idea but the other firm had forty sales people against Praag's two, as well as contacts with wholesalers all around the world. A partnership would provide resources and backing at the same time as it removed one of the major sources of potential competition."

Nievelt believed that the fragmented nature of the industry and the lack of product differentiation were the prime causes of low prices and small or non-existent profits. He hoped that the combined strength of the two firms would enable them to make a much larger impact on the bulb market and eventually claim a significant proportion of Dutch bulb sales at higher margins.

The arrangement worked out on a friendly basis with Van Diemen was that Rediplant NV would be formed as a limited company, with Hans Praag & Co. and Van Diemen Bros. each owning 50 percent of the equity. Rediplant would lease Praag's storage and packing facilities in Hillegom and manufacture for the two sales companies, invoicing them at cost after payment of a royalty to Praag of Fl. 0.04 per strip. Praag would retain the right to all sales anywhere in the world destined for customers via mail order and also to wholesale sales in the United Kingdom, Holland and Switzerland. Van Diemen would cover wholesale sales in all remaining countries. This arrangement meant that there would be little change from past concentration because Praag had had very little wholesale revenue from France or Germany. The direct mail market, moreover, accounted for some 20 percent of Dutch bulb exports for dry sales. Martin Nievelt and the senior Van Diemen agreed to act as commissars for the new firm and to ask John Bryant to act as a third neutral commissar. Solicitors were asked to draw up formal agreements. As of the end of February 1981 the drafts had not yet been received.

Meanwhile, Walter Praag and Dik Van Diemen, son of the Van Diemen president, had agreed to become joint managing directors of Rediplant and had become immersed in detailed planning of the production requirements for the 1981 spring bulb season. The elder Van Diemen had also applied to the Dutch government for a grant to develop the invention and Rediplant had received a non-returnable grant of Fl. 130,000.

MEETING THE DEMAND

The period for selling spring bulbs to intermediate outlets ran from January through August, but delivery requirements would be very tight. Excluding mail order business, 55 percent of all sales had to be packed by mid-August, the next 30 percent by the end of August, and the last 15 percent by the end of September. All United States sales were included in the initial 55 percent because of the need to meet shipping dates, but another week could be saved by air freight although it would increase the freight cost for a standard shipment from Fl. 43.00 per '180' unit to Fl. 129.00. After September, mail order business could then be supplied fairly evenly until early December. Delivery commitments were regarded as very important by all the Rediplant executives. The retail buying season was concentrated and a supplier who failed to meet his commitments would ruin his chance of repeat business. Martin Nievelt considered it would be better to take a limited amount of Rediplant orders in the first season rather than run the risk of not being able to meet orders on time and ruining the Rediplant name.

The supply of bulbs themselves presented few problems. Most bulbs were bought from the growers on a contract basis in the spring while still in the ground. A buyer would contract to buy all the production of a given acreage at a fixed price per bulb. As he sold to his customers before he knew how many bulbs he would receive from this acreage, he had to buy any additional requirements or sell any excess on the free market where the price could fluctuate wildly depending on whether there was a glut or a poor season. Although the average price of bulbs could usually be predicted within 10 percent, a given tulip had fluctuated in price between Fl. 28.00 and Fl. 44.00 per hundred over the previous few years. By industry agreement, payment to growers was required promptly on 1st November. For a merchant to retain a good name amongst suppliers payment could not be delayed.

The real problems in supply stemmed from the short packaging season after the bulbs were taken from the fields. Crocuses might not be ready to be packed until 25th July, narcissi and hyacinths a week later, and tulips between the 25th July and 10th August depending on the variety. Packaging, therefore, had to be very carefully planned.

When the bulbs arrived for packaging they would be inspected and sorted before being placed in the PVC strips by semi-automatic filling machines. The strips would then pass along conveyors to an automatic radio frequency sealing machine and from there to a station where they would be fitted with the cardboard sleeve and packed into cartons. While the vacuum-forming machine making the PVC strips could produce only 900 strips per hour, stocks could be built up before packaging began. The sorting machines worked rapidly and could take large quantities of bulbs so they did not limit the output in any way. The speed of the filling machines could also be increased if needed. Four filling machines, moreover, had been built and these could keep at least four sealing machines busy. The limiting factor, then, seemed to be the number of sealing machines. These operated with an output of 900 strips per hour and at Fl. 33,000 were the most expensive items. One machine had been specially designed for Rediplant. Orders for further units would have to be placed immediately as there was a three month delivery time and orders placed after the beginning of March might not be received in time for the packaging season. The machines were believed to be reliable, but if an electronic component should break down an engineer from the manufacturer would be required.

Praag and Van Diemen were annoyed that the manufacturer of the sealing machine was insisting on payment before delivery, had raised the price to Fl. 33,000 from a verbally agreed figure of Fl. 25,000, and would not make any effort to schedule shorter delivery. They had, therefore, investigated other methods of sealing that did not require expensive equipment. All had major disadvantages. Adhesives and stapling were much slower and stapling spoilt the look of the package, while adhesives attracted the dust from the bulbs and were not 100 percent effective.

Martin Nievelt argued that only one further

sealing machine should be ordered. He pointed out that there was no guarantee that huge volumes of Rediplant could be sold in the first season when the buyers knew it to be experimental; moreover, financial difficulties could limit the opportunity to expand in later years. Hans Praag & Co., had little finance available and this had been a further reason for the partnership with Van Diemen. The total requirement for subscribed capital had to be kept to Fl. 400, 000 (see Exhibit 2) if Praag's share in the partnership was not to fall below 50 percent. There was no chance of credit from the machinery supplier and the bank had said previously that it would advance funds only in exchange for some of the ownership equity.

During the busy season it was usual to work two shifts, seven days a week, using mainly student labour. For the peak period from 27th July until 17th August, Martin calculated that two sealing machines would enable a production of 605,000 strips (21 days × 16 hours × 900 strips × 2 machines). As this period would represent 55 percent of the season's activity this would mean a total production limit of 1.1 million strips. To be on the safe side he set a first tentative limit of 4,750 units (855,000 strips) for the season's selling activity.

Rediplant Sales

While Walter Praag and Dik Van Diemen concentrated on the production planning, Martin Nievelt took on the task of coordinating the Rediplant sale commitments. With Van Diemen's agreement, he had in January allocated the tentative target limit of 4,750 units on the following basis:

1,500	United Kingdom
1,000	United States
1,000	Germany
500	Sweden
250	France
250	Holland
250	Switzerland

EXHIBIT 2
REDIPLANT COSTINGS

Equipment	
Vacuum Forming Plant	Fl. 84,000
Transformer & Electrical Installation	20,000
Moulds	40,000
Sorting Machines 10,000 × 4	40,000
Filling Machines 7,500 × 4	30,000
Transport Lines	20,000
Sealing Machines 33,000 × 2	66,000
	300,000

Packaging Cost	
Electricity & Maintenance	Fl. 10,000
Rent	40,000
Labor (25,000 hours @ Fl. 12)	300,000
Other Overheads	100,000
Depreciation @ 20%	60,000
Interest: on Equipment	30,000
on Materials and Working Capital	20,000
	560,000

Packaged Cost (excl. display stands)	Per Strip	Per Unit (180 Strips)
Bulbs	Fl. 1.24	Fl. 223.2
PVC	0.08	14.4
Sleeve	0.12	21.6
Royalties (all sales)	0.04	7.2
Packaging (@ 1 m strips)	0.56	100.8
Carton Packaging including labour	0.08	14.4
Point of Sale Advertising (display posters and pegs)	0.06	10.8
Packaged cost	2.18	392.4

Martin was quick to admit that these were little more than rough guesses but he felt that the overall demand figures offered even less help. These are shown in Exhibit 3.

By the end of February the sales force was just commencing its main effort and there was still very little sales feedback to go on. One large order of 1,000 units without stands, however, had just been confirmed by the largest garden supply wholesaler in Germany who had placed

EXHIBIT 3
DUTCH BULB EXPORTS, 1979

	Total Exports (Fl. millions)	Exported for Dry Sales* (%)
Germany	236	31
United States	96	70
United Kingdom	70	35
France	68	64
Italy	62	59
Switzerland	42	42
Canada	16	68
Austria	12	64
All other markets	10	55

* Dry sales refer to the proportion of the sales going to the general public either directly or through outlets. Wet sales refer to sales to nurserymen for forcing cut flowers.

this initial order against a request that he be the sole German distributor next year. This firm employed a sizeable sales force calling on both garden supply outlets and major retail chains. The price negotiated by the Van Diemen sales force was Fl. 2.66 per strip net ex Praag warehouse. The German retail mark-up was usually 35 percent on sales and the Van Diemen sales representative had been told that the wholesaler himself would take a 20 percent mark-up on retail price. Transport costs to be met by the wholesaler would be small and there was no duty into Germany.

There had also been other enquiries for large volume supplies but Martin Nievelt had argued against pursuing these for 1981. For example, Beinum, the mail order house who had purchased Praag's mailing lists, had enquired about Rediplant. They would supply their own bulbs and purchase only the packing and packaging but the volumes required could be very large indeed. After initial discussions that ranged around a figure of Fl. 1.20 per strip it was decided not to do anything until the following season. A very large U.S. mail order firm, Henry Field Seed Nursery Co. of Iowa, also showed interest, but would have required delivery for September when their mail order packing com-

menced. Several of the large U.S. retail chains had expressed interest. Other than arrangements for a modified test by A&P, the supermarket chain, however, these were not followed up because the A&P firm alone could absorb all Rediplant output in just one of its regions. This supermarket chain planned to test sales of the product at U.S. $2.69 per strip. Van Diemen's United States salesmen were instead concentrating on the suburban garden centres which mainly purchased loose bulbs. One of them had reported that, by chaining the size of the Rediplant order he would accept to the amount of loose bulbs ordered, he had been able to gain a substantial increase in his sales of loose bulbs.

Martin Nievelt felt that he could safely leave the Van Diemen sales effort to Van Diemen management. They were well organized, with a world-wide sales director and four area managers. He had, however, provided sets of Rediplant brochures and price sheets drawn up in five languages. The prices Van Diemen chose were set to allow them around 20 percent on sales and to meet the usual trade margins in the particular country. In the United States, for example, the standard price for a strip at port of entry had been set at the equivalent of Fl. 3.30 to cover such a margin, 12½ percent duty, and delivery costs.

Van Diemen salesmen were paid a basic salary of Fl. 35,000 plus a commission of 2 percent for the first Fl. 800,000 increasing by ½ percent for each additional Fl. 200,000. Detailed technical training was given and maintained on all aspects of bulb culture, although there was no special sales training. A geographical breakdown of Van Diemen's sales is shown in Exhibit 4, together with the numbers of salesmen concentrating on each country. Scandinavia, with a 5 percent growth rate, was the fastest growing market as well as bringing Van Diemen its largest sales.

UNITED KINGDOM MARKET

Having reserved 1,500 units for the United Kingdom market, Martin Nievelt was anxious to meet

EXHIBIT 4
VAN DIEMEN BROS.—GEOGRAPHICAL PERFORMANCE

	% of 1979 Turnover	No. of Agents
Sweden	20.1	4
W. Germany	19.7	4
Finland	16.7	1 + 1 agent
France	10.7	6 + 3 agents
Italy	8.2	1
Norway	7.0	1 + 6 agents
United States	4.5	5
Denmark	3.8	1
Switzerland	3.0	1
Canada	1.4	—
Austria	1.2	1
Iran	1.1	—
United Kingdom	0.9	1
Greece	0.4	—
South Africa	0.4	—
Belgium	0.4	—
Japan	0.1	—
Portugal	0.1	—
Hong Kong	0.1	—
Rest of World	0.1	—

this figure. He was awaiting news from Jan Straten, Praag's only other salesman, who was currently on a sales trip to Britain. Martin expected him to come back with some good orders for Rediplant, some of which would be test orders from the major chains.

Praag's United Kingdom bulb turnover in 1980 had been £360,000, of which £160,000 was direct mail. At this level of activity Praag was 6th or 7th in the ranking of about 300 Dutch bulb exporters to the United Kingdom. It was this entire turnover that Praag had sold to Sutcliffe Seeds Ltd. at the end of 1980. As part of the agreement Sutcliffe undertook to purchase all their Dutch bulbs from Praag at an agreed formula, whether sold by direct mail or through outlets. Prices were to be set to cover packing and shipping costs and give Praag a 20 percent mark-up on the packaged cost. The suggested retail price would then be set at 100 percent mark-up on the price to Sutcliffe (50 percent on sales). Sutcliffe would give its outlets a discount of 33.3 percent off this sug-gested retail price plus an additional 5 percent for payment within 30 days.

Sutcliffe had been actively looking for ways of expanding their sales of bulbs. They had recently taken over the garden seed division of Charles Gibb & Sons and now held over 30 percent of the retail seed market in the United Kingdom. With a total U.K. seed market of only £24 million, however, further growth would be difficult. Against this, the U.K. bulb market of around £40 million offered more opportunity and Paul Duke, managing director of Sutcliffe, had set his sights on 10 percent of this market by 1985. Although Sutcliffe had bulb sales of only £160,000 at this time and there were a great number of competitors, Duke planned to develop into the quality end of the market using Sutcliffe's name and selling only the best Dutch bulbs. Local bulb growing had expanded considerably in recent years and Dutch mail order firms had been undercut by local suppliers, but there were still many bulb varieties better provided from Holland and direct container shipment in bulk could offset almost all the location advantage.

Paul Duke had also asked if Sutcliffe could have an exclusive distributorship for Rediplant in the United Kingdom. Martin Nievelt knew that Praag would not have the resources to set up a significant sales force and had agreed to Duke's proposal, subject to Praag retaining the right to visit a number of their existing outlets and 20 of the largest chain stores and department stores in the United Kingdom. Nievelt undertook not to sell to these outlets at a price lower than Sutcliffe's net price to its outlets less 2 percent cash discount, on the understanding that Sutcliffe would use the same mark-ups as for loose bulbs.

Nievelt was very pleased with the agreement made with Sutcliffe. He thought that in the first year Sutcliffe's sales force of 60, which called on all the garden centres and hardware and garden stores in the U.K., would take orders for somewhere in the vicinity of 600 units. The top salesmen sold between £200,000 and £240,000 of merchandise each year. Sutcliffe planned, moreover, to spend £80,000 on advertising their bulbs in the ensuing year and was planning to hold a cocktail and dinner party to announce their venture, which would be widely covered in the trade papers.

With the major demands of the Rediplant development, Martin had been unable to manage a selling visit to the major outlets he had retained for Praag, and had sent Jan Straten in his place. Jan Straten had started with Praag eight years ago at the age of eighteen and with the exception of a two-year spell in the Dutch army had worked with them ever since. He was paid a fixed salary of Fl. 35,000 and received £30 a day to cover his expenses while in the U.K. He retained his home in Hillegom, seldom being away from home for more than a month at a time, and had sold £100,000 last year, which Martin Nievelt thought was fairly good for a younger man.

The price at which Jan was seeking Rediplant sales in the United Kingdom was £0.88 per strip delivered to the customer, less 2 percent discount for payment within 10 days. This price was based on a suggested retail selling price of £1.32 per strip, which Martin had decided would be necessary to give Sutcliffe the same mark-up as for loose bulbs and still leave a reasonable profit for Praag. Costs of packing, freight, insurance, duty (10 percent), delivery, etc. would amount to about 20 percent of the packaged cost although this percentage might be reduced for full container deliveries. Martin would have preferred the retail price to be £1.16, which would have about equalled the price for similar loose bulbs in garden stores, but was convinced that at £1.32 Straten should be able to persuade several of the chains to place orders.

APPENDIX: Chronology of Case Events

Late 1979 — Idea for Rediplant conceived by Walter Praag.

May 1980 — Lab testing of Rediplant complete. Relatively crude pack of six bulbs ready for market launch. Vacuum forming machine for strip manufacture purchased.

Summer 1980 — Test sale in three U.K. outlets. All sell 100 strips quickly at £1.30.

Autumn 1980 — Rediplant in "6-pack" featured on cover and 2-page spread of Praag mail order catalogue.

— Continued improvements to Rediplant—redesigned sleeve and instructions, switch to 7 bulbs instead of 6.

— Patent applied for.

— Hans Praag & Co. goes out of mail order business.

— Praag enters marketing agreement with Sutcliffe for U.K. market covering all Praag products.

Late 1980 — Praag approached by Van Diemen Bros. regarding partnership in Rediplant. Friendly agreement reached, but not yet formally signed.

February 1981 — Preliminary production and marketing plans for Spring 1981 season.

— Preliminary selling efforts for Rediplant by Van Diemen salesmen in Germany and U.S., negotiations for mail order with Beinum

— Jan Straten of Praag in U.K. selling to U.K. customers not covered by Sutcliffe.

COMPREHENSIVE ACCOUNTING CORPORATION

Christopher H. Lovelock
Penny Pittman Merliss

Leo G. Lauzen, chairman of the board of Comprehensive Accounting Corporation, was discussing the firm's growth potential with his son, Christopher J. Lauzen, CAC's president. Both men, having scanned numerous spread sheets, agreed that their mutual growth target was 450 franchises to be serving 28,000 clients—double the present number—by the end of 1985.

Leo, looking across his desk at Chris, relaxed and leaned back comfortably in his large leather armchair.

> "Chris, it's already January 1982; how will we obtain this dynamic growth in such a short time?" Should we be rethinking the way in which we recruit both franchisees and clients? I'm interested in the possibility of creating master franchises, covering whole geographic areas which could take on responsibility for recruiting and managing individual franchise units within those areas.

Copyright © 1984 by the President and Fellows of Harvard College, Harvard Business School case 9-585-123.

COMPANY BACKGROUND

The predecessor company of Comprehensive Accounting Corporation was founded by Leo G. Lauzen in 1949. Lauzen, one of four children of Romanian immigrants, grew up in the Chicago area and attended the University of Illinois. During one of his accounting classes, Leo Lauzen asked the instructor, "Why is it that all of the examples we discuss in class are multimillion dollar companies? What about the accounting needs of smaller companies?" The professor replied, somewhat caustically it seemed to his student, that taking care of small businesses was not the concern of the public accounting profession.

Lauzen was dissatisfied with this response, believing that the lack of proper record-keeping procedures and timely financial statements was a major reason why so many small businesses failed. During Christmas vacation, he visited over 30 small- and medium-sized businesses and found that most lacked professional accounting assistance. Here, he felt, was an untapped market waiting for an eager young accountant.

"I was four credits short of a degree, but couldn't wait to get started," Lauzen recalled some 30 years later. "So I dropped out of school and for the next nine months concentrated on developing a reasonably priced accounting service designed to fit the needs of small- and medium-sized companies, typically with 25 employees or fewer."

The service features Lauzen chose included: a profit/loss statement, showing the operating results for both month and year-to-date, with percentages in all categories to make it easily understandable to the client; a balance sheet detailing assets, liabilities, and capital; and a monthly general ledger that itemized all expenses listed in the operating statement by check number, payee, and amount. Bank reconciliation, payroll records, and income tax preparation would also be part of his services, Lauzen decided. And where necessary, he would provide clients with business consultation.

In fall 1949, Lauzen borrowed sixty dollars and founded Leo G. Lauzen & Co. He was ready to start looking for clients willing to pay his fees of $27 a month. The business grew rapidly; however, much of Lauzen's time continued to be devoted to standardization of his accounting systems, so as to facilitate their application to different clients.

By 1959, the company had 500 clients (as compared to 40 for a typical, fully developed, individual accounting practice). By 1965 it had 785 clients and employed four supervising accountants, a general manager, and a clerical staff of four. But to his dismay, Lauzen began to notice that the quality of work provided to clients was not as good as when he personally handled each account. About this time, other accountants approached Lauzen with the suggestion that he rent them his standardized accounting system, which was manifestly more efficient than their own procedures. Industry research in 1965 showed that the average bookkeeper could handle 20 clients,

with an average total billing of $1,000 monthly; the average Comprehensive bookkeeper processed 60 clients and $3,000 monthly.

For the next two years, Lauzen conducted an experiment. Half of his new clients were serviced by his existing company and the other half distributed to several accountants whom he licensed to use his accounting system. At the end of this period, Lauzen decided to divide up the business, offering his existing clients to his supervising accountants in return for payments out of their monthly receipts.

The new licensing approach worked well. Now operating as independent entrepreneurs rather than as employees, the licensees—known as Associates—worked with greater motivation. Lauzen focused his efforts on further improving his accounting systems, recruiting new Associates, and attracting new clients for them. The company adopted the trademarked name "Comprehensive" in 1967, licensing Associates to use it. In 1976, an alternate program was developed. Termed the Affiliates program, this differed in that Affiliates received marketing training, techniques, and support to help them solicit their own clients. Using the same marketing methods, Comprehensive itself continued to generate new clients for the Associates.

Further growth followed. In 1979, the company moved its headquarters to Aurora, Illinois, 50 miles west of Chicago. The 36,000 square feet of office space housed twelve senior executives, including Leo Lauzen and his son Chris, plus 250 staff members, and the firm's computer facility. By early 1982, Comprehensive had a net worth of more than $5 million.

FRANCHISING IN THE UNITED STATES

The 1960s saw an explosive growth of franchise systems in the United States. In theory at least, franchise holders received the expertise and economies derived from belonging to a large, well-known firm, yet retained much of the satisfaction and incentives of working as independent entrepreneurs. The franchisor, meanwhile, obtained a source of highly motivated personnel and new capital.

Traditional types of franchising—otherwise known as *product/trade name franchising*—consisted of distribution arrangements for physical goods in which the franchisee was identified with the manufacturer. Typical of this type of franchise, which accounted for three-quarters of total U.S. franchise sales of $333 billion in 1980, were automobile and truck dealers, gasoline service stations, and soft drink bottlers. Although sales volume was still rising in 1980, the number of establishments had declined to less than 200,000 from 221,000 in 1976.

A newer type of franchising, known as *business format franchising*, involved a fully integrated relationship between franchisor and franchisee. This included not only the product concept (a physical good or service) and trademark, but also training programs, a marketing strategy, advertising and promotional support, operating manuals and standards, quality control, certain supplies, and a two-way management information system. Sales through business format franchises totalled $79 billion in 1980—up from $47 billion in 1976. There were close to 270,000 establishments in 1980, as compared to 222,000 in 1976. Fast-food outlets accounted for more than one-fifth of both sales and establishments.

This rapid growth reflected not only creation of new establishments but also conversion of existing, independently owned businesses to a franchise format. Between 1972 and 1977, for instance, about 8,000 independent real estate firms became franchisees of a half-dozen nationwide realty chains, led by Century 21 Realty Corporation. Another trend, particularly in fast foods, was the rise of multi-unit franchises, whereby a single franchisee (sometimes called a "master franchisee") became responsible for a large number of franchise outlets in a specified geographic area.

Problems for Franchising

Despite the overall success of the franchise concept, a number of problems arose. Certain franchise corporations, such as Howard Johnson's and McDonald's, began to buy back their profitable units. Meanwhile, a number of franchise systems failed. In both instances, lack of control and lack of uniformity were cited as contributing reasons.

Franchisees encountered a variety of difficulties, ranging from inadequate training and absence of continued management and marketing support to what they perceived as excessive control and unfair treatment by franchisors. Many franchisees found themselves with trade names that had no drawing power. Some franchisees claimed that the franchisors had deceived them with unrealistic profit projections, and that the promised advantages of franchising were not always delivered. For instance, instead of being able to purchase supplies less expensively, some franchisees found themselves locked into supply contracts requiring them to pay prices for supplies that netted the franchisor a 200–600 percent profit.

Other sources of dispute included arbitrary terminations of franchise agreements, requirements for sharing advertising costs, penalties for violation of contract, inspections and evaluations by franchisors, minimum performance requirements, royalty payments, territorial limits, and restrictions on products or prices.

Litigation and legislation came to represent major problems during the seventies. Either singly or in class actions, franchisees began bringing suit against franchisors. Although not all suits were successful, the costs of legal fees, damages, and out-of-court settlements were described as "staggering." State legislation was often initiated to curb abuses, requiring full disclosure of franchise information in an unbiased form. "Fair practice" laws prohibited franchisors from terminating or failing to renew franchises without good cause, as well as regulating such practices as the selling of supplies, discrimination among franchisees with regard to royalties, and competing with franchisees in their own market areas.

Franchisors contended that they, too, had their difficulties. A significant problem was franchisees who failed to adhere to agreed standards and procedures. Faced with management control problems, many franchisors preferred a corporate takeover to continuation of franchise arrangements.

Yet franchising continued to flourish. Consultants noted that it offered entrepreneurs a safety net that was unavailable to the typical small business. Service franchise systems were particularly popular. Examples included car and truck rentals, quick service restaurants, hotels and motels, auto repair, real estate brokerages, travel agencies, tax preparation, health clubs, and unisex haircutting. Catering especially to the needs of business firms were printing and copying services, accounting, business counseling, employment services, and credit collection.

THE COMPREHENSIVE SYSTEM

By January 1982, Comprehensive Accounting Corporation was providing accounting practice development consulting and data processing services to 257 franchisees[1] across the United States. These franchisees were independent bookkeeping and accounting firms serving small- and medium-sized business clients. About 95 percent of all clients had 25 employees or fewer, and about 90 percent had total annual revenues of $1 million or less. Collectively, Comprehensive franchisees had 17,743 clients and billings of almost $28 million per year. Annual billings ranged from $15,000 for a recently formed franchise to more than $500,000 for a well-established one. Operating expenses in the average

practice typically amounted to 60–65 percent of revenues.[2]

The system called for clients to fill out special, copyrighted forms each week and send these to their local Comprehensive franchise holder. After checking the figures, and compiling input for the financial statements, the accountant then sent the data to Aurora for processing. Smaller franchisees (typically those with less than 50 clients) mailed their forms; larger ones entered the data into a terminal and transmitted it over phone lines to the Comprehensive computer.

Monthly reports were generated by the computer overnight, and the resulting financial statement was returned to the franchisee for double-checking and distribution to the client. Each Comprehensive accountant was also expected to contact all clients at least once monthly by telephone to assist them in interpreting financial data and to maintain the relationship. In 1981, the average client paid $105 per month plus an additional $315 for preparation of year-end statements and tax forms.

Corporate Services

The corporation appealed to graduate accountants who wanted to run their own businesses and to concentrate on the bookkeeping, accounting, and tax record needs of small- and medium-sized businesses. "Own your own or expand your own Bookkeeping, Accounting, and Tax Service" read the cover of one of Comprehensive's promotional brochures.

By 1980, some 50,000 new accounting graduates were coming on the market each year in the United States, and demand for their services was high. Many joined one of the 700-plus certified public accounting firms, subsequently obtaining certification as CPAs; others went to work in the accounting and financial departments of busi-

---

[1] For simplicity, both Associates and Affiliates will henceforth be described as franchisees.

[2] To these had to be added interest expenses, noncash adjustments, and note payments due.

ness, government, and nonprofit organizations. In time, some attempted to set up their own independent accounting, tax advisory, and bookkeeping practices.[3] There were believed to be more than 130,000 such practices in the U.S.

Comprehensive looked for individuals who were ambitious and hardworking, but not too independently minded. Said Leo Lauzen, himself a self-described "maverick":

> If our organization were made up of true entrepreneurs, we'd be in a hell of a mess! They are not mavericks, because the success of a franchise operation is dependent on the franchisees being held together as a team following a common system. These individuals need to have enough courage to step out on their own, but not completely out on their own; because in a franchise system you're never really alone. Going it alone—together: that's our slogan. What we want is a group of people who will simply take the book, follow it, and work like hell.

The benefits that Comprehensive offered its franchisees included training in the use of its simplified, copyrighted forms and production procedures; data processing; and continuing education seminars. Chris Lauzen considered Comprehensive's marketing assistance its most valuable service to franchisees. "Either we get the clients for them," he commented, "or we show them how to get the clients. Either way, we help build their practice and enhance its value for eventual sale." Franchisees also benefited from use of the Comprehensive corporate name, which was promoted through national advertising, mailings to prospective clients, and various public relations activities.

Comprehensive believed that it had achieved the fastest possible way of performing each account-handling function, while allowing its franchisees to employ less technically skilled

[3] The difference between a certified public accounting firm and an accounting/bookkeeping practice was that only the former was entitled to conduct audits and express an opinion on an organization's financial condition.

bookkeepers than would be needed for a manual system. Research and development efforts sought constantly to improve the system's performance. Noted the chairman:

> Say we have 20,000 clients, and the average client's work is processed by one of our franchises in two and one half hours. If we can cut one minute off the processing of that account, we've cut 20,000 minutes—333 hours—off the production time for all accounts in the system. Multiply that times the average billing rate of our bookkeepers of $30 per hour, and you've got $10,000 clear profit, every single month ad infinitum, to be shared between us and our franchisees.

Additional research focused on increasing the use of minicomputers in financial record-keeping, for both small businesses and their accountants.

Comprehensive management believed that there might be opportunities for the larger franchisees to use minicomputers for processing clients' records and was developing experimental software for this purpose. However, they were concerned that franchisees should not be distracted from the more profitable uses of their time, namely franchise growth and personal attention to existing clients. The growing introduction of microcomputers—also known as personal computers—was not considered significant for Comprehensive, since these machines lacked the power and capacity to process the volume of data flowing into franchisees' offices each month. While it would certainly be possible for clients to process their own records on a personal computer, the corporation targeted its services toward small businesses that actively sought delegation of bookkeeping and tax records to an outside expert; in fact, many Comprehensive clients had microcomputers for functions like billing and payroll checkwriting.

Through a group of practice development specialists at the Aurora headquarters, the corporation sought to help its franchisees manage the growth of their practices in a carefully planned fashion. Thus, when a practice reached 20 clients, the franchisee would be encouraged to hire a bookkeeper; at the 50-client level, use of direct entry data terminals was recommended in place of the mails to transmit client data to Aurora for data processing. Because the corporation knew exactly what volume of business any individual franchise had, it was able to compare this with the averages for practices of a similar age in comparable locations. Special assistance could then be offered to help franchisees who appeared to be floundering.

Chris Lauzen emphasized the importance of compliance with each operating procedure:

> The inside operation of each franchised office is like a gear box. As every franchisee completes his training, he always emphasizes to me his commitment to "following the system." But in three to six months, we find out that what he really meant to say was that he will follow those procedures that he agrees with, and those he does not agree with, he will change. Every time a franchisee changes part of the system, he diminishes his potential for enjoying the same success that others before him have enjoyed. In effect, the franchisee takes out one of the gears in the box, throwing off the total mechanism.
>
> However, we have to recognize the human need for creativity, especially in our entrepreneurs. A point I make in our training programs is that there is a place for creativity in operating an office under a franchise umbrella. Initially, in the first three years, while you're still learning the program, it's in the way that you provide your person-to-person attention to a client. Eventually, if a franchisee proves through performance that he understands the program, he is welcome to serve on our Forms and Procedures committee, which updates the system regularly.

Competition

Among Comprehensive's competitors were other franchised bookkeeping firms. The largest of these, General Bookkeeping Services (GBS), had about 1,000 franchises nationwide. According to Chris Lauzen, small businesses most frequently demanded personal attention and good tax work from their accountants, and he believed that GBS successfully tailored its services to these needs through emphasis on monthly on-site consulting. GBS fees were approximately 30 percent lower than Comprehensive's. On the other hand, the providers of GBS services were rarely degreed accountants, and GBS required its clients to do much of their own bookkeeping, using a relatively unsophisticated single-entry system.

A second form of competition was independent accounting and bookkeeping practices. Leo Lauzen noted that, on average, such practices usually peaked at about 40 accounts and were less profitable to the owner at that level than a Comprehensive franchise—which might easily grow to five times the size, or more. Their fees averaged 10–15 percent less than Comprehensive's.

Computer service bureaus, which generated financial statements from data supplied by the client, were not regarded as direct competition. The younger Lauzen explained:

> Small businesses need personal attention, tax advice, and interpretation of results. The service bureaus don't offer these. They're really designed for firms that are larger than most of our clients. But we do survey their prices once a year and try to set our data processing fees roughly in the middle of their range.

On the other hand, Chris Lauzen saw a potential threat coming from a different direction. Noting that professional restrictions against advertising by certified public accountants had recently been eased, he wondered if CPA firms might represent future competition for Comprehensive:

> A lot of what the CPA does—about 60–70 percent—is write-up work, not the audit function. And advertising of write-up work has never been restricted. As CPAs begin to recognize that 70 percent of their business is something they can compete on, it's going to heat up the marketplace. Some of the CPA firms have already developed divisions to

serve small business. At the moment, however, they charge about 50 percent more than we do—and they lack entrepreneurs within their organization.

Corporate Organization

The Comprehensive organization was split into two broad segments, one reporting to the chairman of the board, the other to the president (Exhibit 1). Leo Lauzen oversaw research and development, Affiliate franchise counselling, and advertising. The latter category included public relations and solicitation of leads for new franchises and new clients for the Associate program by direct mail and telephone.

As president, Chris Lauzen had responsibility for data processing, practice development, personnel, field sales, legal services, and accounting and finance. Field sales generated new clients for franchisees who held Associateships. Practice development helped both Associates and Affiliates to manage their business, with special emphasis on developing marketing skills.

A certified public accountant, the younger Lauzen had graduated from Duke University, where he majored in accounting and management science. After working for two years as supervisor in a franchised Comprehensive office, he had enrolled at the Harvard Business School. On obtaining his MBA in 1978, he joined a large industrial company as assistant to the president. But his career there was cut short in 1979 when his father suffered a severe heart attack. The elder Lauzen recovered but asked Chris to join Comprehensive as executive vice president. His son became president after the previous incumbent retired in the fall of 1980.

ATTRACTING NEW FRANCHISEES

Comprehensive's traditional approach to recruiting new franchisees had been to place advertisements in the business opportunities sections of newspapers and magazines (Exhibit 2). Re-

cently the corporation had also begun a direct mail/telephone solicitation program. A tracking system, involving the use of coded names, facilitated evaluation of different media. Recent experience had shown that each lead received cost between $30 and $100, depending on the form of solicitation employed. However, some leads were of better quality (that is, more likely to result in a sale) than others.

The Recruitment Process

Ted Malone, one of ten franchise counselors, had previously been in fast-foods franchising. While he saw many similarities between franchised accounting services and franchised quick service restaurants, he emphasized that the evaluation procedures at Comprehensive were far more rigorous: "In fast foods, if they can walk money-wise, they're in!" he remarked. By contrast, a candidate for one of Comprehensive's franchise programs had to be a graduate accountant.[4] In qualifying "leads," franchise counselors looked for a strong desire to succeed and a pattern of job stability as well as a high energy level and willingness to work long hours.

Malone stated that out of every 200 inquiries received, about 40 were immediately screened out by an assistant; information packages were then sent by mail to the remainder. Prospective franchisees were initially interviewed over the phone by franchise counselors and a small percentage invited to come to Aurora for further discussions. On average, only about 20 of the recipients returned preliminary applications, of which 14 were rejected on such grounds as insufficient education, low net worth, and (based upon an evaluation by an industrial psychologist) psychological factors such as an insufficient level of drive or stability.

The remaining six applicants were subsequently invited to an initial round of interviews

[4] That is, to hold a bachelor's degree with a major in accounting. About one-third of current franchisees were also CPAs.

EXHIBIT 1
COMPREHENSIVE ACCOUNTING CORPORATION: ORGANIZATION CHART

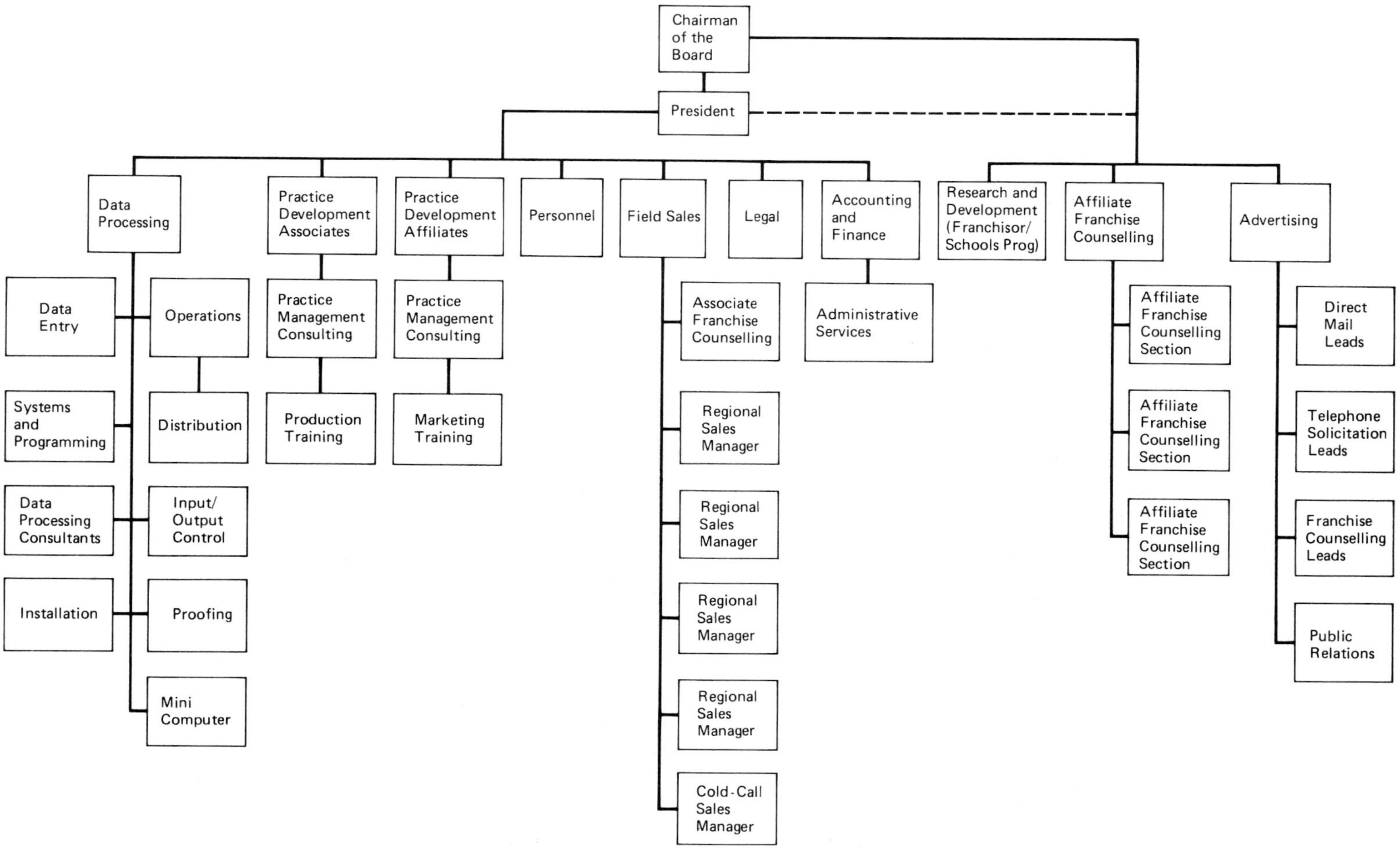

EXHIBIT 2

EXAMPLES OF ADVERTISING USED TO RECRUIT NEW COMPREHENSIVE FRANCHISEES

"Three years ago, I got fed up with slaving for a salary. Now I'm a Comprehensive® accountant, and I've more than <u>tripled</u> my income!"

—Joe Donahue, Denver, Colorado

I'm an accountant. And I'd like to tell you about the opportunities I found with COMPREHENSIVE®.

I always thought my career choices as an accountant were limited to heading for one of the "Big 8" firms, getting lost in a corporation, or going it alone. I'd always wanted to own my own practice, but working for someone else meant I didn't have that core group of clients to get me started.

Then I read about COMPREHENSIVE'S nationwide network of independent local accountants. Local to let me keep in touch with myself and my market, and national to provide all the back-up and support I'd never have if I were strictly on my own.

You might say COMPREHENSIVE helps you be in business for yourself without being in business by yourself.

What is COMPREHENSIVE?

COMPREHENSIVE is the nation's largest franchisor of bookkeeping, accounting and tax services, with more than 19,000 small business clients of all kinds handled every month with a system developed through 30 years of successful experience.

Nearly 200 independent accountants utilize COMPREHENSIVE'S centralized computer system to provide monthly services to their clients. Fast. And with a lot fewer headaches.

With COMPREHENSIVE, I'm backed by a team skilled in accounting systems, practice management, sales and marketing, taxes and more. Plus a national advertising program to attract and pre-sell new clients.

How many clients?

By now, you've probably found the average COMPREHENSIVE accountant has about 90 clients. That's right — 90 clients! And each one receives close, prompt and personalized monthly contact and service.

Many accountants in the system have even more. In fact, my own personal client list now tops 140!

How do I do it? With our exclusive system, it's really not too difficult. And here's what I give *each and every client* every month:

- Operating statement for both the current month and year-to-date, with percentages for both
- Complete bank reconciliations
- All tax returns
- Itemized employee payroll records
- Detailed supporting ledgers by account for each item on the operating statement
- Balance sheets as necessary

What about money?

Before I became a COMPREHENSIVE accountant, my salary was $20,000. That was three years ago, when I was 31. So you know I'm not a remarkable genius.

I'm not one of those Harvard B-School types either. My degree is from Mankato State College in Minnesota. And believe me, there were times I thought I'd never get through. I finally did, though, in 1967, and went to work as an internal auditor with Control Data.

Almost ten years and two jobs later, I'd had it. I was tired of slaving for a salary and going nowhere. The time had come to

Joe Donahue, a COMPREHENSIVE affiliate in Denver, Colorado

make a major decision — both about my career and my life.

What happened?

I quit. And moved my family to Colorado, where I hardly knew a soul.

Most importantly, though, I became a COMPREHENSIVE affiliate and invested in my future.

COMPREHENSIVE trained me to use complete systems, from marketing and sales through production. The system is so sound, it's almost incredible!

All the tools are there. You don't have to be an inventor. And I certainly don't consider myself a super salesman. I'm still nervous whenever I make a new presentation.

Back to money

In my first year, I attained 59 monthly small business clients and was billing at an annualized rate of over $5,500* a month.

By July of 1979, my client list was up to 142 accounts, with annualized billings averaging $17,800* a month.

That means an annualized gross of over $213,000* after only three years!

Cash is important, and it has to be there. But real success is a lot more.

I'm my own boss. I work for myself and own my own practice. I'm building equity for the future. And I have employees who depend on me.

Best of all, I'm committed. And I've proven a lot of things to myself that I always dreamed about.

Legalese

Can you do as well as I did? There are no guarantees. There are certain statements, though, required by the FTC and state regulatory agencies. So here they are:

*These sales, profits or earnings are of a specific franchise and should not be considered as the actual or potential sales, profits or earnings that will be realized by any other franchise. The franchisor does not represent that any franchisee can expect to attain these sales, profits or earnings. There are currently 190 accountants in the franchisor's Associate and Affiliate Programs. Mr. Donahue is in the Affiliate Program, which began in 1976. Of all Affiliates in the program who had completed at least one full calendar year in practice as of January 1, 1979, six of 34 individuals (or 18 percent) achieved annualized billings in excess of $5,500 per month during their first calendar year in practice. Of the six Affiliates in practice for at least three years as of July, 1979, gross annualized billings ranged from a low of $65,969 to a high of Mr. Donahue's $213,543 with a median of $107,497. Of these, only one individual attained billings of less than $100,000.

Now what?

Obviously, you're not going to rush out and invest in becoming a COMPREHENSIVE accountant just on my say so.

So get the facts. Ask for complete information on earnings and profits of *all* current COMPREHENSIVE accountants, including me, Joe Donahue. There's no obligation — and it could be the most important move you'll ever make!

Call M. K. Savage Toll free (800) 323-9000
Anywhere in the Continental U.S. In Illinois, call collect (312) 898-6868

I'd like to know more about my opportunities as a COMPREHENSIVE accountant!

Name _____

Address _____

City _____ State _____ Zip _____

Phone _____ (Best time to call) _____

Mail to: Comprehensive Accounting Corporation
2111 Comprehensive Drive, Aurora, Illinois 60507

COMPREHENSIVE®
accounting corporation
Official Tabulators for the National Easter Seal Telethon

As published in *The Wall Street Journal* and the *Journal of Accountancy*.

EXHIBIT 2 (continued)

Accountants: Start your own practice!

We'll send you The Book on how and why. *Free!*

Programmed for Success is the name—and it has all the facts, figures and background data compiled by COMPREHENSIVE,® the nation's largest franchisor of monthly bookkeeping, accounting and tax services for small and medium-sized businesses of all kinds. If you want to work for yourself, be your own boss, and have the security of being backed by experienced professionals, contact COMPREHENSIVE today.

Programmed for Success

COMPREHENSIVE®

Call S. A. Kucera
Toll free (800) 323-9000
Anywhere in the Continental U.S.
In Illinois, call collect (312) 898-6868

Please send *Programmed for Success*, including complete data on earnings and profits of all current COMPREHENSIVE accountants.

Name _____
Address _____
City _____ State _____ Zip _____
Phone _____
(area code)   (number)   (best time to call)

COMPREHENSIVE®
accounting corporation
2111 Comprehensive Drive, Aurora, Illinois 60507
Official Tabulators for the National Easter Seal Telethon

Shaffer/MacGill & Associates, Inc.

Client: Comprehensive Accounting Corp.
Ad No: CAC-15-80
Title: "Start Your Own"
Size: 150 Lines (2 col x 75)
Publication: Wall Street Journal/Mart

ACCOUNTANTS:
WORK FOR YOURSELF

Start or expand your own bookkeeping, accounting and tax service practice. Our advertising and marketing system helps you get clients. Our proven COMPREHENSIVE® accounting system helps you profitably service those small and medium-sized businesses.

THE SYSTEM

A marketing and accounting system which has been developed through 30 years of experience . . . allowing COMPREHENSIVE accountants to service more than 19,000 monthly business clients.

COMPUTERIZED SUPPORT

Our large scale computer quickly and efficiently provides your clients with complete financial data — every month.

Learn more about how you could start or expand your own practice. Ask for V. A. Cox . . .

Call toll free (800) 323-9000
Anywhere in the Continental U.S.
In Illinois, call collect (312) 898-6868

I'd like to know more about my opportunities as a COMPREHENSIVE accountant!

Name _____
Address _____
City _____ State _____ Zip _____
Phone _____
(area code)   (best time to call)

COMPREHENSIVE®
accounting corporation
2111 Comprehensive Drive, Aurora, Illinois 60507
Official Tabulators for the National Easter Seal Telethon

Shaffer/MacGill & Associates, Inc.

Client: Comprehensive Accounting Corp.
Ad No.: CAC-18-80
Title: "Work for Yourself"
Size: 140 lines (2 col x 70)
Publication: Wall Street Journal/Mart

and testing in Aurora, with the corporation picking up half of their expenses. If this went well, applicants returned for a second interview with their spouses. Leo Lauzen insisted that spouses fully understand the workload and level of commitment that Comprehensive expected of its franchisees—a workload that ran 60–80 hours per week.

Typically, said Malone, three of these six would decide to proceed no further (but no rigorous follow-up had yet been undertaken to determine the reason why). Another two candidates would be terminated by Comprehensive, reflecting corporate doubts about the ability of the candidates to perform at the required level. Thus one sale out of the initial 200 inquiries was likely to be consummated at the end of this process.

Of the ten counselors, one—Malone—worked for the Associates program and the remaining nine for the Affiliates. On average, a franchise counselor could expect to sign up one to three new franchisees per month. The average cost of recruiting, selecting, and training a new Associate or Affiliate was estimated at $18–20 thousand.

Terminations

The other side of the recruitment coin was termination of franchises. Chris Lauzen indicated that approximately 5 percent of all franchises were discontinued each year, most commonly on account of the franchisee's inability to develop and run an efficient practice. This shortcoming ultimately resulted in the franchisee's falling behind on royalty or note payments.

Some franchisees became disenchanted because they did not progress as fast as they had anticipated. "We tell them that it takes several years to build a practice, and that they'll have to work at least 60 hours a week," Chris Lauzen

EXHIBIT 3
GEOGRAPHIC LOCATION OF COMPREHENSIVE ASSOCIATES AND AFFILIATES, EARLY 1981

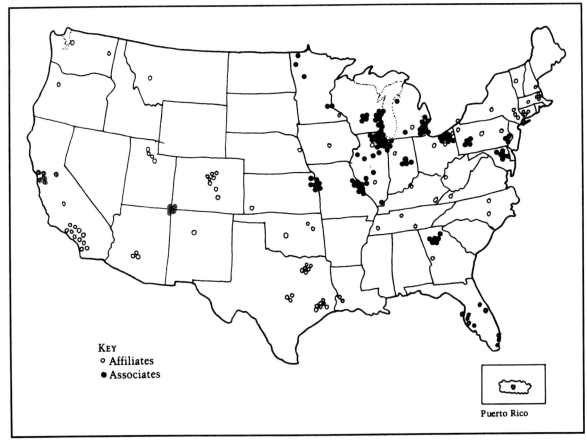

KEY
○ Affiliates
● Associates

Puerto Rico

Source: Company Records

remarked, "but I guess some of them don't take that in."

In 1981, several large franchisees had broken their contracts with Comprehensive, disputing the company's right to insist on controls over quality aspects of data processing. The corporation had recently initiated a lawsuit against these franchisees, retaining a prestigious Chicago law firm to press its case. The Lauzens were confident that Comprehensive would win the suit, thereby demonstrating the validity of the contract and discouraging any further defections. However, they were concerned with the immediate drain on the company's financial resources and management time.

THE ASSOCIATE AND AFFILIATE PROGRAMS

Comprehensive's franchises were divided into two groups, termed Associates and Affiliates.

Both offered clients the same bookkeeping, accounting, and tax record services, and employed the same system for generating reports. The primary difference between the two lay in how their clients were solicited. Affiliate franchises might be located anywhere in the United States and Puerto Rico. Associate franchises, however, were available only in Atlanta, Baltimore, Chicago, Cleveland, Detroit, Minneapolis/St. Paul, Philadelphia, Pittsburgh, and St. Louis. This restriction reflected the need for Comprehensive's field sales personnel to focus their client solicitation efforts on a limited number of geographic areas.

By January 1982, there were 103 Associates and 154 Affiliates. Exhibit 3 shows the locations of these two groups of franchises on a map of the United States. Exhibit 4 shows the growth in the number of clients, franchises, average gross receipts, and net cash flow from 1967–81. Exhibit 5 shows 1981 billings and size of client base by age of franchise.

EXHIBIT 4

COMPREHENSIVE ACCOUNTING CORPORATION: GROWTH IN FRANCHISEES, CLIENTS, RECEIPTS AND PROFITS, 1967–81 *

Year	No. of Associates	No. of Clients	Gross Receipts (000)	Net Op. Profits ($000)	No. of Affiliates	No. of Clients	Gross Receipts ($000)	Net Op. Profits ($000)
1967	4	N/A	156	72	—	—	—	—
1968	10	N/A	521	202	—	—	—	—
1969	13	N/A	1,027	320	—	—	—	—
1970	16	2,000	1,390	389	—	—	—	—
1971	21	4,638	3,363	1,009	—	—	—	—
1972	28	6,292	4,106	1,232	—	—	—	—
1973	43	8,323	5,793	1,738	—	—	—	—
1974	51	8,486	7,506	2,252	—	—	—	—
1975	57	9,150	8,757	2,627	—	—	—	—
1976	66	9,905	9,910	2,973	9	N/A	N/A	N/A
1977	73	11,105	11,964	3,589	22	1,175	1,261	252
1978	96	12,153	14,123	4,427	53	2,676	2,664	415
1979	95	12,253	16,311	4,631	68	3,699	4,761	964
1980	110	11,858	18,671	4,708	104	4,415	6,273	1,294
1981	103	11,303	17,596	4,615	154	6,440	10,306	1,735

* Year-end data excludes financial results of franchisees who may have left the program during the year. 1971–77 extrapolated from other years' data.

Source: Company Records

EXHIBIT 5

COMPREHENSIVE ACCOUNTING CORPORATION: SIZE OF BILLINGS AND CLIENT BASE AT YEAR-END 1981 BY AGE OF FRANCHISE

Year Franchise Instituted	Affiliates				Associates			
	No. of Franchises	Total Clients	Total Billing Volume ($000)	Net Op. Profits ($000)	No. of Franchises	Total Clients	Total Billing Volume ($000)	Net Op. Profits ($000)
Prior to 1976	—	—	—	—	40	5,744	9,365	2,734
1976	9	1,125	2,128	559	7	1,134	1,928	467
1977	9	801	1,476	359	6	888	1,440	378
1978	21	1,554	2,498	604	5	490	811	221
1979	15	915	1,496	361	7	693	1,046	206
1980	42	1,260	1,876	277	21	1,932	2,612	539
1981	58	785	832	(425)*	17	422	394	70

* Partial year's start-up costs.

Note: Interpret this table as follows: At the end of 1981 there were 9 Affiliate Franchises which had been formed in 1976; in total, these Affiliates had 1,125 clients and total billings of $2,128,000.

Franchise Payments

Both Associates and Affiliates were required to make an initial cash payment of $12,500 for a license to use the registered Comprehensive name and systems. The first $1,000 was paid at the time the contract was executed, and the balance at the time the franchisee began training.[5]

Affiliates were required to sign a note for $35,000—to be repaid over a 10-year period—plus a monthly royalty fee. Royalties were set at 2 percent of gross receipts (client billings) in the first year, rising to 6 percent in the second year, and thereafter. Affiliates and new Associates were also required to make payments to the National Advertising Fund on a monthly basis. These payments amounted to 1 percent of gross receipts during the first year, 2 percent during the second, and 3½ percent in the third and subsequent years.

Associates, by contrast, were charged a marketing service fee for each client provided by Comprehensive. This fee amounted to 2.42 times the client's annual billing and was payable over a 12-year period.[6] Associates subsequently paid a 6 percent royalty on the billings of each account that was more than 12 years old.

Both Affiliates and Associates paid a data processing fee averaging 11 percent of each account's monthly billings. When a Comprehensive franchised practice was sold, the corporation received 10 percent of the proceeds if the clients remained within the Comprehensive system.

Comprehensive had developed its Affiliates program in 1976 because the upfront costs of training new Associates, setting them up in business, and supporting a sales staff to provide them with clients were quite substantial, yet the revenue flow from the sale of clients to these Associates extended over 12 years. Financial incentives were built into the repayment schedule to en-

[5] The contract duration was 10 years for Affiliates and 22 years for Associates. Contracts were renewable with the agreement of both parties.

[6] Comprehensive management had found over the years that an ongoing Comprehensive franchise practice could be sold by the franchisee to another accountant for a price averaging 242 percent of total annual billings. Most accounting practices sold at between 80 percent and 120 percent of their annual billings. Comprehensive promoted this differential as evidence of the value and quality of standardization in its franchising system.

courage refinancing of notes due to the corporation with some outside lending institution. However, most Associates remained indebted to Comprehensive, continuing to add new monthly billing and debt as their practices grew through acquisition of new clients.[7] Chris Lauzen noted the importance of internal growth through referrals from existing clients and annual fee increases. "Only in this way," he pointed out, "will Associates successfully service their debt."

The Affiliates program was designed to produce less initial indebtedness by the franchisee, a progressive increase in royalty payments, and—since Affiliates were trained to solicit their own clients—smaller upfront costs to the corporation. Due to the corporation's capital constraints, as well as the fact that the Affiliates program had more potential for rapid market development, the corporate plan was to emphasize attraction of new Affiliates while maintaining current Associates markets.

Recruitment of Clients for Associates

The typical Comprehensive client was a small business with about 10 employees and annual sales of $200–500 thousand, writing 40–50 checks per month. The annual client turnover rate was approximately 10–15 percent, with clients dropping the service being replaced by referrals from the satisfied 85–90 percent. Chris Lauzen estimated that historically a third of the drops had been firms which needed more sophisticated services than the typical Comprehensive franchisee could provide, with the balance being split between clients that went out of business and those that were dissatisfied with a franchisee's services.

The deep recession of 1980–81 had resulted in an increased loss of clients due to business failures. However, with experts forecasting an

economic recovery, Lauzen expected the client retention situation to improve.

Comprehensive executives were reluctant to publicize specific details of how new clients were obtained for Associates, since they regarded this as proprietary information. They noted that the process involved generation of prospective client leads through direct mail and telephone solicitation in the geographic areas open to Associate franchises.

All leads thus obtained were carefully screened. Information on those qualifying as prospective Comprehensive clients was sent directly to one of approximately 20 field salespeople, supervised by three sales managers. A sales representative then visited the prospect and made a standard presentation. Approximately half of the presentations that resulted in sales did so on the first call; the remaining half had to be rescheduled for further follow-up.

The new client signed an agreement that detailed the accountant's and client's responsibilities to the relationship. The field salesperson then arranged for the prospect and Associate to meet. If the Associate decided to accept the client, the latter was "released" and the franchisee agreed to pay Comprehensive 2.42 times the annual billing on the account over the next 12 years. Comprehensive recommended that a new Associate start with up to 30 clients. The primary goal of providing accounts in this way was to construct a base of clientele on which the Associate could grow through fee increases, referrals, and further acquisitions from Comprehensive to a practice size in excess of 200 clients.

This process of client solicitation for Associates was time consuming and expensive. A sales representative averaged only about five new account sales per month. The company estimated that the initial fully allocated cost of obtaining a new client amounted, on average, to about $2,800; this figure did not include significant ongoing practice development support.

It was essential to Associates' success that they grow internally through fee increases and refer-

---

[7] The interest rate on notes due to Comprehensive was a floating one, equal to the prime rate plus several add-on points.

rals from existing clients. To help them, Comprehensive provided sales aids including brochures, audio-visual projectors, filmstrips, and a prospective client presentation manual. Experienced senior Associates were often willing to offer free counsel, and corporate consulting services were available by phone.

Recruitment of Clients by Affiliates

Affiliates were trained by the corporation in marketing techniques, so that they would be able to recruit their own clients wherever they decided to operate. The training program included sessions on locating prospective clients, using the phone to set up appointments, handling objections, recognizing buying signals and closing the sale, arranging callbacks and presenting post-sell items, and understanding competitive services. Following the training program, a Comprehensive marketing consultant worked in the Affiliate's geographic area for one week, helping the new entrepreneur handle actual field situations. An extensive set of marketing support materials was also provided.

Ongoing marketing support was provided through unlimited telephone consultation, included in the franchise fees. For a fee, the Affiliate could have consultants make a site visit; receive assistance in screening, testing, and selecting supplementary sales personnel as the business grew; attend sales training school in Aurora; attend national and regional marketing seminars sponsored by Comprehensive; and receive new advertising supplies and programs.

Peter Szymanski, vice president in charge of Affiliate practice development, believed that it was difficult to teach new Affiliates how to market their services. Central to Comprehensive's sales approach were "cold calls"—unannounced sales calls on prospective clients. Szymanski observed:

> Learning marketing is a traumatic experience for the typical accountant. He's most accustomed—if I remember correctly—to debits left and credits right, and red or black at the bottom of the page. Hard science. He's of an analytical nature, a detail-oriented nature, with each I and T dotted and crossed respectively in that order, because I comes before T.

In support of this contention, one Affiliate observed:

> Accountants are trained to be negative and very questioning. As part of an audit or tax staff, you're looking at past performance and trying to prove things—nitpicking. You're not trained to market, to find clients, to sell yourself. It's hard to find accountants who make good entrepreneurs.

But not all Comprehensive Affiliates resisted the idea of marketing. One successful franchisee in Texas recalled that he used to do quite a bit of cold calling before he could afford to take on a sales representative:

> I loved it! It was like a paid vacation—there's nothing better than talking to prospective clients and seeing all the different ways people make money. Of course, I'm not your typical accountant. In fact, I actually hate accounting—I'm much more of a manager now. I have an office supervisor to handle a lot of the accounting and I can get into public relations, data management, collections—that sort of thing. I can pay clerical help to push the numbers—that's one of the advantages of this system.

On the subject of cold calls, another Affiliate remarked:

> It's difficult to get up and say to yourself, I'll do it! But after half an hour, it's pretty easy. It can be fun. Much depends on who you call on. People in a high visibility shopping center, for instance, see solicitors every day and have their clerks trained to chase you away. I much prefer going to an area that might be half industry and half warehouse, with a group of small businesses that don't get visited by salespeople very often. They're glad to see you.

As their practices grew, Comprehensive encouraged its Affiliates to take on a sales representative to help in generating new clients. This freed the Affiliate to devote more time to management of the practice and maintenance of relations with existing clients. Said one Affiliate:

> I don't hire salespeople with an accounting background. I used to try to find them, but I've found it works better to hire a good salesman and give him a little training about accounting than to try to teach an accountant to sell.

But another Affiliate criticized Comprehensive's relative lack of emphasis on client referrals:

> The Comprehensive system doesn't seem to encourage client referrals. We're told to handle our clients as flapjacks—turn them over once a month—otherwise don't worry about them. We get few referrals that way, because the clients just don't get very excited about that type of service. I'd characterize their reaction to the Comprehensive accountant as kind of a low simmer; they're not disgruntled enough to quit but they're not going to send us any of their friends.
>
> We don't do any more cold calling in my office. We get much better results by "farming" our own clients. What we're talking about is simple account maintenance, which doesn't exist in the Comprehensive program. There the focus is always on new business. Here we open up channels for existing clients—give a person a chance to complain, say what's new, describe his needs for additional or changed services.

Chris Lauzen believed that this Affiliate, Ray Swensen, would eventually try to break his contract. Lauzen noted that Swensen's client turnover rate was the worst in the program, despite deceptively high volume. He attributed this turnover to Swensen's failure to follow simple standardized client financial statement formats and reporting. Swensen had deviated from Comprehensive policies in several other important respects, answering his office phone as Swensen Associates instead of giving the Comprehensive name, and billing clients for services rendered rather than charging a flat fee as stipulated. ("By using fee-for-service billing I can do more com-

plex projects for larger and better clients," Swensen contended.)

Master Franchising

Recently, Leo Lauzen had given some thought to the possibility of introducing master franchising to the Comprehensive operation. He saw an opportunity to offer more responsibility and challenge (as well as greater revenues) to some of the larger franchisees by offering them the option of managing geographic territories on behalf of the corporation.

Fast food franchisees, he noted, had long employed an area franchising concept, selling to master franchisees the right to develop an entire territory. The master franchisee paid an up-front fee, often based upon the population base of the territory, and then recruited and supervised individual franchisees within the area. Fees paid by these individual franchisees were then split between the franchisor and the master franchisee according to a pre-agreed formula that took into account the division of responsibilities between the two supervising parties.

If Comprehensive were to develop such a strategy, top management would have to decide whether to confine prospective master franchisees to virgin territories, in which CAC had no current representation, or to create territories that already contained existing franchisees. Should both Associates and Affiliates be involved in master franchising, Lauzen wondered, or only the latter? What tasks currently performed by the corporation might be assigned to master franchisees? How should royalties and other fees paid by franchisees be split between the masters and the corporation? And what pricing formula should Comprehensive establish for sale of a territory?

THE NATIONAL ADVERTISING FUND

Leo Lauzen had always believed in the importance of active marketing efforts to solicit new clients for Comprehensive. In the process, he largely ignored the accounting profession's long-standing dictum against self-advertising (subsequently relaxed), which he regarded as restraint of trade.

When the Affiliates program was set up, Lauzen decided that it would be necessary to have an umbrella advertising campaign to promote recognition of the Comprehensive name, and thus facilitate the independent client solicitation efforts of Affiliates. This led to creation of the National Advertising Fund (NAF), subsequently renamed the "National Awareness Fund," to which each Affiliate was contractually required to contribute.

The franchise contract stated that the "National Advertising Fund will be applied strictly towards national advertising campaigns (rather than local advertising campaigns) to promote the Comprehensive name and product." A group of six Affiliates was established as the National Advertising Council to advise the chairman and the company's advertising manager on how these advertising moneys should be split. Three Affiliates were elected by the franchisees and three appointed by the corporation.

For several years, the NAF had been a source of conflict between Affiliates and the corporation. NAF revenues had grown steadily, reaching approximately $300,000 in 1981. The goal of the program, as stated in a corporate brochure, was:

> . . . to create national awareness of our name and to establish a quality image for our services. Whenever a Comprehensive practice opens, the goal is for local business owners to recall and respond favorably to the Comprehensive name: "Oh, yes, Comprehensive, I've heard of them." Existing practices profit as well. . . . It serves as a solid foundation upon which Affiliates can build their own local advertising campaign.

Small-format print advertisements had appeared in such publications as the *Wall Street Journal, American Bar Association Journal, Banking, Newsweek,* and *Inc.,* as well as in the inflight magazines of several major airlines, in the publications of civic-oriented associations such as the Elks, Lions, Kiwanis, and Rotarians, and in an assortment of trade, technical and professional journals with a readership of over 4 million small-business owners. (Exhibit 6 shows a representative advertisement.)

Some Affiliates were very critical of the NAF and the way it was administered. Said one successful Affiliate:

> I've paid a total of $20,000 for national advertising in four years and I've gotten two clients from it. During that same time I've spent $1,000 on local advertising and I've also gotten two clients from that. That's a 20-1 yield advantage!

Another Affiliate, based in Texas, was satisfied with the NAF program but critical of the corporation's custom of using leads generated as one measure of advertising effectiveness:

> This gives the impression that advertising is designed only to produce leads—and not many at that. A guy's typical reaction will be: I don't want my moneys going to Oshkosh where there's nobody there to service clients!

An Affiliate in Colorado admitted that a national identity, achieved through exposure in different areas, was important for Comprehensive; but he noted that what franchisees wanted was immediate results. Most Affiliates, he said, felt that they would get business from local radio, TV, or newspaper ads but that national advertising only helped those in other locations. He also addressed the fact that Associates who had joined Comprehensive prior to mid-1979 did not contribute to NAF:

> I don't think it's quite fair. We're giving them benefits and they're not paying for them. I don't see why the corporation can't explain the benefits and make them want to contribute.

Another Colorado Affiliate saw nothing wrong with the concept of the National Advertising Fund, but criticized the way it was used:

EXHIBIT 6
AN EXAMPLE OF ADVERTISEMENT PAID FOR BY NATIONAL
ADVERTISING FUND

Tax time. Without taxing your time.

And we'll trade 16 pages of tax tips for 10 minutes to show you how!

The Comprehensive® system of monthly bookkeeping, accounting and tax services is for small businesses only. To give you the data you need, when you need it. In a usable, easy-to-understand format every month.

Our national network of independent local accountants is backed by a team skilled in financial services, taxes, compensation planning, investments and insurance programs — resources available exclusively to Comprehensive clients.

High speed computers provide operating statements for the current month and year-to-date (with percentages for

both), bank reconciliations, all tax returns (including your own!), payroll records and balance sheets.

To show you how our system works, we'll trade a 16-page booklet of tax tips on the most frequent areas in which business owners overpay taxes or incur penalties for just ten minutes of your time.

And — the cost is surprisingly low. Probably no more than you're paying now. For information on the Comprehensive system . . .

 Call S. E. Ramseth
Toll free (800) 323-9000
In Illinois call collect (312) 898-6868

Please send free information on the Comprehensive system and the name of my local Comprehensive accountant.

Name _____ Title _____

Company _____ Bus. Phone ( ) _____

Address _____

City _____ State _____ Zip _____

COMPREHENSIVE®
business services
2111 Comprehensive Drive, Aurora, Illinois 60507
A Nationwide Network of Independent Local Accountants
Specializing in Small Businesses

SHAFFER/MACGILL & ASSOCIATES, INC.
410 NORTH MICHIGAN, CHICAGO 60611/PHONE 467 0920

Client:	Comprehensive Business Services
Number:	CAC-13-80
Size:	½ page island (4½ × 7½)
Publication(s):	Magazines

I want to see some of those funds used to develop local ads. Right now, any local ads have to be developed individually by Affiliates. We don't know how they tie into a national campaign; we don't even know if they meet legal requirements. I also think that the corporation emphasizes the wrong benefits. The aim shouldn't be to get leads directly. It should be to develop a national image that will enhance the value of a Comprehensive practice when it's sold and make it easier for a franchisee to get loans for expansion.

Leo Lauzen, who often drew analogies to McDonald's and liked to refer to national advertising as "Comprehensive's golden arches," retorted that the corporation had taken several actions to help franchisees undertake local advertising. These included the development of advertisements for the *Yellow Pages* and commercials for use on local radio and TV. Comprehensive's investment in such TV commercials totalled $120,000 in 1980. "Corporate provides the initial productions and placement recommenda-tions," he said. "The franchisee buys the space and/or broadcast time."

THE FUTURE

Leo Lauzen believed that the opportunities facing Comprehensive were almost unlimited. "It's a huge field," he told his son:

> There are 14 million businesses in the United States, and 13.2 million of them are classified by the Small Business Administration as small businesses. Now their definition of a small business is 100 employees or less. Our average client has about 10 employees. So to bring it down to our average account, you're looking at a universe of probably 12 million prospective clients.

"I agree, Leo, the opportunities are tremendous," Chris Lauzen responded. "But we'll still need a specific marketing plan to help us take advantage of them. I'd sure hate to see us get derailed on our way there."

BELMONT ELECTRONICS SWITZERLAND

Jean-Pierre Jeannet

In June of 1981, Peter Moser,* the manager of Belmont Electronics (BE) Consumer Electronics Department, internally known as CED, attended a meeting at the European divisional head office in Brussels. At that meeting, the idea was presented to streamline the existing distribution set-up in Europe. The European divisional group believed that substantial savings could be achieved if shipments were to be made directly to clients in various European countries, thus eliminating much of the present two-stage system whereby products were first shipped from Spain to the sales subsidiary and then sent on to the various retail stores. The meeting ended with the decision to select several of the smaller European countries as the initial markets to phase in such a new system. Peter Moser, as the department manager with responsibility for consumer products in Switzerland, was asked to present a plan to implement this system.

Copyright © 1982 IMEDE (Institut pour l'Etude des Méthodes de Direction de l'Entreprise), Lausanne, Switzerland.

*All names and confidential facts have been disguised.

Over the past 5 years, the department's major business of electronic calculators had become extremely competitive. BE had squeezed the production function to such a high level of efficiency that major improvements in efficiency would have to come from other parts of the department. Already, production and shipment of consumer electronics products had been consolidated in Oviedo, Spain, by eliminating a plant located in Germany. This plant, located in Northern Spain, both produced calculators and acted as a central shipping point to European subsidiaries for finished products shipped from the U.S. The two other major sources of expenses reviewed were administrative overhead and physical distribution. It was this second area that was targeted for further analysis and efficiency improvements.

COMPANY HISTORY

Belmont Electronics Switzerland had been formed about ten years ago and was charged originally with responsibility for marketing BE's consumer electronics products, primarily cal-

255

culators. In the fall of 1980, computers and industrial controllers were added as independent profit centers requiring a restructuring of the Swiss subsidiary. The executive who formerly handled much of the consumer electronics department assumed the overall leadership and Peter Moser was hired to take control of CED, reporting both to his country manager, Mr. Heer, and the European Consumer Electronics Department in Brussels.

CED, the Consumer Electronics Department located at BE's Swiss office in Berne, had a staff of 12, including Peter Moser (see Exhibit 1 for an organization chart). Reporting directly to Peter Moser were the sales manager, the marketing and technical support manager, the operations man-

ager, and the manager for the service department. Three of the department's staff were nominally under the control of CED but in actuality worked up to 50 percent for other departments so that only half of their salary was allocated to CED.

Belmont Electronics' CED sold primarily handheld electronic calculators to consumers, students, businessmen, engineers, and other professionals that might have a need for computing operations. The product line ranged from simpler calculators to some of the most sophisticated models on the market and was priced at average or above average levels as compared to competitors. Calculator sales accounted for over 90 percent of CED's sales in Switzerland.

EXHIBIT 1
ORGANIZATION CHART FOR CONSUMER ELECTRONICS DEPARTMENT (CED) SWITZERLAND

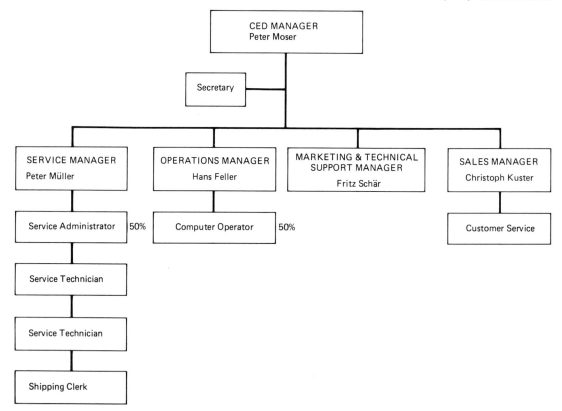

CED OPERATIONS

Under the present system, all operational matters were handled by Hans Feller, CED's operations manager. Included under operations were order entry, shipments, and inventory. Presently, each week one combined order was placed by CED with its European head office in Brussels via a company-owned electronic message system. Having received the orders from all the European subsidiaries, Brussels would ship the required quantity by relaying the orders to BE's factory in Oviedo, again by use of the electronic message system that allowed for virtually instantaneous communications among all of BE's subsidiaries and plants. In shortage situations, the European head office would allocate shipments according to its own established marketing priorities. A notification was sent to each subsidiary about the products to be shipped, and the operations manager compared the confirmation with the original allocation assigned by the European head office. Originally sent by air, the shipments were now transported by truck from Oviedo to Switzerland, which took anywhere from 7 to 12 days. The trucks reached Switzerland at Geneva, its western-most port of entry, where often some delays occurred due to customs procedures. All customs procedures were handled by a forwarding and customs agent, Poseidon AG, which had the shipment forwarded to its own offices near the Geneva airport. (This system was chosen since earlier shipments had come in directly by air to Geneva airport.) At Poseidon's offices, all merchandise received was checked, verified, placed in inventory, and a telex was sent to CED which entered the shipment as inventory on its own in-house computer.

Poseidon AG acted not only as agent but also kept and maintained the inventory for CED. An item by item control on merchandise received was necessary since truck shipments occasionally were reloaded onto a second or third truck, potentially damaging the packaging of the calculators. Sometimes, cartons arrived opened with some calculators missing. It was difficult to determine where the calculators were actually lost.

Shipments to clients were also handled by Poseidon, who received its orders from BE by telex. Poseidon dispatched packages by mail or truck, depending on costs, or made them ready for the larger accounts which typically picked up their orders at Poseidon's warehouse. Poseidon only shipped orders upon written instructions from CED's operations manager, Hans Feller.

For 1980, the total cost of the services performed by Poseidon amounted to about Sfr. 315,000 (see Exhibit 2 for details). About two thirds of these costs were connected with customs duties into Switzerland. Since Swiss duties were determined on a weight basis, special charges arose due to the weighing of each shipment. The other expenses were incurred in connection with the handling of shipments at the

EXHIBIT 2

DISTRIBUTION COSTS FOR POSEIDON A.G. IN 1980
(In Swiss Francs)

Customs Duties	
Air Freight and Customs Clearance	4,370.91
Airport Taxes and Arrival Charges	2,709.24
Tax for Customs Clearance	10,196.95
Customs Duties and Weighing Expenses	205,139.63
Total Customs Duties	222,416.73
Handling Charges	
Transport Airport to Warehouse	7,076.45
Take-out and Take-in at Warehouse	18,783.86
Inspection of Incoming Merchandise	8,550.94
Packing Time and Material for Shipments	57,079.13
Local Transport to Post Office/Railway Station	2,514.66
Postage/Freight to Customer	45,698.16
Other Expenses (Telephone, Telex, etc.)	1,427.71
Subtotal Handling	141,130.91
Minus Postage/Freight Charged to Customers	46,760.14
Total Handling Charges	94,370.77
Overall Distribution Costs	316,787.50

Note: With the switch to truck transport only in 1980, no airport related chrages are expected in the future. All transportation costs are borne by the supplying factory c.i.f. warehouse Poseidon.
One Swiss franc (Sfr. 1.00) = U.S. 0.55.

Poseidon warehouse. Poseidon billed hourly rates and charged BE for all materials used. These rates were renegotiated once each year between the two firms and remained in force for 12 months.

A special situation was freight charges for shipments to retailers. The clients were charged flat fees according to the following schedule:

Order value (Sfr.)	Freight charge (Sfr.)
0–1000	8.00
1,000–2,000	12.00
2,000–3,000	16.00
3,000 +	0.00

Consequently, the actual expenses incurred were offset by charges for the smaller shipments. Since larger customers frequently sent their own trucks to Poseidon to pick up merchandise, they caused no cost to BE.

Pricing and Billing

All merchandise was billed 32 percent off list price. Larger customers could earn a volume bonus of 1 to 3 percent, and an additional 2 percent if paid within 10 days. Consequently, BE's top customers worked on a gross margin of about 37 percent, whereas most smaller accounts achieved a gross margin of only 32 percent. Despite these margin differences, retail prices tended to be set by the large discounters which worked on gross margins of about 20 percent. Consequently, small retailers rarely got the full margin and sold BE calculators at margins below those earned for the majority of their other product lines.

Marketing and Sales Organization

The selling activity was primarily in the hands of Mr. Kuster who visited clients, the larger ones typically once a month and the smaller accounts less frequently. Mr. Kuster as sales manager was assisted by a customer service clerk assigned half-time to CED. As his territory, Kuster was responsible for the German speaking area of Switzerland. The French speaking part was serviced by his assistant. For important visits, they were often joined by the CED manager, Peter Moser.

Sales did not take place as a result of personal visits only, however. In addition to direct calls, some customers called in their orders by telephone to BE's Berne office. From there, shipments were arranged through Poseidon, the forwarding agent. The Consumer Electronics Department also used telephone selling extensively towards the end of each month to ensure that monthly sales quotas imposed by the European head office were met. During such calls, considerable sales pressure was used and net sales to mostly smaller to medium sized customers of anywhere between Sfr. 50,000 to Sfr. 100,000 resulted. A typical approach was to use the ever-existing danger of short supply to get orders now rather than later when merchandise might be hard to get. In case of shortages, CED in Switzerland would allocate merchandise to each customer according to the allocation received by the European head office. BE enforced a rigid policy of minimum order quantity of at least 6 calculators and/or the necessary attachments of Sfr. 200. However, the customer was free to select any configuration of products as long as the minimum amount was met.

Marketing and technical support was handled by Mr. Schär, a trained engineer who had considerable experience in the marketing of consumer electronics. His major responsibility consisted of the creation and organization of advertising and special promotions. However, there was some doubt as to whether this position was really needed given Peter Moser's experience in this area, and it was considered likely that Mr. Schär would eventually be moved out of CED to be reassigned to some of the growing industrial departments of BE Switzerland.

Retail Accounts

BE's Consumer Electronics Department had net sales of about Sfr. 12.8 million for the current fiscal year. Sales were primarily to department stores, discounters, and stationery stores. The top 7 customers accounted for 58 percent of sales, with the next medium group of 45 accounts accounting for about 27 percent. Another group of about 544 small accounts absorbed only 15 percent of sales.

The top seven accounts included two radio and television discount chains, two department store chains, and a smaller chain store, all accounting for some 227 outlets. With the exception of one department store chain, INTERSUISSE, all other chains received only one shipment per month made to one or two points only. Exceptions in one way or another were three of the top seven accounts.

The first exception, INTERSUISSE, was a large department store chain with some 70 outlets, all of which carried BE's products. The stores operated under names that differed by region. INTERSUISSE absorbed about Sfr. 520,000 annually, of which only 40 percent was shipped to the central distribution point. The chain's individual stores had the right to order at regular prices directly from BE, resulting in net sales of about Sfr. 312,000 over and above the shipments to the central distribution warehouse. In total, about 70 shipments were made monthly, one to each outlet.

The second special case was OFFICETECH, a supplier of office products to large companies in Switzerland. This firm had excellent contacts to industry and sold calculators primarily to industrial users. The company achieved sales of about Sfr. 520,000 and required about four shipments per month to its warehouse. OFFICETECH was the only top customer not registered as a whole-

saler or "grossist," thus requiring the addition of Swiss WUST (Warenumsatzsteuer) to its billing amount.[1] This allowed OFFICETECH not to have to settle its accounts with the Swiss WUST authorities and thus simplified its record keeping procedures.

The third and final exception was EDUDISC, a one-man company that specialized in selling large quantities to organizations, particularly schools, at low prices. This client, accounting for about Sfr. 500,000 in annual sales, had only a very brief credit history. Consequently, orders were paid for in advance which guaranteed prompt delivery for this new account, an important consideration for the client when BE's Swiss supplies were limited.

Medium sized customers, of which there were 45, sold BE products through 145 outlets. The majority of these were direct shipments to 113 shipping points. This group included a student organization for university students that annually bought calculators for about Sfr. 65,000.

Small clients, of which there were about 544 active ones with 601 outlets, consisted largely of small stationery stores. This group accounted for 579 shipping points. On average, about 459 shipments were made to this group per month.

COMPETITION

BE's major competitors in the electronic calculator field were Japanese and Far Eastern manufacturers, and one U.S. based company. BE's market share differed substantially by market segment. In the segment "slide rule" (scientific function) BE accounted for about 60 to 70 percent of the market. In the "desk top" segment, BE's share was negligible. In the "programmable" segment, BE had about half of the market. And, finally, in the consumer hand-held segment (four operations) BE was a minor factor with about 10 percent. Overall, BE's sales man-

---

[1] See Appendix at end of case for a description of WUST, the Swiss tax on sales.

ager, Mr. Kuster, estimated his department's share at about 40 percent of the entire electronic calculator market.

BE's major competitors were Casio with 20 percent, and Cannon and Sharp with about 15 percent each. All of these firms were Japanese, though some of their products originated from other Far Eastern countries. The U.S. company, General Instruments (GI), was particularly strong in the more sophisticated segments whereas the Japanese firms dominated the simpler 4-operations segment for consumer hand-held calculators.

With the exception of GI, BE's competitors sold through independent distributors in Switzerland. These distributors also sold other, non-competing products. BE's Asian competitors tended to compete more in the lower price segments. They imposed lower or no minimum order requirements. Casio, e.g., was believed to ship as little as one calculator if requested.

BE'S CONSUMER IMAGE

As one of the pioneers of the calculator business in Europe, BE held a dominating market share due to its prestige and brand image. Though somewhat more expensive than competitive products given the same performance capabilities, there was a strong brand preference for BE products among consumers. The majority of BE's buyers were students of all ages who went to a store and asked for BE's products. The vast majority were judged to be brand loyal. "Eighty percent would go elsewhere if they could not find our products in the store," believed the CED sales manager. In many cases, teachers or professors specified the brand to be used for a course. Frequently, it would be a BE product, further reinforcing the already strong brand loyalty among the public.

Such a preference for BE's products had a strong impact on retailers. Small retailers in particular felt sometimes forced to carry BE products. A retailer could influence the choice of an uncommitted customer. Due to strong sales to

students, BE's sales showed seasonal peaks in the spring and fall coinciding with the beginning of a new school year and semester, respectively.

The billing differed, however, for customers depending on their tax settling status with the Swiss WUST authorities. For such clients who could deposit a WUST declaration with BE, certifying that they would settle with the federal tax authorities directly, no tax had to be added. For the others, BE had to add 8.4 percent to the sales price and remit these funds to the tax authorities via its monthly settlement. It was established that only two percent of BE's volume was done with such small clients. For all others, BE did not have to include WUST in its invoice. A different rate of 5.6 percent was charged to firms purchasing products for their own use rather than for resale. Among those was OFFICETECH, which sold to industrial users and not retailers, and thus was charged 5.6 percent of the invoiced amount. This amount was also remitted by BE to the Swiss WUST authorities. All invoices were payable within 30 days, net. A discount of 2 percent was granted to accounts settling within 10 days.

THE REVISED DISTRIBUTION SYSTEM

The European head office made it clear to the various country sales organizations that they wished to ship directly to large customers in each country since their evaluation showed that the company could incur substantial savings in distribution costs. How the small customers were to be handled had yet to be discussed. Peter Moser was called upon to make a proposal as to how this system might possibly be implemented. From past experience he knew that such a presentation included a thorough review of the entire impact of such change with respect to his organization, sales, costs, and profits. He was aware that cost analyses at the European level had indicated that distribution costs was one of the areas where savings could be achieved without negatively affecting overall performance of BE.

The European head office expected that both shipping and invoicing would be handled directly by the Spanish unit for the top customers. The Swiss unit would more or less act as an agent with respect to sales promotion, credit, collection, and other services. Compensation would be agreed upon once all details were settled. It was planned to assemble all orders via the Berne office which would send them on by the company-owned electronic message system to the Spanish plant. Confirmation of shipments and/or orders to the client would flow back through the same channels.

Some questions arose with respect to customs declarations and Swiss WUST. Since it was the Spanish factory's plan to prepackage each client's shipment in Spain, an individual customs declaration had to be entered for each separate shipment when they were addressed and intended for individual addressees. The basic cost for each of these declarations was Sfr. 50.00 and was identical to the charge made by Poseidon for BE's present declarations. All of these costs were borne by BE under the present system. The Swiss CED's management felt that they could appoint a customs agent in Geneva who would handle all procedures.

A more difficult question was the Swiss WUST. During a visit to the Swiss tax authorities in Berne, the department was informed that the customs agent would have to arrange for the payment of WUST as well. For clients who had declared themselves wholesalers there was no problem since their customs declarations could be submitted with a sticker indicating that they would settle directly with the federal tax authorities. For the others who did not settle directly BE might consider two alternatives:

1 The Spanish company could declare itself a WUST wholesaler with the Swiss tax authorities provided BE's Berne office would promise to keep sufficient records for eventual settlement.

2 The customs agent at the border would pay WUST and bill each client afterwards. Consequently, the WUST liable clients would get two invoices, one from BE and another one from the customs agent covering the amount of WUST owed.

Handling of Top Customers

Based upon CED's sales statistics, there were 26 top customers who appeared to have sufficient business for the direct shipment method. They accounted for about 70 percent of the department's net sales and had accumulated 1,436 orders based upon last year's statistics. The average client had anywhere from one to 5 orders per month, with the exceptions discussed below. Based upon the judgement of both the operations manager and the sales manager, the department head, Peter Moser, concluded that although one monthly shipment would be acceptable to all of these clients, two shipments per month would be the most desirable alternative. The existing trend among mass retailers was to get suppliers to assume a larger burden of merchandising responsibilities. To some extent, this proposal went against this trend.

Problems were posed by three of BE's top clients. OFFICETECH, the supplier of industrial users, had always in the past refused to sign a WUST agreement for direct settlement with the federal tax authorities. Consequently, that client's WUST would have to be prepaid (8.4 percent) at the border with a later bill to OFFICETECH. An additional problem was posed by EDUDISC which up to now had prepaid all its orders. Arrangements had to be made to prepay into an account of the Spanish subsidiary since BE's CED would no longer have any accounts receivables in its name.

A more perplexing problem was the INTER-SUISSE department store chain. Sales could no longer be made directly to the various units. Instead, all orders would have to be centralized and sent to the chain's distribution center. The sales manager, Mr. Kuster, was particularly uneasy about the outcome of such a change with this account. Under the new system he could still call on the various INTERSUISSE units but only to urge them to order from their central distribution center. He judged that to be less effective than to write the order on the spot. Since about two-thirds of INTERSUISSE's annual volume of Sfr. 520,000 were executed directly with the branches, this proposed change might have an effect on future sales. A second impact would center around the margins. If all of INTER-SUISSE's business were to go through the single distribution center, the lower margin (37 percent instead of 32 percent) would then apply for the entire volume affecting the profit margin of the Consumer Electronics Department.

Handling of Small Accounts

The smaller accounts, of which there were about 570 with a total of 918 outlets, accounted for 30 percent of CED's net sales. A total of 6,899 shipments were made last year to these accounts which were typically billed 32 percent off list price. Both the European head office and CED Switzerland were in agreement that these accounts could not be handled profitably directly from Spain. One important reason was the requirement for individual customs declarations and its resulting cost. Another consideration was the WUST billing. The 176 small accounts accounting for 8.5 percent of sales and who had not declared themselves WUST wholesalers required extra billing for each shipment.

As a result, the European head office had asked Peter Moser to come up with alternative plans to handle the small customers. Together with his staff and the Swiss subsidiary's controller, he earmarked four alternative approaches for detailed investigation to make sure that they were actually workable. He included:

1 Poseidon as agent to handle the entire small customer business
2 Poseidon as WUST reporting wholesaler
3 BE Switzerland as handling agent
4 The appointment of an independent distributor

Alternative 1: Poseidon as handling agent.

As under the existing system, the Spanish factory would send twice a month a shipment to Poseidon together with shipments for the 20 top Swiss clients. The shipment would be packed according to the instructions of the Swiss CED. In order to make this system work, BE Spain would have to declare itself a WUST wholesaler under Swiss tax law, allowing for later settlement of the WUST tax between the Spanish subsidiary and the Swiss tax authorities.

This alternative differed from the present system in as much as the bi-monthly shipment would be simply repacked and sent on immediately after receipt, eliminating the inventory presently kept at Poseidon's warehouse. Poseidon would bill the Spanish company for its services instead of the Swiss CED. Billing of retailers could eventually be arranged directly from Spain since the Spanish plant could settle the WUST. Order processing and sales activities of the Swiss office would basically not undergo any changes. The only internal effect under this system, according to Peter Moser, was the likely elimination of the position of assistant to the operations manager who was now employed only half-time by CED. The resulting net savings would amount to approximately Sfr. 15,000 annually, including salary and fringes.

Alternative 2: Turn Poseidon into a WUST reporting wholesaler.

Similar to the first alternative, Poseidon would receive bi-monthly shipments from Spain. But Poseidon would now acquire the entire inventory outright. Sales would still be handled by CED in Berne with orders passed on to Poseidon. Poseidon, while maintaining a self-liquidating inventory, would bill the small clients directly. All costs associated with this effort would be billed to Oviedo. In order to make this alternative operational, Poseidon would have to become a WUST reporting wholesaler. At the present time, Poseidon was not a declared WUST "grossist" under the Swiss tax law.

Since the internal operations at CED would remain identical to those of the first alternative, the same cost savings were expected under the second alternative.

Alternative 3: CED as handling agent. Over the past months, CED and the entire Swiss subsidiary developed some spare capacity with respect to personnel. This was particularly the case in service where changes were instituted that eventually would eliminate one, possibly two positions. Consequently, CED could assume the position of handling shipments to the small retailer segment. Bi-monthly truck deliveries could be made to the offices of BE Switzerland where sufficient elevator and storage capacity existed to handle what would still be a self-liquidating inventory. Packaging, shipping, and invoicing could be handled by CED and billed to BE Spain. Since BE Switzerland was already a declared WUST settling wholesaler, no problems with WUST were to be expected. Billing could be handled either through Spain or Switzerland. In fact, small customers would notice few changes, if any at all.

Alternative 4: Appointment of an independent distributor. This fourth alternative was more sweeping in nature than the three previously discussed. An independent distributor could be appointed to handle all of the small customers and would essentially become the 21st shipping address for BE in Switzerland. The distributor would buy inventory on his own account and be responsible for his own receivables. At this time, Peter Moser had not had a chance to approach any company about this proposal. As a result, he was uncertain as to what kind of a margin a distributor might require. Some estimates he had received centered around 10 percent. After all, BE would continue to handle all promotional matters so that the distributor would not have to assume the entire marketing responsibility. However, Peter Moser believed that BE would not want its subsidiary to sell below the present prices paid by its top customers.

With respect to internal operations, the appointment of an independent distributor would make the position of operations manager unnecessary, yielding an annual cost savings of about Sfr. 50,000. Any orders received by CED in

Berne could be quickly telex-relayed through the firm's private electronic message system by the sales manager, or even Peter Moser himself. With only 27 accounts to handle and billing effected directly from Spain, an additional cost saving of Sfr. 15,000 could result since a part-time person working for the controller's office on CED work would no longer be needed.

Overhead Allocations

The company in Switzerland was structured around product divisions, such as CED, each with P&L responsibility. The subsidiary's overhead, which included office rent, was partially allocated by direct usage of space, personnel, work hours, and sales. While under alternatives 1, 2, and 3 few internal changes were to take place, changes would be more substantial under the 4th alternative (independent distributor). The work in the controller's office would be substantially reduced, and some space now "occupied" by CED would no longer be needed. The company controller, Heini Hemmi, found it difficult to estimate the impact on the CED's overhead allocation, but thought that about Sfr. 10,000 per month would be a good approximation of savings Peter Moser could expect once all of the internal changes had taken place.

DIVERGENT OPINIONS

As was to be expected under the circumstances, the executives involved in the preliminary deliberations were not in agreement as to what CED should propose. Alternative 1, using Poseidon for the small customers only and shipping directly to top clients, was advocated by Hans Feller, CED's operations manager. In his opinion, not even that solution was in the interest of CED. He recounted several instances where "the Spaniards messed us up." In one case, a truck dispatched by the Spanish factory arrived at the Swiss border only to find out that the necessary customs documents had been left behind. The driver decided to return to Oviedo, pick up the documents, and drive all the way back to Geneva. In another case, a truck with shipments destined for Switzerland took off for Holland. The mistake was only noticed once it arrived there. ''What are you going to do about this situation when there is no inventory left in Geneva?'' asked the operations manager.

The third alternative, calling for all handling to be performed by CED itself, was supported by the service manager. He claimed to have spare capacity once the service section was reorganized and that it would not make much sense to pay someone else to do it because CED could do it cheaper in-house. Also, he had to keep a minimum of personnel to handle the service requirements anyway as not all people could perform all jobs that required different skills and knowledge. ''But everybody could pitch in to do the shipping,'' he felt.

Christoph Kuster, the sales manager, was concerned about the impact of any of the proposed changes on sales. He had some preliminary discussion with one major client on direct shipments. ''They don't seem to mind taking over the customs situation since most of them are direct importers anyway. But they want something for it if they have to do it.''

A somewhat different view was held by BE's Swiss subsidiary manager, Peter Moser's superior. Having had several years of experience with the company he judged that they might prefer a clean and more sweeping solution. Consequently, he believed that the 4th alternative, with an independent distributor, was more along the lines of what the European head office expected. He did mention in connection with the pricing issue that, in his opinion, there were still a few percentage points that CED could squeeze out of the margins granted to small retailers. This was based upon his observation that many of them operated without substantial local competition and sold calculators at full margins. With respect

to the entire program he was convinced that whatever Peter Moser was going to present he would have to show higher profits than those achieved under the present setup.

This extensive review had taken several weeks, and Peter Moser was now only a few days away from the crucial meeting with European head office executives who were to fly in for the meeting. At that meeting, he was expected to make a presentation on how he planned to implement the direct shipping and billing for the top customers, and what alternatives he could suggest for the small ones. With respect to the top customers he felt that he had a workable solution. He was much less certain on what to propose for the smaller clients.

From prior experience with the political climate in large multinational companies he knew that it would make little sense to fight head-on against ''corporate wishes'' though in this case he was not quite sure what they were. On the other hand, he wanted to be able to present the European head office executives with an objective and detailed scenario that contained all possible implications with respect to his company's competitive posture, sales and profitability. He felt that these estimates should be realistic so that if he were asked to execute any one of them he would be close to the eventual outcome. In general, he was concerned with presenting a positive attitude toward these changes and did not want to be perceived as a barrier, or stumbling block, in his organization. Having had only 8 months' experience on the job he also viewed this as an opportunity to positively influence his career within the company, though he could not help thinking about what all of these changes meant for his own position. With these thoughts in mind he sat down and began to prepare for his presentation.

APPENDIX: The Swiss Tax on Sales (WUST)

INTRODUCTION

During World War II, a turnover or sales tax [Warenumsatzsteuer (WUST)—Impôt sur le chiffre d'affaires (ICHA)—Imposta sulla ciffra d'affari (ICA)]—was introduced for the first time in Switzerland. By 1980 it provided approximately one-eighth of total tax revenue.

This tax was levied only on deliveries of merchandise, and not on services. It was a single-step tax, that is, on the way from the producer or the importer to the ultimate consumer, only the last delivery was taxable. Export sales were exempt.

The tax was collected through manufacturers, importers, or dealers registered with the tax administration as wholesalers. Their purchases were free of tax and their sales to customers (except to other wholesalers) included tax at the appropriate rate.

For own use of merchandise purchased free of tax, wholesalers had to pay the tax themselves.

A manufacturer or trader was classified as a wholesaler if annual sales (including own use) exceeded Sfr. 35,000 and, for traders, at least one-half was for resale.

RATE OF TAX AND EXEMPTIONS

Turnover tax was levied on net proceeds at the following rates:

	Tax Rate (%)
On deliveries to retailers for resale	8.4
On deliveries to consumers for ultimate use and for own use of items purchased free of tax	5.6

The Government was considering an increase of these rates to 9.3 and 6.2 percent, respectively, as of October 1982.

Deliveries of merchandise belonging to one of the following groups were exempt from turnover tax:

1 Gas, water, electricity, and heating fuel (solid and liquid).
2 Soaps and detergents.
3 Food, non-alcoholic beverages.
4 Cattle, poultry, and fish.
5 Cereals, seeds, flowers.
6 Feedstuffs, fertilizers, plant protection sprays.
7 Pharmaceuticals.
8 Newspapers, periodicals, and books.

On importation, turnover tax was charged at 8.4 percent on the value of the merchandise c.i.f. (cost including freight) Swiss border, including customs duty, but wholesalers could normally obtain exemption from this tax by supplying appropriate guarantees.

COLLECTION AND PAYMENT

Registered wholesalers had to submit tax returns for each calendar quarter and remit the tax due within thirty days, less any tax paid on importation. Returns could be calculated on the collected sales proceeds or billings. In the latter case, discounts, rebates, and bad debts were deductible from billings of the period in which the reduction or loss was recognized in the accounts.

PROPOSED CHANGE TO VALUE-ADDED TAX

It was intended to abolish the present turnover tax and replace it by a value added tax (VAT), which is the system operated in most European countries. This proposed change, however, had been turned down twice in a referendum and was unlikely to be introduced in the near future.

MARKETING COMMUNICATION

Communication, which includes advertising and personal selling, is the most visible or audible of marketing activities, but it has little value unless used *intelligently* in conjunction with other marketing efforts. For example, there is an old marketing axiom that the fastest way to kill a poor product is to advertise that product heavily. Along the same lines, an otherwise well-researched and well-planned marketing strategy is likely to fail if people lack knowledge of the product, its price, or its availability.

Through communications, the marketer is able to inform existing or prospective customers about product, price, and distribution details; to create (where appropriate) persuasive arguments for using the service, buying the goods, or adopting the recommended social behavior; and to remind people of the product—especially at times and in locations where purchase or other desired behavior is particularly relevant or appropriate.

Much confusion surrounds the scope and purpose of marketing communication. Many managers define it narrowly as the use of paid media advertising and professional salespeople, failing to recognize the many other ways in which an organization can communicate with its customers.

Each of the elements in the marketing mix tends to communicate some message. The appearance of a physical product or of service personnel, the way in which a customer is treated, the price that is charged, the location and atmosphere of a service delivery facility all contribute to a general impression that reinforces or contradicts the impression created by the specific messages that the marketer communicates. A hotel may spend much time and money developing an advertising campaign built around the message "We care"—but a single rude or indifferent clerk can shatter that image in an instant.

THE COMMUNICATION PROCESS

Communication involves a *sender* (or *source*) transmitting a message through one or more media to a *recipient,* with the intention of eliciting some form of response. The messages sent, however, may not reach members of the target audience; either they may miss some people altogether or get lost in the general clutter or "noise" of everyday life. Even if a message reaches a specific recipient, it may not be understood as intended or may not be stored in that person's memory long enough to result in the response desired by the sender. Of course, consumers are not necessarily passive factors in this drama. Their interest whetted by need or curiosity, they may be actively seeking new information. While this curiosity increases the chance of their receiving communications on the topic of interest, it does not guarantee it.

Criteria for Effective Communication

What factors determine whether a marketing communication will be effective in stimulating an individual to behave in ways desired by the marketer?

First, a communication strategist must understand the day-to-day behavior of the target audience, so that messages can be delivered in places and at times likely to result in exposure. For mass media advertising, this requires an understanding of the media habits of the target audience—the specific newspapers and magazines that they read (and, if possible, what sections of these they read); the times at which they are likely to watch television and listen to the radio, together with the types of broadcast programs they are most likely to turn to; and the routes and transportation modes that they use for traveling to work and on shopping or recreational trips.

Second, the placement, scheduling, format, and content of the communication must be designed in such a way that it stands out among competing stimuli, thereby gaining the target audience's attention. Success in this area involves skill in copywriting, design, and production. A visual ad that looks different (or an audio ad that sounds different) from other advertisements in the selected medium is one way of achieving this goal.

Next, the message must be couched in terms that the target audience will understand. The symbols used in communication are many; they include verbal language, body language, color, shape, typography, music, and other sounds. But for communication to be effective, both communicator and audience must place similar interpretations on these symbols. Effective salespeople tailor their presentations to the characteristics of the prospect.

It is also very important that the communication imprint itself upon the recipient's mind for long enough to have the desired result. Essentially, the message must be designed to strike some responsive chord in the target audience if it is to elicit the response sought by the communicator. Good copywriting, like effective personal selling, requires an understanding of the needs, wants, concerns, and even fears of the audience.

The final condition for effective marketing communication is that the recipient of the message must be able to respond in the manner desired by the communicator. Many of those who see or hear a message and take note of it are not, of course, prospective customers of the marketing organization. But if a prospective customer is motivated by an advertisement or person-to-person communication, then all the necessary follow-up mechanisms should be in place. For instance, if a phone number is listed as a source of further information, then the line should be staffed or connected to a recorded message. Likewise, the times and locations of service delivery should be easily obtainable (and adhered to in practice), and goods advertised should be in stock at the time the advertising is run or the personal selling effort is made. These may sound like common-sense suggestions (and they are), but it is surprising how often there is a lack of coordination between those who plan and schedule the communication effort and those who are responsible for product execution.

THE COMMUNICATION MIX

The term "communication mix" is sometimes used to describe the array of communication tools and channels available to marketers. Just as marketers need to combine the elements of the marketing mix (including communication) to produce a marketing program, they also need to select the most appropriate ingredients for the constituent communication program.

The elements of the communication mix fall into four broad categories: (1) personal selling, (2) media advertising, (3) public relations/publicity, and (4) promotional or informational activities at the point of sale (or location where the behavior desired by the marketer is expected to take place).

Personal selling involves representatives of the marketer engaging directly in two-way communications with customers, either in person or via electronic media. The latter three elements are all one-way communications—from the marketer to the customers. Advertising messages are designed by the marketer (or an intermediary in the distribution channel) and transmitted through the chosen media in a predesigned format and at a preselected time. PR/publicity, by contrast, involves the creation of information by the marketer for dissemination to the mass media, whose editors then decide whether or not to use it and, if so, how and when to run it. Point-of-sale promotion and information refers to signing, displays, and other forms of nonpersonal communication intended to attract customers' attention and motivate them to act. This element, often coupled with discounted prices or even free use of a service, may be designed to promote immediate action as opposed simply to stimulating awareness and interest.

Personal Communication

Communication between individuals has a powerful advantage over mass-media communication in that the message usually goes directly from sender to recipient. A second major advantage is that personal communications are usually reciprocal, with the recipient being able to ask the sender (salesperson, retail clerk, or telephone operator) for clarification or additional information. A sender can adapt the content and presentation of the message to the characteristics of the recipient, and to that individual's needs and concerns as revealed during the interaction. In fact, communications may be initiated by a prospective customer who has learned about a product from friends, advertising, or other sources and wishes to obtain specific additional information.

Different communication channels may be relatively more effective in moving consumers from one stage of the purchase decision process to another. At the outset of the process, the use of mass media is likely to be the most cost-effective channel for stimulating awareness and providing background knowledge. As consumers move towards evaluation and purchase, however, they may actively seek out two-way personal communications that will enable them to ask specific questions that will help them make their final decisions.

Several types of personal communication are relevant in the development of a communication strategy. They include proactive selling, reactive selling, customer service, and personal advice.

Proactive selling involves the use of trained salespeople or change agents who actively seek out prospective customers or clients and attempt to encourage them to buy something (or adopt the behavior pattern advocated by their organization).

Reactive selling, by contrast, is typified by situations in which the customer seeks out the salesperson, rather than vice versa. Examples might include a retail store clerk or a travel agent. Successful selling usually entails responsibility for closing sales (or for seeing that a specified behavior is adopted). This may involve an element of persuasion—of marshaling the arguments for a particular course of action advocated by the seller.

Not all communications between the customer and representatives of the marketer necessarily involve persuasion or advocacy, however. A related activity, formalized in many service organizations, is the *customer service* function. This is usually concerned simply with giving out information on request (in person, by phone, or by personalized correspondence), responding to routine inquiries, and handling complaints or problems. A well-managed customer service function can lead to increased sales and greater customer satisfaction.

Another type of personal communication is *personal advice* from individuals who are not directly involved in making a "sale," but who are in a position to influence the customer's behavior. These individuals may be family members, friends, other customers, or people whose job it is to offer objective advice—such as guidance counselors or health workers. Word-of-mouth recommendations are often a powerful factor in determining a consumer's behavior, but these communications are not under the direct control of the marketer.

Impersonal Communication

Although personal communication provides a powerful channel for messages, it is also costly and time-consuming. Much information can be delivered far more cheaply through impersonal sources, particularly when the objective is to generate initial awareness.

Impersonal channels normally allow only for one-way communication between marketer and consumer. (In the future, however, we can expect to see more interactive information systems, such as videotext.) The principal impersonal communication channels available to marketers can be divided into three groups—broadcast, print, and outdoor or point-of-activity media. In terms of the communication mix, it is important to distinguish between those communications that are controlled and paid for by the marketer and those that are ultimately controlled by the media in which the information is designed to appear (public relations releases).

Television is a powerful communication medium because it combines both audio and visual images. On the other hand, the high cost of producing quality commercials puts television outside the price range of many smaller or regional firms and nonbusiness organizations, even if donated advertising time can be obtained by the latter. Radio messages are less expensive than television messages, but radio messages leave more to the listener's imagination, because no visual images can be shown. Radio, however, can often reach people at times and in locations where television sets are unlikely to be found—for instance, while they are driving cars or at the beach. In developing countries, where literacy rates are still low, radio is often the most pervasive impersonal advertising medium.

A key characteristic of both television and radio is that broadcast messages are fleeting; without use of recording equipment, they cannot be retained for later reference. Radio advertising is often used for short reminder advertising to encourage people to take action after previous messages, perhaps in other media, have built up awareness and knowledge of the product.

The print medium may be more effective than broadcasting for transmitting messages containing a great deal of information. Newspaper and magazine ads may be clipped for future reference; direct mail not only provides a message in tangible form but also offers the advantage that the content of the message can be personalized to meet the particular situation of the recipient. Like personal communications, a printed message is sometimes used to close the sale—typically, through the use of an order coupon in the body of the ad or an order form and postage paid envelope in a direct-mail communication. Radio and television messages sometimes include an address or phone number to contact, but are less satisfactory because this requires the audience to have pen or pencil ready to quickly copy down the information.

Outdoor advertising, signing, and point-of-sale displays can carry only short messages as a rule, but have the advantage of being geographically quite specific. At the point of purchase, signing and displays can be used to supplement personal communications in telling people where to find a service and how to use it.

The first step in media selection is to recognize the wide array of communication channels available and to be aware of their relative advantages and disadvantages in reaching specific market segments and in communicating certain types of messages. Frequently, it is necessary to use several different communication elements so that these will mutually reinforce each other, with the strengths of one complementing the relative weaknesses of another.

SUMMARY AND CONCLUSION

Communications are used in marketing to inform, persuade, or remind. Messages may be transmitted personally to existing or prospective customers through salespeople (or change agents), through customer-service personnel and other employees in contact with customers, or even through consumers themselves. Alternatively, messages may be transmitted through impersonal channels such as the broadcast and print media, signing, retail displays, and so forth.

Effective communication strategies require that communication objectives be linked to broader marketing objectives. Further, a combined budget should be established for all elements of the communication mix, so that appropriate trade-offs can be made in allocating resources between the different elements. This communication budget should be set within the context of the overall marketing budget and with reference to the value of achieving the goals that have been set. Knowing how communications work and being aware of the wide array of communication tools available are necessary prerequisites to sound decision making.

FEDERAL EXPRESS

Christopher H. Lovelock

It was one o'clock in the morning at Memphis International Airport. The lights of an approaching aircraft grew brighter as it descended toward the runway, while more aircraft lights appeared in the distant sky. "They'll be landing every few minutes from now on," said Heinz J. Adam to the visitor he was showing around the Federal Express distribution hub. Adam, Federal's director of marketing administration, was referring to his company's fleet of 32 Falcon jet "minifreighters" that flew into Memphis, Tennessee, every weeknight from all over the country.

Moments later, a small twin-engined jet taxied noisily up to the huge shed housing Federal's distribution center. Painted a brilliant purple, red, and white, the jet rolled to a stop under the arc lights, parallel to a half dozen identical aircraft. Before the pilot had even cut the engines, an electric truck towing a train of small cargo bins emerged from the distribution center and pulled alongside. The jet's cargo door was

thrown open, revealing a cabin crammed with small packages. While mechanics checked the jet's exterior and an avionics engineer conversed with the captain, a crew of young men went rapidly to work unloading the little aircraft by hand. The unloading was completed within a matter of minutes, by which time another Falcon had parked alongside and been met by a second crew.

Adam led his visitor back inside the busy distribution building, which contained an 800-foot conveyor system. Packages were being unloaded from one of the trains, deposited on moving conveyor belts, and sorted according to destination cities. There were boxes in a variety of sizes, large metal cans, cardboard tubes, envelopes, and an occasional sturdy package marked with the distinctive black and yellow symbol for radioactive materials.

"We're carrying 19,000 packages a day now and have stations in 75 cities throughout the U.S.," said the director. "There's tremendous growth potential ahead for Federal Express, but we'll need to focus our efforts more carefully."

Copyright © 1976 by the President and Fellows of Harvard College, Harvard Business School case 9-577-042.

He leaned over the conveyor belt and plucked up a large purple, red, and white envelope. "This is what we call a Courier Pak," he said. "You can put anything you like in it up to two pounds in weight, and for $12.50 we'll guarantee overnight delivery anywhere in our system. Right now, we're averaging about 1,300 Courier Paks a day but we've never put any real marketing effort behind it. I see no reason why we shouldn't increase that number to at least 6,000 daily."

THE GENESIS OF FEDERAL EXPRESS

Federal Express was the brainchild of Frederick W. Smith, Jr., who at age 27 had incorporated the company in 1971. After combat service as a highly decorated U.S. Marine Corps pilot and two years' successful operation of a business buying and selling used jet aircraft, Smith set about putting into practice a new concept for air transportation of packages. He was convinced that there was significant market potential for a small-package air service, flying primarily at night, on routes that met the needs of freight shippers. Most package airfreight at that time flew on commercial passenger flights.

Smith believed that there were major differences between passengers and packages, and the two required totally different treatment. Most passengers were moving between major business centers and wanted the convenience of daytime flights, whereas shippers needed nighttime service to coincide with late afternoon pickups. Additionally, most people flew round trip, whereas any given shipment of goods flew in only one direction.

Encouraged by the consulting firms' optimistic growth projections for airfreight, Smith subsequently recruited several of the consultants as officers of the new corporation and set about raising almost $90 million in financing. This total included his entire personal worth, $8 million from his family, a $40 million equity capital package from six major corporate investors, plus

another $40 million in bank loans. The privately owned Federal Express Corporation (FEC) thus became the largest single venture capital start-up in the history of American business.

The Federal Express Concept

The company flew small jet freighters over a unique route system, similar to the spokes of a wheel. The hub of this system was a sophisticated sorting facility located in Memphis, Tennessee. Memphis was chosen because it was relatively close to the "center of gravity" of package movements within the United States; its airport's excellent weather record also made it a reliable base point.

Aircraft stationed throughout the United States left their home cities every weeknight with a load of packages and flew into Memphis, often making one or two stops en route. At Memphis, all packages were unloaded, sorted by destination cities, and reloaded. The aircraft then returned to their home cities in the early hours of the morning. Packages were picked up and delivered within a 25-mile radius of the airport by FEC couriers. From door-to-door, the package was in Federal Express hands.

To facilitate handling, Federal Express limited packages to 70 pounds, with a maximum length-plus-girth of 108 inches. In its use of the hub system and limited package size, FEC borrowed heavily from the experience of United Parcel Service, a successful surface package carrier. Many of the new firm's operations managers were recruited from UPS.

For its fleet, Federal Express settled on the French-built Dassault Falcon, a twin-engined executive jet which FEC converted to a minifreighter with a cargo carrying capacity of 6,200 pounds. The use of these small aircraft qualified Federal Express as an air-taxi operator and enabled it to avoid restrictive regulation by the Civil Aeronautics Board.

Operations began on April 17, 1973. On that

night, Federal Express served 22 cities, with 10 aircraft and 150 employees, and carried 15 packages.

Volume increased steadily as additional Falcons were delivered and new cities added, but the company continued to lose money heavily. At one point, Federal Express was technically bankrupt. While top management worked desperately to renegotiate loans, couriers deposited their watches as security when obtaining gas for company trucks, the president sold his personal aircraft, and base personnel hid the Falcons to keep sheriffs from serving attachment papers and chaining the little jets to the ramps. Looking back at the fledgling airline's early difficulties, Smith observed ruefully, "The biggest asset we had going for us was our naiveté. God takes care of fools, you know."

Finally, in mid-1975 Federal Express passed the break-even point. For the fiscal year ended May 31, 1976, the company achieved a net profit of $3.7 million on revenues of $75 million, after paying $65.3 million in operating expenses and $6 million in interest.

In the early summer of 1976, FEC operated 32 Falcons of its own—plus nine other aircraft operated under contract by supplemental carriers—and 500 vans leased from Hertz. It had over 2,000 employees and boasted an average daily volume of close to 19,000 packages. Its flights served 75 cities directly, and pickup and delivery service was provided to 130 cities in the United States. Because of the growth in volume, the company had established a second minihub in Pittsburgh and also operated a shuttle service between Boston, New York, Washington and intermediate cities. Federal Express had 31,000 customers, of whom about 15,000 used the service in any one month.

THE AIRFREIGHT INDUSTRY

A 1975 study estimated that some 1.5 billion tons of freight were shipped annually in the United States by rail, boat, truck, barge, and air. However, air's share of this total was less than 2 percent, mainly because airfreight cost a great deal more than surface freight.

Airfreight offered several advantages in addition to speed. Packaging requirements were fewer and damage and loss rates usually lower. Airfreight shippers also had a lower volume of goods in transit or inventory at any one time than when surface transportation was used.

Typical users of airfreight were producers of time-sensitive, high-priced, finished goods going to widespread locations. Bulk products and commodity goods were rarely sent by air. Indeed, most air shipments were rather small; 55 percent weighed less than 50 pounds while 90 percent of all shipments were composed of individual pieces weighing less than 70 pounds each.

Since the 1960s, airfreight usage had grown faster than any other segment of freight transportation. Domestic airline freight revenues nearly doubled between 1965 and 1970. By 1975 it was estimated that the airfreight market was producing nearly $1 billion in revenue to the airlines, without including the retail mark-up charged by intermediaries.

Only one-fifth of all airfreight was delivered to airports by the shipper or picked up by the consignee. The bulk of the remaining 80 percent was accounted for, in roughly equal proportions, by three major intermediaries.

Air Cargo, Inc. was a trucking service, wholly owned by 26 airlines, that performed pickup and delivery service for the airlines' direct customers. The service was provided by 520 contract truckers at 480 of the 522 airports served by the airlines in the United States.

Freight Forwarders were trucking carriers who consolidated cargo going to the airlines. Basically, they purchased wholesale cargo space from the airlines and retailed it in small amounts. Forwarders catered to small shipment customers, providing pickup and delivery services in most cities, either in their own trucks or through contract agents. Whereas it cost the airlines about $10.00 in 1975 to handle a 50-pound shipment on the ground, forwarders' costs were around $6.80. The freight forwarder industry grew at an average rate of 20 percent annually between 1965 and 1975. There were some 250 firms, with the largest 25 accounting for over 90 percent of the business. Most forwarders were not profitable and only a few of the top firms consistently earned profits. Emery Air Freight was the largest and most profitable, with 1975 domestic billings totaling $164 million and an operating income of $17.9 million.

The *U.S. Postal Service* (USPS) used air services for transportation of long-distance letter mail and air parcel post. It had recently introduced expedited transportation of letters and packages weighing up to 40 pounds through its Express Mail concept. This offered guaranteed overnight delivery or money back (see Exhibit 1).

EXHIBIT 1
EXTRACT FROM U.S. POSTAL SERVICE BROCHURE ON EXPRESS MAIL,
"HERE TODAY . . . THERE TOMORROW"

You can send almost anything by Express Mail.

Anything that's mailable up to 40 pounds—letters, reports, magnetic tapes, merchandise, you name it. And insurance coverage is included at no extra cost. What's more, you can combine letters and merchandise in the same package. For example, you could include regular letters, or data processing runs in the same carton with spare parts, or other merchandise. The Express Mail cost for the entire carton would be the normal weight-and-distance charge with no extra charge for the letters.

Guaranteed overnight delivery.

We will deliver it by 3 P.M. *next day* or, if you prefer, your shipment can be picked up as early as 10 A.M. We will get it there or you get your money back.

It's so easy to use Express Mail.

Just bring your shipment to any Postal facility with an Express Mail window by 5 P.M. Check the enclosed insert for the location nearest you.

You'll get a special Express Mail address label at the window, so there's no need to make out your own shipping label.

You get a receipt for each shipment and a record of delivery is kept at the destination Post Office, if you ever need confirmation.

Programmed service too

If your business depends on quick, *regularly scheduled* intercity shipments of information, financial documents or merchandise, we'll *custom-tailor* a special Express Mail program for you. Pickup and delivery time will be arranged to meet your precise requirements. Service is also available to some foreign countries. For more information, write to: Express Mail, P.O. Box 23555, Washington, DC 20024.

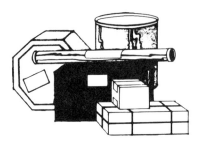

For a 2-pound package, USPS charged a flat rate of $2.25 from post office to post office or $6.25 from post office to addressee.

Because most airfreight was carried in the bellies of passenger aircraft, the operations of these intermediaries were constrained by the airlines, which flew routes and schedules designed to meet the needs of people rather than packages.

Shipping Decisions

Even in the mid-1970s, the purchase of transportation services had yet to receive the same management attention devoted to such company functions as manufacturing, purchasing, engineering, finance, or marketing. It was rare for a traffic executive to rise to top management in any company.

In most organizations, the responsibility for selecting a carrier to handle a specific freight shipment rested with an individual whose title typically was traffic manager, mailroom supervisor, shipping clerk, or dispatcher. Often this person was restricted to use of firms on an approved-carriers list. Sometimes others in the organization insisted upon use of a particular shipping method and even specified the carrier for packages they were sending. Federal Express had found that, for one shipment in four, it was the consignee who specified that FEC service be used.

Competitive Activity

Competition in the aircraft business was intense. It was believed that there were close to 1,000 airfreight forwarder salespeople across the country, to which could be added the representatives of expeditors, couriers, messenger services, REA Air Express, UPS Blue Label service, and the airlines themselves. Every *Yellow Pages*[1] in the larger cities had extensive listings under "Air

[1] The *Yellow Pages* is a directory of suppliers of goods and services, organized by product category and published in each city by the local telephone company.

Cargo Service." (Manhattan had 240 entries), "Delivery Service," or "Messenger Service."

In general, the industry lacked marketing expertise, and companies relied heavily on personal selling efforts. Brochures, sales materials, rate sheets, and routing guides were used to support the sales force. Direct mail was often used to generate sales leads. Only the biggest carriers, such as Emery, Shulman, and REA Air Express, advertised regularly on a large scale. One reason for the limited use of advertising was that most airfreight forwarders had few competitive advantages to offer. Emery Air Freight, by contrast, had spent millions on development of a systemwide computer tracing capability called EMCON and had promoted this in its advertising.

Air Transport World characterized the airfreight industry as "an aggressive, even seamy business." A 1974 marketing study prepared for Federal Express by a consulting firm commented: "The techniques of selling air freight services vary from strictly ethical to outright bribery. Techniques vary from discrediting the competition to kickbacks and payoffs . . . [Name deleted] supports a penthouse and a yacht in New York City."

Some of the forwarding firms focused their attention on shipping for particular industries. Alternatively, salespeople within a given airfreight organization might elect to follow a strategy of industry specialization in their choice of customers and prospects.

THE SMALL PACKAGE MARKET

The market for domestic transportation of small packages could be divided into four groups, categorized by order of speed desired.

Emergency service received maximum speed and was the most costly. This category catered to panic shippers and was not price sensitive. It included courier services, airline baggage services, specialized expeditors, and aircraft charter. Companies active in this field included Purolator Courier Corporation, Shulman Sky

Cab, Delta Dash (a service of Delta Airlines), and other airlines, some air taxis, and many expeditors. This category was generally known as "same day service" (see Exhibits 2 and 3).

Rush service could be described as "fast, within certain limits," was only somewhat price sensitive, and generally involved next-day delivery. Competition included many airfreight forwarders, REA Air Express, some airlines, and Express Mail.

Routine Air was the largest airfreight category. Price competitive, it was often referred to in the trade as "2 + 1" (want it there in two days but can live with three). Competition included Air Parcel Post, UPS Blue Label service, and some airfreight forwarders.

The *Routine* category included all other freight services and involved mostly surface transportation. This segment was by far the largest of the market and highly price sensitive. Major carriers were the U.S. Postal Service (fourth-class parcel post) and United Parcel Service.

The estimated size of the three air markets in 1974 was:

Market	No. of Shipments (mil.)	Avg. per Shipment	Total Volume (mil.)
Emergency	2.5	$30	$ 75
Rush	15.5	10	155
Routine Air	122.3	4	490

All three markets were growing rapidly, together averaging an estimated 20 percent increase each year. The higher priority services were believed to be growing at an even faster rate.

Federal Express Service

The majority of FEC's shipments were for next-day delivery. *Priority One* provided overnight service for packages, with deliveries before noon of the next business day. Special handling, at extra charge, was available for hazardous materials or for *Signature Security*. The latter was de-

signed to provide continuous responsibility for the custody of high-security packages. Another overnight delivery service was *Courier Pak*, which provided transportation of items weighing up to two pounds in special, 12-inch by 15½-inch, waterproof, tearproof envelopes. On average, the contents of a Courier Pak weighed about one pound. Courier Paks could be shipped individually or in a container holding about 30 each.

For shippers who were less rushed, Federal Express offered its less expensive *Standard Air Service*, with deliveries guaranteed on the second business day after pickup. An even lower priority service, *Economy Air*, which offered third-day delivery, had been discontinued in January 1975 when it was found to be losing money.

Rates for Priority One and Standard Air Service were based on weight and distance traveled, with discounts being granted on a sliding scale for consignment of multiple shipments on a single day. Various restrictions discouraged shipment of large packages with a high volume to weight ratio, because the carrying capacity of the Falcons usually cubed out (i.e., filled the aircraft interior) before it grossed out (i.e., reached the maximum loaded weight allowable). The average package weighed about 14 pounds and a rough rule of thumb at FEC was that 10 pounds of cargo took up about one cubic foot of space. A $2.50 surcharge per package was applied to Hazardous Material shipments, and a $5.00 surcharge to Signature Security items. Courier Pak envelopes cost $12.50 for shipment anywhere in the FEC system and had to be purchased in advance in quantities of five or more at a time.

MARKETING AT FEDERAL EXPRESS

Sales and other marketing activities had separate organizational structures at FEC. Contact with customers and prospects was typically made by three groups of employees: sales representatives, termed customer service representatives or senior account managers; couriers; and customer service agents.

Customer service agents, couriers, and cus-

EXHIBIT 2
AMERICAN AIRLINES PRIORITY PARCEL SERVICE ADVERTISING

We're American Airlines. Doing what we do best.

If they left out the research report for tomorrow's meeting...

...you can have it tonight. Tell them to get it on American's Priority Parcel Service.

It's just that simple and just that fast.

When you have a small parcel that has to get somewhere *fast*, just get it on American's Priority Parcel Service and it'll get there...fast.

How small? Pretty big, as a matter of fact. Your parcel can weigh up to 50 pounds and its size can total 90 inches in length, width and height.

With Priority Parcel Service you can ship to 50 cities on American's U.S. and Canadian routes plus San Juan, St. Thomas and St. Croix. Through our interline agreements you can ship practically anywhere in the U.S.

It's easy to get it on American. Just take your parcel to any American airport ticket counter at least 30 minutes prior to the departure time of the flight you want it on. Naturally, American can arrange for pick-up and delivery.

So, when you need to ship a parcel fast, use American's Priority Parcel Service.

Airlines Freight System
633 Third Avenue. New York. N.Y. 10017 U.S.A.

Get it on American
AMERICAN'S PRIORITY PARCEL SERVICE

Source: Advertisement in *American Way,* July 1976

EXHIBIT 3
EXAMPLES OF AIRFREIGHT ADVERTISING BY AIRLINES

Here today. There today.

Eastern Sprints your small package to 85 cities.

If you've got a little package in a big hurry, Eastern's Sprint gives you same-day service on most of the more than 1000 flights to 85 cities in the continental U.S. and Puerto Rico.

Just get your urgent package of 50 lbs. or less with up to 90" overall dimensions, to Eastern's ticket counter at the airport half an hour before flight time. At the destination, your package can be picked up 30 minutes after arrival in the baggage service office.

(For larger shipments ask about Eastern's Air-Express service.)

The cost? $25 per package, $30 coast-to-coast and to Puerto Rico, $35 from West Coast to Puerto Rico. Charge it on your Sprint Credit Card, your American Express Card, or other general purpose credit cards.

For pick-up and delivery in the continental U.S. call: Air Couriers International toll free (800) 528-6075.

For a Sprint Credit Card or information about our downtown drop-off service at selected City Ticket Offices, call Eastern reservations.

EASTERN

On PSA, your cargo gets around California as fast as you do.

Why do most people fly PSA? Probably because we've got more going for you between northern and southern California than any other airline. Over 160 flights a day. Same goes for your aircargo. On PSA, it doesn't sit around. Our expedited service sees that it goes out on the first flight.

Down on the ground, your package is delivered to the plane and to the final destination by our fleet of 800 radio-equipped vehicles serving 438 California communities on a door-to-door basis. Weight limit: 100 lbs. per individual package (35" by 48" max.), but no total-shipment limit. Keep your cargo smiling.

CALL ONE OF OUR AIRCARGO MANAGERS NOW.

San Francisco 761-4061; Los Angeles 646-6897; San Diego 235-7626 San Jose 286-7688; Oakland 562-1664; Sacramento 927-1352; Burbank 377-9533; Long Beach 429-2516; Ontario 983-5016; Fresno 255-1679; Stockton 982-1141.

PSA gives your cargo a lift.

Source: Advertisements in various business publications, 1976

tomer service representatives reported to their local station manager, who was part of the operations chain-of-command. Senior account managers, by contrast, reported through regional sales managers to the vice president–sales. Managers responsible for such areas as market research, marketing administration, and advertising were located in Memphis and reported to the senior vice president–marketing, who had no line authority over the sales function.

Early Marketing Efforts

At the outset, in early 1973, FEC's main problem was finding shippers willing to use its services. Recalled one senior executive:

> We initially served 22 cities. So, we had to go to a shipper who had never heard of us and who had been inundated by fly-by-night operations promising the moon and gone the next day. The shipper is very careful about changing. He's learned the hard way. We came in and said we were flying our own planes and could take certain-sized packages of certain weight going to certain cities. About halfway through our presentation, eyes would start rolling and skepticism became pretty evident. It took a long time to break into major accounts.

The first attempt to develop a systematic marketing plan for Federal Express was made in early 1974. A study by the Aerospace Advance Planning Group (AAPG), a New York consulting firm, highlighted the problems generated by the intense pressure to put FEC on a "pay-as-you-go" basis. These problems, as reported by the consultants, included "reactionary, short-term planning," "failure to follow through on previous programs," and "loss of strategic thinking." In short, AAPG said, the company was crisis oriented.

A major weakness was that available data, while prolific, emphasized operating performance and provided little information on the market, the competition, or the local areas served. Sales incentives emphasized "getting more packages," without regard to profitability.

The resulting recommendations included a change in rate structure, with an increase in most rates; improved coverage of areas served; better account maintenance to ensure that existing customers continued to use Federal Express; more productive use of the sales force; reorganization and expansion of the marketing department; and stronger efforts in advertising and public relations.

Within a month of receiving this report, FEC had hired the principal consultant on the project, J. Vincent Fagan, as senior vice president–marketing. Fagan had been working with AAPG for six years. Prior to that, he had worked with PanAm on its program for marketing the Dassault Falcon in the United States, and with the Mc-Cann–Erickson advertising agency in New York.

Advertising

Fagan determined that an aggressive advertising policy was necessary. Focus group interviews[2] with shipping managers had shown them to be somewhat timid individuals. For the most part they were neither well educated nor particularly ambitious, and their basic job strategy seemed to be one of avoiding problems with their supervisors.

One advertising approach was to use a reliable, well-regarded carrier such as Emery Air Freight, which enjoyed very high awareness. In Vince Fagan's words, "They could use Emery forever and never be criticized."

The New York firm of Carl Ally, Inc., was selected in October 1974 as the company's advertising agency, since it had a reputation of being a "bomb thrower" in the advertising business. Their first advertising for FEC, in early 1975, used both press and television, and was a four- to five-week introductory campaign designed to stimulate awareness.

In April 1975, FEC commissioned the Opinion

---

[2] Focus group interviews involve groups of perhaps five to eight subjects, led by a trained interviewer who directs a discussion on specific topics.

Research Corporation to conduct an impartial test of relative delivery speeds and costs for FEC, Emery, Airborne, and REA Air Express. This study involved rotating test shipments among a variety of different city pairs and different days of the week. The results showed that 93 percent of Federal Express Priority One packages arrived the next day, versus only 42 percent for Emery and even lower percentages for the other two. These results were used as the basis for a new TV and print advertising campaign (see Exhibit 4) initiated during the second half of 1975 and rolled out on a market-by-market basis. This attack positioned FEC firmly against Emery.

Fagan was able to measure the impact of the advertising by running it only in selected cities and then comparing changes in package volume in these test cities with those in the remainder of the FEC system. One flight of advertising was run in the New York and Los Angeles areas between late June and the beginning of September 1975. The average daily package count in these two areas in mid-March 1976 was 89 percent over the April–May 1975 base, versus 48 percent for the rest of the system. A second flight of advertising appeared between early October and mid-November 1975 in Detroit, Cleveland, Philadelphia, and Dallas. The average daily count in these cities in mid-March 1976 was 46 percent higher than the August–September 1975 base, versus 34 percent for the rest of the system.

One of the advantages of advertising, Fagan believed, was that the company maintained complete control, whereas attempting to communicate through couriers or the sales force was subject to the human element.

In March 1976, Fagan had established a new position of director of marketing administration. To fill this spot he had recruited Heinz J. Adam, a marketing executive with the American Can Company in New York. Adam evaluated FEC's various services, with a view to developing strategies for future growth. Working with other staff members, he had begun an in-depth analysis of the market potential for hazardous materials shipments and for Courier Pak.

EXHIBIT 4
FEDERAL EXPRESS: PRINT ADVERTISING 1975–1976

If you've been fairly satisfied with Emery Air Freight, you'll be completely satisfied with Federal Express.

Because in a test, we were faster and cheaper than they were, and the test was as fair and as realistic as could be devised.

We hired an independent research organization to send identical packages between 47 cities via Emery and Federal Express at each company's regular rates.

To be fair, we told our employees nothing of this test.

And also in the interest of fairness, we told Emery nothing of it either.

The numbers above tell the story. Emery, for years regarded as the best in the business, delivered an average of 42% of their packages by the next day.

Federal Express' average: 93%.

And we were cheaper.

Let's see, faster and cheaper than who you're using now.

Kinda makes you want to pick up the phone and call us, doesn't it?

Source: Company records

Personal Contact with Customers

In the summer of 1976, FEC had some 35 senior account managers (SAMs) and 75 customer service representatives (CSRs). Federal Express recruited about 50 percent of the SAMs from sales positions with airfreight forwarders, and promoted 10 percent from among its own CSRs; the remaining 40 percent had other sales experience. By contrast, four-fifths of the CSRs were recruited from the ranks of the company's couriers and customer service agents.

Craig Bell, vice president–sales, saw the task of CSRs more as account maintenance than as selling. They should, he said, be able to generate new leads and to assist station operations with such activities as following up on missing or damaged packages, checking on billing problems and procedures, and ensuring that delivery and pickup schedules were satisfactory for the customer. These tasks were more appropriately included under operations than sales, he believed. On average, CSRs made 8 to 10 calls daily, by phone and in person, and were paid $11,000–$13,000 a year, plus bonus. The total annual cost of maintaining a CSR in the field, including salary, expenses, and overheads, averaged about $18,000.

Bell saw the role of the SAMs as more sophisticated. Identifying the decision maker in a large firm was often a difficult task. Clarifying what had to be done to win the business (or a greater share of an existing customer's business) might require skillful probing and analysis. The task could involve, among other things, working with shippers to determine their long-term needs and providing advice in such areas as packaging and logistics.

The SAMs typically earned a base salary of $15,500–$22,000. Bonuses added an average of 10 percent to this base and were calculated on the individual's performance in three areas—improving volume on present accounts, generating new business, and accurately forecasting account volumes. Bell placed a lot of emphasis on forecasting ability: "Once an individual is able to forecast his business accurately, that tells you

that he understands his customers and their business. Once he knows about his basic accounts, then he knows the questions that should be asked." The total annual cost of maintaining a SAM in the field averaged $31,000. Typically, a SAM was expected to make five to eight customer calls daily.

LOCAL OPERATIONS AND SALES

A sense of what took place at the end of one of the spokes extending from FEC's Memphis hub could be obtained from a visit to the Boston station which, for its size, was representative of FEC station operations.

Federal Express operations in the greater Boston area were based at Hanscom Field in Bedford, about 15 miles west of downtown Boston. Federal leased half a large hangar for light maintenance and package sorting operations; adjoining offices housed the station manager, Denis Spina, the sales staff, and a radio-dispatch facility.

One senior FEC executive described the job of station manager as "the key to company operations." These individuals, he said, had profit and loss responsibility for what might be as much as a $5 million business in large stations. They had to watch costs carefully, supervising performance in both the station office and the field.

Each weekday morning, a Federal Express Falcon flew in from Memphis, scheduled to arrive at 7:30 A.M. Two supplemental carriers, operating under contract to FEC, flew in packages from the recently established Pittsburgh minihub and from several East Coast cities.

At .7:25 one summer morning, a crew of Federal Express couriers could be seen busily unloading the Pittsburgh supplemental flight, a white Hansa Jet. This task was almost complete when at 7:40 the second supplemental, an old-fashioned, propeller-driven Twin Beech, arrived at the end of its milk run from Washington, via Baltimore, Philadelphia, and Newark. There was still no sign of the Memphis flight and a check over the teletype established that it had been delayed half an hour leaving its home base. Spina indicated that such a delay occurred about once every three weeks. Finally, at 7:55 the purple Falcon touched down and taxied quickly over to be unloaded.

In the hanger, two lines of vans, all painted in FEC colors, had been backed up against a line of rollers. As the packages trundled along the rollers, each courier picked out those destined for consignees on his or her route and positioned them carefully inside a vehicle. About 7 percent of the packages were marked "Hold at Airport," for individual collection by the consignee.

The station manager noted that there was an imbalance between outbound and inbound loads in the Boston area. A check of the previous day's totals yielded the following typical figures:

	Priority One	Standard Air	Courier Pak	Total
Outbound	911	227	39	1,177
Inbound	539	133	22	694

However, the couriers had actually made more delivery stops (363) than pickup stops (326). The daily report indicated that 151 of these pickup stops were regular daily visits to frequent shippers, while the remaining 175 had been scheduled in response to telephone call-ins by customers. About 12 percent of outbound packages were brought directly to the airport by the shipper.

Because of the imbalance in loads, there were four flights out of Hanscom Field in the evening, which required routing a second FEC Falcon into Boston at night. Flights left for Memphis at 6:30 and 10:00 P.M., for Pittsburgh at 10:30 P.M., and for the East Coast milk run at 10:55 P.M.

A Morning with a Courier

Working fast, the couriers had loaded all the vans by 8:35 A.M. and had made up some of the time

lost by the late arrival of the Memphis flight. Ken Barlow, a cheerful man in his early 30s, jumped into the driver's seat of his van and within minutes pulled out of the main gate of Hanscom Field onto the road to Lexington. His regular route covered five suburban towns near Boston; he made a delivery run in the morning, a pickup run in the afternoon, and usually finished work around 6:30 P.M.

Ken's first stop, at 8:45, was to deliver a small package at the suburban plant of a large chemical company. It was signed for by the head shipper at the plant's loading dock. As the courier got back in the van, his radio crackled, asking his estimated time of arrival at a particular address.

Five minutes later he was pulling into the receiving dock of a well-known office machinery firm, where he delivered two boxes and a Courier Pak to the receiving dock. At 9:02, another radio call came through.

"Do you have a package for Raytheon there?"

"Yeah, I've got it, Jean. Should be in Waltham around 11:30."

There was a pause, then,

"What's your next stop?"

"I'm on the way to Xerox, then Hewlett-Packard in 20 minutes."

"He'll meet you there."

At 9:05 Ken stopped at the Xerox plant, delivered a package downstairs at the receiving office and a Courier Pak to the receptionist in the office upstairs. As Ken left the parking lot a green car met the van and the driver waved Ken to a stop. It was the man from Raytheon, who signed quickly for a small package which, he explained, was a product part long overdue from the suppliers.

The morning continued with stops every few minutes, typically at new suburban plants and office buildings. Most deliveries consisted of one or two small packages. Two of the larger boxes in the van, both relatively light, were delivered to a major computer firm and bore labels showing that they had been dispatched from the same company's plants in Pennsylvania and California.

Ken exchanged a cheery word or two with

many of the shipping clerks, traffic managers, and receptionists who signed for his packages, but he never dallied at any location. At one plant, the traffic office was empty. "The receiver here's an oldtimer—he's never around," muttered Ken, looking quickly for somebody else to accept delivery. By 11:00 he was driving through a run-down, industrial area of Watertown and was expressing concern that he might not be able to complete all his deliveries before noon. He was annoyed that his route that morning included two deliveries in Arlington, a slow 20 minutes away. For the first time, he had to use his handcart to transport several bulky parcels from the van. At another stop, he dropped off 10 new Courier Paks, which a firm needed for forthcoming shipments of engineering prints.

It was past noon before the courier arrived in Arlington for his last two shipments. At 12:15 he delivered a package to a Datsun dealer and five minutes later a box marked "laboratory specimens" to a doctor's office, but neither showed any awareness that the delivery had been made after the 12 o'clock standard. Heaving a sigh of relief, Ken walked across the street to a small restaurant and bought a large submarine sandwich and a soft drink. He had driven about 30 miles, made 37 stops, and delivered some 60 packages, including three Courier Paks.

An Afternoon with a Sales Representative

John Griffin had been with FEC since June 1973. Then an undergraduate at Boston University, he had taken time out from school to earn extra money by working as a courier for the fledgling Boston operation. Persuaded to stay on, he had been promoted to Lead Courier and was made responsible for assigning the areas to be covered by individual couriers. Next came a year and a half as night operations supervisor. In 1975, he had accepted a position as a CSR, feeling that the long-term opportunities outweighed the immediate, sharp drop in salary. His optimism appeared justified by a promotion to SAM 11 months later.

Griffin explained that he was in a transition between his old and new job. His future assignment would be to focus on 70 key accounts in the Boston/Worcester area. Presently, he had 101 accounts in the Boston area alone and would be transferring the smaller ones to other CSRs. Although he described Federal Express as an easy product to sell, he believed that more effort was needed to develop the market. In particular, he felt that CSRs should report to SAMs rather than to station managers. It was difficult, he said, to get support for a better CSR program, improved secretarial assistance, and more information on who was shipping what to whom.

Griffin's first call after an early lunch was to the corporate headquarters of a large retailing firm, located just outside Boston. The previous week, he and the regional sales manager had made an hour and a half presentation to the firm's traffic manager and three traffic supervisors. Their interest in Federal Express lay in obtaining rapid transportation of small rush orders—"where we needed delivery yesterday"—from vendors and the firm's own warehouses to its numerous stores. Among the concerns raised at this first meeting was that some vendors and stores were located more than 25 miles from a Federal Express station, and hence outside the normal pickup and delivery area. What extra charges, they asked, would be incurred for use of a supplementary carrier to serve these out-of-area locations?

Griffin parked his car, entered the attractive modern building, and gave his name to the receptionist. A secretary came out and led him to the traffic manager's office where a well-dressed man in his late thirties shook hands and waved him to a seat. The salesman had researched store and vendor locations and was able to identify for his prospective client which stores and vendors were located out-of-area. For the next hour they discussed the costs and logistics of servicing these locations and how to resolve the stores' preference for paying c.o.d. rather than being billed separately. Griffin said that he would raise the c.o.d. issue with FEC's accounting office. The meeting concluded with the traffic manager's request for a complete proposal within a month.

From the suburbs, John Griffin drove into Boston for his next appointment. A traffic manager had called the Federal Express office asking that a salesman visit; since Griffin already had a later appointment in the immediate area with an existing client, he had agreed to take this call.

The address turned out to be a gloomy warehouse building, with boxes of all sizes stacked in tall racks. The prospect's office was in a small, green, hut-like structure built out from one of the walls. A middle-aged man, tieless and in shirtsleeves, could be seen through the cracked glass door working at a cluttered desk. Spotting the salesman, he waved him in. Griffin introduced himself. For a moment the man at the desk looked puzzled, then his face cleared. "Oh, yeah," he said. "You're the people with the purple planes. Tell me all you know, kid!"

Griffin began by asking about the company's business, what its products were, where they were shipped, how important delivery times were, and to what extent airfreight was presently employed.

Shipments went in spurts, the manager indicated in response. They used several airfreight firms, most shipments went to Texas and the Midwest, and second-day delivery was usually sufficient. As he spoke, he was sorting waybills into piles on his desk, pausing only to flick ash from his cigarette onto the worn linoleum floor.

"How much do you know about Federal Express?" asked the salesman.

"I watched you on the television versus Emery."

The traffic manager raised his hands, palms down, one a foot above his desk and the other high above his head. Griffin remembered the television commercial (similar in content to Exhibit 4), which had last run in Boston some four months before.

"Is that how you found out about us?"

"Yeah."

The manager went back to his sorting while the salesman briefly described the Federal Express operation and how it worked, outlining the procedures for calling a courier, billing arrangements, and FEC size limitations. The latter would evidently be restrictive, because many of the shipper's packages exceeded Federal's maximum limit, but the traffic manager just shrugged and stubbed out his cigarette in a dirty saucer. When the salesman offered to have a courier call that afternoon, the traffic manager said that he didn't need anything today, thanks, but he'd be calling.

John Griffin shook hands and saw himself out. "That was a rum one," he murmured to himself as he walked out onto the street again. "But I think we'll be seeing some business from him."

His 3:15 appointment was with the operations manager of a medical firm that ran a number of specialist treatment centers around the country. The corporate offices in Boston were responsible for most of the financial work; management apparently placed great importance on shipping financial and statistical reports quickly to local treatment centers for immediate review. The firm had been using Federal Express since 1974 for shipping boxes of reports; it had tried several airfreight forwarders and settled on Federal as providing the best service. In late 1975, finding Special Delivery mail increasingly unreliable after cutbacks in airline schedules, the firm began using Courier Paks for shorter reports. They currently sent 50 Courier Paks and 30 packages each month.

Griffin made a point of calling on this account once every two or three months, following up any problems, and explaining any changes in Federal Express service or prices. On this occasion, he brought a supply of new Courier Paks with him. The operations manager was a woman in her thirties, whose office was a large, windowless room piled with stacks of boxes, documents, and computer printouts. She and the salesman spent about 20 minutes discussing the implications of her firm's planned move to the new John Hancock Tower in central Boston. Griffin mentioned that Federal Express was thinking of installing a drop-box for Courier Paks on the ground floor of the new building, so that the courier could make a late afternoon collection after the offices had closed.

Leaving the building at 3:40, the salesman sought out a pay phone and called his office to check if there were any messages. A prospective customer, located about 10 minutes away, had phoned asking for a presentation, he was told. Griffin obtained the name, address, and phone number, called the prospect, and set up an appointment for four o'clock.

The new prospect was the director of office services for an advertising agency. The decor of the office was arty, modern, and expensive, with several prize-winning advertisements in frames on the walls. The director, a smartly dressed woman in her fifties, shook hands and thanked the SAM for responding to her enquiry so promptly. She paid all the agency's bills, she said, and used airfreight for shipping items like films and artwork, research materials, and even office stationery. Recently, she had noticed that the research department had been receiving packages shipped by Federal Express and returning materials to their clients via this carrier. Her interest had been stimulated by Federal's recent television advertising—"I know you have your own planes," she remarked.

Griffin explained the nature of FEC service and emphasized the importance of having one's own aircraft. He then showed her a Courier Pak and fielded several questions about billing and insurance. Upon being told that the agency frequently shipped film insured for $5,000, he explained that the maximum insurance on Courier Pak was currently only $200 but that arrangements for higher coverage could be made with Priority One. When the director mentioned that Delta Dash charged $26.50 for express document handling between Boston and New York, he told her that using Courier Pak would save her $14.00. She appeared impressed.

The interview concluded with the salesman's leaving a booklet containing information on rates and billing, as well as a supply of airbills (combined bill and shipping order), and explaining procedures for completing the latter. He also sold the director five Courier Paks. Descending in the elevator, John Griffin checked his watch. It was 4:40. With luck, he'd be onto the turnpike and heading back to his office before the traffic built up.

THE SITUATION IN JUNE 1976

In the early summer of 1976 FEC management looked ahead to continued growth. With the average flight carrying 4,900 pounds of freight and loaded to 85 percent of volume capacity, the company was seeking legislation in Congress to allow it to operate larger aircraft. However, it was recognized that this change might take a long time to achieve.

A January 1976 survey showed that awareness of FEC among prime prospects (i.e., airfreight shippers not presently using FEC) had increased significantly, with FEC ranking third out of 10 airfreight companies. Among these prospects, 75 percent recalled the Federal Express name on prompting. However, among these prospects, prompted awareness of Emery was close to universal and for Airborne it was 85 percent. Unprompted recall figures were: Emery, 61 percent; Airborne, 22 percent; and FEC, 12 percent.

These figures were important to Heinz Adam, who had been with Federal Express just three months. While still adjusting to the move to Memphis after living some 20 years in New Jersey and working in New York City, he was enthusiastic about his new position. He described it as demanding but very stimulating. "It's the first time I've really had fun in a job!" he remarked.

Adam termed Federal Express "a very people-oriented organization: people are what make things work here; the loyalty of its employees has been very important to the company." In addition to high wages and good benefits, FEC also operated a profit-sharing plan for employees. A recent attempt by the Teamsters to unionize FEC employees was voted down by a four-to-one margin. On the other hand, Adam did not see Federal Express as a customer-oriented business. "It's operations-oriented," he said, "and as a marketing man this drives me up the wall sometimes."

As he reviewed the company's performance since the beginning of 1975, Heinz Adam became increasingly convinced that Courier Pak had great, but unfilled, potential. Sales had almost doubled in the past year (see Exhibit 5), but still represented less than 10 percent of total overnight package volume for FEC and barely 5 percent of overnight dollar volume. Studies by the cost accounting department showed that the average Priority One package generated a 55 percent contribution margin on an average price of $23.56, while Standard Air yielded a 27 percent contribution on an average unit price of $12.62. Courier Paks, priced at $12.50 each since March 1976, yielded a 66 percent contribution margin.

An analysis of Courier Pak usage by customer type produced the profile shown in Exhibit 6. A spring 1976 survey of Priority One and Courier Pak usage by FEC's top 1,400 customers found that 24 percent used both products, less than 1 percent used only Courier Pak, while the rest used only Priority One. The key attribute separating Courier Pak from Priority One service in the customer's mind was the expectation that the former would be delivered to the addressee and not just to the receiving dock. Another analysis showed that 57 percent of Courier Pak volume came from the 14 top FEC stations and 20 percent from the top 3; the same analysis figures for Priority One were 44 percent and 15 percent,

respectively.[3] On average, users sent 0.45 Courier Paks per day.

A review of the market size for "emergency," "rush," or "special handling" delivery of documents or other small items suggested that the market was almost 870,000 pieces per day (see Exhibit 7). Heinz Adam discussed the situation with Vince Fagan; the two men concluded that a target of 6,000 Courier Paks per day within six months would not be unrealistic, although it represented a 350 percent increase over current levels.

A Marketing Plan for Courier Pak

The next task Adam faced was to develop an appropriate marketing strategy for Courier Pak. In particular, there was a question as to what type and level of advertising and selling effort to put behind this service.

The company's advertising plan for 1976–1977 included television commercials promoting Federal's overall competitive advantages (see Exhibit 8). The planned press and magazine advertising included two different full-page advertisements for use in *Business Week, U.S. News & World Report, Time, Newsweek,* and the *Wall Street Journal,* as well as various trade publications. One of these ads mentioned Courier Pak in the text and showed a small picture of it (see Exhibit 9). The only attempt already planned to promote Courier Pak specifically was an advertisement on the cover of FEC's upcoming July/August routes and tariffs brochure (see Exhibit 10). Would this suffice, Adam wondered, or should a more aggressive policy be adopted, involving advertising, sales activity, and other promotions? One possibility was to install a nationwide "Hotline" for Courier Pak information, using an "800" area code telephone

[3] In rank order, the 14 largest airfreight markets in the United States were: New York, Los Angeles, Chicago, San Francisco, Boston, Philadelphia, Detroit, Atlanta, Dallas, Milwaukee, Minneapolis, Cleveland, Houston, and Miami.

EXHIBIT 5
FEDERAL EXPRESS: VOLUME/REVENUE TREND ANALYSIS, 1974–1976

Week Ended	Average daily package volume				Average daily revenues ($ thousands)			
	Priority One	Standard Air Service	Economy Air	Courier Pak	Priority One	Standard Air Service	Economy Air	Courier Pak
1974[a]								
1/4[b]	2,096		1,001	140	28		5	<1
2/1	2,986		1,571	195	39		7	<1
3/1	3,436		2,365	268	45		11	1
4/5	4,115		3,430	481	53		14	2
5/3	4,010		3,991	411	55		17	2
6/7	4,451		4,850	481	64		20	2
7/5[b]	3,952		4,159	525	56		18	3
8/9	4,950		5,436	527	70		23	3
9/6[c]	5,955	2,825	3,617	547	97	33	18	5
10/4	6,350	2,465	4,229	502	103	28	20	4
11/8	6,745	2,003	4,466	511	107	23	21	4
12/6	6,694	2,351	3,033	534	111	28	18	5
1975								
1/10[d]	6,599	2,556		559	119	38		5
2/7	7,033	2,395		575	129	35		6
3/7	7,630	2,266		592	140	34		6
4/4	7,116	2,056		661	132	30		7
5/2	7,553	2,204		764	140	31		8
6/6	7,663	2,252		794	153	31		8
7/4	7,489	2,257		805	148	30		8
8/1	8,076	2,159		745	161	30		7
9/5	9,372	2,142		859	200	33		8
10/3[e]	10,032	2,289		982	215	34		10
11/7	10,384	2,203		987	221	32		10
12/5	11,177	2,600		1,034	238	36		10
1976								
1/9	11,128	2,772		1,090	232	32		11
2/6	11,056	2,918		1,156	230	33		11
3/5[f]	11,248	3,053		1,194	248	35		12
4/2	12,820	4,979		1,370	287	48		13
5/7[g]	13,400	6,022		1,304	298	65		16

Source: Company records
[a] Courier Pak volumes tended to be higher in the first and last weeks of the month than at mid-month.
[b] Four-day week.
[c] Priority One prices increased, Standard Air Service introduced, Courier Pak prices increased from $5 to $8.50.
[d] Economy Air discontinued, Courier Pak prices increased to $10.00.
[e] Standard Air Service prices reduced.
[f] Courier Pak prices increased to $12.50.
[g] Figures inflated by United Parcel Service strike.

EXHIBIT 6

FEDERAL EXPRESS COURIER PAK: CUSTOMER USAGE PROFILE, MAY 1976

Category	Number of Accounts[a]	Number of Courier Paks Used Monthly	% of Total Usage
Manufacturing and distribution, general	639	4,945	17.1
Advertising industry	140	2,285	8.2
Printing and publishing	80	1,558	5.6
Data processing equipment, mfg. and sales	125	1,160	4.1
Office and business equipment (Xerox = 862)	22	1,024	3.7
Marketing research (Burke)	61	886	3.2
Mortgage and investment banking	98	733	2.6
Computer service bureau	50	686	2.5
Electronic parts and components	76	679	2.4
Communications (telephone electronics)	34	631	2.3
Law firms	94	598	2.1
Insurance companies and agents	38	568	2.0
Service and leasing	76	537	1.9
Medical/dental/optical equipment and supplies	41	476	1.7
Aviation manufacturing and sales	57	448	1.6
Internal Revenue Service	36	443	1.6
Freight forwarders and transport	51	380	1.4
Engineering firms	44	346	1.2
Construction	37	318	1.1
Pharmaceuticals manufacturing	28	304	1.1
Medical/dental labs	16	252	0.9
Motion picture/film industry	30	238	0.8
Real estate	48	233	0.8
Chain store	42	225	0.8
CPA—accounting	45	222	0.8
Consultants (management and research)	53	196	0.7
Import/export brokers	13	190	0.7
Banks	23	181	0.6
Stocks and bonds brokers	14	147	0.5
Record industry	18	120	0.4
Architects and designers	14	114	0.4
Medical care (hospitals)	15	90	0.3
TV stations	16	83	0.3
TV broadcasting	8	47	0.2
Trade associations	5	37	0.1
Subtotal	2,187	21,380	76.3
Miscellaneous categories	na	946	3.6
Unclassified[b]	na	5,632	20.1
Total	na	27,958	100.0

Source: Company records

[a] Some companies had more than one account, representing several departments at a single location or several locations of the same company.

[b] These were sales by users without an FEC account (either infrequent users or new users not yet assigned an account number).

EXHIBIT 7

MARKET STATISTICS FOR SELECTED EMERGENCY, RUSH, AND SPECIAL HANDLING PACKAGES

	Pieces per Day
Express mail[a] (Estimated @ $6.00/piece)	4,400[c]
Registered mail[b] (Estimated @ $3.00/piece)	256,960
Certified mail[b] (Estimated @ $.50/piece)	295,156
Special delivery mail[b] (Estimated @ $1.50/piece)	301,232
Airline over the counter[a] (Estimated @ $50.00/piece)	11,000
Skycab and VIP services[a] (Estimated @ $90.00/piece)	1,000
Total	869,748

Source: Company records

[a] Estimates from FEC marketing plan.

[b] Actual figures 1974–1975 *Annual Report* of the Postmaster General, p. 52.

[c] USPS was expanding its Express Mail network rapidly. By June 1976, this service was available at major post offices in 410 cities nationwide.

number, which would be free to callers. Estimated monthly costs, including WATS rental at $1,670, employee wages, and other costs, were $2,770.

To help evaluate alternatives, Adam's assistant had collected data on advertising rates for a number of periodicals (see Exhibit 11), and for leading daily newspapers and television stations in certain large cities (see Exhibit 12).

Although Federal Express management was pleased with the company's progress, they knew that the competitive climate had toughened. The better carriers had improved their service and were becoming more aggressive, while Express Mail was believed to be doing well. A few days earlier, Adam had opened his *Wall Street Journal* to a double-page advertisement for Emery Air Freight promoting that company's size and resources. He would have to take this overall situation into account in deciding how to proceed on Courier Pak.

EXHIBIT 8 FEDERAL EXPRESS: TV STORYBOARD FOR 1976 ADVERTISING

Carl Ally Inc.
437 MADISON AVENUE, NEW YORK, N.Y. 10022
MURRAY HILL 8-5300

Client: FEDERAL EXPRESS
Product: FEDERAL EXPRESS
Title: "OVERNIGHT"
Commercial No.: QFAS6304 - 30 SECONDS
Date Approved: 6/28/76

1. ANNCR: When a freight forwarder like Emery or Airborne

2. promises to deliver your packages overnight, he's relying on the passenger airlines.

3. But 80% of their planes spend the night on the ground.

4. When Federal Express promises to deliver your packages overnight,

5. we're relying on no one but ourselves.

6. Because we own our own planes. And they fly when we say so,

7. overnight.

8. (SFX: VVVVRRRR-OOOOMMMM.)
ANNCR: (VO) Federal Express.

FEDERAL EXPRESS
Take away our planes,
and we'd be just like everybody else.

9. Take away our planes, and we'd be just like everybody else.

Source: Company records

TAKE AWAY OUR PLANES, AND WE'D BE JUST LIKE EVERYBODY ELSE.

Take away our planes and we'd be just another air freight forwarder.

And since there're already 250 of them, the world didn't need one more.

What the world did need when we went into business 3 years ago was a fast, low cost, dependable way to get packages delivered from one city to another overnight.

A ROUTE SYSTEM FOR PACKAGES. NOT PEOPLE.

So instead of shipping packages on airlines designed for people, we created a system especially for packages.

With a route structure designed for packages. To and from big cities like New York and Los Angeles. And smaller cities like Macon and Albuquerque, and 5,000 other combinations, many of them impossible to connect with on the passenger airlines.

And we fly when packages need to fly, overnight, when more than 80% of the passenger planes are "asleep" on the ground.

It's a totally enclosed system. The packages are picked up by our trucks, flown on our planes,

and delivered by our trucks.

Unlike the air freight forwarder/passenger airline system, *the package never leaves our hands.*

This is why our claim rate is so low: two hundredths of one percent.

And in a test conducted by an independent research organization, our delivery rate was twice as good as Emery's.*

Not only that, our prices are the same and sometimes less than theirs.

But Federal Express is more than the best way to send a package.

It's also the best way to send an envelope.

DELIVERED VIRTUALLY ANYWHERE IN THE COUNTRY OVERNIGHT FOR $12.50.

The Federal Express COURIER PAK™ is a waterproof, tearproof envelope that holds up to 2 lbs. of documents, contracts, tapes, etc. And anything you put in it can be almost anywhere in the country overnight, for only $12.50.

Another application of our system is the Federal Express PartsBank.

It does away with the need for a lot of regional warehouses and the expensive inventory that's had to go into them. Located in Memphis, the "air center" of the country, it's a warehouse and an airline combined. And once you put your parts there, there's no faster, more efficient way for machines scattered all over the country to get the parts they need.

If you took away our planes, none of this would be true.

We'd be just another "me too" system of sending packages.

We'd have to come up with some jingle, or some clever line in our advertising like, "Here today, there tomorrow" or something equally vague.

The planes are the whole idea behind Federal Express.

Take them away and you might as well call somebody else.

FEDERAL EXPRESS

*Test conducted April, 1975, by Opinion Research Corporation, involving identical 9-lb. packages sent door to door. Summaries and other information available upon request from Vincent Fagan, Senior V.P., Federal Express Corporation, AMF Box 30167, Memphis, Tennessee 38130.

Source: Company records

EXHIBIT 10
FEDERAL EXPRESS: COURIER PAK PROMOTION ON CUSTOMER BROCHURE, SUMMER 1976

COURIER PAK®
When you'd give a million to get something somewhere overnight... we'll do it for $12.50.

Our regular services, Priority One and Standard Air Service were designed for the shipper in a hurry.

Then we developed Courier Pak®. For the businessman in a hurry.

Here's how it works.

Courier Paks are sold at $12.50. You simply keep the prepaid envelopes in your office. Whenever you have sales orders, contracts, blueprints, tapes, samples or anything weighing up to two pounds, just put them in the Courier Pak envelope, fill out the label and give us a call. Your Courier Pak will be delivered next morning anywhere in our nation-wide system.

Courier Paks are fast, low-cost and safe. The 15½" x 12" waterproof envelope can't be torn and will hold bulky reports and data printouts.

There are just a few minor restrictions. You must comply with U.S. Postal regulations and apply the proper amount of postage covering any first-class (letter) material contained in the Courier Pak. Courier Paks are prepaid (like postage) and must be purchased in minimum quantities of five at a time. No service is provided outside the 130 major metro areas served by Federal Express.

That's all there is to it. For $12.50 we'll pick up, fly and deliver your important business documents next morning, anywhere in our nation-wide system.

If you're using Federal Express on your shipping dock, chances are your front office or mailroom will have a need for Courier Pak.

Your local sales representative can give you more information.

Courier Pak is the Registered trade mark of Federal Express Corporation.

Source: Company records

EXHIBIT 11

COST OF ONE PAGE ADVERTISING IN SELECTED
PERIODICALS, 1976

	Cost of One Full Page Insertion	Circulation
Vertical Publications		
Advertising Age	$ 5,200	68,063
Broadcasting	2,800	32,267
Journal of Marketing	520	16,669
Graphic Arts Monthly	3,350	76,245
Banking	2,390	43,816
Savings & Loan News	3,200	63,174
ABA Journal (law)	5,000	200,755
Insurance Magazine	725	14,256
Journal of Accountancy	1,890	186,382
The Secretary	950	49,135
General Publications		
Newsweek	22,650	3,028,000
Wall Street Journal	27,972	1,733,000
Time	31,925	3,502,000
Business Week	11,920	1,564,000
U.S. News and World Report	15,690	1,885,000
Sports Illustrated	20,290	2,353,000

Source: Company records

EXHIBIT 12

PRESS AND TV ADVERTISING COSTS IN SELECTED MAJOR MARKET AREAS

Cost of one full page advertisement in leading daily newspapers, 1976

Newspaper	Cost of One Full Page Insertion	Circulation
New York Times	$12,192	806,495
Chicago Tribune	10,769	750,707
Washington Post	8,207	534,400
Los Angeles Times	9,840	1,000,866
San Francisco Chronicle	8,211	457,310

Cost of 30-second TV spot on leading stations in selected cities, 1976

TV Station	City	Prime Time Cost	Prime Time Audience Males 18–49	Late Evening Cost	Late Evening Audience Males 18–49
WAGA	Atlanta	$ 900	108,000	$ 340	77,000
WNAC	Boston	1,500	212,000	750	94,000
WFAA	Dallas	2,200	365,000	550	100,000
WPLG	Miami	1,222	160,000	540	87,000
WCCO	Minneapolis	900	86,000	450	111,000
WCBS	New York	6,050	964,000	1,500	398,000
WCAU	Philadelphia	1,500	216,000	1,200	137,000
WTOP	Washington, D.C.	1,500	189,000	550	79,000
WCPO	Cincinnati	450	63,000	275	63,000
KHOU	Houston	1,150	107,000	1,000	127,000

Source: Company records

CASTLE COFFEE COMPANY, I

William F. Massy
David B. Montgomery
Charles B. Weinberg

In May of 1982, Adrian Van Tassle, Advertising Manager for the Castle Coffee Company, tugged at his red mustache and contemplated the latest market share report. This was not one of his happier moments. "I've got to do something to turn this darned market around," he exclaimed, "before it's too late for Castle—and me. But I can't afford another mistake like last year. . . ."

Indeed, William Castle (the President and a major stockholder of the Castle Company) had exhibited a similar reaction when told that Castle Coffee's share of the market was dropping back toward 5.4%—where it had been one year previously. He had remarked rather pointedly to Van Tassle that if market share and profitability were not improved during the next fiscal year "some rather drastic actions" might need to be taken.

Adrian Van Tassle had been hired nearly two years ago by James Anthoney, Vice President of

© 1985 by the Board of Trustees, Leland Stanford Junior University. This case does not depict an actual company. Reprinted from *Stanford Business Cases 1985* with permission of the publisher, Stanford University Graduate School of Business; specially revised for inclusion in this book.

Marketing for Castle. Prior to that time he had worked for companies in Montreal and Toronto and had gained a reputation as a highly effective advertising executive. Now, he was engaged in trying to reverse a long-term downward trend in the market position of Castle Coffee.

CASTLE'S MARKET POSITION

Castle Coffee was an old, established company in the coffee business, with headquarters in Squirrel Hill, Pennsylvania. Its market area included the East Coast and Southern regions of the United States, and a fairly large portion of the Midwest. The company had at one time enjoyed as much as 15 percent of the market in these areas. These were often referred to as the "good old days," when the brand was strong and growing and the company was able to sponsor such popular radio programs as "The Castle Comedy Hour" and "Castle Capers."

The company's troubles began when television replaced radio as the primary broadcast medium. Although Castle Coffee was an early television advertiser, the company experienced increasing competitive difficulty as TV production and time costs increased over time. Further problems presented themselves as several other old-line companies were absorbed by major marketers. For example, Folgers Coffee was bought by Procter and Gamble and Butter Nut by Coca Cola. These giants joined General Foods Corporation (Maxwell House, Sanka, and Yuban brands of coffee) among the ranks of Castle's most formidable competitors. Finally, the advent of freeze-dry and the increasing popularity of instant coffee put additional pressure on the company, which had no entry in these product classes.

The downward trend in share continued during the 1970s; the company had held 12 percent of the market at the beginning of the decade but only about 5½ percent at the end. Share had held fairly stable for the last few years. This was attributed to a "hard-core" group of loyal buyers plus an active (and expensive) program of consumer promotions and price-off deals to the trade. Anthoney, the Vice President of Marketing, believed that the erosion of share had been halted just in time. A little more slippage, he said, and Castle would begin to lose its distribution. This would have been the beginning of the end for this venerable company.

OPERATION BREAKOUT

When William Castle succeeded his father as president four years ago, his main objective was to halt the decline in market position and, if possible, to effect a turnaround. While he seemed to have achieved success in reaching the first objective, both he and Anthoney agreed that the same strategy, i.e., intensive consumer and trade promotion, would not succeed in winning back any appreciable proportion of the lost market share.

Both executives believed that it would be necessary to increase consumer awareness of the Castle brand and develop more favorable at-

titudes about it if market position were to be improved. This could only be done through advertising. Since the company produced a quality product (it was noticeably richer and more aromatic than many competing coffees), it appeared that a strategy of increasing advertising weight might stand some chance of success. A search for an advertising manager was initiated, which culminated in the hiring of Adrian Van Tassle.

After a period of familiarizing himself with the Castle Company and the coffee market and advertising scene in the United States, Van Tassle began developing a plan to revitalize Castle's advertising program. First, he "released" the company's current advertising agency and requested proposals from a number of others interested in obtaining the account. While it was generally understood that the amount of advertising would increase somewhat, the heaviest emphasis was on the kind of appeal and copy execution to be used. Both the company and the various agencies agreed that nearly all the advertising weight should go into spot television. Network sponsorship was difficult because of the regional character of Castle's markets, and no other medium could match TV's impact for a product like coffee. (There is a great deal of newspaper advertising for coffee, but this is usually placed by retailers under an advertising allowance arrangement with the manufacturer. Castle Coffee included such expenditures in its promotional budget rather than as an advertising expense.)

The team from Ardvar Associates, Inc., won the competition with an advertising program built around the theme, "Only a Castle is fit for a king or a queen." The new agency recommended that a 30 percent increase in the quarterly advertising budget be approved, in order to give the new program a fair trial. After considerable negotiation with Castle and Anthoney, and further discussion with the agency, Van Tassle decided to compromise on a 20 percent increase. The new campaign was to start in the autumn of 1981, which was the second quarter of the company's

1982 fiscal year (the fiscal year started July 1). It was dubbed "Operation Breakout."

PERFORMANCE DURING CURRENT YEAR

Castle had been advertising at an average rate of $2.0 million per quarter for the last several years. Given current levels of promotional expenditures, this was regarded as sufficient to maintain market share at about its current level of 5.4 percent. Castle's annual expenditure of $8 million represented somewhat more than 5.4 percent of industry advertising, though exact figures about competitors' expenditures on ground coffee were difficult to obtain. This relation was regarded as normal, since private brands accounted for a significant fraction of the market and these received little or no advertising. Neither Van Tassle nor Anthoney anticipated that competitive expenditures would change much during the next few years regardless of any increase in Castle's advertising.

Advertising of ground coffee followed a regular seasonal pattern, which approximated the seasonal variation of industry sales. The relevant figures are presented in Exhibit 1. Total ground coffee sales in Castle's market area averaged 22 million cases per quarter and were expected to remain at that level for several years. Each case contained 12 pounds of coffee in one, two, or three pound containers. Consumption in winter was about 15 percent above the yearly average, while in summer the volume was down by 15 percent.

Advertising expenditures by both Castle Coffee and the industry in general followed the same basic pattern, except that the seasonal variation was between 80 percent and 120 percent—somewhat greater than the variation in sales. The "maintenance" level of expenditures on advertising, shown in Exhibit 1, was what Castle believed it had to spend to maintain its "normal" 5.4 percent share of the market in each quarter. Van Tassle had wondered whether this was the right seasonal advertising pattern for Castle, given its small percentage of the market, but decided to stay with it. Therefore, the 20 percent planned increase in quarterly advertising rates was simply added to the "sustaining" amount for each quarter, beginning in the second quarter of the year, as shown in Exhibit 1.

In speaking with Castle and Anthoney about the proposed changes in the advertising program, Van Tassle had indicated that he expected to increase market share to 6 percent or perhaps a little more. This sounded pretty good to Castle, especially after he had consulted with the company's controller. Exhibit 2 presents the controller's memorandum on the advertising budget increase. While a fraction of a share point might seem like a small gain, each additional share point was worth nearly $4 million in annual gross contribution (before advertising) to the company.

Van Tassle, had, of course, indicated that the hoped for 6 percent share was not a "sure thing"

EXHIBIT 1
INDUSTRY SALES AND CASTLE'S ADVERTISING BUDGET

Quarter	Industry Cases*	Sales Index	Maintenance advertising		Planned advertising	
			Dollars*	Index	Dollars*	% Increase
1 Summer	18.7	0.85	1.6	0.80	1.60	0%
2 Autumn	22.0	1.00	2.0	1.00	2.40	20%
3 Winter	25.3	1.15	2.4	1.20	2.88	20%
4 Spring	22.0	1.00	2.0	1.00	2.40	20%
Average	22.0	1.00	2.0	1.00	2.32	16%

* in millions

EXHIBIT 2
AUGUST MEMO

August 1, 1981

CONFIDENTIAL

Memo to: W. Castle, President
From: I. Gure, Controller
Subject: Proposed 20 Percent Increase in Advertising

I think that Adrian's proposal to increase advertising by 20 percent (from a quarterly rate of $2.0 million to one of $2.4 million) is a good idea. He predicts that a market share of 6.0 percent will be achieved compared to our current 5.4 percent. I can't comment about the feasibility of this assumption: that's Adrian's business and I presume he knows what he's doing. I can tell you, however, that such a result would be highly profitable.

As you know, the wholesale price of coffee has been running about $17.20 per twelve-pound case. Deducting our average retail advertising and promotional allowance of $1.60 per case, and our variable costs of production and distribution of $11.10 per case, leaves an average gross contribution to fixed costs and profit of $4.50 per case. Figuring a total market of about 22 million cases per quarter and a share change of from 0.054 to 0.060 (a 0.006 increase), we would have the following increase in gross contribution:

$$\text{Change in gross contribution} = \$4.50 \times 22 \text{ million} \times .006 = \$0.60 \text{ million}$$

Subtracting the change in advertising expense due to the new program and then dividing by this same quantity gives what can be called the advertising payout rate:

$$\begin{aligned} \frac{\text{Advertising}}{\text{payout rate}} &= \frac{\text{change in gross contribution} - \text{change in advertising expense}}{\text{change in advertising expense}} \\ &= \frac{\$0.20 \text{ million}}{\$0.40 \text{ million}} = .50 \end{aligned}$$

That is, we can expect to make $.50 in net contribution for each extra dollar spent on advertising. You can see that as long as this quantity is greater than zero (at which point the extra gross contribution just pays for the extra advertising), increasing our advertising is a good deal.

I think Adrian has a good thing going here, and my recommendation is to go ahead. Incidentally, the extra funds we should generate in net contribution (after advertising expense is deducted) should help to relieve the cash flow bind which I mentioned last week.

and in any case, that it might take more than one quarter before the full effects of the new advertising program would be felt.

The new advertising campaign broke as scheduled on October 1, the first day of the second quarter of the fiscal year. Adrian Van Tassle was somewhat disappointed in the commercials prepared by the Ardvar agency and a little apprehensive about the early reports from the field. The bi-monthly store audit report of market share for September–October showed only a fractional increase in share over the 5.4 percent of the previous period. Nevertheless, Van Tassle thought that, given a little time, things would work out and that the campaign would eventually reach its objective.

The November–December market share report was received in mid-January. It showed Castle's share of the market to be 5.6 percent. On January 21, 1982, Van Tassle received a carbon copy of the memorandum in Exhibit 3.

On Monday, January 24, Anthoney telephoned Van Tassle to say that the president wanted an immediate review of the new advertising program. Later that week, after several rounds of discussion in which Van Tassle was unable to convince Castle and Anthoney that the program would be successful, it was decided to return to fiscal 1981 advertising levels. The television spot contracts were renegotiated and by the middle of February advertising had been cut back substantially toward the $2.4 million per quarter rate that had previously been normal for the winter season. The advertising agency complained that the efficiency of their media "buy" suffered significantly during February and March, due to the abrupt reduction in advertising expenditure. However, they were unable to say by how much. The spring 1982 spending rates were set at the normal level of $2.0 million. Market share for January–February turned out to be slightly under

5.7 percent, while that for March–April was about 5.5 percent.

PLANNING FOR FISCAL 1983

So, in mid-May of 1982, Adrian Van Tassle was faced with the problem of what to recommend as the advertising budget for the four quarters of fiscal 1983. He was already very late in dealing with this assignment, since additional media buys would have to be made soon if any substantial increase in advertising weight were to be implemented during the coming summer quarter. Alternatively, fast action would be needed to reduce advertising expenditures below their tentatively budgeted "normal" level of $1.6 million.

During the past month, Van Tassle had spent considerable time reviewing the difficulties of fiscal 1982. He had remained convinced that a 20 percent increase in advertising should produce somewhere around a 6 percent market share level. He based this partly on "hunch" and partly on a number of studies that had been performed by academic and business market researchers with whom he was acquainted.

EXHIBIT 3
JANUARY MEMO

January 20, 1982

Memo to: W. Castle, President
From: I. Gure, Controller
Subject: Failure of Advertising Program

I am most alarmed at our failure to achieve the market share target projected by Mr. A. Van Tassle. The 0.2 point increase in market share achieved in November–December is not sufficient to return the cost of the increased advertising. Ignoring the month of October, which obviously represents a start-up period, a 0.2 point increase in share generates only $200,000 in extra gross contribution on a quarterly basis. This must be compared to the $400,000 we have expended in extra advertising. The advertising payout rate is thus only -0.50: much less than the breakeven point.

I know Mr. Van Tassle expects share to increase again next quarter, but he has not been able to say by how much. The new program projects an advertising expenditure increase of nearly half a million dollars over last year's winter quarter level. I don't see how we can continue to make these expenditures without a better prospect of return on our investment.

One such study which he believed was particularly applicable to Castle Coffee's situation indicated that the "advertising elasticity of demand" was equal to about ½. He recalled that the definition of this measure when applied to market share was:

Advertising elasticity of demand =

$$\frac{\text{percent change in market share}}{\text{percent change in advertising}}$$

One researcher, whose judgment Van Tassle trusted, assured him that it was valid to think of "percent changes" as being deviations from "normal levels" (also called maintenance levels) of advertising and market share. However, any given value of advertising elasticity would be valid only for moderate deviations about the norm. That is, the value of ½ he had noted earlier would not necessarily apply to (say) plus or minus 50 percent changes in advertising.

Van Tassle noted that his estimate of share change ($6.0 - 5.4 = 0.6$ percentage points) represented about an 11 percent increase over the normal share level of 5.4 points. Since this was to be achieved with a 20 percent increase in advertising, it represented an advertising elasticity of $11\%/20\% = 0.55$. While this was higher than the 0.5 found in the study, he had believed that his advertising appeals and copy would be a bit better than average. He recognized that his ads may not actually have been as great as expected, but noted that, "even an elasticity of 0.5 would produce 5.94 percent of the market—within striking distance of 6 percent. Of course, the study itself might be applicable to Castle Coffee's market situation to a greater or lesser degree."

One lesson which he had learned from his unfortunate experience the last year was the danger inherent in presenting too optimistic a picture to top management. On the other hand, a "conservative" estimate might not have been sufficient to obtain approval for the program in the first place. Besides, he really did believe that the effect of advertising on share was greater than implied by performance in this past autumn. This judgment should be a part of management's information set when they evaluated his proposal. Alternatively, if they had good reason for doubting his judgment he wanted to know about it—after all, Castle and Anthoney had been in the coffee business a lot longer than he had and were pretty savvy guys.

Perhaps the problem lay in his assessment of the speed with which the new program would take hold. He had felt it "would take a little time," but had not tried to pin it down further ("That's pretty hard, after all"). Nothing very precise about this had been communicated to management. Could he blame the controller for adopting the time horizon he did?

As a final complicating factor, Van Tassle had just received a report from Ardvar Associates about the "quality" of the advertising copy and appeals used the previous autumn and winter. Contrary to expectations these ads rated only about 0.90 on a scale which rated an "average ad" at 1.0. These tests were based on the so-called "theater technique," in which the various spots were inserted into a filmed "entertainment" program and shown to a sample of consumers brought together in a theater. The effect of an ad was tested by a questionnaire designed to measure brand purchasing behavior. Fortunately, the ads currently being shown rated about 1.0 on the same scale. A new series of ads scheduled for showing during the autumn, winter, and spring of 1983 appeared to be much better. Theater testing could not be undertaken until production was completed during the summer, but "experts" in the agency were convinced that they would rate at least as high as 1.15. Van Tassle was impressed with these ads himself, but recalled that such predictions tended to be far from perfect. In the meantime, a budget request for all four quarters of fiscal 1983 had to be submitted to management within the next week.

GENERAL ELECTRIC APPLIANCES

Richard W. Pollay
John D. Claxton
Rick Jenkner

Larry Barr had recently been promoted to the position of District Sales Manager (B.C.) for G.E. Appliances, a division of Canadian Appliance Manufacturing Co. Ltd. (CAMCO). One of his more important duties in that position was the allocation of his district's sales quota amongst his five salesmen. Barr received his quota for 1978 in October 1977. His immediate task was to determine an equitable allocation of that quota. This was important because the company's incentive pay plan was based on the salesmen's attainment of quota. A portion of Barr's remuneration was also based on the degree to which his sales force met their quotas.

Barr graduated from the University of British Columbia in 1969 with the degree of Bachelor of Commerce. He was immediately hired as a product manager for a mining equipment manufacturing firm because of his summer job experience with that firm. In 1972 he joined Canadian General Electric (C.G.E.) in Montreal as a product manager for refrigerators. There he was responsi-

Copyright © 1978 by Richard W. Pollay, John D. Claxton, and Rick Jenkner.

ble for creating and merchandising a product line, as well as developing product and marketing plans. In January 1975 he was transferred to Coburg, Ontario, as a sales manager for industrial plastics. In September 1976 he became Administrative Manager (Western Region) and when the position of District Sales Manager became available, Barr was promoted to it. There his duties included development of sales strategies, supervision of salesmen, and budgeting.

BACKGROUND

Canadian Appliance Manufacturing Co. Ltd. (CAMCO) was created in 1976 under the joint ownership of Canadian General Electric Ltd. and General Steel Wares Ltd. (G.S.W.). CAMCO then purchased the production facilities of Westinghouse Canada Ltd. Under the purchase agreement the Westinghouse brand name was transferred to White Consolidated Industries Ltd., where it became White-Westinghouse. Appliances manufactured by CAMCO in the former Westinghouse plant were branded Hotpoint.

The G.E., G.S.W., and Hotpoint major ap-

EXHIBIT 1
ORGANIZATION CHART

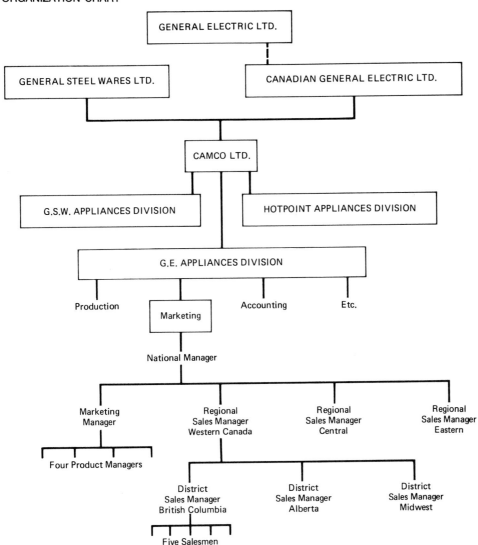

pliance plants became divisions of CAMCO. These divisions operated independently and had their own separate management staff, although they were all ultimately accountable to CAMCO management. The divisions competed for sales, although not directly, because they each produced product lines for different price segments.

COMPETITION

Competition in the appliance industry was vigorous. CAMCO was the largest firm in the industry, with approximately 45 percent market share, split between G.E., G.S.W. (Moffatt & McClary brands), and Hotpoint. The following three firms each had 10–15 percent market share: Inglis (washers and dryers only), W.C.I. (makers of White-Westinghouse, Kelvinator, and Gibson), and Admiral. These firms also produced appliances under department store brand names such as Viking, Baycrest, and Kenmore, which accounted for an additional 15 percent of the market. The remainder of the market was divided among brands such as Maytag, Roper Dishwasher, Gurney, Tappan, and Danby.

G.E. marketed a full major appliance product line, including refrigerators, ranges, washers, dryers, dishwashers, and television sets. G.E. appliances generally had many features and were priced at the upper end of the price range. Their major competition came from Maytag and Westinghouse.

THE BUDGETING PROCESS

G.E. Appliances was one of the most advanced firms in the consumer goods industry in terms of sales budgeting. Budgeting received careful analysis at all levels of management.

The budgetary process began in June of each year. The management of G.E. Appliances division assessed the economic outlook, growth trends in the industry, competitive activity, population growth, and so forth in order to determine a reasonable sales target for the next year. The president of CAMCO received this estimate, checked and revised it as necessary, and submitted it to the president of G.E. Canada. Final authorization rested with G.E. Ltd., which had a definite minimum growth target for the G.E. branch of CAMCO. G.E. Appliances was considered an "invest and grow" division, which meant that it was expected to produce a healthy sales growth each year, regardless of the state of the economy. As Barr observed, "This is difficult, but meeting challenges is the job of management."

The approved budget was expressed as a desired percentage increase in sales. Once the figure had been decided it was not subject to change. The quota was communicated back through G.E. Canada Ltd., CAMCO, and G.E.

Appliances, where it was available to the District Sales Managers in October. Each district was then required to meet an overall growth figure (quota) but each sales territory was not automatically expected to achieve that same growth. Barr was required to assess the situation in each territory, determine where growth potential was highest, and allocate his quota accordingly.

THE SALES INCENTIVE PLAN

The sales incentive plan was a critical part of General Electric's sales force plan and an important consideration in the quota allocation of Barr. Each salesman had a portion of his earnings dependent upon his performance with respect to quota. Also, Barr was awarded a bonus based on the sales performance of his district, making it advantageous to Barr and good for staff morale for all his salesmen to attain their quotas.

The sales force incentive plan was relatively simple. A bonus system is fairly typical for salesmen in any field. With G.E., each salesman agreed to a basic salary figure called "planned earnings." The planned salary varied according to experience, education, past performance, and competitive salaries. A salesman was paid 75 percent of his planned earnings on a guaranteed regular basis. The remaining 25 percent of salary was at risk, dependent upon the person's sales record. There was also the possibility of earning substantially more money by selling more than quota. (See Exhibit 2.)

The bonus was awarded such that total salary (base plus bonus) equalled planned earnings when the quota was just met. The greatest increase in bonus came between 101 and 110 percent of quota. The bonus was paid quarterly on the cumulative total quota. A holdback system ensured that a salesman was never required to pay back previously earned bonus by reason of a poor quarter. Because of this system, it was critical that each salesman's quota be fair in relation to the other salesmen. Nothing was worse for morale than one man earning large bonuses while the others struggled.

EXHIBIT 2
APPLICABLE INCENTIVE EARNINGS SCHEDULE
Sales Incentive Earnings Schedule: Major Appliances & Home Entertainment Products

Sales Quota Realization %	% of Base Salary Total	Sales Quota Realization %	Incentive % of Base Salary Total
70	0	105	35.00
71	0.75	106	37.00
72	1.50	107	39.00
73	2.25	108	41.00
74	3.00	109	43.00
75	3.75	110	45.00
76	4.50	111	46.00
77	5.25	112	47.00
78	6.00	113	48.00
79	6.75	114	49.00
80	7.50	115	50.00
81	8.25	116	51.00
82	9.00	117	52.00
83	9.75	118	53.00
84	10.50	119	54.00
85	11.25	120	55.00
86	12.00	121	56.00
87	12.75	122	57.00
88	13.50	123	58.00
89	14.25	124	59.00
90	15.00	125	60.00
91	16.00	126	61.00
92	17.00	127	62.00
93	18.00	128	63.00
94	19.00	129	64.00
95	20.00	130	65.00
96	21.00	131	66.00
97	22.00	132	67.00
98	23.00	133	68.00
99	24.00	134	69.00
100	25.00	135	70.00
101	27.00	136	71.00
102	29.00	137	72.00
103	31.00	138	73.00
104	33.00	139	74.00
		140	75.00

Quota attainment was not the sole basis for evaluating the salesmen. They were required to fulfill a wide range of duties including service, franchising of new dealers, maintaining good relations with dealers, and maintaining a balance of sales among the different product lines. Because the bonus system was based on sales only, Barr had to ensure that the salesmen did not neglect their other duties.

A formal salary review was held each year for each salesman. However, Barr preferred to give his salesmen continuous feedback on their performances. Through human relations skills he hoped to avoid problems which could lead to dismissal of a salesman and loss of sales for the company.

Barr's incentive bonus plan was more complex than the salesmen's. He was awarded a maximum of 75 annual bonus points broken down as follows: market share, 15; total sales performance, 30; sales representative balance, 30. Each point had a specific money value. The system ensured that Barr allocate his quota carefully. For instance, if one quota was so difficult that the salesman sold only 80 percent of it, while the other salesmen exceeded quota, Barr's bonus would be reduced, even if the overall area sales exceeded the quota. (See Appendix, "Development of a Sales Commission Plan.")

QUOTA ALLOCATION

The total 1978 sales budget for G.E. Appliances division was about $100 million, a 14 percent sales increase over 1977. Barr's share of the $33 million Western region quota was $13.3 million, also a 14 percent increase over 1977. Barr had two weeks to allocate the quota amongst his five territories. He needed to consider factors such as historical allocation, economic outlook, dealer changes, personnel changes, untapped potential, new franchises or store openings, and buying group activity (volume purchases by associations of independent dealers).

Sales Force

There were five sales territories within B.C. (Exhibit 3). Territories were determined on the basis of number of customers, sales volume of customers, geographic size, and experience of the sales-

EXHIBIT 3
G.E. APPLIANCES—SALES TERRITORIES

Territory Designation	Description
9961 Greater Vancouver (Garth Rizzuto)	Hudson's Bay, Firestone, K-Mart, McDonald Supply, plus seven independent dealers
9962 Interior (Dan Seguin)	All customers from Quesnel to Nelson, including contract sales (50 customers)
9963 Coastal (Ken Block)	Eatons, Woodwards, plus Vancouver Island north of Duncan and upper Fraser Valley (east of Clearbrook) (20 customers)
9964 Independent and Northern (Fred Speck)	All independents in lower mainland and South Vancouver Island, plus northern B.C. and Yukon (30 customers)
9967 Contract (Jim Wiste)	Contract sales Vancouver, Victoria. All contract sales outside 9962 (50–60 customers)

man. Territories were altered periodically in order to deal with changed circumstances.

One territory was comprised entirely of contract customers. Contract sales were sales in bulk lots to builders and developers who used the appliances in housing units. Because the appliances were not resold at retail, G.E. took a lower profit margin on such sales.

G.E. Appliances recruited M.B.A. graduates for their sales force. They sought bright, educated people who were willing to relocate anywhere in Canada. The company intended that these people would ultimately be promoted to managerial positions. The company also hired experienced career salesmen in order to get a blend of experience in the sales force. However, the typical salesman was under thirty, aggressive, and upwardly mobile. G.E.'s sales training program covered only product knowledge. It was not felt necessary to train recruits in sales techniques.

Allocation Procedure

At the time Barr assumed the job of D.S.M., he had a meeting with the former sales manager, Ken Philips. Philips described to Barr the method he had used in the past to allocate the quota. As Barr understood it, the procedure was as follows:

The quota was received in October in the form of a desired percentage sales increase. The first step was to project current sales to the end of the year. This gave a base to which the increase was added for an estimation of the next year's quota.

From this quota, the value of contract sales was allocated. Contract sales were allocated first because the market was considered the easiest to forecast. The amount of contract sales in the sales mix was constrained by the lower profit margin on such sales.

The next step was to make a preliminary allocation by simply adding the budgeted percentage increase to the year end estimates for each territory. Although this allocation seemed fair on the surface, it did not take into account the differing situations in the territories, or the difficulty of attaining such an increase.

The next step was examination of the sales data compiled by G.E. Weekly sales reports from all regions were fed into a central computer, which compiled them and printed out sales totals by product line for each customer, as well as other information. This information enabled the sales manager to check the reasonableness of his initial allocation through a careful analysis of the growth potential for each customer.

The analysis began with the largest accounts, such as Firestone, Hudson's Bay, and Eatons, which each bought over $1 million in appliances annually. Accounts that size were expected to achieve at least the budgeted growth. The main reason for this was that a shortfall of a few percentage points on such a large account would be difficult to make up elsewhere.

Next, the growth potential for medium sized accounts was estimated. These accounts included McDonald Supply, K-Mart, Federated Cooperative, and buying groups such as Volume

Independent Purchasers (V.I.P.). Management expected the majority of sales growth to come from such accounts, which had annual sales of between $150 thousand and $1 million.

At that point, about 70 percent of the accounts had been analyzed. The small accounts were estimated last. These had generally lower growth potential but were an important part of the company's distribution system.

Once all the accounts had been analyzed, the growth estimates were summed and the total compared to the budget. Usually, the growth estimates were well below the budget.

The next step was to gather more information. The salesmen were usually consulted to ensure that no potential trouble areas or good opportunities had been overlooked. The manager continued to revise and adjust the figures until the total estimated matched the budget. These projections were then summed by territory and compared to the preliminary territorial allocation.

Frequently, there were substantial differences between the two allocations. Historical allocations were then examined and the manager used his judgment in adjusting the figures until he was satisfied that the allocation was both equitable and attainable. Some factors which were considered at this stage included experience of the salesmen, competitive activities, potential store closures or openings, potential labor disputes in areas, and so forth.

The completed allocation was passed on to the Regional Sales Manager for his approval. The process had usually taken one week or longer by this stage. Once the allocations had been approved, the District Sales Manager then divided them into sales quotas by product line. Often, the resulting average price did not match the expected mix between higher and lower priced units. Therefore, some additional adjusting of figures was necessary. The house account (used for sales to employees of the company) was used as the adjustment factor.

Once this breakdown had been completed, the numbers were printed on a budget sheet, and given to the Regional Sales manager (R.S.M.). He forwarded all the sheets for his region to the central computer, which printed out sales numbers for each product line by salesman, by month. These figures were used as the salesmen's quotas for the next year.

Current Situation

Barr recognized that he faced a difficult task. He felt that he was too new to the job and the area to confidently undertake an account by account growth analysis. However, due to his previous experience with sales budgets, he did have some sound general ideas. He also had the records of past allocation and quota attainment (Exhibit 4), as well as the assistance of the R.S.M., Anthony Foyt.

Barr's first step was to project the current sales figures to end of year totals. This task was facilitated because the former manager, Philips, had been making successive projections monthly since June. Barr then made a preliminary quota allocation by adding the budgeted sales increase of 14 percent to each territory's total (Exhibit 5).

Barr then began to assess circumstances which could cause him to alter that allocation. One major problem was the resignation, effective at the end of the year, of one of the company's top salesmen, Ken Block. His territory had traditionally been one of the most difficult, and Barr felt that it would be unwise to replace Block with a novice salesman.

Barr considered shifting one of the more experienced salesmen into that area. However, that would have involved a disruption of service in an additional territory, which was undesirable because it took several months for a salesman to build up a good rapport with customers. Barr's decision would affect his quota allocation because a salesman new to a territory could not be expected to immediately sell as well as the incumbent, and a novice salesman would require an even longer period of adaptation.

Barr was also concerned about territory 9961.

EXHIBIT 4
SALES RESULTS

Territory	1975 Budget (x1,000)	% of Total Budget	1975 Actual (x1,000)	Variance from Quota (V%)
9967 (Contract)	2,440	26.5	2,267	(7)
9961 (Greater Vancouver)	1,790	19.4	1,824	2
9962 (Interior)	1,624	17.7	1,433	(11)
9963 (Coastal)	2,111	23	2,364	12
9965 (Ind. dealers)	1,131	12.3	1,176	4
House	84	1.1	235	—
TOTAL	9,180	100	9,299	1

Territory	1976 Budget (x1,000)	% of Total Budget	1976 Actual (x1,000)	Variance from Quota (V%)
9967 (Contract)	2,587	26.2	2,845	10
9961 (Greater Vancouver)	2,005	20.3	2,165	8
9962 (Interior)	1,465	14.8	1,450	(1)
9963 (Coastal)	2,405	24.4	2,358	(2)
9965 (Ind. dealers)	1,334	13.5	1,494	12
House	52	.8	86	—
TOTAL	9,848	100	10,398	5

EXHIBIT 5
SALES PROJECTIONS AND QUOTAS, 1977–1978.

	Projected sales results 1977				
Territory	Oct. 1977 Year to Date	1977 Projected Total	1977 Budget	% of Total Budget	Projected Variance from Quota (V%)
9967	$2,447	$ 3,002	$ 2,859	25.0	5
9961	2,057	2,545	2,401	21.0	6
9962	1,318	1,623	1,727	15.1	(6)
9963	2,124	2,625	2,734	23.9	(4)
9965	1,394	1,720	1,578	13.8	9
House	132	162	139	1.2	—
TOTAL	$9,474	$11,677	$11,438		2

	Preliminary allocation 1978		
Territory	1977 Projection	1978 Budget*	% of Total Budget
9967	$ 3,002	$ 3,422	25.7
9961	2,545	2,901	21.8
9962	1,623	1,854	13.9
9963	2,625	2,992	22.5
9965	1,720	1,961	14.7
House	162	185	1.3
TOTAL	$11,677	$13,315	

*1978 Budget = 1977 territory projections + 14% = $13,315.

The territory comprised two large national accounts and seven major independent dealers. The buying decisions for the national accounts were made at their head offices, where G.E.'s regional salesmen had no control over the decisions. Recently, Barr had heard rumors that one of the national accounts was reviewing its purchase of G.E. Appliances. If they were to delist even some product lines, it would be a major blow to the salesman, Rizzuto, whose potential sales would be greatly reduced. Barr was unsure how to deal with that situation.

Another concern for Barr was the wide variance in buying of some accounts. Woodwards, Eatons, and McDonald Supply had large fluctuations from year to year. Also, Eatons, Hudson's Bay, and Woodwards had plans to open new stores in the Vancouver area sometime during the year. The sales increase to be generated by these events was hard to estimate.

The general economic outlook was poor. The Canadian dollar had fallen to 92 cents U.S. and unemployment was at about 8 percent. The government's anti-inflation program, which was scheduled to end in November 1978, had managed to keep inflation to the 8 percent level, but economists expected higher inflation and increased labor unrest during the post-control period.

The economic outlook was not the same in all areas. For instance, the Okanagan (9962) was a very depressed area. Tourism was down and fruit farmers were doing poorly despite good weather and record prices. Vancouver Island was still recovering from a 200 percent increase in ferry fares, while the lower mainland appeared to be in a relatively better position.

In the contract segment, construction had shown an increase over 1976. However, labor unrest was common. There had been a crippling eight-week strike in 1976, and there was a strong possibility of another strike in 1978.

With all of this in mind, Barr was very concerned that he allocate the quota properly because of the bonus system implications. How should he proceed? To help him in his decision, he reviewed a note on development of a sales commission plan which he had obtained while attending a seminar on sales management the previous year (see Appendix at end of case).

APPENDIX: Development of a Sales Commission Plan

A series of steps are required to establish the foundation upon which a Sales Commission Plan can be built. These steps are as follows:

A. Determine Specific Sales Objectives of Positions to be Included in Plan

For a Sales Commission Plan to succeed, it must be designed to encourage the attainment of the business objectives of the component division. Before deciding on the specific measures of performance to be used in the Plan, the component should review and define its major objectives. Typical objectives might be:

- Increase sales volume
- Do an effective balanced selling job in a variety of product lines
- Improve market share
- Reduce selling expense to sales ratios
- Develop new accounts or territories
- Introduce new products

Although it is probably neither desirable nor necessary to include all such objectives as specific measures of performance in the Plan, they should be kept in mind, at least to the extent that the performance measures chosen for the plan are compatible with and do not work against the overall accomplishment of the component's business objectives.

Also, the *relative* current importance or ranking of these objectives will provide guidance in selecting the number and type of performance measures to be included in the Plan.

B. Determine Quantitative Performance Measures to be Used

Although it may be *possible* to include a number of measures in a particular plan, there is a *drawback to using so many as to overly complicate it, and fragment the impact of any one measure on the participants.* A plan that is difficult to understand will lose a great deal of its motivation force, as well as being costly to administer properly.

For components who currently have a variable sales compensation plan(s) for their salesmen, a good starting point would be to consider the measures used in those Plans. Although the measurements used for *sales managers* need not be identical, they should at least be *compatible* with those used to determine their salesmen's commissions.

However, keep in mind that a performance measure that may not be appropriate for individual salesmen may be a good one to apply to their manager. Measurements involving attainment of a share of a defined market, balanced selling for a variety of products, and control of district or region expenses might well fall into this category.

Listed below are a variety of measurements that might be used to emphasize specific sales objectives.

Tailoring Commission Plan Measurements to Fit Component Objectives

Objectives	Possible Plan Measurements
1 Increase sales/orders volume	Net sales billed or orders received against quota
2 Increase sales of particular lines	Sales against product line quotas with weighted sales credits on individual lines
3 Increase market share	Percent realization (%R) of shares bogey
4 Do balanced selling job	%R of product line quotas with commissions increasing in proportion to number of lines up to quota
5 Increase profitability	Margin realized from sales Vary sales credits to emphasize profitable product lines Vary sales credit in relation to amount of price discount
6 Increase dealer sales	Pay distributor salesmen or sales manager in relation to realization of sales quotas of assigned dealers
7 Increase sales calls	%R of targeted calls per district or region
8 Introduce new product	Additional sales credits on new line for limited period
9 Control expense	%R of expense to sales or margin ratio Adjust sales credit in proportion to variance from expense budget
10 Sales teamwork	Share of incentive based upon group results.

For most components, all or most of these objectives will be desirable to some extent. The point is to select those of *greatest* importance where it will be possible to establish measures of standard or normal performance for individuals, or at least small groups of individuals working as a team.

If more than one performance measurement is to be used, the relative weighting of each measurement must be determined. If a measure is to be effective, it must carry enough weight to have at least some noticeable effect on the commission earnings of an individual.

As a general guide, it would be unusual for a plan to include more than two or three quantitative measures with a *minimum* weighting of 15–20 percent of planned commissions for any one measurement.

C. Establish Commission Payment Schedule for Each Performance Measure

1 Determine Appropriate Range of Performance for Each Measurement The performance range for a measurement defines the percent of standard performance (R%) at which commission earnings start to the point where they reach maximum.

The minimum point of the performance range for a given measurement should be set so that a majority of the participants can earn at least some incentive pay: and the maximum set at a point that is possible of attainment by some participants. These points will vary with the type of measure used, and the degree of predictability of individual budgets or other forms of measurement. In a period where overall performance is close to standard, 90–95 percent of the participants should fall within the performance range.

For the commission plan to be effective most of the participants should be operating within the performance range most of the time. If a participant is either far below the minimum of this range, or has reached the maximum, further improvement will not affect his commission earnings, and the plan will be largely inoperative as far as he is concerned.

Actual past experience of R%'s attained by participants is obviously the best indicator of what this range should be for each measure used. Lacking this, it is better to err on the side of having a wider range than one which proves to be too narrow. If some form of group measure is used, the variation from standard performance is likely to be less for the group in total than for individuals within it. For example, the performance range for total District performance would probably be narrower than the range established for individual salesmen within a District.

2 Determine Appropriate Reward : Risk Ratio for Commission Earnings This refers to the relationship of commission earned at standard performance, to maximum commission earnings available under the Plan. A Plan that pays 10 percent of base salary for normal or standard performance, and pays 30 percent as a maximum commission would have a 2:1 ratio. In other words, the participant can earn twice as much (20 percent) for above standard performance as he stands to lose for below standard performance (10 percent).

Reward under a sales commission plan should be related to the effort involved to produce a given result. To adequately encourage above standard results the reward:risk ratio should generally be at least 2:1. *The proper control of incentive plan payments lies in the proper setting of performance standards,* not in the setting of a low maximum payment for outstanding results that provides a minimum variation in individual earnings. Generally, a higher percentage of base salary should be paid for each 1%R above 100 percent than has been paid for each 1%R up to 100%R to reflect the relative difficulty involved in producing above standard results.

Once the performance range and reward-risk ratios have been determined, the schedule of payments for each performance measure can then be calculated. This will show the percentage of the participant's base salary earned for various performance results (R%) from the point at which commissions start to maximum performance.

Example: For measurement paying 20 percent of salary for standard performance.

% Base Salary Earned		% of Sales Quota
1% of base salary for each +1%R	0%	80% or below
	20%	100% (standard performance)
1.33% of base salary for each +1%R	60%	130% or above

D. Prepare Draft of Sales Commission Plan

After completion of the above steps, a draft of a sales commission plan should be prepared using the outline below as a guide.

KEYS TO EFFECTIVE COMMISSION PLANS

1 *Get the understanding and acceptance of the commission plan by the managers who will be involved in carrying it out.* They must be convinced of its effectiveness in order to properly explain and "sell" the Plan to the salesmen.

2 In turn, *be sure the plan is presented clearly to the salesmen* so that they have a good understanding of how the plan will work. We find that good acceptance of a sales commission plan on the part of salesmen correlates closely with how well they understood the plan and its effect on their compensation. *The salesman must be convinced that the measurements used are factors which he can control by his selling efforts.*

3 *Be sure the measurements used in the commission plan encourage the salesmen to achieve the marketing goals of your operation.* For example, if sales volume is the only performance measure, the salesman will concentrate on producing as much dollar volume as possible by spending most of his time on products with high volume potential. It will be difficult to get them to spend much time on introducing new products with relatively low volume, handling customer complaints, etc. Even though a good portion of their compensation may still be in salary, you can be sure they will wind up doing the things they feel will maximize their commission earnings.

4 One good solution to maintaining good sales direction is to put at least a portion of the commission earnings in an "incentive pool" to be distributed by the sales manager according to his judgment. This "pool" can vary in size according to some qualitative measure of the sales group's performance, but the manager can set individual measurements for each of his salesmen, and reward each man according to how well he fulfills his goals.

5 If at all possible, you should test the Plan for a period of time, perhaps in one or two sales areas or districts. To make it a real test you should actually pay commission earnings to the participants, but the potential risk and rewards can be limited. No matter how well a plan has been conceived, not all the potential pit-falls will be apparent until you've actually operated the plan for a period of time. The test period is a relatively painless way to get some experience.

6 Finally, after the plan is in operation, take time to analyze the results. Is the plan accomplishing what you want it to do, both in terms of business results produced and in realistically compensating salesmen for their efforts?

MONTECITO STATE COLLEGE: DIVISION OF EXTENSION STUDIES

Christopher H. Lovelock

"We need to take a hard look at how we're going to promote our extension programs and courses next year." Dr. Rosemary Shannon, Dean of Extension Studies at Montecito State College, was meeting in March 1983 with her assistant, Harry Fourman, to discuss plans for advertising and other communications for the 1983–84 school year.

BACKGROUND

Montecito State College (MSC) was located in Montecito, a suburb of the large western city of Sherman. The City of Sherman had a population of 755,000, while the metro area had a population of 1.8 million. On average, there were 2.6 persons per household.

The College, one of several in the Jefferson State College System, was comprised of the undergraduate day division, the graduate school, and the Division of Extension Studies. MSC had

Copyright © 1983 by the President and Fellows of Harvard College, Harvard Business School case 9-584-011.

been created in 1952 from the merger of Montecito Polytechnic College and Sherman Teachers' College. The facilities of the two institutions were finally combined in 1958 with the completion of a major expansion program at the 90-acre campus of the old "Poly."

In 1982–83, MSC enrolled a total of 6,200 students in the day division, 2,950 in extension studies, and 1,100 in the graduate school. Its undergraduate courses emphasized a variety of technical and business-related subjects, education, and the liberal arts. The graduate school offered MA, MS, and M. Ed. degrees in a number of fields, and had a good regional reputation for its programs in education, management, hotel administration, and psychology.

EXTENSION STUDIES

The Division of Extension Studies was responsible for a wide range of undergraduate and graduate courses offered during the late afternoon, weekday evenings, and Saturday morning hours, as well as for day and evening courses during two intensive summer sessions. Although these offerings were directed primarily at people holding jobs or having other responsibilities that made it difficult to attend on a full-time basis during the day, about 15 percent of the enrollees in extension courses were full-time undergraduates.

In addition, the division also sponsored a range of continuing education (CE) programs— short, noncredit workshops, courses, and seminars. Certificates were awarded upon satisfactory completion of selected courses. The structure and format of these ranged from one- to two-day workshops and seminars, to courses of five two-hour sessions given at weekly intervals, to twelve three-hour sessions offered twice weekly over a six-week period.

The tuition for degree courses in the Extension Division was $45.00 per credit hour for state residents and $75.00 for nonresidents and foreign students; auditors (noncredit) paid $35.00. Tuition fees were set by the Regents of the Jefferson State College System and had to be approved by the State Legislature. These fees were the same for all seven colleges in the system. Although degree courses ranged in length from 2 to 5 credits, the great majority carried 3 credits. After excluding cancellations, a total of 185 extension degree courses were offered at MSC in 1982–83. Fees for the continuing education programs ranged from $45–200—depending on the nature and length of the offering—and were at the discretion of the dean, subject to the approval of the president of the College.

The division had substantial autonomy with the College. It was required to be self-supporting, but was not assessed for many institutional costs, such as classroom space. Courses were taught by both full-time and adjunct faculty who, in most instances, were paid a fixed stipend per course. Part-time faculty were paid a flat rate of $1,500 to $1,800 per semester for a 3-credit course, depending on rank. Typically, courses met once a week for 2½ hours, although a few had two 75-minute classes each week.

The 1982–83 brochure listed 109 different extension courses for credit, many of them offered in both semesters. But, with a few exceptions, courses were automatically cancelled if student registrations failed to reach a pre-defined minimum. Some 900 of the students in Extension Studies in 1982–83 were participants in continuing education programs. (This figure excluded participants in one- and two-day seminars or company-sponsored programs.) The balance of 2,050 accounted for a total of some 5,200 course registrations during fall and spring semesters. Not all students were enrolled both semesters.

Dr. Shannon, a tenured associate professor of political science, was appointed dean of extension studies in July 1982 and had essentially inherited her predecessor's strategy for the current school year (including the two summer sessions). She expressed the view that MSC needed to devote greater commitment to its extension program, whose quality she regarded as uneven.

SATELLITE CAMPUSES

In addition to the permanent campus in Montecito, where all day undergraduate and graduate courses were offered, MSC also operated four "satellite" campuses in the evenings for its degree courses. These consisted of high school facilities, made available to MSC free of charge, in Sherman City, and the suburban towns of North Sherman, San Lucas, and Puget. Course registration in these four satellite campuses accounted for 20 percent of the total; enrollments per course were lower than at the main Montecito campus and there was a much higher rate of course cancellations. Exhibit 1 summarizes enrollments in extension studies at MSC over the past five years, while Exhibit 2 shows the geographic breakdown of students' home locations in 1982–83.

Continuing education programs were generally held at the Montecito campus, although a few had been held at one or other of the satellites. Periodically, CE courses would be commissioned from MSC by a large employer or other

EXHIBIT 1
COURSE REGISTRATIONS IN DIVISION OF EXTENSION STUDIES,
MONTECITO STATE COLLEGE, 1978–79 to 1982–83

Campus	1978–79	1979–80	1980–81	1981–82	1982–83
Montecito	3,775	3,829	4,006	4,218	4,163
Sherman City	615	603	545	421	481
North Sherman	—	110	213	246	232
Weston	68	96	—	—	—
Puget	—	—	—	113	98
Arvin	118	—	—	—	—
San Lucas	—	165	198	214	209
Total academic course registrations*	4,576	4,803	4,962	5,312	5,203
Total continuing education enrollments**	628	714	773	820	903

*About 80 percent of these registrants sought academic credit; the balance enrolled as auditors.
**Not broken out separately by campus since almost all continuing education courses were held at MSC's main campus in Montecito.
Source: Division of Extension Studies, Montecito State College.

organization. In this case the employer's offices or a nearby hotel would be used.

MSC had operated a satellite campus in Sherman City ever since the full-time operations of "Teachers" had been consolidated in Montecito.

EXHIBIT 2
HOME LOCATION OF EXTENSION REGISTRANTS AT MONTECITO STATE COLLEGE, 1982–83*

Location**	Students Enrolled for Credit in Extension Courses	Participants in Continuing Education Seminars
City of Sherman	29%	17%
Balance of Sherman County	7	8
North Sherman	9	11
Balance of Orezona County	30	23
Santa Rosa County	9	22
Wendell County	14	16
Other	2	3

*This included students taking courses at the satellite campuses.
**See Exhibit 3.
Source: Division of Extension Studies, Montecito State College.

For many years, this had been the only satellite operation, but from 1979 onwards the College began to experiment with different locations, some of which had subsequently been closed due to lack of success in attracting students. Past experience had shown that satellite campuses tended to draw from a much smaller radius than did the main campus. In selecting specific facilities, the division now looked for easily accessible sites situated near major highways. Availability of adequate parking was essential, while access to public transportation services was a strong plus.

After careful appraisal of the performance of the different satellite campuses in fall semester 1982, Dean Shannon had decided to close the existing Puget campus and to look for a new location in northwest Sherman County. She believed she had identified a promising site in Pine Creek.

One of the objectives of the satellite campuses was to attract students who might begin their studies at a satellite and then later go on to complete their degrees by taking more advanced courses at Montecito. However, few appeared to be doing this. On the other hand, students who lived near a satellite would sometimes travel all the way into Montecito to take courses there which were available at the satellite. Dean Shannon was not entirely sure why this happened (but surmised that it might reflect the greater use of part-time, adjunct faculty at the satellites). She noted that this practice indirectly led to cancellation of courses at satellites, because course registrations there had often been only one or two students short of the minimum (typically 15 students).

COMPETITION

Dean Shannon described the market for evening credit courses in the Greater Sherman area as "highly competitive," with strong competition coming from the University of Sherman and Wallace College (both private institutions), Sherman State College, Lakeview Junior College, and Valley Junior College. Additional competition came from the University of Jefferson and two county-financed community colleges in the metropolitan area. The dean did not consider the two proprietary schools in Sherman City to be direct competitors, since they were oriented primarily towards vocational education in fields such as computer programming and dental hygiene.[1]

Like Montecito State, a growing number of both public and private institutions operated satellite campuses in the suburbs and in outlying towns. Typically, the facilities used were local high schools whose classrooms were available for evening use. Exhibit 3 shows the location of all main and satellite campuses in the Greater Sherman area.

Tuition at private institutions was sometimes twice as high per credit hour as MSC's. Wallace College, which emphasized business and the social sciences, had been very aggressive in promoting its offerings, making extensive use of radio and newspaper advertising. Although enrollments had risen steadily at their main campus

---

[1] Proprietary schools are run as profit-making businesses offering vocationally oriented courses. Typically, they do not offer courses for academic credit (although certificates are awarded on completion of a course) and are not accredited.

in Santa Rosa, Dean Shannon had heard that their three satellite campuses were not doing especially well.

The two proprietary schools, one owned by a major industrial conglomerate, advertised widely on TV. The *Sherman Monitor* had recently published an exposé of one of these schools charging that its advertising deliberately misled prospective students. It was rumored that the state attorney general's office would soon undertake an investigation.

COMMUNICATIONS

The principal approaches used to promote the Extension Division had been to undertake advertising in the *Monitor* and selected suburban papers, and to publish a catalog. Some 20,000 copies of the catalog were prepared and printed each summer at a total cost of $10,800. About 4,000 were mailed out to a variety of organizations and agencies, including public libraries and company personnel departments. Others were sent out in response to requests or distributed at various locations on campus. The unit cost of printing an extra copy was 16.3 cents, and bulk rate mailing costs were 5.2 cents per copy. The catalog was printed in black and white on medium quality stock.

For its 1982–83 advertising, the division had used the *Sherman Monitor* and selected local newspapers. Although some competitors took full-page newspaper advertisements, and used these to list each and every course offered, MSC's strategy had been to take smaller format advertisements (between one-eighth and one-fourth of a page) which promoted the Montecito State name, listed the locations of the main campus and the various satellite campuses, highlighted the fields in which extension courses were offered, and provided a clip-out coupon and a telephone number which could be used to obtain further information.

In early December 1981, the Extension Division had joined forces with other divisions of the College to develop a four-page newsprint bro-

EXHIBIT 3

MAP OF GREATER SHERMAN AREA SHOWING CITIES IN WHICH ACADEMIC EXTENSION COURSES WERE OFFERED

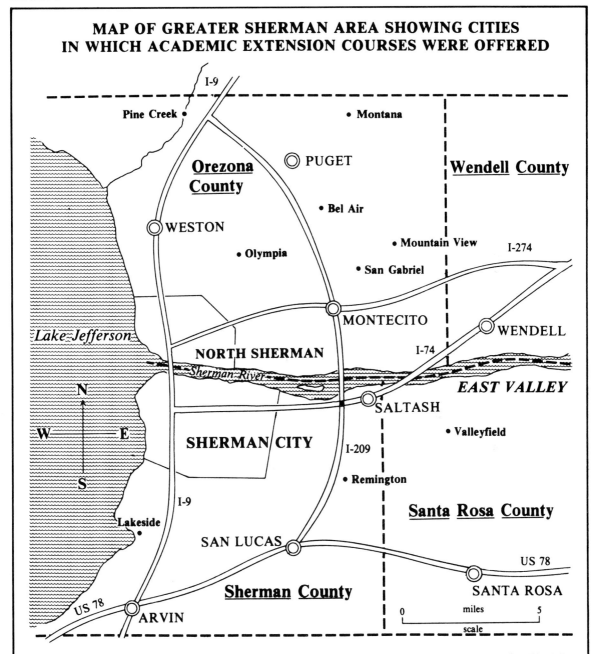

NOTE: The Greater Sherman Metropolitan Area includes all Sherman and Orezona Counties, plus SW Wendell County and NW Santa Rosa County. There are over 40 separate towns and municipalities in the Metro area (which is heavily urbanized), but only selected town names are shown on the map, which also shows the major freeways serving the Metro area. The largest suburban centers outside Sherman City and North Sherman are marked with a double circle.

chure, mailed to 100,000 homes in Montecito and surrounding towns. This included a listing of all spring semester extension courses. The total costs of this mailing (of which Extension Studies paid one-third), were $3,900 for production and printing, plus $5,700 for preparation and mailing. A certain amount of radio advertising had been used by the division of extension studies;

1982–83 costs amounted to about $5,000. However, Dean Shannon expressed doubts about the value of radio advertising. Few registrants could be traced to radio advertising in a recent survey (Exhibit 4), nor was radio often mentioned when telephone enquirers were asked by extension staff how they had learned of Montecito State.

In February 1983, the division had conducted

EXHIBIT 4

RESPONSES TO MAIL SURVEY OF FALL 1982 EXTENSION DIVISION STUDENTS AT MONTECITO STATE (ALL CAMPUSES) WHO DID NOT RE-REGISTER IN SPRING 1983

Total Number of Courses for Which you Registered in Fall 1982
One	126
Two	45
Three	3
Four	2

Your Primary Purpose in Registering Last Semester
Degree credit	105
Professional advancement	44
Desire for knowledge	21
General interest	15
Self improvement	11
Meet new people	5

Your Primary Source of Learning About the Course(s)
A friend or relative	45
Employer/employment agency or education/training office	20
Advertisement in *Sherman Monitor*	16
Advertisement in local suburban newspaper	16
A student enrolled in the program	11
Receipt of unsolicited pamphlet, bulletin, brochure	10
Solicited pamphlet	10
Instructor/counselor at another institution	8
Official pamphlet, bulletin, brochure seen at work	7
Advertisements/information on radio/television	7
Close to home	5
Other	9

*Did All the Courses You Took Last Fall Measure Up to the Description in College Material Received By You?**
1 Completely	96
2 Reasonably So	57
3 To some degree	17
4 Not at all	12

Did You Feel that All the Courses You Took Last Fall Were Effectively Taught?†
1 Very effective	84
2 Fairly Effective	43

EXHIBIT 4 *(continued)*

3 Average	25
4 Rather Ineffective	12
5 Very Ineffective	10

Principal Reason for Not Attending Spring 1983

Job responsibilities conflicted	36
Financial difficulties	30
Moved too far to travel	21
Program required more time than am prepared to invest right now	17
Couldn't find any course of interest	14
Family problems or conflicts	13
Health problems (mine or in family)	12
Veterans benefits discontinued	9
Wanted more advanced courses	8
Completed all degree requirements	5
Did not fit schedule	5
Course not offered	4
Other	20

Planning to Register Again in Evening Division?

Next summer	24
Next fall	44
No—attending a private institution	8
No—attending another public institution	19
No—planning to attend a private institution	9
No—planning to attend another public institution	13
No	21
Uncertain	38

Your Sex

Male	97
Female	109

Your Present Age

17–19	4
20–24	51
25–29	48
30–34	36
35–39	22
40–44	10
45–49	6
50–54	5
55 or over	2

Highest Level of Educational Achievement

Master's Degree or higher	13
Bachelor's Degree	48
More than 2 years of college	35
Associate Degree	25
Some college but less than 2 years	56
High School graduate/equivalency	9

* 4-point scale.
† 5-point scale.
Note: Survey was conducted February 1983. 206 completed questionnaires were received, giving a response rate of 32%. Selected questions only are listed below and non-responses are not shown.
Source: Division of Extension Studies, Montecito State College.

a mail survey of evening degree students registered in fall 1982 who did not graduate at the end of that semester and had not reregistered in January for the spring semester. Among other things, this asked respondents their primary source of learning about the courses they took. Of the 638 questionnaires mailed, 206 had been completed and returned. Selected responses are shown in Exhibit 4. Friends and relatives were given as the primary source of information about courses, followed by professional referrals, *Monitor* advertising, and advertisements in local suburban newspapers.

In addition to being listed in the catalog, most of the 70 continuing education courses offered in 1982–83 were also promoted by direct mail. The division had developed or purchased several mailing lists, enabling it to target brochures promoting specific courses or seminars at groups likely to be interested in the programs in question. These lists included: members of professional organizations (e.g., accountants, lawyers); employers (divided into several categories, according to size, location and activities or product of the organization); school superintendents, chambers of commerce, public libraries throughout the state, and past participants.

Mailings were running at the level of 200,000 a year. The unit cost of producing and printing a brochure ranged from one cent to six or seven cents, depending on length and format, paper stock, and use of color in printing. Bulk mailing costs were 5.2 cents per unit. No mass media advertising had been used to promote continuing education (CE) courses, although press releases promoting specific courses were sometimes picked up by the newsletters and other periodicals published by state and local professional associations. CE mailing expenditures in 1982–83 were budgeted at $18,100.

Several changes were planned for 1983–84. Dean Shannon had assigned primary responsibility for advertising decisions to her assistant, Harry Fourman, and had also placed him in charge of the satellite campus program. Fourman, who

held an MBA from the University of Jefferson, combined his appointment as assistant dean of Extension Studies with a half-time appointment as instructor in management at MSC. As a start, Fourman had compiled some information on the nature of the extension programs offered at MSC and each of its competitors (Exhibit 5).

Advertising and Publicity at MSC

The responsibility for advertising and publicity at Montecito State was in the hands of Roberta Jensen, director of public information. The public information office served every department on campus, including alumni activities. It handled all news items for the College and developed publicity to promote major events. Jensen headed up a group of four people, including a publications editor and a news bureau coordinator. Her own background included a degree in communications, work for the *Chicago Tribune* and a Sherman advertising agency, and three years as assistant director of public relations for a major hospital in Sherman. She had joined MSC in fall 1981.

Total expenditures on publications at MSC amounted to some $100,000 a year. The Division of Extension Studies accounted for about 30 percent of this. Although large pieces, such as catalogs and the annual report, were sent to outside printers, Jensen noted that more work was being done in-house than before, with small flyers being designed, pasted up and typeset on campus. The public information office did not know the total costs incurred by the College for mailing of publications, since mailings were handled on a departmental or division basis. Certain items were bulk-mailed by third class mail, and the College also had two second class mailing permits enabling it, as a nonprofit organization, to mail items such as catalogs more cheaply but supposedly faster. However, various constraints and restrictions had to be observed to qualify for this reduced rate.

MSC did not use a public relations agency for

publicity and news releases, preferring to handle such activities in-house. For media advertising, though, the College used a local advertising agency. The total advertising budget was relatively small compared to that of some of the private junior colleges and proprietary schools in the area. Including both media purchases and production costs, MSC's advertising expenditures in 1982–83 were projected to total just over $90,000. The Division of Extension Studies accounted for over 50 percent of this total.

Rather than working on a commission basis with the advertising agency (whereby the latter's remuneration came from a 15 percent commission received from the media with whom the advertising was placed), MSC had put the agency on a retainer of $1,300 per month and had arranged for it to rebate the commissions directly to the college. This retainer covered consulting services and development of media campaigns, including design of copy and artwork. The advantage of the retainer from the agency's standpoint was that it provided a guaranteed income which would not be affected by fluctuations in the college advertising expenditures. From MSC's standpoint, it meant that there was no incentive for the agency to recommend additional advertising outlays with a view to boosting its commission income.

In an effort to maximize exposure for Montecito State, the public information office used public service announcements (PSAs) on radio and television to promote college events and programs, as well as seeking newspaper listings in the "Calendar" sections. However, Jensen felt that the media were generally reluctant to accept PSAs to promote academic courses. Commenting on the different media in the Greater Sherman area, she observed:

Sherman has one major, metropolitan daily paper, the *Sherman Monitor*. There used to be both morning and evening editions, but now it's only published mornings. Frankly, it's not one of the great newspapers of America, but it is quite widely read,

and gives us an opportunity to hit a wide variety of people.

We have a half-dozen varying quality suburban dailies, and a terrific number of weekly papers, both independent and chain. Most of the suburban dailies are published in the evening. Some households subscribe to both the *Monitor* and a suburban daily. The further you get from Sherman City, the more likely people are to buy a local daily rather than the *Monitor*.

The problem with advertising in suburban papers is that the costs really mount up—collectively, they nickle and dime you to death. The advertising agencies all tell me that the *Monitor* is more effective, though sometimes I have my doubts. But the agencies tell you to use those suburban papers for publicity. They'll nearly always run your news stories, since they need "filler." The *Monitor* doesn't.

We've not purchased television time at all. We wouldn't settle for anything less than first-rate commercials. Just to produce two different 30-second television spots and two different 10-second spots could run anywhere from ten to fifteen thousand dollars. The cost of running the ads would be relatively inexpensive by contrast, depending on what station and time slot you use. My question is whether any return we might generate would justify the cost.

We've used radio for extension studies, but always in conjunction with other media, such as newspapers, and direct mail. The theory behind this is that one medium reinforces another. We tend to use radio towards the end of a campaign—for instance during the last two weeks of a six-week campaign. We believe that it provides a good reminder, a final "push" to make your prospects act. Our extension students are mostly employed, working people, so we often go after "drive time," which is expensive.[2] There are a large number of different radio stations in this area and most of them tailor their programs to fairly specific market segments.

We haven't been able to trace many enquiries to those radio ads. However, advertising agencies will

---

[2] "Drive Time" is time during the morning and evening commute periods when large numbers of people are listening to the radio in their cars as they drive to or from work.

EXHIBIT 5
EXTENSION PROGRAMS AT DEGREE-GRANTING INSTITUTIONS IN THE SHERMAN METRO AREA

Institution	Type	Main Campus Location	1982-83 Satellite Campus Locations	Extension Course Registrations (1982-83)	Fee per Credit Unit	Academic Calendar	1983 Fall Classes Begin	Principal Communications Efforts (1982-83)
Montecito State C.	Public 4-Year Some Grad Programs	Montecito	North Sherman Puget San Lucas Sherman City	5,312	$45	Semester (finishes before Xmas)	Sept. 19	Direct Mail *Sherman Monitor* Local Newspapers Radio (some)
Arvin Comm. C.	Public 2-Year	Arvin	—	2,102	$35	Quarter	Oct. 3	Direct Mail Local Newspapers
Lakeview Jr. C.	Private 2-Year	Weston	Bel Air Puget Olympia North Sherman	5,100	$80	Semester (finishes before Xmas)	Sept. 7	*Sherman Monitor* Local Newspapers OCT Buses Radio
Orezona Comm. C.	Public 2-Year	Mountain View	Montana	2,311	$35	Quarter	Oct. 3	Local Newspapers Radio
St. Anne's C.	Private 4-Year	Bel Air	—	484	$85	Semester (finishes after Xmas)	Sept. 21	Local Newspapers (?)

Institution	Type	City	Feeder Areas	Enrollment	Fee	Calendar	Date	Media
Sherman State C.	Public 4-Year	Sherman City	—	2,950	$45	Semester (finishes before Xmas)	Sept. 19	Sherman Monitor
U. of Jefferson	Public 4-Year Many Grad Programs	Lakeside	Arvin, Sherman City, Remington	6,442	$55	Quarter	Sept. 12	Direct Mail, Sherman Monitor, Local Newspapers, Radio
U. of Sherman	Private 4-Year Many Grad Programs	Sherman City	North Sherman, Olympia, Puget, Valleyfield, Weston	7,106	$75	Quarter	Sept. 26	Direct Mail, Sherman Monitor, Local Newspapers, Radio, Television, Buses
Valley Jr. C.	Private 2-Year	Saltash	Mountain View, Remington, San Gabriel, San Lucas	6,421	$70	Semester	Sept. 19	Radio, Sherman Monitor, Television, Billboards, San Lucas Post
Wallace College	Private 4-Year Some Masters Programs	Santa Rosa	Saltash, San Lucas, Wendell	500	$95	Semester (finishes before Xmas)	Sept. 12	Direct Mail, Radio, Sherman Monitor, San Lucas Post
Wendell College	Private 4-Year	Wendell	—	1,244	$90	4-1-4	Sept. 7	Local Newspapers

tell you that people don't always remember accurately where they learned about a specific product. We've surveyed people on where they first heard about our programs, and often they'll list a newspaper in which we *didn't* advertise!

Two things we haven't used are car cards on the buses and billboards. I have noticed that Lakeview advertises quite heavily on the buses—their ads have little brochures you can tear off and mail in for further information. Nobody around here except the proprietary schools and Valley Junior seem to use billboards, although I know colleges in other cities do.

Developing a Communications Program

In early March 1983, the extension studies staff was evaluating alternative communications strategies for 1983–84. Although the start of the fall semester was still over six months away, a long lead time was required. Meetings were also being held with the director of public information, Roberta Jensen, and would be held later with MSC's advertising agency.

At their first meeting together, Roberta Jensen told Harry Fourman:

One of the things MSC hasn't done as well as it might is to figure out the effectiveness of different advertising approaches. I suspect that habit and intuition have played a significant role in making advertising decisions. Candidly, it looks as though the advertising agency has played a very passive role in media selection in recent years.

Harry Fourman looked thoughtful. "The trouble," he said, "is that we don't have one single funnel through which all our responses flow." He paused, then continued:

We do know that the phone starts to ring as soon as advertising begins. We've also found that while we get good response rates from return of newspaper coupons and self-mailer cards asking for information, the ultimate registration rates resulting from these enquiries have been relatively low.

In 1982–83, the division's budget for promot-

ing degree and continuing education programs offered during the fall and spring semesters had been set at $88,800 (the budget for the summer sessions was set separately). Expenditures were broken down as follows:

Printing of catalogs, brochures, etc.	$20,800
Postage costs	12,600
Radio advertising	5,000
Labor (mailroom, labeling, etc.)	7,000
Newspaper advertising:	
Sherman Monitor	33,700
Selected suburban dailies	6,800
Advertising production costs	2,900
Total Budget	$88,800

Despite rising costs, the vice president–finance had indicated that this budget figure would have to remain unchanged in 1983–84.[3] The question was how to allocate these expenditures among the different alternative media. Of particular interest to the dean and assistant dean of Extension Studies was the relative emphasis that should be given to promoting the satellite campuses and the many continuing education programs. To help him in analyzing the situation, Harry Fourman had compiled a table highlighting the home locations of extension students for 1982–83 (Exhibit 2). At his request, Roberta Jensen had provided some basic cost data on advertising in Sherman area newspapers (Exhibit 6), and also sent him a short memo concerning advertising costs for radio, television, billboard, and transit advertising (Exhibit 7).

Enrollment figures had dropped slightly for extension courses over the past year, but risen for continuing education (CE) programs. The goal

---

[3] Although bulk rate mailing costs were expected to remain at 5.2 cents per unit for the current year, it was estimated that printing and production costs in 1983–84 would be 5 percent higher than during the 1982–83 academic year and that labor costs at MSC would be 6 percent higher. The newspaper and radio advertising costs shown in Exhibits 6 and 7 were about 7 percent above the rates paid by MSC in 1982–83.

EXHIBIT 6

SAMPLE ADVERTISING RATES FOR NEWSPAPERS CIRCULATING IN GREATER SHERMAN AREA

Newspaper	Rate per Line[1]	Lines Per Page[2]	Total Circulation (thousands of copies)
Major Dailies			
Wall Street Journal, (western edition)	$7.80	1,776	2,003[3]
Sherman Monitor	5.45	2,400	511
Suburban Local Dailies[4]			
Arvin Independent	.38	2,400	9
East Valley Star Advocate	.50	2,400	40
Montecito Sun	.79	2,400	55
Pine Creek Enquirer	.29	2,352	11
San Lucas Post	.91	2,464	73
Weston Journal	.30	2,352	14
Suburban/Local Weeklies[5]	.27–.55		

[1] The agate line is the basic advertising cost unit for newspapers. (There are 14 agate lines per column inch in classified advertising.) Although rates tend to vary according to location in the paper and discounts may be given for large format ads or multiple insertions, for the purposes of case analysis, please work from these line rates and assume no discounts.

[2] This provides some sense of the format and size of the paper's pages. The Sherman Monitor page format of 2,400 lines represents approximately 13½″ × 21″ (284 sq. ins.) of space within the printed margins. In making rough calculations for case analysis, take 12 lines as equivalent to 1″ × 1″ of display advertising space.

[3] Estimated circulation in Sherman Metro area: 69,000

[4] Most of these suburban dailies also circulated in adjoining towns and cities.

[5] Thirty-one of the towns and cities within or near Greater Sherman had their own local weekly newspaper.

Source: Newspaper Rates and Data, Standard Rate and Data Service, Inc., January 1983.

that Shannon and Fourman had agreed on for 1983–84 was to increase CE enrollments from 900 to 1,000 and to increase the number of extension course registrations from 5,200 to 5,500.

A NEW DEVELOPMENT

As Fourman sat working at the desk in his rather cramped little office with the door ajar, he heard his name called. It was Dean Shannon. "Hi, Rosemary!" he said. "What's up?"

Shannon pulled over a chair and sat down.

I just got out of a meeting with the president. He agreed to increase our communications budget for next year when he heard that we had signed up Pine Creek High for our new satellite campus. He lives up that way himself and agrees with me that the north county area has real growth potential. The problem with our Puget campus was that access was difficult, whereas Pine Creek is just two blocks from a freeway exit and also has very good bus service.

But he's not happy with MSC's satellite program and told me that next year may be our last chance. Unless we can get course registrations up to a total of 1,200 at the four satellites, he says he'll be forced to consider eliminating them, except the Sherman one, which he has to keep for political reasons.

Fourman leaned forward, anxiously. "So how much money is he willing to let us have next year?"

Ninety-five thousand, but it's not exactly carte blanche. On the one hand, he said that we should

EXHIBIT 7

MONTECITO STATE COLLEGE MEMO ON RADIO, TELEVISION, BILLBOARD, AND TRANSIT ADVERTISING COSTS

March 3, 1983

TO: Harry Fourman
FROM: Roberta Jensen

It's easier said than done to give you "representative" advertising rates for radio and television stations in the Greater Sherman area, since these rates are subject to so many variations, but I'll try to give you some feel at least for the numbers involved.

Television

There are five commercial television stations which can be received in the Sherman metro area. Four have their transmitters in or near Sherman City, while the fifth broadcasts from Wendell and its signal can be picked up in most parts of the metro area, but the quality of reception varies. These stations are:

KZBA-TV	Channel 3	CBS affiliate
KCCL-TV	Channel 4	NBC affiliate
KFFO-TV	Channel 8	ABC affiliate
KSSM-TV	Channel 12	NBC (Wendell)
KIRM-TV	Channel 23	Independent

Rates for each of these stations vary substantially by time of day and nature of program, reflecting both type and size of audience reached. The table below should give you some feel for the ranges of rates charged for different stations at different times of day. All rates are for a single 30-second spot, based upon the purchase of 10–12 such spots. Exact times for running the spots cannot be specified but are at the discretion of the station. Smaller purchases would cost more on a per-unit basis.

			Times		
TV Channel	**Early AM**	**Local Daytime**	**Evening Prime Time**	**Late Evening**	**Late Night**
3, 4, 8	$80–150	$200–500	$1,300–3,200	$350–500	$100–250
12	50–120	150–210	700–1,500	300–450	65–90
23	40–70	50–150	300–600	150–250	40–70

Radio

We certainly have a lot of radio stations in the metro area. There are 15 AM stations and 9 FMs. Some of these, such as KQFD and KRPC-FM, are National Public Radio affiliates, and accept no advertising. Below, I've listed some sample advertising rates for a 30-second radio spot (assuming, again, a purchase of 10–12 such spots). I've confined the list to AM stations—FMs are usually cheaper, but tend to reach a smaller audience; among other things, not that many people have FM car radios, and FM transmissions—being UHF and usually lower power—tend to reach a smaller geographic area than AM.

EXHIBIT 7 *(continued)*

Station	Programming	Principal Target Audience	Drive Time (AM)	Drive Time (PM)	Mid-day/ Evening	Late Night
			Times			
KEFJ	Music, easy listening	Adults 35–49	$ 45	$ 35	$32	$27
KHHD	Talk, sports, news, music	Adults 18–65	125	95	50–80	50
KMPC	Top 40s, rock	Teens, adults 18–35	40	30	22	12
KROQ	Rock, etc.	Teens, young adults	110	75	55–125	45–65
KJIM	Talk shows, popular music for adults	Adults 35 +	110	85	60–100	30
KHRP	Classical music	Adults 18 +	60	55	53	50
KCSB*	Black oriented	Black adults	30	25	22	*
KMNC	Continuous news and information, traffic reports	Adults 18–49	190	130	55–115	30–55
KCHX	Spanish language (talk and music)	Spanish-speaking adults 18 +	35	25	25	15

* Goes off air at sundown.

Outdoor Advertising

It's a bit easier to give an answer on billboards. (I'm assuming you are not interested in the fancy painted variety, just the type you stick paper on.) Billboard rentals vary somewhat according to location and whether or not they're illuminated. A typical cost in the Sherman area would be $315 per month. To this, you've got to add design and production costs of 15–40 percent, plus the cost of putting them up. At a very rough guess, I'd say that a three-month campaign involving ten billboards would cost you a total of about $11,500; for one month, the cost would be around $5,400.

Transit Advertising

As you probably know, there are two transit districts in the metropolitan area—the Sherman Santa Rosa Transit Authority, which operates south of the river, the Orezona County Transit which serves all Orezona County and has commuter services into Sherman City. The SSRTA has 500 buses and a daily ridership of 220,000 passengers; OCT has 300 buses and 100,000 riders. OCT is generally regarded as the better run of the two. Most of their buses are fairly new, they attract a lot of commuters, and there's relatively little vandalism (I know all this because my husband Jack takes OCT to work every day!). Both sell 11″ × 28″ car cards for interior display in the vehicles. They usually charge $10 per card per month and you've got to specify at the outset how many months you want; I should be able to get us a 25 percent discount because we're a public operation. Each transit district has a minimum placement of 50 cards, and you have to take pot-luck on which routes they appear on. But they won't put in more than one car card per bus unless you request it. To print up a three-color card averages $4.30 per card on a print run of 200 cards. After that, the incremental cost is about $1.45 per card.

try to be innovative, that he thinks the division has been in a rut as far as its communications are concerned. Then in the next breath he said that he feels our advertising should be ''dignified''—whatever *that* may mean—and shouldn't make us look like one of those proprietary schools. He also had to overrule Harvey Stimson, the VP–Finance, who was furious about our increased budget—he feels advertising is a waste of money.

She pulled a face, then continued:

The main thing is, he wants to go over the division's marketing plan for fall and spring semesters with us personally next month. He says it is high time he educated himself as to what marketing is all about!

MEDIQUIP, S.A.

Kamran Kashani

On January 18, 1981, Kurt Thaldorf, a sales engineer for the German sales subsidiary of Mediquip, S.A., was informed by Lohmann University Hospital in Stuttgart that it had decided to place an order with Sigma, a Dutch competitor, for a CT scanner. The hospital's decision came as disappointing news to Thaldorf, who had worked for nearly eight months on the account. The order, if obtained, would have meant a sale of DM 1,580,000 for the sales engineer. He was convinced that Mediquip's CT scanner was technologically superior to Sigma's, and overall a better product.

Thaldorf began a review of his call reports in order to better understand the factors that led to Lohmann University Hospital's decision. He wanted to apply the lessons from this case to future sales situations.

Note: All names and financial data have been disguised.
Copyright © 1981 by IMEDE (Institut pour l'Etude des Méthodes de Direction de l'Entreprise), Lausanne, Switzerland.

BACKGROUND

The computer tomography (CT) scanner was a relatively recent product in the field of diagnostic imaging. The medical device, used for diagnostic purposes, allowed examination of cross sections of the human body through display of images. CT scanners combined sophisticated X-ray equipment with a computer to collect the necessary data and translate them into visual images.

When computer tomography was first introduced in the late 1960's, radiologists hailed it as a major technological breakthrough. Commenting on the advantages of CT scanners, a product specialist with Mediquip said, "The end product looks very much like an X-ray image. The only difference is that with scanners you can see sections of a body that were never seen before on a screen—like the pancreas. A radiologist, for example, can diagnose the cancer of pancreas less than two weeks after it develops. This was not possible before the CT scanners."

Mediquip was a subsidiary of Technologie

Universelle, a French conglomerate. The company's product line included, in addition to CT scanners, X-ray, ultrasonic and nuclear diagnostic equipment. Mediquip enjoyed worldwide a reputation for advanced technology and competent after-sales service.

"Our competitors are mostly from other European countries," commented Mediquip's Sales Director for Europe. "In some markets they have been there longer than we have and they know the decision makers better than we do. But we are learning fast." Sigma, the subsidiary of a diversified Dutch company under the same name, was the company's most serious competitor. Other major contenders in the CT scanner market were FNC, Eldora, Magna and Piper.

Mediquip executives estimated the European market for CT scanners to be in the neighborhood of 200 units per year. They pointed out that prices ranged between DM 1–2 million per unit. The company's CT scanner sold in the upper end of the price range. "Our equipment is at least two years ahead of our most advanced competition," explained a sales executive. "And our price reflects this technological superiority."

Mediquip's sales organization in Europe included eight country sales subsidiaries each headed by a managing director. Within each country, sales engineers reported to regional sales managers who themselves reported to the managing director. Product specialists provided technical support to the sales force in each country.

BUYERS OF CT SCANNERS

A sales executive at Mediquip described the buyers of CT scanners as follows:

Most of our sales are to what we call the public sector, the health agencies that are either government-owned or belong to non-profit support organizations such as universities and philanthropic institutions. They are the sort of buyers who buy through formal tenders and who have to budget their purchases at least one year in advance. Once the budget is allocated it must then be spent before the end of the year. Only a minor share of our CT scanner sales goes to the private sector, the profit oriented organizations such as private hospitals or private radiologists.

Between the two markets, the public sector is much more complex. Typically, there are at least four groups who get involved in the purchase decision: the radiologists, the physicists, the administrators and the people from the supporting agency—usually those who approve the budget for purchase of a CT scanner.

Radiologists are users of the equipment. They are doctors whose diagnostic services are sought by other doctors in the hospital or clinic. Patients remember their doctors, but not the radiologists. They never receive flowers from the patients! A CT scanner could really enhance their professional image among their colleagues.

Physicists are the scientists in residence. They write the technical specifications which competing CT scanners must meet. The physicists should know the state of the art in X-ray technology. Their primary concern is the patient's safety.

The administrators are, well, administrators. They have the financial responsibility for their organization. They are concerned with the cost of CT scanners, but also with what revenues they can generate. The administrators are extremely wary of purchasing an expensive technological toy that becomes obsolete in a few years' time.

The people from the supporting agency are usually not directly involved with decisions as to which product to purchase. But since they must approve the expenditures, they do play an indirect role. Their influence is mostly felt by the administrators.

The interplay among the four groups, as you can imagine, is quite complex. The powers of each group in relationship to the others vary from organization to organization. The administrator, for example, is the top decision-maker in certain hospitals. In others, he is only a buyer. One of the key tasks of our sales engineers is to define for each potential account the relative powers of the players. Only then can they set priorities and formulate selling strategies.

The European sales organization at Mediquip had recently put into use a series of forms designed to help sales engineers in their account analysis and strategy formulation. A sample of the forms, called Account Management Analysis, is reproduced in Exhibit 1.

LOHMANN UNIVERSITY HOSPITAL

Lohmann University Hospital (LUH) was a large general hospital serving Stuttgart, a city of one million residents. The hospital was part of the university's medical school. The university was a leading teaching center and enjoyed an excellent reputation. LUH's radiology department had a variety of X-ray equipment from a number of European manufacturers including Sigma and FNC. Five radiologists staffed the department, which was headed by a senior and nationally known radiologist, Professor Steinborn.

Thaldorf's Sales Activities

From the records he had kept of his sales calls, Thaldorf reviewed the events for the period between June 5, 1980, when he learned of LUH's interest in purchasing a CT scanner and January 18, 1981, when he was informed that Mediquip had lost the order.

June 5, 1980   Office received a call from a Professor Steinborn from Lohmann University Hospital regarding a CT scanner. I was assigned to make the call on the professor. Looked through our files to find out if we had sold anything to the hospital before. We had not. Made an appointment to see the professor on June 9.

June 9, 1980   Called on Professor Steinborn who informed me of a recent decision by university directors to set aside funds next year for the purchase of the hospital's first CT scanner. The professor wanted to know what we had to offer. Told him the general features of our CT system. Gave him some brochures. Asked a few questions which led me to believe other companies had come to see him before I did. Told me to check with Dr. Rufer, the hospital's physicist,

regarding the specs. Made an appointment to see him again in ten days' time. Called on Dr. Rufer who was not there. His secretary gave me a lengthy document on the scanner specs.

June 10, 1980   Read the specs last night. Looked like they had been copied straight from somebody's technical manual. Showed them to our Product Specialist who confirmed my own hunch that our system met and exceeded the specs. Made an appointment to see Dr. Rufer next week.

June 15, 1980   Called on Dr. Rufer. Told him about our system's features and the fact that we met all the specs set down on the document. He looked somewhat unimpressed. Left him with technical documents on our system.

June 19, 1980   Called on Professor Steinborn. Had read the material I had left with him. Looked sort of pleased with the features. Asked about our upgrading scheme. Told him we would undertake to upgrade the system as new features became available. Unlike other systems, Mediquip can be made to accommodate the latest technology. There will be no risk of obsolescence for a long time. He was quite impressed. Also answered his questions regarding image manipulation, image processing speed and our service capability. Just before I left he inquired about our price. Told him I would have an informative quote for him at our next meeting. Made an appointment to see him on July 23 after he returned from his vacation. Told me to get in touch with Carl Hartmann, the hospital's general director, in the interim.

July 1, 1980   Called on Hartmann. It was difficult to get an appointment with him. Told him about our interest in supplying his hospital with our CT scanner which met all the specs as defined by Dr. Rufer. Also informed him of our excellent service capability. He wanted to know which other hospitals in the country had pur-

EXHIBIT 1

MEDIQUIP, S.A. ACCOUNT MANAGEMENT ANALYSIS FORMS

Key Account: _____

ACCOUNT MANAGEMENT ANALYSIS

The enclosed forms are designed to facilitate your management of:

1 A key sales account

2 The *Mediquip* resources that can be applied to this key account

Completing the enclosed forms, you will:

- Identify installed equipment, and planned or potential new equipment
- Analyze purchase decision process and influence patterns, including:
  — Identify and prioritize all major sources of influence
  — Project probable sequence of events and timing of decision process
  — Assess position/interest of each major influence source
  — Identify major competition and probable strategies
  — Identify needed information/support
- Establish an account development strategy, including:
  — Select key contacts
  — Establish strategy and tactics for each key contact, identify appropriate *Mediquip* personnel
  — Assess plans for the most effective use of local team and headquarters resources

KEY ACCOUNT DATA

☐ Original (Date:_____) Account No.:_____ Type of Institute:_____

☐ Revision (Date:_____) Sales Specialist:_____ Bed Size:_____

　　　　　　　　　　　　　　　Country/Region/District:_____ Telephone:_____

1. CUSTOMER (HOSPITAL, CLINIC, PRIVATE INSTITUTE)

　Name:_____

　Street Address:_____

　City, State:_____

2. DECISION MAKERS – IMPORTANT CONTACTS

INDIVIDUALS	NAME	SPECIALTY	REMARKS
Medical Staff			
Administration			
Local Government			
State Government			

This exhibit presents a condensed version of the forms, which comprised eight 8½ x 11 inch sheets for entry of relevant information.

3. INSTALLED EQUIPMENT

TYPE	DESCRIPTION	SUPPLIED BY	INSTALLATION DATE	YEAR TO REPLACE	VALUE OF POTENTIAL ORDER
X-ray Nuclear Ultrasound RTP CT					

4. PLANNED NEW EQUIPMENT

TYPE	QUOTE NO.	QUOTE DATE	% CHANCE	EST. ORDER DATE 1980	EST. ORDER DATE 1981	EST. DELIVERY 1980	EST. DELIVERY 1981	QUOTED PRICE

5. COMPETITION

COMPANY/PRODUCT	STRATEGY/TACTICS	% CHANCE	STRENGTH	WEAKNESS

6. SALES PLAN   Product: _____   Quote No: _____   Quoted Price: _____

KEY ISSUES	*Mediquip's* PLAN	SUPPORT NEEDED FROM:	DATE OF FOLLOW-UP/REMARKS

7. ACTIONS – IN SUPPORT OF PLAN

SPECIFIC ACTION	RESPONSIBILITY	DUE DATES ORIGINAL	DUE DATES REVISED	DUE DATES COMPLETED	RESULTS/REMARKS

8. ORDER STATUS REPORT

REVISION DATE	ACCOUNT NAME AND LOCATION	ISSUES/COMPETITIVE STRATEGY	ACTIONS/STRATEGY	RESPON-SIBILITY	% CHANCE	EXPECTED ORDER TIMING	WIN/LOSE

chased our system. Told him I would drop him a list of buyers in a few days' time. Asked about the price. Gave him an informative quote of DM 1,900,000—a price we had arrived at with my boss since my visit to Professor Steinborn. He shook his head saying, "Other scanners are cheaper by a wide margin." I explained that our price reflected the latest technology which was incorporated in it. Also mentioned that the price differential was an investment that could pay for itself several times over through faster speed of operation. He was noncommittal. Before leaving his office he instructed me not to talk to anybody else about the price. Asked him specifically if it included Professor Steinborn. He said it did. Left him with a lot of material on our system.

July 3, 1980 Took a list of three other hospitals of a similar size that had installed our system to Hartmann's office. He was out. Left it with his secretary who recognized me. Learned from her that at least two other firms, Sigma and FNC, were competing for the order. She also volunteered the information that "prices are so different, Mr. Hartmann is confused." She added that the final decision will be made by a committee made up of Hartmann, Professor Steinborn and one other person whom she could not recall.

July 20, 1980 Called on Dr. Rufer. Asked him if he had read the material on our system. He had. But did not have much to say. Repeated some of the key operational advantages our product enjoyed over those produced by others including Sigma and FNC. Left him some more technical documents.

On the way out, stopped by Hartmann's office. His secretary told me that we had received favorable comments from the hospitals using our system.

July 23, 1980 Professor Steinborn was flabbergasted to hear that I could not discuss our price with him. Told him of the hospital administration's instructions to the effect. He was not convinced especially when Sigma had already

revealed to him their quote of DM 1,400,000. When he calmed down he wanted to know if we were going to be at least competitive with the others. Told him our system was more advanced than Sigma's. Promised him we would do our best to come up with an attractive offer. Then we talked about his vacation and sailing experience in the Aegean Sea. He said he loved the Greek food.

August 15, 1980 Called to see if Hartmann had returned from his vacation. He had. While checking his calendar, his secretary told me that our system seemed to be the "radiologists' choice," but that Hartmann had not yet made up his mind.

August 30, 1980 Visited Hartmann accompanied by the regional manager. Hartmann seemed bent on the price. He said, "All companies claim they have the latest technology." So he could not understand why our offer was "so much above the rest." He concluded that only a "very attractive price" could tip the balance in our favor. After repeating the operational advantages our system enjoyed over others, including those produced by Sigma and FNC, my boss indicated that we were willing to lower our price to DM 1,740,000 if the equipment was ordered before the end of the current year. Hartmann said he would consider the offer and seek "objective" expert opinion. He also said a decision would be made before Christmas.

September 15, 1980 Called on Professor Steinborn who was too busy to see me for more than ten minutes. He wanted to know if we had lowered our price since the last meeting with him. I said we had. He shook his head saying laughingly, "Maybe that was not your best offer." He then wanted to know how fast we could make deliveries. Told him within six months. He did not say anything.

October 2, 1980 Discussed with our regional manager about the desirability of inviting one or more people from the LUH to visit the Mediquip headquarter operations near Paris. The three-day trip would have given the participants a chance to see the scope of the facilities and become better acquainted with CT scanner applications. The idea was finally rejected as inappropriate.

October 3, 1980 Dropped in to see Hartmann. He was busy but had the time to ask for a formal "final offer" from us by November 1. On the way out, his secretary told me of "a lot of heated discussions" around which scanner seemed best suited for the hospital. She would not say more.

October 25, 1980 The question of price was raised in a meeting between the regional manager and the managing director. I had recommended a sizeable cut in our price to win the order. The regional manager seemed to agree with me. But the managing director was reluctant. His concern was that too much of a drop in price looked "unhealthy." They finally agreed to a final offer of DM 1,580,000.

Made an appointment to see Hartmann later that week.

October 29, 1980 Took our offer of DM 1,580,000 in a sealed envelope to Hartmann. He did not open it, but commented he hoped the scanner question would be resolved soon to the "satisfaction of all concerned." Asked him how the decision was going to be made. He evaded the question but said he would notify us as soon as a decision was reached. Left his office feeling that our price had a good chance of being accepted.

November 20, 1980 Called on Professor Steinborn. He had nothing to tell me but "the CT scanner is the last thing I like to talk about." Felt he was unhappy with the way things were going.

Tried to make an appointment with Hartmann in November, but he was too busy.

December 5, 1980 Called on Hartmann who told me that a decision would probably not be reached before next January. He indicated that our price was "within the range," but that all the competing systems were being evaluated to see which seemed most appropriate for the hospital. He repeated that he would call us when a decision was reached.

January 18, 1981 Received a brief letter from Hartmann thanking Mediquip for participating in the bid for the CT scanner and informing it of the decision to place the order with Sigma.

THE DIFFUSION GAME

Charles B. Weinberg
Christopher H. Lovelock
Molly Lovelock

Diffusion is the process by which a tangible or intangible item spreads through a society. An area of particular interest to marketers is the diffusion of *innovations,* where an "innovation" is defined as a product, process, behavior pattern, idea or entity which is new to a person or a society. People may be unwilling to adopt an innovation for a variety of reasons, not least because it may involve changes in present habits or beliefs.

Organizations seeking to promote change are sometimes referred to as change agencies and those who work for them as change agents. The latter are professionals who try to get others to adopt innovations. Typically, they work by contacting individuals or groups in person. However, their efforts may also be augmented and supported by nonpersonal communications. Examples of change agents are teachers, health workers, agricultural extension agents, Peace Corps volunteers, salespeople and political precinct workers.

This game asks you to assume the role of a change agent working in a rural village, and to concentrate on two of a change agent's functions—developing a strategy to introduce an innovation into a society and implementing that strategy in a simulated environment.

HOW TO PLAY THE DIFFUSION GAME

Scenario

You are a change agent in a rural village. Exhibit 1 shows a map of this village, which consists of 100 farm households. These households are divided into 10 cliques. Each has a different number of followers, headed by one opinion leader. The degree of influence exerted by each opinion leader varies. In some instances, this influence may extend to villagers outside the opinion

Note: The Diffusion Game is an enlarged, computerized version of a concept originally developed by Professor Everett M. Rogers, Department of Communications, Stanford University, under the title of "The Change Agent Game."

Copyright © 1977 jointly by the Board of Trustees of the Leland Stanford Junior University and the President and Fellows of Harvard College, Harvard Business School case 9-577-181.

EXHIBIT 1
MAP OF VILLAGE #1

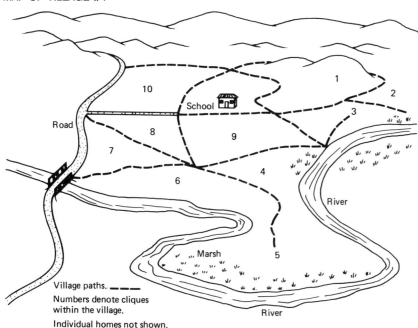

leader's immediate clique. You know little about the village, but have one year to obtain information about the villagers' behavior and to encourage them to adopt an agricultural innovation.

Information about the characteristics of the villagers takes time to obtain, but should help you in developing the diffusion strategies needed to spread the innovation, a new hybrid seed corn, which can be planted at many times throughout the year in this climate. The objective is to secure adoption of this innovation among a specified percentage of village households within 365 days (or less).

You will find yourself engaging in two kinds of activities: (1) obtaining *information* about the village and (2) selecting appropriate *diffusion steps* to motivate villagers to adopt the innovation you are advocating. The information and diffusion strategies available to you and the time "cost"

associated with each are detailed in Exhibits 2 and 3.

Each time you take an information step or a diffusion step, the cost is subtracted from the work days available for completion of the task. The game ends when you have used up all your work days (or have fewer than five) or else have reached the specified level of adoption.

The scoring system rewards players who seek out pertinent information about the villagers' behavior and then use this to choose wisely among the different diffusion strategies. Additionally, the sequence in which diffusion strategies are employed can affect the score.

After visiting Village #1, you may visit Village #2 in a different region where a similar task awaits you. Exhibit 4 shows a map of this second village, which also consists of 100 farm households divided into 10 cliques.

EXHIBIT 2
INFORMATION STEPS AND THEIR COST

Step	Cost
#1 OPINION LEADERSHIP: Identify the opinion leader in a given clique and find out how much influence this individual has.	7 days
#2 NEWSPAPER EXPOSURE: Learn the percentage of villagers reading newspapers.	7 days
#3 RADIO EXPOSURE: Learn the percentage of villagers listening to radio.	7 days
#4 MEETING ATTENDANCE: Learn the percentage of villagers who will attend a public meeting.	7 days
#5 DEMONSTRATION ATTENDANCE: Learn the percentage of villagers who will attend a demonstration.	7 days
#6 LITERACY: Learn the percentage of villagers who can read and write.	3 days
#7 FEEDBACK: Learn the percentage of village households that have adopted the innovation to date	2 days

EXHIBIT 3
DIFFUSION STEPS

Step	Cost	Prior Info. Step Needed
#1 Talk to a specific opinion leader.	20 days	#1
#2 Use newspapers to create knowledge of the innovation.	10 days	#2
#3 Use the radio to create knowledge of the innovation.	10 days	#3
#4 Talk to a villager at random.	10 days	none
#5 Give a lecture at a public meeting about the innovation.	30 days	#4
#6 Show a film about the innovation at a public meeting.	30 days	#4
#7 Conduct a demonstration of the innovation on a specific opinion leader's farm. (You must first talk to an opinion leader before you can hold a demonstration on that person's farm. Only one demonstration is permitted per farm.)	40 days	#1 & #5

Information Steps

The decision on how much information to obtain before initiating diffusion strategies is left to you. Thus, you may make a diffusion step immediately after asking for a specific piece of information (for example, seeking information about an opinion leader, and then taking a diffusion step which involves talking to that opinion leader); or you may first ask for as much information as you want about the village (like opinion leadership, radio exposure, literacy, etc.) and then proceed to take a number of diffusion steps. When you get information, it covers the entire village.

Diffusion Steps

There are several ways in which you can communicate information about the innovation to the villagers. Although you can reasonably assume that each of these diffusion steps is a feasible alternative (for example, you and the villagers

speak the same language, there is a local newspaper and a radio station in the vicinity), some steps may be more effective than others.

It is important to note that you cannot implement most diffusion steps until you have first obtained the relevant information, as shown in Exhibit 3. For example, you cannot plan to select a diffusion strategy of talking about the innovation with a specific opinion leader in the village unless you have already obtained information about that individual.

Each diffusion step has some value in terms of the number of village households who will adopt the innovation as a result of that step. By periodically seeking feedback (information step #7)

EXHIBIT 4
MAP OF VILLAGE # 2

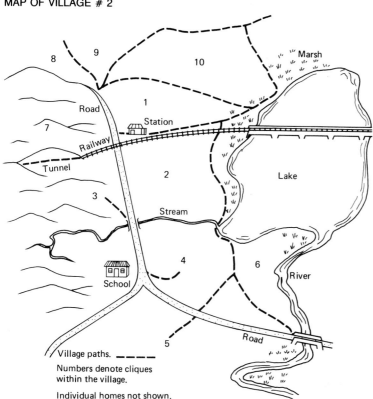

8   9   10   Marsh

Road
7   Station
Railway   1
Tunnel
3   2   Lake
Stream
4   6   River
School
5   Road

Village paths. _ _ _ _

Numbers denote cliques
within the village.

Individual homes not shown.

about your performance, you should be able to assess the relative effectiveness of different steps.

With the exception of diffusion step #7 (see Exhibit 3) there is no limit to the number of times a specific diffusion step may be implemented. The effectiveness (value in terms of new adopters obtained) of some steps will vary with frequency of use. The only way to find out whether this is so is by obtaining regular feedback.

Chance Events

Various chance events affect your success. These events, generated randomly by the computer program, correspond to the sorts of unexpected events that happen in real life. These may be to your advantage or disadvantage. The outcomes of such chance events are disclosed to you at the time they occur. Diffusion steps #1, #2, #3, #5 and #6 each have a set of chance events associated with them.

You cannot lose adopters through chance events. However, for diffusion step #1, a chance event may decrease the usual value of that step. The print-out will indicate when this occurs. The number of adopters obtained by future use of a step is not affected by this chance event.

After each diffusion or information step is complete, you will be notified of the number of work days remaining. At the end of the game, you will be told how many adopters you have gained. At any point in the game, you may ask (through use of information step #7) for feedback on how many adopters you have obtained so far.

SUGGESTIONS FOR PLAYING THE GAME

First develop a strategy and begin to collect the information needed for that strategy. Your objective is *70 percent adoption* in *365 days*.

Remember to use what you know about diffusion, especially the relative importance of different channels of communication at different stages in the innovation decision process.

Don't forget the value of feedback, even if it costs time. This helps you to learn the effectiveness of your strategy.

Play the game, visiting Village #1. Record your results.

Evaluate your strategy and consider what you have learned from your visit to Village #1. Develop a revised plan of action.

Proceed to Village #2 (see Exhibit 4) which is similar but by no means identical to Village #1. Again, play the game and record your results.

The Appendix (see end of case) shows the format for a sample run of the game as it appears when printed out by the computer.

If you wish to abort your game for any reason, use the "S" (stop) action step.

APPENDIX: Sample Run of the Diffusion Game

```
YOU ARE ABOUT TO PLAY THE DIFFUSION GAME, VILLAGE #
AND ARE NOW ENTERING VILLAGE #  POPULATION 100 HOUSEHOLDS


WHAT IS YOUR FIRST NAME?  (PLEASE TYPE)
 ? BETH
WHAT IS YOUR LAST NAME?  (PLEASE TYPE)
 ? SARI

HOW MUCH TIME (DAYS) DO YOU PLAN ON STAYING WITH US  MR/MS SARI  ?
 ?365

WHAT PERCENT OF THE VILLAGERS MUST YOU CONVERT?
 ?70
YOU ARE WELCOME TO OUR VILLAGE, BETH  !
DAYS LEFT:  365

**ACTION: INFORMATION STEP (TYPE: I), DIFFUSION (D), OR STOP (S)
 ?I
WHICH INFORMATION STEP?
 ?1

WHICH CLIQUE WOULD YOU LIKE TO STUDY TO DISCOVER
THE IDENTITY AND INFLUENCE OF THE OPINION LEADER?
 ?5
THE OPINION LEADER IN CLIQUE NUMBER 5
HAS          INFLUENCE

DAYS LEFT:  358

**ACTION: INFORMATION STEP (TYPE: I), DIFFUSION (D), OR STOP (S)
 ?1
WHICH INFORMATION STEP?
 ?1

WHICH CLIQUE WOULD YOU LIKE TO STUDY TO DISCOVER
THE IDENTITY AND INFLUENCE OF THE OPINION LEADER?
 ?7
THE OPINION LEADER IN CLIQUE NUMBER 7
HAS          INFLUENCE

DAYS LEFT:  351

**ACTION: INFORMATION STEP (TYPE: I), DIFFUSION (D), OR STOP (S)
 ?D
WHICH DIFFUSION STEP?
 ?1
WHICH OPINION LEADER DO YOU WANT TO TALK TO?
 ?5
OUTCOME AS EXPECTED
DAYS LEFT:  331

**ACTION:  INFORMATION STEP (TYPE: I), DIFFUSION (D), OR STOP (S)
 ? I
WHICH INFORMATION STEP?
 ?7
CUMULATIVE PERCENTAGE OF ADOPTERS =  _____
```

(Middle portion of game is not shown.)

```
**ACTION: INFORMATION STEP (TYPE: I), DIFFUSION (D), OR STOP (S)
 ?D
WHICH DIFFUSION STEP?
 ?5
SUPPORT INFORMATION FAILS TO ARRIVE IN TIME
OUTCOME AS EXPECTED, BUT IT TOOK AN EXTRA 5 DAYS.
DAYS LEFT:  123

**ACTION: INFORMATION STEP (TYPE: I), DIFFUSION (D), OR STOP (S)
 ?D
WHICH DIFFUSION STEP?
 ?1
WHICH OPINION LEADER DO YOU WANT TO TALK TO?
 ?7
VILLAGERS ASSOCIATE YOU WITH AN UNACCEPTABLE POLITICAL
MOVEMENT. YOU HAD TO SPEND 10 EXTRA DAYS; OUTCOME AS EXPECTED.
DAYS LEFT: 93

**ACTION: INFORMATION STEP (TYPE: I), DIFFUSION (D), OR STOP (S)
 ?D
WHICH DIFFUSION STEP?
 ?5
OUTCOME AS EXPECTED.  NO PENALTY OR BONUS.
DAYS LEFT:  63

**ACTION: INFORMATION STEP (TYPE: I), DIFFUSION (D), OR STOP (S)
 ?D
WHICH DIFFUSION STEP?
 ?5
LOCAL EXPERT VOLUNTEERS TO HELP YOU
SO YOU GAIN 5 DAYS.
DAYS LEFT:  38

**ACTION: INFORMATION STEP (TYPE: I), DIFFUSION (D), OR STOP (S)
 ?D
WHICH DIFFUSION STEP?
 ?3
LOCAL GROUP UNEXPECTEDLY GIVES SUPPORT.
SO YOU GAIN 5 DAYS
DAYS LEFT:  33

**ACTION: INFORMATION STEP (TYPE: I), DIFFUSION (D), OR STOP (S)
 ?D
WHICH DIFFUSION STEP?
 ?5
MORE PEOPLE RECEIVE INFORMATION THAN YOU ANTICIPATED
GAIN 10 DAYS, BETH
DAYS LEFT:  13

**ACTION: INFORMATION STEP (TYPE: I), DIFFUSION (D), OR STOP (S)
 ?D
WHICH DIFFUSION STEP?
 ?4
DAYS LEFT:  3
TOO FEW TO COMPLETE ANOTHER STEP
CUMULATIVE PERCENTAGE OF ADOPTERS =
```

PART SIX

PRICING

The foundations underlying pricing strategy can be described as a tripod, with the three legs representing (1) the costs incurred by the marketer, (2) the prices charged by competitors, and (3) the value of the product to prospective purchasers.

Through pricing, management attempts to recover the costs of the separate elements in the marketing mix—the product itself, associated advertising and personal selling expenses, and the various services provided to consumers by the channels of distribution—as well as to generate profits and the funds necessary to operate the company.

From a consumer viewpoint, the price of a product is the amount paid or to be paid for the benefits offered by the "bundle" of attributes represented by the product and its supporting services. Changes in the nature of this bundle may increase or reduce not only the marketer's costs, but also the product's perceived value and thereby the price that the consumer is willing to pay.

Consequently, pricing policy should be seen in perspective as one of several interdependent elements in the marketing mix. Economic theorists have historically tended to overemphasize the role of price as a determinant of demand, at the expense of such nonprice variables as product attributes, communication activities, and distribution. The economic concept of pricing generally emphasizes the *level* of price charged, overlooking such important marketing considerations as *how* prices are paid by consumers. "Can I charge it?" or "What terms can you give me?" may be equally or more important to consumer purchase decisions than the basic "How much is it?"

An organization's pricing objectives are normally derived from its overall marketing strategy and may change over time in response to changing conditions, both in the marketplace and in the firm's own resources. A common trade-off conflict is between short-run profits versus sales and market-share targets which may enhance profits in the long run.

Pricing strategies must take into account not only the response of the ultimate consumer or industrial buyer but also the needs and characteristics of intermediaries in the channels of distribution. Sufficient margins must be offered at each level of distribution to make it financially attractive for the distributor to carry the goods or to represent the service organization in question.

Finally, pricing policies may reflect a communications objective. Many firms cultivate a "value-for-money" image and are anxious to ensure that each item in the line reflects this image, even if some are only marginally profitable as a result. Taking this policy a step further, some firms may offer one or more "loss leaders"—perhaps on just a temporary basis—to attract attention to the entire product line. At the other end of the spectrum are situations in which the marketer seeks to enhance the quality image of the product by deliberately charging a relatively high price.

FACTORS INFLUENCING GENERAL PRICING DECISIONS

Apart from organizational goals, a number of other factors also influence prices and pricing policies. Key elements include: the cost structure of the firm, the price elasticity of both primary and selective demand, and the competitive structure of the industry in which the firm is competing. Other important considerations include product characteristics and the availability of supply relative to demand considerations.

Cost Structure

Several aspects of an organization's cost structure need to be considered: (1) the level of variable costs per unit and the extent to which these are likely to form a high proportion of selling price, (2) the level of fixed costs, (3) the potential for economies of scale, (4) the possibility of changing cost structures over time, and (5) the firm's costs relative to those of its competitors.

When an organization has high fixed costs and relatively low costs per unit of sale, such as with a computer service bureau or airline, the incremental cost of accommodating new customers or sales is comparatively little in relation to the prices charged. Under such circumstances, earnings may rise sharply if sales increase. Alternatively, for some businesses the reverse may be true; fixed costs may be comparatively low and variable costs per unit, fairly high. Clothing products and certain foodstuffs are examples of products which may require substantial material or labor cost, or both. In these cases, since competition tends to force prices down, unit contribution is often low and even substantial increases in sales volume by itself may not improve earnings dramatically. However, even here, the potential for economies of scale presents opportunities for some organi-

zations, since manufacturing, marketing, or administrative efforts toward efficiency may result in reduced costs per unit as the scale of operations increases.
This situation provides an opportunity to enhance both profits and unit market
share. In some industries, such as electronics, increasing cost savings over time,
due to technological advances and other factors, have an important influence on
both short- and long-term pricing strategies.

Price Elasticity of Demand

A key factor influencing pricing decisions for any product is the sensitivity of
demand to changes in selling prices. If demand rises sharply when prices are
lowered (or falls when they are increased), then demand is said to be highly
elastic. Conversely, if demand is little affected by price changes, it is said to be
inelastic.

The price sensitivity of demand for a particular product category reflects the
importance of the product for consumers, the income level of present consumers,
the existence of substitute products, the extent to which potential exists for
increasing consumption (i.e., whether demand is close to saturation), and
whether or not the product demand is dependent on sales of another product
(such as for part of the undercarriage gear in an airliner). Price elasticity may vary
sharply between market segments. For instance, business travelers are likely to be
less sensitive to a change in hotel prices than are tourists, since the former may
have little choice but to travel and, in any case, their employers may be paying
the bills.

The price sensitivity for a given product category is not necessarily the same as
that for an individual brand within that category. The less that individual brands
are differentiated in consumers' eyes the more difficult it is for a marketer to
charge premium prices without losing substantial market share. Conversely, a
small price cut by one organization may lead to substantial increases in *selective*
demand. Such situations tend to lead to destructive price competition unless one
of the firms in the industry is able to act as a price leader and stabilize prices at a
realistic level.

Competitive Structure of the Industry

The number of firms in an industry often has a direct effect on pricing policy.
When many competitors are selling an undifferentiated product—such as agricultural produce—individual marketers have little discretionary power to influence the prices at which they sell. In the absence of government regulation or the
presence of a cartel, price is set by free-market conditions and the marketer has
little option but to accept it.

At the other extreme are those marketers who face no direct competition for a
much needed product. In theory, monopolists have complete discretionary power
to establish their own selling prices. However, in practice, government regulatory
bodies (as in the case of public-utility commissions overseeing electricity and

telephone companies) often set a rate structure which the company has to accept. Even where no regulations exist, many monopolists choose not to set prices which will maximize profits, either for ethical reasons or for fear of attracting new regulatory controls or new competitors.

In oligopolistic situations, where there are relatively few competitors, one or two of the principal firms may act as price leaders. Other firms are often content to follow their lead, settling for a stable market share in return for an acceptable margin of profits. Although the industry leaders have some discretionary influence over selling prices in such situations, they risk losing this role if their own prices stray too far from those dictated by underlying supply and demand forces in the industry.

In addition to evaluating the nature and extent of existing competition, the marketing manager must also evaluate the possibility of new organizations entering the market. If barriers to entry are high—because of the need for substantial capital investments and/or access to scarce resources or expertise—then the prospect of new entrants may be remote. However, high prices and high earnings within an industry may attract new competitors who are prepared to make the necessary investment for entry. Recognizing this, many firms in oligopolistic industries adopt low, "keep-out" prices, preferring lesser earnings now to the future prospect of additional competitors.

Typically, a firm attempts to escape from the constraints that the industry structure imposes on general pricing policy by differentiating other elements of the marketing mix. An analysis of competitive offerings, distribution channels, and consumer needs can provide insights into the realistic and operational feasibilities of such differentiation.

A final consideration concerns the level of the firm's costs relative to those of the competition. A low-cost situation makes it possible to choose among such alternatives as (1) enjoying extra profits, (2) allocating more resources to marketing activities in an effort to build sales and satisfy consumers better, or (3) initiating an aggressive, low-price strategy. A firm with relatively high costs lacks this flexibility and will probably seek to avoid a low-price strategy which will put it at a financial disadvantage relative to competitors.

PRICING POLICIES FOR NEW PRODUCTS

In establishing the price for a new product, managers should recognize that the characteristics of the product itself play a central role. If it is merely a "me-too" item, not strongly differentiated from competitive offerings, then the level of existing prices may prove the crucial determinant. However, greater price discretion may be available to the marketer of a distinctively different product which has no close substitutes and is unlikely to be imitated in the short term.

Other inputs to the pricing decision include an analysis of the market, prospective consumer segments, existing or potential competitors, and the needs of intermediaries in the distribution channel. Management must estimate the potential volume of demand in each major segment and the speed with which this demand will develop. Demand may be sensitive to changes in both price and the level of marketing effort. Sometimes a new product may be test-marketed at different prices in matched cities in order to obtain a better feel for the sensitivity and demand to these variables. An evaluation of competitive activity, if any, will provide details of the competitors' price range and the terms they offer to intermediaries. It may also help the marketer evaluate the possibility of price retaliation by firms that are marketing products likely to be displaced by the newcomer.

Communications and distribution decisions likewise have implications for pricing. The larger the communications budget, the higher fixed costs will be; further, the margin requirements of different distribution channels may impact upon the ex-factory selling price and/or the recommended retail selling price.

By reviewing all these factors and undertaking a sensitivity analysis of the economic implications of alternative strategies, the marketing manager may be able to resolve the question of whether to adopt a "skim" or "penetration" policy.

Skimming is usually limited to distinctively different products. It involves setting a high initial price which skims the cream of demand at the outset, yielding high profits during the period before competition enters the market and prices start to fall. (High initial prices are sometimes also employed as a means of restricting demand at a time when supplies of the product are limited.)

Market penetration is the opposite approach. It involves use of a low price to stimulate market growth and enable the firm to gain a dominant position; the goal is to preempt competition and ensure long-run profitability.

As the product matures and competitive activity increases, periodic evaluations are necessary to ensure that the pricing policy is realistic in the light of market conditions and the objectives of the firm.

CONCLUSION

When establishing pricing policies, marketing managers must be aware of the costs to be recovered, the prices charged by competitors for broadly similar products, and the value of the product to prospective purchasers. Profit-seeking firms must do more than cover just the variable costs of each product: the price set must yield a sufficient contribution so that, at the anticipated volume of sales, it will cover fixed costs and yield a satisfactory profit.

CASCADE FOODS

Charles B. Weinberg

Sylvia Boaz, product manager for the newly formed fruit drinks division of Cascade Foods,[1] was addressing her product management team in early March 1984.

> We've now completed the last of the test market experiments for the new line of fruit drinks in aseptic packages or "paper bottles," as many people call them. Although this packaging system is new to our market, it's been well accepted in Europe for a number of years and has gained market share rapidly in several U.S. cities. We've all agreed that the test market results are favorable for launching the product, but we can't make a final recommendation to top management until we settle on a pricing strategy. We might like to charge a premium for these fruit drinks but not if it'll damage sales too severely or open up the market for competition. It's ironic: here's a drink that tastes better than fruit drinks in cans, but is actually cheaper to package and ship in aseptic cartons. Do we price on cost or on value?

[1]The data in this case are based on real data, but are disguised, as is the setting.
Copyright © 1984 by Charles B. Weinberg.

With these comments, Boaz began a meeting with Harold Mann, market research manager for Cascade Foods; Carol Gomez, her product assistant; and Scott Green, an experienced marketing consultant who had worked for Cascade Foods a number of times in the past. Cascade had been considering entering the fruit drink market for a number of years, but had not been able to find a profitable niche in the market. The advent of aseptic packaging methods in which a container was made of laminated paperboard appeared to offer the opportunity that Cascade had been waiting for.

COMPANY BACKGROUND

Cascade Foods was founded in 1959 by Benjamin Adam, the son of the controlling owner of Adam Food Stores, a leading supermarket chain in the midwest. Benjamin Adam, a college graduate and World War II veteran, had worked in various executive positions, becoming president of Adam Food Stores in 1952. In 1958, the Adam supermarkets were sold to an expanding national company that wanted to establish a strong presence in the midwest. Although asked to remain as chief executive of the parent company's midwest division, Benjamin Adam resigned shortly after the takeover. He neither wanted to move from his home city nor work as an employee in a large company.

Benjamin Adam began Cascade Foods as a regional marketer of branded packaged goods to supermarkets and other food stores. While many product categories—such as cereals, cake mixes, detergents, and toothpastes—were dominated by a few large companies that competed nationally, other product categories—such as many dairy products, baked goods, and several varieties of fruit juices—did not have nationally dominant brands. This situation is commonly observed by people who move from one region of the country to another and cannot find their favorite brands available. In the early 1980s, for example, Mott's Apple Juice, a leading brand on the East Coast, and Tree Top, a leader in the West, were generally not available in each other's main markets.

Based on his years in the supermarket business, Benjamin Adam believed that there was considerable opportunity for a good regional marketer in many product categories. Some of the companies that sold to Adam Food Stores were professionally managed, but others maintained their position mainly due to a lack of effective competition.

Cascade Foods soon prospered. Its first products were baked goods (breads, rolls, cakes, etc.) and paper products (paper towels, napkins, toilet tissue, paper plates, etc.) but it soon developed a wider range of products. Different brand names were used in different product categories. Adam's strategy was to concentrate on the marketing of branded supermarket products and to use contract packers to manufacture the products sold by Cascade. Cascade presently used more than two dozen contract packers and monitored them under very tight quality control standards.

Cascade used brand advertising, primarily on regional television and in newspapers, to establish strong brand images for its products. Coupled with an efficient distribution system, the company had earned a favorable reputation with the supermarket chains and food stores in the area. Although Cascade had experienced some costly failures, such as its brand of packaged cookies and its line of tomato sauces, more than 60 percent of its product introductions were still in the market. Two product lines had been bought by a national food manufacturer who desired to use the brand name and positioning strategy to launch nationwide brands. Similar strategies had been used by a number of national companies; Duncan Hines cake mixes and Charmin toilet paper were two examples of small regional companies bought by Procter & Gamble and developed into leading national brands.

At present, Cascade Foods marketed only one beverage product, apple juice. That product had been marginally successful with an approximately 7 percent market share in Cascade's region over the past five years. Although total volume of apple juice sold had grown in recent years, Cascade's market share had remained flat. About a year ago, a representative of Brik Pak Inc., the major supplier of aseptic packages ("paper bottles") in North America, had demonstrated the advantages of its packaging system to Cascade for its apple juice. Cascade management, however, had quickly recognized the opportunity that being first in the region's fruit drink market to use this system presented to Cascade.

ASEPTIC PACKAGING

Aseptic packaging was a dramatically different process for packaging milk, wine, fruit juices and drinks, and other liquid and semi-liquid products (See Exhibit 1). Tetra-Pak, a family owned, Swedish company with almost $1.5 billion in sales in 1983, was the inventor of this packaging system and the dominant supplier of aseptic packages worldwide. In Western Europe, almost 50 percent of all milk was sold in Tetra-Pak containers which allowed milk to be kept unrefrigerated for up to five months without loss of nutritional value or flavor. Not only did this provide a benefit for

EXHIBIT 1
EXAMPLES OF BRIK PAK CONTAINERS

These were examples of the 250 mL and 1 liter containers used by a Canadian wine company.

customers, but there were important savings in not having to use refrigerated shipment and storage. Up to 60 percent of a typical supermarket's energy bill was for refrigeration.

Although the refrigeration savings and longer shelf life were of limited application in the fruit juice and fruit drink industries, aseptic paper cartons cost less than bottles and cans. One liter aseptic boxes were estimated to cost only about 30 percent as much as bottles and 50 percent of the cost of cans. Although the filling process for aseptic containers was more complicated (both the container and contents needed to be sterilized), one research firm estimated that the cost of filling juice concentrate in 8 ounce Brik Pak boxes was 18 percent less than that for bottles or metal cans. Similar savings prevailed for larger sizes.

Cost savings were just one of the advantages for fruit drinks of the compact Brik Pak container, Tetra-Pak's most popular shape, which came in two main sizes—a 250 milliliter box (8.4 oz.), with a drinking straw attached, for the convenience market and a one liter container. (Other sizes were available and in 1984 Tetra-Pak was working on advancements such as a resealable half-gallon package for milk.) Aseptic packaging required only flash sterilization during packing, rather than the longer heating process for canned and bottled goods (juice was usually pasteurized after bottling). Consequently, for fruit juices and drinks, the flavors were reported to be truer than in cans and bottles. On the other hand, some people felt that the sterilization process for milk gave it a slightly "cooked" flavor. The rectangular shape of the Brik Pak (whose shape fit its name quite well) allowed it to be easily stacked. Twelve Brik Paks in the one liter size took only about two-thirds as much supermarket display space as twelve one-liter bottles. However, Brik Paks lacked the rigidity necessary for packaging carbonated beverages.

The convenience in use factor was particularly critical for the quarter-liter Brik Pak carton that measured approximately 2½" wide × 4" tall × 1½" deep. It appeared to be just the right size for lunch boxes and snacks and was being sold in specially designed vending machines in some markets. According to a senior executive of Ocean Spray Cranberries Inc., the first company to feature aseptic packaged drinks (such as Cranapple) nationally, "The kinds of products we offer suddenly become portable." One company reported a 20 percent increase in fruit drink sales due to aseptic packaging and classified these volume gains as almost completely incremental. Some soft drink bottlers had begun selling aseptic packages of fruit drinks and stocking them next to soda in supermarkets.

Brik Pak Inc., the U.S. subsidiary of Tetra-Pak, built a manufacturing plant near Dallas, Texas, that produced nearly 1 billion aseptic packages in 1983. In addition there were several other U.S. companies either producing or planning to produce aseptic packages in the near future. After a review by Scott Green of the aseptic packaging industry, Cascade had decided to use Brik-Pak cartons for its proposed entry into the fruit drink market. Cascade, in fact, would not do the manufacturing itself but would buy the finished product from a contract packer who would prepare the product according to Cascade's specifications. Cascade had successfully used this contract packer for several other product lines and had been extremely pleased with the quality and service provided by this firm.

FRUIT DRINK MARKET

Background

Fruit drink sales in Cascade's market area had grown 80 percent in the past five years (see Exhibit 2). Fruit drinks were only one type of bev-

EXHIBIT 2
FRUIT DRINK SALES IN CASCADE MARKET AREA

	Quarter	000s of Cases*
1979	1	428
	2	415
	3	452
	4	413
1980	1	456
	2	463
	3	532
	4	479
1981	1	502
	2	543
	3	627
	4	568
1982	1	715
	2	699
	3	732
	4	701
1983	1	768
	2	750
	3	791
	4	731

*1 case = 12 liters of fruit drinks.

erage refreshment. The most immediate competitors were fruit juices (which had a higher fruit content than fruit drinks) and powdered fruit drink mixes, to which a consumer added water and sometimes sugar. Other competitors included carbonated beverages, plain and flavored milks, and plain water. Few brands competed in more than one of these markets, although some companies had brands in more than one of these markets.

The fruit drink market was very competitive with a number of national and regional brands available; market share data are reported in Exhibit 3. Among the familiar brand names in the category were Hawaiian Punch and Hi-C. Despite its competitive intensity, the market seemed to hold high potential profitability. At current prices, a national brand was estimated to have a gross contribution margin of $3.00 per case (before advertising, promotion, and other marketing costs).

Although the brands differed in number of flavors offered and competed, at times, by introducing new flavors, three flavors accounted for the bulk of sales. These were an apple drink, a grape drink, and a mixed fruit drink. The fruits combined in the mixed fruit drink differed from brand to brand, and some consumers showed a strong preference for the taste of a particular brand's mixed fruit drink. Often, the mixed fruit drink was the company's main focus in advertising and the basis on which the brand had been launched. The apple, grape and other drink flavors often had been introduced to provide variety and to satisfy the taste preferences of consumers.

The national brands were heavily advertised. Although Carl Gomez, the product manager's assistant, could not obtain estimates of advertising and promotion levels on a regional basis, he was able to obtain estimates of expenditures for one national brand for three recent years:

	Cases Sold (000's)	Advertising (000's)	Promotion (000's)
1980	970	$ 950	$680
1981	1,300	1,340	870
1982	1,560	1,500	950

About 25 percent of the market was accounted for by store brands. These brands competed primarily on price; one liter of a store brand fruit drink would typically sell for about $.20 less than a nationally advertised brand retailing at $1.29. Store brands were more successful in the grape and apple flavors than in mixed fruit flavors.

Entry into the Market

Sylvia Boaz had led a new product team that had investigated the possibility of using aseptic packaging systems as a vehicle for entry into the fruit drink market. Although some products, such as the Ocean Spray Cranberry drinks, were already sold in Cascade's market, as yet there was only limited availability of fruit drinks in aseptic packages. By moving quickly, Boaz had estimated that Cascade would develop the first major brand in its area to use the Brik Pak system. The major consumer benefits to be featured were the flavor of the product and the convenience of the package. Senior management approval had been given to carry the project through the test market stage and Boaz was appointed product manager in charge of the product.

Cascade had tentatively decided on an initial three flavor (mixed fruit, grape, and apple) line in 250 milliliter and one liter Brik Pak cartons. In

EXHIBIT 3
MARKET SHARE DATA FOR FRUIT DRINKS (ALL SIZES AND FLAVORS), BASED ON VOLUME IN CASCADE'S MARKET AREA

	1980	1981	1982
Brand A	26%	26%	25%
Brand B	12	13	13
Brand C	12	9	7
Brand D	1	5	10
Store brands and private labels	21	24	26
Other brands	28	23	19

consultation with its contract packer, Cascade had developed the fruit drinks. Harold Mann, the market research manager, had conducted a number of taste tests for the new product and found that the Cascade drinks were favored, on average, by about 65 percent of respondents in paired comparison taste tests in which subjects did not know the brand name of the product they were drinking. This was considered to be a very strong score.

The marketing plan for the first year called for an aggressive advertising and promotion budget of $500,000 for advertising and $350,000 for consumer and trade promotion. (Generally, Cascade budgeted about 50 percent more funds to a new brand introduction than would be required to maintain an established brand at the same volume of sales.) Sales force costs were estimated at $225,000; distribution costs were included in the production costs and not charged against the contribution. The only other charge against the contribution margin was the $250,000 budget for the new product management team, which included the salaries of Boaz and Gomez, costs for market research and consultants, and similar expenses that were incurred by Boaz and her group. At Cascade, entries into new product categories were not expected to break even until the second or third year of marketing.

Pricing Decisions

Sylvia Boaz and her team had recognized that pricing was one of the most critical decisions that had to be made. If Cascade priced on a par with other branded versions of fruit drinks (equivalent to $1.29 per liter and $.40 per 250 mL carton), the cost savings from aseptic packaging would allow a gross contribution margin of $4.00 per case, $1.00 per case greater than that presently estimated to be earned by the leading advertised brands. Assuming the introductory advertising and promotion policy described above, market research tests conducted under the supervision of Harold Mann and Scott Green had estimated a market share of 10 percent of the fruit drink mar-

ket at the end of the first year. Cascade had developed a relatively sophisticated market research, simulation, and test market system to forecast the sales of new products. In the past, that system had estimated the share of market obtained by the new entrant at the end of one year within 1.5 percent of the actual share 80 percent of the time. In other words, Cascade believed there was an 80 percent probability that Cascade fruit drinks would have a market share between 8.5 percent and 11.5 percent at the end of one year with the planned introductory campaign.

Parity pricing was not the only alternative. Gomez had argued strongly that Cascade should charge a premium price for the product. Cascade's real strength, he suggested, was its ability to market branded products in its regional area. Here was a product with superior flavor and convenience, so the customer should be willing to pay more for it. Gomez had claimed that "If it cost more to manufacture than canned drinks, we would charge a higher price without question. Why shouldn't Cascade take the extra profit for itself? Furthermore, a premium price will help convey to consumers the superiority of the product. With a strong advertising campaign, we can position ourselves at the top of the market. If we set the price as the first entrants, others will price at our level. There's very little price variation among major brands at present."

Scott Green had questioned that approach. "High prices only provide an umbrella for competition to enter the market. Besides, why would consumers pay more? A high price could really depress sales. The package itself is novel enough, without imposing a price barrier as well for consumers. Pricing below current prices for canned drinks might even provide an incentive for initial trial, but Cascade shouldn't have to do that in the long run."

The product management group recognized that the pricing decision was too important to be left to guesses. Market research data might help narrow down some of the issues. Harold Mann, the market research manager, had over time built

Cascade management's appreciation of both the value and limits of market research. While market research could not eliminate all uncertainty, it could often reduce some of it.

Two years ago, Cascade had run an experiment for its apple juice brand on the effect of short-term price promotions on sales. This study is summarized in the Appendix. It clearly showed that price reductions had a significant impact on sales, especially when combined with special supermarket displays.

However, the apple juice test, while helpful, was not directly relevant to the fruit drink market. Here Cascade was concerned with a permanent price for a new product. As a result, Boaz asked Mann to use the test market not only to assess the likely success of the product and its expected first year market share, as reported earlier, but also to test the effect of different prices on sales of fruit drinks. As a group, the product management team helped design an experiment. Three price levels were tested:

Low: $1.19/liter; $.35/250 mL
Regular: $1.29/liter; $.40/250 mL
High: $1.39/liter; $.45/250 mL

A change in the retail price of $.10/liter and $.05/250 mL was equivalent to a change of $.90 in Cascade's contribution per case, given the mix of sizes likely to be sold.

In addition, there was considerable discussion as to the effect of advertising on price sensitivity. Some believed that higher levels of advertising decreased price sensitivity by establishing a strong brand image. Others, however, felt that higher advertising expenditures expanded the potential market for the brand as compared to lower advertising expenditures, but that the additional potential consumers were more price sensitive. Hence, they argued for a strategy of high advertising and low prices. Recognizing the importance of this factor, Cascade designed the test market to test two levels of introductory advertising:

Normal: annual rate of $ 500,000
High: annual rate of $1,000,000

These six different price and advertising (3 price times 2 ad budget) levels were tested in 24 supermarkets in four cities. Two cities received high advertising levels and two cities received low advertising levels. Because price could be set individually by store, high, regular, and low prices were tested in two stores in each of the four cities used. Sales in units (normalized for store volume) were recorded bimonthly for each size and flavor for the four months that the test ran. However, there were no major differences in sales among flavors and sizes, so the data were summarized more compactly as shown in Exhibit 4. These data showed a clear effect of price and

EXHIBIT 4
PRICE AND ADVERTISING EXPERIMENT

Sales in Units for Months 1 & 2	AVE.	Sales in Units for Months 3 & 4	AVE.	Price	Advertising
331		280		L	N
394		256		L	N
329	364.3	279	258	L	N
403		217		L	N
662		430		L	H
478	589.3	357	399.5	L	H
552		337		L	H
665		474		L	H
253		247		R	N
289		190		R	N
276	288.3	270	227.5	R	N
335		203		R	N
351		224		R	H
535		394		R	H
409	429.75	203	281.5	R	H
424		305		R	H
252		220		H	N
293		151		H	N
255	252.5	181	177	H	N
210		156		H	N
221		148		H	H
321		254		H	H
310	291.0	172	205.75	H	H
312		249		H	H

Note: Sales in each store were adjusted for the overall volume of fruit drinks sold in each supermarket. The prices tested were *Low* ($1.19, $.35), *Regular* ($1.29, $.40), and *High* ($1.39, $.45); the advertising budgets tested were *Normal* ($500,000) and *High* ($1,000,000). See the text for a description of the experiment.

advertising on sales, but did not fully resolve the issue of the price and advertising levels to use.

A week after receiving these data, Boaz convened a meeting of the product management group. She had asked both Gomez and Green independently to prepare recommendations on a pricing strategy for Cascade fruit drinks in aseptic packages. The purpose of the meeting was to hear both presentations and to resolve the issue of the right pricing strategy to use. Following that, Boaz would need to prepare a report for senior management with a recommendation whether or not to enter the fruit drink market and, if so, with what marketing plan and goals.

APPENDIX: Apple Juice Experiment

In conjunction with one supermarket chain, Cascade had conducted an extensive test of the impact of price promotions and display space on sales of its Cascade brand of apple juice. In brief, Cascade tested three price levels—its regular price level of $1.59 per quart of apple juice and prices of 10 cents off and 20 cents off—and two display conditions, regular shelf space and a special end-of-aisle display. Thus there were six different conditions (3 price levels times 2 display levels). The experiment was conducted in six stores over a twelve week time period. In weeks 2, 4, 6, 8, 10, 12 each store was randomly assigned one of the six treatments and over the six experimental weeks, each store received each combination of price and display once. In the alternative weeks, price and display space were set at their normal levels. The impact on units sold was as follows:

	Normal Display	End-Aisle Display
Regular price	100	131
10 cents off	124	143
20 cents off	136	157

where 100 represents the level of sales at the regular price and with the normal display. In the week immediately following an experimental treatment, sales of apple juice declined about 10 percent in all cases except for the combination 20 cents off and end-of-aisle display where sales in the week following the experiment declined almost 20 percent. After the experiment ended Cascade apple juice sales returned to their normal levels.

NATIONAL CONTAINER CORPORATION

Alan R. Beckenstein
H. Landis Gabel
Robert G. Dykes

In the spring of 1977, James S. Schultz, vice-president in charge of the Container Division, was perplexed by a credit report given him by Robert Crane, his vice-president of sales. It was not at all customary for Schultz to review an application for credit from a prospective customer of the sister Paper Division. After receipt of an application from a new customer account, the credit department generally made preliminary evaluations, then circulated the report among sales personnel of all divisions for any additional information. If a salesperson had any pertinent knowledge of the applicant's financial standing or reputation, he or she would write them on this report. Crane would then initial and route the report back to the credit department, usually without comment.

On this application for the Foldex Corporation, however, Crane had written, "In spite of the preliminary rejection by Credit, I believe that it is in the best interest of this company to approve the new credit account. Foldex, one of our com-

petitors in the container business, is a new company which has shown a remarkable facility for gaining new orders in this depressed market. Its financial condition should improve markedly with sales generated this quarter and projected for the remainder of the year, particularly if general market conditions improve. In view of the Paper Division's operating rate of less than 90 percent and need for additional output, this credit application should be approved." On a separate sheet Crane had written, "Your concurrence on my evaluation, if noted on this report, should assure positive action by Credit."

This commentary struck Schultz as unusual in two respects. First, it was very much unlike Crane to have any great concern for the welfare of the company's other two divisions, Paper and Forest. In fact, to a large degree his compensation was made up of bonuses based on three factors: total Container Division sales, Container Division operating profits, and a subjective evaluation of Container Division performance in relation to the other divisions. Second, and even less characteristic, was Crane's unseemly concern for a competitor. The paper and paperboard supplied

Copyright © 1977 by the Colgate Darden Graduate School of Business Administration Sponsors, University of Virginia. Used by permission. Disguised data.

to Foldex would be converted into folding paper cartons that would compete with National's container sales efforts. This unusual intervention by Crane demanded further explanation.

Schultz sat idly for several minutes after a subsequent meeting with Crane. As he had suspected, other factors had motivated Crane on the Foldex application. St. Paul Converting and the Covington Paper Companies had previously supplied Foldex with its paper and board needs. St. Paul, a leader in the container industry, and Covington were both integrated companies. Foldex, solely a converted products manufacturer, was thus a customer for paper and paperboard, but a competitor for containers and other converted products. The way Crane explained it, Foldex had consistently undercut St. Paul and Covington in competitive bidding. First St. Paul, then Covington refused to supply Foldex with paper and paperboard, claiming delinquent accounts as the motivating factor. Foldex had been refused by still another supplier before approaching National. Crane then received a phone call from his counterpart at Foldex, who charged that there was a conspiracy to drive his company out of business. He warned that if National did not supply them, they would have to conclude that National was part of the conspiracy and that appropriate legal action would be taken.

Schultz considered three alternatives: (1) con- cur with Crane's recommendation and strongly approve the application, (2) concur with the preliminary rejection of the Foldex account, or (3) make no comment and simply route the application back to the credit department. Schultz wondered about the probable consequences of each action. Still more, he worried that any decision he would make could be misconstrued. He reflected on the events that had preceded the decision he must make.

THE COMPANY AND THE INDUSTRY

National Container Corporation was engaged in the manufacture and distribution of all forest products. An integrated processor, its three major product lines were logs, paper and paperboard, and converted products. Corresponding to the product lines, the company had three divisions: Forest, Paper, and Container. The converted products, principally paper folding cartons, had long been the primary contributor to total sales and earnings. Recently, however, the paper and paperboard line had become increasingly profitable and surpassed the converted products line in earnings. Exhibit 1 shows the sales and income data by operating divisions for the period 1972–1976.

Folding cartons and other containers had been extremely profitable items for National in the

EXHIBIT 1

SALES AND INCOME FOR THE YEARS ENDING DECEMBER 31, 1972–1976
(In millions of dollars)

	1976	1975	1974	1973	1972
Container Division					
Sales	66.9	58.4	63.6	55.1	50.4
Net income after tax	1.4	3.0	4.9	3.9	3.7
Paper Division					
Sales	49.8	40.8	28.9	27.7	25.4
Net income after tax	2.9	2.5	1.7	1.9	1.7
Forest Division					
Sales	14.2	11.4	12.6	12.2	11.2
Net income after tax	0.9	0.5	0.8	0.7	0.7

early 1970s, prompting expansion from four plants to five, plus additions to the other plants. Investment in plant and equipment steadily increased from 1971 to 1976, until expansion plans were substantially completed in early 1976. Exhibit 2 shows these expenditures, as well as shipments and capacity utilization for the five-year period, 1972–1976.

The paper container industry was loosely concentrated in terms of the national market, with the four largest companies typically accounting for 20 to 25 percent of total sales. By year end 1976, there were 612 plants in the United States producing folding boxes and other paperboard containers. An abundance of raw materials and a rather simple production process made entry into the industry easy. An equity investment of $125,000 to $200,000 was sufficient to start up a competitive container plant.

While containers varied as to dimensions, weight, and color, they were substantially identical, no matter who produced them, when made to particular specifications. To the purchaser the product was homogeneous; the dominant competitive dimension was price. There was substantial geographical differentiation. High transportation costs, because of the low value of the product in relation to its bulk, coupled with numerous producing mills, created regional markets. Recently there had been some substitution from paper to plastic packaging although no long-term trend appeared clear. The substitution seemed directly related to changes in the price of paper packaging.

Almost 35 percent of total tonnage sales was made on the basis of negotiated contracts, usually for periods of a year or longer. Spot transactions comprised the other 65 percent of total tonnage sales; a spot transaction was a sale resulting from an order for a stated kind and quantity of containers to be delivered on a specified date. The price was generally determined by competitive bidding. It was common for purchasers to buy from two or more suppliers concurrently.

Because packaging was such a small percentage of the cost of the final product, industry demand was inelastic. Industry-wide price changes would not, up to a certain point, visibly affect the total quantity purchased. In periods of generally rising container prices, purchasers were able to absorb costs as well as pass on the increased costs to the ultimate consumer. This resulted partly because of the low cost percentage of the final product but also because the final product, for example, a box of cereal, was generally a consumer staple which was relatively price insensitive. On the other hand, in a period of level demand, the primary effect of price changes among competitors was a reallocation of market share among the producers.

Market Conditions

Schultz was promoted to head the Container Division in March of 1975, when his predecessor left to become president of St. Paul Converting Company, a major competitor. Schultz had been vice-president of production in the division, an office which now reported directly to him. Also

EXHIBIT 2
PLANT EXPANSION, SHIPMENTS AND OPERATING RATES FOR THE YEARS
ENDING DECEMBER 31, 1972–1976

Container division	1976	1975	1974	1973	1972
Additions to plant and equipment (millions of dollars)	6.7	10.2	8.9	6.3	1.5
Shipments (thousands of tons)	161.2	149.8	165.1	154.0	142.5
Operating rate (%)	82.7	78.2	96.8	95.3	92.4

working closely with and subordinate to Schultz was the divisional vice-president of sales, Robert Crane. Crane supervised six district sales managers and a marketing manager.

Market demand for all paper and allied products turned soft in early 1975, just as Schultz assumed his new office. While tonnage and sales dollars remained relatively constant, rising costs cut deeply into earnings. At National, only the Paper Division was able to better the industry-wide trend because of improvements in its coated book and kraft papers. By 1976, market conditions had improved for most of the industry, but folding paper carton prices remained stagnant, and profit margins were further eroded. Demand was slack in part because of increased substitution of plastic containers. On the cost side, in a few short years, energy costs had increased by 400 percent and both raw material prices and labor rates grew at a faster pace than container prices. In addition, similarly to the increased investment in plant and equipment at National, capacity had been greatly extended throughout the carton industry. This led to intense price competition which reduced Container Division's profits to a 10-year low.

In large measure the difficulties were beyond Schultz's control. The overcapacity condition at National resulted from the decisions of his predecessor. Further, the high fixed costs in the container plants required a high operating rate for profitability, yet with slack demand and rigorous competition in an undifferentiated product line, the only way to load the plant was to lower price. Even this response was self-defeating, as a cut by one producer was soon matched and bettered by competitors.

It was against this backdrop that the September 1975 Western States Paper Trade Association's Annual Meeting was conducted. Early on in the proceedings, the president of St. Paul, his former boss, and a small group of executives representing the other industry leaders, had approached Schultz and suggested, without much subtlety, that the only way to save themselves from ruinous price competition was to work to-

gether to increase prices. The plan suggested was a simple bid rigging enterprise.

In the paper container industry short-term contracts in spot transactions were entered into on an almost daily basis, usually for 50,000 to 500,000 units per contract. The manufacturers detailed their needs for bids among the container producers. By the use of "cover bids," producers could act among themselves to accommodate one another. For instance, National could tell other competing carton companies that it had made a bid at a certain price on a new carton container for a certain facial tissue. The other carton manufacturers would agree to bid higher so that National would be awarded the contract. St. Paul would agree to bid at the higher price because in return St. Paul would expect to receive similar assistance from National.

Though not thoroughly versed in the antitrust laws, Schultz suspected that a price fixing attempt such as this was a direct violation of the Sherman Antitrust law. He knew of two instances in the past five years in which some of his competitors had been indicted for price fixing, with some of the officers eventually going to jail. In fact, because of this awareness of the increasing enforcement activity by the Department of Justice, he had previously sought a company policy statement to be distributed among all sales personnel, the marketing personnel, and the purchasing agents. This statement was subsequently authorized and distributed. The text of this statement is reproduced in Exhibit 3.

Schultz recalled quickly extricating himself from the gathering, grabbing Crane by the arm, and retreating to the safe confines of the bar. The penalties for violations of the antitrust laws could be severe and were further strengthened by recent legislation. Formerly a misdemeanor, the violation was now a felony offense with a maximum jail sentence of three years.

The Situation in 1976

In the year following that meeting, however, market conditions worsened for the Container

EXHIBIT 3

NATIONAL CONTAINER CORPORATION CORPORATE POLICY

SUBJECT: Compliance with antitrust laws

National Container Corporation considers strict compliance with all provisions of the antitrust laws as an integral part of company policy. It is the responsibility of the manager of each division or unit to see that this policy is known and observed by all those under his supervision, particularly in the area of sales, marketing, and purchasing.

Violations of the Company policy and the underlying antitrust laws can have a serious, adverse, and lasting effect on the company, its operations, and its growth. Therefore, a deliberate and willful violation of this policy, in the absence of mitigating circumstances, will be sufficient grounds for dismissal. In addition, violation of the antitrust laws could result in criminal or civil proceedings against the responsible employee and the Company.

Your attention is particularly directed to the prohibitions of the antitrust laws against concerted action with competitors on such subjects as prices, customers, terms of sale, and other competitive matters. It is especially important that you avoid both any actual violation and any conduct which might be misconstrued as such a violation.

When an employee who has acted in good faith upon the advice of counsel for the Company nevertheless becomes involved in an antitrust proceeding, the Company will be prepared to assist and defend the employee. However, if an employee is convicted of violating the law, the Company cannot, as a matter of law, save the employee from whatever criminal penalty the court may impose upon the employee as a consequence of such conviction.

This policy applies to the Company, which, as used in this policy statement, includes all of its affiliated companies and subsidiaries.

Division. Schultz feared that an actual loss was possible for the calendar year 1976. Prices for the carton products had to improve, and Schultz felt the only way this could occur would be to control production and raise prices. Prices could not be fixed, but at the least the story had to be told.

One of the section panels at the trade association annual meeting provided for industry projections and analyses by various operating officers. At the very least, Schultz felt compelled to comment on the overcapacity situation and remark on the deleterious effects of recent price warfare. As long as he steered an independent course—let the others take any tack they wanted—he could avoid price-fixing problems. He consulted with Crane several times on the content of the speech. Crane agreed the speech was a good idea and also made a few suggestions.

At the September 1976 annual meeting of the trade association, Schultz carefully avoided contacts with the group that had approached him the prior year. Indeed, those members seemed to avoid him. The main issue at the meeting was a proposed modification of trade association activities, consisting primarily of the addition of a statistical reporting service, called the "open competition plan." This plan is reproduced in Exhibit 4. The major argument of the proponents was that implementation of the plan would reduce market uncertainties and allow management to plan more efficiently. The cost of errors in market judgments based on sketchy information would hence be minimized. After cursory discussion of the proposed changes, and with little opposition, the modification was approved. National Container voted in favor of the modification.

Schultz felt that his presentation, reproduced in

EXHIBIT 4
OPEN COMPETITION PLAN

Statement of Purpose

The purpose of this plan is to disseminate among members accurate knowledge of production and market conditions so that each member may gauge the market intelligently instead of guessing at it; to make competition open and above board instead of secret and concealed; to substitute, in estimated market conditions, frank and full statements of our competitors for the frequently misleading and colored statements of the buyer.

The Open Competition plan is a central clearinghouse for information on prices, trade statistics, and practices. By keeping all members fully and quickly informed of what the others have done, the work of the plan results in a certain uniformity of trade practice. There is no agreement to follow the practice of others, although members do naturally follow their most intelligent competitors, if they know what these competitors have been actually doing.

Membership Requirements

Each member shall send to the Secretary:

1 A daily report of all sales actually made, with the name and address of the purchaser, the kind, grade and quality of cartons sold and all special agreements of every kind, oral or written with respect thereto.

2 A daily shipping report, with exact copies of the invoices, all special agreements as to terms, grade, etc. The classification shall be the same as with sales.

3 A monthly production report, showing the production of the member reporting during the previous month, with the grades and thickness classified as prescribed elsewhere in this plan.

4 A monthly stock report by each member, showing the stock on hand on the first day of the month, sold and unsold, with the total of each kind, grade, and thickness.

5 Price lists. Members must file at the beginning of each month price lists showing f.o.b. shipping point, which shall be stated. New prices must be filed with the association as soon as made.

6 Inspection reports. These reports are to be made to the association by a service of its own, established for the purpose of checking up grades of the various members. The association will provide for a chief inspector and sufficient assistants to inspect the stocks of all members from time to time.

7 All of these reports by members are subject to complete audit by representatives of the association. Any member who fails to report shall not receive the reports of the Secretary, and failure to report for twelve days in six months shall cause the failing member to be dropped from membership.

Association Duties

The Secretary is required to send to each member:

1 A monthly summary showing the production of each member for the previous month, subdivided as to use, grade, kind, thickness, etc.

2 A weekly report, not later than Saturday, of all sales, to and including the preceding Tuesday, giving each sale and the price, and the name of the purchaser.

3 On Tuesday of each week the Secretary must send to each member a report of each shipment by each member, complete up to the evening of the preceding Thursday.

4 He must send a monthly report, showing the individual stock on hand of each member and a summary of all stocks, sold and unsold. This report will be referred to by the managing statistician as the monthly inventory of the stock of each member.

5 Not later than the 10th of each month the Secretary shall send a summary of the price lists furnished by members, showing the prices asked by each, and any changes made therein must be immediately transmitted to all the members.

6 A market report letter shall be sent to each member of the association pointing out changes in conditions both in the producing and consuming sections, giving a comparison of production and sales and in general an analysis of the market conditions.

7 Meetings shall be held once a month in St. Louis or at points agreed upon by members. It is intended that the regular meetings shall afford opportunity for the discussion of all subjects of interest to the members.

Later Amendments to the Plan

1 In order that members may more conveniently attend, there shall be four districts, in each of which a monthly meeting will be held.

2 A questionnaire will be sent to all members prior to the meeting. From the replies received, supplementing the other reports, the statistician will compile his estimate of the condition of the market, actual and prospective, which will be distributed to the members attending each meeting and mailed to those not present.

Among the questions are the following:

What was your total production during the last month?
What do you estimate your production will probably be the next two months?
Do you expect to shut down due to any shortage or for any reasons?
If so, state how long you expect your mills to be idle.
What is your view of market conditions for the next few months?
What is the general outlook for business?

State all reasons for your conclusions.

Exhibit 5, was very well received, and he returned from the meeting gratified with having vented some frustration and expressed his concerns. Crane stayed at the meeting site several days longer, having stated a desire to follow up some contacts made with customers at the meetings.

Crane's Phone Call

In early October 1976, Schultz received a phone call from Crane. The call concerned a problem that affected not only National but the industry as a whole, particularly in the past two years of soft demand. The problem was the age-old game of playing two ends against the middle. Purchasing agents would detail their order requirements and phone a number of salespeople for bids. The purchasing agent might then call all the salespeople who had delivered higher bids, informing them of the low bid. The salespeople would then have the option of beating that price or losing out on the order. This practice might continue through three or four iterations until a final bid was reached. The problem was further heightened for the producers when the purchasing agent threw out a "phantom" bid, a low bid which did not actually exist. If in the first round of bidding, purchasing agents could not get other salespeople to beat the low bid, they might approach the low bidder and tell of a lower bid they might have to meet to get the order. Because of the antitrust laws, any exchange of price information between competitors on specific bids could be a violation; hence, competitors were hesitant to contact one another on information delivered by the purchasing agents. Only later, on an informal basis, would a salesperson sometimes learn that a bid was fraudulent by checking with a

EXHIBIT 5
SPEECH DELIVERED TO WESTERN STATES PAPER ASSOCIATION, ANNUAL MEETING
SEPTEMBER 15, 1976, "OUTLOOK FOR 1977."
By James S. Schultz

I think I would have to start by saying what I am sure a substantial portion of other industry executives will be saying: that on balance we have been disappointed that the general level of activity in the North American paper and container industry has not picked up in 1976 as much as one would have hoped from the vantage point of a year ago. Looking at 1977, specifically in the paper folding container area which is the mainstay of National's business, we have to view the approaching year with some caution as it certainly looks now as if a major pickup in general demand is not likely to occur before 1978.

The experiences of the past few years—rapidly escalating raw material costs, fourfold increases in power costs, shortages, and violent changes in market demand—have forced us to reassess some treasured assumptions and have helped us to conclude that some very basic changes in our future planning are essential. Cost problems in the areas of energy, labor, materials, and pollution regulations will continue to be acute. While paper and board companies, and paper divisions, have been able to increase their prices in the past year, gains in carton prices have been nominal at best. This stems from overcapacity which has prompted cutthroat bidding practices in futile efforts to load plants. It can't be done with current demand—it just cuts container margins. Improvement in margins is of paramount concern to National. Price increases across broad product lines are essential in order to recover some of these sharp cost increases. This also reflects upon our ability to attract capital to increase capacity which provides, in turn, increased employment. But capacity additions are in the long term. As far as my company is concerned, we will be extremely cautious in making any substantial additions to current plant. The ROI is just too low for new mill construction. Attacking cost problems can be extremely profitable, and that's our current game plan. If there is no increase in production, generally, then there is going to be good business. No company is safe in increasing their production. If they do, they will be in bad shape, because demand will not support the additional production. Certainly, National Container Corporation is adjusting its production scheduling appropriate to current demand.

Historically, change has always been resisted mightily. This will never be truer than in 1977. The greatest thing managers in the paper industry can do in 1977 is to know the facts and make the best possible decisions out of the information that they have gathered. This is the stuff of success, and there is no other.

competitor. The result was that even a low bidder would occasionally beat its own bid in order to win the bid, and there was little the salespersons could do to defend themselves against the practice.

As well as Schultz could recall, the conversation lasted only several minutes:

Crane: Those blasted P.A.s have been at their games again this past week. In two regions where we had good competitive bids we were informed of a low bid that we had to beat to get the business. In the Pacific Region in particular, I have good reason to believe we had the lowest bid, though I'm not so sure about the Mid-East bid.

Schultz: They just don't let up, do they? Say, in that Mid-East bid, was that for the new market penetration in Indiana?

Crane: Yeah, the Clarksville area where they have a lot of those small independent suppliers. That's what I mean. Even if we felt there was another low bid and we still wanted to fill the order at a lower price, we still can't indiscriminately undercut the independents because of a possible charge of price discrimination. The only defense the Robinson-Patman Act gives us here is a good faith attempt to meet competition. And we can't really rely on that unless we verify prices of our competition. We've batted this around long enough, don't you think? We've got

EXHIBIT 6

WESTERN STATES PAPER TRADE ASSOCIATION—MONTHLY REPORT ON BIDDING
AND PRICES
(cumulative)

Bid date	Quantity ordered	National	St. Paul	Covington	Mar-Vel	Foldex	Harrington
Sept. 27	180,000	$.0156	$.0160	$.0148	$.0156		$.0170
Sept. 30	100,000	.0156	.0148	.0150			.0170
Oct. 4	50,000	.0160	.0156	.0150	.0148		.0170
Oct. 8	160,000	.0148	.0160	.0150	.0150		.0156
Oct. 15	275,000	.0156	.0146	.0148	.0148		.0148
Oct. 16	300,000	.0148	.0146	.0148			.0144
Oct. 18	150,000	.0142	.0144	.0148	.0150		.0144
Oct. 22	250,000	.0160	.0160	.0150	.0150		.0148
Oct. 26	320,000	.0160	.0160	.0160	.0158		.0160
Oct. 29	80,000	.0160	.0162	.0160	.0160		.0158
Nov. 2	400,000	.0160	.0162	.0162	.0162		.0164
Nov. 12	380,000	.0162	.0160	.0164	.0162		.0162
Nov. 14	45,000	.0162	.0162	.0162	.0160		.0164
Nov. 16	85,000	.0162	.0164	.0162	.0162		.0160
Nov. 19	240,000	.0164	.0164	.0162	.0164		.0164
Nov. 19	160,000	.0166	.0162	.0166	.0164		.0164
Nov. 26	110,000	.0162	.0166	.0164	.0164		.0164
Nov. 28	425,000	.0160	.0166	.0166	.0162		.0166
Dec. 3	280,000	.0166	.0166	.0166	.0162		.0158
Dec. 4	315,000	.0166	.0166	.0156	.0158		.0166
Dec. 8	140,000	.0166	.0168	.0166	.0154		.0166
Dec. 15	380,000	.0168	.0164	.0168	.0154		.0168
Dec. 17	250,000	.0168	.0144	.0168	.0154		.0168
Dec. 27	150,000	.0166	.0170	.0170	.0170		.0170
Jan. 3	260,000	.0170	.0168	.0170	.0170		.0170
Jan. 7	120,000	.0170	.0172	.0170	.0170		.0168
Jan. 10	65,000	.0172	.0172	.0172	.0170		.0172
Jan. 13	375,000	.0172	.0172	.0170	.0172		.0172
Jan. 15	140,000	.0170	.0174	.0172	.0172		.0172
Jan. 20	80,000	.0174	.0172	.0174	.0174	.0166	.0174
Jan. 24	170,000	.0174	.0172	.0174	.0174	.0166	.0174
Jan. 27	140,000	.0174	.0164	.0174	.0174	.0166	.0174
Jan. 31	180,000	.0164	.0164	.0164	.0164	.0166	.0162
Feb. 3	260,000	.0164	.0164	.0164	.0162	.0166	.0164
Feb. 6	70,000	.0164	.0164	.0162	.0164	.0160	.0164
Feb. 11	390,000	.0164	.0172	.0162	.0164	.0172	.0164
Feb. 14	280,000	.0170	.0172	.0172	.0172	.0172	.0172
Feb. 21	350,000	.0172	.0170	.0172	.0172	.0172	.0172
Feb. 24	175,000	.0172	.0172	.0172	.0172	.0172	.0170
Feb. 25	130,000	.0172	.0172	.0172	.0170	.0172	.0172
Feb. 28	125,000	.0172	.0174	.0172	.0172	.0170	.0172
March 3	260,000	.0174	.0174	.0172	.0174	.0168	.0174
March 6	180,000	.0174	.0174	.0164	.0174	.0168	.0174
March 10	90,000	.0162	.0174	.0174	.0174	.0164	.0164
March 14	360,000	.0158	.0174	.0174	.0160	.0160	.0162
March 17	95,000	.0160	.0156	.0160	.0160	.0154	.0156
March 19	285,000	.0160	.0148	.0160	.0158	.0152	.0156
March 24	470,000	.0150	.0144	.0154	.0150		.0152
March 26	380,000	.0144	.0150	.0152	.0152		.0160
March 28	240,000	.0160	.0166	.0154	.0150	.0174	.0160

to get some control over this phantom bidding. Look, all it takes is a simple phone call to the supposed low bidder. If the P.A.s learn we're verifying the information they give us, they'll play it straight. Cutthroat competition is bad enough without having to beat imaginary competitors.

Schultz: O.K., look, you know the pressure we're under to meet our profit targets, and if we don't meet them our year-end bonus is shot. I would say to put an end to it where you can use verification for an excuse in checking with competitors, but it's sticky. Maybe you should check with our general counsel. Still, we should stop their cheating. Look, you've got a job to do—as far as I go, I know nothing. All right?

Crane: O.K. I can take it from there.

THE SITUATION IN 1977

Schultz heard nothing more from Crane on the subject. Several months later he asked Crane how the new program was working out. Crane reported that it was the best thing they could have done. They detected three fraudulent bids, in several regions, in the first month of the verifica-

tion program. Thereafter, according to Crane, they had had no such problems, and it was this that accounted for very recent price improvements.

Prices continued to improve marginally for most container orders, and despite some softness in March, prices beginning in April 1977 were substantially improved over the previous year's levels. Operating rates were up and Schultz felt that increased demand for containers was finally mitigating the overcapacity problem of the past two years.

Schultz had been reviewing the Trade Association's monthly summary of prices and production by members, when the credit evaluation on Foldex was delivered to his desk. After conferring with Crane, he was clearly worried about the antitrust threat posed by Foldex. Before deciding on the disposition of the credit report, Schultz poured over the trade association statistics once more. Among other things that worried him was the data on bids for facial tissue containers. The cumulative summary of the last six monthly reports is shown in Exhibit 6.

SOUTHWEST AIRLINES

Christopher H. Lovelock

"Y'all buckle that seat belt," said the hostess over the public address system, "because we're fixin' to take off right now. Soon as we get up in the air, we want you to kick off your shoes, loosen your tie, an' let Southwest put a little love in your life on our way from Big D to Houston." The passengers settled back comfortably in their seats as the brightly-colored Boeing 737 taxied down towards the takeoff point at Dallas's Love Field airport. Moments later, it was accelerating down the runway and then climbing away steeply into the Texas sky on the 240-mile flight to Houston.

On the other side of Love Field from the airport terminal, executives of Southwest Airlines ignored the noise of the departing aircraft, which was clearly audible in the company's modest but comfortable second-floor offices next to the North American-Rockwell hangar. They were about to begin an important meeting with representatives from their advertising agency to discuss the alternative strategies open to them in

Copyright © 1975 by the President and Fellows of Harvard College, Harvard Business School case 9-575-060.

response to an announcement by their major competitor, Braniff International Airways, that it was introducing a 60-day, half-price "sale" on Southwest's major route effective that same day, February 1, 1973.

COMPANY BACKGROUND

Southwest Airlines Co., a Texas corporation, was organized in March 1967. The founder, Rollin W. King, had graduated from the Harvard Business School in 1962 and was previously an investment counselor with a San Antonio firm. From 1964, King (who held an airline transport pilot's license) had also been president of an air taxi service operating from San Antonio to various smaller South Texas communities.

From the middle 1960s, Rollin King and his associates became increasingly convinced that there was a need for improved air service between Houston, Dallas/Fort Worth, and San Antonio. These four cities were among the fastest growing in the nation. By 1968 the Houston standard metropolitan statistical area had a popula-

367

tion of 1,867,000. Dallas's population was 1,459,000, San Antonio's 850,000, and Fort Worth's 680,000. The cities of Dallas and Fort Worth were located 30 miles apart in northeastern Texas but were frequently thought of as a single market area; although each had its own airport—with Dallas's Love Field the busier of the two and the only one served by the airlines—construction had recently begun on the huge new Dallas/Fort Worth Regional Airport, located midway between the two cities and intended to serve both.

Air service between these market areas was provided primarily by Braniff International Airways and Texas International Airlines. In 1967, Braniff operated a fleet of 69 jet and turboprop aircraft on an extensive route network, with a predominantly north-south emphasis, serving major U.S. cities, Mexico, and South America. Total Braniff revenues in that year were $256 million and it carried 5.6 million passengers. Texas International Airlines (then known as Trans-Texas Airways) was a regional carrier serving Southern and Southwestern states and Mexico. In 1967, it operated a fleet of 45 jet, turboprop, and piston-engined aircraft on mostly short-haul routes, carrying 1.5 million passengers and generating total revenues of $32 million. Both Braniff and TI were headquartered in Texas.

Service by these two carriers within Texas represented legs of much longer, interstate flights; travelers flying from Dallas to San Antonio, for example, might find themselves boarding a Braniff flight which had just arrived from New York and was calling at Dallas on its way to San Antonio. Local travel between Dallas and Houston (the most important route) averaged 483 passengers daily in each direction in 1967, with Braniff holding an 86 percent share of this traffic (Exhibit 1).[1] Looking back at the factors which had first stimulated his interest in developing a

new airline to serve these markets, Mr. King recalled:

> The more we talked to people, the more we looked at figures of how big the market was and the more we realized the degree of consumer dissatisfaction with the services of existing carriers, the more apparent the opportunities became to us. We thought that these were substantial markets, and while they weren't nearly as large as the Los Angeles-San Francisco market, they had a lot in common with it. We knew the history of what PSA had been able to do in California with the same kind of service we were contemplating.[2]

On February 20, 1968, Southwest was granted a Certificate of Public Convenience and Necessity by the Texas Aeronautics Commission, permitting it to provide intrastate air service between Dallas/Fort Worth, Houston, and San Antonio, a triangular route structure with each leg ranging in length from roughly 190 to 250 miles (Exhibit 2). Since the new airline proposed to confine its operations to the State of Texas, its executives maintained that it did not need certification from the federal Civil Aeronautics Board.[3]

The next day, Braniff and Texas International asked the Texas courts to enjoin issuance of the Texas certificate. These two airlines already served the proposed routes and considered market demand insufficient to support another airline. The resulting litigation proved extremely costly and time-consuming, eventually reaching the U.S. Supreme Court. However, the case was finally decided in Southwest's favor.

During the summer of 1970, Rollin King was

---

[1] Local travel figures excluded passengers who were traveling between these cities as part of a longer journey.

[2] Pacific Southwest Airlines had built up a substantial market share on the lucrative Los Angeles-San Francisco route, as well as on other intrastate operations within California. Southwest executives subsequently studied PSA carefully when designing their own operations.

[3] The Civil Aeronautics Board regulated all interstate airlines in matters such as fares and routes, but had no authority over airlines operating exclusively within a single state. (The CAB should not be confused with the Federal Aviation Administration [FAA], which regulated safety procedures and flight operations for all passenger airlines, including intrastate carriers.)

EXHIBIT 1

SOUTHWEST AIRLINES AND COMPETITORS: AVERAGE DAILY LOCAL PASSENGERS CARRIED IN EITHER DIRECTION, DALLAS-HOUSTON MARKET[1]

	Braniff[2]		Texas Int.[2]		Southwest		Total Market
	Psgrs.	% of Mkt.	Psgrs.	% of Mkt.	Psgrs.	% of Mkt.	Passengers
1967	416	86.1	67	13.9	—	—	483
1968	381	70.2	162	29.8	—	—	543
1969	427	75.4	139	24.6	—	—	566
1970							
1st half	449	79.0	119	21.0	—	—	568
2nd half	380	76.0	120	24.0	—	—	500
Year	414	77.5	120	22.5	—	—	534
1971							
1st half	402	74.7	126	23.4	10	1.9	538
2nd half	338	50.7	120	18.0	209	31.3	667
Year	370	61.4	123	20.4	110	18.2	603
1972							
Jan.	341	48.3	105	14.9	260	36.8	706
Feb.	343	47.6	100	13.9	277	38.5	720
March	357	47.5	100	13.3	295	39.2	752
April	367	48.3	97	12.8	296	38.9	760
May	362	48.5	84	11.3	300	40.2	746
June	362	46.8	81	10.5	330	42.7	773
1st half	356	48.0	93	12.5	293	39.5	742
July	332	48.1	74	10.7	284	41.2	690
Aug.	432	53.7	56	6.9	317	39.4	805
Sept.	422	54.9	55	7.2	291	37.9	768
Oct.	443	53.1	56	6.7	335	40.2	834
Nov.	439	50.6	55	6.3	374	43.1	868
Dec.	396	52.1	56	7.4	308	40.5	760
2nd half	411	52.1	59	7.5	318	40.4	788
Year	384	50.1	77	10.0	306	39.9	767
1973							
Jan.[3]	443	51.5	62	7.3	354	41.2	859

[1] Passenger figures should be doubled to yield market statistics for travel in both directions.

[2] These figures were calculated by Mr. Muse from passenger data which Braniff and TI were required to supply to the Civil Aeronautics Board. He multiplied the original figures by a correction factor to eliminate interline traffic and arrive at net totals for local traffic.

[3] Projected figures from terminal counts by Southwest personnel.

Source: Company records.

approached by M. Lamar Muse, an independent financial consultant, who had resigned the previous fall as President of Universal Airlines—a Detroit-based supplemental carrier—over a disagreement with the major stockholders on their planned purchase of Boeing 747 jumbo jets. Mr. Muse had read of Southwest's legal battles and told Mr. King and his fellow directors that he would like to help them transform the company from "a piece of paper" into an operating airline.

EXHIBIT 2
SOUTHWEST AIRLINES ROUTE MAP

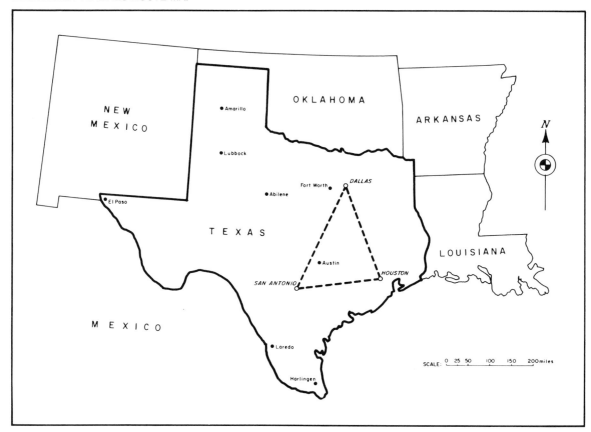

The wealth of experience which Lamar Muse could bring to the new airline was quickly recognized. Before assuming the presidency of Universal in September 1967, he had served for three years as President of Central Airlines, a Dallas-based regional carrier. Prior to 1965 he had been Secretary-Treasurer of Trans-Texas Airways, Assistant Vice President-Corporate Planning of American Airlines, and Vice President-Finance of Southern Airways. After working informally with Southwest for a couple of months, Mr. Muse became an employee of the company in October 1970 and was elected President, Treasurer and a director on January 26, 1971. Mr. King was named Executive Vice President-Operations at the same time.

One of the reasons he was attracted to Southwest, Lamar Muse explained, was that

> I felt the interstate carriers just weren't doing the job in this market. Every one of their flights was completely full—it was very difficult to get reservations. There were a lot of cancelled flights; Dallas being Braniff's base and Houston, TI's base, every time they had a mechanical problem it seemed like they always took it out on the Dallas-Houston service. From Dallas south to San Antonio and Houston is the tag end of Braniff's system; everything was turning around and going back north to Chicago or

New York or wherever. There was so much inter-line traffic that most of the seats were occupied by those people. While Braniff had hourly service, there really weren't many seats available for local passengers. People just avoided flying in this market—they only went when they had to.

Muse added that Braniff's reputation for punctuality was so poor that it was popularly referred to by many travelers as the "World's Largest Unscheduled Airline."

Optimistic about the outcome of Southwest's legal battles, Messrs. Muse and King spent many weeks on the West Coast in late 1970 and early 1971, prospecting for new aircraft. There was a recession in the airline industry at the time and prospective aircraft purchasers were being courted assiduously. High pressure negotiations were therefore initiated by Southwest with representatives of McDonnell-Douglas, Boeing, and several airlines for the purchase of new or used jet aircraft.

Finally, the Boeing Company, which had overproduced its Boeing 737 twin jet (in a speculative assessment of future orders which had failed to materialize), offered both a substantial price reduction and also very favorable financing terms. In March 1971, Southwest signed a contract for three Boeing 737-200 aircraft, some months later increasing the order to four. The total purchase price for the four 737s was $16.2 million, compared with a previous asking price of approximately $4.6 million each.

Muse and King regarded the 737s as better aircraft for their purposes than the McDonnell-Douglas DC-9s operated by Texas International or the larger, tri-jet Boeing 727s flown by Braniff on their Texas routes.

PREPARING FOR TAKEOFF

Back in Texas, Muse and King faced some urgent problems and an extremely tight deadline. The start of scheduled operations had been tentatively set for June 18, a little over four months away.

During this period, Southwest had to raise additional capital to finance both start-up expenses and what might prove to be a prolonged period of deficit operations. The existing skeleton management team had to be expanded by recruiting several new specialist executives. Personnel had to be hired and trained for both flight and ground operations. Meantime, numerous marketing problems had to be resolved and an introductory advertising campaign developed to launch the new airline. Finally, Braniff and Texas International were continuing their legal battles to stifle Southwest.

Once again, legal matters were left to the company's lawyers while the Southwest executives moved quickly to attend to financial, personnel, and marketing problems. An urgent need was to improve the airline's financial position, since at year's end 1970 the company had a mere $183 in its bank account (Exhibit 3). Between March and June 1971, Southwest raised almost $8 million through the sale of convertible promissory notes and common stock.

Vacancies on the existing management team were soon filled by four executives with many years' airline experience. Three of them had previously worked for either Braniff or TI and had recently been fired by those carriers—a fact which Mr. Muse considered one of their strongest recommendations for employment with Southwest.

Decisions on route structure and schedules had already been made. Initially, two of the three Boeing 737s would be placed in service on the busy Dallas-Houston run and the third would fly between Dallas and San Antonio. For the time being, Southwest did not plan to exercise its rights to operate service on the third leg of the triangle between Houston and San Antonio.

Schedule frequency was constrained by aircraft availability. Allowing time for turning around the aircraft at each end, it was concluded that flights could be offered in each direction between Dallas and Houston at 75-minute inter-

EXHIBIT 3

SOUTHWEST AIRLINES: BALANCE SHEET AT DECEMBER 31, 1972, 1971, AND 1970

	1972	1971	1970
Assets			
Currrent assets:			
Cash	$ 133,830	$ 231,530	$ 183
Certificates of deposit	1,260,000	2,850,000	—
Accounts receivable:			
Trade	397,664	300,545	—
Interest	14,691	35,013	—
Other	67,066	32,589	100
	479,441	366,127	100
Less allowance for doubtful accounts	86,363	30,283	—
	383,078	337,844	100
Inventories of parts and supplies, at cost	154,121	171,665	—
Prepaid insurance and other	75,625	156,494	31
Total current assets	2,006,663	3,747,533	314
Property and equipment, at cost:			
Boeing 737-200 jet aircraft	12,409,772	16,263,250	—
Support flight equipment	2,423,480	2,378,581	—
Ground equipment	346,377	313,072	9,249
	15,179,629	18,954,903	9,249
Less accumulated depreciation and overhaul allowance	2,521,646	1,096,177	—
	12,657,983	17,858,726	9,249
Deferred certification costs less amortization	371,096	477,122	530,136
Liabilities and Stockholders' Equity			
Current liabilities:			
Notes payable to banks (secured)	950,000	—	—
Accounts payable	124,890	355,539	30,819
Accrued salaries and wages	55,293	54,713	79,000
Other accrued liabilities	136,437	301,244	—
Long-term debt due within one year	1,226,457	1,500,000	—
Total current liabilities	2,493,077	2,211,496	109,819
Long-term debt due after one year—			
7% Convertible Promissory Notes	—	1,250,000	—
Conditional Purchase Agreements—			
Boeing Financial Corporation (1½% over prime rate)	11,942,056	16,803,645	—
	11,942,056	18,053,645	—
Less amounts due within one year	1,226,457	1,500,000	—
	10,715,599	16,553,645	—
Contingencies:			
Stockholders' equity—Common stock, $1.00 par value, 2,000,000 shares authorized 1,108,758 issued (1,058,758 at December 31, 1971)	1,106,758	1,058,758	372,404
Capital in excess of par value	6,062,105	6,012,105	57,476
Deficit	(5,343,798)	(3,752,623)	—
	1,827,065	3,318,240	429,880
	$15,035,741	$22,083,381	$539,699

Notes to financial statement not shown here.
Source: Southwest Airlines Company Annual Reports, 1971 and 1972.

vals, and between Dallas and San Antonio at intervals of every two and a half hours. Both services were scheduled for 50 minutes. The Monday-Friday schedule called for 12 round trips daily between Dallas and Houston and six round trips daily between Dallas and San Antonio. Saturday and Sunday schedules were more limited, reflecting both the lower travel demand at weekends and the need for downtime to service the aircraft.

The pricing decision, meantime, had been arrived at after talking with PSA executives in California. Rollin King recalled:

> What Andy Andrews [President of PSA] said to Lamar and me one day was the key to our initial pricing decision. Andy told us that the way you ought to figure your price is not on how much you can get or what the other carriers were charging. He said, "Pick a price at which you can break even with a reasonable load factor, and a load factor that you have a reasonable expectation of being able to get within a given period of time, and that ought to be your price. It ought to be as low as you can get it without leading yourself down the primrose path and running out of money."

After estimating the amount of money required for pre-operating expenditures and then carefully assessing both operating costs and market potential, Muse and King settled on a $20 fare for both routes, with a break-even point of 39 passengers per flight. This compared with existing Braniff and TI coach fares of $27 on the Dallas-Houston run and $28 on the Dallas-San Antonio service. The two executives felt that an average of 39 passengers per flight was a reasonable expectation in light of the market's potential for growth and the frequency of flights Southwest planned to offer, although they projected a period of deficit operations before this break-even point was reached. They anticipated that while Braniff and TI would probably reduce their own fares eventually, Southwest could expect an initial price advantage.

Early in 1971, Lamar Muse got together with the VP-Marketing, Dick Elliott, to select an adver-

tising agency (the company already employed a public relations agency to handle publicity). The account was given to The Bloom Agency, a large regional advertising agency conveniently headquartered in Dallas. Their assignment: come up with a complete communications program—other than publicity—within four months. "We've got no hostesses and no uniforms and no airplanes and no design and no money," Muse told the agency people, "but we're going to have an airline flying in 120 days!"

The agency approached Southwest Airlines "as though it were a packaged-goods account." The first task was to evaluate the characteristics of all American carriers competing in the Texas markets. To facilitate comparisons, a two-dimensional positioning diagram was prepared, rating each airline's image on "conservative-fun" and "obvious-subtle" dimensions (Exhibit 4). This was based primarily on a content analysis of recent airline advertising, with a view to determining the image conveyed by each carrier.

Texas International was immediately dismissed as dull and conservative, with a bland image (Exhibit 5). Braniff's advertising, however, presented an interesting contrast in styles. From 1965 to 1968, Braniff had employed the New York agency of Wells, Rich, Greene, which had developed an innovative marketing and advertising strategy for their client, with a budget that exceeded $10 million in 1967. Braniff's aircraft were painted in a variety of brilliant colors covering the entire fuselage and tailfin. Hostesses were outfitted in "couture costumes" created by an Italian fashion designer, and the advertising sought to make flying by Braniff seem a glamorous and exciting experience. This strategy proved extremely successful and was believed by many observers to have been an important factor in Braniff's rapid growth during the second half of the 1960s. However, Bloom executives concluded that by 1971 Braniff's image was changing; it had abandoned its initial fun image in favor of a subtler, more conservative style (Exhibit 6), with an advertising budget reduced to

EXHIBIT 4
SOUTHWEST AIRLINES: ADVERTISING AGENCY'S POSITIONING DIAGRAM OF U.S. AIRLINES ADVERTISING/COMPETING IN TEXAS MARKETS

Obvious
SOUTHWEST
BRANIFF*
DELTA
TEXAS INTERNATIONAL
AMERICAN
Conservative
Fun
FRONTIER
UNITED
OZARK
TWA
EASTERN
BRANIFF†
PAN AM
Subtle

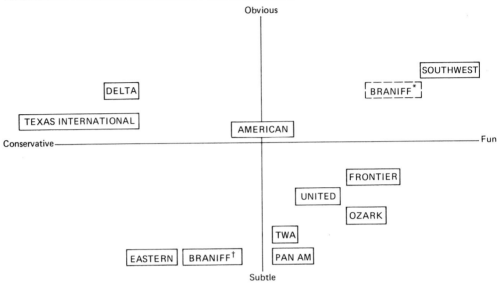

*Former advertising by Wells Rich Green ("The End of the Plain Plane," "The Air Strip")
†Current advertising by Clinton Frank

EXHIBIT 5
EXAMPLE OF TEXAS INTERNATIONAL NEWSPAPER ADVERTISING 1970–71

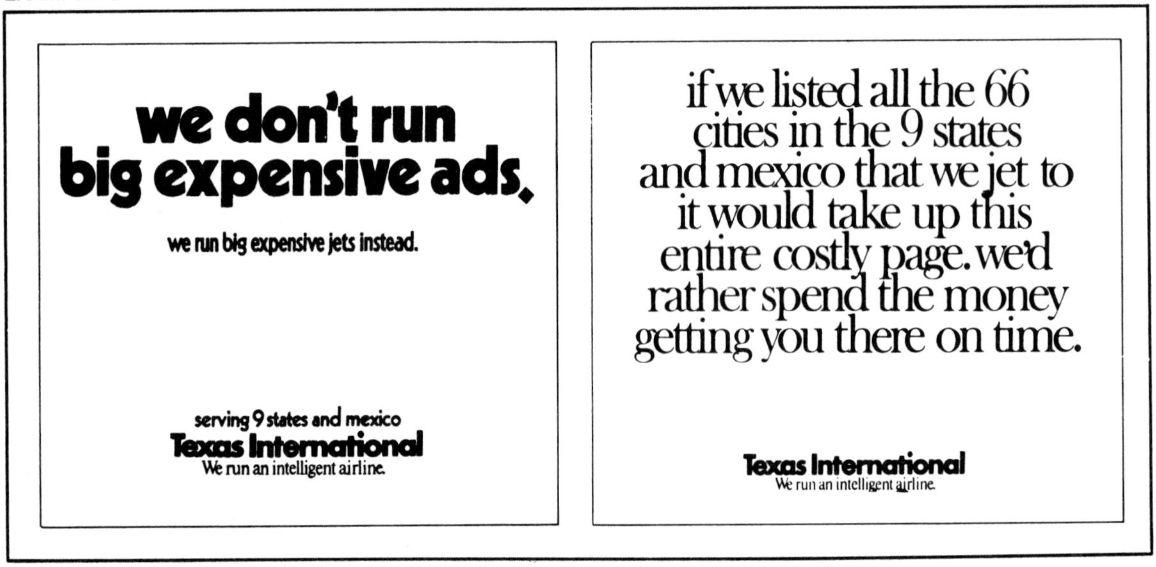

we don't run big expensive ads.
we run big expensive jets instead.
serving 9 states and mexico
Texas International
We run an intelligent airline.
if we listed all the 66 cities in the 9 states and mexico that we jet to it would take up this entire costly page. we'd rather spend the money getting you there on time.
Texas International
We run an intelligent airline.

EXHIBIT 6
EXAMPLE OF CLINTON E. FRANK PRESS ADVERTISING FOR BRANIFF INTERNATIONAL, 1970

EXHIBIT 7
SOUTHWEST INTRODUCTORY ADVERTISING

At last, there's somebody

The planes are new. The pilots are not. We've talked to, tested, and evaluated very good, reputable, reliable pilots that any major airline would hire. Out of them all we've selected a group — maybe an elite — of the very best in the business, with an average of 15,200 hours in the air.

Our ground crew is no small potatoes, either. They're well-trained in dozens of skills that insure your comfort aboard Southwest Airlines.

It's us, Southwest Airlines.

Us, with our brand new Boeing 737's.

We fly to Dallas/Ft. Worth, Houston and San Antonio. Your choice, all flights non-stop.

In that time you're going to feel there really is somebody else up there who loves you.

By sharing a lot of little things with you. Big, little things that mean a lot to travelers.

Three years ago the Boeing 737 was introduced to the public all over the world. Today — as of this morning — the Boeing 737's have accumulated 1,000,000 flight hours, carrying nearly 70 million passengers approximately 430 million miles. The Boeing 737 is the super reliable jet specially designed for short haul traffic. Obviously, it is more than just a beautiful body. No other airlines will be flying 737's on these routes. And Southwest Airlines won't be flying anything else

And we give trading stamps. Not the ordinary kind. Ours are Love Stamps. You get one from our hostess if for any reason she finds you unhappy in any way with our service. The basic idea is that we want you to trade in your bad feelings for good ones. The Love Stamp hopefully will make amends—with a free drink or something, and then you'll feel better about us right away. And want to ride our airplanes again, and again.

JUNE 18

LOVE STAMP

Dallas/Ft. Worth to Houston (and back)
Dallas/Ft. Worth to San Antonio (and back)
All flights non-stop.

else up there who loves you.

By paying attention to you, giving efficient service, and getting you there on time.

And, if for some reason, you don't get all the love we've got to give, we'll make it up by giving you a Love Stamp. Why are we doing all this? Because we need your love, too. And we know we won't get it unless we give it.

She will not plee-aze you. Plee-aze is stiff, formal and very affected English for please. It is usually accompanied by a gleaming toothpaste smile. People who say plee-aze are trying very, very hard to be nice to you. Too hard. And it isn't real. It's like plastic flowers vs. real flowers. You can feel the difference. That's why in our hostess school we haven't taught our girls how to be nice to you. We figure if they didn't already know, they weren't for us. In our school we teach other things. Mostly how to take care of you. Then we dress them in our exciting new hot pants designed for Southwest Airlines by Lorch of Dallas. That really ought to please you.

$20

Save from $14 to $16 per round trip. Eventually, the other airlines may meet our price, but remember, you can't buy love.

Love Potions for the very weary. Order by numbers 1-10, and they're only $1.00 each, not $1.50. That's what happens when you have somebody else up there who loves you.

A love machine which issues you tickets in under 10 seconds. Another way we prove our love: love machines in two great locations — at the ticket counter and at the departure gate, take your pick. Then you give your $20 (or any one of five charge cards) to our people stationed behind the love machines and you're on your way.

DALLAS 826-8840 • HOUSTON 228-8791

SAN ANTONIO 224-2011 • FORT WORTH 283-4661

This is another Southwest Airlines exclusive — our phone number. Keep it on file in your head or elsewhere because it's not in the phone book yet! Use this number to call ahead for reservations if you want to. If you don't want to that's o.k. too. You don't need reservations to board the plane. Just come, plunk down $20 and out pops your ticket from our Love Machine. We plan to make waiting in line a thing of the past.

SOUTHWEST AIRLINES
The somebody else up there who loves you.

approximately $4 million. This left a vacuum for Southwest Airlines to move into. The agency decided to position Southwest even further out on the "fun"/"obvious" side of the old Braniff image.

With this in mind, the account group developed what they termed "an entire personality description model" for the new airline. The objective was to provide the agency's creative specialists with a clear understanding of the image that Southwest should project, so that this might be reflected consistently in every facet of the communications campaign they had to design. This personality statement, which was also used as a guideline in staff recruiting, saw Southwest as "young and vital . . . exciting . . . friendly . . . efficient . . . dynamic."

One constraint which restricted marketing activities in the period prior to passenger operations was the planned issue of over $6 million worth of Southwest stock on June 8. The company's lawyers had advised that a media campaign promoting the airline prior to the stock issue might violate Securities and Exchange Commission regulations against promotion of stock. Virtually the only advertising conducted prior to this date, therefore, was for personnel.

Recruitment advertising in one area proved outstandingly effective, with over 1,200 young women responding to advertisements placed in national media for positions as air hostesses with Southwest. Forty were selected for training and while airline officials made no secret of the attractive looks of the successful candidates, it was also pointed out that their average scores on the required FAA proficiency test placed the Southwest hostesses among the highest ranked in the nation.

The prohibition on advertising did not entirely keep Southwest out of the news. The airline's continuing legal battles with Braniff had TI received wide press coverage in the mass media, while Southwest's public relations agency put out a number of press releases which subsequently, appeared as news or feature stories.

INAUGURATION OF SERVICE: THE FIRST SIX MONTHS

On June 10, 1971, The Bloom Agency's advertising campaign for Southwest finally broke. It began modestly with small "teaser" advertisements in the newspapers, containing provocative headlines such as "The 48-Minute Love Affair," "At last a $20 ticket you won't mind getting," "Love Can Change Your Ways," and "A Fare to Remember." The ads were unsigned, but contained a telephone number for the reader to call. On phoning, a caller in Dallas would hear the following message:

> Hi. It's us. Southwest Airlines. Us with our brand new, candy-colored, rainbow powered Boeing 737 jets. The most reliable plane flying today. And we start flying June 18, to Houston or San Antonio. You choose—only 45 minutes non-stop. In that time, we'll be sharing a lot of big little things with you that mean a lot. Like love potions, a lot of attention, and a new low fare. Just $20. Join us June 18. Southwest Airlines. The somebody else up there who loves you.

Approximately 25,000 telephone calls resulted from these ads.

On Sunday, June 13, all newspapers in the three market areas ran a four-color doubletruck[4] advertisement for Southwest (Exhibit 7). Each day for the next two weeks, full-page newspaper ads were run in all markets focusing on the various advantages Southwest Airlines offered the traveler—new aircraft, attractive hostesses, low fares, fast ticketing, and inexpensive, exotically-named drinks. Television advertising was also heavy and included 30-second spots featuring the Boeing 737, the hostesses, and what was referred to as the "Love Machine" (Exhibit 8). Whereas the competition used traditional, handwritten airline tickets, Southwest counter staff accelerated the ticketing process by using a

---

[4] A "Doubletruck" is a printer's term used to describe material printed across two full pages. A "halftruck" ad is one printed across two half pages.

EXHIBIT 8
SOUTHWEST AIRLINES INTRODUCTORY TV ADVERTISING, JUNE 1971

SOUTHWEST AIRLINES

CODE NO: SWA-3-30-71
TITLE: "TV Love Machine"

TELEVISION STORYBOARD
THE BLOOM AGENCY

1. (Natural sfx, people talking up and under)...

2. ...

3. ...

4. ...

5. (Wm Anncr VO) If you're standing in line...

6. ...you're not flying...

7. ...Southwest Airlines.

8. Because our Love Machine gives you a ticket...

9. ...in under ten seconds.

10. HOSTESS: Have a nice flight.

11. (Sfx: music and jet engine) 12 flights each day to Houston...

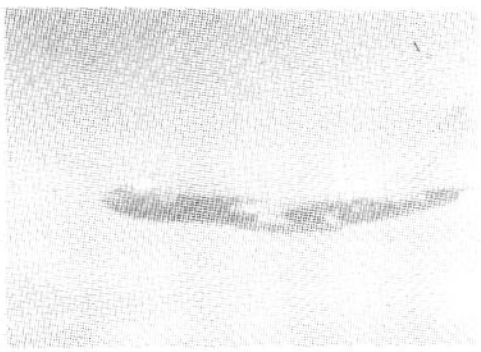

12. ...6 to San Antonio, for a loveable $20...

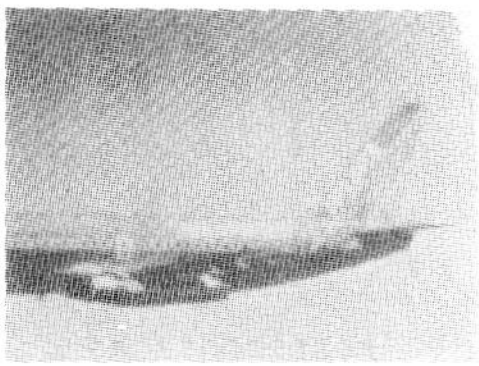

13. ...on Southwest Airlines.

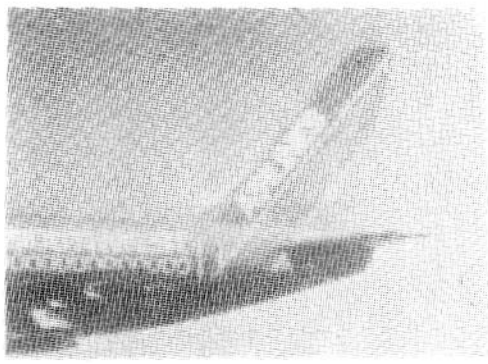

14. "The somebody else up there...

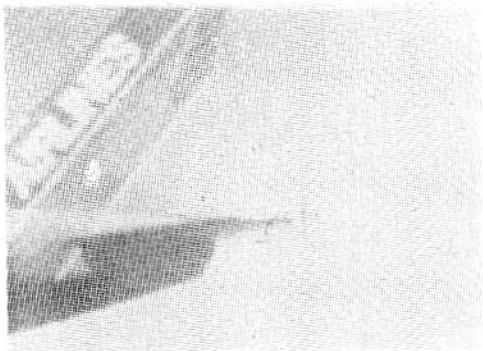

15. ...who loves you."

machine to print out tickets and a pedal-operated tape recorder to record the passengers' names for the aircraft manifest as they checked in—both of these ideas having been copied from PSA. Rounding out the advertising campaign were strategically located billboards at entrances to all three airports served by Southwest. Nearly half the year's promotional budget was spent in the first month of operations (Exhibit 9).

Scheduled revenue operations were inaugurated in a blaze of publicity on Friday, June 18, but it soon became evident that the competition was not about to take matters lying down. In halftruck and full page newspaper ads, Braniff and TI announced $20 fares on both routes. The CAB had disclaimed authority over intrastate fares and Texas law barred jurisdiction by TAC over carriers holding Federal Certificates of Public Convenience and Necessity; thus, the CAB carriers were free to charge any fare they wanted. Braniff's advertising stressed frequent, convenient service—"every hour on the hour," hot and cold towels "to freshen up with," beverage discount coupons and "peace of mind" phone calls at the boarding gate; it also announced an increase in frequency of service between Dallas and San Antonio, effective July 1 (Exhibit 10). TI, meantime, announced that on July 1 it would inaugurate hourly service on the Dallas-Houston route, leaving Dallas at 30 minutes past each hour. TI also introduced "extras" such as free beer, free newspapers and $1 drinks on those routes competing with Southwest (Exhibit 11). Southwest countered with advertising headlined "The Other Airlines May Have Met Our Price But You Can't Buy Love."

Advertising and promotion continued with regular television advertising and frequent publicity events, usually featuring Southwest hostesses. A direct mail campaign was targeted at 36,000 influential business executives in Southwest's service areas. Each of these individuals received a personalized letter from Lamar Muse describing Southwest service and enclosing a voucher good for half the cost of a round-trip ticket; about 1,700 of these vouchers were subsequently redeemed.

Surveys of Southwest passengers departing from Houston showed that a substantial percentage would have preferred service from the William P. Hobby Airport, 12 miles southeast of downtown Houston, rather than from the new Houston Intercontinental Airport, 26 miles north of the city. Accordingly, arrangements were completed in mid-November for seven of Southwest's 14 roundtrip flights between Dallas and Houston to be transferred to Hobby Airport (thus reopening this old airport to scheduled commer-

EXHIBIT 9

SOUTHWEST AIRLINES: ADVERTISING AND PROMOTIONAL EXPENDITURES, 1971 AND 1972

	1971			1972
	Pre-Operating	**Operating**	**Total**	
Advertising				
Newspaper	$139,831	$131,675	$271,506	$ 60,518
Television	36,340	761	37,101	127,005
Radio	5,021	60,080	65,101	95,758
Billboards	26,537	11,670	38,207	90,376
Other publications	710	20,446	21,156	28,139
Production costs	52,484	43,483	95,967	83,272
Other promotion and publicity	29,694	27,200	56,894	48,366
	$290,617	$295,315	$585,932	$533,434

Source: Company records.

Prepared by: Clinton E. Frank, Inc.

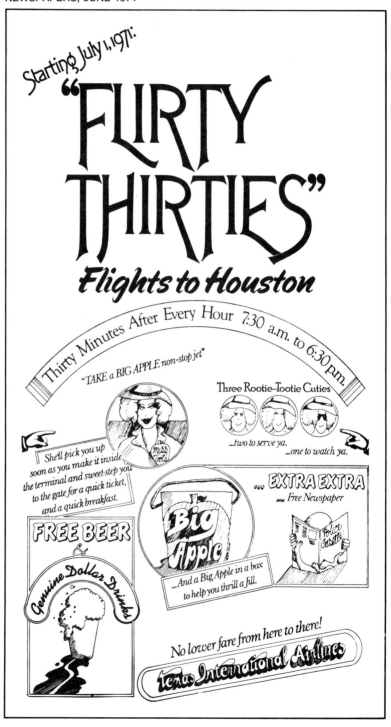

cial passenger traffic). Additional schedule revisions made at the same time included a reduction in the number of Dallas-San Antonio flights to four roundtrips each weekday, inauguration of three roundtrips daily on the third leg of the route triangle between Houston (Hobby) and San Antonio, and elimination of the extremely unprofitable Saturday operation on all routes. These actions contributed to an increase in transportation revenues in the final quarter of 1971 over those achieved in the third quarter, but Southwest's operating losses in the fourth quarter fell only slightly, from $1,006,000 to $921,000 (Exhibit 12). At year's end 1971, Southwest's accumulated deficit stood at $3.75 million (Exhibit 3).

The Second Six Months

In February 1972, Southwest initiated a second phase of the advertising campaign, hired a new Vice President-Marketing and terminated its public relations agency. At the same time, the Company recruited the agency's publicity director to fill a newly-created position as Public Relations Director at Southwest.

The objective of this new phase was to sustain Southwest's presence in the marketplace after eight months of service. Heavy frequency advertising, with a wide variety of messages, was directed at the Airline's primary target, the regular business commuter. Surveys had shown that 89 percent of Southwest's traffic at that time was accounted for by such travelers. Extensive use was made of television in this campaign, which featured many of Southwest's own hostesses.

Mr. Elliott, whom the President described as having performed a "Herculean task" in getting Southwest off the ground, had resigned to take a position with a national advertising agency. The new Vice President-Marketing, Jess R. Coker,

EXHIBIT 12
SOUTHWEST AIRLINES: QUARTERLY INCOME STATEMENTS

Income Statements	1971		1972			
($'000)	Q3	Q4	Q1	Q2	Q3	Q4
Transportation revenues[1]	887	1,138	1,273	1,401	1,493	1,745
Operating Expenses						
Operations & maintenance[2]	1,211	1,280	1,192	1,145	1,153	1,156
Marketing & gen. admin.	371	368	334	366	313	351
Depreciation & amortiz.	311	411	333	334	335	335
Total	1,893	2,059	1,859	1,845	1,801	1,842
Operating profit (loss)	(1,006)	(921)	(586)	(444)	(308)	(97)
Net interest revenues (costs)	(254)	(253)	(218)	(220)	(194)	(204)
Net income (loss) before extraordinary items	(1,260)	(1,174)	(804)	(664)	(502)	(301)
Extraordinary items	(571)[3]	(469)[3]	—	533[4]	—	—
Net income (loss)	(1,831)	(1,643)	(804)	(131)	(502)	(301)

[1] Includes both passenger and freight business.
[2] Incremental costs per flight were $226 during the second half of 1971, $231 in the first half of 1972, and $244 in the second half of 1972. In addition, management estimated that variable costs per passenger carried amounted to $2.53 during the first half of 1972 and to $2.80 during the second half of the year. These variable costs per passenger included $.13 for passenger beverages and supplies in the first half and $.43 in the second half.
[3] Write off of pre-operating costs.
[4] Capital gain on sale of one aircraft.
Source: Company records.

had spent ten years in the outdoor advertising business after graduating from the University of Texas. His most recent assignment, before joining the airline, had been as Vice President of Southern Outdoor Markets, a company representing 85 percent of all outdoor advertising facilities in the 14 southern and southeastern states. Mr. Coker now became responsible for all marketing functions of the airline, including advertising, sales, and public relations (Exhibit 13). Jess Coker typically met weekly with the account executive from The Bloom Agency to discuss media advertising, and the numerous other small activities handled by the agency. These included preparation and execution of pocket timetables, point-of-sales materials for travel agents, and promotional brochures.

Although the majority of ticket sales were made over the counter at the airport terminals, sales were also made to travel agents and corporate accounts. Travel agents received a 7 percent commission on credit card sales and 10 percent on cash sales. Corporate accounts—companies whose personnel made regular use of Southwest Airlines—received no discount but benefited from the convenience of having their own supply of ticket stock (which they issued themselves) and of receiving a single monthly billing. Jess Coker was responsible for a force of six sales representatives, whose job was to develop and service both travel agents and corporate accounts, encouraging maximum use of Southwest through distribution of point-of-sale materials, development of package arrangements, distribution of pocket timetables, etc. Sales representatives also promoted Southwest's air freight business, which featured a special Rush delivery service for packages. Each representative, as well as most com-

EXHIBIT 13
SOUTHWEST AIRLINES: PARTIAL ORGANIZATION CHART, 1972–73

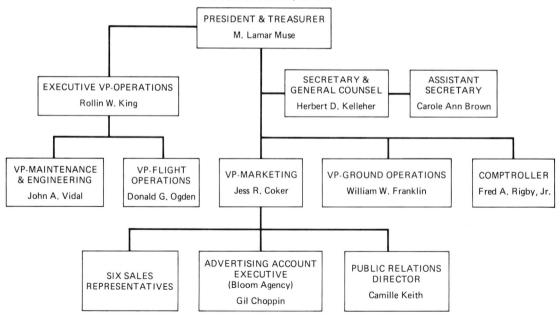

Source: Company Records.

pany officers, drove an AMC Gremlin car, strikingly painted in the same color scheme as Southwest's aircraft.

Also reporting to Coker was Southwest's new Public Relations Director, Camille Keith, formerly publicity director of Read-Poland, Inc., the public relations agency which had up till then handled the airline's account. Keith's responsibilities focused on obtaining media coverage for the airline, and also included publication of Southwest's inflight magazine and development of certain promotions jointly with the advertising agency.

Between October 1971 and April 1972, average passenger loads systemwide increased from 18.4 passengers per flight to 26.7 passengers. However, this was still below the number necessary to cover total costs per trip flown, which had been tending to rise. It had become evident that the volume of traffic during the late morning and early afternoon could not realistically support flights at hourly intervals. It was also clear that most Houston passengers preferred Hobby Airport to Houston Intercontinental. Over time, the number of Southwest flights to Hobby had been steadily increased and the decision was now taken to abandon Houston Intercontinental altogether.

On May 14, a new schedule was introduced, which reduced the total number of daily flights between Dallas and Houston from 29 to 22, primarily by reducing service in the 9:30 a.m. to 3:30 p.m. period from hourly to two-hourly. There were still 11 flights daily on the Dallas-San Antonio route and six between San Antonio and Houston, with some minor schedule modifications. Hobby Airport was to be used exclusively for all flights to and from Houston. Braniff quickly retaliated by introducing its own service from Dallas to Hobby and undertaking an extensive publicity program promoting this airport.

From a financial viewpoint, the most significant aspect of Southwest's actions was that the new schedule made it possible for the company

to dispose of its fourth Boeing 737. Experience had shown that the 737s could be turned around (i.e. loaded and unloaded) at the gate in as little as 10 minutes. This meant that an hourly schedule on the Dallas-Houston run could be maintained with only two aircraft, instead of three. With the slack provided by the reduced mid-day frequencies and a schedule which involved periodically flying an aircraft around all three legs of the route triangle, management concluded that three aircraft would suffice and that the fourth could be sold. By mid-1972, the airline industry had recovered from its 1970–71 slump and aircraft manufacturers had waiting lists for their more popular models. Southwest had no trouble finding a ready buyer for its now surplus 737 and made a profit of $533,000 on reselling it. The combination of this capital gain, lower operating costs, and a continued increase in revenues resulted in a reduction of the quarterly net loss from $804,000 to $131,000 between the first and second quarters of 1972 (Exhibit 12).

For some months, Southwest had been experimenting with a $10 fare on Friday evening flights after 9:00 p.m. In May, this reduced fare was extended to post 9:00 p.m. flights on a daily basis. The result was sharply higher load factors on these discount flights relative to the average achieved on standard price flights (Exhibit 14).

June 1972 saw Southwest Airlines celebrating its first birthday. This gave Camille Keith an opportunity for more of the publicity stunts for which the airline was already becoming renowned. Posters were hung inside the aircraft and in the waiting lounges, the aircraft cabins were decorated and there was an on-board party every day for a week, with birthday cake for the passengers and even balloons for the children. This activity, promoted by newspaper advertising, generated considerable publicity for the airline and, in management's view, reinforced Southwest's image as the plucky, friendly little underdog which had now survived an entire year against powerful, entrenched competition.

EXHIBIT 14
SOUTHWEST AIRLINES: DISCOUNT VS. REGULAR FARE FLIGHTS
All routes

Month	Regular Flights		Discount Flights[1]		Price Changes
	Psgrs.	Flights	Psgrs.	Flights	
June 1971[2]	5,530	424	—	—	
July	15,459	988	—	—	
Aug.	16,121	1,026	—	—	
Sept.	16,440	939	—	—	
Oct.	21,044	1,146	—	—	
Nov.	19,042	963	73	3	$10 fares on some evening weekend flights
Dec.	20,178	981	198	5	
1971 Total	113,814	6,467	271	8	
Jan. 1972	20,694	899	170	4	
Feb.	20,696	912	216	4	
March	24,656	1,014	702	10	
April	24,077	916	573	8	
May	23,112	869	2,189	51	$10 fare on all flights after 9 p.m.
June	22,972	784	4,636	78	
July	18,994	740	5,720	78	Basic fare raised to $26
Aug.	21,257	819	5,739	81	
Sept.	19,020	717	5,358	83	
Oct.	21,894	786	6,599	98	
Nov.	19,825	648	12,141	197	Half-price fares weekdays after 8 p.m. and on all weekend flights
Dec.	17,142	604	10,617	176	
1972 Total	254,339	9,708	54,660	868	
Jan. 1973[3]	18,893	599	13,635	239	Half-price fares on all Dallas-San Antonio flights

[1] Includes flights on which gifts were offered.
[2] Part-month only.
[3] Estimated figures.
Source: Company records.

Not all public relations activity was just hoopla, Keith stressed, mentioning that she worked quite closely with the advertising agency to coordinate the airline's mass communication strategy.

One example of a specialized promotional campaign involving inputs from both Camille Keith and The Bloom Agency was the Southwest Sweetheart's Club. Using a specialized mailing list, a direct mail piece was sent to executive secretaries in Southwest's market area, offering them membership in this club. For each reservation on Southwest she made for her boss, the secretary received a "sweetheart stamp," and for each 15 stamps, she obtained a free ride on Southwest. Additional bonuses for members included a twice-yearly drawing for a big Mexico City vacation.

INTRODUCTION OF NEW PRICING STRATEGIES

After a year of operation, Southwest management decided it was time to take a hard look at the fare structure and its relationship to costs and revenues. They soon concluded that the airline could no longer afford a $20 fare on daytime flights. New tariffs were therefore filed with the Texas Aeronautics Commission, effective July 9, 1972; these raised Southwest's basic one-way fare from $20 to $26, established a round-trip fare of $50 and offered a $225 Commuter Club Card providing unlimited transportation for the purchaser on all routes for a 30-day period.

One problem was how to break the news of the increased fares to the public. At a strategy session with representatives of The Bloom Agency, Camille Keith suggested that Southwest announce a new Executive Class service on all full-fare flights, offering passengers new amenities. The idea was quickly refined: two rows of seats would be removed from the aircraft, reducing its capacity from 112 to 104 seats but increasing legroom; additionally, passengers would be offered free drinks (it was felt that the hostesses would not have time to serve more than two drinks per passenger on such short flights). Full-page newspaper advertisements were then run announcing Southwest Airlines' New Executive Class service, with first-class legroom for everyone and free cocktails. The $26 price also absorbed the security check charges introduced the previous month.

The key consideration was how the competition would react. "For a few days," admitted Jess Coker, "we were really sweating." Braniff's initial response was to devote an additional aircraft to its Dallas-Hobby Airport flights on July 11, thus permitting them to offer on-the-hour service most hours of the business day. However, on July 17, Texas International increased their fares to the same level as Southwest's; then on July 21 Braniff met all aspects of the fare and on-board service charges, also adding a $10 "Sundowner" flight to Hobby at 7:30 p.m. As a result of Bra-

niff's increased service and the higher fares, as well as cutbacks in the number of Southwest flights, Southwest passenger counts fell on all three routes (Exhibit 15). Overall, Southwest's patronage fell back by 2 percent in the third quarter of 1972, compared with that in the second quarter, but transportation revenues increased (Exhibit 12).

During September a third phase of the advertising campaign was launched, based on the slogan "Remember What It Was Like Before Southwest Airlines?" which the agency saw as a war cry to rally consumers. The principal media used were television (Exhibit 16) and billboards.

At the end of October, another major change was made in pricing strategies. The $10 discount fares, which had never been advertised, were replaced by half-fare flights ($13 one-way, $25 round-trip) in both directions on the two major routes each weekday night after 8 p.m. Saturday flights were reintroduced and *all* weekend flights were offered at half-fare. An intensive, three-week advertising campaign accompanied this new schedule and pricing policy change, using one-minute radio commercials on country and western, top forty, and similar type stations.[5] The response was immediate: November 1972 traffic levels were 12 percent higher than those in October—historically the best month of the year in Southwest's commuter markets.

In the new year, management turned its attention to its largest single remaining problem. The company was now actually making money on its Dallas-Houston flights but incurring substantial losses in the Dallas-San Antonio market, where passenger volume was much lower (Exhibit 15). Southwest offered only eight flights a day on this route, versus 33 by its major competitor, and was averaging a mere 17 passengers on each full-fare flight. Southwest management concluded that unless a dramatic improvement in patronage was

---

[5] A "top forty" station is one which specializes in playing currently popular rock music recordings.

EXHIBIT 15

SOUTHWEST AIRLINES: MONTHLY FLIGHTS AND PASSENGER COUNTS ON EACH ROUTE

Month	Dallas-Houston		Dallas-San Antonio		San Antonio-Houston	
	Psgrs.	Flights	Psgrs.	Flights	Psgrs.	Flights
June 1971[1]	3,620	276	1,910	148	—	—
July	10,301	642	5,158	346	—	—
Aug.	11,316	672	4,805	354	—	—
Sept.	11,674	612	4,766	327	—	—
Oct.	14,552	764	6,492	282	—	—
Nov.	14,060	654	4,167	240	888	72
Dec.	14,665	687	4,004	165	1,707	134
1971 Total	80,188	4,307	31,302	1,962	2,595	206
Jan. 1972	16,122	634	2,788	141	1,954	128
Feb.	16,069	640	2,755	142	2,088	134
March	18,285	669	4,270	209	2,803	146
April	17,732	605	4,617	189	2,301	130
May	18,586	584	4,254	198	2,461	138
June	19,782	521	5,198	201	2,628	140
July	17,596	494	5,011	193	2,107	131
Aug.	19,620	546	4,978	208	2,398	146
Sept.	17,472	489	4,734	184	2,172	127
Oct.	20,776	545	5,197	200	2,520	139
Nov.	22,461	507	6,640	199	2,865	139
Dec.	19,080	468	6,211	186	2,468	126
1972 Total	223,581	6,702	56,653	2,250	28,765	1,624
Jan. 1973[2]	21,948	505	7,710	197	2,870	136

[1] Part-month only.
[2] Estimated figures.
Source: Company records.

quickly achieved on this route, they would have to abandon it. They decided to make one last attempt to obtain the needed increase and on January 22, 1973, announced a "60-Day-Half-Price-Sale" on *all* Southwest Airlines flights between Dallas and San Antonio. This sale was announced by advertising on television and radio (Exhibit 17). If successful, it was Lamar Muse's intention to make this reduced fare permanent, but he felt that announcing it as a limited period offer would stimulate consumer interest even more effectively, while also reducing the likelihood of competitive response.

The impact of these half-price fares was even faster and more dramatic than the results of the evening and weekend half-price fares introduced the previous fall. By the end of the first week, average loads on Southwest's Dallas-San Antonio service had risen to 48 passengers per flight and continued to rise sharply at the beginning of the following week.

On Thursday, February 1, however, Braniff employed full-page newspaper advertisements to announce a half-price "Get Acquainted Sale" between Dallas and Hobby on all flights, lasting until April 1 (Exhibit 18).[6]

Lamar Muse immediately called an urgent

[6] Braniff flights to Houston Intercontinental continued to be priced at the higher fare.

EXHIBIT 16

SOUTHWEST AIRLINES' TV ADVERTISING: "REMEMBER WHAT IT WAS LIKE BEFORE
SOUTHWEST AIRLINES?" SEPTEMBER 1972

SOUTHWEST AIRLINES

CODE NO: SWA-34-30-72
TITLE: "Executive Class"

TELEVISION STORYBOARD
THE BLOOM AGENCY

1. HOSTESS: Remember what
it was like...

2. ...before there was somebody
else up there who loved you?

3. There was no such thing as
executive class service to Dallas,
Houston and San Antonio.

4. With first class leg room,
free cocktails for everyone,...

5. ...and a schedule you could
depend on.

6. (Sfx: jet taking off)...

7. ...

8. ...

9. Remember?

10. (Natural sfx up and out)

EXHIBIT 17

SOUTHWEST AIRLINES: RADIO ADVERTISING FOR HALF-FARE FLIGHTS

All San Antonio Flights, January 1973

Number: 118–23–2   Length: 60 secs.   Date: 12/21/72, revised 12/29/72

Music: Clinky piano

Announcer: It's time for Captain Moneysaver, the man who knows how to save your dough!

Captain Moneysaver: Hello, money-savers! Since Southwest Airlines introduced its half-price sale on all flights every day between Dallas and San Antonio, many listeners have asked that age-old question: Can I get there cheaper? Cheaper than $13? Sure!

   You can strap five thousand pigeons to your arm and fly yourself. Or propel your body with a giant rubber band. Put a small motor on a ten-speed bike. . . .

Music: Light, happy

Hostess: Southwest Airlines announces the 60-day half-price sale between Dallas and San Antonio. It's good on all flights every day. Just $13 one way. $25 round trip. So what are you waiting for?

SFX: Street

Cowboy: You mean I kin fly between San Antonio and Dallas on a real jet airplane fer only $13?

Announcer: That's right! On any Southwest Airlines flight, every day.

Cowboy: They still gonna have them pretty girls and all?

Announcer: Same Southwest Airlines love service. And it's cheaper than the best bus service.

Cowboy: Howzit compare to my pickup?

Music: Light, happy

Hostess: Fly now while it's half fare on every Southwest Airlines flight every day between Dallas and San Antonio. All our love at half the price.

Voice: Half price? Can they do that?

Second voice: They did it!

Prepared by: The Bloom Agency.

---

meeting of the management team, including Rollin King, the Marketing VP, the Public Relations Director, the company's attorneys, and the account people from The Bloom Agency, to decide how Southwest should respond to Braniff's move.

Braniff's 'Get Acquainted Sale'

Half-price to Houston's Hobby Airport.

$13 Coach
$17 First Class

To Hobby			Back to Dallas-Fort Worth		
Leave		**Arrive**	**Leave**		**Arrive**
7:30 a.m.	Non-stop	8:20 a.m.	8:00 a.m. (Ex Sun)	Non-stop	8:50 a.m.
9:30 a.m.	Non-stop	10:20 a.m.	9:00 a.m. (Ex Sun)	Non-stop	9:50 a.m.
11:30 a.m.	Non-stop	12:20 p.m.	11:00 a.m.	Non-stop	11:50 a.m.
2:30 p.m.	Non-stop	3:20 p.m.	1:00 p.m.	Non-stop	1:50 p.m.
3:30 p.m. (Ex Sat)	Non-stop	4:20 p.m.	4:00 p.m.	Non-stop	4:50 p.m.
5:30 p.m.	Non-stop	6:20 p.m.	5:00 p.m. (Ex Sat)	Non-stop	5:50 p.m.
6:30 p.m. (Ex Sat)	Non-stop	7:20 p.m.	7:00 p.m. (Ex Sat)	Non-stop	7:50 p.m.
			9:00 p.m.	Non-stop	9:50 p.m.

Sale lasts 'til April 1

From now until April 1, all Braniff International flights to Houston's Hobby Airport are priced to go. Half price to be exact. 50% off.

A one-way ticket in coach is $13.00. Round-trip is an even better bargain at $25.00. And in first class, $17.00 one-way, $34.00 round-trip.

We believe we have the best service to Hobby Airport. But not enough people know about it. So, we're offering you a chance to sample our big 727 Wide-Body jets to Houston's Hobby at half the regular price. We call it our "Get Acquainted Sale."

Half price and a reserved seat, too. Call Braniff International at 357-9511 in Dallas; 335-5811 in Fort Worth.

You'll like flying Braniff Style.

BRANIFF
US MAINLAND   HAWAII   MEXICO   SOUTH AMERICA

CROWE CHEMICAL DIVISION

M. Edgar Barrett
Charles T. Sharpless

Michael Demming, executive vice-president of the Crowe Chemical Division of Majestic Tool Company, Inc., was sitting in his Beaumont, Texas, office. It was late in the evening on a midweek day in July 1976. Demming had stayed late at the office in order to be able to spend some time assessing the ramifications of a recently announced price cut by a major competitor. The competitor, Cajun Chemical Corporation, was the industry leader in the region of the country and the market segment served by Crowe Chemical. The Louisiana-based firm was both larger and more profitable than Crowe.

THE COMPANY

Crowe Chemical was a wholly owned subsidiary of Majestic Tool. It was a small concern, with manufacturing and administrative facilities located in or near Beaumont, Texas. The firm was engaged in the production of industrial chemicals which were used primarily in the oil refining

Copyright © 1978 and 1979 by M. Edgar Barrett.

process. Although it was far smaller than most firms in the chemical industry, Crowe had managed to survive, and, in fact, stay quite competitive.

Crowe's divisional strategy was built on the premise that the firm would concentrate its efforts in the marketing, manufacturing, and distribution of specialty chemicals. The manufacturing process for each of the firm's products was nearly identical. With a few minor exceptions, the productive plant and equipment could be used for the manufacture and packaging of all three products.

The firm's three products were also closely related in that they required similar raw materials. One of the raw materials used to produce one of the three products (Sa 11) was itself a by-product resulting from the manufacture of another of the firm's products (Sa 10). The amount of this by-product which resulted from the manufacture of Sa 10 at the current level of production was well in excess of the firm's current and projected needs as an input to the Sa 11 production process. The excess amount of by-product was sold on the open market and treated as a reduction in Sa 10's overall raw material costs.

The sales and marketing efforts of the Crowe Chemical Division were concentrated in three Gulf Coast states. Salaried salespeople were assigned to specific geographic regions in Texas, Louisiana, or Mississippi. Price was a major consideration for the smaller refineries with which the Crowe Chemical Division often dealt. However, some degree of brand loyalty had been created as a result of long-standing customer relationships developed by the regional salespeople. The management of Crowe Chemical estimated that they held an average market share of 16 percent for Sa 10, 14 percent for Sa 11, and 8 percent for Sa 12 within the three-state region served by the firm.

Some History

Crowe Chemical Company was founded in 1939 by John Lewis Crowe. The firm benefited handsomely from the wartime economic boom. By 1946, annual sales had reached the level of $5 million. The firm continued its pattern of gradual but steady growth over the next three decades. Record sales of nearly $42 million were recorded in 1974.

J. L. Crowe resigned from his management position in mid-1973. The resignation had been planned for some time as a result of Crowe's explicit desire to free most of his time for use in family-related interests and personal real estate ventures. The presidency of the firm was handed to Crowe's son-in-law, George Thompson. Crowe, however, did not totally withdraw from the ongoing activities of the firm. He had, for example, played an important role in the merger negotiations that took place during 1975.

ACQUISITION BY MAJESTIC TOOL

Due in large part to spiraling production costs, 1975 was not a very profitable year for either Crowe Chemical or the industry as a whole. In fact, 1975 was an exceptionally poor year for the entire chemical industry. Raw material prices rose considerably. Rising labor costs and sharply higher utility rates took their toll in terms of reduced levels of profit. Finally, it was widely acknowledged that production capacity had recently grown in a manner disproportionate to increases in demand.

Crowe's common stock, traded over the counter, fell considerably in price during the year. After being the target of two unannounced takeover bids, Crowe's management sought out a friendly partner. Majestic Tool, a Louisiana-based supplier of high-technology products and services to the energy sector, ultimately entered into merger discussions with the firm.

The acquisition talks centered, at one point, on what role George Thompson would play in the emerging subsidiary. It was finally agreed that he would remain in his present capacity as chief executive officer, with responsibility for planning and personnel. The agreement stipulated, however, that one of Majestic's own people was to be brought in as executive vice-president. This person, Michael Demming, had had extensive experience in industrial products and was to be in charge of day-to-day operations.

ANALYSIS OF OPERATING RESULTS

Demming assumed his new position in early 1976. Several days after his arrival, he and Thompson met to review the firm's 1975 operations. The two men inspected the income statement for the year just ended (Exhibit 1), as well as several other documents recently computed by the controller's department. One of these other documents was a product line profitability analysis for the calendar year 1975 (Exhibit 2). Another document provided information about the particular characteristics of individual product costs, including some written comments regarding their projected behavior (Exhibit 3).

While no action was taken as a result of the discussion that took place between the two men,

EXHIBIT 1

INCOME STATEMENT
(FOR THE YEAR ENDED DECEMBER 31, 1975)

Gross sales	$37,985,788
Less: discounts	690,343
Net sales	37,295,445
Cost of goods sold	19,655,641
Gross margin	17,639,804
Operating expenses	16,980,765
Operating income	659,039
Less: interest	357,143
Divisional profit (before tax)	301,896

Thompson did express his concern about the loss shown on Sa 11. Excerpts from the conversation are included below.

George Thompson: It looks to me like we're losing our shirt on Sa 11. The results have never been great on this product, but now they've really turned bad. I wonder if we shouldn't cut back on our production and sales efforts on this one.

Michael Demming: According to the records, we've never shown a very substantial profit

EXHIBIT 2

PRODUCT LINE PROFITABILITY ANALYSIS
(For the year ended December 31, 1975)

	Sa 10		Sa 11		Sa 12	
	Thousands of dollars	**Per unit**	**Thousands of dollars**	**Per unit**	**Thousands of dollars**	**Per unit**
Gross sales	$115,514	$7.7500	$13,517	$9.0000	$8,954	$9.5000
Discounts	194	.0969	304	.2024	192	.2037
Net sales	$ 15,320	$7.6531	$13,213	$8.7976	$8,762	$9.2963
Cost of goods sold:						
Direct labor	$ 2,035	$1.0165	$ 3,352	$2.2319	$1,579	$1.6753
Direct material[a,b]	1,919	.9586	1,701	1.1326	1,439	1.5268
Indirect labor	1,087	.5430	1,189	.7917	907	.9623
Fringe benefits	81	.0405	134	.0892	64	.0679
Insurance	104	.0519	79	.0526	49	.0519
Repair service	336	.1678	254	.1691	157	.1666
Power	124	.0619	94	.0626	58	.0615
Property taxes	204	.1019	154	.1025	94	.0997
Supplies	507	.2533	1,109	.7384	845	.8965
Total	$ 6,397	$3.1954	$ 8,066	$5.3706	$5,192	$5.5085
Gross margin	$ 8,923	$4.4577	$ 5,147	$3.4270	$3,570	$3.7878
Operating expenses:						
Administrative	$ 970	$ .4846	$ 628	$ .4181	$ 534	$ .5666
Advertising	1,706	.8522	1,213	.8076	797	.8456
Depreciation	2,396	1.1969	1,906	1.2690	1,089	1.1554
Interest	164	.0819	116	.0772	77	.0817
Research and development	1,745	.8717	1,241	.8263	814	.8636
Allocated overhead	892	.4456	634	.4221	416	.4413
Total	$ 7,873	$3.9329	$ 5,738	$3.8203	$3,727	$3.9542
Divisional profit (before tax)	$ 1,050	$ .5248	($ 591)	($ .3933)	($ 157)	($ .1664)
Unit sales (in barrels)	2,001,842		1,501,885		942,512	

   [a] The sale of the excess by-product resulting from the production of product Sa 10, as well as the internal transfer of by-product to product Sa 11, resulted in a reduction in the recorded direct materials cost for product Sa 10.
   [b] The Sa 10 by-product used in the production of Sa 11 was charged to Sa 11. It was valued at the market price of the by-product in the outside (of Crowe Chemical Division) market.

EXHIBIT 3
CONTROLLER'S ANALYSIS OF MANUFACTURING COSTS

Variable costs:

Direct labor:	Direct labor costs have been historically treated as varying with volume of production. An identifiable number of workers, however, are paid their full weekly wages regardless of units produced.
Direct materials:	Purchased at market price. The market is highly susceptible to the relative forces of supply and demand, but prices tend to change on a quarterly basis. See also the notes to Exhibit 2.
Fringe benefits:	Included are compensation insurance, group health plan, and group life insurance. These programs are mandatory and the amount paid is most directly related to the amount of direct labor costs.
Supplies:	Supplies are purchased from company offering most favorable terms. Cost is net of discounts.
Repair service:	Has historically varied with level of production. Repair people are available on short notice in case of unforeseen downtime.
Power:	Charged industrial rates. The total bill tends to be directly related to production volume.

Fixed costs:

Indirect labor:	This consists largely of supervisory labor. A few laborers available to relieve workers or substitute for those on holiday and sick leave are also included.
Depreciation:	This represents a fixed amount assigned to each product.
Interest:	Total interest charges are divided among the products on the basis of a formula largely derived from expected unit sales.
Administrative:	These costs represent salaries paid to executive and office personnel.
Advertising and research and development:	The total amount of expenditures is fixed at yearly budget meetings. They may be augmented during the year at management's discretion. The total is allocated to specific products based on the same formula used for interest.
Insurance and property taxes:	Fire, property, and vehicle insurance charges are assigned to each product line. Property taxes are based on assessed values and are considered to be fixed. They do, however, tend to rise slightly each year.
Allocated overhead:	Other overhead costs. This category includes such things as heat, water, and janitorial services.

on this product. With the disaster of a year we've had, the loss may have been unavoidable.

George Thompson: You may be right, Mike. But, I just don't see any feasible way to lower manufacturing costs by 39 cents a barrel. We also ought to look at Sa 12. We're off-budget on that one as well.

Michael Demming: Let's hang on for another quarter, George. Making drastic changes may well do us more harm than good. If things don't improve with time, we'll have to address the issue head-on later during this year.

First-Quarter Results

Around the middle of April, Demming received an income statement for the first three months of 1976 (Exhibit 4). Much to his satisfaction, the division had managed to earn a modest profit. A week or so later, Demming received the first quarter's version of a new product line profitability analysis form that he had specifically requested from the divisional controller (Exhibit 5). Demming inspected the report and compared the results to the previous year's operations.

EXHIBIT 4
INCOME STATEMENT
(For the quarter ended March 31, 1976)

Gross sales	$9,913,923
Less: discounts	180,309
Net sales	9,733,614
Cost of goods sold	4,985,357
Gross margin	4,748,257
Operating expenses	4,343,212
Operating income	405,045
Less: interest	89,124
Divisional profit (before tax)	315,921

CAJUN CHEMICAL'S PRICE ANNOUNCEMENT

During the second quarter of 1976, the Gulf Coast chemical industry suffered from the results of circumstances quite similar to those that had existed in 1975. The Crowe Chemical Division managed to keep a tight grip on their market share. Nonetheless, profits for the three-month period declined.

Even before the release of the second quarter operating data, events took what Demming per-

EXHIBIT 5
PRODUCT LINE PROFITABILITY ANALYSIS
(For the quarter ending March 31, 1976)

Majestic Tool, Inc.: Form 640

Copies to:	Standard per unit	Total at standard cost and actual units (000s)	Total at actual (000s)	Variance (000s)
		Product Sa 10		
Revenue (net sales)	$7.6533	$3,973	$3,973	—
Variable Costs:				
Direct labor	1.0775	559	545	14
Direct materials	.9585	498	509	(11)
Fringe benefits	.0405	21	19	2
Repair service	.1680	87	88	(1)
Power	.0620	32	33	(1)
Supplies	.2535	132	131	1
Total variable costs	2.5600	1,329	1,325	4
Fixed costs:				
Indirect labor	.5430	282	272	10
Depreciation	1.1969	621	599	22
Interest	.0819	43	41	2
Insurance	.0519	27	26	1
Administrative	.4846	252	243	9
Research & development	.8717	453	436	17
Advertising	.8522	442	437	5
Property taxes	.1019	53	51	2
Allocated overhead	.4456	231	224	7
Corporate overhead	.0720	37	36	1
Total fixed costs	4.7017	2,441	2,365	76
Divisional profit (before tax)	.3916	203	283	80
Unit sales (in barrels)		519,140		
Expected sales (in barrels)		500,000		

ceived to be an even more somber tone as Cajun Chemical announced a price decrease. This decrease, to be effective immediately, meant that Cajun's version of product Sa 10 would carry a net list price of $7.15 a barrel. It was this price cut that Demming had now focused upon for analysis.

Demming recalled that he and George Thompson had speculated several weeks ago that a price cut by Cajun was a possibility that they should consider. At that time, Thompson had stressed that he did not wish to sell Sa 10 below cost. He had based his view on the fact that the product was currently the division's major source of profit.

Demming also recalled a conversation of earlier in the same day with the divisional sales director. The director, Bill Sharpless, predicted that the sales volume for Sa 10 during the second half of 1976 would approximate 1 million barrels. When pressed, however, he admitted that this estimate was based on an assumption of price parity with the Cajun Chemical product. He said that sales would probably fall to around 875,000 barrels if the Cajun price cut was not met. Thompson believed it was time to make a decision about Sa 11 and to decide whether to meet the Cajun price cut.

EXHIBIT 5 (continued)

	Product Sa 11				Product Sa 12		
Standard per unit	Total at standard cost and actual units (000s)	Total at actual (000s)	Variance (000s)	Standard per unit	Total at standard cost and actual units (000s)	Total at actual (000s)	Variance (000s)
$8.7975	$3,265	$3,265	—	$9.2957	$2,495	$2,495	—
1.6754	622	764	($142)	1.6752	450	453	($3)
.9486	352	366	(14)	1.5268	409	409	—
.0670	25	29	(4)	.0678	18	18	—
.1680	62	60	2	.1666	45	51	(6)
.0626	23	23	—	.0615	17	17	—
.7384	274	273	1	.8965	241	231	10
3.6600	1,358	1,515	(157)	4.3944	1,180	1,179	1
.7919	294	297	(3)	.9045	243	227	16
1.2690	471	476	(5)	1.0888	292	272	20
.0772	29	29	—	.0771	21	19	2
.0526	19	20	(1)	.0495	13	12	1
.4180	155	157	(2)	.5430	146	137	9
.8260	307	310	(3)	.8139	218	203	15
.8165	303	308	(5)	.7986	214	201	13
.1025	38	38	—	.0940	25	23	2
.4221	157	158	(1)	.4135	111	103	8
.0693	26	26	—	.0681	18	17	1
4.8451	1,799	1,819	(20)	4.8510	1,301	1,214	87
.2924	108	(69)	(177)	.0503	14	102	88
	371,185				268,413		
	375,000				250,000		

FRASER COMPANY

Charles B. Weinberg

Alice Howell, president of the Columbia Plastics Division of the Fraser Co., leaned forward at her desk in her bright, sunlit office and said, "In brief, our two options are either to price at a level that just covers our costs or we face losing market leadership to those upstart Canadians at Vancouver Light. Are there no other options?" Tamara Chu, Columbia's marketing manager, and Sam Carney, the production manager, had no immediate reply.

Columbia Plastics, based in Seattle, Washington, had been the area's leading manufacturer of plastic molded skylights for use in houses and offices for almost fifteen years. However, two years earlier Vancouver Light, whose main plant was located in Vancouver, British Columbia, Canada, 150 miles to the north of Seattle, had opened a sales office in the city and sought to gain business by pricing aggressively. Vancouver Light began by offering skylights at 20 percent below Columbia's price for large orders. Now

Vancouver Light had just announced a further price cut of 10 percent.

COMPANY BACKGROUND

The primary business of the Fraser Co., which had recently celebrated the fiftieth anniversary of its existence, was the supply of metal and plastic fabricated parts for its well known Seattle neighbor, Boeing Aircraft. Until the 1960s Boeing had accounted for more than 80 percent of Fraser's volume, but Fraser then decided to diversify in order to protect itself against the boom and bust cycle which seemed to characterize the aircraft industry. Even now, Boeing still accounted for nearly half of Fraser's $50 million[1] in annual sales.

Columbia Plastics had been established to apply Fraser's plastic molding skills in the construction industry. Its first products, which still accounted for nearly 30 percent of its sales, included plastic garage doors, plastic gutters, and

Copyright © 1985 by Charles B. Weinberg.

[1]All prices and costs are in U.S. dollars.

plastic covers for outdoor lights, all of which had proved to be popular among Seattle home builders. In 1968 Columbia began production of what was to be its most successful product, skylights for homes and offices. Skylights now accounted for 70 percent of Columbia's sales.

THE SKYLIGHT MARKET

Although skylights varied greatly in size, a typical one measured 3' × 3' and would be installed in the ceiling of a kitchen, bathroom, or living room. It was made primarily of molded plastic with an aluminum frame. Skylights were usually installed by homebuilders upon initial construction of a home or by professional contractors as part of a remodelling job. Because of the need to cut through the roof to install a skylight and to then seal the joint between the roof and skylight so that water would not leak through, only the most talented of "do-it-yourselfers" would tackle this job on their own. At present 70 percent of the market was in home and office buildings, 25 percent in professional remodelling, and 5 percent in the do-it-yourself market.

Skylights had become very popular. Homeowners found the natural light they brought to a room as being quite attractive and perceived skylights to be energy conserving. Although opinion was divided on whether the heat loss from a skylight was more than the light gained, the general perception was quite favorable. Homebuilders found that featuring a skylight in a kitchen or other room would be an important plus in attracting buyers and often included at least one skylight as a standard feature in a home. Condominium builders had also found that their customers liked the openness that a skylight seemed to provide. Skylights were also a popular feature of the second homes that many people owned on Washington's lakes or in ski areas throughout the Northwest.

In Columbia Plastics' primary market area of Washington, Oregon, Idaho, and Montana, sales of skylights had levelled off in recent years at about 45,000 units per year. Although Columbia would occasionally sell a large order to California homebuilders, such sales were made only to fill slack in the plant and, after including the cost of transportation, were only break-even propositions at best.

Four homebuilders accounted for half the sales of skylights in the Pacific Northwest. Another five bought an average of 1,000 each, and the remaining sales were split among more than 100 independent builders and remodellers. Some repackaged the product under their own brand name; many purchased only a few dozen or less.

Columbia would ship directly only to builders who ordered at least 500 units per year, although it would subdivide the order into sections of one gross (144) for shipping. Most builders and remodellers bought their skylights from building supply dealers, hardware stores, and lumberyards. Columbia sold and shipped directly to these dealers, who typically marked up the product by 50 percent. Columbia's average factory price was $200 when Vancouver Light first entered the market.

Columbia maintained a sales force of three persons for making contact with builders, remodellers, and retail outlets. The sales force was responsible for Columbia's complete line of products which generally went through the same channels of distribution. The cost of maintaining the sales force, including necessary selling support and travel expenses, was $90,000 annually.

Until the advent of Vancouver Light, there had been no significant local competition for Columbia. Several California manufacturers had small shares of the market, but Columbia had held a 70 percent market share until two years ago.

Vancouver Light's Entry

Vancouver Light was founded in the early 1970s by Jennifer McLaren, an engineer, and Carl Garner, an architect, and several of their business associates, in order to manufacture skylights. They believed that there was a growing demand for skylights, but there was no ready source of supply available in western Canada. Their assessment proved correct and their business was successful.

Two years ago the Canadian company had announced the opening of a sales office in Seattle. McLaren came to this office two days a week and devoted her attention to selling skylights only to the large volume builders. Vancouver Light announced a price 20 percent below Columbia's with a minimum order size of 1,000 units to be shipped all at one time. It quickly gained all the business of one large builder, True Homes, a Canadian owned company. In the previous year that builder had ordered 6,000 skylights from Columbia.

A year later one of Columbia's sales representatives was told by the purchasing manager of Chieftain Homes, a Northwest builder who had installed 7,000 skylights the previous year, that Chieftain would switch to Vancouver Light for most of its skylights unless Columbia was prepared to match Vancouver's price. Columbia then matched that price for orders above 2,500 units, guessing that smaller customers would value highly the local service that Columbia could provide. Chieftain then ordered 40 percent of its needs from Vancouver Light. Two smaller builders had since switched to Vancouver Light as well. Before Vancouver's latest price cut had been reported, Tamara Chu, Columbia's marketing manager, projected that Vancouver Light would sell about 11,000 units this year, compared to the 24,000 that Columbia was now selling. Columbia's volume represented a decline of 1,000 units per year in each of the last two years, following the initial loss of the True Homes account.

Columbia had asked its lawyers to investigate whether Vancouver Light's sales could be halted on charges of export dumping, i.e., selling below cost in a foreign market, but a quick investigation revealed that Vancouver Light's specialized production facility provided a 25 percent savings on variable cost, although a third of that was lost due to the additional costs involved in importing and transporting the skylights across the border.

THE IMMEDIATE CRISIS

Alice Howell and her two colleagues had reviewed the situation carefully. Sam Carney, the production manager, had presented the cost accounting data which showed a total unit cost of $135 for Columbia's most popular skylight. Vancouver Light, he said, was selling a closely similar model at $144. The cost of $135 included $15 in manufacturing overheads, directly attributable to skylights, but not the cost of the sales force nor the salaries, benefits, and overheads associated with the three executives in the room. General overheads, including the sales force and executives, amounted to $390,000 per year at present for Columbia as a whole.

Tamara Chu was becoming quite heated about Vancouver Light by this time. "Let's cut the price a further 10 percent to $130 and drive those Canadians right out of the market! That Jennifer McLaren started with those big builders and now she's after the whole market. We'll show her what competition really is!"

But Carney was shocked: "You mean we'll drive her *and* us out of business at the same time! We'll both lose money on every unit we sell. What has that sales force of yours, Tamara, been doing all these years if not building customer loyalty for our product?

"We may lose most of our sales to the big builders," cut in Howell, "but surely most customers wouldn't be willing to rely on shipments from Canada? Maybe we should let Vancouver Light have the customers who want to buy on the basis of price. We can then make a tidy profit from customers who value service, need immediate supply, and have dealt with our company for years."

PART SEVEN

SEVEN

MARKETING RESEARCH

Sound marketing decisions require accurate, timely information about markets, competitors, and consumer behavior. Marketing research, which is one form of marketing information, is primarily concerned with special-purpose research projects, although the same techniques may be used repeatedly on similar or different classes of problems. Every marketing research project should begin with a clear understanding of the organization's specific information needs. Given the uncertain, dynamic, and competitive nature of the marketing environment, no manager can hope to gain perfect understanding of the organization's market. Rather, the goal of marketing research is to reduce uncertainty to tolerable levels at a reasonable cost.

STEPS IN THE MARKETING RESEARCH PROCESS

Marketing research is properly viewed as a sequence of steps which can be termed the *research process*. A summary of the research process is presented in Exhibit 1. When beginning a study, managers are often tempted to go straight to the instrument design and data collection stages, without thinking through the prior steps. This is a serious mistake and often leads to market research reports which are not useful because the wrong questions—or not enough questions—are asked and the data collected then turns out to be unreliable, inaccurate, or incomplete.

EXHIBIT 1
THE MARKET RESEARCH PROCESS

1 Defining the purpose of the research—Why is information to be gathered?

2 Statement of research objectives—What information is needed?

3 Review of existing data—What is already known?

4 Value analysis—Is the research worth the cost?

5 Research design.
   a Exploratory.
   b Descriptive.
   c Causal.

6 Methods of primary data collection.
   a Communication.
   b Observation.

7 Research tactics—sampling procedures and instrument design.
   a Target population.
   b Sample selection.
   c Sample size.
   d Instrument design.
   e Pretesting.

8 Field operations—Collection of the data.

9 Data analysis.

10 Completion of the project.
   a Interpretation of data.
   b Recommendations.
   c Final report.

Defining the Purpose of the Research

The primary questions to be asked before beginning any marketing research project are "Why is this information needed?" and "What will the implications of this research be?" Only if the findings can influence management decisions should the research be carried out.

The reasons for conducting marketing research can be categorized by examining the process of decision making. A useful three-stage model is (1) recognizing and defining problems, (2) generating and selecting alternative courses of action, and (3) monitoring performance.

The first stage of any decision is recognition that a problem exists. Often, the initial signals that managers receive are only vague indications or symptoms of a problem. But once the problem is detected, marketing research can be very useful in defining and understanding it.

With marketing research, managers can better understand the problem or opportunity, as well as search for and evaluate alternative courses of action after the stage of problem recognition. Much of the work done in this area is characterized by formal research procedures. Indeed, the careful gathering of descriptive data and the evaluation of specific alternatives through questionnaire and observational studies is probably the area in which the most money is spent. Market surveys and test marketing are both examples of such studies.

Once a marketing plan is implemented, its progress should be measured against the original purpose through performance monitoring. The information gathered should help ascertain not only whether the program is meeting its goals but also *why* it is succeeding or failing. Performance monitoring may indicate a need for changes in a specific plan or its execution; moreover, it enables managers to learn from their mistakes and successes and to redirect the business accordingly.

Statement of Research Objectives

After establishing that the research will serve a useful purpose, the next step is to state explicitly the research objectives—what specific information is needed? In other words, this stage involves going from the general to the particular.

Information requirements should be stated in writing. These requirements can then be reviewed to see if they are specific enough to provide guidance to the researchers, set forth the issues to be investigated, and include all the relevant questions to be asked. Some managers determine their information requirements by stating their beliefs about the market as a set of hypotheses. For example, a brand manager might wish to test the hypothesis that increasing the advertising budget by 25 percent will expand sales by at least 20 percent. It is often helpful to prepare samples of possible outputs and see what issues the sample report raises. Are other data needed before the results can be used? For example, is it enough to know that an ad budget should be increased, or must the media be specified as well?

Review of Existing Data

Before gathering new data, researchers should investigate the possibility of using data that already exist. Market researchers divide information into two classes, primary data and secondary data. *Primary* data are new information collected especially for the research project being undertaken; *secondary* data, in contrast, have previously been collected separately for other purposes. An organization's own internal record-keeping system, the observations of staff, easily accessible published data, reports from the trade, and other kinds of information can often be readily assembled to give a good deal of valuable information. Federal, state, and local governments gather and publish voluminous amounts of statistical data; government agencies also publish studies on a wide range of topics. A good general rule to follow is not to gather primary data until it becomes clear that no satisfactory secondary data are available. Even then, it is best to start with secondary data and restrict primary data collection to topics that remain unresolved.

Value Analysis

Management's next task is to ask whether the research is worth doing in terms of the value of the information obtained for decision making. Not all information is worth the monetary and time costs associated with its collection. No research project should be implemented unless management is committed to using the findings as an input to decision making. Before carrying out a research project, a manager should be satisfied that its findings will be useful in reducing the likelihood either that a bad (and costly) mistake will be made or that a marketing program will lack the fine-tuning necessary to achieve its full financial potential. By relating the cost of the research to the estimated incremental value of improved decision making, a manager can then determine whether the proposed study represents a worthwhile investment.

A second consideration in value analysis is timeliness. Because of market dynamics and competitive pressures, marketing decisions often must be made quickly. Partial information that can be obtained next week may be worth more than detailed information that will be available next quarter. Similarly, a more expensive research project may be justifiable if it can deliver the required data more quickly.

Research Design

A research design guides the collection and analysis of data. Although each study has its own specific purpose, the marketing research may be broken down into three broad groupings: (1) exploratory studies, (2) descriptive studies, and (3) experiments and other causal studies.

Exploratory studies are most often used in the problem-discovery and definition phases of decision making. They are more informal and less rigidly controlled than standardized questionnaire interviews, and they include such methods as (1) review of related literature, (2) interviews with experts, (3) in-depth interviews of small samples of typical consumers, and (4) detailed case histories.

Managers should not overgeneralize from the results of exploratory research. Caution is necessary since the results are not based on a representative sample of the population and cannot be projected to the entire market. The semistructured nature of the research, the role of the interviewer in directing the responses, and the subjectiveness of the answers do not usually allow for a rigid interpretation of the results. Qualitative research should be used to gain insights into the consumer perspective and suggest hypotheses for further testing.

Descriptive studies are used (1) to portray the attitudes, behavior, and other characteristics of persons, groups, or organizations; (2) to determine the extent of association among two or more variables and to draw inferences about these relationships; and (3) to make predictions about the future or about the results of different management actions, or both.

In general, descriptive studies can be subdivided between cross-sectional and longitudinal studies. Cross-sectional studies examine the population of interest at one point in time. For example, one appliance company carried out a survey to determine whether such characteristics as income, number and age of children, and wife's employment status were associated with owning microwave ovens and other kitchen appliances. By contrast, a longitudinal study, or panel, investigates a fixed sample of people who are measured at a number of points in time. While cross-sectional, or aggregate, data describe total consumption, a panel allows researchers to monitor an individual's behavior over time, such as for a customer's brand loyalty.

Experiments provide the best means for establishing a causal relationship. In an experiment, various levels of the causal factor—the treatment—are assigned on a statistically random basis to subjects. Then differences in response between those receiving the different treatments and those receiving no treatment—the controls—are measured and analyzed to see if there is evidence of a causal relationship.

The goal of *test marketing,* one form of experiment, is to determine how consumers react to a new product under market conditions. Test markets can be used to estimate the likely sales of a new product in order to help decide whether to launch the product nationally. Another use of test marketing is to evaluate several marketing plans. For instance, a company uncertain as to whether to use a standard- or high-promotion budget may test these alternatives in different cities. Test markets also help a company to study wholesaler and retailer response to its marketing program and to observe consumer purchasing patterns and possible problems that occur when the product is bought and used under normal buying conditions.

Competitive reactions to a test market, however, are somewhat problematic. A competitor who makes no reaction to a test market may later compete actively, perhaps with an imitative product. Other competitors may react aggressively to disrupt a test market in order to lower the value of information gained and to discourage a company from implementing its new product plans. Despite the costs and difficulties in producing them, test markets are usually helpful in increasing a good product's likelihood of success and avoiding major failures.

Methods of Primary Data Collection

The two major methods of data collection are communication and observation (oral and written). Observation involves the recording of behavior or the identification of readily observable personal characteristics such as age or sex. In some cases subjects may not even be aware that they are being observed. Other characteristics, such as a person's awareness and attitudes, can only be obtained by asking—communication. Also it is usually cheaper and faster to ask people about their behavior through interviews or questionnaires than it is to observe it.

One advantage of observation is that it does not depend on the ability or willingness of the respondent to provide data. Some people may seek to hide from interviewers the fact that they buy cheaper, generic brands; others may try to overclaim their thriftiness. Observation describes actual behavior.

Research Tactics

In choosing the subjects for a study, the researcher must distinguish between the target population, or universe; the sampling frame; the sample; and the respondents. The *target population* is the group we wish to study. For example, if a bank is planning a financial services program for people over 65, then that is the target population.

The *sampling frame,* which specifies the members of the population to be surveyed, is not always easy to identify. For the bank's program, the sampling frame might be a list of all those who receive Social Security checks. However, the frame may not be a perfect representation of the population, since not everyone who is over 65 receives Social Security payments and some younger, and disabled workers also receive Social Security payments.

In *probability samples,* every person in the frame has a known chance of being selected; the actual choices will be made probabilistically. (A random sample is one kind of probability sample in which each person has an equal chance of being selected.) The great advantage of probability sampling is that this known chance of selection allows the researcher to make a statistical estimate of the size of the sampling error, and thereby determine how far the findings might differ from those that would be obtained by studying the entire population.

In *nonprobability samples,* the interviewer has more discretion in selecting respondents. Convenience samples are composed of subjects who volunteer or who are readily available to the researcher, such as people walking through a shopping center, church groups, or students in class. Quotas may be established to ensure that respondents reflect a mix of prespecified characteristics, such as being equally split between men and women.

One danger associated with giving interviewers control over the choice of respondents is that they will tend to choose those individuals who are easiest to interview—people who look friendly or live in convenient locations, e.g., apartment houses in "good" neighborhoods. Such respondents may not be representative of the population as a whole, even though they may share some of that population's readily measurable characteristics.

In practice, researchers use nonprobability designs quite frequently. They are the logical choice for informal exploratory research and can save time and money in other studies. Also such samples may provide better control of any error due to factors other than sampling.

Sample Size   "How large should the sample be?" is one of the most frequently asked and seemingly simple questions raised in planning research studies. The answer depends on the purpose of the research, the sampling design used, the characteristics being studied and their variation within the population, the precision desired from the estimate, the desired level of confidence in the accuracy of the estimate, the cost of the study, and the time available. Mathematical formulas can be used to help determine the optimal sample size.

In general, precision increases with the square root of the increase in the sample size, so that doubling precision requires multiplying the sample size by four. Other factors, such as the nature of the analysis to be performed on the data, can be very important in setting sample sizes. Too small a sample in segmentation studies, for example, may make it impossible to conduct meaningful analyses of cross-tabulated data.

Response Rate   People fail to respond to surveys for two reasons—either they are not reached by the researchers (not-at-homes in interviews, wrong addresses in mail surveys), or they refuse to participate. Mail questionnaires typically achieve response rates in the 10 to 50 percent range; personal and telephone interviews (with three or four callbacks) reach 50 to 80 percent of subjects. High response rates are needed to limit nonresponse bias because responders and nonresponders generally differ. Women who do not answer morning telephone calls, for instance, may be employed outside the home, in contrast to housewives who are easier to reach. The researcher needs to determine how significant these differences are and to make adjustments where appropriate.

Large sample sizes do not in themselves compensate for biases resulting from low response rates. Often, greater validity is achieved by increasing the response rate than by increasing the number of people sampled. Special incentives, prior mailings, a well-written, well-designed questionnaire, a combination of interview methods, and intensive follow-up efforts can lead to higher response rates.

Methods of Administration   Telephone and personal interviews and mail questionnaires are the three major ways of collecting information, although various combinations of these methods can be used. While mail is usually the cheapest of the three, the cost of data collection and analysis per completed mail questionnaire usually exceeds $5.00. Telephone can be two to four times as expensive, and personal interviews even more so. In addition to costing less, *mail questionnaires* offer the advantage of uniformity of administration, since the interviewers themselves may add variation to personal and telephone surveys. However, considerable time must be allotted for the mailing and return of questionnaires.

Although *personal interviews* are costly, they provide the researcher with considerable flexibility and control. Samples of the product can be shown. An interview is particularly appropriate for revealing information about complex, emotional subjects and for probing sentiments underlying expressed opinions.

Telephone interviews are less expensive than personal interviews and quicker to complete. Political candidates, for instance, often use telephone interviews to monitor voters' changing opinions before an election. Telephone interviews combine many of the advantages of the mail and personal methods. Of course, telephone interviews do not lend themselves to the use of graphical materials and cannot be as rich in content or as long as personal interviews.

Content and Wording of the Questions   Those who design questionnaires must be certain that each individual question is carefully constructed, in order to obtain accurate data. For example, in wording questions, clear, simple words should be used and leading or biased questions avoided. Answers to socially sensitive or personally embarrassing questions are potentially unreliable and particular care must be taken in asking for such information. Additionally, it's important to consider whether the respondent knows the answer or can get the requested information without too much time and effort. While unnecessary questions should be avoided, the researcher should make sure that all needed information is obtained.

Pretesting The researcher should never expect that the first draft of a questionnaire will be usable. After completion, it must be reexamined as a whole and revised. Even then the design is far from complete; the key test of a questionnaire is how it performs in practice. Two types of pretesting are required. The first is conducted through personal interviews with a convenience sample to identify major errors. More critical is a pretest that simulates the actual administration of the questionnaire. Those who design a questionnaire are much closer to a topic than the respondents will be, and the pretest identifies problems that may arise because of these vast differences in perception. Additionally, the researcher should attempt to tabulate the data from the pretest to see if, in fact, the analyses that were planned can and should be carried out. In brief, pretesting is a *must*.

Field Operations

Field operations include those parts of the research process during which the data are collected and coded. Since a number of professional market research firms specialize in these tasks, many organizations contract out all or part of the field work. As with all such tasks, management must ensure that it has an effective way to monitor the quality and performance of data collection and coding. Otherwise errors can occur. In one study of theater attendance, 35 percent of the nonsubscribers were falsely classified as new subscribers because the analysts interpreted no reply to a question as equivalent to a check by the number zero, an answer which represented a new subscriber.

Data Analysis

Data analysis often involves complex, sophisticated techniques. The manager should not reject a specific technique just because it is complex, since it may contribute new insights to understanding a market. On the other hand, not all useful analysis techniques are necessarily complicated.

Although data analysis is one of the last steps in the market research process, its impact appears much earlier. For example, the type of analysis to be done often influences the content and form of the questions. It is often a good idea to create dummy versions of the tables that are expected to appear in the final report and to make sure that the questions included (and their format) lend themselves to the sort of analysis required to complete those tables.

Interpretation of Data, Recommendations, and Report Writing

Depending upon their skills, interests, and organizational policies, researchers and managers may share a good deal of the writing and interpretation, or they may not. Two cautions are in order. First, the interpretations of the data should be based on an analysis of what the survey actually discovered, not on what managers and researchers hoped would be found. Second, the report should be written clearly and concisely so that the newly discovered information and insights are communicated to the relevant decision makers. Graphic presentations of data are often more easily understood by decision makers than are tables.

SUMMARY

Successful market research requires a disciplined approach to problem specification and data collection and analysis; it is not simply a matter of asking questions. Many market research projects fail to influence decision making because of weaknesses in planning, execution, analysis, and presentation. Both managers and researchers are more likely to obtain findings that will be useful for decision making if they follow a systematic approach to doing market research.

INFO-MED

George S. Day

Tim Findlay was troubled as he studied the PMR proposal on his desk. He had expected a much more detailed outline of the market research task that Precision Market Research would do and had found the proposal provided few details. Furthermore, he had just received a phone call from the author of the PMR proposal, asking that they meet next week to begin planning the project. The researcher added that he hoped Findlay would give further thought to the objectives of the study, as well as provide reactions to the proposed design. Findlay now decided to go back over the pilot research study in order to see whether a second study was really needed and, if needed, what kind of study it should be.

BACKGROUND

The PMR research was to guide the formation of a new business, called INFO-MED. The concept of the new business came from Dr. Arthur Lam,

This case was provided through the courtesy of Dr. Robert V. Illa of the Medical Abstract Retrieval Service.
Copyright © 1979 by George S. Day.

who envisioned a new method of supplying physicians with up-to-date medical information: a computerized medical abstract retrieval system. Doctors would have a computer CRT terminal in their offices that would allow them to search a carefully selected data base for abstracts of articles dealing with problems faced by the practicing doctor. An on-line, "natural language" keyword search technique would allow the doctor, quickly and simply, to find and read the abstracts dealing with new developments in the treatment of the case in hand.

The Need for INFO-MED

Dr. Lam felt such a service should be aimed at the practicing "primary" physician—those doctors practicing general medicine who were the first line of medical care (general and family practitioners and internists). Most cases were treated by the primary physician, but it was often necessary to know when and where to send patients when they required the attention of a specialist.

Because medical knowledge had a half-life of

about five years, doctors who had been out of medical school for five years and had not attempted to keep up-to-date would find 50 percent of their knowledge to be obsolete. With the many pressures of running a private practice, few physicians had time to read medical journals. Furthermore, journal articles were reports of problems and solutions as they occurred and were therefore difficult to access when needed by the doctor.

Lam found that, while some doctors keep large literature indices on their bookshelves, these indices often were outdated and required a trip to the library to read the actual article. More often, a physician relied on colleagues or on literature from drug companies to keep informed about recent developments. This was especially true in rural areas. Because of these factors, Lam felt that INFO-MED could satisfy a significant need.

INFO-MED: The Service

Because Dr. Lam knew little about computers, he interested a systems analyst, Fred Junkin, in assisting him to develop the idea. The heart of INFO-MED was to be the data base, containing abstracts of articles appearing in selected medical journals. The articles would be selected for their problem-solving relevance, by a board of prestigious doctors. The data base would be updated continuously.

By operating the computer terminal, the doctor could access all abstracts containing the key words chosen. Generally, the abstract alone would be sufficient to solve most problems. The terminals would be connected by phone lines to the INFO-MED computer, so that the service would be available throughout the country. While conventional computer services usually charged by hour of terminal time (e.g., $100 per hour). Junkin felt that this would make most doctors nervous. A better alternative seemed to be a modest monthly charge of $60 per month to cover the terminal rental and a charge of $8.00 per completed search.

Market and Financial Analysis

Since neither Lam nor Junkin had any business experience, they turned to Tim Findlay, a local accountant, for help in establishing the new venture. Findlay thought the idea was a good one and contacted a few companies that he thought might be interested. These contacts pointed out that past attempts to market computer services often had been disastrous and that the mix of computers and doctors was even worse. Findlay felt that it was too early in the development of this idea to be able to make a persuasive case that this service would be any different.

With the help of Lam and Junkin, Findlay was able to develop estimates of break-even volume. In addition to start-up costs of $650,000, primarily to prepare the data base and absorb initial losses, there would be fixed operating costs of $135,000 per month. It was estimated that the contributions[1] from 1,260 terminals would cover this fixed cost. This was encouraging inasmuch as the available data from the American Medical Association indicated a very large market, as follows:

Segment I (group practices): There were 12,200 groups in either general practice or multiple specialties; each group had an average of five doctors.

Segment II (small hospitals with inadequate medical library facilities): There were 8,000 hospitals with less than 150 beds.

Segment III (solo physicians): There were 81,200 doctors in general practice or internal medicine not associated with a group.

Preliminary Market Study

It was clear to Findlay that a direct assessment of the doctors' interest in this service was necessary

---

[1] The contribution was estimated on the assumption that each terminal would be used for 30 searches per month and 10 abstracts would be accessed during each search.

before any company would invest any money into developing this idea. Consequently, a pilot assessment of market acceptance was conducted by sending 200 doctors in the Chicago area a letter (Exhibit 1) and return postcard (Exhibit 2), asking them for their opinions. Their names were taken from lists of doctors affiliated with three large medical centers in the area.

The overall response rate was 52 percent, yielding 104 usable responses. There were 63

EXHIBIT 1
LETTER TO CHICAGO AREA DOCTORS

Arthur Lam, M.D.
Harrison Road
Oakbrook, Illinois
April 5, 1979

Dear Sir:

I am interested in your opinion of the possible utility of the system described in the following abstract:

"On-Line Continuing Education for the Primary Physician"
by Lam, A. and Junkin, F.

Participation in programs of continuing education by the busy practitioner has been impeded by a number of factors, such as time, geographic location, financial considerations and, in some instances, course content, which he may judge to be irrelevant. We propose as a partial solution to this problem the installation in the physician's office of a computerized literature retrieval system which would allow quick, convenient and relevant access to that portion of the medical literature for which he would have the greatest need. We discuss the feasibility of such a system, and suggest advantages over traditional methods of access.

Within this system, a physician in his office operates a keyboard-video display terminal, whereby groups of keywords can be combined to carefully select abstracts from the computer files of articles from selected medical journals in the data base. The physician is continually advised of the number of abstracts stored that correspond to his current request. For example, by combining the key words "DIGOXIN" and "ARRYTHMIA," the physician might find that there are ten relevant abstracts. At that point, he can then request a display of the abstracts of interest.

In addition to abstracts of articles from the current medical literature, the data base would include abstracts of reviews, and other important past articles. The service would provide advantages over current MEDLINE searches, in terms of ready accessibility, ease of use, specificity and quality of information provided.

Please note your response on the enclosed postcard.

Thank you for your cooperation.

Yours truly,

Arthur Lam, M.D.

Enclosure

EXHIBIT 2
QUESTIONNAIRE RETURN CARD

＿＿＿＿ I am interested in the idea.
＿＿＿＿ I would probably use such a system in my office.
＿＿＿＿ I would probably use such a system in my office if the cost were below $300 per month.
＿＿＿＿ Please send me a copy of the paper.
＿＿＿＿ I would have no use for such a system.
Other comments:
＿＿＿＿＿＿＿＿＿＿＿＿＿＿＿＿＿＿＿＿＿＿＿＿＿＿＿＿＿
＿＿＿＿＿＿＿＿＿＿＿＿＿＿＿＿＿＿＿＿＿＿＿＿＿＿＿＿＿
＿＿＿＿＿＿＿＿＿＿＿＿＿＿＿＿＿＿＿＿＿＿＿＿＿＿＿＿＿
＿＿＿＿＿＿＿＿＿＿＿＿＿＿＿＿＿＿＿＿＿＿＿＿＿＿＿＿＿

respondents who said they were interested; among this group 13 indicated they "would probably use such a system" and a further 11 respondents indicated they would "probably use such a system if the cost were below $300 per month."

Research Proposal

At this point, it seemed that too much weight was being placed on the pilot market survey, so Findlay decided to investigate the possibility of having a market research firm conduct a full-scale study. Findlay felt a private market research firm would be a relatively objective source with the credibility necessary to convince potential investors that there was a reasonable chance of success for the business.

Consequently, Lam, Junkin, and Findlay decided to invest up to $10,000 in a market survey. Findlay contacted Precision Market Research (PMR) and asked that a research proposal be developed for the introduction of INFO-MED. PMR said a survey of about 40 doctors could be done in three geographic clusters in Illinois and Ohio for a little over $10,300 and submitted this proposal to Lam, Junkin, and Findlay for approval (Exhibit 4).

The PMR study was given initial approval by Findlay and the others. PMR was anxious to get started and requested a planning session where the objectives and methods of the project could be decided. So far, it was agreed that the best way to conduct the survey would be to have Junkin demonstrate the service in the doctor's office during the interview with a portable CRT terminal. This demonstration approach was thought necessary because a working prototype would help greatly to communicate the concept.

Aside from the demonstration idea during a personal interview, however, little else had been decided. Even so, Findlay was not completely convinced that personal interviews were the most cost-effective method. He still had no idea as to how to structure the interview questionnaire, what segments to contact, and how to interpret the results. As he thought about the upcoming planning session with PMR the following week, he kept wondering whether this was the best way to spend $10,300 of their capital. He knew that further funding for research was very unlikely.

EXHIBIT 3
PROPOSAL BY PRECISION MARKET RESEARCH

PRECISION MARKET RESEARCH, INC.

Proposal No. RPP79-257

September 12, 1979

Mr. Tim Findlay, F.C.A.
966 Franklin Ave., Suite 501
Chicago, Illinois 21402

Dear Mr. Findlay:

The following is a proposal to perform research for a new venture, INFO-MED. The proposal is divided into three sections: Our Approach to the Problem, Estimated Time, and Estimated Costs.

Our Approach to the Problem

PMR has conducted several studies in the past that appear to parallel this form of new venture in the medical industry. Based on our knowledge of the existing market and the potential in the future (1985), we view this assignment as having three major phases.

The first phase will be to interview on a personal basis key decision-makers in hospitals and group and solo practices in Illinois and Ohio. The purpose of these interviews is to assess the likely reaction to such a service among potential purchasers in terms of current needs and pricing.

The second phase is an analysis of the perceived present and future competition. This step involves interviews with executive sources at firms and associations, i.e., nonprofit groups, who currently operate, or have the potential to develop, a service competitive with that contemplated by INFO-MED.

At the conclusion of the first two phases, PMR will prepare and deliver a brief (10-page) written report of the findings, conclusions, and recommendations.

The third phase of the assignment will involve limited ongoing assistance and consultation in marketing and financial areas until the final decision is made in late December.

Estimated Time

Given our present workload and experience with projects of a similar nature, we are prepared to perfom this work according to the following schedule:

Phase	Description	Timing	Estimated days of Professional and Research Assistant work
1	Perform field interviews and evaluate response	10/7/79 to 10/25/79	15
2	Assess competitive environment	10/21/79 to 10/30/79	5
	Prepare, deliver, and discuss report	11/4/79	5
3	Provide ongoing consultation	11/5/79 to 12/31/79	5

EXHIBIT 3 *(continued)*

-2-

This schedule allows a minimum of two weeks for field interviews of key decision-makers. During these interviews, an INFO-MED employee will assist the PMR staff in the demonstration of a CRT device using a product algorithm similar to that which is currently contemplated.

The project will be conducted under the direction of Bill Skelly. The project leader will be Sam Kellner. Brief descriptions of their professional backgrounds and related experience are attached.

Estimated Cost

The charge for the proposed project is $10,300 including personnel, travel, and related charges. To provide the working capital required for this project, the initial payment due on acceptance of the proposal is $5300 to be followed by two monthly payments of $2,500 each.

This proposal will remain in effect until October 1, 1979; we will be pleased to consider an extension if requested.

We feel that our qualifications will meet with your approval. We look forward to this most interesting and challenging assignment and await your authorization to proceed.

Respectfully yours,

Sam Kellner

Approved:

Pat Pepall, General Manager

Accepted: _____ Date: _____

HINESBURY MILLS, I

Christopher H. Lovelock
Gerald J. Eskin

Marjorie Halstein, group product manager at Hinesbury Mills, Inc., a leading foods manufacturer, was concerned over competitive developments which posed a potentially severe threat to her brand's share of the United States cake mix market. Hinesbury was one of three major brands in this market; it also faced competition from several minor brands and private label brands.

Until recently, all brands had been selling essentially the same product line of regular cake mixes in which shortening cake predominated. Each brand offered a basic core of staple flavors, such as chocolate, yellow and white cakes, to which were added a variety of minor flavors which changed periodically. The strategy of the three major brands was essentially one of flavor proliferation; minor and private label brands offered less choice, competing primarily on the basis of price six months earlier. Hinesbury Mills

(HM) had introduced a new line of premium cake mixes, containing superior quality ingredients which included real butter. However, before the company had time to evaluate the impact of the new line on the market and conduct any meaningful market research, its two major competitors both introduced new cake mixes. The new entrants looked as though they might also offer the higher quality appeal of HM's new premium line, achieved in their case through requiring purchasers to add their own butter.

THE CAKE MIX MARKET

Consumers had three major sources of cake available: (a) ready-make cakes purchased from bakeries or supermarkets; (b) entirely home-made cakes; (c) cakes prepared at home from manufactured mixes. Total cake consumption per capita had remained fairly constant over the years, with cake mixes accounting for about one-third of all cakes consumed. Three main types of cake mix products were available: regular two-layer size, loaf or one-layer size, and angel/chiffon type.

Reprinted from *Stanford Business Cases 1985* with permission of the publishers, Stanford University Graduate School of Business. Specially revised for inclusion in this book.

Copyright © 1985 by the Board of Trustees, Leland Stanford Junior University.

The product category of immediate concern to Hinesbury executives was the two-layer type which, with an annual market of some thirty million 12-pack cases, accounted for the major portion of the total cake-mix market. Although experiencing a modest annual growth rate, the long-term outlook for the two-layer cake mix market suggested that the product might be reaching the mature stage in its life cycle. Halstein knew that the per capita consumption of this type was declining gradually in the face of increasing competition for the consumer's dollar from other prepared desserts.

Hinesbury's Market Strategy

Hinesbury Mills had pioneered the development of modern cake mixes. Over the years, the company had faced strong competition from Allied Foods Corporation and Concorn Kitchens, Inc. and, to a lesser extent, from a number of regional and private label brands—generally referred to as "price brands" since this formed the main basis of their competitive strategy. The other two major brands (Allied and Concorn) focused their marketing efforts on a strategy of heavy and consistent promotion aimed at building up distinctive images of themselves in consumers' minds. Allied Foods emphasized the moistness characteristic of cakes made with its mix, while Concorn's advertising concentrated on the flavor quality of its product. Hinesbury's response to these competitive attitudes was to adopt a strategy of proliferating its product line by offering an even wider range of flavors and by building markets through widespread use of deals.[1] By combining a continuous program of product improvement with new flavor introductions and heavy promo-

[1] Deals are cut-price offers to consumers, such as "5 cents off," "three for the price of two," etc. Dealing is widely practiced in the packaged foods industry as well as in certain product areas of the drug and cosmetics industries, notably when there are several large brands competing with essentially similar products.

tional expenditures, HM had been able to maintain its position as the market leader.

Eventually, however, Hinesbury began to find itself faced with a disturbing loss of market share and weakened distribution. The company fought back with strategic actions that included curtailing the proliferation of flavors, intensively pushing sales, and making heavy promotional expenditures with an emphasis on price deals. Most important of all, in the view of HM executives, was the introduction of a premium line of high quality cake mixes with superior ingredients including real butter and a guaranteed shelf life of 24 months. This was a technological breakthrough and was designed to appeal to an identified consumer need, capitalizing on that large section of the existing market whom research had shown to want a moister, higher quality cake. It was also the first product innovation to disturb the existing structure of the market.

Although it retailed at a recommended price of $1.19, as against a recommended 79 cents for the standard mix, initial acceptance of the premium line appeared very favorable and the decision was soon made to expand distribution nationwide. Like all cake mixes, heavy emphasis was placed on price deals. However, it was anticipated that six months would be needed to build up the product and obtain conclusive data on its impact on both regular cake mix sales and HM's overall market share.

Competitive Actions

To the dismay of Halstein and other Hinesbury executives, their premium line had only been in national distribution seven weeks when both major competitors countered with strategic moves that posed a severe threat to Hinesbury's own strategy. Virtually identical product lines were launched within a few days of each other by Concorn (into a midwestern test market) and by Allied Foods (which immediately went national). Their entries were both regularly priced (recommended retail price of 79¢) cake mixes in two flavors called Butter Chocolate and Butter Yellow. Unlike the standard mix, which contained an inexpensive shortening, or Hinesbury's premium mix with its butter content, these new products contained no shortening at all. Instead, they called for consumers to add their own butter to a "specially prepared formula," thus allegedly producing the same end product for which Hinesbury was asking consumers to pay an extra forty cents. In practice, there were certain distinguishable differences between the premium and add-butter end products. Premium mix cakes, while perceived by many as being of higher quality and more moist than the standard mix versions, still retained the latter's light and fluffy consistency. The add-butter cakes, by contrast, tended to have a somewhat denser and closer-grained texture, more akin to brownies or cupcakes. Again, it was believed that many consumers regarded the add-butter end product as of higher quality than standard mix cake.

Halstein assumed that if the initial move with chocolate and yellow flavors was successful, the two competitors would subsequently introduce add-butter versions to other flavors. Moreover, Halstein noted three significant strengths to the competition's approach. First, ingredient costs to the manufacturer were reduced in that no shortening need be placed in the mix; since the add-butter product sold at the same price as the standard mix, this meant higher unit profits. Second, the new products possessed a similar appeal to Hinesbury's premium line—that of the higher quality resulting from inclusion of butter as an ingredient—but with the further characteristic of allowing each consumer to add butter to the prepared mix and thus "individualize" the cake. On the other hand, of course, this method lacked the convenience inherent in a complete mix. Third, it seemed likely that many consumers would not see the addition of butter, which they already had in the home, as an incremental cost. If the cost of butter were added to the price of the

competitive mix, this would bring the total cost of the cake up to the same level as Hinesbury's premium offering, but it seemed probable that in many cases the consumer would still see the cost of the cake as 79 cents.

HINESBURY MILLS DEBATES ITS RESPONSE

HM was now offering two lines of cake mix (standard and premium) while its two major competitors were offering standard and add-butter lines. No information existed on how market share might break down among these three lines and among the different brands once the situation stabilized. The principal question for Halstein was how the introduction of the new add-butter line by the competition would affect its own brand standing; but there were other problems too. Would the add-butter line appeal to the same consumers as HM's premium line? Should Hinesbury Mills also offer an add-butter product? To what extent would consumers be willing to pay a higher pack price for a better quality, convenience product? In essence HM could pursue a myriad of possible alternatives in terms of the flavor, texture, quality, price, and convenience of the mix itself. Beyond that, a wide variety of marketing strategies might be employed. Halstein felt it was imperative to respond quickly to the competitive threat, but wondered how to obtain quickly sufficient information to permit an early strategic decision. At that point, nobody really had any firm information at all on the current state of the market.

Following an all-day conference with other marketing executives, Halstein took three immediate actions. First, she told the Research and Development department to begin developing an add-butter line in case it was subsequently decided to offer such a product on the market under the Hinesbury Mills label. Second, she contracted with the A.C. Nielsen Company to monitor the performance of both the Allied Foods and Concorn Kitchens add-butter lines in the market. Last, she and her colleagues decided to undertake development of a computer model of the cake market. They believed that by actually simulating, in a computer-based model, the decision process that various types of consumers made in buying a cake, they could develop an understanding of the purchase process and how decisions were arrived at under different circumstances. This might then permit predictions of the market performance of standard, premium, and add-butter lines. The simulation approach had the added advantages of being much faster and cheaper than actual market testing of different product formulations under differing marketing strategies, as well as keeping HM actions secret from the competition.

Halstein assigned the marketing research department the task of building the simulation model. After some discussion, it was agreed that they should begin by developing an explicit but fair representation of the consumer decision process involved in the purchase of a cake mix. At the same time, it was decided to identify clearly some of the principal needs that a consumer might have concerning cakes. To help them in this task, the director of marketing research proposed to draw on transcripts of some interviews with consumers on their cake-buying and cake-making habits. These interviews had been conducted recently for the company by a well-known research firm. Some extracts from the interviews are shown in Exhibit 1.

EXHIBIT 1
RESEARCH COMPANY'S REPORT ON CONSUMERS' CAKE-BUYING AND -MAKING HABITS
Extracts from interviews conducted with consumers

---

1 "Yes, I use quite a lot of cake mixes. You known how it is with three young boys—they like to have something sweet at dinnertime, so I often quickly whip up a cake for them. My husband likes them too, but I won't let him have too much if it's one of those rich, heavy ones: he's really got to watch his weight these days (laughs). . . . I guess I bake about one cake a week, sometimes two. Generally I get Concorn's. I think their flavors are nicer than the other brands, and the quality's good, too. But usually I'll look first to see if any of the main brands have got any special offers. My husband's been on short-time at the plant for nearly three months now, so I have to watch the pennies. Can't afford to be too extravagant. Cake's quite a good buy really."

2 "No, I don't buy cake mixes that often—usually it's just for some special occasion and when I do I like to get the best, and then take a bit of time and trouble over it. You know, even with a good brand like Hinesbury or Concorn you've got to be prepared to put in a few ingredients of your own. I've got a special recipe I use adding sour cream—makes a delicious cake, you know, rich and moist."

3 "I bake a lot of cakes. We often have them with the evening meal. Most times we prefer to have a light spongy cake which I serve with ice cream. For special occasions though, I'll make an extra fancy one and decorate it really nicely. I enjoy doing my own cooking, but with a full-time job I just can't give it the time that I'd like to. So I want something that's quick and fairly foolproof."

4 "I've got two kids—and they're always demanding sweet things, so I try to have some sort of cake around most of the time. Mostly, I just put it on the table at dinnertime and let them have as much as they want. Don't care for it much after a meat dish myself, but sometimes I'll make myself a snack during the day and have a sandwich and some cake with a glass of milk when the kids are off at school and I can't be bothered to cook myself lunch. . . . No, I really don't worry about the brand, can't say I can tell the difference myself, especially when there's a frosting on top. They're all good enough. I just look to see if any brand has a few cents off, same as I do with detergent."

EXHIBIT 1 *(continued)*

5 "I'm pretty choosy about the brands I buy—the quality does vary. Allied Foods makes the best lemon I think, but I don't like their chocolate so well—Hinesbury is much the nicest there. . . . One thing, though, I like to put in a few extra touches of my own—makes me feel it's my cake and not just some home economist's. That way I feel I can still take some of the credit for the way it turns out. I've still got all of my mother's old cookbooks and sometimes I get ideas out of these, particularly if I want to make a really rich cake for some special occasion."

6 "Yeah, I guess we occasionally have cake with the evening meal. They're pretty quick and easy to make and my nine-year-old likes putting on the topping. Usually I pick up two or three packages of mix at the market whenever I notice there's a good deal on. Quality? No I don't think there's really much difference between the main brands, though I guess some of the others mightn't be too hot. I tried a private label once because it was cheaper, but it was pretty bad. Came out all heavy and tasteless. So now I stick with brands like Concorn, Hinesbury and Allied. Better to be safe than sorry, I guess."

7 "I reckon the only time we have cake is just three or four times a year when it's someone's birthday or something. I'm not much of a cook, but if you stick with one of the quality brands and get a flavor you know people like, it's pretty hard to go wrong if you just follow the instructions. Mind you, there was the time I forgot to set the timer. . . ." (laughs)

8 "My husband says I spend more on gas driving around the different markets than I save on discounts and special offers. But I get a real charge out of looking for bargains. If I see something like Concorn cake mix with a really good offer on it, I just can't resist it. D'you know, last week I bought six packets of some new flavors they were bringing out—they were offering ten cents off a pack. I guess we'll all be eating cake now every day for the next three weeks."

9 "I like to make a rich fudge cake as a treat for my grandchildren when they visit me, but personally I prefer something lighter and not so sweet to have with coffee around mid-morning."

10 "There are four of us sharing this apartment, see, and we take turns doing the cooking. It's really neat the way it works out—we each do a week at a time. I can never get over how good the two boys are at it. I'm the only one who makes cake though—it's a fun thing to do and I like experimenting with different types of cake and adding little touches of my own. . . ."

11 ". . . I like a cake with a nice fluffy consistency. Not one of those heavy ones you get in some flavors . . ."

12 "Generally, I make a cake about once a month. My husband has a sweet tooth and likes cake at dinner sometimes or for a quick bite when we get home from afternoon classes. I like a fairly moist consistency, not too sickly sweet with lots of flavor and a pretty appearance. I guess they're all fairly easy to make. Usually, I get Hinesbury, except I watch out for specials—I'd buy any major brand on special. Some of the really cheapo ones haven't much taste. Too dry, too."

13 "We often have cake for dinner. Personally, I prefer buying the frozen kind—the ready-made ones. They taste nicer and they're much easier. My daughters'll bake a cake from a mix recipe sometimes. I really don't know why, because they always seem to manage to have them crumble all over. So if I'm buying a mix, I just look for something cheap."

14 "The two things I look for in a good cake are taste and consistency. I don't like eating something that looks like a bathroom sponge, but want a cake I can get my teeth into."

ETHICAL DILEMMAS IN MARKETING RESEARCH

Charles B. Weinberg

Marketing managers and marketing researchers in businesses, nonprofit organizations and government agencies are frequently confronted by ethical problems and dilemmas. Gathering, analyzing, and presenting information all are procedures that raise a number of important ethical questions in which the manager's need to know and understand the market in order to develop effective marketing programs must be balanced against an individual's right to privacy. The interpretation and use of data can also raise ethical questions.

The following scenarios present a set of ethical dilemmas that might arise in marketing research. Your assignment is to decide what action to take in each instance. You should be prepared to justify your decision. Bear in mind that there are no uniquely right answers; reasonable people may choose different courses of action.

Reprinted from *Stanford Business Cases 1977* with permission of the publisher, Stanford University Graduate School of Business. Copyright © 1977 by the Board of Trustees of the Leland Stanford Junior University.

1 As market research director of a pharmaceutical company, you are given the suggestion by the executive director that physicians be telephoned by company interviewers under the name of a fictitious market research agency. The purpose of the survey is to help assess the perceived quality of the company's products, and it is felt that the suggested procedure will result in more objective responses.

What action would you take?

2 Your company is supervising a study of restaurants conducted for an agency of the federal government. The data, which have already been collected, include specific buying information and prices paid. Respondent organizations have been promised confidentiality. The federal agency demands that all responses be identified by business name. Their rationale is that they plan to repeat the study and wish to limit sampling error by returning to the same respondents. Open bidding requires that the government maintain control of the sample.

What action would you take?

3 You are the market research director in a manufacturing company. The project director requests permission to use ultraviolet ink in precoding questionnaires on a mail survey. He points out that the accompanying letter refers to a confidential survey, but he needs to be able to identify respondents to permit adequate cross-tabulation of the data and to save on postage costs if a second mailing is required.

What action would you take?

4 Your company, along with several other well-known market research companies, has been asked to prepare a research proposal to study the trial and repeat rates of buyers of state lottery tickets. The lottery proceeds, which help to support the state's welfare program, have fallen short of the original goals. The director of the lottery is unsure if this is because too few people have ever bought tickets or because not enough of those who try the lottery repeat their purchases on a regular basis. In particular, the director wants to relate geographic and socioeconomic factors to lottery ticket purchases. The director claims that the lottery takes revenue away from illegal numbers rackets; others claim that it induces participation from those who can least afford to gamble. Because the state takes at least 40 percent of the total receipts for social welfare programs, many illegal numbers games return more to the bettors than does the state lottery.

As president of the company, what do you do?

5 You are employed by a marketing research firm and have conducted an attitude study for a client. Your data indicate that the product is not being marketed properly. This finding is ill received by the client's product management team. They request that you omit that data from your formal report—which you know will be widely distributed—on the grounds that the verbal presentation was adequate for their needs.

What do you do?

6 You are a project director on a study funded by a somewhat unpopular federal agency.

The study is on marijuana use among young people in a community and its relationship, if any, to crime. You will be using a structured questionnaire to gather data for the agency on marijuana use and criminal activities. You believe that if you reveal the name of the funding agency and/or the actual purposes of the study to respondents, you will seriously depress response rates and thereby increase nonresponse bias.

What information would you disclose to respondents?

7 You are employed by a market research company. A clothing manufacturer has retained your firm to conduct a study for them. The manufacturer wants to know something about how women choose clothing, such as blouses and sweaters. The manufacturer wants to conduct group interviews, supplemented by a session which would be devoted to observing the women trying on clothing, in order to discover which types of garments are chosen first, how thoroughly they touch and examine the clothing, and whether they look for and read a label or price tag. The client suggests that the observations be performed unobtrusively by female observers at a local department store, via a one-way mirror. One of your associates argues that this would constitute an invasion of privacy.

What action would you take?

8 You are a study director for a research company undertaking a project for a regular client of your company. A study you are working on is about to go into the field when the questionnaire you sent to the client for the final approval comes back drastically modified. The client has rewritten it, introducing leading questions and biased scales. An accompanying letter indicates that the questionnaire must be sent out as revised. You do not believe that valid information can be gathered using the revised instrument.

What action would you take?

9 A well-respected public figure is going to face trial on a conspiracy charge brought by the U.S. Justice Department. The defense lawyers have asked you, as a market research specialist, to do a research study to determine the characteristics of people most likely to sympathize with the defendant and hence to vote for acquittal. The defense lawyers have read newspaper accounts of how this approach has been used in a number of instances.

What do you do?

10 You are the market research director for a large chemical company. Recent research indicates that many customers of your company are misusing one of its principal products. There is no danger resulting from this misuse, though the customers are wasting money by using too much of the product at one time. You are shown the new advertising campaign by the advertising agency. The ads not only ignore this problem of misuse, but actually seem to encourage it.

What action would you take?

BAY-MADISON, INC.

C. B. Johnston

Shortly after the first of the year, George Roberts, research director of Bay-Madison, Inc., a large advertising agency, was faced with the problem of how best to conduct a study on Rill, a product of the Ellis Company, one of the agency's clients.

Rill, a powdered cleanser, was first introduced by the Ellis Company in 1923. Its original use was as a heavy-duty cleansing agent for removing dirt and stains from porcelain, metal, and ceramic tile surfaces. A unique bleaching property of the product eliminated the necessity for scrubbing, and it contained no abrasive material. In 1936, the company's research department developed and added to the product an ingredient which imparted a light, fluffy texture to textile products washed in a mild solution of Rill. Recognizing the problem of keeping such articles as baby clothes, towels, and blankets soft through repeated washings, the company had promoted Rill both as a cleanser and as a laundry wash water additive since 1937. Over the years, about 50 percent of the company's advertising had fea-

Copyright © 1984 by The University of Western Ontario.

tured the product solely as a cleanser, 30 percent as a laundry additive, and 20 percent as a dual-purpose product.

Rill was nationally distributed in a concentrated form in three can sizes—4 ounces, 8 ounces, and 1 pound. Six other nationally distributed cleansers and two nationally distributed laundry additives posed formidable competition.

The product had sold well during the earlier years, but during the past five years unit sales had declined considerably apparently because of competition, although dollar volume over this period had remained fairly constant.

Company and agency personnel were in basic disagreement as to whether the product should be promoted as a cleanser, a laundry additive, or a dual-purpose product. In order to formulate marketing and advertising strategy for the coming year, the agency personnel believed it was necessary to supplement the quantitative information they had on unit sales, outlets, margins, and distribution with information of a more qualitative nature on consumer attitudes toward the product, usage patterns, and opinions on different product characteristics such as strength or concentration, odor, and package size.

Research Proposal

In November, two months earlier, Mr. Roberts and his staff had drawn up a research proposal which they had forwarded to six marketing research firms for detailed information regarding the following:

1 An appraisal of the proposal and suggestions for any changes.
2 A price quotation on the project (a) as outlined and (b) including any suggested changes.
3 A brief description of the staff who would handle the project.
4 Time required for preparation, implementation, tabulation, and final presentation.
5 Pilot testing suggested.
6 Detailed explanation of suggested sample size.
7 Information on the firm's executive personnel, interviewing staff, and the projects handled over the preceding two years.

The research proposal contained a description of the product's marketing problems, the objectives of the proposed research, broad suggestions regarding research methodology, and a proposed questionnaire.

In his proposal, Roberts outlined the major marketing problems as follows:

1 We really want to know how many people would buy Rill because (a) it is a cleanser, (b) it is a laundry additive, or (c) it is a dual-purpose product.
2 How do people buy products like Rill? Is it better to have a strong product or a weaker one? What size package should we have? Should it smell like soap or like perfume? At what price should it be retailing?
3 Do people see Rill as being a good, average, or poor product? What do they like about it? What don't they like about it?

4 Do people want a one-use product or a multi-use product?

By early January, Roberts had received the submissions of all six marketing research firms requested to bid on the job.

Three of these firms were eliminated after preliminary consideration of their submissions revealed either inadequate staffs, superficial recommendations, or excessively high costs.

In considering the three remaining firms, Roberts felt that he was hampered by his lack of knowledge of the techniques proposed by two of the firms and by his inability to decide whether it was reasonable to expect that a detailed plan could be drawn up from the information he had provided in his proposal.

Two of the firms under consideration, National Research Associates and The Progressive Research Group, had outlined quite comprehensive plans for the research (See Exhibits 1 and 2). The third, H. J. Clifford Research, had merely stated that it would not attempt to formulate any research plans from what it considered inadequate information. It believed that the only way a detailed plan could be formulated was "through a continuing cooperation, based on mutual confidence, between the research firm, the advertising agency, and the client."

Roberts knew that many marketing research executives considered the third firm to be the outstanding marketing research company in the country and because of this, he did not believe it could be overlooked.

DISCUSSION

In discussing these proposals with his assistant, Mr. Jacks, Mr. Roberts wondered whether his own staff could not answer some of the questions if a thorough study of past consumer panel reports were conducted. For some 10 years Bay-Madison had received full reports from an independent research company which ran a consumer panel, but these had only been used for day-to-day planning. Never, for instance, had a long-term, thorough study of the trends in Rill sales been compared with the various advertising and promotional campaigns the company had used or with the various price levels that had existed from time to time. Jacks was particularly enthusiastic about the idea as he had long maintained that the agency was not getting full value from the panel data. He said that he would personally like to work on such a project.

Roberts, in considering the idea further, estimated that such an analysis could be done for approximately $9,000. He had checked with the research company and found that all past reports were kept on automatic data processing cards. The company was most interested in the idea as an experiment and estimated that all the data required by the agency could be compiled for about $2,500. Roberts thought he could release Jacks from his other duties for a period of two months and that the cost of Jacks' salary, statistical and secretarial help, and other expenses would not exceed $5,500.

He knew a decision had to be made quickly as the client was very anxious to get the Rill situation straightened away.

Exhibit 1

Submission of National Research Associates

INTRODUCTION

The present research proposal is based upon the assumption that it is crucial to obtain answers to the following marketing problems:

1 Is it advisable to continue to promote Rill as a multipurpose product?
2 If it is, should its various uses be promoted simultaneously or separately, and what are the promotional approaches which would be most effective?
3 If it is not advisable to continue its promotion as a multipurpose product, for what uses could Rill be most successfully promoted?
4 What would be the most effective promotional approaches for the uses decided upon?

5 Would it be advisable to launch another product, or possibly the same product under a different name, for either of its uses?
6 What are the ways in which Rill distribution, packaging, pricing, and merchandising could be improved?

RESEARCH OBJECTIVES

To be able to plan a sound and effective marketing policy for Rill it will be essential to know:

1 The present market position of Rill in relation to its competitors in each of the fields in which it is used.
2 The reasons why Rill is in its present position in each of these markets.

I Consumer habits and practices

The study will provide as complete a description as possible of the cleanser and laundry additive markets. Data will be provided in regard to (1) users and nonusers, (2) brand usage, (3) purchasing habits, and (4) usage habits.

This information will be cross-analyzed by age, socioeconomic status, community size, and level of education of the respondent.

II Consumer attitudes, opinions, and motivations

The study will thoroughly explore the underlying reasons for the market strengths and weaknesses of Rill in each of the usage categories as completely as possible under the broad headings of:

1 The underlying attractions or resistances to using any product for each of the purposes with which Rill is concerned.
2 The comparative strength of attractions to using Rill and to using competing brands for each of these purposes.
3 The comparative strength of resistances to using Rill relative to competing brands.

Some of the specific topics which will be investigated under these general headings are discussed below:

1 The perceived uses of Rill and its major competitors.
2 Factors affecting the perception of Rill, i.e.,

confusion regarding usage, incompatibility of uses, one use more efficient than the other, and where the attitudes toward the product originated.

3 Attributes of the most desirable product for each of the uses.

4 Common knowledge of the attributes of various brands now on the market.

5 Associations evoked by the brand name Rill and the brand names of competing products.

III Consumer knowledge of and attitudes toward relevant advertising

1 How far the terms and phrases currently used in promoting Rill and competing brands are seen as (a) meaningful, and (b) appropriate to the product and its uses.

2 What copy points and adjectives might be most effective for the promotion of each use.

IV An evaluation of the advertising themes and approaches used by Rill

The research will attempt to determine whether the themes and approaches used in past and present Rill advertising are likely to operate toward overcoming resistances to Rill and capitalizing on sources of attraction.

V An assessment of the Rill package

The Rill package will be tested to determine:

1 Its visual effectiveness as evidenced by its attention-getting ability, its legibility, its memorability, and its apparent size.

2 Its psychological effect on the consumer's perception of the brand.

METHODOLOGY

I Market survey

Face-to-face interviews will be conducted with 2,275 homemakers who will be asked to give factual information about the products they use for each purpose. This survey will show the competitive position of Rill but will not attempt to provide "reasons why."

II Intensive interview study

The "reasons why" Rill is in its present position will be explored in 200 1½- to 2-hour depth interviews which will attempt to discover at-

titudes, perceptions, and feelings toward the product and its uses.

The depth interview is designed to prompt the revelation of true attitudes and reasons for them by employing projective techniques which, instead of emphasizing personal behavior, invite comment on the behavior of others.

In-depth interviewing takes place in a relaxed, information atmosphere. Interviews are usually conducted in the respondent's home, and her verbatim responses to questions are noted.

The interview schedule contains a large number of open-ended and close-ended queries.

In addition, it employs a variety of techniques, most of which are taken from or patterned after standard psychological tests. A description of some of these techniques is given below.

1 *The Personification Test.* This is essentially an extension of the projective technique employed in psychological testing. It involves an attempt on the part of the respondent to describe certain products in human terms. Such an approach provides an opportunity for the expression of attitudes and opinions not otherwise easily obtainable.

2 *The Thematic Apperception Test* (TAT). Like the Personification Test, this test is similar to the TAT in psychological projective testing. It consists of presenting to the respondent an unstructured drawing of a particular situation and asking him to "make up a story" of what is happening.

3 *Word-Association Tests.* Respondents are asked to relate what comes to mind when a given word or phrase is read to them. This technique aids in throwing light on areas which may warrant fuller investigation.

4 *The Semantic Differential Test.* This method, developed by us, has been designed to provide insights and information in regard to the perception of company and product attributes.

Fundamentally, the test consists of having the respondent rate a series of products on specially designed scales. The scales are so designed as to provide an extremely sensitive measure in regard to many dimensions as applied to the various products.

The manner in which these data (along with the data obtained through the use of other techniques) are analyzed makes it possible to determine:

  a The extent to which a given product's image is correlated with the perceived "ideal" product.
  b The desirable direction of change in the perceived product attributes, if such change is found necessary.

Other techniques which may be employed include: (a) rank-ordering tests, (b) sentence completion tests, (c) forced choice tests, (d) paired comparison tests, and (e) true-false tests.

III Laboratory study Our visual laboratory is equipped to evaluate the relative effectiveness of various merchandising and advertising stimuli. By means of specially designed instruments it will be possible to evaluate the relative effectiveness of the Rill package and label in comparison with those of major competitors.

The various tests which will be conducted include:

  1 Attention-getting tests.
  2 Product recognition tests.
  3 Brand identification tests.
  4 Visibility and legibility tests.
  5 Memorability tests.
  6 Apparent size tests.
  7 Color preference and association tests.

SAMPLE

I Market survey
For the purposes of economy it is suggested that a quota-controlled, weighted, national sample of 2,275 housewives be employed. The accompanying table presents an unweighted sample in proportion to household figures and the proposed weighted sample (see Table 1).

The unweighted sample exceeds the number of interviews necessary to ensure reasonable reliability.

However, to allow for a cross analysis of white and black and urban and rural respondents, a total of 3,113 interviews would be required. The weighted sample cuts by 50 percent the number of interviews in the Midwest and the West. The data from these areas will be mathematically converted to representative proportions in the final tabulation.

II Intensive study
Quota-controlled samples of 450 white and 150 black homemakers will be used.

III Laboratory study
The number of respondents varies from test to test, but the samples will be designed to ensure statistical reliability.

TABLE 1

| | Rural | | | | Urban | | Total | |
| | Farm | | Nonfarm | | | | | |
	Unweighted	Weighted	Unweighted	Weighted	Unweighted	Weighted	Unweighted	Weighted
Southeast	44	44	76	76	132	132	252	252
Northeast	101	101	110	110	614	614	825	825
Midwest	126	63	139	70	837	436	1,102	569
West	179	90	107	53	324	162	610	305
South Central	22	22	60	60	242	242	324	324
Total	472	320	492	369	2,149	1,586	3,113	2,275

FIELD STAFF

I Market survey

Our field staff of 455 interviewers located across the country will conduct the interviews and will be specially briefed and trained for this survey.

II Intensive study

Our staff of 88 university-trained depth interviewers will conduct an average of seven interviews each.

BRIEF DESCRIPTION OF FIRM

National Research Associates has conducted almost 400 separate and varied research projects since its establishment in 1954. The success of the organization is portrayed by its rapid growth from a small unknown company to a recognized leader in the field in the United States. Further attestation has been the establishment of "continuing relationships" with many clients. The company is an "official training ground" for graduate students in the Department of Social Psychology at a prominent university.

The following individuals will be involved in this project:

R. J. Morrison, Ph.D., research coordinator and major client and agency contact; academic training—B.Sc., M.Sc., and Ph.D., 1944 to 1959, major universities; research experience—wide experience in research as study director, consultant, and research associate in four U.S. universities from 1944 to 1956; teaching experience—seven years of lecturing in psychology at two American universities.

A. Milton, study director, graduate in economics with 10 years' experience in the research field, including 3 years with a prominent United Kingdom research firm and a number of years with other English companies.

H. W. Rolland, associate study director; senior staff psychologist who will coordinate the intensive study phases of the research; M.Sc. working on Ph.D.

R. W. Brown, associate study director; university graduate in sociology and statistics—10 years' experience in research—will handle tabulation and statistical analysis.

(Four additional staff members were listed, all of whom were university graduates.)

TIME AND COST ESTIMATES

The research can be completed in 12 weeks after finalization of the research design. The cost is estimated at $62,000, 50 percent payable upon initiation of the study and 50 percent upon completion.

Exhibit 2

Submission of The Progressive Research Group

NATURE OF THE PROBLEM

It is possible that the two major uses of Rill may, in combination, affect the market negatively. Women may think of it primarily in one sense or the other, and those who regard it as a cleanser may not be willing to use it as a laundry additive, or vice versa.

In addition to this possible overall problem, there are certain marketing specifics which may also be important.

1 Is the product right?
2 What about its physical characteristics (strength or concentration, odor, physical form)?
3 What about its psychological connotations?
4 What about the packaging (size of package, nature of package, labeling, and package)?

We propose a consumer study covering the major areas of behavior and attitude, including:

1 Brand personality and image for each of several cleansers (including Rill).
2 Brand personality and image for each of several laundry additive products (including Rill).
3 Habit pattern on home cleaning (including products used).
4 Habit pattern on laundry additives (including products used).

SCOPE OF THE STUDY

We see this as a national study, as it is entirely possible that varying areas may display differing habits and attitudes.

The section of this proposal dealing with the sample will show the reasons underlying our recommendations. We suggest a total of 750 interviews in this consumer study, and the sample will be of a "tight" nature.

THE SAMPLE

I Type of sample

The sample will be of such a nature that it properly represents the homemaker population in terms of region, socioeconomic group, urban-rural, and the like.

The sample design will be a known probability sample. Primary sampling units will be selected proportionately across the country, and randomly selected starting points will be chosen from which a predetermined path of interviewing will be followed.

II Size of sample

We recommend a total sample of 750 housewives.

There are several reasons. The first concerns our belief that no subsample on which results are based should have fewer than 150 cases.

The other reason concerns overall accuracy with a sample of 750 cases. Better than 9 times out of 10, results based on this total sample should be accurate within some 2.4 percent; this level of sampling accuracy on an overall basis seems highly acceptable for the purposes of this particular study.

The numerical distribution of interviews is indicated in the accompanying table (Table 2).

FIELDWORK

Our field staff is of highest quality. It has been built over a 10-year period, and we spend a sizable amount of money each year on maintenance and development of this staff.

The field staff totals 723 workers, and all states and community sizes are represented.

SUPERVISION

We maintain a staff of 20 salaried regional supervisors across the country. With the exception of a few small, remote areas, this means that every interviewer works under the direct control of a regional supervisor.

QUALIFICATIONS OF INTERVIEWERS

The average interviewer on our staff has been working for the firm for approximately four years. For our consumer work, we make use of women who, on the average, have the following characteristics: (a) they fall between the upper middle and lower middle socioeconomic group; (b) they have completed some or all of high school; (c) they are extroverted; and (d) they are above the average in intelligence.

THE QUESTIONNAIRE

It is difficult to evaluate your questionnaire without considerable field testing. in the present case, there has been no effort at all to do so. We would save our "criticism" for (a) detailed discussion with the agency and (b) considerable field testing.

We have conducted a group interview with the subject matter pretty much in its present sequence, though the questions asked were more of an open-minded variety than contained in the questionnaire draft submitted with your specifications.

We do know that the sequence of questions will work. We also know that women can and will

TABLE 2

	Natural proportional distribution of sample	Proposed sample distribution	Weighting factor	Weighted cases
Southeast	77	125	2	250
Northeast	211	211	3	633
Midwest	265	177	5	885
West	130	130	3	390
South Central	67	107	2	214
Total	750	750		2,372

answer these questions, despite their nature, if the right approach is used. We further know that while the questionnaire form is quite lengthy, it is still feasible in terms of its length. So it is not as if we know nothing about feasibility of the instrument.

FIELD TESTING

As a result of the group interview, it will be possible—though we have not taken the time to utilize it in such a manner—to study the consumer response to the interview so carefully as to make sure that the phrasings used in the questionnaire follow the words and phrases used in the consumer's actual thinking. The group interview thus means that we are that much further ahead in the phrasings of this questionnaire, even though it so far has not been utilized for such a purpose.

We plan a field test—or perhaps several—with a total of 100 homemakers distributed among people of varying socioeconomic groups, largely concentrated (for efficiency of handling) in the Chicago Metropolitan Area to make sure that the sequence and phrasing are of such a nature as to be understandable, to get cooperation, and to obtain unbiased replies.

DESCRIPTION OF THE FIRM

The Progressive Research Group began operations in 1948 and, as such, is one of the oldest marketing research companies. Over the years the company has handled a large number of projects and has among its clients many of the largest consumer goods manufacturers.

The company possesses the most advanced computer equipment in the country, and constant improvements are being adopted to speed up and make more economical, complete, and detailed client reports.

The following persons will direct the project:

A. W. Willis, B.A., overall project coordinator; president of The Progressive Research Group and a graduate in economics from a large university.

B. K. Walker, M.B.A., project director and client contact; vice president and a graduate in business administration from a major university.

R. C. Moffatt, Ph.D., project adviser; major in sociology—five years' research experience as project director with large U.S. advertising agency before joining The Progressive Research Group in 1957; three years spent as lecturer and consultant at two large American universities.

TIME AND COST

Our report should be available 12 weeks after the finalizing of the project details. Our estimate of the cost of this project is $38,900 plus or minus 10 percent. It is our practice to bill one half of the estimated cost at the time of authorization, with the final half billed on delivery of the report.

PART **EIGHT**

STRATEGIC MARKET
PLANNING

Managers often devote inadequate attention to strategic market planning because they are overly busy reacting to immediate market situations. This neglect often results in long-term decline of the company's established market position and inadequate development of profitable new opportunities.

At the highest level of the organization, strategic planning involves defining the corporate mission or purpose; setting objectives; and formulating strategy. However, many layers of strategy are necessary in a large company, each layer being progressively more detailed to provide operational guidance for the next level of subordinate managers. At each level of the company (business unit, product line, market, brand, etc.) the strategy must be coordinated with those above and below. Critical to success of a strategy is the marketing plan, which summarizes the strategy and its development as well as laying the framework for its implementation.

STRATEGIC PLANNING PROCESS

Mission

Fundamental to a firm's overall strategy is a definition of its mission or purpose, a basic long-term statement of what the organization seeks to do, and the rationale for its existence. A company's mission is determined by answering such basic questions as what business are we in, who are our customers, and what value do we provide to our customers? Profit making itself is not the purpose of a company but the outcome that accrues from successful fulfillment of its mission.

Probably the most important test for a mission statement is that it be both externally and internally oriented. Many organizations define themselves solely in product or technological terms, not in market terms, and suffer from so-called "marketing myopia." For instance, many metal-can manufacturers ran into difficulties because they defined themselves in just that way—not as being in the packaging business—and thus could not cope with innovations in materials and changes in customer needs. Of course, in using a market definition, an organization must be careful not to move too far away from its resources and abilities. Thus, defining a metal-can manufacturer as being in the packaging business does not mean that it should be supplying paper bags to supermarkets.

Objectives and Goals

Once defined, the purpose should be translated into a set of goals or objectives that indicate the specific accomplishments to be attained in fulfilling it. Objectives, which should be based on a realistic assessment of what can be accomplished, can have varying time horizons, degrees of interrelatedness, and levels of priority. However, too many goals for a manager result in an effort that is not well-focused. Without a few key, specific, measurable objectives, strategy becomes merely a statement of good intentions. Efficient achievement of objectives within the available resources is the key criterion of strategic choice.

Strategy

If the objectives specify what is to be accomplished, the strategy specifies how. Strategic decisions include both where to commit resources and how to use the resources, once committed.

There are a number of analysis tools available that can help management to formulate strategy. For example, a product-market growth matrix categorizes opportunities for growth in terms of the business's current products (or technologies) and markets. A growth-oriented company can then look for expansion through *market penetration* (increased usage of current products by present market segments), *product development* (adding new products that appeal to current markets), *market development* (offering existing products to new markets), or *diversification* (growth strategies encompassing both new markets and new products). When considering any growth strategy, even those based on diversification, management should look for attractive opportunities that use at least some of the firm's strengths and have some link to current activities.

Portfolio management can also be a useful aid to making strategic resource allocation decisions. In portfolio analysis, organizational subunits are typically evaluated along two dimensions, the overall attractiveness of the market and the unit's relative strength in the market. For instance, one popular approach, the growth-share matrix, uses growth to represent market attractiveness and share to represent competitive strength. Portfolio analysis helps to highlight critical strategic issues and aids in deciding whether to invest, maintain, or withdraw resources from a unit.

COMPETITIVE MARKETING STRATEGY

Competitive marketing strategy focuses on determining the critical factors necessary for success in the chosen markets and determining the means by which to compete. Once the critical success factors are identified, management must objectively evaluate its strengths and weaknesses in meeting those requirements as compared to that of present and potential competitors. True strength is usually based on accumulated experience and substantial success; occasional flashes of brilliance are rarely dependable in the long run.

Strategies can be broadly summarized as being the overall low-cost producer and/or establishing a differential competitive position [through (1) product or other forms of differentiation and (2) market segment specialization—employed either alone or in combination]. However, the next questions to ask are how is cost leadership to be attained and what are the bases for a differentiation or segmentation strategy, which in turn leads to a long list of alternatives. Ultimately, strategy formulation is a creative process; no analyst can really claim to offer a complete list of strategy types.

The proposed strategies must be evaluated on such criteria as (1) direct economic analysis, (2) ability to meet the objectives set, (3) external and internal consistency, and (4) degree of risk undertaken and robustness of the strategy in the light of market and environmental uncertainty. One reason strategic choice is difficult is that it is unlikely that one alternative will uniformly exceed the others on all criteria. Once adopted, the strategy becomes the basis for resource allocation and the development of annual marketing plans.

DEVELOPING A MARKETING PLAN

The marketing plan is a systematic way of structuring an analysis of a market, an organization's position in that market, and a program for future marketing activities. The elements of a plan are interrelated, so that its development may involve cycling through its components several times before satisfactory results are achieved. The following discussion briefly highlights selected portions of the marketing plan format suggested in Exhibit 1.

Situation Analysis

The situation analysis examines the relevant external and internal environments. The situation analysis typically includes a historical summary, an evaluation of previous marketing efforts, an analysis of the present situation, and an assessment of future trends.

The identification and assessment of threats and opportunities is the key output of a situation analysis. A momentum forecast of year-end position, which assumes that present conditions continue, can be constructed on the basis of the situation analysis. This forecast is then compared with the desired year-end position, and the gaps between the forecast and the desired position are identified.

EXHIBIT 1
MARKETING PLAN FORMAT

EXECUTIVE SUMMARY
Situation Analysis (Where are we now?)
　External
　　Environment (political, regulatory, economic, social, technical, and other relevant areas)
　　Consumers and markets
　　Employees
　　Suppliers and distributors
　　Competition
　Internal
　　Objectives
　　Strengths and weaknesses
　Problems and opportunities
　　Forecasting momentum
　　Identifying gaps

MARKETING PROGRAM GOALS (Where do we want to go?)

MARKETING STRATEGIES (How are we going to get there?)
　Positioning
　　Target segments
　　Competitive stance
　　Usage incentive
　Marketing mix
　　Product
　　Price
　　Distribution
　　Marketing communication
　Contingency strategies

MARKETING BUDGET (How much do we need and where should we allocate it?)
　Resources (money, people, time)
　Amount and allocation

MARKETING ACTION PLAN (What do we need to do?)
　Detailed breakdown of required activities
　Responsibility by name
　Activity schedule in milestone format
　Tangible and intangible results expected from each activity

MONITORING SYSTEM (Are we performing?)

Marketing Strategy

As discussed earlier, strategy specifies the means by which the marketing goals are to be achieved. It is the core of the marketing plan.

　Positioning may be defined as the fundamental statement of what the organization and its products represent to chosen market segments. The first step in positioning is defining the target segments. Next is setting the organization's competitive stance, the degree to which its products will be similar or different in each of the target segments. Depending on the segment and the competition, the most profitable competitive stance can vary considerably. The final step in positioning is to establish the usage incentive, that is the primary benefits to be offered to current and potential users in each segment. The positioning strategy is vital not only for reaching the consumers; it also provides a focus for management efforts and ultimately channels the efforts of the entire marketing organization.

The *marketing mix* (product, price, distribution, and communication) is a convenient way of summarizing a set of activities that support the marketing goals of the organization. People new to the field often consider these activities, especially advertising, to be all of marketing; on the contrary, they are just one part of marketing.

A marketing plan also should include *contingency strategies*. Since it is difficult to predict the future precisely, the manager should anticipate and be prepared for major surprises. Having well-thought-out, timely contingency strategies can provide a competitive advantage in a crisis situation.

Marketing Budget

For each element in the plan, the resources required to operate at different levels and the results at these different levels should be determined and evaluated. Trade-offs must often be made and interrelationships among marketing elements need to be considered.

Marketing Action Plan

The marketing action plan is a detailed breakdown of the activities necessary to achieve each of the goals. Planning without implementation is worth little; much effort in planning is wasted because of inadequate execution.

Monitoring Systems

The monitoring system is concerned with whether assumptions about the external environment are valid, whether the organization is carrying out the plan in the desired manner, and whether the specified milestones and goals are being achieved. Significant deviations from the marketing plan and unanticipated events may require management to make adjustments to the original plan or substitute a contingency strategy.

SUMMARY

Strategy at all levels of the organization is the means of guiding management action and resource allocation. It is rooted in a clearly articulated mission and a well-defined set of objectives. For long-run profitability, planning is needed to help the organization overcome the vagaries of the immediate environment and do more than merely react to competitive initiatives. A well-conceived, creative marketing plan that recognizes the capabilities and limitations of the organization, as well as any potential environmental threats and possible opportunities, is often a critical tool for successful marketing management.

LA QUINTA MOTOR INNS

Penny Pittman Merliss
Christopher H. Lovelock

La Quinta Motor Inns had organized its presentation to Boston security analysts with characteristic flair. The luncheon meeting—one of a series being presented by top La Quinta[1] management in major financial centers during 1980—was held aboard the vessel *Discovery*, anchored in Boston Harbor beside the New England Aquarium. Twenty-two analysts had appeared to learn more about the lodging chain boasting one of the highest average occupancy rates in the U.S. Now, as Sam Barshop, La Quinta's founder and president, made his way to the podium, an expectant hush fell over the group. Barshop smiled at his audience and declared:

> Ladies and gentlemen, let me begin by telling you what we *don't* have at La Quinta. We don't have night clubs, we don't have ballrooms, we don't have jungles of tropical plants, we don't have atriums with birds flying around. We've got clean, comfortable rooms targeted to the business traveler

[1] Pronounced "La Keen-ta."

Copyright © 1980 by the President and Fellows of Harvard College, Harvard Business School case 9-581-038.

that we sell at prices 20–25 percent below competition. And that's as close to inflation-proof and recession-proof as you can get.

COMPANY BACKGROUND

The first La Quinta Motor Inn opened in San Antonio, Texas, in 1968. It was planned to accommodate travelers attracted to the World's Fair, Hemisfair 68. Although the developers, Sam and Philip Barshop, had previous experience in the lodging industry, neither planned to develop La Quinta into a chain. As Sam Barshop put it: "We were going to build two motels in San Antonio and that would be that."

But success proved difficult to resist. The first and then the second La Quinta "took off like rockets," as Barshop recalled, and developers began to call with tempting site offers. By late 1980, La Quinta had expanded into a 95-unit chain with over 11,000 rooms, serving travelers in 23 states. Eighty-one of these inns were company owned; the remaining fourteen were licensed to franchisees. One inn was affiliated

439

EXHIBIT 1
LA QUINTA OPERATING STATISTICS, 1976–1980

	Year ended May 31				
	1976	**1977**	**1978**	**1979**	**1980**
Inns owned, start of year*	45	49	49	55	64
Opened	4	3	8	10	13
Purchased	1	—	—	1	—
Sold	(1)	(3)	(2)	(2)	(1)
Inns owned, end of year	49	49	55	64	76
Inns licensed, end of year	11	14	13	14	14
Total	60	63	68	78	90
Number of rooms, end of year:					
Inns owned*	5,183	5,355	6,161	7,288	8,791
Inns licensed	1,388	1,776	1,638	1,770	1,775
Total	6,571	7,131	7,799	9,058	10,566
Percentage of occupancy:*					
All inns	80.5%	85.8%	88.6%	88.1%	83.8%
Inns over one year old	82.1%	86.6%	89.1%	90.6%	87.7%
Average daily rate per occupied room*	$14.56	$15.80	$17.80	$20.21	$23.25

* Inns owned by the company and by joint ventures owned at least 50 percent by the company.
Source: La Quinta annual report.

with the Ramada Inn chain and six with Rodeway Inns; the others operated under the La Quinta name. Operating statistics for fiscal 1976–80 are presented in Exhibit 1, which also shows existing and planned inns as of June 1980.

Average occupancy for the fiscal year ending May 31, 1980, was 83.8 percent; total revenues stood at a record $61.8 million; and the company's five-year compounded growth rate exceeded 27 percent for revenues and 42 percent for net earnings (Exhibit 2). La Quinta paid no cash dividends to investors, but had had four 10 percent stock dividends, the most recent in January 1979. The company planned to open fourteen more properties in fiscal 1981, entering three new states (Exhibit 3).

The La Quinta Service Concept

The typical La Quinta Motor Inn was located on an interstate highway or major traffic artery and contained 106–122 rooms. Approximately 85 percent of La Quinta inns were located in metropolitan areas of 100,000 people or more; the rest were in smaller cities (many of them in Texas) within existing market areas. All La Quintas offered guests a 24-hour switchboard, free parking, same-day laundry service and a swimming pool. Lobby space was minimal and there were no banquet or meeting rooms; furthermore, no restaurant was operated within the building. La Quinta was thus able to offer what industry observers termed "Holiday Inn-standard rooms" at up to 25 percent less cost to guests. During fiscal 1980, the average daily room rate in company-owned units was $23.25, up from $20.21 the previous year (Exhibit 1).

La Quinta rooms were relatively large, averaging 310 square feet (the industry standard for similar "garden"-style motor inns was 300 square feet). All-concrete construction ensured relative quiet. Each room came equipped with queen-sized beds, guest-controlled air conditioning, and free color television with built-in

EXHIBIT 2
LA QUINTA INCOME STATEMENT AND OTHER FINANCIAL DATA FOR FISCAL YEARS
1976–80 (in $000's)

	Year ended May 31				
	1976	**1977**	**1978**	**1979**	**1980**
Revenues:					
Motor inn	$22,173	$27,256	$35,580	$44,682	$57,746
Restaurant rental	990	1,127	1,545	1,881	2,200
Restaurant and club	1,084	960	1,029	1,094	1,139
Other	437	551	541	567	740
Total revenues	24,684	29,894	38,695	48,224	61,825
Operating costs and expenses:					
Motor inn direct	12,762	15,139	18,410	22,958	28,336
Restaurant and club direct	1,113	1,013	988	1,038	1,076
Selling, general and administrative	1,836	2,292	3,450	4,512	6,102
Depreciation and amortization	2,554	2,964	3,743	4,438	5,896
Total operating costs and expenses	18,265	21,408	26,591	32,946	41,410
Operating income	6,419	8,486	12,104	15,278	20,415
Other income (deductions):					
Interest income	156	229	498	700	1,238
Interest, expense, net of capitalization	(3,499)	(3,922)	(4,946)	(6,172)	(8,410)
Gain on sale of assets, principally motor inns	215	501	553	1,477	818
Partners' equity in earnings and losses:					
Operations	(385)	(897)	(1,719)	(2,437)	(3,373)
Sales of motor inns	—	—	—	(589)	—
Total other income (deductions)	(3,513)	(4,089)	(5,614)	(7,021)	(9,727)
Earnings before income taxes	2,906	4,397	6,490	8,257	10,688
Income taxes	1,205	1,939	2,759	3,385	4,276
Net earnings	$ 1,701	$ 2,458	$ 3,731	$ 4,872	$ 6,412
Total assets	$63,167	$77,974	$97,247	$131,167	$178,545
Shareholders' equity	9,958	12,427	16,487	22,817	29,390
Partners' capital	3,054	3,573	5,102	8,892	10,785
Long-term debt	$43,675	$53,935	$66,055	$ 87,423	$119,054

Source: La Quinta annual report.

AM/FM radio. Interior decor was muted orange, brick red, and dark brown, carrying out the company's Spanish theme ("la quinta" means "country house" in Spanish). In order to accomodate guests who wished to use their rooms as temporary offices, folding doors in each room separated the large dressing area with sink from the work-ing/sleeping area. Immediately adjacent to each property was a restaurant, open 24 hours; many had been built by La Quinta and leased to national restaurant operators such as Denny's or jojo's.

La Quinta properties were managed by husband-and-wife teams, many of whom had retired

EXHIBIT 3
LOCATIONS OF PLANNED AND EXISTING LA QUINTA INNS, JUNE 1980

Alabama
Mobile

Arizona
Phoenix
Tucson

Arkansas
Little Rock (2)

California
Costa Mesa

Colorado
Denver (3)
▲Denver

Florida
Jacksonville
Tallahassee

Georgia
Atlanta
Columbus

Illinois
▲Champaign

Indiana
Indianapolis
▲Merrillville
▲Indianapolis

Kansas
Kansas City
Wichita

Kentucky
Louisville
▲Lexington

Louisiana
New Orleans (2)

Mississippi
Jackson

Missouri
St. Louis

Nebraska
▲Omaha

Nevada
Las Vegas
▲Reno

New Mexico
Albuquerque
▲Albuquerque

Ohio
Columbus

Oklahoma
Oklahoma City
Tulsa

South Carolina
Columbia
▲Charleston
▲Greenville

Tennessee
Memphis
Nashville

Texas
Abilene
Austin (3)
Beaumont
Brazosport
Brownsville
College Station
Corpus Christi
Dallas Metro Area (8)
Denton
El Paso
Houston (7)
Killeen
Laredo
Lubbock
San Antonio (7)
Texas City
Waco
Wichita Falls
▲Dallas Metro Area (3)
▲El Paso
▲Fort Worth
▲Houston
▲Odessa
▲San Antonio

Utah
Salt Lake City

Wyoming
Casper
▲Cheyenne

**Licensed La Quinta
Motor Inns**

Arizona
Flagstaff
Kingman

Florida
Orlando (2)
Tampa

Illinois
Moline

Ohio
Cincinnati
Dayton (2)

Texas
Corpus Christi
Fort Worth
Galveston
McAllen
San Angelo

Ramada Inn

Louisiana
Lafayette

Rodeway Inns

Texas
Dallas
Houston (3)
San Antonio (2)

▲ Denotes Planned
Inns

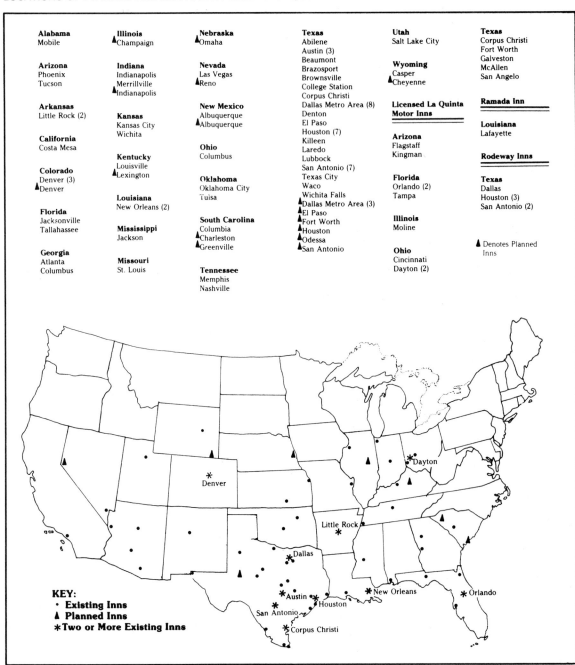

KEY:
• **Existing Inns**
▲ **Planned Inns**
✳ **Two or More Existing Inns**

from earlier jobs and had no previous lodging experience. Management couples were given three weeks' classroom instruction and six weeks' on-the-job training. Sam Barshop summarized their duties:

> We have a very simple concept. What we're doing is selling beds. Not operating restaurants, not running conventions—just selling beds. Which means the managers have three things to do. One, run the desk. Two, keep the rooms clean and the building maintained. Three, give an accurate report at the end of the day.

In addition to their salaries, management couples received free lodging in one-bedroom apartments on the premises, substantial discounts on food at the adjacent restaurant, free laundry and local telephone service, and a monthly car allowance. On a typical day shift, the husband-and-wife team managing a 122-room property supervised one housekeeper, eight maids, three laundry workers, two general maintenance people, and a desk clerk. Approximately 90 percent of La Quinta's 2,500 employees were hourly workers; none were represented by labor unions.

La Quinta's senior management saw distinct advantages to the company's manager-couples system. One corporate executive declared:

> Our system gives each property its own distinct personality. Is that important? Sure it's important, because you have people who stay with you every other week, all year long. We're growing fast, and I don't want us to become so professional that professional means cold and cruel to the guests. The manager-couples make it feel like home, because it *is* their home.

A mail survey of 10,000 customers conducted in March 1978 revealed that 80 percent of La Quinta's guests identified themselves as business travelers. Sixty-five percent arrived at their destination by car. The survey, which generated a 56 percent response, was designed and tabulated by an independent market research firm and administered by La Quinta. Managers at each property were instructed to select 250 names from the guest book over a ten-day period, and send the names to the company's marketing department. A questionnaire (with return postage paid) was then sent to the address (either business or home) listed by each guest. The survey was introduced by a letter from Barshop; both questionnaire and letter are reproduced in Exhibit 4.

Establishing the Product

Every La Quinta site was chosen personally by Sam Barshop. In his opinion, site selection was the key to success: "You can change anything about a motel except where it sits," he declared. "You can change the decor, you can change the management, but once you've made a bad site decision, it's irrevocable."

Barshop looked for sites within areas where La Quinta was already established, as well as sites located no more than 300 miles from existing inns on connecting interstate highways. The plan was that inns located in more distant sites would become the nuclei for development of additional inns in those same areas, eventually resulting in a series of clusters. Barshop preferred busy highways on which La Quinta's distinctive architecture and prominent sign would be highly visible (as well as accessible). He ranked his location priorities in the following order: (1) airports; (2) interstate highways; (3) office complexes and industrial parks; (4) medical centers; and (5) major universities. In Barshop's words:

> In site selection, we look to see if we can derive the bulk of our business from that three-to-five mile radius accessible within a five-minute drive. One of the first things people look for in a motel is location. Is it convenient to the next day's work? Visibility is probably even more important than accessibility, because once they see you, they can always get to you. And we also have to choose our location with a good restaurant in mind, because we don't operate our own restaurant.
>
> There's no art to all this, it's gut feeling, and that's really based on years and years of experience. What you've always got to remember to do is find

La Quinta

MOTOR INNS, INC.

Dear La Quinta Guest:

Will you help us serve you better?

Please take a few minutes to reflect on your most recent visit at a La Quinta Motor Inn and fill out this marketing research questionnaire. This research will tell us more about you and your travel habits and needs.

From this information, we will try to determine if we are meeting your expectations. It will help us, also, to be aware of what kind of service you want in the future.

Please help us improve our services to you by returning your completed questionnaire in the enclosed stamped, self-addressed envelope.

The attached 25¢ is our way of saying "thanks" for your help. That way, your next *Wall Street Journal* can be on us.

Sam Barshop
President

1a. On about how many different occasions have you stayed at La Quinta during the past twelve months? 10.2 (10-/11-)

1b. How many nights did you stay at La Quinta Motor Inn on your most recent visit? 2.6 (12-)

2. What was the purpose of that trip? (CHECK AS MANY AS APPLY)
Personal 9.5 (13-1) Pleasure 12.2 (3) Vacation 2.0 (5)
Business 79.8 (2) Convention 3.5 (4)

3. Was that your first stay in a La Quinta Motor Inn? Yes 27.0 (14-1) No 70.1 (2)

4. How often do you stay in motels or hotels?
Once a week or more 39.0 (15-1) About once a month 16.4 (3)
Once every few weeks 21.7 (2) Less often than every few months 21.2 (4)

5. What motel or hotel do you visit **most** often in the South or Southwest? (CHECK ONE)
La Quinta 45.4 (16-1) Sheraton 4.3 (6) Ramada 9.6 (X)
Howard Johnson 3.7 (2) Quality 1.6 (7) Hyatt 1.2 (Y)
Days Inn 4.7 (3) TraveLodge 2.6 (8) Hilton 4.3 (17-1)
Holiday Inn 28.7 (4) Rodeway 4.2 (9) Other 9.3
Marriott 2.5 (5) Best Western 11.7 (0) (write in)

6. On your most recent visit to La Quinta, was it a: (CHECK ONE)
Business trip paid for by the company 65.7 (18-1)
Business trip paid for by yourself 16.4 (2)
Pleasure trip paid for by yourself 18.0 (3)

7. On that trip, did you rent a car? Yes 23.1 (19-1) No 75.9 (2)

8. On that trip, did you: Fly into the city 34.0 (20-1) Drive into the city 64.8 (2)

9. Why did you choose the particular La Quinta Motor Inn at which you stayed? (CHECK AS MANY AS APPLY)
Close to next day's activities 47.5 (21-1) Price 36.6 (6)
Saw it when ready to stop 5.7 (2) Stayed here before 40.9 (7)
Recommended by friend, relative, etc. 15.4 (3) Friendly/Courteous personnel 27.9 (8)
Specified by your company 7.3 (4) Other motels full 3.1 (9)
Personal preference based on previous experience 48.1 (5)

10. Who made your reservations?
Yourself 55.4 (22-1) Travel agency 2.7 (4) Relative, friend, etc. 4.7 (6)
Your secretary 13.3 (2) Association/Convention 2.2 (5) No reservations 10.4 (7)
Your company 10.4 (3)

---

11. On that trip, did you share your room with others? (CHECK AS MANY AS APPLY)
Spouse 21.6 (23-1) Business associates 4.1 (4)
Children 5.2 (2) No 68.9 (4)
Friends 3.4 (3)

12. For each of the following statements, please check those which you feel are particularly true about the motel/hotel chains listed below. Check as many motel/hotel chains as you feel apply to each statement.

	Holiday Inn	Marriott	La Quinta	Ramada
Hotels are not conveniently located	8.0 (24-1)	20.3 (25-1)	6.0 (26-1)	13.0 (27-1)
Employees are not courteous, efficient	24.3 (2)	4.5 (2)	3.0 (2)	14.9 (2)
Room sizes are not satisfactory	7.2 (3)	1.9 (3)	1.9 (3)	6.5 (3)
Have not had a disappointing experience with one of their motels/hotels	23.4 (4)	25.0 (4)	49.7 (4)	23.2 (4)
Motel/hotel is not kept clean	23.1 (5)	1.4 (5)	2.2 (5)	20.1 (5)
Rooms are not always clean and ready when they're supposed to be	22.8 (6)	3.3 (6)	5.1 (6)	14.6 (6)
One of my favorite places to stay	14.7 (7)	15.3 (7)	52.5 (7)	9.6 (7)
Try to avoid when I can	30.2 (8)	9.7 (8)	1.0 (8)	23.6 (8)
Room too noisy	21.1 (9)	2.7 (9)	5.0 (9)	14.3 (9)
No Answer	26.2	48.3	23.6	35.7

13. When you try to make a reservation at a La Quinta Motor Inn, can you get a room: (CHECK ONE)
All the time 27.6 (28-1) Most of the time 49.5 (2) Sometimes 7.3 (3) Not very often 2.7 (4)

14. When you make a reservation at a La Quinta Motor Inn, is your reservation: (CHECK ONE)
Always waiting for you when you get there 73.6 (29-1)
Waiting for you most of the time 12.2 (2)
Waiting for you only sometime 1.9 (3)
Very often not waiting for you .6 (4)

15. What is your likelihood of staying at a La Quinta Motor Inn the next time you visit the city?
Extremely likely 54.2 (30-1) Not very likely 2.6 (4)
Very likely 30.3 (2) Not at all likely 1.0 (5)
Somewhat likely 11.0 (3)

16. What is your likelihood of staying at a La Quinta Motor Inn if one were available in another city you visit?
Extremely likely 45.5 (31-1) Not very likely 2.3 (4)
Very likely 35.4 (2) Not at all likely .7 (5)
Somewhat likely 15.3 (3)

Would you please answer just a few more questions about yourself for purposes of classification only:

A. Are you: Male 89.0 (32-1) Female 10.1 (2)

B. How old are you? 42.0 (years) (33-/34-)

C. What is your occupation? (PLEASE CHECK ONLY ONE)
Craftsperson/Technician/Mechanic/Factory Worker 3.4 (35-1)
Executive/Manager 25.7 (2) Office Worker/Clerk/Secretary 1.8 (7)
Government employee 7.3 (3) Salesperson/Buyer 26.7 (8)
Homemaker 2.0 (4) Self employed/Owner of business 10.2 (9)
Active Duty/Military 1.4 (5) Retired 4.1 (0)
Professional 16.6 (6) Teacher/Professor/Student 3.4 (X)

D. Where do you live?
___ 38% Texas ___
(City)   (State) (36/37)   (Zip Code) (38/42)

E. What is your approximate annual family income including all members of your household?
Up to $10,000 1.8 (43-1) $25,001-$35,000 28.9 (5)
$10,000-$15,000 6.8 (2) $35,001-$50,000 17.6 (6)
$15,001-$20,000 12.3 (3) $50,001-$75,000 5.8 (7)
$20,001-$25,000 17.1 (4) $75,001 or more 2.6 (8)
Mean $31,620

F. Do you buy and sell stock in one or more public companies regularly?
Yes 25.3 (44-1) No 69.9 (2)

G. If yes, do you buy stock in companies whose products or services you use?
Yes 78.2 (45-1) No 17.7 (2)

out what business is going to be available in the neighborhood. You can't create business when it's not there. You're not going to bring someone from the south side of town to the north side of town just because you're La Quinta and they like to stay at La Quinta.

By analyzing the business traveler's needs, which Barshop described as "a clean quiet room and a convenient location, with friendly, courteous service, at a price that offers good value," La Quinta management had developed what they considered an infallible formula for consistent success. In Barshop's opinion, La Quinta was positioned to fill the void between "the big Holiday Inns-type garden motels and the so-called budgets." He explained:

A chain like Holiday Inns is so huge now that it's easier for them to get a $100 million, thousand-room hotel together than it is to put ten 100-room motels together. The budget chains, on the other hand, don't use the quality construction that business travelers will accept. We're giving business travelers what they want, and if we tried to give them more, we'd be going outside our concept.

Financing and Pricing

Historically, La Quinta had not relied on the public equity market for much of its capital needs. In the past two years, the company had obtained mortgage commitments from eight of the ten largest U.S. life insurance companies. La Quinta had financed many of its properties through joint ventures with strong financial partners who provided the majority of the required capital, each partner owning one-half of the property in question. Typically, these partners contributed capital or land and La Quinta constructed and operated the inn, receiving development and management fees. Profits, losses, and residual real estate values were shared. Because of after-tax returns on equity of 25–30 percent, the combined mortgage plus equity return to a lender at La Quinta was substantially greater than the return on conventional hotel-motel loans.

La Quinta management felt that joint venturing enabled the company to expand to a greater extent than would otherwise be feasible, while maintaining a degree of operational control over quality of service that was not possible with franchising. The company had discontinued domestic franchising in February 1977, after licensing fourteen properties (see Exhibit 1). Revenues from license fees and room royalties amounted to less than 1 percent of the company's total revenues in fiscal 1980.

Barshop's efforts were central in financing, according to one senior company manager: "Sam has the contacts with the project finance people, the institutions, the potential joint venture partners, and the restaurants, and he puts a deal together." Barshop himself confirmed this view: "I'm good at that, and it's what I love. But I wouldn't know how to check a customer in and out of a motel properly."

The average new La Quinta property cost $3.2 million to construct in 1980. It was a rule of thumb in the lodging industry that room rates should be pegged to construction costs by a ratio of 1:1,000—one dollar charged per room/night for each thousand spent in financing, constructing, and furnishing it. In mid-1980, La Quinta was spending approximately $25,000 per room. Management, however, was more concerned about competition than construction costs in setting rates. Explained Barshop: "We want to stay 20–25 percent lower than our competition, and they keep raising their prices so high that it's not difficult to do that." Summarizing his position on pricing, Barshop commented:

Price is important but I don't think it's as significant for a motel as a lot of other things. The most important thing is location; the second is cleanliness. People will forgive service to some extent—though we would love to always have good, cheerful, efficient service at the front desk—but they won't forgive a dirty room or a property that's not maintained. Especially business travelers—men look under the beds to see if the carpet has been vacuumed more often than women do.

Quality Control

Quality control over La Quinta properties was supervised by Robert S. Noyes, senior vice president of operations and a 36-year veteran of the lodging industry. Noyes' inspectors made four unannounced visits to each property annually, each time arriving at 4:30 a.m. and staying about eight hours. They conducted a general inspection of the entire property, inspected 25 percent of the rooms in detail, and reviewed front-office and bookkeeping operations. The ratings resulting from these visits had a direct impact on the salaries and bonuses of the inn-keeping teams. In addition, La Quinta's internal audit department performed a yearly operational audit of each property's front desk, examining cash control, adherence to prescribed procedures, and service to guests.

COMPETITION AND GROWTH

La Quinta management viewed lodging as a classic service industry in which no one company dominated the market. Holiday Inns, the largest single competitor, controlled only 12–15 percent of the nation's 2.25 million beds. Moreover, as David B. Daviss, La Quinta's senior vice president for administration, told the Boston security analysts:

Sixty percent of those 2¼ million beds are over ten years old and must be replaced. Today, La Quinta has less than one-half of 1 percent of those lodging rooms—maybe 10,000—and is represented in only forty-seven of the 247 SMSAs in the United States.[2] Travel in the past 15–20 years has grown by about 3 percent annually, and it is projected to continue to grow at 3 percent for the next 15–20 years. That provides us with an exceptional opportunity to increase market share.

Barshop added:

[2] SMSA (Standard Metropolitan Statistical Area) was a term used to identify densely inhabited areas of 50,000 or above in population.

Our concept seems simple, but as I always tell everybody, simple isn't easy. Our stroke of genius is that we build fewer rooms and so we fill more of them up. It's easier to sell 120 rooms than it is 300. That's why our occupancy is so high. If you're going to run a service business, you just do the simplest things, and you do them over and over again. I keep telling all these business school graduates—try not to make things complicated. You can't be everything to everybody. We've got a simple concept, and we're going to cookie cut, and cookie cut, and cookie cut, until there aren't any more cookies left to cut.

By fall 1980 it appeared that many corporate travel managers were seeking better ways to control expenses, but the future effect of rising costs on business travel was hard to predict. Some companies, such as consulting firms, billed their clients for travel expenses. Others saw travel as a necessary evil—and pointed out that if the economy worsened, executives and sales representatives might have to spend even more time on the road trying to drum up business.

Telephone survey findings released by the U.S. Travel Data Center in April 1980 revealed that two-thirds of domestic vacations would be taken by car, truck, or recreational vehicle. On all but the most competitive routes, increased airline fares meant that flying remained more costly than driving for a family of four.

Appraising La Quinta's potential for growth within the current travel environment, one industry analyst observed that the quality of the company's management was very high, "stronger than needed for a company this size."

MARKETING

La Quinta's marketing effort was divided among several departments of the company (Exhibit 5). Barshop had informally dubbed himself "senior vice president of marketing" because of his role in site selection, which he considered La Quinta's most important marketing task. Joyce Wilson, who held the title of vice president-mar-

EXHIBIT 5
LA QUINTA CORPORATE ORGANIZATION, 1980

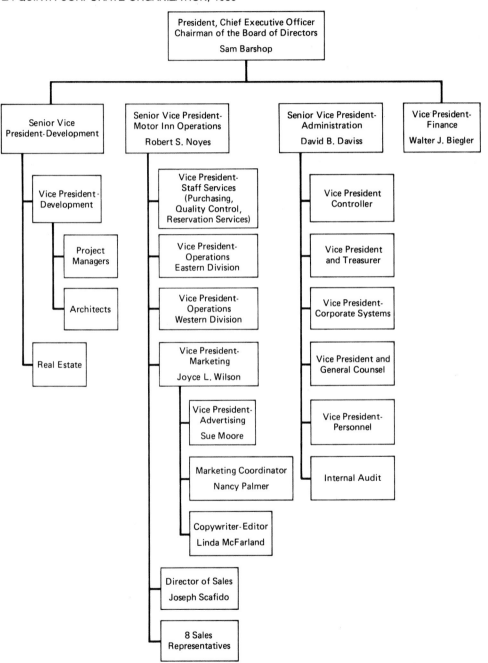

keting, directed advertising, public relations, and research, and reported to Bob Noyes, senior vice president of operations. Joseph Scafido, director of sales, worked outside Wilson's department and also reported to Noyes. Appraising this structure, David Daviss commented:

> Marketing is kind of a misnomer in our organization, in my mind. I see it as primarily a public relations function. . . . I think there's some perception on the part of our marketing people that they ought to be involved in marketing in a broader sense, as they define the term, but we really haven't defined it for them in that way.

Communications

Joyce Wilson, La Quinta's vice president of marketing, had worked in radio, television, advertising and public relations for 26 years. She had joined La Quinta in 1975, created the marketing department, and hired the first sales representative. La Quinta's corporate headquarters was located in San Antonio. But Wilson's department was in a small Dallas office park 270 miles away—45 minutes by commuter airline. Initially, La Quinta management had decided to locate Wilson in Dallas (where she lived when she was hired) because, as she reflected later, "The company wasn't too sure what role this function was going to play." Later, when a move to the home office was discussed, it was decided that both news sources and creative resources—such as artists, printers, and copywriters—were more plentiful in Dallas or Houston than in San Antonio and that the marketing department could operate more efficiently and more objectively from a vantage point outside corporate headquarters.

Wilson's key staff consisted of four people: herself; Sue Moore, vice president-advertising and director of La Quinta's in-house advertising agency; Nancy Palmer, who supervised publicity; and Linda McFarland, editor of the company's internal magazine. All four also created

and produced a variety of brochures, visual presentations, information packets, direct mail programs, and specialty items, not only for sales promotion purposes but also for the use of various corporate departments.

The in-house advertising agency had been set up in 1977 to extend the buying power of the budget. Moore estimated that because she could eliminate standard outside agency fees and markups, and use media commissions to buy more space, La Quinta's buying power for fiscal 1980 would be $89,000 greater than what the company could have purchased through an outside agency.

In fiscal 1980, $401,000 was generated for La Quinta's national advertising fund by assessing each property 12 cents per room per day. Of this, $114,000 went to overhead expenses for the marketing department, market research, and special public relations promotions, $199,000 was earmarked for national advertising, and $88,000 designated for the semi-annual La Quinta directory, which listed the names, rates, and locations of all company properties. Senior management believed the work turned out by the marketing department was very cost-effective and had created considerable awareness of the chain.

Moore's current advertising campaign—a series of four ads which appeared a total of fifteen times in *Business Week* and the national executive editions of *Newsweek* and *Time*—emphasized La Quinta's positioning concept. Headlines focused on price, location, or service mix, as illustrated in Exhibit 6. A new advertising program was under development for 1981. Other projects directed by Wilson's group included the Caballero club, which comprised 8,500 regular customers of La Quinta. The club was started to give inn managers an opportunity to "introduce" their regular customers to other managers in the chain; benefits included promotions directed to club members and a quarterly newsletter.

Although Barshop praised the marketing department as the most cost-efficient group in the

EXHIBIT 6
LA QUINTA NATIONAL ADVERTISING, 1980

"I DON'T NEED CONVENTION MOBS, LONG CHECK IN AND CHECK OUT LINES, FANCY LOBBIES OR NIGHTCLUBS. I JUST WANT A CLEAN, QUIET ROOM AND PERSONAL SERVICE.

THAT'S WHY I STAY AT LA QUINTA."

At La Quinta, you'll never be jostled aside by conventioneers because we don't book conventions.

You won't be disturbed by a noisy nightclub, because we don't have nightclubs. Or any unnecessary frills for that matter.

We do have what the experienced business traveler really wants:

Comfortable, clean, quiet rooms with color TV and phone.

Same-day laundry service. 24-hour coffee shop. Swimming pool.

And a staff trained to give you personal attention, supervised by husband and wife managers who live on the premises.

By cutting out the things you don't need, La Quinta can afford to give you lower rates. Up to 25% less in most cases.

No wonder 4 out of 5 of our guests are business travelers. La Quinta: 7,500 rooms in 17 states. And growing.

For free directory and other information, write La Quinta Marketing, Dept. T, 1625 Regal Row, Suite 170, Dallas, Texas 75247.

Toll free reservations: 800-531-5900
From Texas: 800-292-5200

Reservations guaranteed with all major credit cards.

© 1978. La Quinta Motor Inns, Inc
Listed on American Stock Exchange (LQM)

"OUR SALESMEN ARE ON THE ROAD MORE THAN EVER. BUT OUR TRAVEL EXPENSES ARE DOWN.

WHERE ARE WE STAYING? LA QUINTA."

An independent survey of La Quinta guests proved 4 out of 5 are business travelers.

They know every motor inn on the road. And they prefer La Quinta over their second choice almost two to one!

Which shows us we're giving our preferred guests, business travelers, what they really want:

Metro locations close to business centers and transportation.

Big, comfortable, quiet rooms with color TV and phone. Same-day laundry service. Swimming pool. 24-hour coffee shop next door.

And a helpful, courteous staff. (Headed by husband and wife managers who live on the premises.)

We don't book conventions. Nor court the vacation trade.

By cutting out the things you don't use, La Quinta can afford to give you lower rates. Up to 25% lower in most cases!

Business travel? Think La Quinta. Now 7,500 rooms in 17 states. And growing.

For free directory, write La Quinta Marketing, Dept. B, 1625 Regal Row, Suite 170, Dallas, Texas 75247.

Toll free reservations:
800-531-5900
From Texas:
800-292-5200
Reservations guaranteed with all major credit cards.

©1978. La Quinta Motor Inns, Inc
Listed on American Stock Exchange
(LQM)

company, Wilson felt that much of marketing's potential at La Quinta remained untapped. In her words:

> I think marketing is the process of ascertaining what your customer needs, presenting an image to your various publics, listening to customers, and communicating their ideas to the rest of the company's planning staff. The company's perception of where marketing input is needed has not been defined.
>
> Let me give you an example. Sue Moore heard recently that La Quinta was planning to build an addition to a property in San Antonio in which they were going to put king-size beds and just showers —not shower and tub. We were surprised that the plans were that far along without our knowing about them. So I asked, have we made plans on how this change in product should be presented to our customers? Will the price be different? Will they be told at the desk that they have a choice?
>
> I'm not saying they're wrong. Our customers may love the concept. I'm saying let's plan it a little, let's figure out how to tell them when they make reservations that we have two different types of accommodations and what the differences are. Let's not throw somebody who is used to the room we've got into a different room without letting him know.

Wilson also believed that La Quinta was overlooking significant opportunities for market research. She observed:

> We need to add to our personal opinions and experience. We have had two research projects. Both built customer profiles and indicated that the reasons people chose La Quinta were (1) location; (2) personal preference for the chain; and (3) price. Those projects were nearly three years apart, but nevertheless the findings were consistent. We need to keep up research.
>
> I also think the company needs more marketing input about possible changes in our concept. I spend a great deal of time keeping people stuck to this concept, in agreement with Sam's theory that if it isn't broken, don't fix it, but at the same time, our job, as I envision it, is to be aware that there may be some changes down the road. I don't see the necessity for drastically changing our concept—we've been highly successful—but if our customers' needs, perceptions, or habits are changing, we

need to be prepared to make a decision on how to cope with them. Subtle changes may or may not portend a trend.

Wilson's department played no role in La Quinta's pricing decisions, which were made every six months by a rate committee consisting of Barshop, Noyes, Daviss, and the company's senior vice president-development and vice president-finance. According to Noyes, "A lot of these decisions are made from a marketing standpoint. We may feel that we should charge more on a certain property, but we'll hold rates down for a while to build occupancy."

Sales

La Quinta's sales department had been reorganized five times between 1976 and 1980. Commenting on the sales task, Bob Noyes stated:

> Sales in our organization are a very intangible thing. Our sales reps are selling an idea—our unique lodging value—and they can't come back in and tell their superior, "Well, I sold a quarter of a million dollars worth of business today," because we don't have convention facilities to accommodate those packages. We use a lot of gung-ho young people who expect to see concrete results, and we expect a lot of turnover because some of them get frustrated.

La Quinta's sales were directed by Joseph Scafido, who had joined the company in 1976 as one of its first sales representatives. From his office in San Antonio, he supervised eight sales reps, based in Atlanta, New Orleans, St. Louis, Houston, Dallas, San Antonio, and Denver. Sales objectives, in order of importance, included: (1) increasing occupancy, especially in new markets; (2) developing national corporate business; (3) maintaining accounts; and (4) increasing occupancy in soft periods like weekends. His key responsibility, Scafido explained, was preparing for the opening of new properties:

> About six to eight months in advance, a sales or marketing person goes out and surveys the site.

How far are we from the airport? What are the major companies? What's the general economic climate? How many miles from the feeder cities? Some of this work is done during site selection. We also determine our position in the market—we check rates and conditions of competition. We flag where billboards can do us the most good.

Our reports go to Bob Noyes, Joyce Wilson, Sue Moore, and the regional sales rep. Then I'll sit with Joyce and Sue to formulate a timetable, coordinating advertising, public relations, and personal sales calls. Sometimes we'll set up a sales blitz—bringing a few of the reps to one area for a limited time to knock on doors to qualify accounts. Then, three to four weeks after the property opens, the local sales rep starts the follow-up calls.

Scafido saw other opportunities for La Quinta's sales and marketing staff to contribute to management decision making. For example, he had stressed to the operations department (to which he reported), the importance of having courtesy cars at inns that were close to airports:

We stress in our advertising and our sales calls that we offer the basic services. One of the primary services offered by lodging facilities located near the airport—other than budget motels—is airport transportation. This helps occupancy—not just because the car is available, but because it runs around the airport with our name on it and we can advertise that service in the baggage claim areas of the terminal.

A recent disappointing opening experience for La Quinta had occurred in Abilene, a city of 100,000 in central Texas, 180 miles west of Dallas. Scafido recalled:

We tried to open Abilene as though it were a property in Dallas, where we put a sign, open the doors, and count on recognition. Well, it's been three months since we opened the doors and occupancy is still 20–30 percent, the lowest in the chain. It's the first time that's happened to us in Texas—now we have to investigate why.

Marketing input has been limited at La Quinta. That's because it didn't seem necessary at first—Sam's own marketing genius in picking sites did all our marketing for us. But as we expand away from

the Southwest, we have found that not all markets are alike. Identity and awareness of the chain are key ingredients to the success of a property. Accessibility and visibility are very important components, too, but until we inform the local market just who we are and what they can expect from us, they won't be knocking our doors down.

The company's attitude toward the marketing function has become more open in the past year, as the sales and marketing departments have grown and increased credibility. Now management seems to be listening when we describe the difference in marketing a product in Jacksonville, Florida, and one in Houston, Texas. In a new market, we don't have the identity, the awareness, and the customer base to draw from.

Scafido, like Wilson, wondered whether the company was paying enough attention to changes in the travel market. Though he totally supported La Quinta's service concept—"I have location, service mix, and price branded on my forehead," he declared—Scafido was concerned over the company's lack of research on possible changes in the travel market. "Somebody needs to step back," he said, "and see if the recession, airline deregulation, and similar new trends are going to give us problems."

Weekend Occupancy Concerns

The gasoline shortage in the summer of 1979 had a marked impact on the lodging industry. Although management feared La Quinta properties would be affected, the chain dropped only 3 percentage points in occupancy from comparable 1978 figures in June, 5 points in July, and 2 points in August. However, a sharp increase in gasoline prices in 1980, combined with a recession, led to a further softening in occupancy rates (Exhibits 1 and 7). To rebuild occupancy, many properties seeking leisure travelers began advertising discounted weekend packages. Barshop had frequently urged Wilson, Moore, and Scafido to develop similar weekend programs.

Currently, La Quinta was running no advertisements targeted toward weekend travelers.

EXHIBIT 7 OCCUPANCY DATA,
SUMMER 1978–79, FOR A REPRESENTATIVE CROSS-SECTION OF LA QUINTA INNS

	June '78		July '78		August '78		September '78	
	Fri.–Sat.	Sun.	Fri.–Sat.	Sun.	Fri.–Sat.	Sun.	Fri.–Sat.	Sun.
Austin #1	100.4	81.2	100.5	75.7	100.2	80.5	97.2	68.2
Austin #2	100.5	83.5	100.7	86.2	100.4	91.1	92.6	66.4
Austin #3	91.6	93.7	98.2	84.6	100.6	89.9	98.7	81.0
Dallas/Ft. Worth Airport	114.5	109.9	111.9	95.5	110.2	85.7	103.8	88.0
Dallas #2	101.0	102.0	100.0	99.8	100.8	100.8	95.3	96.0
Dallas #3	100.4	94.5	98.0	94.1	100.5	90.7	99.6	95.8
Dallas #4	97.2	95.8	93.5	88.7	99.3	90.6	79.7	73.7
Denver #1	91.4	93.5	99.5	98.3	100.7	94.2	96.3	89.1
Houston #1	95.4	77.9	101.9	84.4	97.0	74.6	90.5	67.5
Houston #2	99.6	79.1	96.7	76.9	95.7	76.5	89.7	85.5
Houston #3	99.6	97.8	100.2	96.6	100.4	97.2	101.5	84.4
Houston #4	100.0	98.5	100.5	98.0	100.0	96.0	97.5	79.0
Kansas City	86.6	60.4	84.2	51.5	92.2	50.5	76.6	56.9
Las Vegas*								
Little Rock #1	101.6	94.2	100.2	94.2	100.6	92.9	82.5	65.2
Merrillville* (Indiana)								
Nashville*								
New Orleans #1	99.1	87.8	98.5	84.7	96.9	78.5	94.0	79.5
New Orleans #2	98.1	100.2	99.9	94.0	100.5	100.2	96.7	98.8
Phoenix	93.8	93.9	83.2	84.4	86.2	70.7	78.4	61.8
St. Louis	92.5	71.8	95.6	70.8	89.2	60.9	71.1	57.6
Tucson	82.4	40.2	75.4	52.2	64.4	48.3	65.5	47.8
Tulsa	95.7	73.1	99.5	75.3	89.3	64.2	97.2	75.3

*Open one year or less.
Note: Occupancy greater than 100 percent indicates that room was occupied twice in one 24-hour period.
Source: Company records.

Sales reps pursued some weekend group business—such as university athletic teams—but as Noyes pointed out, "It's hard for us to put together a so-called package deal because we don't have bars and restaurants and similar facilities." Noyes considered weekend group business hard to handle; many school groups, he felt, were not well-chaperoned, "and at $23 a night we can't afford much damage." Wilson also had objections:

We don't *have* anything to package, nor do we have any money to promote that package. Our occupancy figures proved that the places where people wanted to go for the weekend—like Dallas, Houston, New Orleans, Austin, San Antonio—were still running 95 percent to 100 percent full on Fridays and Saturdays. Sure, we could use more business on Sunday nights everywhere, but you can't entice people to travel on Sunday nights. We could use weekend business in smaller Texas cities like Denton and Killeen, but there are no attractions for people there. We determined from the weekend occupancies that the newer, and therefore weaker, properties were hardest hit; the established ones remained pretty strong, in most cases. And let's not forget what it will cost to promote such a package.

EXHIBIT 7 *(continued)*

June '79		July '79		August '79		September '79	
Fri.–Sat.	Sun.	Fri.–Sat.	Sun.	Fri.–Sat.	Sun.	Fri.–Sat.	Sun.
101.0	76.3	99.7	64.8	100.2	74.8	99.3	66.2
100.1	75.9	99.3	62.1	100.0	78.0	96.5	82.2
100.3	85.6	100.6	75.2	100.4	91.4	100.3	72.5
116.9	108.3	116.8	110.1	116.7	107.3	105.6	91.8
98.5	83.0	97.9	82.6	100.0	83.2	98.9	83.1
100.8	98.4	100.3	98.5	101.1	94.5	102.4	97.9
91.7	91.7	90.6	89.7	89.9	88.9	76.7	61.6
98.1	78.1	93.7	89.6	99.2	91.6	92.7	91.2
91.5	64.1	94.8	78.3	98.9	83.5	94.2	67.8
88.2	85.3	88.9	91.0	94.4	86.9	79.4	79.7
99.8	88.7	98.2	95.3	98.0	91.1	98.1	89.9
98.2	65.0	100.9	89.0	102.0	97.0	96.3	75.3
89.9	58.5	84.8	54.3	90.5	63.9	56.6	49.5
84.9	50.5	86.9	47.8	93.6	51.9	89.5	47.6
73.9	52.7	76.2	60.7	89.3	71.2	74.4	59.8
60.1	41.1	69.5	42.8	84.6	48.1	57.3	34.2
96.3	46.7	102.1	50.9	97.2	69.3	87.0	49.5
100.5	92.9	94.1	81.6	100.6	91.1	88.8	93.6
100.4	88.1	100.8	85.4	99.9	95.3	95.5	85.9
86.0	51.0	73.8	72.6	67.8	63.9	67.1	55.4
64.9	47.2	55.8	46.0	68.7	56.8	53.6	53.5
63.2	45.1	50.6	40.2	56.0	37.3	61.2	45.1
84.1	50.5	87.5	67.2	97.2	66.4	83.0	66.4

We have a very small advertising budget as it is. Are we going to take money away from promoting our chain's image nationally to promote something that may not solve the problem?

I'm convinced that there's nothing in the world I can do to get people to go to Jackson, Mississippi, or Tulsa, Oklahoma, for a weekend unless they have family there. A package is especially expensive when you don't have a restaurant or a bar. People like Marriott can afford to offer two nights for the price of one because their high rate allows more flexibility in discounting and because they hope to make it up in the bar, the restaurants, and the gift shops—all their little profit centers. We don't have these things. All we've got to sell is that room, and it's already discounted because our rates are low. Are we going to give it to people for $10? For what purpose? I say let's spend more on building awareness nationally for our chain and its marketing position. Once people get to know our product, they're going to use us on weekends, on vacations, whenever they're traveling with their families and want a better lodging value.

THE FUTURE FOR LA QUINTA

To more than one observer of the lodging industry, La Quinta's future appeared bright. In August

EXHIBIT 7 *(continued)* OCCUPANCY DATA,
SUMMER 1978–79, FOR A REPRESENTATIVE CROSS-SECTION OF LA QUINTA INNS

	June			July		
	Mon.–Thurs.	**Fri.–Sat.**	**Sun.**	**Mon.–Thurs.**	**Fri.–Sat.**	**Sun.**
Austin #1	98.9	100.4	74.0	99.9	101.3	77.0
Austin #2	98.5	99.3	74.0	98.1	96.7	59.0
Austin #3	100.5	100.2	75.0	100.4	100.2	75.0
Dallas/Ft. Worth Airport	112.4	109.6	94.0	118.0	119.0	93.0
Dallas #2	90.4	97.5	78.0	86.7	96.4	85.0
Dallas #3	101.0	101.0	88.0	100.9	101.2	89.0
Dallas #4	95.9	90.8	77.0	93.8	77.0	78.0
Denver #1	99.0	97.7	93.0	96.7	99.6	92.0
Denver #2—Airport	99.8	97.4	94.0	98.6	98.5	98.0
Houston #1	99.5	93.6	77.8	95.5	92.2	73.2
Houston #2	99.6	85.6	77.0	96.4	83.1	83.6
Houston #3	100.1	100.1	96.2	100.2	100.1	92.4
Houston #4	99.5	98.7	86.0	98.0	98.9	81.0
Kansas City	95.9	82.1	66.9	93.9	85.1	54.7
Las Vegas	74.6	92.7	57.0	76.2	95.4	54.3
Little Rock #1	99.5	67.8	51.7	96.9	74.2	79.7
Little Rock #2*	97.4	67.3	50.9	94.8	75.3	66.9
Merrillville (Indiana)	89.0	73.0	25.4	92.0	94.1	41.8
Nashville	85.5	94.8	57.0	84.5	96.0	61.0
New Orleans #1	99.5	97.0	82.0	99.9	100.9	93.3
New Orleans #2	101.1	99.8	98.0	100.2	101.0	100.1
Phoenix	97.9	73.0	70.3	89.3	53.0	68.5
St. Louis	93.4	65.9	51.9	86.3	57.7	37.2
Tucson	96.6	74.4	51.9	82.4	57.9	44.1
Tulsa	102.0	92.1	53.9	100.4	97.3	61.7

*Open one year or less.
Note: Occupancy greater than 100 percent indicates that room was occupied twice in one 24-hour period.
Source: Company records.

1980, the brokerage firm of Donaldson, Lufkin & Jenrette, Inc. declared La Quinta's stock potential to be the best among all lodging companies. The question most frequently heard from security analysts by La Quinta management was, "If your idea is so great, what's to keep someone else from copying it?" Pointing to La Quinta's 11,000-room head start, Barshop's response was:

It could be done, but who's going to do it? Capital investment is a real barrier to entry now. Holiday Inns can't do it; their license and franchise network

is so extensive that they'd be competing with themselves.

Management generally professed to see no barriers to unlimited growth, other than the internal problems of expanding what had started as a small entrepreneurship into a professionally managed giant. The company's sales, earnings, and occupancy figures for the fiscal year ending May 31, 1980, were highly encouraging, with revenues up 28 percent and net earnings up 32 percent, although systemwide occupancy had

EXHIBIT 7 (continued)

August			September		
Mon.–Thurs.	Fri.–Sat.	Sun.	Mon.–Thurs.	Fri.–Sat.	Sun.
99.7	100.2	92.0	98.3	96.0	64.0
98.6	97.2	74.0	98.4	88.3	63.0
99.7	99.9	92.0	98.8	91.9	66.0
110.0	102.2	95.0	110.5	113.2	79.0
97.1	98.9	91.0	77.0	82.0	64.0
100.2	100.2	99.0	98.4	100.0	90.0
93.5	96.7	88.0	94.4	63.4	61.0
96.4	97.2	88.0	96.2	93.3	84.0
100.3	100.8	101.0	98.5	93.8	95.0
99.4	94.5	70.2	94.4	79.8	59.2
97.9	89.6	81.1	76.0	72.1	69.9
101.2	102.2	94.3	99.1	101.4	75.4
99.2	98.5	88.0	95.8	96.6	93.0
94.9	90.2	57.5	90.3	67.3	44.3
76.7	87.5	65.7	58.9	73.4	57.0
99.8	84.2	56.2	93.2	71.4	48.2
98.6	75.2	71.6	93.2	74.8	54.7
98.9	97.8	50.0	94.0	81.1	49.1
61.0	82.2	98.0	70.0	57.1	34.0
100.1	102.2	95.2	100.5	94.9	98.1
100.1	100.6	97.0	97.8	98.1	88.1
88.8	65.8	54.6	88.2	62.3	60.1
95.4	72.2	42.4	79.5	47.4	27.3
87.8	60.3	42.1	91.7	54.7	46.0
102.5	89.7	70.5	97.0	84.3	49.0

dipped from 88.1 percent to 83.8 percent (Exhibit 1). One of the factors pulling down the average occupancy rate in FY 1980 had been the large number of new inns opened by La Quinta during that year. Still, management noted that the reported industry average was about 70 percent, and that La Quinta's 1980 occupancy was 84 percent, the highest reported by any chain in the industry.

Further analysis in early October showed that demand on weekends in recent months had been somewhat weaker than during the previous year Inns owned). Some La Quinta executives began to wonder again whether the company should more aggressively pursue weekend business. Any discussion of a strategy designed to raise weekend occupancy kept returning to the same point: Would an attempt to attract tourists, families, and other weekend guests alter La Quinta's positioning too drastically? Was Wilson correct in assuming that La Quinta had already penetrated all the weekend markets it could realistically hope to enter? Some members of management felt the potential rewards of such a strategy were not worth the risk involved.

But beneath this immediate question lay what others perceived as a deeper issue: the future role of marketing at La Quinta and how its functions should be defined and organized. It was expected that a new senior vice president-operations would join the company before Thanksgiving as Noyes turned his attention exclusively to quality performance, and that Wilson would continue to report to operations.

WATER CONSERVATION IN PALO ALTO

Peter T. Hutchison
Don E. Parkinson
Charles B. Weinberg

Mr. Alan Jay, Chief Engineer of the Department of Water, Sewage and Gas (DWSG) in Palo Alto, California, did not know how to react to the first rain in weeks in drought-stricken California. It was the beginning of March 1977 and close to the end of what was normally considered the "wet" season in the region.

He wondered whether a few days of rain would result in a decrease in water conservation efforts. One thing the Chief Engineer knew for certain was that he could not continue to rely on the effect of the strong and extensive newspaper stories that had announced the launching of the initial water conservation campaign in January with headlines such as *"Save Water or Else . . . Area Warned"* and *"Water Cut Target 10 percent."*

THE DROUGHT OF 1977

For the second year in a row, Northern California had experienced record drought conditions, with

Reprinted from *Stanford Business Cases 1977* with permission of the publisher, Stanford University Graduate School of Business. Copyright © 1977 by the Board of Trustees of the Leland Stanford Junior University.

rainfall less than 50 percent of normal and reservoir levels at record lows.

Shortly after the start of 1977, most people, and particularly weather forecasters, realized that the unseasonable warm and dry weather that the Western portion of the United States was enjoying had the potential to change people's lifestyles, to cause industrial problems, and to threaten the existence of numerous farms and ranches that depended upon irrigated water.

In the early months of 1977, *Time, Newsweek,* and many other national magazines had reported extensively on the drought. The television networks had brought films and reports on the drought to Eastern viewers suffering from record cold and snow falls. People generally smiled at solutions such as the use of pipelines to send Eastern snow west and at slogans like "Save Water—Shower with a Friend," while trivia buffs prospered with such gems as "The toilet accounts for 40 percent of all indoor household water usage (up to seven gallons a flush)." However, the lack of rain had serious consequences for both the nation and the West.

Because 85 percent of the water used in California was consumed by farmers supplying 40 percent of the country's fresh vegetables and fruits, the reduced water supply was expected to result in shortages and higher prices for all. Utilities in the Pacific Northwest, which used hydroelectric energy as a major source of power, would have to turn to more expensive sources. Forest rangers were worried about fire hazards; outdoors enthusiasts, about the loss of fishing and boating opportunities; and homeowners, about keeping lawns and gardens green. Although long-term solutions such as weather modification, better irrigation techniques, and desalting water were being discussed, no amount of talk or money could change the fact that many reservoirs had gone dry, and there was no chance of any change in that condition until the end of 1977. No one had dared to consider the consequences of a third drought year.

Public Opinion in California

In March 1977, the California Poll conducted a representative statewide survey of 962 California residents and published the results in newspapers throughout the state. (The California Poll, which had operated since 1947, was an independent media-sponsored, public opinion news service which regularly carried out personal interview surveys on socially significant issues.) Eighty-five percent of those surveyed believed the drought was either "extremely serious" or "somewhat serious." When asked which user class should be cut the most if mandatory rationing became necessary, respondents replied as follows:

User Class	% Saying Cut This Group Most
Business and Industry	50
Households	33
Health and Safety	3
Agriculture	3
No opinion	11

With regard to reduction of household water

usage by 25 percent, only 10 percent of respondents said it would cause severe problems: however, 51 percent said a 50 percent cutback would cause severe problems. Finally, 93 percent claimed to be practicing some form of water conservation, such as using less water for bathing (70 percent), watering lawns less (67 percent), and washing cars less frequently (58 percent). Twenty-four percent claimed to have installed devices in their toilet tanks to reduce the amount of water used to flush, and 16 percent said they had installed water flow restrictors to reduce the rate of water flow in showers.

PALO ALTO AND THE SAN FRANCISCO BAY AREA

The population of the City of San Francisco was 700,000, and that of the nine-county San Francisco Bay Area totalled some 4.5 million. The Bay Area's generally mild climate had an average temperature range of from 54°F to 77°F (in summer) and from 39°F to 58°F in winter. The average annual rainfall of 15.5 inches occurred mainly from October through March. It almost never rained in June, July, and August. In 1975–76 and 1976–77, the rainfall had been less than one half of normal.

Palo Alto, a city of 55,000 people located about 35 miles south of San Francisco and 15 miles north of San Jose, was one of a number of cities which formed an extensive urban corridor along the length of the San Francisco Peninsula (Exhibit 1). The surrounding area offered a number of desirable features. Four hours' drive to the East, the Sierra Nevada mountains offered some of the best skiing, camping, and backpacking country in the United States. And 30 minutes to the West, across the foothills of the Peninsula, were the inviting but chilly beaches of the Pacific.

Palo Alto residents tended to be highly educated and had a median income level among the highest in the nation. They took an active interest in city affairs, and their city government was

EXHIBIT 1
MAP OF SAN FRANCISCO BAY AREA SHOWING PIPELINES AND RESERVOIRS

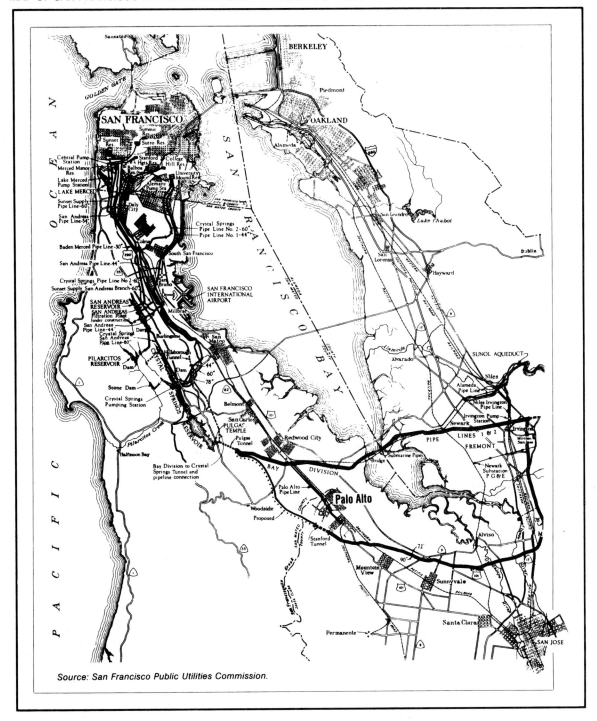

Source: San Francisco Public Utilities Commission.

considered to be very well run. The *Palo Alto Times,* with a circulation of 50,000 in Palo Alto, Los Altos, Menlo Park, Mountain View, and the surrounding area, reported extensively on the actions of the local city governments. Palo Alto fell within the circulation area of the *San Francisco Chronicle,* the *San Francisco Examiner,* and the *San Jose Mercury-News.* City residents could receive broadcasts from six VHF television and 58 radio stations.

Adjacent to the city, but not within city limits, was Stanford University. The presence of Stanford, as well as other factors, had stimulated the development of a high technology emphasis in many companies located in Palo Alto. Firms such as Hewlett-Packard, Varian, and Syntex had headquarters offices, research centers, and manufacturing operations in the city. The business community of Palo Alto had in the past been supportive of most community projects and had also demonstrated an effective response to the initial water conservation program. Civic groups, such as the Chamber of Commerce, had also been supportive of community conservation projects.

THE WATER SYSTEM IN PALO ALTO

The Palo Alto Department of Water, Sewage and Gas (DWSG) was responsible for the planning, production, and marketing of the water supply service of the city.[1] This department was directly responsible to the Utilities Director, who in turn was responsible to the City Manager (see Exhibit 2).

Mr. Jay, the Chief Engineer, was in charge of the operations of the DWSG. He supervised an administrative assistant plus a planning and de-

[1] The City of Palo Alto supplied electricity, gas, and water to all residents and commercial or industrial customers in the city. One monthly bill for all three utility services was mailed to all customers by the city. Usage and billing rates for each utility were separately itemized. In addition, the City of Palo Alto also provided garbage collection, but this service was administered and billed separately from the other three services.

sign team of six people. The customer service department of the city was divided into two parts: first, the clerical function, which reported to the City Treasurer; and second, the technical function (complaints regarding quality or quantity of the water supply), which was administered by the field supervisors.

In connection with the water supply function, the DWSG had three goals:

1 To serve the populace with an adequate supply of drinking water for domestic, industrial, commercial, and public needs;

2 To provide this service at rates comparable to those charged by the utilities of neighboring cities and towns; and

3 To provide revenue to the general fund of Palo Alto by operating efficiently and earning a reasonable (5 percent–8 percent) return on investment. (Profit maximization was *not* a goal; nor was more than a prudent return on investment sought.)

These broad goals had been effectively translated into measurable operating goals. Examples stated by the DWSG were: (1) The DWSG strived to maintain water pressure within narrow tolerances. (Numerical standards were set and monitored.) (2) There was a constant monitoring of the quality of the potable water supplied, which was checked against a pre-set quality standard. (3) The customer service department had a goal of 15-minutes response time to a customer complaint. Currently a service crew arrived on the scene to investigate a complaint within 30 minutes of notification.

In addition, the DWSG provided such complementary services as technical advice on methods and new devices that could be employed by industrial and manufacturing customers to conserve water and consequently reduce costs. Mr. Jay and his staff had worked successfully with a number of local companies in developing efficient water usage programs well before the current crisis arose. In recent years, a number of local companies had achieved significant reduc-

EXHIBIT 2
PALO ALTO UTILITIES: PARTIAL ORGANIZATION CHART

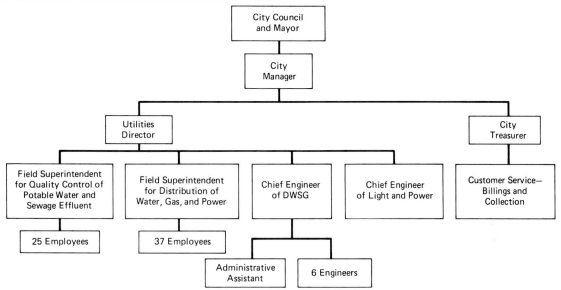

tions in water consumption by recycling water used for cooling, by watering grounds at night when less evaporation took place, and by preventive maintenance programs.

Palo Alto's Water Supply

The source of supply for Palo Alto was the San Francisco Water Department (SFWD) System, which served the City of San Francisco and over 30 communities in the Bay Area. The primary sources for the SFWD were the Hetch Hetchy, Lake Eleanor, and Lake Lloyd Reservoirs in Yosemite National Park, nearly 200 miles away. Rain and snow melt in the Yosemite area of the Sierra Nevada mountain range filled these reservoirs and the water was conveyed to the Bay Area through a series of tunnels and pipelines. The DWSG had a contract with the SFWD that expired in 1982. Although there were no specific provisions in the contract for renewal, there was no reason to believe that there would be any difficulties in doing so, as there had been none in

the past. The contract did not specify any guaranteed supply to Palo Alto, but the city had been able to obtain as much water from SFWD as it had needed.[2] The total amount of water supplied by SFWD to Palo Alto was metered, and monthly dollar sales were determined at a pre-set rate. Monthly sales figures (volume of water) for the six year period 1971–76 are given in Exhibit 3.

As an alternative source of supply, the DWSG could draw on groundwater from its own well network. This source, which could supply about 40 percent of current demand, was used as a standby and had been used in 1976 when the supply from San Francisco was reduced because of a short strike by city workers. The quality of the groundwater was inferior to that supplied by the SFWD and required a considerable amount of softening. Prior to 1962, when Palo Alto began receiving its entire water supply from the SFWD,

---

[2] If there was insufficient water in the SFWD, the contract provided that all users (including the City of San Francisco) would have the amount of water supplied cut back by a uniform percentage of the previous year's usage.

EXHIBIT 3
WATER SUPPLIED BY SFWD TO DWSG 1971–76
(million cubic feet/month)

	1971	1972	1973	1974	1975	1976	Average
January	40	46	47	45	48	52	46
February	50	46	45	45	52	58	49
March	45	52	44	46	47	55	48
April	60	71	60	54	53	67[1]	61
May	66	83	79	74	67	82[1]	75
June	86	92	94	94	100[2]	98	94
July	93	95	104	89	99[2]	101	97
August	98	100	95	95	100[2]	97	98
September	92	90	89	100	89	82	90
October	73	71	71	72	73	67	71
November	65	49	54	63	58	66	59
December	48	44	45	48	56	50	49
Average	68	70	69	69	70	73	70

[1] Includes 5 and 7 million cu. ft. supplied from groundwater in April and May respectively.
[2] Original data adjusted by summing three months supply and spreading equally to each month.
Source: DWSG records.

the DWSG had used the well system as its source of supply. At that time, the groundwater table was considerably drawn down, a condition that led to problems of subsidence and fears of salt water intrusions into the aquifers (water bearing ground). The latter was a very real and present threat, since some intrusion had already occurred on the eastern side of the San Francisco Bay. Prolonged use of the ground well system would threaten to "sink" neighboring cities.

The Demand for Water

Because the city's population was stable, the demand for water in Palo Alto had been practically static for several years (Exhibit 3); no increase in demand was projected in the future.

The DWSG categorized its customers by usage into the following categories: domestic, commerical, industrial, and public. The domestic consumers were further broken down into single family and multiple family (apartment and condominium type) units. In the latter case, each family was not metered separately; instead the complex as a whole was metered. Customer data are shown in Exhibits 4 and 5.

Pricing Policy

The pricing policy for water in Palo Alto was based on the following criteria:

1 Providing an equitable allocation of revenues and cost for the various classes of customers;
2 Providing a reasonable return on investment;
3 Providing the minimum basic requirement of a family for water at the lowest possible price (this was termed a lifeline rate);
4 Encouraging conservation.

The level of prices was based primarily on the cost of the supply from SFWD (which accounted for approximately 63 percent of total revenue). Other costs such as distribution, administration, and general expenses accounted for approximately 19 percent of revenues.

The scale of charges was approved by the City

EXHIBIT 4
NUMBER OF CUSTOMERS AND ANNUAL WATER USAGE BY USER CLASS

	Number of customers fiscal year ending June 30					
	1971	**1972**	**1973**	**1974**	**1975**	**1976**
Single Family	14,083	14,150	14,178	14,146	14,251	14,268
Multifamily	1,235	1,261	1,281	1,240	1,252	1,253
Commercial	1,321	1,332	1,425	1,490	1,496	1,513
Industrial	227	228	265	271	272	271
Public Facility	198	200	218	213	208	203
City	121	124	71	207	259	260
Total	17,185	17,295	17,438	17,567	17,738	17,768
	Annual CCF per customer					
Single Family	224	236	225	209	210	204*
Multifamily	435	415	398	410	431	413*
Commercial	709	768	744	662	890	855*
Industrial	7,886	7,835	7,410	7,734	8,211	8,229*
Public Facility	3,924	4,144	3,495	4,319	2,601	2,827*
City	2,571	2,608	3,426	1,497	1,212	991*
Total	436	452	444	443	448	455*

* Estimated.
Source: DWSG.

Council, based on the DWSG's recommendation. The current scale of charges had been in effect since July 1, 1976. Until that date, the scale of charges had been such that the marginal cost decreased with increased consumption. The new structure made the unit price greater as consumption increased, so that a user of more than 1,000 CCF (1 CCF = hundred cubic feet) per month would pay about 10 percent more per CCF above 1,000 than would a user of 50 CCF per month.[3] In addition, a general price increase of 8 percent was made. Careful analysis had shown that demand for water was not materially affected by this pricing strategy.

The extent to which the DWSG met its goal of maintaining its prices at levels comparable to those of neighboring utilities is shown in Exhibit 6. The average residential water bill was 4 percent above to 45 percent below adjacent cities,

---

[3] Water consumption is measured in terms of "units" of one hundred cubic feet. One unit = 1 CCF = 748 gallons.

and average industrial bills were 6 percent above to 32 percent below adjacent cities.

THE WATER SHORTAGE PROBLEM

Despite the two years of record drought, on January 6, the general manager of the San Francisco Water Department (SFWD) informed Mr. Jay in Palo Alto that no curtailment of local water use would be necessary. Mr. Jay was somewhat surprised, therefore, when two weeks later, he heard on the radio that Bay Area suburban users would need to cut water consumption by 10 percent. The need for reduced water usage immediately received extensive coverage in the *Palo Alto Times* and the San Francisco newspapers.

Palo Alto's Water Conservation Program

Following the SFWD's request of a voluntary curtailment of 10 percent in water consumption, the

EXHIBIT 5
WATER DEMAND IN PALO ALTO—MONTHLY AND QUARTERLY AVERAGE FOR 1975-76
(thousands of units—one unit = 1 CCF)

	Quarter I				Quarter II				Quarter III				Quarter IV			
	Jan.	Feb.	Mar.	Tot.	Apr.	May	June	Tot.	July	Aug.	Sept.	Tot.	Oct.	Nov.	Dec.	Tot.
Industrial	146	170	163	479	168	183	196	537	213	216	197	626	201	177	156	534
Public Facility	42	45	45	132	50	66	84	200	86	85	85	256	68	55	44	167
City Depts.	16	22	16	54	14	32	42	88	46	41	39	126	24	23	16	63
Domestic Single Family	180	163	167	510	190	273	379	842	406	363	361	1130	243	194	176	613
Domestic Multifamily	41	43	38	122	39	42	52	133	54	51	53	158	43	40	40	123
Commercial	77	88	83	248	75	90	110	275	123	120	110	353	93	79	71	243
Total	502	531	512	1545	536	686	863	2075	928	876	845	2649	672	568	503	1743

Source: Derived from DWSG—Monthly Sales Report.

EXHIBIT 6
AVERAGE MONTHLY WATER BILL FOR PALO ALTO AND OTHER BAY AREA CITIES

	Usage* (CCF)	Palo Alto	San Jose	Mountain View	Sunnyvale	San Mateo	San Francisco
Residential	18	$ 8.00	$ 8.14	$ 7.66	$ 11.71	$ 9.31	$ 7.71
Commercial	60	22.78	25.84	, 24.05	34.41	31.52	24.61
Industrial	630	224.58	238.97	238.70	289.81	296.74	241.65
Industrial Large (1)	2,500	889.33	938.50	940.50	886.47	1,167.69	950.65
Industrial Large (2)	5,000	1,784.78	1,883.00	1,761.00	1,574.04	2,338.20	1,827.40
Industrial Large (3)	10,000	3,567.28	3,751.00	3,329.70	2,909.66	4,661.25	3,496.20

* Average usage in Palo Alto for different user classes.
Source: DWSG Staff Report 3/18/76.

DWSG developed a conservation program aimed at all users, with special emphasis on domestic and industrial users. The thrust of the campaign was the conservation of water for the benefit of the community in general. After the Palo Alto City Council had adopted a resolution on water usage curtailment (see Exhibit 7A for supporting Staff Report), all Palo Alto residents were sent a message from the Mayor (Exhibit 7B), some informational materials (Exhibit 7C) and two water flow restrictors.[4] The industrial water conservation program is outlined in Exhibit 7D.

Mr. Jay felt that it was too early to assess the long run effect that DWSG's campaign would have. However, owing to the extraordinary publicity given to the water shortage problem by the press as well as radio and television, the community was well aware of the problem; it had reacted by reducing consumption 17 percent compared to 1976, since the emergence of the water shortage problem. The figures, in fact, were so satisfactory that there was a temptation to complacency. However, other resource crises (such as the fuel one of 1973) had shown the public's memory to be very short, and Mr. Jay feared that if the issues were no longer of interest to the media, the public would very rapidly return to its previous levels of consumption. The current shortage was clearly not just a short term problem. Because there was little expectation of significant amounts of additional rainfall before summer, the water shortage problem would probably last until the end of 1977 at least.

Mr. Jay knew that 70 percent more water usage occurred in the summer months when people tended their gardens and watered their lawns, and companies maintained the extensive landscaping around their factories, laboratories, and research centers (see Exhibit 5). He wondered whether those who conserved water when it was supposed to rain would also conserve when it was not supposed to rain. In addition, he felt that

[4] A water flow restrictor, a disc installed on the pipe leading to the shower head, reduced the flow of water by as much as half when showers were taken. (See Exhibit 7D).

San Francisco would soon raise the water reduction order to at least 25 percent less than the previous year's consumption.

The only comfort Mr. Jay had—which was not much—was that his colleagues in Menlo Park, Mountain View, and the other Bay Area cities served by the San Francisco Water Department and the City of San Francisco itself were faced with the same problem. Even worse off were some San Francisco communities that did not use the SFWD System; for example, Marin County, just north of San Francisco, faced a 57 percent reduction target. Because there were no Federal, State, or County conservation goals, each area user (or groups of users) had to set its own goals in accordance with its perception of its own demand and supply condition. Mr. Jay knew there were literally hundreds of officials who needed to design programs in response to the drought and, although he personally knew and had communicated with many of them, none had solutions to the problem.

The Need for Further Conservation Efforts

Though there was awareness of a water shortage problem in the community, Mr. Jay was concerned that the nature of the problem might not have been fully understood. Thus, he wanted to develop a plan that would ensure that the public had the correct perception of the long term nature of the problem and was provided with the information, motivation, and methodology they needed to help overcome the problem. Mr. Jay had a budget of $12,000 for a water conservation program. Nearly $7,000 had already been invested in the current campaign.

The Chief Engineer had to devise and implement a second water conservation plan that would reinforce the impact of the initial conservation campaign and encourage greater conservation in the immediate future. Although some had suggested a "mandatory" water conservation program, he was not sure that the City Council or

February 10, 1977

THE HONORABLE CITY COUNCIL
Palo Alto, California

San Francisco Water Curtailment

Members of the Council:

Since the request from the San Francisco Water Department to curtail water consumption was reported to you on January 24, 1977, staff has been working closely
with the City of San Francisco, members of the Bay Area Water Users Association,
and water agencies of Northern Santa Clara County to develop a uniform program
for water conservation. Resolutions similar to the attached one, which is submitted for your consideration, have been adopted by the Bay Area Water Users
Association representing contract users of San Francisco water. An almost
identical resolution has been approved by the treated water purveyors of Santa
Clara County and the Board of Directors of the Santa Clara County, and the Board
of Directors of the Santa Clara Valley Water District. The purpose of this report
is to request Council approval of the attached resolution, and to advise Council
of steps that are being taken to reduce water consumption in Palo Alto.

Background

Due to two successive years of record drought, the snow-melt inflow to the San
Francisco Hetch Hetchy system has dropped to 40 percent of normal. As a result,
storage in the Hetch Hetchy Reservoir is only 10 percent of capacity and water
production from the Tuolumne River watershed cannot meet the San Francisco
Water Department's goal of providing a minimum thirty-billion gallons (three-
months' supply) of local storage to serve the City of San Francisco and
Peninsula cities. (See Exhibit A). This water deficit has prompted the San
Francisco Public Utilities Commission to request all San Francisco water users
to reduce water consumption by at least 10 percent. Your Utilities Department
staff had developed such a program and the initial phases of it have already
been implemented.

Water Conservation Program - City Facilities

Initially, a memorandum was circulated to all City Department and Division
Heads requesting each to review their operation for opportunities to conserve
water   This memo evoked changes in operations in several departments that will
result in water savings. Notable efforts in conservation were the following:

> The annual water-main flushing program was canceled. Mains will be flushed
> selectively if required.

CMR:153:7

Page Two

. The hydrant-flow program has been curtailed to that required for ascertaining that no valves servicing fire hydrants are inadvertantly closed.

. Annual flower plantings in the City's parks will be eliminated.

. Flow restrictors will be installed on all City facilities where feasible.

. Use of the City Hall fountain has been curtailed.

. Engineering on facilities to deliver reclaimed wastewater to the Golf Course for irrigation needs have been expedited.

. Consideration is being given to the installation of tensiometer control on the Foothills Park irrigation system.

. Flow restrictors will be installed on all City showers and flushometer settings adjusted to reduce flow.

. The use of water for the cleaning of tennis courts and other paved areas has been discontinued.

. The level of irrigation required for the City's parks is being reviewed by maintenance personnel.

. A series of Wednesday night classes in water conservation have been offered by the Utilities Department staff members together with outside speakers.

Palo Alto Unified School District's Conservation Program

The Maintenance and Operations Coordinator of the Palo Alto Unified School District was contacted and responded promptly with an excellent program designed to substantially reduce the water consumption at School District's facilities.

Residential Conservation Program

It is proposed to send a mailing to all utility customers with the following material included:

. A letter from the Mayor requesting the participation of all citizens in the water conservation program (Exhibit B).

. A document showing areas where principal residential water uses occur and where savings may be achieved by the residential consumer (Exhibit C).

. An envelope containing two flow restrictors for showers.

. A sheet instructing the consumer how to install the flow restrictors and how to accomplish savings by installing plastic bottles in the flush tanks of toilets (Exhibit D).

CMR:153:7

Page Three

- Additionally, it is proposed to send a monthly reminder to all utility consumers that a continuation of the water conservation program is imperative. This program will be coordinated with other water purveying agencies in this area.

Industrial Water Conservation Program

The industrial water conservation program proposed by City staff is enclosed herewith (Exhibit E). This program was presented to the Chamber of Commerce's Utilities Task Force and many industrial facility managers on Thursday, February 3, 1977. This program appeared to be well received and stimulated a good exchange of information between representatives of industry, the School District and the City. Your staff is particularly encouraged by the fact that several industries are studying the feasibility of using slightly degraded cooling water for irrigation purposes. This proposed reuse, in addition to saving water, will reduce the hydraulic load on the Wastewater Treatment Plant.

Financial Impact

The total financial impact of the water conservation program will be reported to Council at a later date. Direct expenses of approximately $10,000 are anticipated over a period of one year for the purchasing and mailing of material to the public. It is anticipated that this can be financed from the current budget; thus a budget amendment will not be necessary. Less tangible impacts, such as reduced water sales and purchases, and reduced sewer-use charges and treatment costs, will require more time to properly evaluate.

Recommendation

It is staff's recommendation that Council adopt the attached resolution urging the citizens of Palo Alto to observe the water conservation practices outlined during the drought period.

Respectfully submitted,

Director of Utilities

Assistant City Manager

Attachments

CMR:153:7

A MESSAGE TO THE RESIDENTS OF THE CITY OF PALO ALTO

FROM THE MAYOR

Two successive drought years have reduced the inflow to San Francisco's Hetch Hetchy water supply system by more than 60% and drawn accumulated reserves of water down to an undesirably low level. As a result, the San Francisco Public Utilities Commission, on January 25, 1977, requested all water purveying agencies served by Hetch Hetchy Water to effect a voluntary overall 10% reduction in consumption for at least the next 16 months. If this action fails to bring about the desired reduction in a short period of time, a mandatory program of water rationing will be imposed upon all users of San Francisco water.

As a contracting agency for San Francisco water, the City of Palo Alto is vitally affected by this request to conserve. It is essential that water savings are accomplished as soon as possible. I would therefore urge all Palo Altans to review their present water use practices, to discontinue all nonessential uses and to reduce essential uses wherever possible.

Palo Alto has long been known for its beautifully landscaped homes and parks, but here too we must curb our uses of water by refraining in our planting of water intensive annual flowers, and in the use of water hoses for the aesthetic wash down of cars, windows, houses and driveways, until the weather cycle again makes water more abundant.

Industrial processes that are wasteful of water should be reviewed and methods devised to recycle and conserve water wherever possible.

I am certain that with the cooperation of our citizens and industries, Palo Alto can achieve a saving in water consumption in excess of the 10 percent requested. Please look at the enclosed information which will help you reduce the consumption of water in your home.

Respectfully submitted,

STANLEY R. NORTON
Mayor

YOUR PERSONALIZED WATER SAVING PLAN

Use the chart below to determine where the water is used in your house each day and where you want to cut back.

How many times a day do you use water ??

Directions:

1. Locate in the "water use" column all the ways you use water.

2. On the row next to each water use write the number of times per day you use water in that way.

3. Multiply the number of gallons indicated for that water use by the number of times per day. Enter the answer in the "gallons per day" column.

4. After you finish filling in the "gallons per day" column, add up the total number of gallons in that column.

5. The total gallons per day can be used to devise your own water saving plan. If you wish to save 10% of the water you use, multiply the total by .10. (For example: a family of four found that they used 563 gallons per day. 563 x 0.10 = 56 gallons per day) The total for your water saving plan should be 10% less than your old total (in this example, 563 - 56 = 507).

6. Now go back to the chart and figure out how you can save that number of gallons. Put the ways you plan to use your water in the columns under "water saving plan". For example, the family of four took four showers per day. For their water saving plan they decided to insert a flow restrictor in their shower. The first line in the chart is what their entries for "shower" would look like.

WATER SAVING PLAN

Water Use		Typical Gallons per use	No. of times per day	Gals. per day	Water Saving Plan # of times per day	Gallons per day
Example Shower	Normal, water running	25	4	100		
	Flow restrictor, water running	17			4	68
	Wet down, soap up, rinse off	4				
Shower	Normal, water running	25				
	Flow restrictor, water running	17				
	Wet down, soap up, rinse off	4				
Bath	Full	36				
	Minimal water level	11				
Brushing Teeth	Tap running	10				
	Wet brush, rinse briefly	½				
Shaving	Tap running	20				
	Fill basin	1				
Dishwashing	Tap running	30				
	Wash & rinse in dish pan or sink	5				
Automatic Dishwasher	Full cycle	16				
	Short cycle	7				
Washing Hands	Tap running	2				
	Fill basin	1				
Toilet Flushing	Normal	5				
	Water saving toilet	3				
	Toilet with displacement bottles	4				
Other						
			No. of times per week			
Washing Machine	Full cycle, top water level	8*				
	Short cycle, minimum water level	4*				
			No. of min. per week			
Outdoor Watering	Average hose (10 gallons per minute)	1*				

Note: To compare this with your utility bill, 748 gallons are equal to one unit.

Total gallons per day_____
10% saving (total gallons x .10)_____   Water saving
Water saving goal _____   total_____

* The figures are the average per day for once a week use.

Industrial Water Conservation Program

. Flushometers – Set the rate of closing of these devices to use only that amount of water required for a proper flush of the apparatus served.

. Flow Restrictors – Install these devices wherever possible to limit flow to showers, lavatory basins, wash sinks, etc.

. Faucet Aerators – Install these devices on sinks, lavatory basins and where rinsing is commonly done.

. Area Wash Downs – The use of the wastewater stream to convey wastes to the Regional Water Quality Control Plant is still looked upon with favor, but the use of potable water to wash leaves and debris from lawns and parking lots is not. This job of cleanup can be achieved with more environmental favor by use of brooms or air blowers.

. Fountains – The use of ornamental fountains during periods of drought is a questionable use of water. If used at all, these facilities should utilize recycled water in a nonwasteful manner.

. Cooling Waters – If cooling waters are used in quantity then cooling tower should be utilized. If cooling tower wastewaters are seriously degraded, they should go to sanitary sewer after filing for industrial waste permit. Nondegraded water may pass to storm sewer or be used for irrigation.

. Rinse Baths – If possible, use the cascade rinse approach to minimize water waste. If water is not seriously degraded, consider storing it for irrigation of landscaping.

. Landscape Irrigation – Serious consideration should be given to converting shrubbery irrigation to the drip method. This method can cut use of water for this purpose by 20 to 50 percent. If this system is operated on a time clock, an overriding tensiometer may be installed to limit irrigation to times when soil moisture content is low.

. Turf Irrigation – Sprinklers

  – Pressure at the heads should be proper (normally 35 psi). Excess pressure may cause atomization and hence waste due to evaporation and wind drift

  – Sprinkling in the rain is of no real value to either the turf, the storm sewer system, the water conservation program, or the pocket book, but is a regular activity engaged in by many of the industries on the hill. A good cure for this illness is the installation of a tensiometer, moisture sensory device to override the time-clock programming sprinkler irrigation. It is claimed that a savings of 25 percent or more may be achieved by irrigating when water is needed instead of when the clock says "go". These devices have been used successfully for many years to control irrigation of citrus groves in Southern California. Recent installations have been made in Palm Park in Redwood City, and four more are due to be installed in the Redwood Shores development.

the public would accept an extreme approach. Even in a mandatory program, allocations for different user classes would have to be made and decisions about how to treat unmetered apartment dwellers would be required.[5]

With regard to households, a mandatory limit on water consumption could be stated as a flat amount per person resident in the household or as a percentage reduction from usage in the same month of the previous year. The first approach was insensitive to variation in individual needs; the second approach would penalize those who had been efficient in previous years.

Past experience had suggested that a small price increase would have little effect, and even

---

[5] Typically, apartment buildings had one central water meter, so that it was not possible to determine how much water was being used by each separate unit.

the doubling of the current water rates would only raise the average household bill to $16.00. It was very unlikely that the City Council would approve a policy banning the watering of lawns and, even if approved, the enforcement of such a ban would be exceedingly difficult.

As Mr. Jay sat pondering the problem and looking out of his window at the rain, his telephone rang with the news that the San Francisco Water Department had imposed a 25 percent mandatory reduction in water consumption throughout its service area. Mr. Jay realized he had a few weeks to prepare a water conservation plan for the City Council to discuss and, hopefully, adopt at its March 31, 1977, meeting. In presenting this plan, the Chief Engineer knew that not only would he need to defend it against alternative proposals, but he would also have to indicate why he believed that his plan would work.

TRANS AMERICA CABLE

Frederick C. Livingston
Christopher H. Lovelock

Herb Pomeroy, marketing director for the Alabama division of Trans America Cable (TAC), was jolted out of some deep thinking by the bark that came over the intercom, "Pomeroy, get in here!" It was his boss, Barry Smith, the general manager. As Pomeroy walked down the hall to Smith's office he suspected that this was going to be his first "crisis" meeting since joining Trans America four months earlier, in November 1982.

Entering the office Pomeroy observed that the general manager was somewhat agitated. As Pomeroy sat down, Smith got right to the point:

> I just got a call from Pendergast [president of TAC]. He's concerned that with numbers like February we aren't going to make the sales targets promised in our loan commitments. When I told him that the first half of March showed a net increase of 200 basic subscribers in Kingston and only 28 in Brighton, I thought he was going to croak. He said he and Bradford, the V.P. marketing, would be down from Philadelphia on Tuesday and that we

Copyright © 1983 by the President and Fellows of Harvard College, Harvard Business School case 9-583-150.

better have some new marketing ideas to get this operation back on budget.

Sharing this information with Pomeroy seemed to take some of the tension out of Smith. After a moment of silence he commented, "I hope you didn't have any plans for the weekend."

THE CABLE TELEVISION INDUSTRY

Cable television was originally developed in the late 1940s to serve rural areas which were unable to receive over-the-air television broadcasts because of distance or obstructions such as hills. Community antenna television (CATV) systems used tall antennas placed on geographic high points to capture and process signals from remote broadcast transmitters, and then fed these signals by cable to local households.

The growth of cable television was stimulated by such technological innovations as the development of microwave transmissions and the advent in 1974 of satellite broadcasting. These steps allowed CATV systems to greatly expand their

473

programming. By the early 1980s, many cable systems offered more than 30 channels of programming. These channels typically included: (1) broadcasts from unaffiliated local television stations; (2) "community access" programming in such fields as local government, health care and education (where responsibility for program content was assigned to such institutions as local government agencies, hospitals, and school boards); (3) network broadcasts via local affiliates of CBS, NBC, and ABC, and local PBS stations; (4) satellite-transmitted broadcasts from "super-stations," such as Turner Broadcasting System's WTBS, and from special interest networks such as CNN (Cable News Network), the Christian Broadcasting Network, and ESPN (22 hours of sports and 2 hours of business reporting each day); (5) textual services that provided news, weather, and programming information in text format only; and (6) premium (or pay) services for which subscribers paid an extra fee—these included Home Box Office (first-run movies without cuts plus Broadway plays and special shows), Showtime (movies and shows), Cinemax (principally movies), and Home Theater Network.

Services in categories 1, 4, and 5 were often offered to the cable system at a monthly fee based on the number of subscribers, although some were offered free of charge. Suppliers of premium services (category 6) charged the system a percentage of the monthly fee paid by each subscriber. Services in category 2 were supplied by the system itself with programming being developed by local intermediaries. Services in category 3 were free to the system.

By early 1983, some 5,000 cable systems supplied cable programming (both basic and pay) to approximately 27.5 million U.S. households. The monthly rates for basic services ranged from $6 to $12, with premium services costing an extra $5 to $15 each per month. Most cable systems offered subscribers two or three premium services. Some systems offered discounts on subscriptions to multiple premium services. Although many homes opted only for the basic

service, cable users in "dual pay" systems subscribed on average to 1.4 pay services and those in "triple pay" systems to 1.6 pay services.

Operators of cable systems included both small companies operating a single CATV system and multiple system operators (MSOs), such as American Television and Communications, Continental Cablevision Inc., Tele-Communications Inc., Trans America Cable, and United Television Corp.; each of these corporations operated more than 50 systems that jointly reached a total of over half a million subscribers.

The MSOs had grown rapidly during the past ten years, primarily by developing new systems or acquiring existing ones. However, by 1983, the prospects for growth via these routes, especially the former, were becoming quite constrained. Instead, growth-oriented MSOs found themselves examining opportunities for other ways to expand their revenues. Some of the larger systems were placing increased emphasis on selling advertising time on those programs that they controlled directly; however TAC's efforts in this direction had been very limited thus far.

THE TRANS AMERICA CABLE ORGANIZATION

Trans America was the twelfth largest multiple system operator (MSO) in the United States cable television industry. As of March 1983, TAC served 565,000 basic and 490,000 pay subscribers through a total of 68 systems. Exhibit 1 provides a summary of key operational and financial statistics for TAC from 1976–1982. The firm's management philosophy was to invest autonomy and responsibility for operation of these systems in each of six operating divisions encompassing the following states: Pennsylvania, Indiana/Kentucky, Georgia/Florida, Alabama, Missouri/Arkansas, and Texas.

The general managers of each division ran their operations much like independent companies. These managers were evaluated qualitatively in terms of their ability to get proj-

EXHIBIT 1
KEY OPERATIONAL AND FINANCIAL STATISTICS FOR TRANS AMERICA CABLE, 1976–1982

	Operational data			Financial data (000s omitted)		
Fiscal Year Ending	No. of Systems	No. of Basic Subscribers	No. of Pay Subscribers*	Gross Revenues	Net Profits before Tax & Minority Interest	Total Assets
12/82	66	542,000	476,000	$87,417	$6,928	$171,602
12/81	52	382,000	281,000	56,364	4,370	118,780
12/80	34	286,000	152,000	36,647	4,643	87,146
12/79	29	233,000	100,000	25,651	3,355	49,164
12/78	26	193,000	66,500	18,675	2,864	36,938
12/77	25	167,000	39,000	14,228	1,632	30,769
12/76	23	146,000	11,000	10,772	812	31,120

* Pay subscribers were those who paid an extra monthly fee to obtain one or more premium services such as Home Box Office, Showtime, and Cinemax.

ects completed on time, manage labor relations satisfactorily, and perform effectively. The key financial performance measure was the operating margin (expressed as a percentage of gross revenues) contributed to the parent corporation. However, acceptable performance varied according to the size and maturity of the systems contained within each division; the more mature divisions were regarded as cash cows that could be used to cross-subsidize expenditures in the newer development properties. For fiscal 1983, the Alabama division had a target operating margin of 37 percent.

The division general managers had broad discretion in terms of operating expenditures subject to the constraints imposed by the target operating margin. However, capital expenditures in excess of $100,000 required informal review by corporate management.

There were 30 people working in the Trans America Cable corporate office in Philadelphia. The chairman and president split responsibility between themselves for the six divisions. A 15-person marketing department, under the direction of George Bradford, vice president-marketing, acted as a staff resource to the operating divisions. Among the services provided were ad-

vertising concepts and materials (including newspaper, direct mail, and image campaigns), customer service and sales training, market research, sales and marketing consulting, and programming recommendations. The operating divisions could choose to use the assistance of corporate marketing as much or as little as they wished, and they were "billed" (through intercompany transfers) for such services as were provided. The corporate office also included an eight-person finance department.

TRANS AMERICA CABLE OF GULF CITIES

TAC of Gulf Cities (TAC/GC) was formed in January 1978 when the Alabama division of TAC was granted a 15-year franchise to operate a new system in Brighton, Alabama. A second franchise was awarded to TAC in June 1979, by the nearby city of Kingston. In September 1981, TAC acquired from a competitor the franchise rights for cable service operation in the third Gulf Cities community of Hove. TAC of Gulf Cities operated under the name of "Gulf Cable" in all three cities. TAC/GC had total assets of $40.4 million; plant, property, and equipment were valued at

$39.9 million gross, less accumulated depreciation of $7.6 million. From 1978–82, TAC/GC had accumulated net losses of $6.4 million.

THE GULF CITIES

The Gulf Cities metropolitan area, located on the Gulf of Mexico, comprised three primary cities—Kingston, Brighton, and Hove—as well as the surrounding suburban area of Kingston county (Exhibit 2). At the time of the 1980 census, the metropolitan area had a population of about 800,000 with the bulk being in Kingston (275,000), Brighton (175,000), and Hove (52,000). For analytical and record-keeping purposes, TAC/GC divided each city into numbered "management areas," each comprised of clusters of two or three adjacent census tracts.

Kingston was the largest and most urban of the three cities; it had a large downtown area and in 1983 its harbor was the second biggest port in the southeastern United States. The city's population

EXHIBIT 2
GULF CITIES METROPOLITAN AREA: LOCATION OF MANAGEMENT AREAS

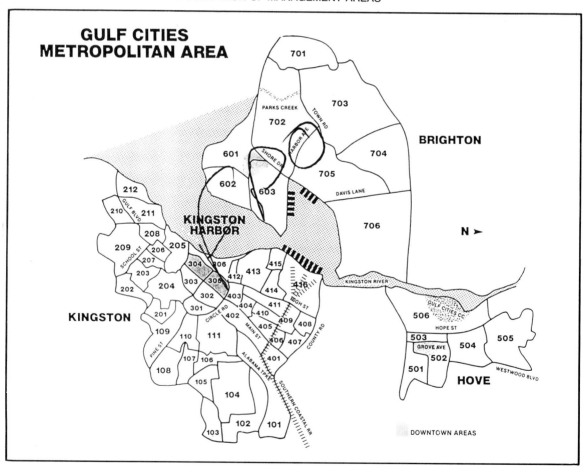

Source: U.S. Bureau of the Census and TAC/Gulf Cities. (Note: names are disguised.)

was more than 50 percent black, and some areas were more than 95 percent black. However, although some neighborhoods were quite run down, there was no area which could be called a ghetto as the term was used in northern cities.

Brighton's population was composed primarily of middle class blue- and white-collar families, including a considerable number of black residents. A number of oil service companies were located in Brighton as well as several shipping companies.

Hove had the highest income of the three Gulf Cities and was almost exclusively white. It was characterized by medium-sized to large homes with nicely manicured lawns. Gulf Cities Country Club was located in Hove.

In early 1983, the Gulf Cities designated market area (DMA) had a total of 320,000 households, making it the sixth largest in the Deep South. The TAC franchise area embraced 180,000 of these households. Single or duplex (two-unit) homes comprised 72 percent of this total; the balance was composed of multi-unit dwellings. Products shipped through the Gulf Cities were primarily agricultural; they were transported to Kingston or Brighton by rail and transferred there to freighters. Other important industries in the Gulf Cities ranged from offshore oil service to various manufacturing businesses, including hand tools and vinyl upholstery.

There were three television stations in Kingston/Brighton. Channel 6 was a CBS affiliate, Channel 9 carried ABC, and Channel 25 (a UHF outlet) offered NBC. In addition, homeowners with large, sophisticated antennas (estimated at 5–10 percent of all households) could get three network affiliates, one independent, and a PBS station from New Orleans plus additional stations from other southern cities. The reception on these distant signals, however, was of very inconsistent quality.

The principal newspaper in the area was the *Gulf Cities Chronicle,* a daily morning paper that also had a Sunday edition. The daily circulation of the *Chronicle* was 220,000 and the Sunday edition, 195,000. Contract ad rates for the daily edition were $15 per column inch and for the Sunday edition, $22.[1] There were also a number of weekly papers in the area, including two in Kingston and one each in Brighton and Hove. Advertising rates for these papers ranged from $4.50 to $7.00 per column inch.

Eleven radio stations offered Gulf Cities residents a wide variety of programming formats, including "middle-of-the-road" music, all news, country, classical, and soul. The audiences for these stations tended to be segmented along such demographic lines as age, race, and education. A representative radio advertising schedule (125 household GRPs) cost about $2,000 per week.[2] A television campaign which delivered 200 household GRPs per week (120 GRPs adults 18–49) cost approximately $5,000 per week.

Gulf Cities residents could choose between a number of entertainment alternatives. There were twelve movie theatres offering a total of twenty-five screens, plus five drive-ins with another seven screens. The Gulf Cities Coliseum offered an event approximately 225 days each year—including rock concerts, country music, Kingston State Baseball, a circus, and the Alabama Symphony. A minor league baseball team, an affiliate of the Houston Astros, was located in Kingston; on fall weekends, a number of college football games took place at various locations within one hour's drive of downtown Kingston.

CABLE SERVICE IN THE GULF CITIES

In spring 1977, the cities of Brighton and Hove independently issued requests for proposals for development of new cable services. Each community attracted considerable interest from cable companies—with Brighton receiving seven proposals and Hove five. After lengthy deliberations, Brighton granted a 15-year franchise to Trans

---

[1] The *Chronicle's* format comprised 189 column inches per page.
[2] GRP (gross rating points) is a measure of advertising reach times frequency.

America in January 1978. Two months later Hove granted a 15-year franchise to Republic Cablevision.

Kingston first requested proposals in May 1978. However, considerable infighting developed between the mayor and the cable commission chairman who was an ally of the chairman of the city council. These problems delayed the process and it was not until February 1979 that the original seven applicants were asked to file amended applications. A number of applicants, TAC included, bid 400 megahertz, 52 channel systems. The franchise was awarded to TAC in June 1979 and the first subscriber was turned on in August 1980.

Once the Kingston franchise was awarded to TAC, Republic Cablevision quickly lost interest in the Gulf Cities area. Republic had hoped to use Hove as a springboard to the Kingston franchise (much as TAC had, in fact, done with Brighton). Hove alone was not large enough to justify Republic's operating in the Gulf Cities since that company's next nearest system was over 500 miles away. Within a matter of months, Republic entered into negotiations to sell Hove to TAC, accomplishing the sale in September 1981. Hove had a 35-channel system like Brighton's, but equipment, programming, and pricing were different. In each of the three systems, there was a one-time installation fee of $20 when a new customer was first supplied with service. However, this was sometimes waived as a promotional device during major marketing campaigns. No installation charges had been imposed during the initial introductory marketing campaigns following system turn on. When additional premium services were requested by existing customers, there was a $15 charge per visit. However, no charges were levied for service deletions.

The incremental costs of providing basic service to a new subscriber were quite modest (approximately $1.85 per month) once the initial installation and connection task (which cost TAC/GC about $50) had been completed. A cost of about $18 was incurred on each occasion that a formerly served home was reconnected or an existing subscriber added one or more premium services. Disconnecting service or downgrading (eliminating one or more premium services) cost the company $15. TAC/GC paid a monthly royalty fee to the suppliers of premium services; in 1983 these fees were set at 44 percent of the monthly subscription charge for HBO, 41 percent for Showtime, and 39 percent for Cinemax.

Marketing and Penetration

Marketing experience in the Gulf Cities had been mixed. Exhibit 3 gives quarterly data on the number of subscribers and penetration for each service in the three cities since turn on. On balance, the Brighton results were considered to be good, as were the basic subscriber numbers in Hove. However, Kingston had proved to be a difficult market to penetrate.

To head up the marketing effort in TAC of Gulf Cities, Barry Smith had hired Frank DeFelice as sales manager for Brighton, subsequently extending his responsibilities to Kingston and Hove. Prior to selling the Hove system to TAC, Republic had subcontracted marketing efforts to outside sales firms. DeFelice was a cable veteran, having started in the industry as a salesman in 1973; he had served as a sales manager in several locations since 1976.

In all three systems, cable was introduced through door-to-door sales. As was typical in newly constructed cable systems, sales levels reflected the construction crews' progress in extending the cable into new areas. In Brighton it took 12 months from the April 1979 turn-on date to market the system to all households in the city. Hove, being smaller, proved slightly faster and the construction task to make cable available to all households was completed within six months of the July 1979 turn on. The sales performance in Brighton, marketed through 1979 and into

EXHIBIT 3
QUARTERLY SUBSCRIBER DATA FOR TRANS AMERICA CABLE, 1979–82

	Kingston						Brighton					Hove (since acquisition by TAC/GC)				
	No. of Homes Passed	Subscribers					No. of Homes Passed	Subscribers				No. of Homes Passed	Subscribers			
		Basic	% Pen.	HBO*	Show-time*	Cine-max*		Basic	% Pen.	HBO*	Cine-max*		Basic	% Pen.	Show-time*	HBO*
6/79							5,479	1,455	26.5	1,260	193**					
9/79							9,953	2,968	29.8	2,525	516**					
12/79							18,009	4,413	55.1	3,587	933**					
3/80							26,653	6,576	24.6	5,342	1,407**					
6/80							36,562	9,725	26.5	7,867	1,770**					
9/80	1,072	63	5.8	49	33	17	47,547	12,763	26.8	10,309	2,142**					
12/80	8,697	1,353	15.5	1,073	563	253	50,771	15,600	30.7	12,536	2,769**					
3/81	21,788	2,829	12.9	2,312	1,196	518	59,331	18,549	31.2	14,467	4,878					
6/81	35,030	4,717	13.4	3,734	2,703	1,382	59,331	21,259	35.8	15,927	6,464	19,975	5,992	29.9	2,369	1,798
9/81	51,194	8,205	16.0	6,708	5,315	2,596	61,413	24,803	40.3	18,539	8,746	19,975	5,713	28.6	2,302	1,216
12/81	62,426	13,627	21.8	11,007	9,063	4,444	62,680	27,668	44.1	20,293	10,473	20,225	5,925	29.2	2,587	1,492
3/82	74,864	18,263	24.3	14,414	11,692	5,823	62,956	27,951	44.3	20,488	9,925	20,415	6,309	30.9	2,902	1,836
6/82	88,218	22,889	25.9	17,901	13,797	7,180	63,474	28,188	44.4	19,917	9,770	20,663	6,683	32.3	3,213	2,365
9/82	90,626	27,013	29.8	20,689	15,596	7,936	63,702	27,986	43.9	19,865	9,536	20,903	6,901	33.0	3,350	2,499
12/82	91,797	28,903	31.4	21,655	15,998	8,104	63,874	28,207	44.1	19,154	9,679	20,929	7,058	33.7	3,629	2,733

* By definition, all subscribers received basic service (the percentage in the following column show the basic penetration of homes passed). They had the option to subscribe to HBO, Showtime and Cinemax separately. The data in these columns are a subset of the basic service totals.

** Prior to February 1, 1981, Brighton subscribers could receive Home Theater Network (HTN), but this option was replaced by Cinemax on that date.

Source: TAC of Gulf Cities.

1980, was viewed as very good by TAC's Alabama division, but results in Kingston, sold between August 1980 through mid-1982, were regarded as quite disappointing, yielding a penetration of slightly more than 30 percent. As of March 1983, virtually all single-family homes and apartment complexes in all three cities had been approached at least once by door-to-door salespeople.

The "remarket" (a second round of intensive marketing efforts) proceeded on a parallel course in all three systems. In each case (including Hove since it was acquired) direct sales was the primary means of remarket, with sales reps sweeping methodically through the entire territory. Installation charges were waived for a few days only while the cable sales representative was in the immediate neighborhood. In 1982, the sales force employed in the three systems averaged a total of approximately 25 persons (against a target sales force of 30), all of whom were employed on a full-time basis. Most sales reps were recruited locally; the majority were in their twenties. All had participated in a one-week training and familiarization program. Much of their time was spent selling to new addresses and participating in apartment sweeps, as opposed to making return visits to homes previously contacted. Compensation was "commission only" with an average sales representative making $250–$350 per week, and the best salespeople making $500 or more. The expectation was that each sales rep would contact 20 addresses ("cards") per day. Cards were assigned geographically on a neighborhood-by-neighborhood basis. TAC/GC management was disappointed in the remarket results. Sales effectiveness, as measured by "sales to cards" (see Exhibit 4) was low in all 3 markets, but Kingston, where the remarket had begun in early 1982, was the weakest. To supplement the direct sales effort, acquisition and upgrade direct mail campaigns—supplied by the Philadelphia marketing department—were run in 1982. The results were considered satisfactory, but not outstanding (Exhibit 5).

Programming

As of March 1983, the programming lineup in the three cities varied considerably, reflecting their different histories. Exhibits 6 and 7 indicate the current channel availability and prices for each system, and the dates when new services were added. No further rate increases could be imposed in any of the three systems before April 1984. In terms of premium services, which required an additional subscription fee, each system was different. The Kingston system was launched with Home Box Office (HBO), Showtime, and Cinemax, which remained the lineup in 1983. In Brighton, the original offerings were HBO and Home Theater Network (HTN). On February 1, 1981, Cinemax was offered to HTN users as a replacement on a negative option basis (i.e., HTN subscribers were offered Cinemax as a substitute at the HTN rate for one month and then had to call TAC if they did *not* want to continue receiving Cinemax). In Hove, Showtime was the foundation service from turn on, but HBO was added within three months of launch to replace HTN after the latter performed poorly in initial marketing.

Reflecting the differences in services offered and variations in penetration rates for the premium services, the revenue breakdown for each of the three systems varied quite widely (Exhibit 8).

The Loan Commitment

In the process of obtaining financing for the three Gulf Cities cable systems, Trans America Cable had committed itself to meet budgets for both number of subscribers and number of revenue units.[3] These targets were respectively 74,000 basic subscribers and 178,300 revenue units by December 1983. The financial results of TAC/GC in 1981 and 1982 (Exhibit 9) had been disap-

---

[3] Each service, basic or premium, constituted one revenue unit. Thus a household which subscribed to basic service plus two premium services represented three revenue units.

EXHIBIT 4

1982–83 REMARKET SALES RESULTS IN GULF CITIES 2 FOR TRANS AMERICA CABLE

	Kingston					Brighton					Hove				
	No. of New Subs.[1]	Sales/Cards %[2]	% Contact[3]	% Pay[4]	Pay %[5]	No. Sales[1]	Sales/Cards %[2]	% Contact[3]	% Pay[4]	Pay %[5]	No. Sales[1]	Sales/Cards %[2]	% Contact[3]	% Pay[4]	Pay %[5]
'82 June	1209	31	73	74	164	308	15	77	77	119	252	19	82	79	135
July	460	23	77	81	162	165	16	79	74	115	363	18	85	70	132
Aug.	750	19	80	76	173	157	14	81	75	115	329	15	88	80	135
Sept.	733	18	88	71	154	251	13	82	73	112	315	19	90	78	133
Oct.	426	11	85	56	122	256	11	79	70	111	307	21	82	82	136
Nov.	510	14	81	57	126	227	15	85	67	112	296	19	83	77	129
Dec.	483	12	82	55	125	199	14	86	72	115	215	17	84	76	125
'83 Jan.	516	9	86	60	134	215	13	89	75	116	274	15	86	78	135
Feb.	582	11	81	65	141	243	12	88	80	122	289	14	88	82	141

[1] Number of homes sold that month by the remarket salesforce (excludes other sources of new subscriptions).
[2] Number of sales expressed as a percentage of the addresses ("cards") within the geographic area being marketed (sold).
[3] Number of households contacted expressed as a percentage of the addresses (see above).
[4] Percent of new subscribers taking one or more premium services (e.g. HBO) in addition to basic.
[5] Total number of premium services sold as a percentage of the number of new subscribers.
Source: TAC of Gulf Cities.

481

EXHIBIT 5
DIRECT RESPONSE CAMPAIGN RESULTS, 1982, FOR TRANS AMERICA CABLE

Date		Kingston			Brighton			Hove		
		Revenue Units Acquired[1]	% Response[2]	Cost per Unit Acquired[3]	Revenue Units Acquired	% Response	Cost per Unit Acquired	Revenue Units Acquired	% Response	Cost per Unit Acquired
Feb.	Direct mail campaign (New sub. acquisition)	1,504	3.39	$8.99	288	1.92	$14.52	—	—	—
April	HBO free preview (Upgrade)	—	—	—	262	3.51	8.73	239	3.93	$8.23
June	Summer reruns (New sub. acquisition)	990	0.52	5.32	—	—	—	—	—	—
Sept.	WTBS campaign (New sub. acquisition)	1,333	2.69	16.29	—	—	—	862	3.47	9.62
Oct.	HBO free preview (Upgrade)	—	—	—	—	—	—	267	4.16	7.96
Oct.	Cinemax free preview (Upgrade)	615	2.49	11.96	677	2.43	12.04	—	—	—
Nov.	Showtime free preview	793	2.32	12.13	—	—	—	296	4.43	8.17

[1] Units acquired include all basic and premium service units. All campaigns will attract both new subscribers and additional pay units.
[2] The response rate refers to the number of households that respond to a promotion as a percentage of the total potential. Each responding household may take more than one revenue unit.
[3] Cost per unit acquired is derived by dividing the total cost of the campaign by the number of revenue units acquired.
Note: All campaigns included direct mail with newspaper and radio support—except the "Summer Reruns" campaign which included only newspaper.
Source: TAC of Gulf Cities.

pointing. This was primarily due to the shortfall in basic and pay subscribers in Kingston and Hove. Exhibit 10 outlines the cumulative monthly subscriber budget projections for all three systems in 1983. Management recognized that these month-end numbers reflected only one of several alternative ways of meeting the year-end loan commitment figures. However, there were no system extensions planned for 1983, nor any possibility of gaining new franchise territory, so that all revenue units must come from the 176,000 homes currently passed by the cable.

The poor historical results and optimistic loan commitments resulted in management's setting some very ambitious objectives for 1983. However, the goal of obtaining new revenue units had to be achieved within the constraints of maintaining acceptable operating margins.

THE 1983 MARKETING PLAN

In August 1982, Barry Smith had assigned Frank DeFelice the task of developing 1983 subscriber projections and a marketing plan. DeFelice submitted a marketing plan which emphasized door-to-door sales, but also included a telephone upgrade campaign, a direct mail acquisition campaign (at a cost of $0.65 per mailer, including media support), and preview weekends that enabled existing cable subscribers to receive a sample of premium service programming free of charge; the preview program would cost TAC/CG $0.51 per prospect, including media support. The sales commission on telephone sales was set at $4.50 per revenue unit, with overhead costs estimated to average $0.35 per unit. At the urging of Barry Smith, acting on feedback from George

EXHIBIT 6
CHANNEL LINE-UPS IN MARCH 1983, TRANS AMERICA CABLE

Channel	System		
	Kingston (Turned on 8/80)	**Brighton** (Turned on 4/79)	**Hove** (Turned on 7/79)
2	Cinemax	Cinemax (2/81)	CNN Headline News
3	Nickelodeon/Arts	Nickelodeon/Arts	CTV-3-Local
4	Program Guide	Program Guide	Time & Weather
5	WBRT-Brighton-NBC	WBRT-Brighton-NBC	ESPN
6	WKAL-Kingston-CBS	WKAL-Kingston-CBS	WKAL-Kingston-CBS
7	CTV-7-Local	CTV-7-Local	Program guide
8	WGLF-Kingston-ABC	WGLF-Kingston-ABC	WGLF-Kingston-ABC
9	The Weather Channel (10/82)	The Weather Channel (10/82)	The Weather Channel (10/82)
10	Cable News Network	Cable News Network (9/81)	Satellite Program Network
11	Satellite Program Network	Satellite Program Network	WAET-Brighton-PBS
12	WSFA-Montgomery-ABC	WSFA-Montgomery-ABC	WSFA-Montgomery-ABC
13	—	—	WBRT-Brighton-NBC
14	HBO	HBO	—
15	USA Network	USA Network (3/80)	CBN Network
16	Community Access	Community Access	—
17	WTBS-Atlanta-Ind.	WTBS-Atlanta-Ind.	Showtime
18	UPI News	UPI News	HBO
19	Cable Classifieds	Cable Classifieds	—
20	WAET-Brighton-PBS	WAET-Brighton-PBS	—
21	Dow Jones News (10/82)	Dow Jones News (10/82)	Dow Jones News (10/82)
22	—	Educational Access	USA Network
23	—	—	Government Access
24	ESPN	ESPN (3/80)	Cable News Network
25	C-SPAN	C-SPAN (9/81)	WGN-Chicago-Ind.
26	WGNO-New Orleans-Ind.	WGNO-New Orleans-Ind.	WGNO-New Orleans-Ind.
27	CBN Network	CBN Network	WTBS-Atlanta-Ind.
28	Government Access	Government Access	Nickelodeon/Arts
29	—	—	C-Span
30	—	—	Educational Access
31	—	—	Government Access
32	—	—	Health Access
33	Music Television (10/82)	Music Television (10/82)	Music Television (10/82)
36	Modern Satellite Network	—	—
41	Educational Access	—	—
42	Library Access	—	—
44	Community Bulletin Board	—	—
45	Alabama News	—	—
49	World News (UPI)	—	—
50	WCTV-Tallahassee-CBS	—	—
51	Sports News (UPI)	—	—
55	Showtime	—	—

Note: Dates in parentheses refer to start-up dates for new services added to those available at the time of system turn on.

EXHIBIT 7
TRANS AMERICA CABLE'S PRICES FOR CABLE
SERVICE IN THE GULF CITIES

Service Option	Kingston	Brighton	Hove
Basic	$7.50	$8.25	$7.95
HBO	$7.50	$8.95	$9.50
Showtime	$7.50	NA	$9.50
Cinemax	$7.50	$8.95	NA
Discount	—	—	$2.00 for dual pay
Additional outlet (for second TV set)	$1.95	$2.50	$2.50
FM	$1.95	$2.50	$2.50
Converter*	$2.50 for remote;	$2.50 for remote	$1.95 for remote; $3.95 for wireless
Guide	NA	$1.25	NA

* A converter is a piece of equipment that replaces the customary channel selection controls on the television set with a control tied to the specific channels supplied by the cable system. Remote controls were connected to the set by wire; wireless controls had no direct connection. TAC purchased converters in bulk from a manufacturer at $80 each.
Source: TAC of Gulf Cities.

Bradford in Philadelphia, an acquisition/retention marketing campaign was added to be implemented in television and newspaper. The advertising for this campaign stressed the quality and variety of programming available on cable, as well as Gulf Cable's commitment to customer service. This campaign was slated to run in the

EXHIBIT 8
TRANS AMERICA CABLE: REVENUE BREAKDOWN BY
SYSTEM, 1982

	Kingston	Brighton	Hove
Basic service	31.5%	40.1%	44.6%
HBO	30.2	33.4	17.8
Cinemax	19.9	15.1	—
Showtime	9.6	—	24.8
Advertising	7.8	5.4	6.2
Other income	0.6	3.7	4.2
Installation income	1.4	2.3	2.4
Total	100.0%	100.0%	100.0%

EXHIBIT 9
TAC OF GULF CITIES OPERATING STATEMENTS FOR
1981 AND 1982
(000s omitted)

	1981	1982
Revenues		
Basic income	$3,598	$ 6,307
Premium service income	3,894	7,636
Installation income	219	354
Other income	719	1,429
Total	$8,430	$15,726
Costs and expenses		
Operating expenses	2,056	3,704
General and administrative	1,171	3,220
Premium service fees	1,655	3,207
Marketing	705	823
Program production	190	399
Total	6,323	11,293
Operating income before depreciation	2,107	4,433
Depreciation	$2,217	$ 2,406
Interest	$3,710	$ 4,619
Total	5,927	7,025
Loss before income taxes	(3,820)	(2,592)
Provision (credit) for income taxes	(802)	(609)
Net profit (loss)	($3,018)	($ 1,983)

Source: TAC of Gulf Cities.

Gulf Cities for the balance of 1983. Costs were estimated at $7,500 for a two-week flight of television commercials and $4,500 for the newspaper campaign. The complete marketing plan is summarized in Exhibit 11.

By October, Smith had concluded that it was time for a change. It was clear to him that a strategy of relying primarily on a direct sales approach to the market with some support from other techniques, under the direction of a sales manager like Frank DeFelice, was not producing a meaningful improvement in penetrations. To develop a new marketing approach he undertook a search for a divisional marketing director, which proved fruitful with the mid-November hiring of Herb Pomeroy, previously a regional

EXHIBIT 10
CUMULATIVE MONTHLY SUBSCRIBER PROJECTIONS FOR TAC GULF CITIES, 1983: ACTUAL vs BUDGET, FEBRUARY 1983

Kingston

		January	February	March	April	May	June	July	August	September	October	November	December
Basic	Budget	30,500	31,000	31,500	32,000	32,600	33,000	33,500	34,000	34,600	35,000	35,500	36,000
	Actual	29,215	29,840										
HBO	Budget	22,875	23,250	23,625	24,000	24,475	24,750	25,125	25,500	25,975	26,250	26,625	27,000
	Actual	21,865	22,363										
Showtime	Budget	18,300	18,600	18,900	19,200	19,600	19,800	20,100	20,400	20,800	21,000	21,300	21,600
	Actual	16,178	16,638										
Cinemax	Budget	9,150	9,300	9,450	9,600	9,800	9,900	10,050	10,200	10,450	10,500	10,650	10,800
	Actual	8,244	8,633										

Brighton

		January	February	March	April	May	June	July	August	September	October	November	December
Basic	Budget	28,100	28,200	28,300	28,400	28,600	28,600	28,150	28,750	28,950	28,950	29,050	29,200
	Actual	28,282	28,555										
HBO	Budget	19,300	19,600	19,900	20,200	20,600	20,800	21,100	21,400	21,800	22,000	22,300	21,600
	Actual	19,224	19,474										
Cinemax	Budget	10,250	10,500	10,750	11,000	11,350	11,500	11,750	12,000	12,350	12,500	12,750	13,000
	Actual	9,804	10,084										

Hove

		January	February	March	April	May	June	July	August	September	October	November	December
Basic	Budget	7,200	7,350	7,500	7,650	7,900	7,950	8,050	8,200	8,450	8,500	8,650	8,800
	Actual	7,238	7,492										
Showtime	Budget	3,650	3,800	3,950	4,100	4,350	4,400	4,550	4,700	4,950	5,000	5,150	5,300
	Actual	3,764	3,981										
HBO	Budget	2,850	3,050	3,250	3,450	3,750	3,850	4,000	4,200	4,500	4,600	4,800	5,000
	Actual	2,863	3,072										

Source: TAC of Gulf Cities.

EXHIBIT 11
MONTHLY SCHEDULE OF PROPOSED MARKETING ACTIVITIES FOR GULF CITIES REGION: TRANS AMERICA CABLE, 1983

System	Jan.	Feb.	Mar.	April	May	June	July	Aug.	Sept.	Oct.	Nov.	Dec.
Kingston	D/S	D/S TV	D/S PREV-H,C	D/S	D/S TV/NAC	D/S	D/S	D/S O/P-C,S	D/S FULL	D/S PREV-C	D/S TV FOS	D/S FOS
Brighton	D/S	D/S TV	D/S PREV-H,C	D/S	D/S TV/NAC	D/S	D/S	D/S O/P-C	D/S FULL	D/S PREV-C	D/S TV FOS	D/S FOS
Hove	D/S	D/S TV	D/S PREV-H	D/S PREV-S	D/S TV/NAC	D/S O/P-S,H	D/S O/P-S,H	D/S O/P-S,H	D/S FULL	D/S PREV-H	D/S TV FOS	D/S FOS

KEY:
D/S: Direct sales (remarket).
O/P: Outgoing telephone upgrade (H = HBO) (C = Cinemax) (S = Showtime).
FULL: Full direct mail campaign.
PREV: Preview weekend (H = HBO) (C = Cinemax) (S = Showtime) (P = Outgoing phone support).
FOS: Front office sales (a front office training program for customer service representatives).
TV: Television acquisition campaign.
NAC: Newspaper acquisition campaign.
Source: TAC of Gulf Cities.

marketing manager with Columbia Cablevision. Feeling that he had been passed over for the marketing job, Frank DeFelice resigned, effective January 15, 1983.

Pomeroy held a BA from Tulane University and an MBA from Northwestern. Prior to joining Columbia in 1977 he had worked as promotion manager for Six Flags Amusement Park outside of St. Louis. From 1977 to 1982 he had held various positions with Columbia Cablevision, including marketing trainee, system marketing manager and regional marketing manager. Columbia was considered to be one of the most sophisticated cable firms in terms of marketing and Pomeroy had been exposed to a variety of marketing concepts and techniques.

To help him in redirecting the marketing effort at TAC/GC, Pomeroy spent a considerable amount of time looking at both TAC/GC's past marketing efforts and data on the Gulf Cities markets. His assessment of the previous marketing effort was not very positive. The figures told the story. Basic penetration in Kingston was well below the accepted industry minimum standard of 40 percent of all homes passed. Premium penetration was barely acceptable in Kingston (158 percent pay to basic was not too bad for triple pay), but the premium to basic levels in Brighton (102 percent) and Hove (90 percent) were clearly unacceptable for dual pay systems.[4] He had also broken down the three markets according to the percentage of subscribers with basic service only and with basic plus one, two, and three premium services (Exhibit 12).

Pomeroy had looked at churn rates which averaged 1.8 percent for basic, 3.2 percent for the first pay, 4.7 percent for the second pay, and 6.0 percent for the third over the three systems and found them to be lower than the industry average.[5] However, no analysis had been done to determine what types of subscribers were terminating or downgrading service. House sales (those coming in from people moving to homes in the area) and those sold by word of mouth seemed to be on target. On balance Pomeroy figured that these two components would result in a net monthly decline of 0.5 percent in basic, 0.9 percent in the first pay, 1.4 percent in the second, and 1.8 percent in the third without any consistent marketing effort. This was well within industry tolerance.

[4] Premium service penetration is calculated by summing the number of homes subscribing to each premium service and dividing this by the number of basic subscriptions. A figure of 158 percent indicates that *on average* each subscriber to the basic service also pays for 1.58 premium services (out of the three available in this "triple pay" system).

[5] The churn rate is the percentage of current subscribers who terminate basic or pay service each month.

EXHIBIT 12
PENETRATION BREAKDOWNS IN GULF CITIES MARKETS, FEBRUARY 1983

	Kingston	Brighton	Hove
Basic	3,379 (.11)	8,569 (.30)	1,908 (.25)
Basic + 1 pay	12,801 (.43)	10,414 (.36)	4,115 (.55)
Basic + 2 pay	6,227 (.21)	9,572 (.34)	1,469 (.20)
Basic + 3 pay	7,433 (.25)	—	—
Total subscribers	29,840	28,555	7,492
Total homes passed	91,797	63,874	20,929

Source: TAC of Gulf Cities.

EXHIBIT 13
TRANS AMERICA CABLE: MEMORANDUM ON DIRECT SALES COMMISSION AND GOALS FOR GULF CITIES

To: Herb Pomeroy   December 8, 1982
From: Frank DeFelice
Re: Direct Sales Commission and Goals

Kingston and Brighton/Hove both have direct sales forces. Since most homes in the franchise areas have been marketed, this current effort is primarily "remarket." As you know, the "remarket" sale is more difficult because many consumers have already decided against receiving the service. The following sales targets and commission rates were established:

Sales targets:	**Kingston**	**Brighton/Hove**
Contact % (people contacted/cards issued)[1]	88%	88%
Close % (people who take service/all people contacted)	19%	18%
Pay penetration (percentage of customers who take at least one pay)	80%	82%
Pay sales index (number of pay units sold expressed as a percentage of all new customers)[2]	175%	145%

Commission rates:
$7.00 per revenue unit (basic or each pay = 1 unit)

Cancellations:
1 All commissions will be deducted if order is cancelled before installation.
2 Commission will be deducted for downgrades and disconnects during the first thirty days of service.

One problem was that no minimum standard was set. We *assumed* that a commission structure would be enough to motivate all salespeople. However, it seems that poor individual performance was dragging down overall system performance. Therefore, in addition to the sales commissions and targets, a minimal quota and bonus program was instituted. Including overhead, we projected a total cost of $8.25 per revenue unit acquired.

Individual quota:
1 50 total units per week.
2 Failure to sell at least 50 units for several weeks is grounds for probation.

Individual bonus:
Goals and bonus vary according to monthly objective of sales manager.

---

[1] "Cards issued" referred to the list of prospects to be contacted given to sales reps during each sales period.
[2] That is, if 100 new customers subscribed to 175 pay units, the percentage would be 175 percent.
Source: TAC of Gulf Cities.

The problem seemed to be in acquiring new subscribers and upgrading existing subscribers to additional pay units. Pomeroy knew that the current approach to door-to-door remarket was not working. He did not know whether this was due to the sales force itself, the nature of the market (demographics, etc.), or a negative attitude toward cable. He sensed that a monolithic "blunderbuss" approach to sales was at least part of the problem. Before leaving TAC/GC, Frank DeFelice had summarized in a memo the sales targets and commission rates established for the direct sales force (Exhibit 13). At Columbia Cablevision, Pomeroy had had experience with a better-paid, more targeted sales force which had sold very successfully in an upper income community that had hitherto been poorly penetrated. Perhaps something similar would work in Gulf Cities, he thought.

In addition to looking at penetration data, sales results, and campaign results, Pomeroy had collected some demographic information on each of the management areas[6] in the three cities (Exhibit 14), and had commissioned a telephone survey, the purpose of which was to determine the attitude of Gulf Cities residents concerning cable television; the results of this survey are summarized in Exhibit 15. Pomeroy also had access to various industry research studies; one of these had studied likeliness to subscribe among current nonsubscribers in three separate and relatively diverse cable systems (Exhibit 16).

THE SEARCH FOR A TURNAROUND STRATEGY

As they sat together in the general manager's office, Smith and Pomeroy both realized that meeting the year-end budget numbers was a "do

[6] Management areas represented consolidations by TAC/GC of two or more U.S. census tracts.

or die" situation. TAC had been operating in Gulf Cities for nearly four years, and there could really be no excuse for missing the 1983 projections. Both men recognized that their jobs were probably on the line, based on the next nine months' performance. After a short silence Barry Smith spoke again, "You've been here for about four months now, Herb. What do you think it is going to take to turn this market around?"

Pomeroy thought briefly. He realized that a timely decision and quick turnaround were important if the problem was to be solved and the year-end numbers met. Then he told Smith:

> I reckon that a new marketing program will have to be in place within six weeks—say May 1—to give TAC/GC a fighting chance. Rather than shooting from the hip, I'd like to outline a provisional strategy for you on Monday morning. I've spent quite a bit of my time during the last few months trying to get a handle on what's going on in the Gulf Cities market.

Barry Smith looked a little more cheerful. "Have a nice weekend!" he said with a perverse grin.

EXHIBIT 14
DEMOGRAPHIC DATA BY TAC MANAGEMENT AREAS*

Management Area	Households	Penetration 12/82	House Income	% Black, Other	Medium Age	% Apartment
Kingston:						
101	364	28.1%	$11,389	38.8%	49.3	0.0%
102	4,980	31.1	20,058	6.1	54.1	8.5
103	1,516	36.5	21,233	99.3	26.8	28.2
104	6,026	34.5	21,969	25.8	49.2	31.9
105	1,444	38.0	31,205	88.3	32.4	22.2
106	1,742	44.9	31,461	96.9	34.2	27.7
107	2,364	36.8	20,322	98.6	28.5	3.2
108	3,252	37.4	26,717	94.4	28.1	1.6
109	2,624	50.1	22,184	94.4	27.9	2.2
110	2,722	37.9	22,441	98.4	30.6	19.6
111	2,576	35.2	28,981	94.7	26.0	7.4
201	1,464	27.0	13,385	99.0	16.1	20.6
202	3,419	28.3	13,162	99.9	18.0	13.6
203	1,892	30.1	14,632	99.7	29.6	2.6
204	2,580	43.1	16,391	97.2	19.1	26.2
205	1,898	38.0	12,485	84.2	24.8	22.2

EXHIBIT 14 *(continued)*

Management Area	Households	Penetration 12/82	House Income	% Black, Other	Medium Age	% Apartment
Kingston: *(continued)*						
206	1,464	50.6	13,755	97.7	28.2	1.0
207	1,178	42.2	13,199	99.6	28.0	4.6
208	1,812	33.3	14,320	89.4	24.2	15.2
209	2,706	34.0	15,971	99.1	25.4	11.0
210	1,452	36.2	27,292	57.5	43.3	14.4
211	490	35.5	13,868	48.7	29.4	2.3
212	1,258	36.5	24,607	53.0	38.2	0.0
301	2,264	12.9	9,228	98.7	17.9	44.5
302	1,664	14.6	12,509	97.1	45.2	5.4
303	2,160	15.0	23,323	32.3	40.4	87.1
304	641	16.6	6,692	28.0	22.3	37.5
305	640	16.3	18,716	35.6	59.7	0.0
306	603	15.0	12,313	65.8	34.1	0.0
401	445	23.6	15,761	7.4	42.5	12.6
402	1,600	21.3	13,755	96.7	35.4	3.6
403	711	21.2	20,763	32.9	20.6	55.3
404	4,458	21.9	24,754	8.7	29.2	58.2
405	4,077	15.0	28,576	10.9	43.9	54.9
406	1,939	23.6	23,474	6.8	41.6	61.5
407	2,953	22.9	18,407	2.0	48.6	37.4
408	1,712	22.2	23,196	16.4	48.3	15.3
409	2,423	21.9	21,571	28.2	41.4	28.9
410	3,199	13.4	27,542	4.3	39.9	29.2
411	3,410	11.1	14,218	65.4	32.5	13.8
412	954	39.5	13,754	4.8	31.1	31.1
413	1,233	35.5	38,809	69.1	38.4	38.4
414	1,691	34.2	22,140	93.9	32.2	32.2
415	935	32.9	27,390	99.4	33.0	33.0
416	862	33.3	12,821	98.7	26.4	26.4
City totals, averages	91,797	31.4%	$19,500	64%	34	22%
Brighton:						
601	6,803	28.4%	$20,509	80.7%	28.2	7.4%
602	8,169	36.6	30,603	30.5	34.4	36.2
603	3,366	48.2	22,138	3.3	50.2	3.5
701	815	45.3	24,082	47.7	29.9	0.0
702	6,621	51.5	27,933	47.6	27.4	12.1
703	9,145	54.0	28,076	21.7	26.3	16.3
704	5,952	46.7	25,061	29.3	25.7	0.0
705	8,525	50.4	22,046	32.0	31.1	0.8
706	14,478	40.5	25,804	33.7	25.4	21.0
City totals, averages	63,874	44.1%	$25,000	59%	33	20%
Hove:						
501	3,966	31.2%	$25,725	1.7%	44.1	28.5%
502	4,728	26.7	24,679	1.0	48.8	6.6
503	2,367	23.6	28,662	0.8	56.2	48.8
504	3,485	38.8	39,062	12.7	38.5	1.8
505	3,803	42.8	74,693	1.9	25.5	3.5
506	2,580	39.6	94,980	1.6	46.6	9.9
City totals, averages	20,929	33.7%	$48,000	3%	43	16%

* Management areas represented consolidations of two or more U.S. Census Tracts.
Source: U.S. Bureau of the Census and TAC/Gulf Cities.

EXHIBIT 15

PRINCIPAL FINDINGS OF TELEPHONE SURVEY ADMINISTERED TO A RANDOM SAMPLE OF 309 GULF CITIES RESIDENTS, JANUARY 1983

	Cable Subscribers, %	Former Subscribers, %	Non-Subscribers, %
Have you ever heard of cable television before?			
Yes	97.6	91.7	97.8
No	2.4	.0	1.4
Don't know	.0	8.3	.8
How would you describe Cable to a friend?			
Offers wide variety of programs	62.2	50.0	39.7
Offers movies	31.1	41.7	23.7
Offers specials	6.7	16.7	2.3
Offers sports	11.6	.0	9.9
Good reception	1.2	.0	2.3
Too expensive	.0	.0	3.8
Poor service	.0	.0	4.6
Other	20.7	75.0	22.1
As a Gulf Cities subscriber, what types of programming do you think are available to you?			
Movies	84.1	66.7	74.8
Sports	63.4	91.7	45.0
Entertainment specials	25.6	16.7	9.9
Programs for adult audiences	6.1	8.3	14.5
Foreign films	3.7	8.3	.8
24 hours a day	33.5	.0	19.8
Local Gulf Cities stations	7.9	.0	3.1
TV stations from Georgia/Louisiana	14.0	16.7	6.9
Cultural shows	12.8	8.3	6.9
Children's shows	14.0	8.3	13.7
Religious shows	7.9	.0	8.4
Documentaries	1.8	.0	.0
Educational shows	1.8	.0	.0
Other	17.1	41.7	10.7
Don't know	1.8	8.3	13.7
Overall, what would you say your opinion of Cable programming is?			
Very favorable	45.1	50.0	31.3
Somewhat favorable	47.1	25.0	36.6
Not very favorable	4.3	16.7	11.5
Not favorable at all	1.2	8.3	10.7
Don't know	2.4	.0	9.9
Based on what you know about Cablevision, how likely would you be to hook into the cable system during the next 12 months?			
Very likely	NA	50.0	23.7
Somewhat likely	NA	16.7	16.6
Not very likely	NA	.0	23.1
Not at all likely	NA	33.3	31.3
Don't know	NA	.0	5.3

EXHIBIT 15 *(continued)*

	Cable Subscribers, %	Former Subscribers, %	Non- Subscribers, %
Why will you be unlikely to hook up to Cablevision?			
Too expensive	NA	25.0	-36.4
Don't watch television	NA	50.0	42.4
Don't like programming	NA	.0	4.5
Adult movies	NA	.0	7.6
Other	NA	25.0	27.3
What do you think the costs of having Cablevision are? First, how much do you think the installation charge would cost?			
$1 –$ 4.99	NA	NA	1.5
$5 –$ 9.99	NA	NA	2.3
$10–$14.99	NA	NA	3.1
$15–$19.99	NA	NA	13.7
$20–$24.99	NA	NA	.0
$25–$29.99	NA	NA	14.5
$30–$34.99	NA	NA	5.3
$35–$39.99	NA	NA	6.1
$40–$44.99	NA	NA	.8
$45–$49.99	NA	NA	.8
$50 & over	NA	NA	14.5
Don't know	NA	NA	37.4
What do you think the monthly subscriber fee would be?			
$1 –$ 4.99	NA	NA	.8
$5 –$ 9.99	NA	NA	10.7
$10–$14.99	NA	NA	13.7
$15–$19.99	NA	NA	20.6
$20–$24.99	NA	NA	11.5
$25–$29.99	NA	NA	8.4
$30–$34.99	NA	NA	4.6
$35–$39.99	NA	NA	2.3
$40–$44.99	NA	NA	.8
$45–$49.99	NA	NA	.0
$50 & over	NA	NA	.8
Don't know	NA	NA	26.0
Thinking now of other service or utility companies, how would you rate the customer service of Trans America Cable?			
Very favorable	16.5	12.5	NA
Somewhat favorable	42.7	37.5	NA
Not very favorable	18.1	25.0	NA
Not favorable at all	13.0	18.8	NA
Don't know	9.8	16.2	NA
Have you been contacted about cable?			
Yes	NA	NA	73.7
No	NA	NA	26.3

Note: Total number of sampling: cable subscribers = 132; former subscribers = 16; non-subscribers = 161.

EXHIBIT 16
STUDY OF LIKELINESS TO SUBSCRIBE AMONG NON-SUBSCRIBERS OF CABLE TV
IN CURRENTLY SERVED AREAS*

	Percentages		
	Likely to Subscribe	**Unlikely to Subscribe**	**Don't Know**
Age:			
18–39	45	52	3
40–59	33	66	1
60+	21	73	6
Race:			
Black	55	43	2
White	34	63	3
Sex:			
Men	43	55	2
Women	29	66	5
Children at home:			
Yes	40	55	5
No	25	72	7
Household income:			
$15,000	38	58	4
$15,000–30,000	41	55	6
$30,000	33	65	2

* 200 non-subscribers were surveyed by telephone in 3 diverse cable systems between August 27 and September 30, 1981.
Source: TAC of Gulf Cities.

LAKESHORE ELECTRIC COMPANY

Caroline M. Henderson
Christopher H. Lovelock

Richard Krisak spread out on his desk the many exhibits collected by the steam heat task force over the previous eight months. There were sales and operating cost data, consumption figures for the company's major customers, trends in prices, and costs for different types of fuel.

The youngest individual ever to head a task force at Lakeshore Electric, Krisak had been placed in charge of undertaking a comprehensive analysis of the company's steam business. This business had been suffering a declining customer base and poor financial performance for a number of years, a situation which appeared to be based on the changing economics of different fuels.

From his office window on the nineteenth floor of the Fraser Bank Center, Krisak could see the two tall stacks of the Kane Street station down by the lakefront. From this and Lakeshore Electric's other three steam plants, steam flowed through an underground network of pipes to pro-

vide energy for heating, cooling, and other purposes to more than 400 commercial and institutional customers in the city of Fraser.

The months of spadework were over for the task force, but as yet nothing had been written. On returning to the office from the long Labor Day weekend in September 1980, Krisak had received a phone call from Andrew McDowall, the senior vice president responsible for overseeing the study. After enquiring about the status of the project, McDowall had suggested it was time to start writing. "You'd better get going, Rich," he said. "I want you to make a presentation to our strategic management council on October 1."

THE COMPANY

Incorporated in 1890, Lakeshore Electric was an investor-owned public utility engaged primarily in the generation, transmission and sale of electrical energy. The company served the city of Fraser and many of its surrounding suburbs, reaching a population of 1.6 million with a net-

Copyright © 1981 by the President and Fellows of Harvard College, Harvard Business School case 9–582–081.

work extending some 20 miles along the shoreline of one of the Great Lakes.

In 1979, sales were approximately $700 million, and the company had over 4,000 employees, of whom 180 worked for the steam business. Total sales were divided into: residential (32 percent of total sales and comprising 550,000 households), commercial (35 percent), industrial (14 percent), and uses such as wholesaling to other electric utilities (19 percent).

Like many large electric utilities, Lakeshore Electric had been criticized for high costs. Contributing to this problem were high local property taxes, fuel costs (particularly imported oil), and a substantial investment in underground lines. Industry observers generally concluded, however, that Lakeshore was progressive and well managed. The company spent heavily on research and was also known for voluntarily searching out effective methods of pollution control; it had instituted stack scrubbers before environmental legislation required it.

DISTRICT HEAT

District heat was a mechanism for distributing energy from a central source. It involved the provision of hot water or steam through a network of pipes from a central generating station to a large number of separate buildings. There were three types of systems: steam, pressurized high temperature hot water (over 300° F), and hot water. At the station, fuel—generally oil, gas, coal, or most recently, municipal refuse—was burned under a boiler of water and the potential energy in the fuel converted to heat and pressure in the steam. The output was typically measured in thousands of pounds (Mlb). In some instances, the steam was cogenerated with electric power. The steam or hot water flowed through pipes or mains buried beneath city streets.

The steam or hot water was used within buildings for "space conditioning"—heat and air conditioning. For heating, steam was passed through a heat exchanger, heating water which circulated throughout the building before being returned to the heat exchanger again to maintain the required water temperature. Cooling involved the creation of chilled water, which was then circulated building wide, cooling air for work area comfort. Chilled water was produced by either a centrifugal chiller driven by a steam turbine or a steam absorption chiller in which the steam served as the energy input to a refrigeration process. Large buildings required a substantial amount of cooling equipment—including cooling towers on the roof.

History

The first district heating system in the United States was constructed in 1877 in Lockport, New York. Early systems used boilers which generated steam exclusively, but by the turn of the century technology existed for cogeneration of both electricity and steam. This technology led to the rapid development of district heating systems in many cities and by 1909 there were 150 electric utilities in the U.S. selling heat in this way. As electric service grew and new technologies were introduced, these cogeneration economies decreased; in part this was because electric turbines did not exhaust steam at a temperature high enough for production of district heat through what was termed "turbine topping." In addition, newer electric plants tended to be located away from urban centers, whereas district heat systems needed to be contained within a two- to three-mile radius. As city populations shifted to the suburbs and took advantage of inexpensive oil and gas heat, some district systems were discontinued. In Europe, however, district heat systems never suffered this decline, since central planning boards searched for the most economical heating methods for entire urban areas. During the 1970s the Europeans led in technological advances in district heat—particularly in the development of hot water systems of greater efficiency and lower installed cost than steam. Scandinavia, in particular, relied heavily on district heat; by the late 1970s 25 percent of total heating requirements in Denmark were being met by district heating systems.

The Industry

Except for university or military systems, district heat was considered a public utility in the U.S. Some systems were operated as separate companies but many were owned by electric or gas utilities. By 1980, there were about 50 steam heat companies reporting operating statistics to the industry trade association (Exhibit 1); another 19 organizations (mostly colleges) had affiliated status. About half of these systems were under the regulatory control of a state or municipal public utility commission which set the rates after public hearing. Lakeshore Electric's steam heat business was not regulated, although its electrical business was.

The number of customers served by these systems ranged from as few as 5 to over 2,500, but had been decreasing yearly. Many systems were operating in the red and for others profitability was quite low. Despite European advances in technology and the interest taken in district heat by government policy makers and energy specialists, the general consensus was that district heat was in trouble in the U.S.

THE LAKESHORE STEAM SYSTEM

The district heat system had historically grown up alongside the electric business but had been dwarfed as electricity demand surged ahead. In 1979, the steam business comprised only about 6.5 percent of total Lakeshore sales. Nationwide, Lakeshore was one of the top ten largest district steam providers.

The system employed four plants (Kane Street, Anglia, Miller and 15th Street) and 22 miles of underground piping. Most of the steam was used for space conditioning; in 1980, all 417 customers used steam for heat and 40 of them also used

EXHIBIT 1
REPORTED STATISTICS FOR U.S. MEMBER
COMPANIES OF INTERNATIONAL DISTRICT
HEATING ASSOCIATION, 1979

Total steam production delivered:	94,700 million pounds
Sold	80,300
Loss	14,400
Total hourly production capacity:	
Capacity total	46.2 million pounds/hour
Maximum send out*	32.8
Energy source used in steam production†:	
Coal	15,000 million pounds
Gas	20,200
Oil	58,100
Prices charged by steam utilities:	
Maximum	$10.59 dollars/Mlb
Average	6.77
Minimum	1.61

* The difference between this figure and "capacity" is the allowance for back-up capability.
† 37% of steam production was derived from cogeneration through "turbine topping."
Source: International District Heating Association, "Statistical Committee Board of Industry Statistics."

it for cooling. Steam was used by some customers to heat hot water; one such user was the Fraser Aquarium, which heated the water for its fish tanks with steam. In addition, there were a few process steam users—one gelatin factory, a few laundries, some garment manufacturers, and several restaurants. The four hospitals in the city were particularly dependent on the reliability of the Lakeshore steam system, since they used it for space heating and cooling, hot water, and sterilization of surgical equipment and garments.

The bulk of Lakeshore Electric's steam system had been constructed in the mid-1930s, although certain elements of the system were even older. Net assets were about $27 million or 2.5 percent of Lakeshore's total, although the cost of replacing the entire system was estimated in 1974 at $100 million. In 1979, additions to the steam plant totaled $310,000 while maintenance expense was $2,786,460. Much of the latter figure was for replacement of the insulation around the underground conduits. By mid-1980, more than

a third of the system had been reinsulated with new materials that were much more resistant to deterioration.

Operating Results

In 1979 4,390,000 thousand pounds (Mlbs) of steam had been sold by Lakeshore at an average price of $8.84 per Mlb. While this represented an increase in revenues, management was particularly concerned with the decreasing profitability of the steam business (Exhibit 2). Historically, steam had shown a higher return on equity than electricity, but this situation had changed over the past few years.

Theoretically, steam did not have an upper limit on its profit potential since, unlike the electric side of the business, steam rates were not regulated. Every year like clockwork, however, the Building Owners and Managers Association (BOMA) of Fraser filed legislation at the state capitol to regulate district steam. Although these

---

EXHIBIT 2
LAKESHORE ELECTRIC COMPANY: STEAM ALLOCATED INCOME AND COST STATEMENT

	1975	1976	1977	1978	1979
Revenues	$32,786,543	$37,207,042	$38,818,876	$35,580,735	$39,022,142
Fuel expenses	22,669,920	22,930,436	25,222,500	24,073,411	26,867,957
Operations and maintenance (including distribution)	3,668,252	3,851,276	3,972,580	4,546,396	4,549,310
Depreciation	956,967	1,152,042	1,332,742	1,360,371	1,382,864
Indirect operations and maintenance*	1,652,074	1,764,723	2,011,025	2,450,696	1,045,865
Taxes (excluding income)	2,474,536	2,617,214	3,451,041	3,773,120	3,728,603
Net utility operations before interest charges and taxes	1,364,794	4,891,351	2,826,987	(623,259)	1,447,543
AFUDC†	471,086	523,704	4,780	611	291
Interest	1,435,217	1,443,316	1,713,395	1,649,817	1,546,053
Net income before income tax	(541,509)	2,924,331	1,108,812	(2,273,687)	(98,801)
Income taxes	(249,094)	1,345,192	500,456	(1,045,896)	(45,448)
Income available for dividends	(292,415)	1,579,139	608,356	(1,227,791)	(53,353)
Dividends	867,856	982,683	1,315,466	1,197,720	1,172,165
Balance after payment of dividends	$ (1,160,271)	$ 596,456	$ (707,110)	$ (2,425,511)	$ (1,225,518)

* Indirect Operations and Maintenance charges were dependent on company allocation formulas. In 1979, the allocation had changed.
† Allowance for Funds Used During Construction.
Source: Company records.

initiatives had always been rejected in the past, company executives were not convinced that the situation would remain unchanged in the future.

Operations

There was a load imbalance between the different seasons of the year, with steam usage peaking in the winter. Spring and fall had very low utilization since neither heat nor air conditioning was required. Special lower steam rates were offered to customers during the summer. In 1979, expenses for operating the four steam plants had totaled about $29.7 million, of which $23.4 million was fuel costs. Each of the plants in the Lakeshore steam system was different (Exhibit 3).

The *15th Street plant* had been constructed in 1898 as an electric generating station, and in 1967, was converted to steam with electricity as a by-product. Currently, 60 employees were needed to run 15th Street.

The *Anglia and Miller stations* were formerly electric plants which had been converted to steam. Unlike 15th Street, these plants were used only for peak loads and did not require a large operations staff on a day-to-day basis. When these stations were needed, employees were sent from other locations to operate the equipment.

The *Kane Street station* was built in 1931 for the purpose of generating steam. Originally fired by coal, this station had been converted in 1960 so that its four boilers could use either #6 oil or natural gas. In 1979, natural gas supplied 25 percent of total fuel consumption. A special contract had been negotiated for this gas and the price obtained was 20 percent below #6 oil. Kane Street, which employed an operations and maintenance staff of 65, was considered the heart of the steam-generating system.

THE MARKET FOR STEAM

Historically, steam had been the first choice for space conditioning in new construction in the city of Fraser. Through the 1960s, 90 percent of all new buildings had selected steam. At that time Fraser had been experiencing a boom in development and steam sales expanded at a rate of 12 percent annually. In 1969, the system reached a peak of 626 customers. Thereafter, however, the customer base began to decline at an annual rate of 2–3 percent, reaching 537 in 1975. During the

EXHIBIT 3
1979 OPERATING DATA BY PLANT

	Miller	Anglia	Kane Street	15th Street	Total
Days utilized	3	15	365	330	—
Annual maximum potential output at 100% capacity (000 Mlb)	2,190	2,716	9,286	6,570	—
Actual production (sendout) (000 Mlb)	3	32	3,006	2,123	5,164
Sales price per Mlb sendout†	$7.51	$7.51	$7.51	$7.51	—
Sales revenues ($ 000)	$23	$240	$22,575	$15,944	$38,872*
Total operating and maintenance expenses‡ ($ 000)	107	348	16,378	12,853	$29,686
Net income (loss)§ ($ 000)	$ (84)	$(208)	$8,325	$2,691	$9,336

 * Additional income of $240 thousand was not attributable to particular plants.
 † Because of transmission losses of 15%, Lakeshore could only charge customers for 85% of the steam generated at the plants. In 1979, customers consumed 4,390,000 Mlbs of steam at $8.84 per Mlb, but Lakeshore actually "sent out" 4,390,000/.85 = 5,164,700 Mlbs, resulting in a net yield of $8.84 × .85 = $7.51 per Mlb of send out.
 ‡ Includes fuel but excludes distribution.
 § Before depreciation and allocations.
 Source: Company records.

EXHIBIT 4
STEAM SALES BY LAKESHORE ELECTRIC, 1969–79

Year	Sales (Mlbs)	Heating Degree Days*	Average Number of Customers Billed
1969	4,734,850	5,631	626
1970	4,946,786	5,848	613
1971	5,527,961	5,738	587
1972	5,564,564	5,932	574
1973	5,567,374	5,188	560
1974	5,410,174	5,648	559
1975	5,293,503	5,315	537
1976	5,490,435	5,289	510
1977	5,372,588	5,301	482
1978	5,040,000	5,880	457
1979	4,390,000	5,391	437

* Degree days are the sum of the number of degrees that the average daily temperature falls below 65°F. during the course of the calendar year. For example, if the average daily temperature for three days was 55°F, this would total [3 × (65 − 55)] = 30 degree days for this three-day period.
Source: Company records.

following five years, the decline accelerated, although sales revenues increased each year. By 1979, 437 customers remained (Exhibit 4); this figure had fallen to 417 by the fall of 1980.

Many of the customers who left the system were small users who had been able to reactivate or install oilburning boilers within their buildings or whose buildings had been razed in urban renewal projects. These customers were not an important factor in sales revenues, as it was estimated that 58 customers accounted for 82 percent of sales. Nevertheless, the sales loss amounted to 450,000 Mlbs on an annual basis. Exhibits 5 and 6 show an analysis of the customer base in 1979, as compiled by the task force under Richard Krisak's direction.

During the 1970s, Lakeshore steam had attracted only one large new user and a few small ones, adding only 190,000 Mlbs in additional sales. The last two major construction projects had selected electricity from Lakeshore Electric for their space conditioning needs. But company executives did not see this loss of business to their other product as entirely benign, since large new

EXHIBIT 5
LAKESHORE ELECTRIC COMPANY: STEAM AND ELECTRIC CONSUMPTION
FOR THE TEN LARGEST STEAM CUSTOMERS, 1979

	Steam Consumption Mlbs (000)	Steam Revenue (000)	Electric Consumption Kilowatt Hours (000)	Electric Revenue (000)	Total Steam and Electric Revenue (000)
Fraser Hospital	485	$ 3,969	47,090	$ 2,398	$ 6,367
Methodist Hospital	215	1,905	20,068	979	2,884
Midwestern Oil Building	191	1,695	55,639	3,087	4,782
Fraser Bank Center	144	1,179	35,923	1,930	3,109
Cole Memorial Hospital	188	1,557	19,797	969	2,526
Fraser State University	156	1,387	25,087	1,245	2,632
Lakeview Hilton	163	1,381	16,011	803	2,184
State Office Building	114	946	10,737	639	1,585
Olson Medical Center	147	1,306	23,911	1,239	2,545
Northwest Housing Project	113	969	3,545	239	1,208
Total	1,916	$16,294	257,808	$13,528	$29,822

Source: Company records.

EXHIBIT 6
LAKESHORE ELECTRIC COMPANY: KEY ACCOUNT ANALYSIS
(Lakeshore's 58 largest steam users)

Segment	Number of Customers	1979 Sales (000 Mlbs)	Estimated Conservation Potential*
Commercial real estate	29	1,542.8	8.8%
City government	6	354.1	2.0
Federal government	4	135.4	6.1
State government	6	277.1	8.4
Nonprofit	6	270.3	10.0
Hospitals	7	1,031.6	16.0

* Task force estimate.
Source: Company records.

electric cooling systems created peak load problems that led to incremental losses for the electric side of the business. Under the current regulatory climate, complete recovery of costs was not forthcoming.

In 1980, the Fraser area was looking forward to new growth. A number of large new construction projects were planned—condominiums, office buildings, retail complexes, and hospital and university expansion. But as one executive in the Lakeshore steam division put it, "Our people call on the engineers and architects and the first thing they hear is, 'Don't try to sell me steam.' "

Sales projections for 1980 continued the steady decline experienced in recent years (Exhibit 4). During the past five years, there had been a cumulative net sales loss of 1,890,000 Mlbs; 77 percent of this total was attributed to conservation. In part, this reflected government-mandated temperature restrictions that public buildings should be kept no warmer than 65° F. in the winter or no cooler than 78° F. in summer. In addition, several large customers had found it financially worthwhile to install more efficient equipment, resulting in energy savings ranging from 25 percent–40 percent. The three sales engineers working on steam accounts were very involved in helping customers use computer controls and other devices to achieve such savings.

Energy conservation was expected to become even more important in the future as the development of the electric heat pump, in the words of one Lakeshore executive, was expected to "revolutionize" the heating and cooling business.[1] Reliable versions had been available since 1975, permitting users to save up to 50 percent of their previous space heating costs.

Economics of Self-Generation

Based on changes in input costs, Lakeshore could no longer sell steam to new customers at a cost competitive with heat sources such as onsite steam or hot water boilers, or centrally generated electricity. There were two components to the steam price: fuel costs and base costs (Exhibit 7). Base costs were the expenses associated with owning, operating (excluding fuel), and maintaining the steam plants and distribution system. They also included customer and revenue-related expenses. Number 6 oil had historically been sold at a price far below #2 oil—the fuel gener-

[1] The heat pump works on the simple principle that heat can be moved from cold places to warmer places, the principle used in refrigeration. Thus, the relative temperature differences between the inside and outside of buildings provide the energy source. Electric power is used for the motor or the heat pump, and the system is reversible to allow for both winter heating and summer cooling.

EXHIBIT 7
HISTORICAL STEAM PRICES AT
LAKESHORE ELECTRIC

| | Price per Mlb (Annual Average*) | | |
	Base Price	Fuel Price	Total
1975	$2.56	$3.64	$6.20
1976	2.89	3.55	6.44
1977	2.95	4.28	7.23
1978	2.99	4.06	7.05
1979	3.48	5.36	8.84
1980 (projected)	3.74	8.43	12.17
1981 (forecast)	4.24	9.74	13.98

   * The fuel price was adjusted monthly based on Lakeshore's actual costs for purchasing fuel oil. The fuel price shown, and thus the total, are annual *averages*. The base price remained constant from month to month except for planned price increases. The most recent increase had taken place in October 1979, when the base price was raised by 20%.
   Source: Company records.

EXHIBIT 8
LAKESHORE ELECTRIC COMPANY: FUEL PRICES
IN $/MILLION BTUs*

| | Fuel Oil | | |
Historical†	No. 2 Fuel	No. 6 (5% Sulphur)	No. 6 (2.8% Sulphur)
1972	$ .93	$ .67	N/A
1973	1.20	.82	N/A
1974	2.03	1.96	N/A
1975	2.08	2.09	N/A
1976	2.30	1.97	N/A
1977	2.61	2.28	N/A
1978	2.83	2.22	N/A
1979	4.17	3.63	N/A
Projected‡:			
1980	$ 5.80	$ 5.18	3.84
1982	7.44	5.49	4.49
1985	9.77	7.39	6.16
1990	16.98	12.77	10.65
1995	26.92	20.19	16.83
2000	40.57	30.29	25.24

   * Prices are shown in units of one million BTUs because oil grades contain differing amounts of BTUs per unit of volume. The prices shown are on a comparable basis.
   † Source is company records (price actually paid by Lakeshore).
   ‡ Source is consultant's report.

ally used in on-site boilers. After the rapid price increase for all petroleum products in the 1970s, the percentage advantage for #6 had been almost eliminated by 1980. However, projections for future years showed the prices of the two diverging again (Exhibit 8). An additional problem for Lakeshore had been created by the need to switch to 0.5 percent sulphur fuel because of environmental restrictions in the downtown area. This change had further narrowed the fuel cost differential, as the low sulphur oil cost $2–$3 more per barrel than the oil previously burned.

   The total cost of generating steam on-site (capital, space, operation and maintenance, fuel delivery, etc.) was calculated on a cost comparison analysis; since fuel costs represented a major part of that analysis company officials had, in the past, used the ratio of #6 to #2 oil as a guide to competitiveness. A favorable ratio, last seen in 1969, was felt to be 70 percent. As an aid to planning, Lakeshore analysts had commissioned estimates from a consulting firm (Exhibit 8) on future oil costs, and the task force had worked out some price comparisons between fuel alternatives (Exhibit 9).

   Base costs included both direct and indirect

EXHIBIT 9
LAKESHORE ELECTRIC COMPANY: COST TO
USER OF Mlb EQUIVALENTS IN 1979
CONSTANT DOLLARS*

Year	Gas	Electric	Oil	Steam
1970	$7.02	$14.03	$5.37	$3.67
1971	7.40	14.83	5.60	4.50
1972	7.27	14.23	5.40	4.53
1973	7.07	12.71	5.57	4.59
1974	6.98	16.34	6.16	7.50
1975	7.74	16.10	5.41	8.15
1976	8.21	16.39	6.58	8.08
1977	8.41	16.39	6.67	8.55
1978	8.07	15.65	6.84	7.75
1979	8.46	14.73	7.54	8.84

   * "Mlb equivalents" imply a similar output of BTUs; electricity costs assume that heat pumps are *not* used.
   Source: Company records.

operations and maintenance expense and taxes, including property tax. Customers who had installed steam plants did not generally incur an increase in property tax because of tax assessment practices and regulations.

Other costs incurred by Lakeshore that would not be borne by individual customers' plants were water and sewer charges. Individual plants usually involved closed systems which recirculated the condensate.[2] The Lakeshore system had no condensate return; water accounted for 16¢ of the price of each Mlb of steam. The sewer charges incurred by those individual plants which did discharge the condensate were fairly minimal.

It was estimated that customers installing their own equipment could expect an overall system efficiency of 60–75 percent. In comparison, the efficiency of the Lakeshore system was 56 percent, reflecting not only loss of the unused energy in the condensate, but also the loss incurred in transmission from Lakeshore's generating plants to the customers' sites. However, transmission losses were gradually being reduced as the old insulation was replaced by technologically superior materials.

Individual customers installing their own plants had to have boilers large enough to meet peak usage of steam during the winter heating season, which was often as much as 2.5 times the average consumption per hour over the year; as a result the boiler only operated, on average, at 35–40 percent of capacity.

Recently, several large customers—including Fraser Hospital and the State University—had hired engineering consultants to study the feasibility of conversion to an on-site steam generation plant. These customers had not yet discussed these plants openly with Lakeshore Electric steam officials, but the company was well aware of their activities. A Lakeshore sales engineer reported that one consultant had written to a number of steam customers in an attempt to stimulate their interest in having similar feasibility studies done.

The economics of such conversions varied greatly and depended on three major assumptions: first, the efficiency of the boilers that would be installed (or reactivated); second, the installation cost and the amortization of that investment; and third, expected fuel costs. In recent conversions, installation costs per pound of installed capacity had varied; but assuming that average conversions would cost $12 to $18 per pound of steam per hour of installed capacity (including the associated distribution network), and using a 12 percent interest rate, Krisak calculated the converter's payback period to be between 4 and 7 years. Installation costs had ranged from $5.58 to $28.00 per pound. The higher estimates were for users with multiple buildings who would need more elaborate distribution systems.

One of the major problems in this type of retrofitting lay in acquiring enough space to install the equipment. If a building had originally been built to use steam from the district heat system, there might be no space large enough—either in the basement, or beside the building—to house the new equipment. Additionally, if oil or gas were to be used, a smokestack would be required to carry the hot gases into the air. In a recent customer survey, Lakeshore Electric had tried to identify those customers who would be most space-limited. The findings showed that 79 percent of the federal government customers, 23 percent of commercial property customers, and 12 percent of nonprofit customers could be considered space-limited.

Other nonfinancial considerations included the fact that government officials tended to favor district heat over self-generation for pollution reasons (fewer fuel trucks making deliveries and fewer smokestacks).

Not all current customers would be equally motivated to save nor be aware of all the alternatives available to them. Certain customers might move slowly because of cumbersome in-

---

[2] Condensate is the term for the water condensed from the "used" steam.

ternal decision-making processes. In a few instances, a lot depended on the individual customer's preference and attitudes toward conversion. In small buildings, the responsibility for recommending to the owners that they make such a conversion might lie with the building manager. In larger structures, agreement on conversion would have to be achieved among a number of decision makers.

ORGANIZATION OF THE STEAM BUSINESS

There was a separate division for the steam business and no one executive with overall responsibility. Four groups were involved: Steam Production, Steam Distribution, Steam Meters and Steam Customer Contact (Exhibit 10). Other departments involved in steam included: Rates, Legal, Engineering, Financial, Environmental, System Operations, and Accounting. While the number of employees involved in the steam business had almost doubled in the last 12 years, it was estimated that top management spent only 2.5 percent of their time on the steam side of the business.

Steam Production was under the Steam and Electric organization and had responsibility for steam production at the four stations. About 130 operations and maintenance personnel were used to staff the facilities.

Steam Distribution, a part of the Engineering organization, installed, operated, and maintained the 22 miles of underground piping, as well as various pieces of equipment owned by the company installed on customer property. There were 30 employees in this group.

Steam Meter was composed of 11 employees who maintained and replaced the 800 meters and associated equipment in the system. This group was also in the Engineering organization.

The *Steam Customer Contact* group belonged to the Commercial organization and was responsible for selling steam service and rendering con-

tinuing customer service. There were six employees in this group: one sales engineer, two engineers, one supervisor, an administrative assistant, and the division head, who was part of the task force.

The sales engineer and two engineers were responsible for customer sales and service. The company had recently changed the job description from "engineer" to "sales engineer" and planned to fill any vacancies with individuals meeting the new requirements. The new qualifications were a combination of business and engineering education rather than an engineering degree, and an emphasis on "people skills." The company had no formal sales training program.

The sales force was unionized and divided into two ranks: grade 2 who called on customers with an annual steam revenue potential of $10,000 to $100,000, and grade 1 who called on those below $10,000. In addition, the sales engineers were assigned to geographical areas so that the two grade 1's divided the city between them. The supervisor handled the 40 largest accounts personally.

When major new construction projects were announced, the division head and the administrative assistant sought to interest the project's architect and engineers in using steam. Typically, the consulting engineer was the key individual in the decision process, as his/her recommendation was usually followed by the architect. The administrative assistant reporting to the division head was most active in the selling effort. (The administrative assistant job description defined the position as "accountable for the establishment and implementation of a steam sales program.") The assistant sought to contact the consulting engineer with the objective of obtaining the building's plans, so that these could be used by the technical staff in the commercial department to work up a feasibility study for steam. This study estimated initial costs, and annual owning and operating costs of a steam system. When the study was complete, the

EXHIBIT 10
LAKESHORE ELECTRIC COMPANY: PARTIAL ORGANIZATION CHART

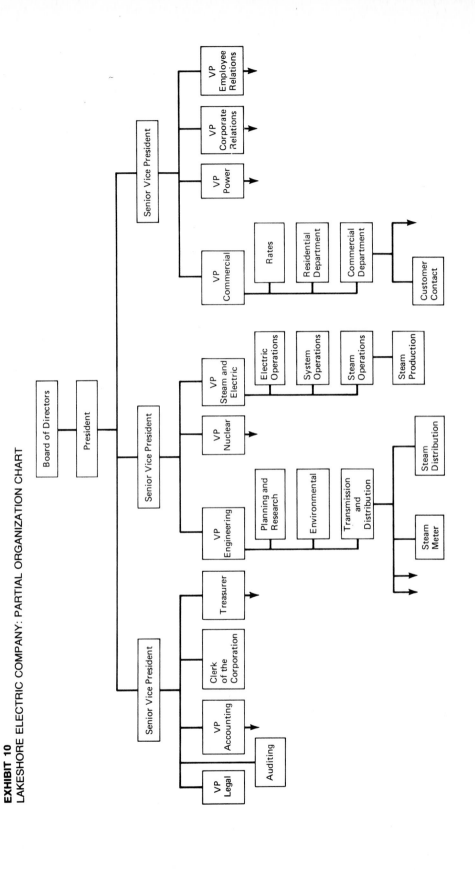

administrative assistant would try to set up a presentation before the consulting engineer.

While no "canned" presentation had been developed for steam, the division head and administrative assistant usually tried to address such benefits as cost, reliability, space savings, air quality, and less management time for the user (oil storage and delivery, labor disputes, antipollution requirements, boiler maintenance, etc.). Lately these efforts had been unsuccessful.

The engineers and sales engineer were really not involved in formal selling as such. Their daily work was devoted to solving operating problems and to helping existing customers conserve. One company executive joked, "This is the only business in which you teach the customer to use less of the product!" He added that company employees emphasized personal attention, and pointed out that when customers purchased steam they also got a plant engineer. To keep customers informed, the department published a newsletter, which was sent to all steam customers.

Pricing

Pricing strategy at Lakeshore Electric was the responsibility of the rate policy committee, a large standing committee composed primarily of executives at the vice president and senior vice president level. Recommendations for price changes originated with the financial organization which, together with the Commercial Department, conducted periodic cost-of-service studies.

The first step was to gather all expenses incurred in the most recent 12-month period, called the "test year." Sales were then forecast and test-year expenses adjusted for the next years' operating environment, thus enabling the department to project revenues and expenses. The required rate of return was then calculated and the shortfall, if any, between expected expenses plus rate of return and forecasted revenues represented the necessary rate increase. Senior management then evaluated the increase

against the probability that some customers might discontinue Lakeshore steam if the increase was implemented. A strategy emphasizing an adequate rate of return might be traded off against one of retaining steam customers.

Eventually, a recommendation would be made to the rate policy committee, which might make some adjustments before approval. Since no regulatory approval was needed, implementation of the increase entailed giving customers 30 days' notice and printing new rate schedules. In October 1979, a base rate increase of 20% had been put into effect. It was the first increase since April 1977 and had an overall effect on total price of 7.5%.

THE STEAM TASK FORCE

The declining customer base and poor profitability of the steam business had been reviewed by a senior executive of Lakeshore's strategic management council at the annual management "retreat" in late 1979. A complete analysis and specific recommendations for improving performance were requested.

Krisak came to this assignment from the Coordinating and Expediting Department, where he had been a division head in charge of offering project management services to company construction projects. Like many other Lakeshore middle- and upper-management employees, his education and eight-year career with the company had been in engineering. Working with him were six management-level employees drawn from each of the divisions of the company responsible for steam. Unlike Krisak, other members of this group devoted only a portion of their time to the task force.

Task Force Activities

Between January and August of 1980, the task force collected a considerable amount of data relevant to the steam business. Five earlier reports, written over the preceding 12 years, had been identified. Each of these made strategic organizational recommendations for Lakeshore steam. However, as far as Krisak could tell, none of their recommendations had been adopted. Engineering studies had also been conducted and most of their specific cost reduction recommendations had been implemented: as a result, Krisak believed that there was little extra fat to be trimmed from the steam system operations in their present form.

Among the recommendations of the non-engineering studies were: (1) establishing a separate organizational unit to consolidate all steam heat activities under one manager; (2) seeking opportunities for major cost reductions, such as closing plants or attempting to negotiate with the city for tax relief or for use of cheaper fuels with a higher sulphur content; and (3) implementing new planning procedures. The authors of a 1977 study were particularly concerned with the lack of goals for the steam system, stating:

> A forty-million dollar business cannot continue to exist without some idea of where its future lies. If this were a regulated business, the company would be hard pressed to answer such questions as, "What plans does the steam heating business have to alleviate the present high costs of producing steam?"

In addition to these documents, the task force put together a set of data on current system operations and finances. The fuel comparison was an example of this type of information.

Identifying and Evaluating Alternatives

Although he had spent much of his time over the summer on resolving operational problems, Krisak believed he had reached a few tentative conclusions. Faced with evidence that the 15th Street station was the cause of the recent operational problems, Krisak had decided to recommend that it be closed. He thought it was worth taking a calculated risk on peak capacity requirements in order to reduce costs.

A decision to close 15th Street would reduce

capacity, but historically, the steam system had been able to operate with minimal reserves until 1974, when a new boiler at the Kane station came on stream. This capacity had proved to be an operational convenience but Krisak felt that customers might be happier not paying for peaking plants. The all-time system peak to date had occurred in the winter of 1977 when 2,042 Mlbs per hour had been required. Customers at the far end of the steam main system—the Natural History Museum and Fraser Hospital—were likely to be the most affected in the event that system pressure could not be maintained. However, by making some minor reconfigurations of the existing electric station adjoining 15th Street, an emergency capacity of another 220 Mlbs per hour could be obtained to help maintain system pressure.

Krisak also believed that the company was committed to staying in the steam business. Through his conversations with Andrew McDowall, he had sensed that this commitment was fairly strong and that only a grim financial forecast would cause consideration of the sale of the business.

Termination was difficult in any case since examples existed of direct local intervention when a public utility had tried to abandon a district heating system. In 1971, Ohio Edison (a regulated steam business) had petitioned the Public Utilities Commission of Ohio to allow abandonment of the Akron system. The petition cited the age of the system (c. 1928) and lack of profitability as the major reasons. Steam users were shocked at the prospect of this loss and formed a "Concerned Steam Users Committee" which successfully prevented Edison's petition from being granted. In 1980, the utility was finally able to sell the system to a new operator, the city of Akron, for $50,000.

Krisak had come to believe that refueling the system was necessary. An entirely new system—both plant and distribution—was out of the question because of the vast expense in replacing the 22-mile distribution system. Without this kind of total replacement it would be impossible to use the new hot water technology that was popular in Europe. The possibility of using coal as a fuel appeared distant, as coal conversion would cost somewhere in the neighborhood of $100 million and would present major air pollution difficulties. It did not seem possible to build a coal plant in or near downtown Fraser. It appeared that only one option remained.

Burning Municipal Refuse

As the average American generated several pounds of trash per day, municipal waste for district heating systems had received a lot of attention—as "resource recovery"—but implementation of the concept had been fairly slow. The first incinerator to produce steam for heat was built in Denmark in the 1920s. In Europe, the idea had caught hold and over 200 such plants were operating, whereas the United States only had 17. Part of this discrepancy was due to the relative economics of waste disposal, as landfill was often the cheapest approach in the U.S. However, with increasing regulations and siting problems, using landfills was expected to become more difficult.

To date, there had been only limited success at generating electricity from trash, but several steam-generating projects were quite successful. For instance, a Saugus, Massachusetts, plant processed daily about 1,000 tons of trash and sold the steam product to a nearby industrial plant. Most refuse plants were smaller, with capacities of only 100–200 tons per day (TPD) and supplied energy to a single large industrial user rather than to a multitude of utility customers.

Based on the experience of current refuse steam plants, the economics appeared favorable. Each ton of trash would generate about 4.2 Mlbs. of steam and would generate revenue from three sources: charges for dumping refuse at the plant, estimated at $10–$15 per ton; recovered materials which would be separated out before burning and sold for scrap at $3–$5 ton, and steam

sales. Capital costs for the four plants starting up in 1979 had varied from $50,000 to $60,000 for each ton-per-day capacity. Krisak was considering a plant with a total capacity of 1,800 tons of trash per day; he anticipated average utilization over the year at 80 percent of capacity. The cost of constructing such a plant in the Fraser area was estimated at $100 million.

A refuse plant was particularly attractive for Lakeshore because of the possibility for sharing or eliminating any capital costs through a joint venture. For the purpose of analysis, Krisak assumed that Lakeshore would not invest in the plant, but would purchase all steam output at a price equivalent to 60 percent of the prevailing cost of the oil needed to produce a similar volume of output. Under this scenario, the actual owner of the plant would receive the dumping charge, and scrap sales in addition to making energy sales would go to Lakeshore. If Lakeshore were to own the plant, these revenues could be used to offset operations expenses. Annual operating and maintenance expenses per Mlb produced would be about equal to the average for the current plants.

If Lakeshore were to go ahead with the project, it would be five years before the plant could come on stream. This time estimate was based on four components of the project: working out a joint venture agreement, resolving the community relations problems of site selection, constructing the facility, and negotiating supply contracts.

WRITING THE REPORT AND RECOMMENDATIONS

The task force was completing the background material for the final report, but the recommendations had yet to be written and a comprehensive presentation planned for top management. This would be the first time that a study of the steam business had been presented to the strategic management council for discussion and action.

In addition to making a broad strategic recommendation for the business, Krisak intended to propose a marketing plan to help implement this strategy. He needed to recommend a specific price for steam service during 1981. Due to fuel adjustment increases, the steam price was currently about $12/Mlb. Krisak also wondered how the current sales force might be used to better advantage. For instance, was Lakeshore overlooking any opportunities for creative new marketing efforts?

He also planned to include organizational recommendations in his report. It seemed clear that steam management needed strengthening but there was a question of just how this might be done. McDowall had mentioned his own concern that the company needed to be moved closer to an entrepreneurial posture in order to succeed at steam. Krisak wondered what specific recommendations might meet this requirement.

Krisak was aware that the way in which he made his recommendations was almost as important as the recommendations themselves. He found the situation frustrating—so many reports had been written in the past and even the notion of a refuse plant had first surfaced seven years previously. Somehow he had to make the problems and opportunities of running what he called Lakeshore's "shoe store" business come alive.

THE GILLETTE COMPANY: TRAC II

Jay E. Klompmaker
Charles M. Kummel

In July 1978, Mike Edwards, Brand Manager for TRAC II,[1] was beginning to prepare his marketing plans for the following year. In preparing for the marketing plan approval process, he had to wrestle with some major funding questions. The most recent sales figures showed that TRAC II had continued to maintain its share of the blade and razor market. This had occurred even though the Safety Razor Division (SRD) had introduced a new product to its line, Atra. The company believed that Atra would be the shaving system of the future and, therefore, was devoting increasing amounts of marketing support to this brand. Atra was launched in 1977 with a $7 million advertising campaign and over 50 million $2 rebate coupons. In less than a year, the brand achieved a 7 percent share of the blade market and about one third of the dollar-razor market. Thus, the company would be spending heavily on Atra, possibly at the expense of TRAC II, still the number one shaving system in America.

Copyright © 1982 by Jay E. Klompmaker.

[1] TRAC II is a registered trademark of The Gillette Company.

Edwards was faced with a difficult situation, for he believed that TRAC II still could make substantial profits for the division if the company continued to support it. In preparing for 1979, the division was faced with two major issues:

1 What were TRAC II's and Atra's future potentials?
2 Most important, could SRD afford to heavily support two brands? Even if they could, would it be sound marketing policy to do so?

COMPANY BACKGROUND

The Gillette Company was founded in 1903 by King C. Gillette, a 40-year-old inventor, utopian writer, and bottle-cap salesman in Boston, Massachusetts. Since marketing its first safety razor and blades, the Gillette Company, the parent of the Safety Razor Division, had been the leader in the shaving industry. The Gillette safety razor was the first system to provide a disposable blade that could be replaced at low cost and that provided a good inexpensive shave. The early ads focused on a shave-yourself theme: "If the time, money, energy, and brainpower which are wasted (shaving) in the barbershops of America were applied in direct effort, the Panama Canal could be dug in four hours."

The Pre-World War Years

With the benefit of a 17-year patent, Gillette was in a very advantageous position. However, it was not until the First World War that the safety razor began to gain wide consumer acceptance. One day in 1917 King Gillette came into the office with a visionary idea: to present a Gillette razor to every soldier, sailor, and marine. Other executives modified this idea so that the government would do the presenting. In this way, millions just entering the shaving age would give the nation the self-shaving habit. In World War I, the government bought 4,180,000 Gillette razors as well as smaller quantities of competitive models.

Daily Shaving Development

Although World War I gave impetus to self-shaving, World War II popularized frequent shaving—12 million American servicemen shaved daily. This produced two results: (1) Gillette was able to gain consumer acceptance of personal shaving, and (2) the company was able to develop an important market to build for the future.

Postwar Years

After 1948, the company began to diversify through the acquisition of three companies which gave Gillette entry into new markets. In 1948, the acquisition of the Toni Company extended the company into the women's grooming aid market. Paper Mate, a leading maker of writing instruments, was bought in 1954, and the Sterilon Corporation, a manufacturer of disposable supplies for hospitals, was acquired in 1962.

Diversification also occurred through internal product development propelled by a detailed marketing survey conducted in the late 1950s. The survey found that the public associated the company as much or more with personal grooming as with cutlery and related products. Gillette's response was to broaden its personal care line. As a result, Gillette now markets such well-known brands as Adorn hair spray, Tame cream rinse, Right Guard antiperspirant, Dry Look hair spray for men, Foamy shaving cream, Earth Borne and Ultra Max shampoos, Cricket lighters, and, Pro Max hair dryers as well as Paper Mate, Eraser Mate, and Flair pens.

Gillette's Current Operations

Gillette was divided into four principal operating groups (North America, International, Braun AG, Diversified Companies) and five product lines. As Exhibit 1 indicates, the importance of blades and

EXHIBIT 1
GILLETTE SALES AND CONTRIBUTIONS TO PROFITS BY BUSINESS SEGMENTS

Year	Blades and razors		Toiletries and grooming aids		Writing instruments		Braun electric razors		Other	
	Net sales	Contributions to profits	Net sales	Contributions to profits	Net sales	Contributions to profits	Net sales	Contributions to profits	Net sales	Contributions to profits
1977	31%	75%	26%	13%	8%	6%	23%	13%	12%	(7)%
1976	29	71	28	15	7	6	21	10	15	(2)
1975	30	73	30	15	7	5	20	8	13	(1)
1974	30	69	31	17	7	6	20	5	12	3
1973	31	64	32	20	7	5	22	10	8	1

Source: Gillette Annual Report for 1977, p. 28.

razors to company profits was immense. In nearly all the 200 countries in which its blades and razors were sold, Gillette remained the industry leader.

In 1977, Gillette reported increased worldwide sales of $1,587.2 million with income after taxes of $79.7 million (see Exhibit 2). Of total sales, $720.9 million were domestic and $866.3 million were international, with profit contributions of $109 million and $105.6 million, respectively. The company employed 31,700 people worldwide, with 8,600 employees in the United States.

Statement of Corporate Objectives and Goals

At a recent stockholders' meeting, the chairman of the board outlined the company's strategy for the future:

The goal of The Gillette Company is sustained growth. To achieve this, the company concentrates on two major objectives: to maintain the strength of existing product lines and to develop at least two new significant businesses or product lines that can

make important contributions to the growth of the Company in the early 1980s.

In existing product lines, the Company broadens its opportunities for growth by utilizing corporate technology to create new products. In other areas, growth is accomplished through either internal development or the acquisition of new businesses.

The Company uses a number of guidelines to evaluate growth opportunities. Potential products or services must fulfill a useful function and provide value for the price paid; offer distinct advantages easily perceived by consumers; be based on technology available within, or readily accessible outside the Company; meet established quality and safety standards; and offer an acceptable level of profitability and attractive growth potential.

THE SAFETY RAZOR DIVISION

The Safety Razor Division had long been regarded as the leader in shaving technology. Building on King Gillette's principle of using razors as a vehicle for blade sales and of associating the name "Gillette" with premium shaving, the Division had been able to maintain its number-one position in the U.S. market.

EXHIBIT 2
THE GILLETTE COMPANY ANNUAL INCOME STATEMENTS, 1963–1977
(Thousands of dollars)

Year	Net sales	Gross profit	Profit from operations	Income before taxes	Federal and foreign income taxes	Net income
1977	$1,587,209	$834,786	$202,911	$158,820	$79,100	$79,720
1976	1,491,506	782,510	190,939	149,257	71,700	77,557
1975	1,406,906	737,310	184,368	146,954	67,000	79,954
1974	1,246,422	667,395	171,179	147,295	62,300	84,995
1973	1,064,427	600,805	155,949	154,365	63,300	91,065
1972	870,532	505,297	140,283	134,618	59,600	75,018
1971	729,687	436,756	121,532	110,699	48,300	62,399
1970	672,669	417,575	120,966	117,475	51,400	66,075
1969	609,557	390,858	122,416	119,632	54,100	65,532
1968	553,174	358,322	126,016	124,478	62,200	62,278
1967	428,357	291,916	101,153	103,815	47,200	56,615
1966	396,190	264,674	90,967	91,666	41,800	49,866
1965	339,064	224,995	75,010	75,330	33,000	42,330
1964	298,956	205,884	72,594	73,173	35,500	37,673
1963	295,700	207,552	85,316	85,945	44,400	41,545

Share of Market

Market share was important in the shaving industry. The standard was that each share point was equivalent to approximately $1 million in pretax profits. Over recent history, Gillette had held approximately 60 percent of the total dollar market. However, the division had put more emphasis on increasing its share from its static level.

Product Line

During the course of its existence, Gillette had introduced many new blades and razors. In the last 15 years, the shaving market had evolved from a double-edged emphasis to twin-bladed systems (see Exhibit 3). Besides Atra and TRAC II, Gillette marketed Good News! disposables, Daisy for women, double-edge, injector, carbon, and Techmatic band systems (see Exhibit 4). Within their individual markets, Gillette sold 65 percent of all premium double-edged blades, 12 percent of injector sales, and almost all of the carbon and band sales.

Marketing Approach and Past Traditions

During 1977, the Gillette Company spent $207.9 million to promote all its products throughout the world, of which $133.1 million was spent for advertising, including couponing and sampling, and $74.8 million for sales promotion. In terms of the domestic operation, the Safety Razor Division used an eight-cycle promotional schedule whereby every six weeks a new program was initiated. During any one cycle, some but not all the products and their packages were sold on promotion. Usually one of the TRAC II packages was sold on promotion during each of these cycles. As stated in the company's 1977 annual report:

> Gillette advertising is designed to provide information to consumers and motivate them to buy the Company's products. Sales promotion ensures that these products are readily available, well located

and attractively displayed in retail stores. Special promotion at the point of purchase offers consumers an extra incentive to buy Gillette products.

In the past the company had concentrated its advertising and promotion on its newest shaving product, reducing support for its other established lines. The theory was that growth must come at the expense of other brands. When TRAC II was introduced, for example, the advertising budget for other brands was cut, with the double-edged portion being decreased from 47 percent in 1971 to 11 percent in 1972 and TRAC II receiving 61 percent of the division budget, or 27% of total market expenditures (see Exhibit 5).

A long standing tradition had been that razors were used as a means for selling blades. Thus, with razors, the emphasis was on inducing the consumer to try the product by offering coupon discounts, mail samples, and heavy informational advertising. Blade strategy had been to emphasize a variety of sales devices—such as discounts, displays, and sweepstakes at pharmacies, convenience stores, and supermarkets—to encourage point-of-purchase sales. In spite of this tradition, razor sales were a very significant portion of division sales and profits.

At the center of this marketing strategy had been the company's identification with sports. The Gillette "Cavalcade of Sports" began with Gillette's radio sponsorship of the 1939 World Series and continued in 1978 with sponsorship of the World Series, Super Bowl, professional and NCAA basketball, as well as boxing. During the 1950s and 1960s, Gillette spent 60 percent of its ad dollars on sports programming. Influenced by research showing that prime-time entertainment offered superior audience potential, the company switched to a prime-time emphasis in the early 1970s. However, Gillette had recently returned in the last two years to its sports formula.

Marketing Research

Research had been a cornerstone to the success of the company, for it had been its means of

EXHIBIT 3
GILLETTE PERCENTAGE OF U.S. BLADE SALES (ESTIMATED MARKET SHARE)

Total

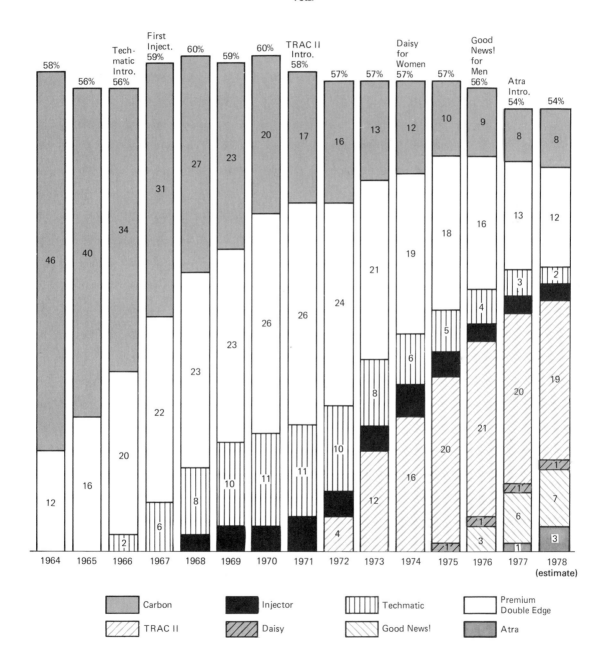

EXHIBIT 4
SAFETY RAZOR DIVISION PRODUCT LINE, JUNE 1978

Product line	Package sizes	Manufacturer's suggested retail price
Blades:		
TRAC II	5, 9, 14, Adjustable 4	$1.60, 2.80, 3.89, 1.50
Atra	5, 10	$1.70, 3.40
Good News!	2	$.60
Daisy	2	$1.00
Techmatic	5, 10, 15	$1.50, 2.80, 3.50
Double-edged:		
Platinum Plus	5, 10, 15	$1.40, 2.69, 3.50
Super-Stainless	5, 10, 15	$1.20, 2.30, 3.10
Carbon:		
Super Blue	10, 15	$1.50, 2.15
Regular Blue	5, 10	$.70, 1.25
Injector:		
Regular	7, 11	$1.95, 2.60
Twin Injector	5, 8	$1.40, 2.20
Razors		
TRAC II	Regular	$3.50
	Lady	$3.50
	Adjustable	$3.50
	Deluxe	$3.50
Atra		$4.95
Double-edged:		
Super Adjustable		$3.50
Lady Gillette		$3.50
Super Speed		$1.95
Twin Injector		$2.95
Techmatic	Regular	$3.50
Three-Piece		$4.50
Knack		$1.95
Cricket Lighters	Regular	$1.49
	Super	$1.98
	Keeper	$4.49

remaining superior to its competitors. For example, Gillette was faced in 1917 with the expiration of its basic patents and the eventual flood of competitive models. Six months before the impending expiration, the company came out with new razor models, including one for a dollar. As a result, the company made more money than ever before. In fact, throughout the history of shaving, Gillette had introduced most of the improvements in shaving technology. The major exceptions were the injector, which was introduced by Schick, and the stainless-steel double-edged blade introduced by Wilkinson.

The company spent $37 million annually on research and development for new products, product improvements, and consumer testing. In addition to Atra, a recent development was a new sharpening process called "Micro-smooth" which improved the closeness of the shave and the consistency of the blade. This improvement was to be introduced on all of the company's twin blades by early 1979. Mike Edwards be-

EXHIBIT 5
GILLETTE ADVERTISING EXPENDITURES, 1965–1978
(Percentage of total market)

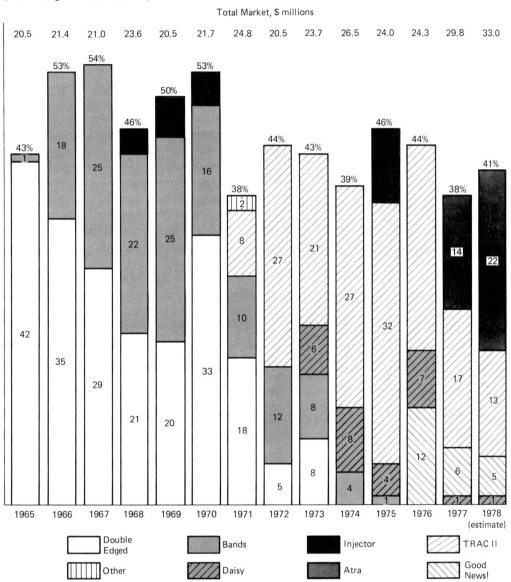

Total Market, $ millions

| 20.5 | 21.4 | 21.0 | 23.6 | 20.5 | 21.7 | 24.8 | 20.5 | 23.7 | 26.5 | 24.0 | 24.3 | 29.8 | 33.0 |

Legend:
- Double Edged
- Other
- Bands
- Daisy
- Injector
- Atra
- TRAC II
- Good News!

lieved that this would help to ensure TRAC II's retention of its market.

At the time of Atra's introduction, Gillette research found that users would come from users of TRAC II and nontwin-blade systems. This projected loss was estimated to be 60 percent of TRAC II users. Recent research indicated that with heavy marketing support in 1978, TRAC II's loss would be held to 40 percent.

THE SHAVING MARKET

The shaving market was divided into two segments: wet and electric shavers. In 1978, the wet shavers accounted for 75 percent of the market. In the United States alone, 1.9 billion blades and 23 million razors were sold annually. Gillette participated in the electric market through sales of electric razors by its Braun subsidiary.

Market Factors

There were a number of factors at work within the market: (1) the adult shaving population had increased in the past 15 years to 74.6 million men and 68.2 million women, (2) technological improvements had improved the quality of the shave as well as increased the life of the razor blade, and (3) the volume of blades and razors had begun to level off after a period of declining and then increasing sales (see Exhibit 6). Although the shaving market had increased slightly, there were more competitors. Yet Gillette had been able to maintain its share of the market—approximately two thirds of the dollar-razor market and a little over half of the dollar-blade market.

Market Categories

The market was segmented into seven components: new systems, disposables, injector, premium double-edged, carbon double-edged, continuous bands, and single-edged systems. In the early 1900s the shaving market consisted primarily of straight-edges. During the past 70 years, the market has evolved away from its single- and then double-edged emphasis to the pres-

EXHIBIT 6
RAZOR AND BLADE SALES VOLUME, 1963–1979

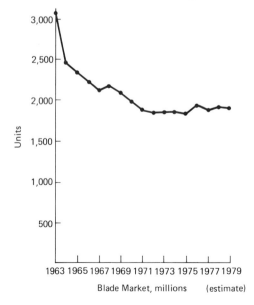

Blade Market, millions   (estimate)

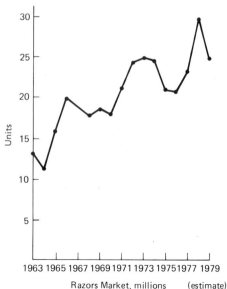

Razors Market, millions   (estimate)

ent market of 60 percent bonded systems (all systems in which the blade is encased in plastic). Exhibit 7 shows the recent trends within the market categories.

Competitors

Gillette's major competitors were Warner-Lambert's Schick, Colgate-Palmolive's Wilkinson, American Safety Razor's Personna, and BIC. Each had its own strongholds. Schick, which introduced the injector system, controlled 80 percent of that market. ASR's Personna sold almost all of the single-edged blades on the market. Wilkinson's strength was its bonded system which appealed to an older, wealthier market. BIC had developed a strong product in its inexpensive disposable system.

Competitive pricing structure was comparable to Gillette within the different system categories. Although all the companies had similar suggested retail prices, the differences found on the racks in

the market were a function of the companies' off-invoice rates to the trade and their promotional allowances. Although not much of a factor at this time, private label covered the range of systems and continued to grow.

Market Segmentation

The success of Gillette's technological innovation could be seen in its effect on the total shaving market. Although there were other factors at play in the market, new product introductions had contributed significantly to market expansion as Exhibit 8 indicates.

TWIN-BLADE MARKET

Research played a key role in the development of twin blades. Gillette had two variations—the current type in which the blades were in tandem; the other type in which the blades' edges faced each other and required an up-and-down scrub-

EXHIBIT 7
RECENT SHARE TRENDS
(In percentages)

Volume	1972	1973	1974	1975	1976	1977	1978, 1st half
Units:							
New systems	8.8%	20.6%	28.8%	36.2%	39.9%	40.8%	43.8%
Injector	20.2	17.6	17.1	16.3	15.7	14.2	12.8
Double-edged:							
Premium	39.4	34.9	30.8	27.4	24.5	21.1	19.0
Carbon	12.0	10.6	9.4	8.1	7.3	7.6	6.6
Bands	13.1	10.3	8.0	6.4	4.7	3.7	2.7
Disposables	—	—	—	—	2.5	6.9	9.7
Single-edged	6.5	6.0	5.9	5.6	5.4	5.7	5.4
Total market	100.0	100.0	100.0	100.0	100.0	100.0	100.0
Dollars:							
New systems	11.8	26.9	36.9	46.0	50.1	50.1	52.1
Injector	21.8	18.6	17.8	16.4	15.0	13.8	12.5
Double-edged:							
Premium	41.5	34.2	28.7	24.0	20.8	18.1	16.1
Carbon	6.1	5.4	4.7	4.2	4.0	4.1	3.5
Bands	15.4	11.8	8.7	6.5	4.8	3.6	2.8
Disposables	—	—	—	—	2.8	7.5	10.5
Single-edged	3.4	3.1	3.2	2.9	2.5	2.8	2.5
Total market	100.0	100.0	100.0	100.0	100.0	100.0	100.0

EXHIBIT 8
NEW PRODUCT INTRODUCTIONS AND THEIR EFFECTS ON THE MARKET, 1959–1977

Year	Product segment	Dollar sales blade/razor market (millions)	Change (%)
1959	Carbon	122.4	Base
1960	Super blue	144.1	+17.7 over 1959
1963	Stainless	189.3	+31.3 over 1960
1965	Super stainless	201.2	+ 6.3 over 1963
1966	Banded system	212.1	+ 5.4 over 1965
1969	Injector	246.8	+16.3 over 1966
1972	Twin blades	326.5	+32.2 over 1969
1975	Disposable	384.0	+17.6 over 1972
1977	Pivoting head	444.9	+15.9 over 1975

bing motion. From a marketing standpoint, and because the Atra swivel system had problems in testing development, TRAC II was launched first. The research department played a major role in the positioning of the product when it discovered hysteresis, the phenomenon of whiskers being lifted out and after a time receding into the follicle. Thus, the TRAC II effect was that the second blade cut the whisker before it receded.

Since its introduction in 1971, the twin-blade market had grown to account for almost 60 percent of all blade sales. The twin-blade market was defined as all bonded razors and blades (e.g., new systems: Atra and TRAC II; disposables: Good News! and BIC). Exhibit 9 shows the trends in the twin-blade market.

During this period many products were introduced. These included the Sure Touch in 1971, the Deluxe TRAC II and Schick Super II in 1972, the Lady TRAC II, Personna Double II, and Wilkinson Bonded in 1973, the Personna Flicker, Good News!, and BIC Disposable in 1974, the Personna Lady Double II in 1975, and the Adjustable TRAC II and Schick Super II in 1976.

Advertising

In the race for market share, the role of advertising was extremely important in the shaving industry. Of all the media expenditures, television was the primary vehicle in the twin-blade market. For Gillette, this meant an emphasis on maximum exposure and sponsorship of sports events. The company's policy for the use of television was based on the concept that television was essentially a family medium and programs

EXHIBIT 9
THE TWIN-BLADE MARKET, 1972–1978
(Millions of dollars)

	1972	1973	1974	1975	1976	1977	1978, estimate	1979, estimate
Razors	29.5	32.1	31.4	31.3	31.5	39.7	53.8	
Disposables	—	—	—	—	14.5	41.5	64.9	
Blades	31.6	72.0	105.7	147.5	176.3	183.7	209.2	
Total twin	61.1	104.1	137.1	178.8	222.3	264.9	327.9	
Total market	326.5	332.6	342.5	384.0	422.2	444.9	491.0	500.0

EXHIBIT 10
ESTIMATED MEDIA EXPENDITURES
(Thousands of dollars)

	1976	1977, 1st half	1977, 2nd half	Total 1977	1978, 1st half	Total 1978 estimate
Companies:						
Gillette	$10,800	$ 4,800	$ 6,400	$11,200	$ 8,100	$13,800
Schick	7,600	3,700	4,300	8,000	4,300	8,900
Wilkinson	2,700	1,400	2,200	3,600	1,400	2,200
ASR	2,600	700	200	900	200	800
BIC	600*	4,300	1,800	6,100	4,000	7,300
Total market	$24,300	$14,900	$14,900	$29,800	$18,000	$33,000
Brands:						
TRAC II	$ 6,000	$ 3,300	$ 1,700	$ 5,000	$ 2,400	$ 4,000
Atra	—	—	4,000*	4,000	4,500	7,500
Good News!	1,900	1,200	600	1,800	700	1,600
Super II	2,600	1,400	2,600	4,000	3,000	4,600

* Product introduction.

should therefore be suitable for family viewing. Gillette tried to avoid programs that unduly emphasized sex or violence.

As the industry leader, TRAC II received a great deal of competitive pressure in the form of aggressive advertising from competitors and other Gillette twin-blade brands (see Exhibit 10). For example, the theme of recent Schick commercials was the "Schick challenge," and BIC emphasized its lower cost and cleaner shave in relation to those of other twin-blade brands. However, competitive media expenditures were such that their cost per share point was substantially higher than TRAC II's.

Despite competitive pressures, TRAC II had been aggressively advertised too. As a premium product, it did not respond directly to competitive challenges or shifts in its own media; rather, the advertising followed a standard principle of emphasizing TRAC II's strengths. As Exhibits 11 and 12 indicate, the TRAC II media plan emphasized diversity with a heavy emphasis on advertising on prime-time television and on sports programs. In addition, TRAC II was continually promoted to retain its market share.

For 1978, the division budgeted $18 million for advertising, with Atra and TRAC II receiving the major portion of the budget (see Exhibit 13). The traditional Gillette approach was for the newest brand to receive the bulk of the advertising dollars (see Exhibit 5). Therefore, it was cer-

EXHIBIT 11
TRAC II MEDIA PLAN, 1976, 1977
(Thousands of dollars)

	Quarter				
	1	2	3	4	Total
1976:					
Prime	935	575	1200	550	3160
Sports	545	305	450	1040	2440
Network total	1480	880	1650	1590	5600
Other	80	85	70	165	400
Total	1560	965	1720	1755	6000
1977:					
Prime	1300	900	300	—	2500
Sports	500	400	400	400	1700
Network total	1800	1300	700	400	4200
Print	—	—	200	200	400
Black	75	75	75	75	300
Military, miscellaneous	25	25	25	25	100
Total	1900	1400	1000	700	5000

EXHIBIT 12
TRAC II MEDIA PLAN, 1978

Media	Jan.	Feb.	March	April	May	June	July	Aug.	Sept.	Oct.	Nov.	Dec.	Totals
Prime TV[a]	$1,055 M[c] — 15 Weeks →							$115M	World Series Promo				$1,170M
Baseball[b]			19 Weeks + All Star, Playoffs, & World Series → $1,278M										$1,278M
Misc. sports[b]	$1,062M — 52 Weeks →												$1,062M
Spot TV											$230M 4 Weeks		$230M
Black, military, Sunday newspaper, misc.			$260M — 40 Weeks →										$260M / $400M

[a]Prime-time TV advertising:
KAZ
ABC Friday Movie
Tuesday Big Event
ABC Sunday Movie
Roots Two
Love Boat
Different Strokes
Real People
Duke
Rockford Files

[b]Sports TV advertising:
Wide World of Sports, Saturday
College Basketball
NBA All Star Game
International Teen Boxing
Wide World of Sports, Sunday
NBA Basketball
History of Baseball
Game of the Week Day
This Week Baseball

[c]M = $1,000.

EXHIBIT 13
RAZOR DIVISION MARKETING BUDGET, 1978

	Atra line	TRAC II line	Good News!	Double-edged blades	Double-edged razors	Techmatic line	Daisy	Injector line	Twin injector	Total blade/razor
Marketing expenses:										
Promotion[a]	42.3	69.4	65.2	92.2	75.4	52.7	58.4	77.5	48.3	60.7
Advertising[b]	55.6	28.8	31.2	4.6	—	—	39.0	—	26.3	36.5
Other	2.1	1.8	3.6	3.2	24.6	47.3	2.6	22.5	25.4	2.8
Total marketing	100.0	100.0	100.0	100.0	100.0	100.0	100.0	100.0	100.0	100.0
Percentage line/total direct marketing	34.1	38.4	14.9	7.6	.4	.3	3.4	.2	.7	100.0
Percentage line/total full revenue sales	20.5	41.8	13.4	16.8	1.4	2.1	2.2	.6	1.2	100.0

[a] Defined as off-invoice allowances, wholesale push money, cooperative advertising, excess cost, premiums, contests, and prizes.
[b] Defined as media, sampling, couponing, production, and costs.

tain that Atra would receive a substantial increase in advertising for 1979. Whether the division would increase or decrease TRAC II's budget as well as whether it would increase the total ad budget for 1979 was unknown.

TRAC II

The 1971 introduction of TRAC II was the largest in shaving history. Influenced by the discovery of the hysteresis process, by the development of a clog-free dual-blade cartridge, and by consumer testing data which showed a nine to one preference for TRAC II over the panelists' current razors, Gillette raced to get the product to market. Because the introduction involved so many people and was so critical to reversing a leveling of corporate profits (see Exhibit 2), the division president personally assumed the role of product development manager and lived with the project day and night through its development and introduction.

Launched during the 1971 World Series promotion, TRAC II was the most frequently advertised shaving system in America during its introductory period. Supported by $10 million in advertising and promotion, TRAC II results were impressive: 1.7 million razors and 5 million cartridges were sold in October; and during the first year, the introductory campaign made 2 billion impressions and reached 80 percent of all homes an average of 4.7 times a week. In addition, a multimillion-unit sampling campaign was implemented in 1972 which was the largest of its kind.

For five years TRAC II was clearly the fastest growing product on the market, and it helped to shape the switch to twin blades. Its users were predominantly young, college-educated, metropolitan, suburban and upper-income men. The brand reached its peak in 1976 when it sold 485 million blades and 7 million razors. In comparison, projected TRAC II sales for 1978 were 433 million blades and 4.2 million razors. During this period, TRAC II brand contribution decreased 10 percent (see Exhibit 14).

Competitors' responsive strategies seemed to be effective. The growth of Super II during the last two years was attributed to certain advantages it had over TRAC II. Super II had higher trade allowances (20 percent versus 15 percent), improved distribution, an increased media expenditure, and generally lower everyday prices.

In preparing the 1979 marketing plans, the objective for TRAC II was to retain its consumer franchise despite strong competitive challenges through consumer-oriented promotions and to

EXHIBIT 14
TRAC II LINE INCOME STATEMENT, 1972–1978

	1972[a]	1973	1974	1975	Base 1976	1977	Estimated 1978
Full revenue sales (FRS):							
Promotional	28	41	71	100	100	110	112
Nonpromotional	38	91	89	83	100	80	65
Total	32	60	78	93	100	99	95
Direct cost of sales:							
Manufacturing	63	77	93	111	100	88	83
Freight	51	80	91	106	100	82	80
Total	62	77	93	111	100	88	83
Standard profit contribution	26	56	75	89	100	101	97
Promotional expenses:							
Lost revenue	26	39	72	100	100	114	126
Wholesale push money	455	631	572	565	100	562	331
Cooperative advertising	27	36	58	71	100	115	133
Excess cost	25	50	59	83	100	63	92
Premiums	3	29	16	28	100	78	217
Contests & prizes	7	21	110	115	100	215	109
Total	26	40	67	90	100	112	129
Advertising expenses							
Media	90	83	110	119	100	96	75
Production	96	128	130	104	100	196	162
Couponing & sampling	470	344	177	112	100	166	131
Other	19	120	68	78	100	54	54
Total	124	110	108	117	100	96	78
Other marketing expenses	108	120	847	617	100	242	86
Market research	122	65	47	34	100	134	91
Total assignable marketing expenses	67	69	87	102	100	106	108
Net contribution:	14	53	81	85	100	100	94
Percentage of promotional FRS/total FRS	56	43	58	76	63	70	74
Percentage of promotional expenses/promo FRS	15	16	16	15	11	17	20
Percentage of promotional expenses/total FRS	9	7	9	10	11	12	15
Percentage of advertising expenses/total FRS	28	13	10	9	7	7	6
Percentage of media expenses/total FRS	17	8	8	8	6	6	5

[a] Each year's data are shown as a percentage of 1976's line item. For example, 1972 sales were 32 percent of 1976 sales.

market the brand aggressively year round. Specifically, TRAC II was:

1 To obtain a 20 percent share of the cartridge and razor market.

2 To deliver 43 percent of the division's profit.

3 To retain its valuable pegboard space at the checkout counters in convenience, food, and drug stores as well as supermarkets.

In 1978, Mike Edwards launched a new economy-size blade package (14 blades) and a heavy spending campaign to retain TRAC II's market share. He employed strong trade and consumer promotion incentives supported by (1) new improved product claims of a "microsmooth" shave, (2) new graphics, and (3) a revised version of the highly successful "Sold Out" advertising campaign (see Exhibit 15). Midyear results indicated that TRAC II's performance had exceeded division expectations as it retained 21.6 percent of the blade market and its contribution exceeded the budget by $2 million.

ATRA

Origin

Research for the product began in Gillette's United Kingdom Research and Development Laboratory in 1970. The purpose was to improve the high standards of performance of twin-blade shaving and, specifically, to enhance the TRAC II effect. The company's scientists discovered that a better shave could be produced if, instead of the shaver moving the hand and face to produce the best shaving angle for the blade, the razor head could pivot in such a way as to maintain the most effective twin-blade shaving angle. Once the pivoting head was shown to produce a better shave, test after test, research continued in the Boston headquarters on product design, redesigning, and consumer testing.

The name "Atra" came from two years of intensive consumer testing of the various names which could be identified with this advanced razor. The choice was based on how easy it was to remember the name, how well it communicated the technology, its uniqueness, and the feeling of the future it conveyed. Atra stood for *Automatic Tracking Razor Action.*

Introduction

Atra was first introduced in mid-1977. The introduction stressed the new shaving system supplemented by heavy advertising coupled with $2 razor rebate coupons to induce trial and 50-cent coupons toward Atra blades to induce brand loyalty. An example of Atra advertising is shown in Exhibit 16. During its first year on the national market, Atra was expected to sell 9 million razors although 85 percent of all sales were sold on a discount basis. Early results showed that Atra sold at a faster level than Gillette's previously most successful product, TRAC II. The Atra razor retailed for $4.95. Blades were sold in packages of 5 and 10. TRAC II and Atra blades were not interchangeable. Because of Gillette's excellent distribution system, it had not had much problem gaining valuable pegboard space.

CURRENT TRENDS AND COMPETITIVE RESPONSES IN THE TWIN-BLADE MARKET

There was quite a bit of activity in the shaving market during the first half of 1978. Atra had increased the total Gillette share in the razor and blade market. During the June period, Atra razors continued to exceed TRAC II as the leading selling razor whereas Atra blades share was approximately 8 percent, accounting for most of Gillette's 4 percent share growth since June 1977. Thus, the growth of Atra had put more competitive pressure on TRAC II. In addition, the disposable segment due to BIC and Good News! had increased by five share points to a hefty 12

EXHIBIT 15

Gillette **TRAC II**®

THE GILLETTE COMPANY
SAFETY RAZOR DIVISION

BBDO

"SOLD OUT"

LENGTH: 30 SECONDS   (MICROSMOOTH-GIRL) SUPER II   COMM'L NO.: GSRD 8033

IRVING: Sold out again!???
(SFX: DING!)

CUSTOMER 1: The new improved
Gillette TRAC II, please.

IRVING: Er . . . say . . . who needs
improved when these twin blades'll do.

CUSTOMER 1: TRAC II has micro-
smooth edges . . . makes the blades
smoother than ever.

IRVING: Shave better than these?

CUSTOMER 1: Better, safer, smoother
. . . and comfortable.

IRVING: Comfort . . . schmomfort . . .
you don't have . . . But . . . but . . . b-b . . .

CUSTOMER 2: Do you have the new
improved Gillette TRAC II?

IRVING: Improved TRAC II??
(INNOCENTLY) Improved TRAC II?

ANNCR: The new improved Gillette
TRAC II. Micro-smooth edges make
it a better shave.

EXHIBIT 16

:30 second commercial   GSRS7013 "Impossible, Yes"   August, 1977

ANNCR (VO): Could Gillette make a razor that does the impossible?

Yes.

Could it shave closer with even more comfort?

Yes.

Gillette introduces Atra . . .

the first razor with a pivoting head . . .

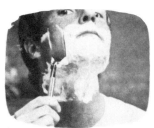

that safely follows every contour of your face.

This Atra face-hugging action keeps the twin-blades at the perfect angle.

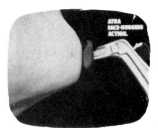

You've never shaved this close with this much comfort.

MAN: Impossible!

ANNCR: The New Gillette Atra Razor.

Yes, it's the impossible shave.

© THE GILLETTE COMPANY, BOSTON, MASS. 1977

percent dollar share of the blade market. Combined with TRAC II's resiliency in maintaining share, competitive brands had lost share: Schick Super II, ASR, and Wilkinson were all down two points since June 1977.

In response to these recent trends, the TRAC II team expected competition to institute some changes. In an effort to recover its sagging share, Edwards expected the Schick Muscular Dystrophy promotion in October 1977 to help bolster Super II with its special offer. The pressure might already be appearing with Schick's highly successful introduction of Personal Touch for women in this year, currently about 10 percent of the razor market, which had to draw TRAC II female shavers. In addition, it appeared inevitable that Schick would bring out an Atra-type razor. This would remove Atra's competitive advantage but increase pressure on TRAC II with the addition of a second pivoting head competitor.

Continuing its recent trends, it appeared that the disposable segment of the market would continue to expand. The first sign of this was the BIC ads offering 12 BIC disposables for $1. Good News! received additional advertising support in the latter half of the year as well as the introduction of a new package size. One of Edwards's major objectives was to emphasize the importance of TRAC II to upper management. Besides the introduction of the microsmooth concept, a price increase on TRAC II products would be implemented soon. It was unclear whether the price change would have an adverse effect on brand sales.

In preparing the 1979 TRAC II marketing plan, Edwards realized that Atra would be given a larger share of the advertising dollars following a strong year, and the disposable market would continue to grow. TRAC II share remained questionable, depending on the level of marketing support it received. Whether TRAC II would be able to continue its heavy spending program and

generate large revenues for the division remained to be seen. All of these factors, as well as the company's support of Atra, made 1979 a potentially tough year for Mike Edwards and TRAC II.

1979 MARKETING PLAN PREPARATION

Edwards had received the following memorandum from the vice-president of marketing:

MEMO TO: Brand Group
FROM: P. Meyers
DATE: July 7, 1978
SUBJECT: 1979 Marketing Plans

In preparation for the marketing plan approval process and in developing the division strategy for 1979, I would like a preliminary plan from each brand group by the end of the month. Please submit statements of objective, corresponding strategy and levels of dollar support requested for the following:

1 Overall brand strategy[2]—target market
2 Blade and razor volume and share goals
3 Sales promotion
4 Advertising
5 Couponing and sampling
6 Miscellaneous—new packaging, additional marketing research, marketing cost saving ideas, etc.

See you at the weekly meeting on Wednesday.

In developing the TRAC II marketing plan, Edwards had to wrestle with some strategy decisions. To get significant funding, how should he position TRAC II in relation to Atra and the disposables? Also, how could he convince the vice-president that dollars spent for TRAC II were more effective than expenditures on Good News! or Gillette's other razors?

---

[2] Brand strategy means positioning the brand in such a way that it appeals to a distinguishable target market.

PART NINE

ORGANIZING AND IMPLEMENTING THE MARKETING EFFORT

Excellence in organizing and implementing the marketing effort is a characteristic of outstanding firms. Organizing the marketing effort requires more than just deciding how to structure the marketing department and assigning specific responsibilities to specific individuals. It includes developing a strong consumer orientation throughout the institution, examining marketing's role in the overall organization, and facilitating marketing's interaction with other functional areas of management.

TOWARD A MARKETING ORIENTATION

Meaningful implementation requires a marketing orientation throughout the organization, starting with the chief executive officer. Managers at all levels in each function must understand what marketing is and how it can contribute to the organization. Employees must be service-oriented and be prepared to act as if they were users instead of providers of the product.

Once market sensitivity has been achieved, maintaining such an orientation is a continuous process. Long-run vitality requires responsiveness to change and maintenance of the external perspective that market-focused management brings.

Marketing is a demanding discipline; even successful organizations face the danger of slipping back into a product- or inward-looking orientation. Executives must constantly be aware of the indicators of product-oriented management. Not tailoring marketing strategies to meet segment needs and seeing the product as being inherently desirable for the target market may cause the organization to blame lack of consumer interest in the offering on ignorance or lack of motivation. Consequently, management places too much emphasis on communication strategies, and uses research, not to understand consumer needs, but to confirm management beliefs. Similarly, generic competition is largely ignored in a product-oriented firm. Successful implementation requires that a business maintain a market orientation at all levels and throughout all functional and management areas that interact directly or indirectly with consumers.

Working with Other Areas

Marketing is just one of several major management functions. Although the importance of these functions varies by the nature of the organization and the types of products offered, successful design and implementation of marketing programs require cooperation and coordination across functional areas. For example, a marketing orientation requires that the finance and control functions provide financial information on a product or market basis so that decisions about changes can be made in a sound way. A food manufacturer needs to know the difference in costs if it offers additional flavors or package sizes; a restaurant should know both the incremental and allocated costs of opening early for breakfast. Because financial executives often have an oversight role on substantial investments and expenditures, they must be educated by the marketing managers as to the need to spend funds on intangibles such as market research and advertising, which are not capitalized as assets on the balance sheet and whose value is realized only after the money is spent.

Coordination with all functional areas is important, but cooperation with the management of production and operations is of particular concern. Especially in a service industry, marketing and operations should be seen as mutually supportive functions. Developing customer demand for a product that cannot subsequently be produced is as harmful as efficiently providing a product nobody needs and for which there is no potential to develop a demand. Successful products make sense from the vantage point of both operations and marketing.

Nevertheless, there are fundamental differences in orientation between marketing and production (or operations) that management must bridge in order to achieve competitive and market success. Marketing management is oriented externally to the needs of the customers and to threats from competition. In response, it tends to offer a wide range of products and to want to update them frequently. Success is defined in terms of customer satisfaction and product utilization. Operations, or manufacturing management, on the other hand, is internally oriented. It wants to offer a few standardized products and is reluctant to make changes. It emphasizes producing these products in an efficient manner. Success tends to be measured in terms of cost minimization and achievement of operating standards that may have no relation to customer concerns. Often there is little recognition that the organization currently or potentially faces either direct or generic competition.

Ultimately, success of a marketing program depends upon the people who come in direct contact with the users; these people are often operations, not marketing, personnel. Many organizations—such as hotels, restaurants, and airlines—produce the final product as it is being consumed. As a result, the marketing function in a service organization must be closely interrelated with, and dependent on, the personnel and operations functions and the people, procedures, and facilities administered by these functions.

The Marketing Organizational Structure

The effectiveness of marketing efforts depends on how well matched the marketing department is to both the external environment and the company's internal characteristics. No single organizational structure can be effective in all settings, and the structure of a marketing department may have to be changed as the corporation evolves.

Marketing departments are generally structured in one of three major ways. A functional system groups together people who carry out similar marketing functions. Thus all those working on advertising would be in one group, those involved in field sales in a second, those responsible for pricing in a third, and so forth. By contrast, a decentralized product-manager system focuses on grouping together managers on the basis of a series of different products. Some have found that a product-manager system provides too much focus on the product and not enough on the market segments served and have, therefore, turned to a market-centered approach.

The choice between a functional versus a product-manager or market-centered system has long been a topic of debate in marketing. Each system has its strengths and weaknesses. Companies rarely install one of these frameworks in a "pure" form, tending to modify the basic structure to meet their own needs. In complex situations, combined product-market manager systems are sometimes needed.

Good Practice in Marketing

There are no magic formulas for good practice in marketing or sure-fire formulas for success. But there are some areas that need to be emphasized, including a consumer orientation throughout the firm and a supportive relationship among the functional areas based on mutual trust and respect.

Particularly important in successfully executing marketing strategies is the establishment of a clear, powerful, shared theme, a vision of what the company does and how with regard to marketing. For example, a company may emphasize customer service so that no consumer problem is too small to be disregarded. Products are to be highly reliable, and virtually instantaneous service is provided nationwide, 24 hours a day, every day of the week. All personnel then know that customer satisfaction comes first in decision making.

Success also requires a high degree of competence in carrying out the marketing-mix functions—advertising, pricing, and distributing the product. Often a company will have one or a few selected functions in which it excels. One consumer-goods firm, for example, dominates its markets through its skill in obtaining display space in stores for its heavily advertised branded products.

In addition to skills in the marketing-mix functions themselves, there needs to be a program to coordinate the functions. In other words, management must make sure the elements operate as an integrated marketing mix, not as individual components. For example, one organization's mail order campaign to sell Christmas gifts was enormously successful in generating orders but produced huge embarrassment to the company when stocks were exhausted early in the campaign, because of someone's failure to ensure access to adequate supplies.

Good implementation requires the development of a monitoring system to measure and control the results of marketing activities. The marketing plan can be the basis of a management-control system. An action plan can detail the specific activities that need to be carried out and list responsibilities, or targets, by name or functional area. The established targets then become the basis for control so that deviations in performance are identified and corrective action, when necessary, is taken. By monitoring against these targets on a continuing basis, usually monthly or quarterly, management has time to make changes before the situation deteriorates to a crisis condition. It would seem easy for managers to get information to keep track of how well they are doing. Nevertheless, many marketing departments do not have reliable, understandable monitoring mechanisms. The marketing strategy may set the direction and excellent execution may carry the organization along, but a reliable, timely monitoring and control system is needed to make sure the program is on the right path.

CONCLUSION

Marketing is concerned not only with the grand design of strategy but also with the implementation of programs and the execution of myriad necessary details. While excellent execution cannot save a misdirected strategy, only good execution can transform a sound strategy from plans on paper to reality. Marketing success depends on all elements of a plan working together to accomplish the organization's goals.

A continuing challenge for any business is to organize its marketing efforts in ways that efficiently leverage its competitive standing in the marketplace. Decisions on whether to structure the marketing organization by marketing function, products, markets, or geographic areas (or a combination of these alternatives) should reflect an understanding of the key success factors underlying the strategy selected by the firm.

Within any firm, marketing has to develop a means of coexisting with other functional areas of management, whose concerns often tend to be cost- and efficiency-centered rather than driven by a desire to satisfy customer needs in a competitive marketplace. One of the responsibilities of the general manager is to act as arbiter in interfunctional disputes, balancing the concerns of both sides. Clearly, this requires that the general manager have a good understanding of all functions.

The organizational structure and procedures to be adopted should reflect the nature of both the firm and its environment. No firm can afford to allow its organization to be cast in concrete. As the role of marketing evolves, and as changes take place in products, markets, and the competition, so should organizational frameworks be allowed to evolve in response.

KNOWLES PRODUCTS: BRAND MANAGEMENT SYSTEM

Charles B. Weinberg

In early 1984, Clive Langdon, Group Vice President—Pharmaceutical Products of Knowles Products, was reviewing a specially commissioned report on his division's brand management system. Knowles, a major marketer of a well-known brand of analgesic and a number of personal care products and owner of a Southern U.S. chain of franchised drug stores, had used a brand management system for more than a decade. This system had worked well for Knowles; however, it seemed to Langdon that a review of this system was appropriate. Consequently, in September he had asked Leslie Nome, a well-regarded marketing consultant, to conduct such a review. After some discussion, Langdon and Nome agreed that the first stage of the project should be to document the way that brand management system operated at Knowles. Langdon was reviewing that report in anticipation of a meeting the next morning with Nome.

© Copyright 1985 by Charles B. Weinberg.

COMPANY BACKGROUND

In the early 1900s Jason Knowles, a pharmacist by training and a travelling salesman by profession, developed a patent medicine that he claimed was beneficial for relieving a variety of ills. Over time, the claims moderated but Knowles' products, sold primarily in tablet form, gained popularity as a headache remedy. Descendants of the original family maintained control of the company until the early 1970s, when the stock was first publicly offered.

PRODUCT LINE

For the fifty years leading up to Knowles' going public in 1973, the firm had essentially been a one product company. Although Knowles analgesic was sold in liquid and tablet form and combined with other ingredients to produce such products as cough syrups and cold remedies, the focus was always on Knowles pills and their promised relief from headaches. Some other brands had been introduced but none had ever accounted for more than 10 percent of corporate sales.

Prior to going public in 1973, Knowles management had begun to plan a major expansion of its product line. In 1975, the company announced a program for growth marked by expansion in four major directions:

1 Health related products
2 Personal care products
3 Franchised drug stores
4 International markets

In the immediately ensuing years, Knowles acquired three companies, each with a major well-known brand name of health related product (an upset stomach remedy, a muscle relaxant, and a treatment for athlete's foot). In addition, Knowles also acquired several small companies that marketed specialty personal care products, such as a dandruff shampoo and a denture cleaner. In the six years ending in 1981, Knowles acquired companies with a total of fifteen significant brand names and introduced three new internally developed brands as well. Although selling a variety of pharmaceutical and personal care products, the majority of the company's sales was made through supermarkets. In 1981, senior management decided to cease acquiring new companies and concentrate on internal development.

In 1979, Knowles acquired a chain of drug stores, named Southern Star, located in Florida and Georgia. About half of Southern Star's outlets were franchised; the rest were wholly owned. Although some additional smaller acquisitions were made, expansion of the Southern Star was accomplished primarily through opening new outlets and increasing sales per store.

Knowles' analgesics had been sold in Western Europe for almost thirty years. Several of the new brands were also manufactured in Europe or Asia, but most overseas markets were served through export sales.

Overall corporate sales had increased by more than tenfold in the past decade to $1.3 billion in 1983. However profits had not kept pace. Exhibit 1 summarizes corporate performance by line of business from 1978 to 1983. An abridged organization chart for the Knowles Products is given in Exhibit 2.

THE BRAND MANAGEMENT SYSTEM

Knowles had been organized along the lines of a very strong product management system, particularly in the Pharmaceutical Products division as

EXHIBIT 1
KNOWLES PRODUCTS: CORPORATE PERFORMANCE
(by line of business; $ millions)

	1983	1982	1981	1980	1979	1978
Net sales:						
Consumer products						
Pharmaceuticals	513	461	399	338	339	251
Personal care	110	94	86	67	39	31
Subtotal	623	555	485	405	378	282
Drug stores	690	678	596	403	240	—
Total	1313	1233	1081	808	618	282
Net income:						
Consumer products	53	49	41	39	32	29
Drug stores	20	18	16	10	7	—
Total	73	67	57	49	39	29

EXHIBIT 2
PARTIAL ORGANIZATION DIAGRAM FOR KNOWLES PRODUCTS

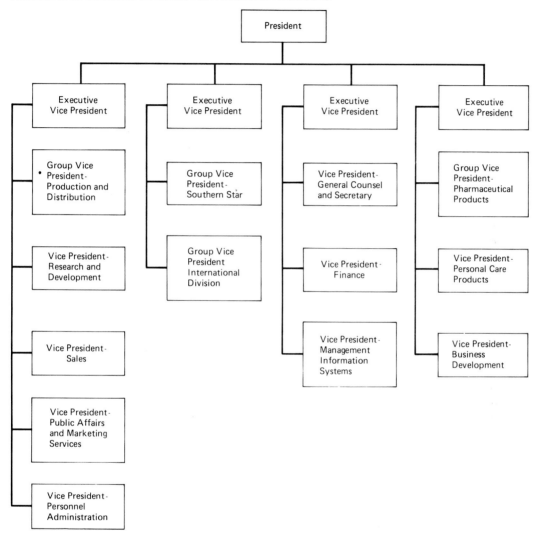

shown in Exhibit 3. There were five job levels in the brand system: brand assistant (BA), assistant brand manager (ABM), brand manager (BM), associate marketing manager (AMM), and marketing manager (MM). The focus of Nome's initial report was on the brand manager and lower levels, i.e., assistant brand manager and brand as-

sistant. (See Exhibits 4, 5, and 6 for relevant job descriptions.)

Although Nome's report did not deal extensively with the MM and AMM levels of management, these managers played a critical role in brand management. The MM managed all aspects of marketing, except sales execution, for

EXHIBIT 3
KNOWLES' MARKETING ORGANIZATION, PHARMACEUTICAL PRODUCTS DIVISION

```
                    ┌──────────────────────────┐
                    │ Group Vice President-    │
                    │ Pharmaceutical Products  │
                    └──────────────────────────┘
                                │
                    ┌──────────────────┐
                    │ Vice President   │
                    └──────────────────┘
                                │
    ┌──────────┬──────────┬──────────┬──────────┬──────────┐
┌────────┐ ┌────────┐ ┌────────┐ ┌────────┐ ┌────────┐
│Manager │ │Manager │ │Manager │ │Marketing│ │Controller│
│Product │ │Manufac-│ │Sales   │ │Manager │ │         │
│Develop-│ │turing  │ │        │ │        │ │         │
│ment    │ │        │ │        │ │        │ │         │
└────────┘ └────────┘ └────────┘ └────────┘ └────────┘
 ┌────────┐  ┌────────┐             │
 │Market  │  │Media   │     ┌──────────────┐
 │Research│  │Manager │     │5 Associate   │
 │Manager │  │        │     │Marketing     │
 └────────┘  └────────┘     │Managers      │
                            └──────────────┘
                                   │
                            ┌──────────┐
                            │15 Brand  │
                            │Groups    │
                            └──────────┘
                                   │
                            ┌──────────┐
                            │Brand     │
                            │Manager   │
                            └──────────┘
                                   │
                            ┌──────────┐
                            │Assistant │
                            │Brand     │
                            │Manager   │
                            └──────────┘
                                   │
                            ┌──────────┐
                            │Brand     │
                            │Assistant │
                            └──────────┘
```

the division. This manager's key objectives were not only achievement of short-term volume and profit goals but also development, testing and expansion of new products, improved products, and line extensions. These latter goals were emphasized by top management to ensure continued corporate growth. The AMMs largely served coordinating, controlling, training and strategic overview roles between the AM and

BMs. They also had final decision-making authority on promotion activities within existing budgets, and handled many of the administrative jobs in the advertising department.

The entry-level job was that of BA. The BA was primarily responsible for monitoring the product budget, developing sales promotions, and analyzing marketing information (e.g., sales data from the company's management informa-

EXHIBIT 4
JOB DESCRIPTION—BRAND MANAGER

Function. To contribute to the overall growth of Knowles through development, recommendation and implementation of effective marketing programs capable of building brand volume, share and profit for assigned brands. The brand manager is charged to:

1 Provide management with relevant data regarding the state of the business, serving as management's antennae in the category to identify problems and opportunities.

2 Develop recommendations which are designed to stimulate brand growth.

3 See that all programs are coordinated and run properly, serving as the focal point for all brand related activity.

4 Ensure that brand personnel learn the skills to handle multifaceted responsibilities of the job.

The brand manager's specific marketing responsibilities are as follow:

1 *Product.* Ensure that the product and package are superior to competition within cost constraints demanded by the marketplace and profit considerations. Requires consumer usage/ attitude and product research, establishment of product improvement objectives, and periodic review of progress toward these objectives.

2 *Positioning.* Position the product to maximize volume within the existing consumer and competitive environments. Periodically review marketing strategy in light of changing consumer needs, wants, and attitudes and competitive product positionings and sales. Develop and test alternative copy and promotion strategies attuned to the marketing strategy to improve the brand's overall positioning.

3 *Copy.* Ensure that copy provides the optimum selling power. Demands an ongoing effort in development and testing of new copy pools, different executional formats and alternative copy strategies.

4 *Media.* Ensure that media plans are designed to deliver advertising in the most effective and efficient manner against the brand's target audience. Requires periodic review of target audience criterion and testing of alternative mixes of media vehicles within budget constraints, as well as testing of different media weights.

5 *Promotion.* Plan, execute and evaluate, with the assistance of the sales department, consumer and trade promotions, which are cost-effective in increasing brand volume. Demands testing of a variety of promotions each fiscal year and testing, on a periodic basis, alternative annual promotion levels and/or alternative consumer/trade promotion splits within existing budgets.

6 *Volume/Control.* Make adjustments as necessary in fiscal year plans to deliver volume base.

The brand manager's specific management information responsibilities are as follows:

1 *Volume.* If fiscal year overshipment or undershipment seems obvious, inform management and recommend action.

2 *Competitive Developments.* Report significant competitive activity and recommend defensive action.

3 *Product Problems.* Analyze and recommend action on any product or package problems which threaten volume.

4 *Problem Markets.* Identify, analyze, and propose remedial action.

5 *Schedule Changes.* Advise promptly when delays from expected test market or expansion dates are encountered and explain reason for delay.

6 *Costs.* Report significant shifts and recommend action (e.g., price increase).

7 *Governmental Actions.* Report on any legislative or regulatory activities that could affect the business and recommend action.

EXHIBIT 5
JOB DESCRIPTION—ASSISTANT BRAND MANAGER

Marketing Responsibilities:

1 *Business Building Plans.* Develop, recommend, and execute those key projects which, long term, will have a major effect on the shipments/consumption of the brand. Examples of these are the introduction of new sizes/products, major distribution building programs or major trial generating promotions.

2 *Copy.* Work with the brand manager in providing direction to the advertising agency in the development of new executional formats (based on current strategy) and the testing of new copy strategies/executions. Also, work with technical and legal to obtain copy clearance/claim support.

3 *Media.* In conjunction with the brand manager, provide the agency with direction on new ways to more efficiently reach the brand's target audience. This may take the form of media mix tests or testing of different media levels.

4 *Product.* Ensure that a product which fulfills consumer needs and wants is marketed within cost constraints.

5 *Market Research Planning and Analysis.* Initiate and analyze those market research projects which will yield information upon which the brand may act to improve current market position or correct an ongoing problem.

6 *Package Design.* Ensure that the package in the marketplace is appealing, eye-catching, and connotes those attributes of the product most important to consumers.

Management Information:

1 *Market Research.* Analyzes research and recommends next steps to correct any problems or capitalize on any opportunities.

2 *Media.* Analyze results of media testing and recommend action to be taken.

3 *Schedule Changes.* Inform brand manager of delays in the progress of key projects in order that management may be apprised of the delay and the reason why.

---

tion system, consumption data from the A.C. Nielsen Company, and additional data from other outside market research services). New projects were added as competence was gained until the BA was sent out for "sales training," a 12-week field sales assignment.

Promotion to ABM followed this selling experience. Emphasis was placed upon learning advertising copy and media, developing long-term business-building programs, and assisting and helping train the BA in the area of sales promotion. ABM was a transition job which could last from one to two and a half years, depending on the capabilities of the person and the needs of the company.

When the ABM was promoted to BM, he or she was given overall marketing responsibility for one or more products, including planning, fore-

casting, and controlling volume and spending for these products. He or she also supervised ABMs and BAs. Due to rotation and normal turnover, not all brand groups were fully staffed with a BA and ABM.

In terms of day-by-day operations, the brand management group considered the other functions as "staff" to them. Nonetheless, brand management had no direct authority over sales, manufacturing, market research and product development. But it did have the responsibility to obtain from staff the inputs necessary for successful marketing. Each functional group, for this purpose, had a representative designated to deal with the brand manager. An integral part of this system of "responsibility without direct authority" was the fact that brand management controlled budgets for areas such as market research

EXHIBIT 6
JOB DESCRIPTION—BRAND ASSISTANT

Marketing Responsibilities:

1 *Sales Promotion.*   Plans, in consultation with other brand group members and the sales department, national and test promotions. Writes promotion recommendations and issues related feasibility requests and production orders. Implements consumer-oriented portions of promotions (e.g., coupon copy and media, sample drops, etc.) and oversees and/or cooperates with sales department in implementing trade-oriented portions of promotions (e.g., preparation of organizers, selection of salesperson's incentives, etc.). Controls all budgeting for promotions. Evaluates promotions.

2 *Budget Administration and Control.*   Reviews and codes invoices. Reconciles the budget with accounting on quarterly basis. Closes out budget with accounting at the end of the fiscal year.

3 *Market Analysis.*   Analyzes Nielsen data and writes bimonthly Nielsen reports. Audits other sources of market information (monthly shipment reports, SAMIs, etc.) and writes analytical reports as necessary.

4 *Shipment Estimates.*   In consultation with assistant brand manager and/or brand manager, prepares monthly shipment estimate which forecasts next three months' shipments with supporting rationale.

5 *Competitive Activity.*   Monitors competitive activity reported by sales (promotion and pricing activity), agency (competitive media spending), and other sources (periodicals, etc.). Writes reports on significant developments.

6 *Public Relations.*   Cooperates with consumer services in handling special consumer-oriented problems which fall outside normal consumer services activities. Works with research services (home economists) and public affairs on brand-related consumer information projects.

Other areas where brand assistant may contribute, depending upon individual brand assignments, are as follows:

1 *Package Design.*   Development of design objectives. Interface with package designers, marketing services, and technical staff on development, consumer testing, and feasibility determination on design. Recommendation, implementation, and evaluation of any test market.

2 *Business-Building Tests.*   Work with assistant brand manager and/or brand manager on one or more of the following aspects of business-building tests—planning, recommendation, implementation, and evaluation.

Management Information: Reports to brand manager on:

1 *Competitive Activity.*   Significant competitive developments.
2 *Budget Variance.*   Any variations from budget forecasts.
3 *Promotion Problems.*   Any problems with implementation of promotions.
4 *Consumer Relations.*   Any product problems which threaten volume.

and package design and represented staff's channel to top management. For example, a departmental request for information or specific action was typically directed to the brand manager who not only had to concur but was the interface with top management. (See Exhibit 7.)

Excerpts from interviews with several brand managers are given in the Appendix at the end of the case.

Corporate Atmosphere

Nome considered Knowles to be an almost classic example of brand management. Brand managers played a "line management" role within the marketing function at Knowles. The reasoning for this was that the BM had direct responsibility for the most critical marketing factor—advertising—and had the broadest exposure to the operations of the company and the

EXHIBIT 7
INTERFACE MATRIX

Brand Manager Responsibilities	Work with These Departments	Brand Role
Product or package improvement	Sales, R&D market research, manufacturing and controller	(a) Develop objectives for product or package development. (b) Approve aesthetics. (c) Develop consumer research objectives, fund research and summarize results. (d) Determine unit profit potential and return on investment. (e) Recommend test market to management. (f) Write manufacturing production orders for test market production of product. (g) Analyze test market results and recommend national expansion.
Positioning	Advertising agency, market research and legal	(a) Develop alternative positionings. (b) Develop consumer research objectives and fund research. (c) Analyze research results and recommend test market. (d) Analyze test market results and recommend national expansion.
Copy	Advertising agency, market research and legal	(a) Review agency copy submissions and select copy to be presented to management. (b) Approve final production for on-air copy testing. (c) Analyze copy test results. (d) Recommend national airing of copy.
Media	Advertising agency and media services	(a) Review agency media objectives and strategies and recommend alternatives. (b) Review and modify agency media plans with help of media services. (c) Forward agency media plan to management. (d) With help of media services monitor implementation of media plan.
Sales promotion	Sales, manufacturing, promotion development and legal	(a) Develop national promotion plan with help of sales department. (b) Recommend plan to management. (c) Write manufacturing production order for production of sales promotion product. (d) Implement consumer portion of promotion (i.e., coupons, samples, etc.) and fund all trade allowances and consumer promotions.
Volume control	Sales	(a) Monitor shipments. (b) If undershipment of objectives seems possible, recommend remedial marketing efforts.

best overall perspective on his product and markets.

Brand managers were able to accomplish their goals through other people by using their control over the product budget, their position as coordinator of all information, and their interpersonal skills. They had to be successful "at getting others to do the job."

But there was even more to the essential nature of the brand manager's job, a perspective that can only be expressed by senior management. These people looked upon brand managers as individuals who could be expected to ask the type of questions a top manager might ask, gather the facts necessary to make a decision, and then recommend a course of action in a very succinct memo. The net effect was that top management's job of managing the marketing of a large number of diverse brands in diverse categories became easier and more effective. The system assured that all brands, even those with small sales, were given attention and that a variety of marketing approaches designed to stimulate growth would at least be explored and recommended.

The power of the brand managers rested largely in their authority to ask questions anywhere in the company and demand carefully thought out, responsible answers, as long as the questions and answers were limited to matters which either directly affected the consumer of their product or affected their brand's contribution margin (revenue less manufacturing and shipping costs and brokerage commission). In addition, successful brand managers had informal authority arising from their superior knowledge, as compared to that of a functional specialist's, of all consumer aspects of their product, and they had the power to discuss their recommendations (in writing, usually) with top management.

Selection and Screening

Typically, brand assistants were recent MBAs from leading business schools with minimum work experience (See Exhibit 8 for a sample recruitment ad.) In recent years, Knowles had hired some graduates with advertising experience as well as some transferees from other company departments, but these were exceptions. Brand managers were almost always promoted from within. In initial hiring, Knowles sought individuals who were intelligent, trainable, competitive, aggressive and hard-working. Ideal candidates

had qualities which were generalized as: analytical ability; communication skills; the ability to plan, organize and follow through; the ability to work well with others; leadership, resourcefulness and ingenuity; decision-making skill; drive and determination; and maturity.

Training

The introduction for the new brand assistant was strenuous. Although the initial jobs might range from planning promotions to writing market research summaries, there was a lot of arduous "number crunching." Hours were long, often including weekends. There were no shortcuts or special courses and readings that could bypass this breaking-in period. Nor was there much sympathy for the neophyte. Everyone in brand management had been through the same experience, recognized its necessity, and knew the work could be done. "Help" was mainly in the form of providing initial direction, pointing out errors, and suggesting new projects as competence increased. The newer projects were invariably more interesting and challenging, which provided additional incentive to master the earlier tasks. And as new BAs were hired, the more mundane jobs could be passed down.

The purpose of this training was to internalize certain "first principles" which were considered necessary to maintain the brand management system:

1 *All information could be derived from numerical data:* Brand people had minimal contact with either customers or suppliers. Customers were normally represented by market research findings and sales results. Suppliers were represented by specific liaison people. Thus there always had to be an analytic justification for a project or program. Results needed to be summarized in terms of cases of product and net revenue (minus all costs except advertising).

2 *Concern for mistakes:* Brand people were trained to be detail-oriented and concerned

EXHIBIT 8
SAMPLE RECRUITING ADVERTISEMENT

**Marketing Careers with
One of the Nation's
Leading Companies**

Knowles Corporation manufactures and markets over 15 major consumer brands. Many are among the country's market leaders.

A limited number of entry level positions are available as BRAND ASSISTANT, working within a Brand Group which has responsibility for one or more individual products and is the driving force behind them.

As a Brand Assistant, you will be assigned to a specific product. Your Brand Manager will give you immediate responsibility for a variety of projects and then look to you for leadership, ideas, and results. Some examples of your assignments will be: planning, executing and evaluating promotions; analyzing business performance; planning and executing a sales presentation for a new market initiative; developing new packaging; and helping to manage your brand's budget.

In addition to individual projects, you will be broadly exposed to all aspects of Brand Management. As you contribute to the management of your brand and demonstrate your ability to handle additional responsibility, you will be assigned more complex and important projects. Your Brand Manager is responsible for your training and will work very hard to accelerate your personal development. The emphasis, however, is always on you . . . your thinking, your ideas, your contributions. Management career development is excellent. At Knowles, promotion is always from within, and based upon individual performance and contribution.

If you are about to obtain an MBA degree or equivalent and are just starting your career, if you have a background of achievement and can exhibit good analytical and communication skills, and if you are interested in talking further with us, send your resume to:

CORPORATE RECRUITING MANAGER
KNOWLES CORPORATION

---

about not making errors. No mistake, particularly in a memo, was too small to be noticed. The feedback was intense since memos were commented on in writing as they were passed up and down the distribution chain. If anyone found a mistake, then everyone who missed it was embarrassed.

3 *Brand manager's budget as a control system:* This principle was a bit deceptive, however. While some staff groups—market research, sales merchandising and package design—were dependent upon brand management for funding of projects, brand management did not use the budget as a club. The range of interrelationships between brand management and staff was too involved to be reduced to the single lever of money control.

4 *Career success required "the Knowles style":* The Knowles style contributed to the climate and mystique which made brand management successful. This style included memo format, job concept, and attitude. Memos conformed to a particular writing style and format and were not supposed to exceed two pages without an attached summary. Brand people had to be the resident experts on everything affecting their products. Brand managers thought of themselves as the general managers of a very small company. Nonetheless, brand people had to maintain their aggressive, competitive attitude without hurting their relations with staff. The BA might achieve a basic competence in one or two years. The competence was recognized by the addition of more complex assignments. As the BA's credibility and influence increased with the staff, he or she conformed more and more to the corporate style. BMs estimated that they spent as much as 25 percent of their time training BAs and ABMS. In fact, the entire brand management system was a training program. There was no such thing as an old BM; there was no place for the person who didn't want to be promoted.

MANAGEMENT INFORMATION SYSTEMS

The BM used current data almost exclusively, even though comprehensive historical files were maintained. Meetings were usually frequent and short. Memos were passed through for comment and review by the BM. Magazines might be scanned for ideas but were seldom read. For many BMs, only the Nielsen chart books, the product fact book, and project folders were kept within easy reach.

Tests were used extensively to determine the accuracy of the information routinely received so that results could be optimized and problems avoided. Brand people went out into the field infrequently, yet they had a strong perception about what was happening through their tests and the management information system.

Emphasis had to be placed on the management information system because the BM changed products about every two years and thus lost personal contacts in the agency and staff groups who tended to remain with the products.

RELATIONSHIP WITH THE "BIG FIVE"

The five groups which brand management dealt with regularly were the advertising agency, sales, market research, manufacturing, and product de-

velopment. With each group, there were conflicts which the BM had to resolve. These conflicts might include work priorities, differences of opinion about strategy or objectives, or disagreements over project timing. Brand managers sometimes argued that they had the responsibility for volume and spending without explicit authority to force staff compliance. These other departments, however, saw brand management as more in control due to its final authority to make recommendations to top management as well as its role in setting initial objectives. The other departments would have preferred a better understanding (by brand management) of their role and problems, yet essentially believed in the brand system as the best way to run the company.

ROTATION AND PROMOTION

Brand people were expected to shift products about every two years. Due to attrition, new hires, and promotions, the time could vary but seldom exceeded three years. It took a BM several months to become familiar with a new assignment and perhaps a year to implement a major strategy. Thus, the typical BM was working on a predecessor's strategy for much of his or her tenure.

Performance was judged on a number of bases:

1 Did the BM prepare a sound annual marketing plan and was he or she able to sell it to management?

2 How well did the product perform against the volume objective in the marketplace (regardless of who prepared the budget)?

3 What sort of major improvements or line extensions were proposed (though not necessarily implemented)?

4 How well did he or she train others?

In addition, part of a BM's evaluation was based on such factors as: communication, analysis, thoroughness, prioritization, productivity, organization, leadership, work with others, reponsibility, ability to accept criticism, motivation, maturity, capacity, judgment and attitude.

SUMMARY

Brand management at Knowles was a total system. The climate, selection, training and promotion all tended to encourage the "best and brightest" people to dedicate themselves to making a product successful.

The people were supported by a management information system and organizational structure that allowed them to be trained on the job and rotate from product to product at frequent inter-

vals. The products were all marketed in a similar enough way, e.g., advertising, sales promotions, supermarkets and retail drug outlets, that the system and organization were the same for each.

The strength of the system lay in the fact that each product had a "champion" who attempted to achieve volume and share objectives, as predicted in an annual plan. The short term was not sacrificed for the long term since the long term generally represented the incumbent's proposed strategy and ongoing business-building tests, and the short term represented a predecessor's strategy. In addition, a pool of potential general management talent was being established and utilized as experienced managers were promoted and new employees added.

APPENDIX: Selected Portions of Interviews with Brand Managers

Question 1: You tyically hire MBAs with a small amount of work experience. What do you look for and how would you describe their jobs as BAs?

Brand Manager No. 1: I find it takes several months for a BA to become acclimated. New people are usually too theoretically oriented; at this level, pragmatic application of judgment to problems is more important. The most important thing for a BA to learn is to pay attention to details. Even "typos" have a dollar impact. The BA should learn to think things through comprehensively.

The BA begins working about ten hours per day plus homework, but the time goes down as the job is learned.

All marketers are pretty much alike—aggressive, detail-minded—and that's what we look for here.

BM No. 2: The biggest problem a new BA has is to learn how to juggle projects and determine priorities. Business schools teach sequential problem solving but "Brand" requires juggling 15 trivial things and 1 major one. The BA's initial problem is establishing credibility. Brand management requires a mixture of talents but no one specific personality is appropriate. Some brand people do consider themselves "prima donnas."

BM No. 3: The BA's problem is simply a lack of experience with our system. The system relies on numbers, and the numbers come from the BA. The BA is constantly calculating and must think in analytic terms. The BA must work very hard, develop rapidly, and learn what brand management is all about. It takes two to six months for the BA to have a good grasp of the job and become acclimated to the system. All training is on-the-job.

The BA is responsible for sales promotions and the budget. It is important for the BA to develop creative ways to solve problems.

The BA must determine what motivates people and use it.

Question 2: What is the relationship between brand management and the other departments?

BM No. 1: Brand managers are considered with respect by the advertising agency but brand managers are committed to the agency because the BM cannot fire the agency. Most of the people in other departments do not want to move as fast as brand management. It is a problem conveying the urgency and importance of timing. The BM is responsible for planning, and the other departments for advice and/or execution.

Knowledge is power and the BM is the resident expert on his or her products.

BM No. 2: Brand management is more a line than a staff function.

Brand management has responsibility for achieving volume objectives and keeping profit/case close to target level, but brand management has no direct authority over many other departments which impact on the ability to achieve objectives.

Senior management recognizes that sometimes performance is beyond the control of brand managers.

A brand manager does not have to be nice to suppliers and sometimes can become a tyrant due to the pressure.

BM No. 3: Brand managers control the money. Many other departments must rely upon brand management for direction and project funding. The advertising agency has account executives who deal with brand people and the agency's creative and media departments. The agency presents a national media plan once a year. Since the marketing budget is mainly advertising, brand and agency personnel write the request. Sales promotions are originated by brand management and proposed to the sales department.

Brand management recommends and analyzes market research test markets. The purpose of these is to avoid "national blunders," although the risk is relatively small with ongoing products.

Question 3: What common characteristics do brand managers have?

BM No. 1: The important attributes are aggressiveness and attention to detail.

BM No. 2: The BM must have an aggressive outlook toward life, be competitive, like to win, and be action-oriented.

It's important to learn to do a thorough analysis of all inputs.

Question 4: How do brand managers spend their time?

.BM No. 1: Daily activities are coordination, fielding short questions with answers on the telephone, and commenting on memos passing through. Wide variation exists, but a day might have one hour for thinking and strategy, one hour for standard reports, one hour for the "In/Out basket," two hours on the phone, one hour with subordinates, and two hours in meetings.

Dealings are mainly with the "Big Five": the account executive at the advertising agency; sales; the manufacturing coordinator; market research; and the product development specialists.

On the average, the BM travels to the field once every three months. Brand management's job is to study the product, determine what is needed, and prioritize projects. The budget for this is set once a year.

BM No. 2: The most important job of a brand manager is the budget request and appropriation. Once each year, a two- to three-hour meeting is held which lays out how and why money is to be spent for the next year. During the period preceding this meeting, much of a BM's time may be spent with the agency. During the remainder of the year, the time falls off with the time spent in once-a-week meetings and telephone calls.

The second major job is the Brand Improvement Objectives meeting which is also held once a year. Brand works with R&D to develop both short-term and long-term product development plans.

Brand strategies require 1½ to 2 years to implement. Long-range planning is important because few changes can be made in the short term due to long lead times in production and media planning.

Most of the BM's time is spent on specific projects.

Heavy use is made of the telephone and many short meetings are held, usually with six people or less.

Brand management has a meeting with the Product Development Center every two weeks.

Question 5: How often does a brand manager change brands?

BM No. 1: All brand people are interchangeable, although it takes about two to four months to become the most knowledgeable. You spend one to two years on a brand.

BM No. 2: Rotation is caused by promotions and departures and occurs every 1½ to 2 years. Continuity is provided by the staggered rotation of BAs, ABMs, and BMs. Once you rotate, you usually do not have time to find out how your old product is doing.

THE PARKER HOUSE, II

Penny Pittman Merliss
Christopher H. Lovelock

"Could I speak to you for a minute, Mac?"

Robert McIntosh, general manager of the Parker House, Boston's oldest hotel, looked up from his desk. William Murphy, the hotel's director of sales, was standing in the doorway. McIntosh smiled. "Any time, Bill," he replied, hoping no more surprises had surfaced since last week, when a group of athletes sponsored by one of the hotel's leading corporate clients had smoked enough marijuana to render their rooms uninhabitable for 24 hours. Or perhaps another VIP was complaining about the need to book early at the Parker House; the hotel was often filled to capacity during the fall season, and early October 1979 was proving to be no exception.

"We have got a problem on our hands with TransAm Tours," Murphy began. "My sales force has been doing its best to cut down on tour groups, especially since the hotel's done such a good job of attracting clients who will pay the full rate. Some of our other properties—I am thinking of the Berkshire Place in Manhattan—can't afford to turn down a lot of tour business."

Copyright © 1980 by the President and Fellows of Harvard College, Harvard Business School case 9–580–152.

McIntosh nodded. He was well aware of the Parker House's 85 percent occupancy rate, significantly above national average and the second highest in the Dunfey Hotels system.

"Well, I just got a call from Harvey Kimball" [Dunfey's national tour sales director], Murphy continued. "He's worked out a deal with TransAm Tours for next summer and fall. They've agreed to block out approximately 2,000 guest nights at the Berkshire Place, weekends as well as midweek, from June through October 1980. The problem is that TransAm is trying to leverage the Berkshire deal into roughly 4,000 guest nights with us during the same period. Now, not only are we trying to avoid tour groups—we're also trying to maximize our room revenues. On the other hand, Mac, the Berkshire is a Dunfey hotel, and it needs our help. What do you think we should do?"

DUNFEY CLASSIC HOTELS

The Parker House, wholly owned by the Dunfey corporation, was the most profitable of the company's 23 hotels. Generally considered to be the flagship of the corporation, it was the premier member of Dunfey's Classic Hotels division, directed by Yervant Chekijian. Management felt that the Classic hotels—each of which was a unique unit—offered discriminating travelers a welcome opportunity to escape the monotony of the chains. The Classics also provided a retreat from the noise and crowds of conventions. As Chekijian explained:

> A Dunfey Classic is not a convention hotel. While we will accommodate small executive and professional groups, our marketing approach is not to pack the house with large groups. We are seeking a quiet, peaceful atmosphere. . . . Our feeling is that corporate travelers who are regular customers of the hotel will appreciate knowing that they can get rooms with us even if the rest of the town is sold out to a convention.

Each Classic hotel was a formerly elegant property located in the city center which had fallen into decay prior to Dunfey's purchase. The renovation process involved more than refurbishment of facilities. In the words of William Dunfey:

> A Dunfey Classic hotel is not just an old hotel that we've slapped a new coat of paint onto. Even though some of the properties may have been neglected or run down when we took over, they all had a tradition of excellence and quality. Turning them into Classic hotels involves restoring that level of service as well as restoring the physical plant.

In keeping with Dunfey management's belief in the individuality of the Classic hotels, each had a very different decorating scheme. The Berkshire Place, in Manhattan, where major renovations were completed in May 1979 at a cost of over $9 million, had a contemporary tone, with large green plants, hand-woven Oriental rugs, and imported Italian marble columns and floors in the lobby. The Ambassador East, in Chicago, restored a year earlier for over $7 million, was decorated in a mixture of eighteenth century English antiques and Oriental and contemporary accessories.

Renovations at the Parker House had been designed to establish the air of understated luxury considered most congenial to cultivated New England tastes. Old oak paneling and rich Oriental carpets decorated the lobby; burnished, ornately patterned brass doors glowed on the elevators; a two-tiered brass chandelier was suspended from the elaborately carved central wooden ceiling. Encouraged by the success of the first round of room renovations, completed in 1975, the Dunfey management began even more luxurious redecorating in 1979. The cuisine served in Parker's Restaurant, reopened in 1975, had become widely recognized for its excellence among Boston diners; according to *Boston* magazine, Parker's was one of the ten best restaurants in the city and offered the best Sunday brunch in town.

Situated on the Freedom Trail, a self-guided walking tour through the heart of historic Boston, the Parker House was closer to Boston's financial, governmental, and trade centers than any other major hotel in the city. Much of the waterfront area, once decayed, now contained new apartments, offices, shopping areas, and parks; the recently restored Faneuil Hall-Quincy Market retail and restaurant complex, which had become enormously popular, was less than a ten-minute walk from the hotel. However, between mid-1981 and late 1982, three new luxury hotels were scheduled to open in the same general area of the city as the Parker House. Offering a combined total of over 1,200 rooms, these new hotels would be operated by Inter-Continental (a subsidiary of Pan Am), Meridien (a subsidiary of Air France), and Marriott Hotels, respectively.

THE PARKER HOUSE: FROM BANKRUPTCY TO REVIVAL

The Parker House was the oldest continuously operating hotel in the United States. The original building, constructed in 1855, quickly attracted a large and cosmopolitan clientele. The hotel had been almost totally rebuilt in 1927, but during the fifties and sixties it fell into decline. By 1969, occupancy at the Parker House was down to 35 percent, and the hotel that had hosted Presidents was forced to declare bankruptcy.

The Parker House was rescued by Dunfey Hotels, a privately owned chain. In 1975, the Dunfey family hired the former head of Sheraton's international marketing, Jon Canas, as vice president of sales and marketing. Canas brought a strong marketing orientation to the organization and recruited a number of experienced hotel executives.

Well aware of the heavy fixed costs of operating a hotel, Canas and his team knew that their major source of profits lay in room sales rather than food and beverage revenue. Accordingly, they went after all the business they could find: tour groups, conventions, training sessions, anything to "keep the lights on." As occupancy rose, they began to upgrade the appearance of the Parker House, renovating, restoring, and finally repositioning rooms, restaurants, and public areas. Room prices rose accordingly, and many of the customers who had initially enabled the hotel to survive were replaced by less price-sensitive corporate clients. Successful renovation of the Parker House, combined with Canas's marketing efforts and the improving national economy, led the Dunfey hotels' revenues to double in three years; chain-wide occupancy rates went from 56 percent in 1975 (when industry average was 62.5 percent) to a projected 76 percent in 1979. At the Parker House, the net earnings of the hotel in 1979 (after deducting all operating costs, depreciation, and amortization), were projected to reach $1.19 million—up from $1.05 million in 1978.

Target Marketing

The key to successful marketing, in the opinion of Dunfey management, was segmentation. Ron Gustafson, Dunfey's manager of sales administration, stated:

What we want to say is, "We are this type of a

hotel: now what do we need to do to reach these segments?" First we canvass an area door to door. We talk to customers and find out their needs. Then we tell them our story, we bring them down and show them the hotel. Then, when business begins to pick up, we try to monitor whether we're taking share from the correct hotels. We want to build our business with the correct market segments—not just fill rooms—because we're building for the future and the profile of customers we take in has a tremendous impact on creating a position for the hotel in the minds of the customers. For example, if our hotel is in the luxury class appealing to the upscale business executive and professional traveler, we don't want the badge-and-bottle conventioneers running around the lobby because, frankly, it destroys the atmosphere.

Extensive segmentation was very unusual in the hotel business. Most hotels segmented their guests into two or three categories: tourists, corporate travelers, and groups. However, the Parker House segmented its clients as follows:

1 *Pure Transient*—the customer, either tourist or corporate traveler, who simply picked up the phone and made a reservation at the rack rate,[1] attracted through general advertising or word of mouth. No direct sales effort reached this person.

2 *Outside Reservation*—the customer whose room (also at rack rate) was arranged through Dunfey's toll-free reservations number, often used by travel agents for their clients. This number, operated for Dunfey Hotels by an independent reservation service, cost the Parker House $100 per month, plus $5.43 for each individual reservation thus made. Management was interested to see how well this service performed.

3 *Executive Service Plan* (ESP)—consisted of executives traveling singly or in groups smaller than ten who reserved their rooms through an unlisted number and paid rack rate. Because this group was, to a large extent, drawn to the Parker House as a direct result of personal sales calls by

---

[1] The published rate charge for each accommodation, as established by hotel management.

ESP representatives, it was important to measure the success of the sales effort.

4 *Special Transient*—a limited category composed of friends of management, favored travel agents, etc. This segment was traced so that the lower rates charged to it would not skew other rate data. The hotel tried to limit these bookings to slow periods, such as weekends or the first quarter of the year.

5 *Patriot*—the government segment. The Parker House had 36 extremely small rooms, each containing a single bed, which were offered to government employees for a price considerably below the rack rate. In 1979 7,000 room nights in this category were billed. This segment was also traced primarily to avoid skewing more significant data.

6 *Mini-Vacation*—a standard weekend package comprising two nights (Friday-Saturday or Saturday-Sunday) and two breakfasts. In spring 1980 its cost would be $88.

7 *Classic Package*—the luxury weekend package, including a wine and cheese platter in the room, Godiva chocolates in the evening, sheets turned down before bedtime, dinner at Parker's Restaurant. In spring 1980 this package would cost $186.

8 *Corporate Groups*—corporate clients reserving rooms at the same time in blocks of ten or more. It was very unusual for the Parker House to book sleeping space for groups of over 150 people, though meetings of up to 500 were accepted.

9 *Associations*—professional associations reserving rooms at the same time in blocks of ten or more. Like those of corporate groups, their rates varied, depending on the time of the year and the desirability of the groups. Medical associations, for example, were highly prized, because they spent heavily on food and beverage and often planned their meetings during the weekends, when the hotel's occupancy dropped.

10 *Bus Tours*—the hotel attempted to limit these groups to weekends and the months of July and August, traditionally slower periods. The Parker House also tried to upgrade its bus tours

from American groups to European, Japanese, and other foreign tourists, who were willing to pay higher rates.

11 *Airline*—these 117 small rooms, overlooking airshafts, were secured through annual contracts with airlines using Boston's Logan International Airport and were occupied seven nights a week. The rate was somewhat cheaper, but European and other foreign airlines were courted because they were willing to pay more for the rooms than American carriers.

The other categories were: *permanent residents* (at present, the Parker House had none); *complimentary rooms,* provided free of charge, sometimes to compensate for a previous error made by the hotel; and *house use rooms,* given to employees who were forced to stay overnight or who wished to appraise the hotel's service. A quarterly breakdown of room revenue by segment is presented in Exhibit 1.

In some cases the market was segmented further by seasons of use, geography, and industry. The hotel also segmented its referrals. When all rooms were full, or when a guest was turned away because of overbooking, management made sure that well-heeled transients and top-rated corporate clients were referred to Boston's best hotels, such as the Ritz, the Copley Plaza, and the Hyatt Regency, the latter across the river in Cambridge. More price-sensitive guests were directed to middle-rank hotels or motor lodges.

Pricing varied for each segment and depended to a great extent on competition. Boston hotel rates in general were much lower than rates at similar hotels in New York City. Competitive information was gathered at regular intervals. Projected rack rates at the Parker House for fall 1980 are reproduced in Exhibit 2.

One of the most important benefits of the detailed segmentation employed by the Parker House management was the guidance it offered to the sales division. Jon Canas commented:

> With the rooms merchandising plan you know what to ask sales and reservation people to do. In general, in the industry, salespeople do not know who

EXHIBIT 1
THE PARKER HOUSE ROOM REVENUE BY SEGMENT, 1978
(quarterly)

Segment	(1) Jan.–Mar.	(2) April–June	(3) July–Sept.	(4) Oct.–Dec.	Total
1 Pure transient	$ 448,087	$ 335,103	$ 387,227	$ 338,141	$1,508,558
2 ESP	382,287	605,889	594,414	594,224	2,176,814
3 Mini-vacation*	45,894	48,855	40,098	67,388	202,235
4 Patriot and airline	243,438	247,121	251,300	252,002	993,861
5 Associations and corporate groups	156,500	314,541	208,669	276,268	955,978
6 Bus tours	12,819	64,914	172,910	83,388	334,031
7 Other†	38,095	21,353	23,276	32,555	115,279
Total	$1,327,120	$1,637,776	$1,677,894	$1,643,966	$6,286,756

* The only weekend package plan available in 1978.
† Includes Special Transients and Outside Reservation System guests.
Source: Company records.

to see, they do not know how many rooms are available, and they definitely do not know what rate to charge. At Dunfey we want to provide these guidelines as closely as possible in order to maximize our profitability and productivity.

The Sales Division

The Parker House sales division was led by Bill Murphy, who had previously directed sales at the Ambassador East in Chicago. He directed a group of five salespeople and eight inhouse telephone and clerical staff. Direct sales efforts were targeted toward the most desirable market segments, according to the hotel's mission statement. The sales manager handled professional asociations; the corporate sales executive covered corporate groups; and the two ESP account executives, Lyssa O'Neill and Pamela Roberge, were responsible for sales to individual business

EXHIBIT 2
PROJECTED PARKER HOUSE ROOM RATES, FALL 1980

Room Category	Number	Rate Single	Rate Double	Furnishings
1 Standard	130	$70	$80	Double bed, clock radio, color TV, Drexel furniture, Thermopane windows, individually controlled heat and air conditioning. The least expensive room available to ESP clients.
2 Deluxe	181	80	90	Similar to standard; larger room.
3 Top of the line	20	90	100	King-size beds; other furnishings similar to standard; larger room.
4 Mini-suite	48	105	115	Very large room (often constructed from two smaller rooms, with a wall removed) with walk-in closets and dividers between living and sleeping areas.
5 Parlor suite	16	$125		Living room, bedroom (1 or more), and some kitchen facilities such as a sink or wet bar.
6 Deluxe suite	2	250		Larger rooms, complete kitchen facilities, luxurious furnishings.

travelers. Since most ESP reservations were made by secretaries or corporate travel managers, O'Neill and Roberge directed the majority of their calls to people in these positions. All three of these sales efforts—corporate, professional, and ESP—were directed only toward room sales; banquets were handled by another representative who also reported to Murphy.

One of the hotel's goals for 1980 was to shift its market base toward customer segments more likely to pay full rates. Very seldom were all 546 rooms in the Parker House sold at the rack rate; most often about 30 percent were discounted. In an attempt to raise room sales efficiency[2] and reduce discounting, management had decided to aim for a lower occupancy rate—83.5 percent—in the hope of bringing in more guests at rack rate and raising revenues and profits. The latest renovations and rate increases were an essential part of this strategy. As Yervant Chekijian put it: "We are going to have no compromises on our product offering, and at the same time, we are not going to apologize for our rates."

Executive Service Plan

Because rates for tours, groups, and associations were often discounted, but ESP clients were always charged the rack rate, the ESP plan was considered the key to the hotel's new room sales efficiency target. Designed to make it convenient for individual corporate travelers to use the hotel, the plan included a direct unlisted telephone number reserved for ESP clients (out-of-town customers could call collect); "preferred" (i.e., larger) rooms; preregistration to ensure easy check-in; an express check-out service; bill-back privileges; a welcome packet, including a complimentary newspaper each morning (to be picked up in the lobby); and a special ESP privilege on Friday and Saturday nights entitling the

spouse of an ESP guest to stay at the hotel free of charge.

Direct sales calls were an essential element of ESP marketing strategy. The Parker House sales division kept files on 710 ESP companies, categorized as red, blue, green, or yellow depending on how frequently their employees used the hotel. Red clients, who booked over 150 room nights annually, were called on monthly; blue clients (75–150 rooms annually), every two months; green clients (25–75 rooms annually), every three months; and yellow clients, once or twice a year. In order to cover these accounts, ESP reps Roberge and O'Neill made approximately 40 calls (including 16 key accounts) weekly.

The ESP job was the hotel's entry-level sales position. Selling to groups and associations, according to Dunfey management, required dealing with experienced travel and convention planners and was handled by more senior members of the sales staff. In fact, since many of the ESP accounts were steady clients of the Parker House, and the demand for hotel space in Boston was high for a large part of the year, the ESP reps tended to view their job as customer service or client education rather than sales. "As salespeople we're not strictly solicitors at all," said O'Neill. "We're more personal contact. We are the company's liaison to the hotel, and they can call us if they have a problem. They know our faces, our names."

During and immediately after the original renovation of the hotel, ESP reps had been given a quota of 25 new accounts per week to solicit. By late 1979, demand for the Parker House had increased to the point that management instituted an account evaluation program. Roberge explained:

It's reached the point where we've had to look at an account and say, OK, these people have only used the hotel three times in the past year—to accommodate them on these three nights we may be shutting out somebody who uses us 1,500 room nights a year. We're going to try to be a little more selective about sales calls.

---

[2] Defined as the ratio of total room sales revenue over a period divided by the potential revenues that might be obtained if all available rooms were sold at full rates during the same period.

Neither ESP representative considered it very difficult to distinguish the hotel's most valuable clients. Commented O'Neill:

> The least desirable people are those who are very price-sensitive and concerned about the rates. For instance, one guy who ran a shoe outlet wanted to have a function here and bring his own liquor and his own dry snacks. People like that—or people who have reservations made on short notice in spring and fall only—I really want to discourage because the hotel is full during that time and their volume is nothing we can put our finger on. I'll bring up rates during the call, which is something a salesperson usually doesn't do. Alternatively, I would encourage such a client to go through the front desk or the 800 number, which offers the smaller, less expensive rooms that we don't sell to ESP guests.

Allocation of Capacity

The sales staff saw one of its major challenges as determining how many rooms should be set aside for clients desiring long lead time, how many rooms should go to shorter lead-time groups, and how much capacity should be saved for walk-in business. Faced with average occupancy rates ranging from 90–97 percent, Monday–Thursday, during many periods in 1978–79, many clients tried to book well in advance.[3] The Parker House, however, refused to quote rates more than six months in advance and had set a 45-day maximum on advance banquet bookings at lunch; such banquets could potentially interfere with the needs of groups booking rooms as well as meal service. Jon Canas summed up the situation:

> Consider New England during the middle of October. For us success at this time is to have 100 percent walk-in transient business at the rack rate— and to have raised the rate the day before! It wouldn't be to our best interest to have booked a group at a very low rate way in advance when we know we're going to get this excellent, high-rated

[3] Occupancy rates Friday–Sunday during the same periods averaged 80–83 percent.

transient business at this time of year. On the other hand, there are cases which crop up when it's necessary to give people a discount in the middle of October—when you could have had the highest rate—in order to get that business back on January 2 when you will otherwise have nothing. So, it's a constant game of balancing.

Customer complaints to the sales division usually centered on one of two problems: room availability or the difficulty of getting through to the ESP office on the phone. Both Roberge and O'Neill made a point of frequently reminding their accounts about the hotel shortage in Boston. There were a total of 6,925 rooms in the city; all major hotels were fully booked for close to 90 days of the year. The sales division published a special quarterly newsletter for ESP clients which publicized problem dates, and also kept a waiting list, again for ESP accounts, after space closed. An extra telephone line had been added to the ESP office in fall of 1979; in February 1980 a recorded announcement would be introduced which would take and hold calls when all reservationists were busy.

The hotel continued to solicit some new business, primarily in New York City, where Roberge and O'Neill had recently traveled on a sales trip. It was hoped that the highly desirable, less price-sensitive accounts solicited there would crowd out smaller, rate-conscious clients and increase the number of ESP guests in the hotel.

ESP Sales Calls

Lyssa O'Neill was the senior Parker House ESP account executive. Her talent for sales had surfaced in grade school; at age eleven, she had sold 165 boxes of Girl Scout cookies in five days. Reviewing her background, she commented:

> In high school and college I waitressed a lot and was an assistant manager at one restaurant, which really brought a lot to this job as far as knowledge of food and beverage is concerned. Being a waitress, I think, is one of the best possible kinds of experience for dealing with people—dealing with their objections, pampering them, understanding their needs.

Minimization is a big part of this job—how we softsoap people, deal with complaints, get them to realize how the hotel's "batting average" outweighs isolated incidents.

O'Neill had begun her career with Dunfey as an in-house ESP reservations manager, answering the phones. After nine months she was promoted to account executive, and she expected to receive another promotion in early 1980, after a year's experience on the job. Her present salary consisted of a base rate plus a quarterly incentive, tied to the occupancy rate of the hotel as well as the number of ESP bookings she brought in through her own calls.

A week of sales calls for O'Neill typically began on the preceding Friday afternoon. After reviewing company files pulled by a secretary, she compiled a detailed itinerary listing the 16 key accounts she planned to cover and her objective in visiting each one. Next to a major accounting firm's name, she noted: "Meet new contact in Personnel: check on volume potential for first quarter." For a medium-sized bank she wrote: "Major contact back from maternity leave; reaffirm and probe future needs." She assessed a small brokerage firm as: "An inactive yellow account; determine potential through contact before killing." A copy of this itinerary was sent to Murphy before the calls began. At the end of the week, when O'Neill had covered all 16 key accounts as well as about 24 others, she sent another copy of the itinerary to Murphy, along with copies of 16 key call reports. The call report was a detailed description of the sales call, followed by a plan for future action. As O'Neill described it:

> We write up a call report on every complaint or problem that comes into the office; we also write up a call report after every sales visit. These enable every person who's picking up an account to know what this customer does, what their travel trends are, which person in the office is making reservations. They also help when you are going out on a call and you are aware that this company has had problems. They feel very good when you go in and

say, I understand you have had difficulties—how is everything going now?

After completing the call reports, O'Neill selected a date for the next sales call, based on the account's volume, and wrote the date in the file and on a separate index card. Through these index cards, filed chronologically, the ESP reps kept the coming weeks' schedules at their fingertips and could tell the secretaries exactly which files to pull.

Except for Friday afternoons, when she planned the upcoming week, and Monday mornings, which she spent in departmental sales meetings, O'Neill was out every day from 10–12 and 2–4, calling on accounts. Her midday lunch period was frequently spent meeting clients and giving them lunch and tours of the hotel. Very often the people she brought in were secretaries. O'Neill felt that by targeting the people who actually made reservations, rather than restricting her contact to those who stayed in the hotel, she pulled in a significantly greater number of ESP rooms.

O'Neill felt she could number her difficult clients almost on the fingers of one hand:

> I feel there are three basic ingredients in dealing with this job: a sense of respect, a sense of discretion, and a sense of humor. I have had only a few really unpleasant experiences since I have been here in which customers were downright rude. Some people, for instance, don't realize that a hotel is a business with a limited capacity. They think of it as a personal service—"Don't tell me you're sold out. Don't tell me there isn't a room in the place."

Managers believed that no other hotel in Boston offered significant competition to the Parker House's ESP account coverage program. The Sonesta, across the river in Cambridge, sent representatives out to corporate accounts about once every two months; other hotels invited clients to occasional public relations functions. As O'Neill saw it, the Parker House corporate plan was by far the most attractive in Boston.

Tour Groups

Although Harvey Kimball, Dunfey's director of tour sales, maintained his office at the Parker House, the greater part of his marketing efforts were directed toward other Dunfey hotels which considered tours an important part of their business mix. His task was to uncover leads; it was the responsibility of the individual hotel's Executive Operating Committee (EOC), aided by the regional director of sales, to decide whether the business was good for the hotel. Kimball received a yearly salary, plus a bonus based on the number of room nights he brought in.

Janet Morin, the Parker House tour coordinator, was a secretary in the general manager's office who received no incentive and made no direct sales calls of any kind. "It really isn't necessary," she stated. "The tour wholesalers call us—in fact, I usually get about 18 calls a day and end up referring most of them to the Park Plaza,[4] which is more eager to get tours than we are." Rates for groups of 15 or more varied according to the time of year, ranging from $44 to $58 (single), with a $10 additional charge per person for double, triple, and quadruple occupancy. The hotel did not encourage tours during the middle of the week, because ESP and transient guests brought in much more revenue. During the weekend, however, ESP guests almost vanished, and as Morin noted, "We need anything we can get." During 1979, tour rooms as a percentage of total rooms sold monthly ranged from 0.3 percent to 11 percent; tour room revenues as a percentage of total monthly revenues ranged from 0.3 percent to 8 percent.

Tours usually reached the hotel in groups of 46, a standard bus load. Most tour group guests were older people who preferred not to drive themselves, and they spent relatively little money in the hotel. "Our restaurants are in the moderate to expensive range," Morin explained, "and tour operators want the least expensive rate they can

---

[4] A large hotel, not part of the Dunfey organization, located on the fringe of the downtown area.

get on everything. They'll put inexpensive restaurants on the itinerary and herd the group in and out." The one meal which tour groups usually ate in the hotel was breakfast, and this had caused problems in the past, according to Morin:

> We charge the tours a prepaid flat rate of $5 for breakfast. We used to omit a service charge, until the waitresses started complaining that the groups would never tip—apparently they assumed that the $5 covered service. Now we add a 15 percent service charge to their bill.
>
> The breakfast scene is at its worst in the fall. We may have several tours in the hotel and they'll all come down for breakfast at 8:15 or 8:30, because their buses leave at 9. You have hundreds of people waiting to eat breakfast, lines in the lobby, buses leaving at 9, people getting edgy, and then if they have to miss breakfast to catch the bus they all want vouchers for another meal. It gets very confusing.

Tour wholesalers also tended to submit their passenger lists to the hotel at the last minute, a habit which both the sales division and the front desk found intensely annoying. "We like to get a rooming list three weeks beforehand for forecasting," Morin explained, "but tour groups will sell space in a tour till the day they leave. They'll send us a list with four names on it to meet the deadline, and then they'll give us any excuse to keep putting more names on. That's okay on weekends, but terrible on weeknights." Tours also often failed to meet their pre-established check-in times of 1 p.m. Groups coming in late were asked to wait in their buses until the lobby was clear of other tours, "but they always get out anyway and end up crowding around the desk," according to Morin.

Despite these frustrations, Morin felt that tour wholesalers offered one advantage to the hotel in addition to raising weekend occupancy: they did occasionally bring in corporate bonus trips. Fifty top sales representatives from a large corporation, for example, might be rewarded with a weekend in Boston and brought to the hotel in a group. Since corporations were less price-sensitive than tourists, the hotel could charge rack rate for each room.

TransAm Tours [disguised name], operated out of the West Coast and put together packaged tours for travel agents and individuals. This firm was considered a relatively "exclusive" tour wholesaler by the Parker House. "They're price-sensitive," Morin commented, "but their customers aren't." TransAm tourists were flown to Boston and then put aboard a bus which would transport them through New England. A typical group would come in late Thursday night, spend Friday exploring Boston and return after dinner, spend Saturday in New Hampshire, return to the hotel Saturday night, and leave early Sunday for Vermont. "They don't spend any money in the hotel, outside breakfast," Morin noted, "because they're never here."

Advertising, Promotion, and Customer Relations

The Parker House advertising strategy, as devised by Bill Murphy and Dunfey's senior marketing executives, was twofold. The hotel was promoted locally, as an individual property, and nationally, as a Dunfey Classic hotel. Although the need for strong promotion had been questioned, Paul Sacco, Dunfey's corporate director of sales, felt the Parker House's high average occupancy rate was very deceptive:

> The hotel is favored with a very heavy demand on Monday, Tuesday, and Wednesday nights. But we fight like hell to get people to stay on Sunday night, and we beg them to stay over Thursday and check out Friday—maybe stay for the weekend, bring their spouse. When we have an occupancy in the high 90s Sunday through Saturday, we will be satisfied. That's not presently the case.

Bill Murphy added:

> It's important not to look at it as though we do not need to sell any more. Actually, we have to work even harder—it's easier to get soft at the top. Our sales reps don't have a quota of 25 new accounts per week any more, but they do have a firm quota

of 40 calls. That's necessary just to keep up with movement within firms and within the city.

All promotion at the Parker House was based on an Advertising Action Plan, again developed jointly by the hotel's EOC and corporate headquarters. This plan, which was revised every four months, set specific advertising and direct sales targets and established the budget and media through which these goals would be reached. Classic hotel advertising, budgeted at close to $800,000 in 1979, promoted the Parker House, the Berkshire Place, and the Ambassador East as a group, and was supervised by Dunfey's director of advertising and public relations.

The Classic hotels advertisement was designed to upgrade and promote the Dunfey corporate image while it simultaneously linked the three hotels as a group. A four-color, one-page ad, it first appeared in mid-1979 in the Boston, New York, Chicago, and Los Angeles editions of leading national news and business magazines. Local promotion of the Parker House as a Classic hotel was particularly important, according to Dunfey's advertising director:

> The Boston market is a very important source of guests for New York and Chicago. The Dunfey corporate image still needs to be supported. And also, though from a rooms point of view and an occupancy point of view they may not seem to need it, the combination of the Parker House with the Ambassador and the Berkshire is helping to further position the Parker House, further upgrade its image . . . as well as positioning Dunfey.

Local promotion for the Parker House was supervised by Bill Murphy, whose combined advertising and sales budget totalled approximately $260,000 in 1979. Except during December, January, and February, when occupancy averaged 75 percent, promotions (such as parties for clients or inexpensive desk items for travel agents) were not a major concern at the hotel.

Management placed a good deal of emphasis on customer reaction to the hotel. Questionnaires were distributed to clients after banquets; they were also placed prominently in every

EXHIBIT 3
TRANSAM'S REQUESTED BOOKINGS AT THE PARKER HOUSE, JUNE–OCTOBER 1980

	S	M	T	W	T	F	S
June					[26][a]	[27][a]	
July			1	2	3	4	5
	6	7	8	9	(10)[a]	(11)[a]	12
	13	14	15	16	17	18	19
	20	21	22	23	[24][a]	[25][a]	26
	27	28	29	30	(31)[a]		
August						(1)[a]	2
	3	4	5	6	(7)[a]	(8)[a]	9
	10	11	12	13	14	15	16
	17	18	19	20	[21][b]	[22][b]	23
	24	25	26	27	28	29	30
	31						
September		1	2	3	[4][a]	[5][a]	6
	7	8	9	10	[11][a]	[12][a]	13
	14	15	16	(17)*	△18[b]	◇19[d]	△20[a]
	(21)[a]	22	(23)*	(24)*	△25*	◇26[c]	[27][a]
	(28)*	(29)*	(30)*				
October				[1]*	△2*	◇3*	[4]*
	(5)*	(6)*	(7)*	△8*	△9*	◇10[b]	[11][b]
	(12)*	(13)*	(14)*	[15]*	△16[b]	◇17[d]	[18][a]

Bookings Requested by TransAm Tours for Specific Dates

○ One group (2 singles, 20 doubles, 1 complimentary for tour escort).

□ Two groups (4 singles, 40 doubles, 2 complimentary).

△ Three groups (6 singles, 60 doubles, 3 complimentary).

◇ Four groups (8 singles, 80 doubles, 4 complimentary).

Parker House's Initial Response to TransAm Requests

[a] All reservations requested for that date were immediately accepted by the hotel.

[b] Only one group of requested bookings was accepted.

[c] Only two groups of requested bookings were accepted.

[d] Only three groups of requested bookings were accepted.

* None of requested bookings were accepted.

Source: Company records

room. The cards were signed by Roy Dunfey, vice president of employee and guest relations, and designed to be mailed directly to him. Although comments were not tabulated by segment, it was McIntosh's opinion that bus tours complained the most. As he put it: "They are on limited budgets, they have high expectations because their vacation is a big thing for them, they have time on their hands for complaining, and they give lots of reinforcement to each other's objections."

THE CONTINUED DEBATE

The Parker House's dislike for tour groups was not totally shared in Dunfey headquarters, and by mid-October 1979, as the deadline for responding to TransAm's offer approached, discussions grew increasingly heated. From the beginning, there had been no doubt that the Berkshire Place business would be accepted. TransAm had originally offered to pay a flat $25 (double), mid-week and weekend, for 2,000 Berkshire guest nights. After bargaining the rate up to $55, Dunfey sales executives felt that the revised contract was almost indispensable, considering the Berkshire's occupancy rate: 60 percent in July 1979, 70 percent in August (breakeven was about 62 percent). Then came a strong intimation from TransAm that the Berkshire business might ultimately depend on a guarantee of all 4,000 guest-nights requested at the Parker House.

In the discussion that followed, Terry Flahive, Dunfey's regional director of sales for New England, argued in TransAm's favor, telling Paul Sacco, the corporate director of sales:

We're desperate for business in New York. From a corporate point of view, we want those room nights to make the Berkshire Place successful. I think we're going to have to bite the bullet at the Parker House, even though it might be bad rooms merchandising.

Sacco tended to agree. As he pointed out to Bill Murphy:

It isn't actually a big bite, because we definitely want the business at the Berkshire Place, and at the Parker House we want the weekends. What we're arguing about is weeknights, midweek, and the question is whether we should cut some of that revenue in order to capture the rest.

Murphy, on the other hand, was strongly opposed. He knew that the Parker House had already accepted a number of other advance tour bookings:

We're already booked very heavily to other tour brokers, and if we accept TransAm for every date they've requested, we're going to be rolling the dice a little bit, hoping we get some cancellations. What is even more important, in my opinion, is that if we add another tour group of this volume, we're going against the entire mission of the hotel.

TransAm's specific Parker House room requests are reproduced in Exhibit 3. Approximately half of these requests were accepted immediately, at a rate of $32/39, single/double (weekend) and $53/61 (weekday). TransAm then requested that the hotel accept the company's remaining tour bookings at a rate of $32/39 (weekend) and $63/73 (weekday); it was implied that all TransAm business would hinge on the hotel's acceptance of this latest offer.

Murphy and Flahive immediately began an intensive review of the specifics of the TransAm proposals, attempting to calculate exactly how much tour space was available and how much revenue the tours might generate, compared with expected transient and corporate business. The key to establishing room availability was the Group Rooms Control Log (GRC), which listed "selective sell targets" for groups broken down by room night. By starting with the total number of rooms in the hotel (546) and subtracting projected transient, ESP, "patriot," and airline business, the sales department could apportion a certain number of rooms each night to be sold to groups of all kinds, including corporate groups, associations, and tours. GRCs for the remaining dates requested by TransAm are reproduced in Exhibit 4.

Potential TransAm revenues were then compared to the revenues to be derived from the sale of comparable rooms at projected summer and fall 1980 rack rates (Exhibit 2). Since it was not possible to know how guests would make their choices between room categories (e.g., standard vs. deluxe vs. top of the line), an average of standard and deluxe rates was used for calculations.

Murphy felt he was faced with three questions. Did the Parker House have space for TransAm on the dates not yet accepted (Exhibit 3)? Would the TransAm business be as profitable as reservations which might be booked simultaneously by other segments? And how many tours could the Parker House accept without altering the desired positioning of the hotel?

As he wrestled with these issues, the phone rang. Harvey Kimball was on the line. "Bill, I just talked to TransAm Tours," he announced. "They told me they're in the process of putting things together for Chicago—and under certain circumstances, might consider booking at the Ambassador East. Can we give them the go-ahead for the Parker House?"

EXHIBIT 4
EXTRACT FROM GROUP ROOMS CONTROL LOG

Type of Group	Number of rooms requested*		Day Aug.	S 17	M 18	T 19	W 20	T 21	F 22	S 23	Rates
	Gross	Net	SST†	193	135	135	135	140	253	258	
Assoc./Corp.‡											
Definite	800	500		125	125	125	125				53/61
Tentative	600	600		100	100	100	100	100	100		NRQ#
Tours											
Definite	52	40						40			28/31/36
Tentative	169	164						47	72	45	NRQ

Type of Group	Number of rooms requested		Day Aug.	S 24	M 25	T 26	W 27	T 28	F 29	S 30	Rates
	Gross	Net	SST†	103	110	75	75	90	233	258	
Assoc./Corp.‡											
Definite	200	160		40	40	40	40				NRQ
Tentative	0	0									
Tours											
Definite	25	20						20			28/31/36
Tentative	632	593		25				67	238	263	28/43

Type of Group	Number of rooms requested		Day Sep.	S 21	M 22	T 23	W 24	T 25	F 26	S 27	Rates
	Gross	Net	SST	128	100	75	75	90	233	258	
Assoc./Corp.‡											
Definite	267	220				70	70	70	70	10	58/68
Tentative	100	80				80					NRQ
Tours											
Definite	50	40						20		20	28/31/36
Tentative	827	769		114				35	311	309	28/43

(continues)

EXHIBIT 4 *(continued)*

Type of Group	Number of rooms requested		Day	S	M	T		W	T	F	S	Rates
			Sep.	28	29	30	Oct.	1	2	3	4	
	Gross	Net	SST	138	90	75		75	75	218	238	
Assoc./Corp.												
Definite	298	293		50	60	50		61	61	11		NRQ
Tentative	0	0										
Tours												
Definite	225	198							20	45	133	NRQ
Tentative	576	500		85	20					185	210	30/43

Type of Group	Number of rooms requested		Day	S	M	T	W	T	F	S	Rates
			Oct.	5	6	7	8	9	10	11	
	Gross	Net	SST	108	75	75	75	75	218	238	
Assoc./Corp.											
Definite	69	54						18	18	18	50/58
Tentative	0	0									
Tours											
Definite	200	170		40				20	45	65	28/43
Tentative	689	650		90	40			25	220	275	28/43

Type of Group	Number of rooms requested		Day	S	M	T	W	T	F	S	Rates
			Oct.	12	13	14	15	16	17	18	
	Gross	Net	SST	148	50	50	60	60	208	188	
Assoc./Corp.											
Definite	120	90							45	45	NRQ
Tentative	0	0									
Tours											
Definite	75	70		20					25	25	28/49
Tentative	717	659		162	20			22	226	229	33/46

*Gross = the number of rooms reserved by a group; net = salesperson's estimate of the number of rooms a group would actually occupy.

†SST = "selective sell target," the optimum number of rooms to be sold to associations, corporate groups, and tours.

‡Assoc./Corp. = professional or special-interest associations and corporate groups.

#NRQ = no rate quoted.

Source: Company records.

CRESTLIGHT PAPER COMPANY

Kenneth Simmonds

The speed of David Farrel's management changes had surprised everyone. Aged 33, David was the first of the firm's graduate M.B.A. recruits to reach the divisional general management level. He always seemed quiet and reserved, but interested in and understanding of others' viewpoints, and his promotion from Assistant Manager in the Forms division to General Manager of the Education division had been a popular one. Three weeks after he took over from the retiring general manager, however, the Education division had a new personnel manager, a replacement for the accountant and two entirely new posts advertised for product managers. Now Farrel was calmly asking Andrew Smythe to take over as Divisional Sales Manager. "Wesley McFarlane expressed his interest in early retirement," said Farrel, "and we agreed that there would be little purpose in a drawn-out handover period. He will formally retire from Crestlight at the end of March, but hand over the reins of the sales force to you as from Friday week, 24th

Copyright © 1979 by Kenneth Simmonds.

February. Unfortunately, I shall be away at the Group Conference all next week, but we can go over the situation in detail as soon as I am back—let's say the afternoon of Monday, 27th February."

Farrel's approach was so unexpected and his manner so direct, that in five minutes Andrew found he had accepted the promotion, agreed to clean up his outstanding commitments at Group Head Office within two days and to spend the next week, Wesley McFarlane's last, learning all he could from Wesley. As he walked back to his office, Andrew was elated with his new appointment; but he had a strange feeling of his future vanishing into a vacuum. Farrel had somehow stopped him asking about where he, Farrel, wished to head the Education division and had avoided any discussion at all about Wesley McFarlane's sales achievements. Had Wesley been good, bad or indifferent? Whatever the answer, this was the sort of opportunity Andrew had been waiting for. In fact, it was beyond his immediate expectations. He had believed his image in Crestlight to be that of a future "comer" who

559

would be given a year or two to prove himself in some assistant sales management post before he would be offered a senior divisional appointment. Farrel had certainly picked Andrew up and put him on the escalator.

ANDREW SMYTHE

Andrew Smythe had joined Crestlight eighteen months ago, on completing his Master of Business Administration degree at Manchester Business School. He had been based at the Group Head Office as assistant to the Group Marketing Director and given a succession of non-repetitive problems to sort out—mainly concerned with matching supply and forecasts for Crestlight lines. Off and on over the past six months he had also participated as a member of a team sorting out a new group acquisition. But at 28 he was becoming restless in a staff position. He felt that he should get into some operating post. Operations seemed the only way to the top at Crestlight. At Business School he had positioned himself as a finance specialist, but then became disillusioned with capital asset pricing theory and rather low finance grades and, anyway, marketing had seemed from outside the function of the future in Crestlight. From within, he was not so sure. He had come to regard the Marketing Director as little more than the Group's senior sales person, with the added concern for investigating major foreign orders and new agency possibilities.

Prior to his two years at Business School, Andrew had been a sales management trainee with a branded food company. There, too, the position had been a misnomer—probably titled to attract graduates. The post had amounted to two and a half years as a field representative, calling on supermarket buyers and store managers and arranging special promotions. He supposed it was good experience, but he had not really enjoyed the job and he could see that his Bachelor's degree in Economics from Nottingham was not

going to move him along in any way at all—he needed an M.B.A. for that.

Andrew shared a flat in London with two other Business School graduates and led an active social life. He still played rugby, turning out for a team in Esher on Sundays, and for the last two years he had taken winter skiing holidays. He had no plans for marriage and the idea of settling into a suburban house in Croydon, as one of his friends had done, did not appeal to him; although he had toyed with the idea of buying a house in order to build up some equity.

CRESTLIGHT EDUCATION DIVISION

Crestlight had grown from a small beginning in the late 1940s, based on a license from the U.S. to manufacture and distribute throughout the U.K. a coated paper used in industrial drawing offices. Over the years the firm had added a whole range of photographic and reproduction papers and supplies, together with a line of equipment for reproduction of large size drawings. Then in 1964 Crestlight had moved onto the acquisition trail and added a specialty paper merchant and a major form printing house. A divisional organisation pattern had emerged almost without planning. There were now five principal divisions—Equipment, Supplies, Paper, Education and Forms—and four non-integrated subsidiaries.

The Education division had been formed in 1970 to give specialist attention to the increasing demand from the education sector for special paper and reproduction supplies and equipment. Nine years later the division carried a range of 1,000 items and sold directly to Local Education Authorities (LEA's), Central Supplies Departments (who usually supplied several authorities), universities, polytechnics and some large schools. Several education wholesalers were also supplied. Some of these carried a much broader line of education supplies than Crestlight—including for example, scientific apparatus—and had very active sales forces calling on similar direct customers.

Profit margins differed from order to order. The standard gross margin for direct supply to Local Education Authorities and individual establishments was 40 percent of total sales value, while on sales to wholesalers and central purchasing stores the average margin was only 26 percent.

LEARNING FROM WESLEY MCFARLANE

Wesley McFarlane was friendly and relaxed when Andrew moved in with him the following Monday. Tall and well-dressed, he reminded Andrew of a trained athlete as he seemed to flow around the office without effort. Although he was only 52, he seemed to have welcomed the early retirement and gave no hint at all that he felt he had been moved out. Andrew rather gauchely tried to sound him out about the internal politics behind the move by asking him whether he minded moving at this stage in his career. Wesley came back without any hesitation, "Should have done it years ago. Sales management will never get you anywhere against the engineers and accountants, and a safe middle-of-the-road salary is a living death in Britain today." He then went on to outline to Andrew his plans for a partnership with his brother in a caravan sales agency south of London. Now that his three children were safely through school and launched on their own careers, he could turn his sales skills to his own advantage without family demands requiring him to draw too much out of the business at the wrong times. Wesley was so convincing with the detail of his own plans that he spent an hour explaining to Andrew the "ins" and "outs" of the caravan business. Andrew couldn't help but feel it more fascinating than selling school supplies.

Wesley finally brought Andrew back to earth by starting on a comprehensive survey of the Education division sales force. As Wesley talked,

Andrew took his own brief notes and asked for photocopies of the annual sales figures and sales force and territory details that Wesley showed him. Exhibit 1 shows the divisional sales figures and Exhibits 2 to 6 the territory and sales force details and performance. Exhibit 7 sets out the notes on individual salesmen as Wesley pictured them—but, as Wesley said, Andrew would get a better picture by meeting them himself. He had, accordingly, arranged the next sales meeting for Wednesday, so that he could introduce the sales force to Andrew before he formally took over.

The remainder of Monday vanished rapidly as Wesley outlined his overall sales philosophy to Andrew:

> Last year's sales of one and a half million were just above a 20 percent increase over 1977. Most of this represented price increases rather than volume and by my guess market penetration has gone up slightly from 19.5 percent. When I say "guess" I am basing this on my estimates of market size for the three product lines. These have been asked for each year for the annual plans and what I do is to identify all the competitors and place a sales figure against each. One or other of the salesmen is bound to have heard something about a competitor's sales levels, and I do some questioning around outside as well and check the competitor's annual reports and published estimates of educational purchasing. There are too many customers to build a figure up from their estimated annual order potential and

EXHIBIT 1

CRESTLIGHT PAPER COMPANY: EDUCATION DIVISION MARKET AND SALES BY PRODUCT (£'000s)

	Market Estimates		Sales	
	1978	1977	1978	1977
Special paper	3,600	3,050	696	560
Reproduction supplies	2,200	1,850	401	337
Reproduction equipment	1,300	1,100	363	311
Total	7,100	6,000	1,460	1,208

EXHIBIT 2
MAP OF SALES TERRITORIES

EXHIBIT 3
SALES TERRITORY DETAILS

Territory	Salesman	Area ('000s sq km)	Secondary and Higher-Level Pupils 1978 (millions)	Estimated Potential Accounts	Home Base
1. Greater London	Halbert	1.6	1.60	570	Twickenham
2. South East	Jennings	25.6	2.27	1,060	Bromley
3. South West & Wales	Bindon	44.6	1.55	934	Cardiff
4. Midlands East	Vereker	28.2	1.18	653	Leicester
5. West Midlands	Prince	13.0	1.24	566	Solihull
6. North West	Anderson	7.3	1.65	699	Liverpool
7. Humberside	Randall	15.4	1.16	531	Bradford
8. North	Thompson	15.4	.83	423	Newcastle
9. Scotland	Campbell	78.8	1.32	529	Glasgow
Total		229.9	12.80	5,965	

EXHIBIT 4
SALES FORCE DETAILS

Salesman	Age	Year Joined Crestlight	Educational Qualifications	Previous Experience
1 Halbert, Russell	54	1965	—	Textile salesmen (10 years) Accounts clerk (7 years)
2 Jennings, Frederick	42	1973	Higher National Certificate	Post Office Teleprinter salesman (4 years) Equipment maintenance (16 years)
3 Bindon, Harold V.	33	1971	B.A. (Geography)	Joined as sales trainee
4 Vereker, John	29	1975	—	Head storeman (3 years) Dispatch clerk (3 years)
5 Prince, Alan	57	1976	—	Salesman, etc. (35 years)
6 Anderson, Graham	37	1969	B. Tech.	Production scheduling (5 years)
7 Randall, John	48	1951	—	Joined as clerk in original Crestlight unit. Appointed salesman 1964
8 Thompson, Herbert	33	1975	B.Sc. (Metallurgy)	Wallpaper sales rep. (4 years) Research technician (2 years)
9 Campbell, Ian	43	1971	B.A. (English)	Teacher (12 years)

EXHIBIT 5
SALES FORCE PERFORMANCE

	1978				1977			
	Sales £('000s)	Accounts Sold	Gross Margin £('000s)	Calls Made	Sales £('000s)	Accounts Sold	Gross Margin £('000s)	Calls Made
Halbert	258	239	75	1,230	217	279	69	1,260
Jennings	239	509	79	1,168	198	539	69	1,194
Bindon	156	476	59	1,051	129	503	48	1,018
Vereker	112	353	41	1,409	98	356	36	1,290
Prince	154	413	55	1,196	123	382	43	1,185
Anderson	112	398	39	1,450	97	412	34	1,410
Randall	142	202	50	1,171	125	198	42	1,293
Thompson	123	364	47	1,220	101	323	39	1,163
Campbell	143	317	53	1,135	123	326	46	1,088
	£1,439		£498		£1,211		£426	

industry figures don't coincide with our narrow line definitions.

They are all good men. There is not a bad egg among the nine and they work willingly if you don't push them too hard. Of course there are differences in sales performance, but these occur in all sales teams. Besides, you have to bear in mind the travel times some of them need to reach quite small accounts as well as the amount of work that has been done in the past to build up our accounts in a territory.

These same factors have to be taken into ac-count in territory sizes. I think we have them about right now. As you can see from the territory varia-tion in numbers of secondary and higher level pupils, the range between smallest and largest is only a factor of two—which is, in fact, very small. But each salesman has plenty of potential to un-cover, no matter what his territory size.

The basic salaries can't be adjusted very much. You have to keep the basic high enough to attract new reps, who might not make much commission for a while, and yet not so high that they have an easy time. Actually, I had been thinking about rais-

EXHIBIT 6
REMUNERATION AND EXPENSES, 1978 EDUCATION DIVISION SALES FORCE (£)

Name	Salary 12/31/78	Commissions 1978	Total Remuneration	Expenses 1978
Halbert	5,800	3,870	9,670	1,980
Jennings	4,800	3,585	8,385	2,810
Bindon	4,200	2,340	6,540	5,010
Vereker	3,800	1,680	5,480	3,820
Prince	4,900	2,310	7,210	2,600
Anderson	5,100	1,680	6,780	1,940
Randall	5,200	2,130	7,330	3,400
Thompson	4,000	1,845	5,845	3,200
Campbell	5,000	2,145	7,145	3,300
	42,800	21,585	64,385	28,060

EXHIBIT 7
WESLEY MACFARLANE'S COMMENTS ON SALESMEN

Russell Halbert	Our star salesman. Very experienced. Knows central area. Reacts well to new ideas and well liked by customers. Has a smooth, competent air about him.
Frederick Jennings	Very sound man, systematic and conscientious and well dressed. Moved across from equipment side, so knows the technical aspects. Had some marital problems last year but apparently straightened them out.
Harold Bindon	Very large area but really gets round it. Presents himself well. Sales coming along nicely. Could go a long way in the company.
John Vereker	Sales not really very high. Young man with a lot to learn. Probably as a young man about town is taking time off for other things.
Alan Prince	Grandad of the team. An old sales lag. Joined only 3 years ago. Will not readily adopt new approaches, but you cannot teach an old dog new tricks. Will not be around for more than five years. No really formal education, so unlikely to make general impact on buyers in the education area. Nevertheless, doing quite acceptably.
Graham Anderson	Has a degree, but very disappointing sales results. Technically competent and extremely conscientious in covering his territory. A good worker and a rather engaging personality.
John Randall	Bright and attractive personality. Good salesman type. Always thinking up new ideas. A bit of a troublemaker. Fairly lazy and sales below what they might be. A good pep talk should move him along.
Herbert Thompson	Only been with us a few years, but keen to perform. Will take time to develop the polish of the true salesman, but the material is there. Needs guidance from sales manager about sales technique.
Ian Campbell	Very solid and unexciting. Always quiet at sales meetings. Suspect he will never make an outstanding salesman. Knows the Scottish educational buying scene very well. A chess player at competition level as a hobby.

ing the commission rates. I think the carrot works a lot better than any pseudo-analytical target that tries to push from behind. Commission rates are only 1½ percent and if we raised them a further 1 percent instead of a salary increase this year, I think we would get five times as much back in gross margin.

Expenses are pretty much under control; I get the daily call reports and I know who they are entertaining and where they are travelling. Harold Bindon spends more time away from home than any of the others and his entertainment goes up as a result, but if life were too dreary we would have problems with that territory.

Tuesday rushed quickly past as Wesley and Andrew waded through the files for each of the product groups in the Crestlight Education range. Eighty per cent of the sales came from internal production in the other divisions but the remaining twenty per cent included a very long list of products. In some of the cases, Wesley had been required as part of the agency agreement to provide detailed reports on the sales efforts and results.

THE SALES MEETING

The Wednesday meeting got underway in the conference room with a great deal of joking and laughter. As Andrew came in, Wesley was called away to the telephone, but the salesmen knew all about the management change and introduced themselves in ones and twos before drifting towards the table with coffee cups in hand. Wesley took the seat at the head of the long table and Andrew drew up a chair towards the other end between John Randall and Ian Campbell.

Andrew could feel that Wesley was genuinely well liked and respected. He admired the way Wesley led the group smoothly through the agenda, starting with a discussion of the January sales figures and the effects that anticipation of a change in political party had had on educational spending. One foreign manufacturer of educational forms had been threatening to withdraw his line from Crestlight and this provoked a comparison of current buyers with those who had rejected the line. Wesley also had a spate of announcements concerning new items and replacements in the line. Under "Other Business" a long discussion boiled up around order procedure problems that had stemmed from some abstruse ruling in the Department of Education.

As the meeting was drawing to a close, John Randall stood up and on behalf of the salesmen made a short farewell speech thanking Wesley for his years of leadership. Wesley acknowledged the round of applause, thanked them warmly and then everybody headed for the "Three Feathers" where Wesley had booked a table for lunch.

The lunch went on rather a long time with numerous rounds of drinks and a series of wild sales stories directed at Wesley. John Randall and John Vereker were the most vociferous. Randall elaborated at great length about a female pur-chasing officer from a Local Education Authority who had him take her out until 3 a.m. every night for a week before placing an order for a gross of protractors—while Vereker seemed the authority on landladies' daughters. At one point, Andrew ventured a story about clam digging that had been told with much hilarity at the Rugby Club. It went reasonably well, but was quickly lost in the stream of wisecracks and competing comments.

Finally, about 2:30 p.m., Wesley looked at his watch and the group began to break up. Andrew and Wesley were separated by the salesmen as they said their farewells. What struck Andrew as strange was that although each salesman used his own words, their message was the same: "If I can be of any help in showing you the ropes, don't hesitate to ask."

THE LIVELY ARTS AT HANSON, I

Kenneth Shachmut
Charles B. Weinberg

"I'm very frustrated about our attendance figures," noted Barbara Lynn, associate director of the Office of Public Events at Hanson University, a well-known privately funded university in Southern California. "Our programming is high quality, and for the whole season we have only about 30,000 seats to sell, but we have a significant seasonal attendance problem. Our Spring quarter attendance has been running at only 50 percent of capacity over the last few years, down from about 85 percent in the Fall. Winter quarter figures are just marginally better than those for Spring, averaging about 60 percent."

Both she and Tom Bacon, who was finishing his fourth year as director of the Office of Public Events, regarded this seasonal attendance pattern as their most pressing management problem in May 1982 as they contemplated possible remedies for the upcoming 1982–83 season and beyond.

Reprinted from *Stanford Business Cases 1985* with permission of the publishers, Stanford University Graduate School of Business. Copyrighted © 1985 by the Board of Trustees of the Leland Stanford Junior University.

PROGRAM CHANGES

Over the past three seasons, Bacon had implemented a number of changes in the "Arts at Hanson" program. Attendance as a percentage of capacity had increased from 54 percent in the three academic years 1976–79 to 68 percent in the most recent three years. These changes are summarized below:

Programming

The number of performances was reduced from 41 in 1978–79 to 31 for the 1979–80 season. This figure rose again to 36 in 1980–81 and was reduced once more to 25 in 1981–82. Additionally, Bacon had attempted to make the program commercially more viable during the last three seasons than it had been previously. He accomplished this by scheduling relatively more performances by string quartets and guitarists, which usually did very well at Hanson. Attendance data by type of programming for the period from Fall 1979 to Spring 1982 were: guitar—104 percent of capacity, chamber music—79 per-

EXHIBIT 1
1981–82 ATTENDANCE STATISTICS FOR LIVELY ARTS

| | Percent of capacity* | | | | |
	Student	Nonstudent	Total	Capacity	Day
	Fall quarter				
Performance:					
Sour Cream (CM)	49%	55%	104%	720	Tuesday
LA 4 (Jazz)	39	59	98	1,694	Friday
Hartford Ballet 1 (Dance)	38	28	66	1,694	Thursday
Hartford Ballet 2	27	27	54	1,694	Friday
Contemporary Chamber Ensemble	19	19	38	720	Friday
Guarneri Quartet 1 (CM)	49	63	112	720	Tuesday
Guarneri Quartet 2	53	62	115	720	Friday
Guarneri Quartet 3	50	71	121	720	Sunday
Ron Thomas (YCA)	22	37	59	350	Friday
Paco de Lucia (Guitar)	39	69	108	1,085	Friday
Breakdown (average figures):					
Chamber Music (5)	44%	54%	98%	720	
Guitar (1)	39	69	108	1,085	
Jazz (1)	39	59	98	1,694	
Dance (2)	33	28	60	1,694	
Young Concert Artist (1)	22	37	59	350	
Totals (10)	38	48	86	10,117	

cent, jazz—75 percent, dance—62 percent, and young concert artists—51 percent. Detailed attendance statistics by quarter for 1981–82 are shown in Exhibit 1.

Personnel

The size of Bacon's staff was increased, permitting more and more effective promotional activities. Even with this increase, however, the total time devoted to the program during the 1981–82 season was not greatly in excess of one person-year, due to the fact that the Office of Public Events was responsible for managing four other University programs in addition to the Arts program during the school year.

The first of these programs was general administration (mainly scheduling) of all public events on the Hanson campus. This function required considerable time and represented a steady workload throughout the academic year. Sec-

ond, the office was responsible for coordinating all university public ceremonies. Most significant of these was the annual Commencement exercise, conducted during June. Although some aspects of Commencement required advance planning and coordination, by far the biggest push came in the two months immediately preceding the event. The third major responsibility of the office was coordination of various university lecture programs, including several endowed lectures. As with general administration, the lecture series imposed a relatively steady workload throughout the year.

In addition, Bacon was responsible for a travel film and lecture series which ran throughout the academic year. Also, during the summer, he scheduled a number of "commercial" attractions (for example, the Preservation Hall Jazz Band) for community emjoyment.

The university administration considered all of these activities to be important in helping fulfill

EXHIBIT 1 *(continued)*

	Winter quarter				
Performance:					
AMAN! (Dance)	31%	69%	100%	1,694	Friday
Music by Three (YCA)	14	37	51	350	Friday
Nicanor Zabaleta (Harp)	38	66	104	720	Friday
Pilobolus Dance Theater 1	6	37	43	1,694	Thursday
Pilobolus Dance Theater 2	26	25	51	1,694	Friday
Tel Aviv Quartet (CM)	19	64	83	720	Friday
Fernando Valente (Harpsichord)	26	68	94	720	Friday
Hiroko Yajima (YCA)	7	41	48	350	Friday
Murray Dance Company 1	7	12	19	1,694	Thursday
Murray Dance Company 2	22	21	43	1,694	Friday
Music from Marlboro (CM)	14	52	66	720	Friday
Breakdown (average figures):					
Chamber Music (2)	17%	58%	75%	720	
Dance (5)	18	33	51	1,694	
Young Concert Artist (2)	11	39	50	350	
Other (2)	32	67	99	720	
Totals (11)	19	41	60	12,050	

	Spring quarter				
Performance:					
Mummenschanz (Mime)	17%	26%	43%	1,694	Tuesday
Early Music Consort of London (CM)	35	69	104	720	Friday
Paul Winter Consort (Jazz)	21	24	45	1,694	Friday
Arthur Renner (YCA)	11	51	62	350	Friday
Breakdown (not applicable)					
Totals (4)	21%	34%	55%	4,458	

* Chamber Music events were held in the 720-seat hall, Dance and Jazz in the 1,694 seat hall, and the Young Concert Artist series in the 350 seat hall. For the Guitar Concert, the balcony and back rows of the 1,694 seat hall were not made available for sale, leaving a capacity of 1,085 seats. Other events were scheduled for either the 720- or 1,694-seat hall depending upon the nature of the event. The average production cost per performance was $3,000 in 1981–82.

the multiple goals of a major university in the community. Tom Bacon knew that whatever new marketing moves he attempted for "The Arts at Hanson" must be accomplished within strict personnel time constraints.

PROMOTIONAL CHANGES

Name

The name of the program was changed to "The *Lively* Arts at Hanson" for the 1979–80 season, in order, hopefully, to attract more attention to the program and to identify it more positively as a *performing* arts program. This new name was incorporated in a redesigned logo used in all media advertising.

Brochure

The season brochure (now entitled "The Lively Arts at Hanson") was made much more elaborate and eye-catching, starting with the 1979–80 season. Its physical size was doubled (to 8½ by 11 inches) and it was printed in three colors on glossy paper stock. These changes increased the costs substantially. By 1981–82 the total cost of the brochure (45,000 copies printed, of which 30,000 were mailed and 15,000 bulk distributed) had risen to $16,800 (including mailing costs) from approximately $6,500 in 1978–79.

The brochure included listings for not only the Lively Arts program, but also performances by various university departments (e.g., drama and music departments). These nonprofessional performances were clearly separated from the Lively Arts offerings within the brochure. In addition, the sponsoring departments were required to fully absorb their pro rata share—$2,000—of total brochure costs. Bacon planned to maintain this policy into the foreseeable future.

The brochure was sent out to a composite mailing list at the beginning of each season in early September. The mailing list was actually composed of three individual lists. The first list included approximately 15,000 individuals who had previously purchased Lively Arts season tickets, who had purchased individual tickets by check (from which a name and address was obtained), or who had specifically requested to be put on the list (by filling out cards available at all performances).

A second list (about 6,000)—the so-called "Sunset Hills Cultural List"—was obtained from the Council for the Arts in Sunset Hills (a large suburban community adjacent to Hanson). The remainder of the mailed brochures (approximately 9,000 for 1981–82) was sent to local Hanson alumni, priority being determined by proximity of residence to the university campus.

These three lists were not cross-checked against each other for duplication. A spokesperson from University Computing Services, which maintained the lists, said that due to their different coding systems, reprogramming and integrating the lists would be costly and time-consuming. Overall, Bacon had no good feeling for the extent to which duplication existed within the lists. However, he noted that he personally received three mailed copies of the brochure each year.

In addition to program information, the annual brochure included a calendar of all performances (professional and nonprofessional), season ticket information, and ticket order forms for all performances.

Additional Brochures

Supplemental one-page brochures in a postcard format were mailed at the beginning of Winter and Spring quarters to the Lively Arts mailing list, briefly outlining the upcoming quarterly program offerings.

Posters and Flyers

When available from the performers' agents, posters and flyers were distributed around the Hanson campus on centrally located information kiosks, in dormitories, and other places about two weeks prior to each performance. Depending upon availability, additional posters were distributed to other college campuses in the area and to willing local merchants. These posters were of varied quality and Public Events staff had no control over their format. Typically the posters included a blank area at the bottom in which was printed program time and location information. The posters did not include the Lively Arts logo or any other mention of the program itself.

Advertising and Other Promotional Activities

Each performance was advertised for about two weeks prior to the performance itself in the local press and, for some performances, on classical music radio stations. Typical newspaper sources were the *Hanson Daily, Los Angeles Times, Sunset Hills News,* and *Orange County Crier.* Additionally, miscellaneous promotional pieces such as Lively Arts bookmarks were printed in large quantities and made widely available on campus at the beginning of each season.

Total approximate promotional expenditures for the 1981–82 season are presented in Exhibit 2.

EXHIBIT 2
APPROXIMATE PROMOTIONAL EXPENDITURES—1981-82 SEASON

Annual costs:			
Season brochure*	$16,800		
Program covers	1,200		
Promotional material (bookmarks, surveys, etc.)	1,650		
		$19,650	
Fall quarter costs:			
Advertising			
Newspaper	$ 7,500		
Radio	900		
Other	300	$ 8,700	
Posters & flyers		600	
Other		300	
			$ 9,600
Winter quarter costs:			
Advertising			
Newspaper	$ 7,650		
Radio	1,050		
Other	450	$ 9,150	
Posters & flyers		600	
Winter brochure*		3,150	
Other		450	
			$13,350
Spring quarter costs (estimate):			
Advertising			
Newspaper	$ 3,750		
Radio	750		
Other	150	$ 4,650	
Posters & flyers		300	
Spring brochure*		1,350	
Other		150	
			$ 6,450
Total promotional costs			$49,050

   * Includes mailing cost.

Pricing

Greater flexibility was introduced to the pricing scheme, with price levels varying across different performances according to program cost, expected drawing power of individual performers, and other factors. For example, during Winter quarter, 1982, the best nonstudent tickets for the Murray Dance Company sold for $9.00, while the Tel Aviv Quartet seats went for $7.00, and Young Concert Artist series performances sold at $5.00 for nonstudents. Additionally, the overall price level was increased to an average ticket price paid (including student and season discounts) of $4.97 for 1981–82, compared to $4.01 for 1979–80.

STUDENT PROMOTIONS

Student Introductory Program (SIP)

Under this program, initiated in 1979–80, each new Hanson undergraduate or graduate student was given a free pass to any one performance during the Fall quarter and also a coupon allowing that student to buy a ticket at 75 cents for any other performance during the year.

Response to the initial free ticket was good, but only a very limited number of students exercised the follow-up 75-cent option. Consequently, the 75-cent coupon was discontinued after only one season. The initial free SIP ticket had been maintained up to the present time, however.

Student Discount Tickets

The price of a ticket to any performance for students was set substantially below the average nonstudent ticket price. During the 1981–82 season the student price was $4.50 per ticket. Bacon felt that this price level was appropriate and equitable and he desired to maintain it as long as possible.

OVERALL ACCOMPLISHMENTS

Tom Bacon was convinced that the program changes represented significant accomplishments for "The Lively Arts at Hanson," notwithstanding the existence of several persistent

problems. Overall, he felt there were two major accomplishments:

• Total program attendance had risen steadily from 1976–77 to 1979–80, declining only in the recession year 1980–81. Further declines in the total attendance for 1981–82 were believed to be due principally to the reduced number of performances.

• Average percentage attendance for Fall quarter had increased markedly from 68 percent in 1976–78 to 85 percent in 1979–81. Bacon attributed this increase to a combination of successful marketing innovations initiated in Fall quarter 1979. These included the expanded brochure, more successful programming and the SIP program.

Together these accomplishments convinced Bacon and Lynn that the Lively Arts was an extremely viable program with a growing base of supporters.

PROGRAM ATTENDANCE

In May 1982 Bacon was undertaking a reappraisal of the entire Lively Arts marketing

EXHIBIT 3a
FALL QUARTER AUDIENCE SIZE
(Audience size by market segment, 1981–82)

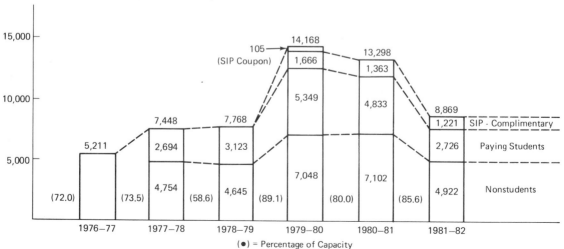

(•) = Percentage of Capacity

EXHIBIT 3b
WINTER QUARTER AUDIENCE SIZE

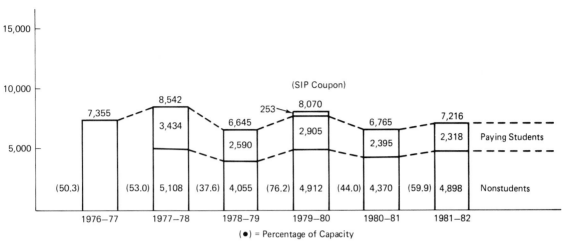

(●) = Percentage of Capacity

program employed over the past three seasons to determine what changes, if any, might be warranted. Although he felt strongly that many of his program changes had been successful, he still faced significant problems. Most worrisome of these was a marked pattern of seasonal attendance. While Fall quarter audiences had been very good, averaging nearly 85 percent of capac-

ity, the comparable figures for Winter and Spring quarters were 60 percent and 50 percent, respectively. To compound this difficulty Mr. Bacon noted that student attendance had slipped from a high of over 45 percent of the audience during the 1979–80 season to an all-time low of 32 percent for the Winter quarter 1981–82 (Exhibits 1, 3 and 4).

EXHIBIT 3c
SPRING QUARTER AUDIENCE SIZE

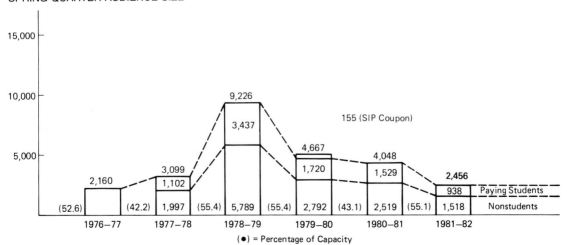

(●) = Percentage of Capacity

EXHIBIT 4
ATTENDANCE BY QUARTERS, 1976–82

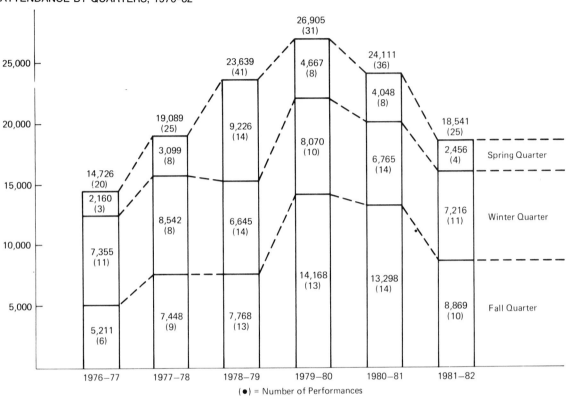

(●) = Number of Performances

Bacon was concerned about both of these trends:

"The Lively Arts at Hanson" presents first-rate artists in a varied program that should appeal to a broad base of individuals. Look at this season's offerings for example: The Guarneri and Tel Aviv string quartets; Music from Marlboro; AMAN! (a folk dance group); Pilobolus and the Murray Company in dance; the Early Music Consort of London. These artists are representative of the best in their fields.

Our Young Concert Artist series brings some of the most promising young talents in the world to the Hanson audience. These are the artists who will be at the top of their profession in a few years. Already they have received laudatory reviews by major music critics. Moreover, our prices are quite low com-

pared to what one would have to pay to see comparable performers in Los Angeles. The average nonstudent ticket price this year was only about $6.00–9.00. Most city performances cost twice that much.

Student attendance also bothers me. As a group, Hanson students should be very interested in the Lively Arts program. However, from a number of sources, I have the strong impression that they're really not as aware of our program as I would like. For example, take the Student Introductory Program (SIP). By and large, new students were very willing to take a complimentary ticket, but very few of them exercised the option to purchase a second ticket for 75 cents plus the SIP coupon, as our statistics show.

There are other indications as well. Not concrete to be sure, but present nevertheless. Somehow we have to get through to the students that "The Lively Arts at Hanson" is something very special and very professional, to be distinguished from the whole host of other performance activities with which we must compete for their attention on campus.

"The Lively Arts at Hanson" was not alone in facing a seasonal attendance problem. The performing arts program at State University experienced similar difficulties. Bacon's counterpart at State U. commented that she had had some success in combating this problem by scheduling relatively more "light" and fewer "heavy" performances during Spring quarter, her toughest attendance period. The "light" category encompassed performances which typically sold well at State U., including string quartets, early music, and anything by Bach. "Heavy," on the other hand, included contemporary music and vocalists, which were always difficult to sell. The State U. manager also tended to favor more well-known performers in the Spring.

PROGRAM GOALS

Bacon felt strongly that the program had—and must of necessity have—multiple goals reflecting the multiple dimensions of managing an arts program. For purposes of control and evaluation of the program's progress, Bacon decided after much thoughtful consideration that the following four goals were paramount:

• Establish "The Lively Arts at Hanson" as a major source of first-rate performing arts talent for the extended county community as well as for the immediate Hanson University community.

• Run the series on a close-to-breakeven basis, incurring only a minimal deficit as approved by the university administration.

• Keep prices as low as possible in order to make performances widely accessible.

• Target the total season for overall attendance at 75–80 percent of capacity. Further, maintain the following overall audience propor-

tions: students, 35 percent; nonstudents, 65 percent.

PROGRAMMING DIFFICULTIES

In order to achieve the first of these goals, which he and his staff felt was probably the most important, Bacon knew it would be imperative to continue to present a varied program of artists each season. This was difficult for two reasons. First, the scheduling problems were impressive. Not only did Bacon have to book the artists more than a year in advance in most cases, but also he had to compete with various departmental and student arts productions (e.g., music department concerts, drama department, and theatrical club productions) for a very limited number of available auditoriums on campus and suitable dates.

However, even more troublesome was a second factor. By maintaining a varied program, Bacon was including each season a number of performance types which did not seem to do very well in drawing large audiences, such as the Young Concert Artist series and dance in general. He had broken down his quarterly attendance statistics for the past three seasons and was upset by them. He knew that he would have to try to ameliorate the contrasts in attendance statistics by performance type for the 1982–83 season if possible, but he wasn't sure of the best way to go about it.

SEGMENTATION

Barbara Lynn, who had been working in the Office of Public Events for two years, had some strong feelings about the potential audience:

> I think we have, basically, three groups of people who come out to our performances. First there are the students—mostly from Hanson, but some from neighboring colleges and secondary schools as well. Our sources on campus seem to indicate that Hanson students are not very aware of our program. The students have heard of the Guarneri Quartet—and they know they will be performing—but they

don't seem to know that the "Lively Arts" is bringing the Guarneri to campus. I don't know, but maybe our posters and *Hanson Daily* advertising aren't doing the job. They sure cost enough, though!

Second is the group I like to call "Hanson affiliated": University faculty and staff members and their spouses. We haven't made any special attempt to get them interested, but feel they should respond to the advertising both on campus and in the local press.

Finally we've got the community at large—mostly in and around Hanson and Sunset Hills. Many of these people receive our annual brochure and the subsequent quarterly postcard mailings. In addition, they probably read both the *Los Angeles Times* and the *Sunset Hills News,* in which we advertise regularly. They're all great fans in the Fall, but when we have to compete with spring weather their loyalty runs thin. Their allegiance during the Winter is also poor.

There are other groups, too. For example, local music teachers and their pupils; maybe even some of the companies up in the Hanson Industrial Park. We could probably do a lot here in the way of group discounts. This also might apply to faculty and staff—especially those living nearby on University land. I've got a million ideas I'd like to try out, but not nearly enough time. Especially now, with Commencement to worry about. . . .

IMAGE ADVERTISING

Both Lynn and Bacon were concerned that the perceived image of "The Lively Arts at Hanson" was not as good as it could be. Precise information was not available on this issue, but a number of informal sources supported this belief:

• The manager of the Campus Ticket Office reported that very few buyers ever mentioned the program when purchasing individual performance tickets. Additionally, she said that over the past few years only one of the many students who had worked part time in the ticket office had heard of the program before beginning work.

• Informal pollings of students in the Hanson Graduate School of Business indicated that only

5–10 percent of them had heard of the program before studying an earlier version of this case in class.

These and other indicators led Bacon and Lynn to consider the possibility of an image advertising campaign during the summer in the local press as well as on campus at the beginning of the academic year in September 1982. Lynn also thought that students in Hanson's several graduate professional schools (Business, Law, Medicine, and Education) might be a good target segment. She reasoned that these students were much more dedicated to a particular field than were undergraduates, and therefore probably were less involved in competing general university activities, of which there are many.

Also, professional school students were generally more isolated from the university at large, she thought, and therefore less likely to be aware of the Lively Arts program. Finally, many of the professional school students were married; Lynn felt that the combination of easily accessible, low priced, high quality performing arts entertainment should have tremendous appeal to young professionals on a student budget.

AUDIENCE QUESTIONNAIRE

In order to try to get a handle on some of the characteristics of the audience and formulate an appropriate marketing plan for next year, Lively Arts staff had prepared an audience survey. This questionnaire (Exhibit 5) was distributed to most of the audience at ten of the Winter quarter performances in early 1982. A random sample of about 100 (when less than 100 questionnaires were turned in, the whole group was used) was selected from each performance (in all, over 850 responses were sampled) and the results were analyzed using the computer program available through the university computer center.

By mid-May Bacon had the results of his analysis (Exhibits 6–9). By and large the questionnaire reconfirmed many intuitive feelings he and his

EXHIBIT 5

QUESTIONNAIRE DISTRIBUTED AT WINTER 1982 PERFORMANCES
(Excludes cover letter to recipients)

1. Age:
   - ☐ Under 18
   - ☐ 18–24
   - ☐ 25–34
   - ☐ 35–44
   - ☐ 45–60
   - ☐ Over 60

2. Number of children: _____

3. Education:
   - ☐ Grammar school
   - ☐ 1–3 years high school
   - ☐ 4 years high school
   - ☐ 1–3 years college
   - ☐ 4 years college
   - ☐ Graduate work

4. Annual family income (before taxes):
   - ☐ Under $3,000
   - ☐ 3,000–4,999
   - ☐ 5,000–6,999
   - ☐ 7,000–9,999
   - ☐ 10,000–14,999
   - ☐ 15,000–24,999
   - ☐ 25,000–49,999
   - ☐ Over $50,000

5. Are you a Hanson
   - ☐ student?
   - ☐ faculty member?
   - ☐ staff member?
   - ☐ alumnus?

6. Is any member of your immediate family a Hanson
   - ☐ student?
   - ☐ faculty member?
   - ☐ staff member?
   - ☐ alumnus?

7. In what community do you live?
   - ☐ Hanson
   - ☐ Sunset Hills
   - ☐ Verona
   - ☐ Parkside/Vista Valley
   - ☐ Verdes/Verdes Hills
   - ☐ Ocean View
   - ☐ Other (please specify)
   _____

8. How many performing arts programs have you attended at Hanson within the past year?
   - ☐ 1–3
   - ☐ 4–7
   - ☐ 8–10
   - ☐ More than 10

9. How far in advance of this performance did you purchase your tickets?
   - ☐ At the door
   - ☐ Day of performance
   - ☐ 1–3 days before
   - ☐ 4–7 days before
   - ☐ 2–3 weeks before
   - ☐ 1 or more months before

10. Are you presently a subscriber to (check as many as apply)
   - ☐ Lively Arts at Hanson?
   - ☐ Los Angeles Symphony?
   - ☐ Los Angeles Opera?
   - ☐ American Conservatory Theater?
   - ☐ Other art series? (please specify)
   _____

11. If you did not buy your ticket on a discount plan, what price did you pay?
   $ _____

12. Did you receive a copy of *The Lively Arts at Hanson* in the mail?
   - ☐ Yes   ☐ No

13. How did you hear of this performance? (check as many as apply)
   - ☐ Brochure by mail
   - ☐ Newspaper advertising
   - ☐ Newspaper story
   - ☐ Newspaper photograph
   - ☐ Radio announcement
   - ☐ Television announcement
   - ☐ Poster or flyer
   - ☐ Word-of-mouth
   - ☐ Other (please specify)
   _____

14. What sources do you usually consult for information about upcoming arts events? (check as many as apply)
   - ☐ *Hanson Daily*
   - ☐ *Campus Report*
   - ☐ *Hanson Observer*
   - ☐ *Los Angeles Times*
   - ☐ *Long Beach News Press*
   - ☐ *Country Recorder*
   - ☐ *Verona Almanac*
   - ☐ *Sunset Hills News*
   - ☐ *Orange County Crier*
   - ☐ KDFC/KIBE
   - ☐ KKHI
   - ☐ KZSU
   - ☐ Other (please specify)
   _____

15. Do you regularly listen to classical music programs on the radio?
   - ☐ Yes   ☐ No

16. If *Yes* to question 15, which station do you listen to most often?
   - ☐ KKBM
   - ☐ KNFC/KIBC

17. What is your favorite restaurant?
   _____

18. What is your occupation?
   _____

19. What kinds of performances do you like to attend? (check as many as apply)
   - ☐ Theater
   - ☐ Contemporary music
   - ☐ Symphony
   - ☐ Modern Dance
   - ☐ Instrumental recitals
   - ☐ Opera
   - ☐ Chamber music
   - ☐ Ballet
   - ☐ Vocal recitals

20. In making a decision to attend a performance, what weight do you give to the following factors?
   Name of performers:
   - ☐ *Important*   ☐ *Unimportant*
   Repertoire to be performed:
   - ☐ *Important*   ☐ *Unimportant*
   Ticket Price:
   - ☐ *Important*   ☐ *Unimportant*
   Ease of finding performance hall:
   - ☐ *Important*   ☐ *Unimportant*

21. What particular artist and/or attraction would you like to see at Hanson?
   _____
   _____

22. Additional comments you might wish to make concerning the "Lively Arts at Hanson" series of performances:
   _____
   _____
   _____

If you do not return this questionnaire on the night of the performance, please staple or seal it and mail to us. If you mail it, please fill in the date and name of performance below. Thank you.

_____   _____
Date   Name of Performance

EXHIBIT 6
AUDIENCE PROFILE

	Students*	Nonstudents
Median:		
Age group	18–24	35–44
Number of children	0	1
Education level	4 years college	graduate work
Annual family income	—	$25–49 K
Hanson affiliation†:		
Students	73%	3%
Faculty	—	10
Staff	1	9
Alumni	3	15
Place of residence		
Hanson	44%	10%
Sunset Hills	26	35
Verona	1	2
Mateo Park	8	15
Parkside/Vista Valley	1	5
Verdes/Verdes Hills	2	7
Ocean View	5	5
Other	13	21
Performing arts performances attended in Hanson within the past year:		
1–3	64%	49%
4–7	27	27
8–10	4	10
Over 10	5	13
Time of ticket purchase:		
At the door	19%	12%
Day of performance	11	9
1–3 days before	23	12
4–7 days before	16	11
2–3 weeks before	11	12
1 or more months before	20	45
Lively Arts at Hanson:		
Current subscribers	8%	34%
Received brochure in mail	21	56
Information sources for this performance (most frequently mentioned)‡:		
Brochure by mail	15%	48%
Newspaper advertising	34	27
Newspaper story	9	14
Poster or flyer	42	14
Word of mouth	46	29

EXHIBIT 6 *(continued)*
AUDIENCE PROFILE

	Students*	Nonstudents
Sources usually consulted for upcoming arts events (most frequently mentioned)‡:		
Hanson Daily	72%	27%
Campus Report	12	17
Hanson Observer	9	14
Los Angeles Times	32	46
Sunset Hills News	21	54
KNFC/KIBC	18	17
KKBM	13	18
Listen to classical music radio regularly	57%	73%
Station most often listened to:		
KKBM	20%	37%
KNFC/KIBC	39	40
Performance preferences:		
Theater	81%	77%
Contemporary music	41	33
Symphony	63	68
Modern dance	58	51
Instrumental recitals	47	51
Opera	25	32
Chamber music	47	55
Ballet	58	62
Vocal recitals	11	17
Factors important in deciding to attend a performance:		
Name of performers	68%	75%
Repertoire	79	87
Ticket price	68	49
Find hall easily	28	29

* Student/Nonstudent categories were developed according to the response to the occupation question (#18, Exhibit 5).

† Multiple responses were possible for this question. For example, an individual might be a Hanson faculty member and alumnus.

‡ All other categories mentioned less than 10% of the time by both students and nonstudents.

Source: Audience survey questionnaire.

staff had had prior to the survey. But they gained several new insights as well. As a result of the questionnaire, Bacon was seriously rethinking some of his marketing strategies for next season.

THE 1982–83 SEASON

Due to the long-range planning horizon implicit in arranging bookings for performing artists, the 1982–83 season was already scheduled (Exhibit 10). Of the 26 performances, nine were scheduled for the fall quarter, 10 for winter, and seven for spring. Within this programming context, Bacon sought to use all the market information he had gathered during the season to formulate a well-integrated, *specific* marketing plan.

To operationalize his strategic planning, he thought it would be a good idea to set a specific attendance objective. After much thought he decided upon a season attendance goal of 75 per-

EXHIBIT 7
MARKET SEGMENTS AND THEIR CHARACTERISTICS
(percent of audience)

	Nonstudent (70.2%)	Hanson Students* and Spouses (19.3%)	Hanson Faculty, Staff and Spouses (15.9%)
Residence in Hanson-Sunset Hills	45.4%	—	—
Attended at least 4 performances within the last year	50.6	42.7%	49.2%
Purchased ticket at least one month before performance	43.9	12.3	53.0
Lively Arts subscribers**	33.6	4.2	36.8
Information source for this performance:			
Brochure by mail	48.3	10.3	58.8
Newspaper advertising	27.4	36.4	35.3
Poster or flyer	14.3	46.1	20.6
Word of mouth	28.9	41.8	30.1
Usual information source:			
Hanson Daily	26.9	87.9	61.8
Campus Report	16.9	13.9	49.3
Hanson Observer	13.8	11.5	14.7
Los Angeles Times	46.2	27.3	44.9
Sunset Hills News	53.5	14.5	61.8

*Student status: undergraduate 42.4%
              graduate student 54.9
**Season ticket purchasers.
Source: Audience survey.

EXHIBIT 8
ATTENDANCE AND TICKET-PURCHASING BEHAVIOR OF PATRONS

	Nonstudents*	Hanson Students and Spouses
Attended 1–3 performances within past year	49.5%	56.1%
Attended at least 4 performances within past year *and* purchased tickets at least one month in advance	34.8	10.2
Attended at least 4 performances within past year and purchased tickets less than one month in advance	15.7	33.7
	100.0%	100.0%

* Within 1–2 percentage points in each category, the figures for Nonstudents also apply to Hanson Faculty, Staff and Spouses, and Hanson Alumni and Spouses, as well.
    Source: Audience survey.

EXHIBIT 9

CROSS TABULATIONS OF TIME OF TICKET PURCHASE BY
NUMBER OF PERFORMANCES ATTENDED WITHIN PAST YEAR

Time of Ticket Purchase	Performances Attended				Row Total
	1–3	4–7	8–10	Over 10	
Nonstudents					
At door	42	12	2	4	60
Day of performance	35	9	2	2	48
1–3 Days before	45	14	3	2	64
4–7 Days before	37	12	2	3	54
2–3 Weeks before	44	15	2	2	63
1 Month or more	68	84	47	59	258
Column total	271	146	58	72	547
Hanson students and spouses					
At door	14	8	2	4	28
Day of performance	12	6	0	0	18
1–3 Days before	23	10	0	1	34
4–7 Days before	20	4	5	2	31
2–3 Weeks before	10	6	2	0	18
1 Month or more	4	12	2	1	19
Column total	83	46	11	8	148

Source: Audience survey.

cent, with a 35–65 percent student/nonstudent mix. This was clearly a stretch target, but by setting his overall season goals high, Bacon hoped to really come to grips with his historically most pressing problem: seasonal attendance. He further thought that, at a minimum, his plan should address the following issues:

- *Brochures* Was the "lavish" annual brochure with quarterly postcard follow-ups sufficient, or should *each* quarterly mailing be more like the current annual elaborate brochure?
- *Advertising* How should he allocate his advertising budget? What media should he expand? Contract? Why? What are the possibilities of image advertising over the summer to develop latent demand?
- *Pricing* How might he alter his pricing policy further? What level of prices would be tolerable and consistent with his goals?

- *Season Tickets* Was the "choose-your-own" program[1] viable? Why or why not? What might be employed as an alternative? For example, should the six Guarneri Quartet performances be packaged as a series to be sold at a discount?
- *Segmentation* What would be an effective way to target his marketing pitch at each of the segments that Lynn had identified? Were there other viable segmentation possibilities?

As Bacon mulled over these issues he recognized that his total promotional budget could not exceed about $50,000 for the 1982–83 season. To assist in formulating the marketing plan, Lynn had put together an estimate of the major adver-

[1] The "choose-your-own" program allowed season ticket purchasers to structure their own discount season, choosing only those performances they wished to attend, as long as a minimum number of performances was selected.

EXHIBIT 10
1982–83 SEASON SCHEDULE

Fall quarter:

October 22	Chamber Music Society of Lincoln Center
October 28	"Are You Now or Have You Ever Been?" (drama)
October 29	Oba Koso (Nigerian opera)
November 5	Roman de Fauvel (medieval secular music drama)
November 9	Music from Marlboro (chamber music)
November 12	Young Concert Artist
November 14, 16, 19	Guarneri String Quartet—Beethoven Quartet Series (chamber music)

Winter quarter:

January 18	"An Evening of George Orwell" with Jose Ferrer (celebrity)
January 21	Young Concert Artist
February 1, 2, 3	Eliot Feld Ballet Company (dance)
February 11	Young Concert Artist
February 18	Bach Aria Group (chamber music)
February 22, 25, 27	Guarneri String Quartet—Beethoven Quartet Series (chamber music)

Spring quarter:

April 1	Narciso Yepes (guitar)
April 7, 8	Utah Repertory Dance Company
April 15	Young Concert Artist
April 17	American Brass Quintet (chamber music)
April 24, 26	Fine Arts Quartet (with viola)—Mozart Quintet Series (chamber music)

tising, brochure, and other promotional expense items for the 1982–83 season (Exhibit 11). Bacon also thought it would not be too early to begin formulating some strategy regarding the more long-term issue of programming selection (i.e., how many of what type of performances to schedule when?). Although he wanted to maintain program diversity, he knew that university financial pressures would force his program's funding implications into prominence in future interdepartmental budget battles.

EXHIBIT 11
ESTIMATED MARKETING EXPENSES—1982–83 SEASON

Newspaper ad rates costs quoted are "per column-inch" for each time the ad is run:

Sunset Hills News	$11.00	
	8.50	(if there are no changes and the ad is run a minimum of four times)
Orange County Crier	17.25	
Hanson Daily	5.00	
Los Angeles Times	54.00	

Radio ad rates—costs for a 30-second announcement:

KKBM	$43.00
KIBC/KDOC	24.00
KBIG	36.50

Lively Arts brochure—annual:

Typesetting	$165 per page		
Printing	150 per page		
Fixed cost (plates)			
Variable cost per page:			
First 10,000 copies	$.022		
Next 20,000 copies	.007		
Next 30,000 copies	.005		
Labels and bulk mailing	.11 per brochure		
Typesetting	$165 × 20 pages		$ 3,300
Printing:			
Fixed (plates)		$3,000	
Variable			
$.022 × 10,000 × 20		4,400	
$.007 × 20,000 × 20		2,800	
$.005 × 15,000 × 20		1,500	11,700
Labels and bulk mailing	$.11 × 30,000		3,300
			15,000

Winter and Spring Quarter Brochures ("Snake Mailers"):

Printing	
Fixed cost (plate)	$15.00
Variable cost per item	
First 25,000	.03
Next 50,000	.022
Labels and bulk mailing	.09 each

Bookmarks:

Printing	$ .019 each

Notes: (1) A typical Lively Arts ad in 1981–82 was 2 columns wide and 3 inches long, or 6 column-inches. In the Sunset Hills *News* these ads typically ran for about two weeks prior to the performance.
(2) Los Angeles *Times* advertising for 1981–82 was restricted to the Sunday "Datebook" section.
(3) For the 1981–82 season the brochure was 20 pages; 45,000 copies were printed and 30,000 bulk-mailed at a total cost (including mailing) of $16,800.

THE LIVELY ARTS AT HANSON, II

Charles B. Weinberg

In the fall of 1983, Tom Bacon and Barbara Lynn of Hanson University's Office of Public Events began planning the 1984–85 season for the Lively Arts at Hanson (LAH) program. In December, they would go to the annual booking meeting in New York, at which time almost all the commitments for 1984–85 would be made.

In preparation, the two managers had prepared a list of events they might wish to schedule for LAH. Exhibits 1 to 5 list the performers that were being actively considered, a brief description from promotional brochures about the performer, the month the performer was available, and the seating capacity of the hall they would perform in if they were to be booked as part of the LAH program.[1] Each performer listed went on a national or regional tour and would be available for Hanson at different times of the year, although sometimes performers could adjust their schedule to be available at another time.

The LAH season generally ran from October to early May. Most of December and early January were excluded because of winter holidays at the university; much of March, because of spring holidays.

As in the current year, LAH planned to offer approximately 25 performances. In general, performers made only one appearance on campus during a year. However, because of the expense of setup, any dance group that was booked appeared a minimum of two times and usually three times. In addition, the Guarneri String Quartet, which had become virtually a Hanson tradition (and a sellout), performed three times and it was possible to book one other chamber music group for more than one night. Booking too many groups for more than one night would detract from LAH's objective of presenting a mix of events.

It was decided to abandon the "Young Concert Artist" designation for 1984–85. Such a designation seemed to create a self-fulfilling

Copyright © 1985 by Charles B. Weinberg.

[1] The seating capacity of the large hall was approximately 1,700 (usually 1,694) seats. When the balcony and back rows were closed off, then approximately 1,100 (usually 1,085) seats were available for sale.

584

EXHIBIT 1
CHAMBER MUSIC

Name	Description	Month Available	Seating Capacity
1 Tokyo String Quartet	Four young musicians who burst on the musical scene eight years ago and are now ranked with the nation's top-flight quartets. "If you care at all about chamber music, you won't want to miss them."	October	720
2 Guarneri String Quartet	The talents of the Guarneri need little description, so supreme is the Quartet's playing. Played at the university every year since 1970.	November	720
3 Juilliard String Quartet	As veterans of more than 3,000 sold-out concerts, participants in every major music festival around the world and with a repertory of more than 375 works, it's no wonder that the Juilliard is hailed as one of America's first families of chamber music.	November	720
4 Pittsburgh Symphony Chamber Players with Barry Tuckwell, French Horn	Tuckwell has subjected one of the most difficult instruments to a degree of obedience that approaches perfection. His performance with the principal players of the Pittsburgh Symphony Orchestra provides a delightful evening of music.	January	720
5 Bartok Quartet	Acclaimed worldwide as one of the most distinguished chamber groups on the concert scene. "The sense of ensemble could hardly be more intimate and the tonal blend of the instruments more homogeneous."	January	720
6 Music from Marlboro	Join us for what has become a tradition at Hanson; the annual visit of Music From Marlboro. Performing with the ensemble on its 1979 tour will be Isidore Cohen, famous violinist with the Beaux Arts Trio.	March	720
7 Chilingirian String Quartet	Four polished musicians who produce an elegant, exquisite sound. "Once you've heard them, you'll never forget them."	April	720

prophecy of low attendance. Consequently, younger artists would not be separately identified but would be described by type of performance.

Bacon and Lynn were trying to develop a 25 event schedule. They had already scheduled the following 10 performances:

Edward Albee, Playwright	October (to open the season)	1 night
Guarneri String Quartet	November	3 nights
Misha and Cipa Dichter, Pianists	January	1 night
Nicanor Zabaleta, Harpist	February	1 night
Repertory Dance Theatre	February	3 nights
Michael Lorimer, Guitar	May	1 night

While the financial aspects could not be ignored, at this stage LAH management was more concerned with scheduling a season that would help LAH to meet its non-financial objectives. Indeed, the artistic fees of the performers listed in Exhibits 1 to 5 were such that LAH would have a deficit of between $1,000 and $2,000 if ticket sales were at the historic average level for the type of event. Ticket prices were expected to be in the $9 to $10 range, but the decision on prices would not be required for some time.

In planning for next year, LAH management had available an interactive computer model, called ARTS PLAN, to help forecast attendance and choose events to schedule. A brief report

EXHIBIT 2

DANCE

Name	Description	Month Available	Seating Capacity
1 Bella Lewitzky Dance Company	Lewitzky is a revelation . . . a major choreographer . . . a great dancer . . . a superb teacher. With herself and her company, there is a body awareness that transcends mere muscular discipline.	October	1,700
2 Kathryn Posin Dance Company	One of the bright new stars on the dance horizon. "Posin's choreography is simply brilliant, employing both space and body in fresh, formful ways. She uses a wide range of dance idioms that are molded like putty to her purpose."	October	1,700
3 AMAN*	Colorful, authentic costumes, exotic instruments and an exciting repertory of more than 70 folk dances from the Balkans, Middle East, North Africa and the U.S. AMAN, the American International Folk Ballet, has become one of the nation's most respected performing arts companies.	January	1,700
4 Joffrey II	The best small classical ballet company in the country. Their remarkable control and technique will dazzle you.	January	1,700
5 Repertory Dance Theatre	Utah's exciting dance company includes in its repertory some 60 works by the greatest names in modern dance. From the classics to exciting new choreography, this company of nine excels in its art.	February	1,700
6 Alvin Ailey American Dance*	Modern, jazz and classical dance technique which reflects America's heritage, black and white.	March	1,700
7 Pilobolus	An ever-changing flow of linked body shapes that mold and re-mold in space with skill and sophistication. Pilobolus is gymnastics, acrobatics, applied physics, theories of leverage and contemporary dance!	March	1,700

* Can be considered a "well-known" dance group.

EXHIBIT 3

GUITAR

Name	Description	Month Available	Seating Capacity*
1 Eugenia Zukerman, Flutist/Carlos Bonell, Guitarist	Zukerman, one of the finest flutists to be found anywhere, teams up with Bonell, one of Europe's leading guitarists, for a program of works primarily from the Baroque period.	February	1,085
2 Ronald Radford, Flamenco Guitar	One of the few American masters of the Flamenco guitar shares Spanish gypsy music with you through performance and dialogue.	April	1,085
3 Michael Lorimer, Guitarist	A protégé of Andres Segovia, Lorimer has carved an enviable reputation as a classical guitarist.	May	1,085

*Guitarists usually perform in the 1,700 seat hall, but some 600 of these seats are not made available for sale.

EXHIBIT 4
JAZZ

Name	Description	Month Available	Seating Capacity
1 New England Conservatory Ragtime Ensemble with Gunther Schuller	The toe-tapping sounds of Joplin, Morton, Marshall, Hampton and others are played by this very famous ensemble. Gunther Schuller himself will be at the podium, conducting and discussing this marvelous period in our country's musical history.	October	1,700
2 Richard Stoltzman, Clarinet	Consistently acclaimed as "an artist of indescribable genius." Often compared to the legendary Reginald Kell. Pianist/Bassoonist Bill Douglas will perform with Stoltzman.	October	720
3 Billy Taylor Trio	Jazz pianist, composer, arranger, teacher and actor, Billy Taylor performs in company with a drummer and bassist. Taylor is among those musicians who have elevated jazz to new heights of recognition and appreciation.	December	1,700
4 Toshiko Akiyoshi/Lew Tabackin Big Band	An outstanding jazz orchestra in the tradition of the great Duke Ellington: each musician's individual sound and style becomes an integral part of the ensemble's musical identity. Akiyoshi is composer, conductor, pianist. Tabackin plays tenor sax and flute and is the principal soloist.	February	1,700
5 Sonny Rollins, Tenor Saxophone	"A giant speaking. A man who has altered the course of music to which he still contributes mightily." Hear the musician who has converted a new generation to the meaning and joys of jazz!	February	720
6 Dizzy Gillespie, Trumpeter	Revered throughout the world as one of the giants of jazz, an artist with absolute mastery of his instrument and seemingly unlimited musical ideas.	March	1,700

describing this system is included in the Appendix. The system had provided accurate forecasts when previously used by LAH management.

Tom Bacon and Barbara Lynn expected to use ARTS PLAN as an aid in developing next year's schedule. However, from past experience, they knew it was best to develop a limited list of alternative schedules before using the computer system. They also found it more efficient to prepare the fall, winter and spring schedules separately at first, and then, after some test computer runs, to consider a full schedule. One year, when the computer was unavailable, Bacon and Lynn simply used the ARTS PLAN forecasting rule (see page 592) with a pocket calculator to test scheduling alternatives.

Meeting attendance goals was just one of the tasks that they faced. They had to deal with the pragmatic problems of when performers were available and the need to have a schedule that presented a relatively even number of events in the major months of October, November, January, February and April. Beyond this, the programming schedule also had to help achieve the goal of establishing LAH as a major source of first-rate performing art talent in a variety of fields.

EXHIBIT 5
OTHER ARTISTS

Name	Description	Month Available	Seating Capacity
Theater			
1 Edward Albee, Playwright	Edward Albee is one of the world's most important contemporary playwrights. A cast chosen and directed by Albee will present "The Zoo Story" and "The American Dream." The former was Albee's first play and won the Vernon Rice Award in 1960; the latter was written in 1960 and won the Foreign Press Association Award in 1961.	October	1,700
2 The World of Gilbert & Sullivan	Artists from the famous D'Oyly Carte Opera Company present in concert some of Gilbert & Sullivan's finest tunes and patter. Produced in cooperation with the university chorus and orchestra.	October	1,700
3 The Acting Company	Presenting the "White Devil," a work by John Webster, author of the Elizabethan classic, "The Duchess of Malfi."	January	1,700
4 Ruby Dee & Ossie Davis, Theater	Two of America's foremost black performers share their love of stories, poems, legends and experiences in "Inside/Out," a project of personal love and dedication that has become one of our nation's theatrical riches.	April	720
Soloists and Duets			
1 Elly Ameling, Soprano	Truly one of the foremost masters of the art of song in the world.	October	720
2 Clamma Dale, Soprano	The toast of the musical world last season for her brilliant portrayal of Bess in the Houston Grand Opera's Broadway production of "Porgy and Bess."	October	720
3 Igor Kipnis, Harpsichordist	The foremost harpsichordist of today. "He need bow to no one in the intelligence and scrupulousness with which he approaches the various stylistic requirements of Renaissance, Baroque and Classical music."	November	720
4 Misha and Cipa Dichter, Pianists	Husband and wife, Misha and Cipa Dichter win accolades wherever they perform for their assurance, virtuosity and unique sense of musical spirit.	January	720
5 Nicanor Zabaleta, Harp	The harp virtuoso of our era. A veteran of more than 4,000 concerts around the world and a sellout at every previous Lively Arts concert.	February	720
6 Robert Cohen, Cello	Winner of the 1978 Gregor Piatigorsky Award, Cohen is known for his combination of high virtuosity and genuine eloquence.	March	720
7 Charles Rosen, Piano	"His playing is all one could wish for. It has taste, intelligence and artistic insight."	April	720

EXHIBIT 5 (continued)

OTHER ARTISTS

Name	Description	Month Available	Seating Capacity
	Groups		
1 Sour Cream	Frans Brueggens' avant garde recorder trio. Join him, Kees Boeke and Walter van Hauwe for an informal session of music making, featuring works from the Renaissance to the present.	October	720
2 Il Divertimento	Eight master woodwind players performing on 18th-century instruments. Hear Haydn, Beethoven and Mozart played the way the composers themselves heard it.	November	720
3 Waverly Consort	Hear gentle pastorales and madrigals, ribald drinking songs, lusty cries of chimney sweeps, delicate airs for the recorder and viheula, gay gigues and galliards, sedate minuets—all played on instruments of the Medieval, Renaissance and Baroque periods.	March	720
4 Greenwood Consort	Music of the late Middle Ages and Renaissance delivered with verve, enthusiasm, humor and top-notch musicianship. The Boston-based Greenwood brings early music to life by combining voices with flute, recorder, lute, pipe and tabor, krummhorns and viols.	April	720

APPENDIX: Excerpts from a Report Describing the Development and Use of ARTS PLAN

As part of an effort to get a better understanding of the factors influencing attendance at Lively Arts at Hanson (LAH) events, LAH management asked a marketing faculty member at Hanson University for help. By employing a statistical technique known as regression analysis, a fairly accurate attendance forecasting system was developed. Moreover, the professor and a student assistant were able to transform the technical statistical analysis into a "user-friendly" computer system, called "ARTS PLAN," that LAH management had used to help plan a season. The remainder of this appendix describes briefly the development and usage of the system.

DEVELOPMENT OF A FORECASTING MODEL

A number of factors beyond the distinctive appeal of an individual performer could influence the attendance at any given performance. The first step was to determine these factors and to measure their importance via the use of regression analysis. The resulting model forms a preliminary base case forecast for a planning model. The manager can override the forecast, if necessary, because of factors not captured in the model.

Data were available on attendance by performances for 93 LAH performances over three years. Preliminary analyses of these data revealed that there were seasonal effects in attendance. An average performance drew 85 percent of capacity in the fall, 60 percent in the winter, and 50 percent in the spring. Similarly, there were effects by type of performance. Chamber music performances drew 80 percent of capacity, dance 60 percent, guitar 105 percent (seats on the stage or tickets for standing room were sometimes sold), and jazz 75 percent. Performers classified as Young Concert Artists (YCA) drew 50 percent of capacity. These five performance types accounted for 81 of the 93 performances. The remaining 12 events averaged 60 percent of capacity. It was also believed, although not specifically tabulated, that performances on Friday nights drew better than performances during the week. There are too few Saturday night or Sunday performances to examine other weekend nights.

Approximately 15 percent of the performers who were booked appeared for more than one performance. There were a number of reasons for multi-performance bookings. Some groups had a varied repertoire and fairly broad appeal. Dance groups were generally booked for multiple performances because of the fixed costs involved in bringing such a group to campus. The number of performances for some groups was determined by their availability or the availability of auditoriums on campus. Because of the various reasons for having multiple performances, the effect on attendance was problematic. Multiple performances could spread out a limited audience over several days, provide opportunities for word-of-mouth to build second or third day audiences, and allow devotees to attend several times.

Examination of the data revealed that there was only one group that appeared more than five times over the three years. A specific variable was set up to represent this group.[2] Although no dance group appeared more than five times, there appeared to be a subset of dance groups that were particularly well known. A specific variable was established for dance groups belonging to this subset.

The performances were held (with three exceptions in 93 performances) in three different halls on campus with capacities of approximately 350, 720, and 1,700 seats. Thus, the capacity of the hall could be a factor in the actual attendance obtained; however, the hall chosen was dictated by the musical and technical requirements of the performance type and not by an estimate of attendance. Thus, for example, chamber music concerts usually are held in a 720 seat hall, and dance groups always perform in a 1,700 seat hall. Because of the direct association between type of performance and capacity of hall, it was not possible to separate the effect of capacity from performance type. Thus the performance type "dance" actually refers to dance held in a 1,700 seat auditorium; if a dance performance were to be held in a 2,000 seat auditorium, some extrapolation would be required.

Data on several other potentially important factors (such as competing events being held on the same night and different weather conditions) were not readily available in LAH records. For example, attendance might suffer if a basketball game were being played that night. Also, the effect of any special promotion was not included. However, to account for any temporal shift, variables to represent year were included.

Statistical Model

The mathematical model tested was the following:

$$Y = a_O + a_W W + a_S S + a_{T1} T_1 + a_{T2} T_2 + A_{T3} T_3 + a_{T4} T_4$$
$$+ a_{T5} T_5 + a_{F1} F_1 + a_{M1} M_1 + a_{G1} G_1 + a_{G2} G_2 + a_{Y1} Y_1 + a_{Y2} Y_2,$$

[2] Code named the Gala Quartet in the computer analysis, this group is actually the Guarneri String Quartet.

where Y = attendance
  W = 1, if held in winter, 0 otherwise,
  S = 1, if held in spring, 0 otherwise,
  T_1 = 1, if chamber music, 0 otherwise,
  T_2 = 1, if dance, 0 otherwise,
  T_3 = 1, if guitar, 0 otherwise,
  T_4 = 1, if jazz, 0 otherwise,
  T_5 = 1, if young concert artist, 0 otherwise,
  F = 1, if held on Friday, 0 otherwise,
  M = 1, if part of a series of multiple performances, 0 otherwise,
  G_1 = 1, if by group performing more than five times, 0 otherwise,
  G_2 = 1, if by well-known dance group, 0 otherwise,
  Y_1 = 1, if held during year 1, 0 otherwise,
  Y_2 = 1, if held during year 2, 0 otherwise.

The independent variables are all 0, 1 dummy variables in order to represent different effects and, as is usual, are defined to omit one class in order to preserve the non-singularity of the independent variables.

Statistical Results

When regression analysis was run, five variables, Y_1 for year 1, M for multiple performances, F for Friday, W for winter, and T_1 for chamber music were not statistically significant at the 0.05 level. When these variables were deleted, all the remaining variables were significant at the .05 level. The regression results are shown in Exhibit A1. The adjusted R^2 was 0.79. When a split-half double cross over validation was run, the R^2 turned out to be 0.70. These results are considered to be very good and are superior to what has been expected by both management and the analyst. All the significant effects were in the expected direction.

There was a clear effect for performance type, four of the five dummy variables for performance type were significant and, in addition, were significantly different from each other. Although the dummy variable for chamber music did not achieve significance, this

EXHIBIT A1
REGRESSION RESULTS FOR PREDICTING ATTENDANCE

	Coefficient	Beta Weight	Value of F*
Variable:			
S (Spring)	−127	−0.12	5.5
T_2 (Dance)	231	0.22	12.3
T_3 (Guitar)	481	0.26	27.0
T_4 (Jazz)	732	0.46	79.6
T_5 (YCA)	−400	−0.30	33.0
G_1	178	0.10	4.1
G_2	804	0.50	74.1
Y_2 (Year 2)	−113	−0.12	6.0
Constant	647		

* As discussed in the text, all coefficients are significant at the 0.05 level or above.

only implies that its attendance is not significantly different from that for the 12 non-classified performances. The attendance estimate for chamber music is significantly different than that for the other four performance types.

Year 3 was the base case for the annual effects. No particular explanation for the comparative drop-off in year 2 attendance, but not in year 1, has been developed. In the absence of an apparent trend, it was decided to assume $Y_2 = 0$ in the forecasting model.

Forecasting Rule

In brief, the forecasting model was:

$$
\begin{aligned}
\text{attendance} = 647 & \\
-127 & \text{ (if spring)} \\
+231 & \text{ (if dance)} \\
+481 & \text{ (if guitar)} \\
+732 & \text{ (if jazz)} \\
-400 & \text{ (if YCA)} \\
+178 & \text{ (if Guarneri)} \\
+804 & \text{ (if popular dance group)}
\end{aligned}
$$

For example, the base case forecast for a dance event to be held in the spring is $647 - 127$ (Spring) $+ 231$ (Dance) $= 751$; the forecast for jazz in the fall would be $647 + 732$ (Jazz) $= 1,379$.

PLANNING MODEL

The planning model is designed to help the manager determine whether a tentative or planned schedule will meet attendance objectives for the year and what the impact of promoting certain events would be on the attendance predictions.

The model has three main stages. The first stage establishes a base case forecast for the season being planned, using the forecasting model discussed in the previous section. The second stage allows the manager to *override* the regression forecast because of unique factors of which the manager is aware. For example, although the expected attendance for jazz groups booked in the fall was 1,379 people, one group may be expected to do particularly well at the university because of its local reputation or a previous successful appearance. The manager may wish to test alternative estimates for groups falling in the "other" category. When this stage is completed, a forecast of attendance by performance, season, or year is available.

In the third stage, the manager can then test the impact of alternative strategies. The strategic options are to make scheduling changes (add, omit, or substitute a performance) and to promote particular performances. For example, if the manager wants to schedule a dance company instead of a guitarist as the second performance of the season, the impact of this scheduling change on attendance can be assessed.

A routine for suggesting performances to promote has also been developed. The manager's choice is primarily whether to promote a given performance, rather than the level of promotional effort. Not all performances are equally responsive to promotion. For each performance, using the regression forecast (possibly adjusted) as a base, the manager estimates the percentage attendance with promotion. After the estimate is given for all performances, an optimizing routine then calculates the impact of promotion on attendance and produces an ordered list of performances in which the sequencing variable is increases in attendance due to promotion of the performance. The manager then chooses the performances to promote. The model substitutes the forecast of percentage attendance with promotion for the previously utilized attendance forecast and then develops a projection of attendance for the season.

IMPLEMENTATION EXPERIENCE

The ARTS PLAN system has been used at LAH as an aid in the management of an on-going season and in the planning of a future season. Before the start of the last season, attendance forecasts were made for the 26 performance schedule. A few adjustments were made to the regression analysis forecast to account for several factors that the manager thought were important. Selected performances in the winter and spring were scheduled for intensive promotion. In December, results to date were checked. At the end of the season, the actual and predicted attendances were compared. An R^2 of 0.80 between actual and predicted was obtained. Further, the total attendance prediction was within 5 percent of the actual attendance.

SAMPLE APPLICATION OF USAGE

Exhibit A2 is an illustration of the usage of the ARTS PLAN system. The number of options considered is relatively small because of space limitations, and fictitious names are used for the performances. Attendance forecasts are made in terms of percentage of seating capacity to make the system easier for the manager to use. Although this procedure introduces some small rounding errors of 10–20 seats, these are judged to be inconsequential by the manager. In actual usage, the exact seating capacities are used. The exhibit is largely self-explanatory. The following comments briefly describe the use of the model in this example.

After identifying the time period to be examined and setting the number of performances, the program prints out the historical record. The program then requests the user to identify each performance by name and type, give the capacity of the hall it is in, and indicate any special effects that may exist. If the performance is not one of the five types, the user has the immediate option to override the attendance forecast. This is because the "other" category includes a wide mix of performance types. When all the required information has been submitted, the program provides a forecast of attendance.

An option is then provided to override the base case projections because of additional information that the manager has available. For example, the jazz group Sari may be particularly well-known and consequently may be expected to do better than the average jazz group, even without special promotion. The adjustment may either be upwards or downwards. The manager can also examine the impact of adding, deleting, or replacing a performance with another. When all the adjustments are completed, a planning base forecast for the quarter is established.

The manager has the opportunity in the next phase of the program to investigate the impact of allocating promotional effort to one or more performances. First, the manager is asked what would be the impact of promotion on the percentage of capacity sold for each

EXHIBIT A2
EXCERPTS FROM A SAMPLE RUN

```
ARTS PLANNING MODEL
DO YOU WISH TO INVESTIGATE AN ENTIRE SEASON, OR A
SINGLE QUARTER?  (S = SEASON; Q = QUARTER)?Q
WHICH QUARTER DO YOU WISH TO INVESTIGATE
    (FALL = 1, WINTER = 2, SPRING = 3)     ?3
NO. OF PERFORMANCES PLANNED FOR QUARTER (MAX = 17)?4
THE FOLLOWING TABLE PRESENTS THE BASE-CASE ATTENDANCE
PERCENTAGES WHICH WILL BE USED IN GENERATING THE
FIRST-ROUND ATTENDANCE PROJECTION

                    ESTIMATED ATTENDANCE PERCENTAGES (HISTORICAL)*
                        FALL            WINTER          SPRING
(1)   CHAMB MUSIC       90              90              72
(2)   DANCE             52              52              44
(3)   GUITAR            104             104             92
(4)   JAZZ              81              81              74
(5)   YCA               71              71              34
(6)   OTHER-(720)       90              90              72
(7)   OTHER-(1700)      38              38              31
*IN ADDITION THE FOLLOWING SUPPLEMENTARY EFFECTS HAVE BEEN OBSERVED
    (G)   GALA QUARTET          +22 PERCENT
    (P)   POPULAR DANCE GROUP   +47 PERCENT
AT THIS STEP YOU ARE ASKED TO PROVIDE SPECIFIC INFORMATION ON
THE PROGRAM YOU ARE PLANNING.
********************************************************************
PERFORMANCE NUMBER 1
ENTER PERFORMANCE NAME (MAXIMUM 12 CHARACTERS)?BETH
ENTER PERFORMANCE TYPE (USE CODE NUMBER:)
    1=CHAMBER MUSIC   3=GUITAR  5=YOUNG CONCERT ARTISTS(YCA)
    2=DANCE           4=JAZZ    6=OTHER-(720)  7=OTHER-(1700)
?2
ENTER CAPACITY OF HALL?1700
    POPULAR DANCE GROUP  (Y=YES, N=NO)?Y
********************************************************************
 † (Remainder of initial input deleted)

ATTENDANCE PREDICTIONS FOR SPRING QUARTER
PERFORMANCE     PERFORMANCE     PERCENTAGE      CAPACITY
NUMBER          NAME            ATTENDANCE      OF HALL      ATTENDANCE
  1             BETH            91              1700         1547
  2             SARI            74              1700         1258
  3             AMY             34              350          119
  4             MICHELLE        72              720          518
-------------------------------------------------------------------------
TOTALS          *               77              4470         3442
*********************************************************************
DO YOU WISH TO MAKE ANY CHANGES?  (Y=YES, N=NO)?Y
ENTER NUMBER OF PERFORMANCE YOU WISH TO CHANGE?2
CURRENT STATUS OF PERFORMANCE NUMBER 2
    NAME        SARI
    TYPE        (4) JAZZ
 PCT ATTEND     74
 CAPACITY       1700
 ATTENDANCE     1258
INDICATE BY CODE NUMBER THE PARAMETER YOU WISH TO CHANGE
ENTER ONE ONLY  1=PERFORMANCE NAME  3=PERCENTAGE ATTENDANCE EXPECTED
                2=PERFORMANCE TYPE  4=CAPACITY OF HALL
?3
OLD PERCENTAGE ATTENDANCE IS:       74
NEW PERCENTAGE ATTENDANCE EXPECTED: 85
ANY OTHER CHANGES TO THIS PERFORMANCE  (Y=YES, N=NO)?N
```

EXHIBIT A2 *(continued)*

```
ATTENDANCE PREDICTIONS FOR SPRING QUARTER
PERFORMANCE      PERFORMANCE         PERCENTAGE      CAPACITY
NUMBER           NAME                ATTENDANCE      OF HALL         ATTENDANCE
   1             BETH                    91          1700              1547
   2             SARI          RV        85          1700              1445
   3             AMY                     34           350               119
   4             MICHELLE                72           720               518
----------------------------------------------------------------------------
TOTALS           *                       81          4470              3629
****************************************************************************
DO YOU WISH TO MAKE MODIFICATIONS TO THE PLANNED
SEASON?        (Y=YES, N=NO)?Y

INPUT TYPE OF CHANGE DESIRED.  (ONE ONLY)

     1 - ADD A NEW PERFORMANCE
     2 - DELETE AN EXISTING PERFORMANCE
     3 - REPLACE AN EXISTING PERFORMANCE WITH ANOTHER
     4 - MAKE CHANGES TO AN EXISTING PERFORMANCE
?2

WHICH PERFORMANCE DO YOU WISH TO DELETE (ENTER PERFORMANCE NUMBER)?2


DO YOU WISH TO EXAMINE PROMOTIONAL IMPACT  (Y=YES, N=NO)?Y

AT THIS STAGE YOU ARE ASKED TO ESTIMATE THE IMPACT OF DEVOTING
CONSIDERABLE PROMOTIONAL EFFORT TO A PARTICULAR PERFORMANCE.

PERFORMANCE             PROJECTED           ESTMATED % ATTENDANCE
NAME                    % ATTENDANCE        WITH PROMOTION
BETH                    91                  ?95
AMY                     34                  ?34
MICHELLE                72                  ?95

THE FOLLOWING TABLE LISTS PERFORMANCE BY ORDER OF INCREASE
IN ATTENDANCE DUE TO PROMOTION

PERFORMANCE      PERFORMANCE         PROJECTED      INCREASE      ATTENDANCE WITH
NUMBER           NAME                ATTENDANCE     FROM PROMO    PROMOTION
   3             MICHELLE              518            166            684
   1             BETH                 1547             68           1615
   2             AMY                   119              0            119

WHICH PERFORMANCE, IF ANY, DO YOU WANT TO PROMOTE?   INDICATE BY
   PERFORMANCE NUMBER OR ZERO IF NO MORE . . . .?3
PERFORMANCE NUMBER OR ZERO IF NO MORE . . . .?0
ATTENDANCE WITH PROMOTIONS CHOSEN IS NOW ESTIMATED
****************************************************************************
ATTENDANCE PREDICTIONS FOR SPRING QUARTER
PERFORMANCE      PERFORMANCE         PERCENTAGE      CAPACITY
NUMBER           NAME                ATTENDANCE      OF HALL         ATTENDANCE
   1             BETH                    91          1700              1547
   2             AMY                     34           350               119
   3             MICHELLE                95           720               684
----------------------------------------------------------------------------
TOTALS           *                       85          2770              2350
****************************************************************************
```

performance. The performances are then ranked in order of increase in attendance. This ranking reflects the promotional responsiveness of a performance, capacity of the hall, and attendance without promotion.

The user then selects the performances to be promoted in light of the above results and any other information available. An attendance projection by performance and by quarter, including the effect of promotion and a variety of summary statistics, are then displayed. The user has the option to revise estimates or make programming changes before terminating the program.

ILLINOIS CENTRAL GULF RAILROAD

Christopher H. Lovelock

"Harry, I think you're making a terrible mistake!" declared the senior vice president-law of the Illinois Central Gulf Railroad (ICG). He continued earnestly:

> I've been in this business a long time, Harry, and I know what it's like in all the other railroads. They've got sales offices everywhere just teeming with people and yet you're talking about closing more than a third of our offices, cutting back our field sales force and having a few folks in the remaining offices trying to sell over the telephone. The accounting department tells me that we've got 22,000 customers at the ICG. How can we possibly hope to hold on to them all with a sales force that's smaller, relative to our size, than nearly all our competitors? We need more people out there, not less!

Harry J. Bruce, senior vice president-marketing, listened quietly, waiting for reactions from his other colleagues. He had just concluded a presentation to senior staff members of the ICG at their regular monthly meeting in June 1979. His

Copyright © 1982 by the President and Fellows of Harvard College, Harvard Business School case 9-583-083.

topic concerned a proposed reorganization of the railroad's sales force. Based upon findings from an in-depth study of present sales activities, plans were now well advanced for a major restructuring of the sales territories and a redirection of the sales effort. Bruce hoped to publish the final report and recommendations in early August.

COMPANY BACKGROUND

The Illinois Central Gulf (ICG) Railroad was a wholly owned subsidiary of IC Industries, Inc., a large holding company which also owned a diverse group of consumer and industrial firms. The ICG was a consolidation of more than 100 railroads and had adopted its present name following the merger of the Illinois Central (IC) and the Gulf, Mobile and Ohio (GM&O) railroads in 1972.

The senior of these two roads, the Illinois Central, was chartered in 1851. It enjoyed the distinction—rare in transportation—of never having been in receivership, undergone a reorganization, or defaulted on its bonded debt. With lines extending from the Great Lakes to the Gulf of Mexico and with short but important east and west lines traversing both the upper and lower Mississippi Valley, the IC System was appropriately nicknamed the Main Line of Mid-America. The merger resulted in a 9,657 mile rail system that dominated the center of the nation along its north-south axis (Exhibit 1). Nearly every ton of rail freight moving eastward or westward across the country passed over or crossed ICG tracks somewhere along the way. However, the railroad had a serious load imbalance on north-south lines, with southbound load factors almost double the northbound ones.

DIVERSIFICATION OF THE ILLINOIS CENTRAL

By the 1960s, the U.S. railroad industry, especially lines in the northeast and midwest, was in a serious state of decline. Lack of investment in maintenance and upgrading and continuing loss of market share to other transportation modes had taken their toll. Many observers blamed government policy for the industry's plight. Subsidies for construction of interstate highways, modernization of key waterways and expansion of airports stimulated truck, automobile, barge, and airline traffic. Yet no comparable aid was given to railroads to help them improve their facilities. Regulation by the Interstate Commerce Commission (ICC) tightly controlled the rates charged for different commodities and made it difficult for U.S. railroads to set up their own trucking, shipping, or airline subsidiaries as the Canadians had done.

The Illinois Central fared better than many railroads. However, in 1963 a holding company, IC Industries, was formed to reduce dependence on railroad fortunes. Management subsequently announced four priorities: (1) to modernize the Illinois Central Railroad; (2) to strengthen the railroad through mergers; (3) to develop the valuable real estate held by the railroad; and (4) to diversify by acquiring companies in other indus-

tries. IC Industries' first investments were in the field of industrial manufacturing. Subsequently, the holding company added other commercial products and branched into consumer goods and services.

By 1976, railroad operations (excluding the ICG's real estate activities) represented only 37 percent of IC Industries' gross revenues of $1.69 billion and contributed a net loss of $6.5 million on the holding company's pretax income of $60.8 million. In its annual report management noted:

> There are many uncertainties relating to the railroad industry, and to the ICG in particular. . . . It is possible that the ICG may, at some time in the future, be merged with or sold to another railroad system, not part of IC Industries, or otherwise disposed of.

Prospects brightened with passage of the Railroad Revitalization and Regulatory Reform Act of 1976, which paved the way for U.S. railroads to obtain loans and grants for new investment, more equitable tax treatment, regulatory reform, more favorable financing, and a more liberal approach to mergers. The ICG took advantage of the act's provisions to substantially increase capital and operating expenditures for track maintenance and equipment. Rates were increased, marketing efforts strengthened, and costs reduced.

This program had a positive impact on ton-miles, revenues, and profits (Exhibit 2). Line abandonments reduced the ICG system to 8,400 miles by mid-1979, yielding further savings. By encouraging major shippers to invest in their own cars the ICG was able to reduce the expense of maintaining its own fleet. Contributing to the improved financial picture was the railroad's marketable real estate, conservatively valued at over $150 million and including many surplus freight yards in urban areas.

On the horizon was the prospect of deregulation. The Carter administration initiated moves to deregulate the nation's interstate transportation services, beginning with air freight in 1978 and

EXHIBIT 1
MAP OF ICG SYSTEM

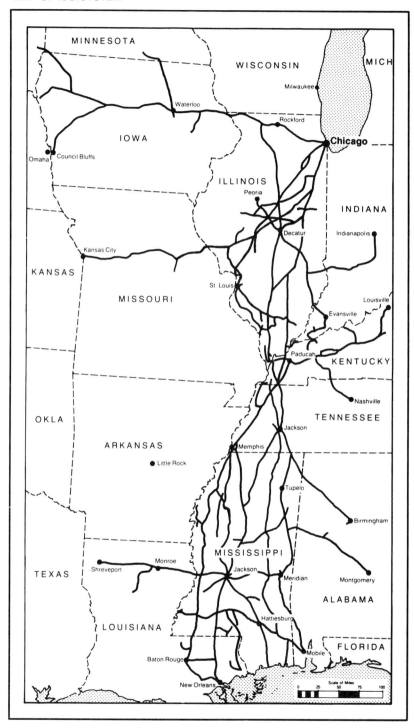

EXHIBIT 2
KEY PERFORMANCE INDICATORS FOR ICG RAILROAD AND IC INDUSTRIES, 1970–1978

	ICG Railroad*			IC Industries	
Year	Net Freight Revenue (Ton miles, billions)	Total Sales Revenues ($ millions)	Pre-Tax Profit (loss) ($ millions)	Total Revenues ($ millions)	Pre-tax Profit ($ millions)
1970**	N/A	355	25.5	837	59.1
1971**	N/A	370	26.8	872	62.9
1972**	31	427	29.0	979	73.1
1973	34	548	39.4	1,191	80.3
1974	32	605	36.2	1,375	82.6
1975	27	577	(5.4)	1,475	52.2
1976	29	654	13.9	1,650	94.9
1977	30	704	23.6	1,832	114.9
1978	33	786	26.0	2,671	153.2

* ICG Railroad revenues include income from sale of real estate.
** Pre-1973 figures for ICG Railroad represent pooled data from Illinois Central Railroad and Gulf, Mobile & Ohio Railroad; pre-1973 figures for IC Industries exclude GM&O Railroad revenues and pre-tax contribution.
Source: Annual Reports of IC Industries.

commercial passenger aviation in 1979. Many observers anticipated that 1980 would see passage of legislation to deregulate the railroad and trucking industries, although no one was sure just how far such actions might go.

FORMATION OF THE MARKETING DEPARTMENT

In 1975, ICG management decided that a major reorganization of the commercial activities was needed if the recently enlarged railroad were to return to profitability and remain competitively viable. To this end, they hired Harry J. Bruce as senior vice president-marketing, to replace the vice president-traffic, who had left the railroad to join Amtrak; one of Bruce's first acts on joining ICG was to rename the Traffic Department as the Marketing Department.

Trained in transportation and industrial engineering, Bruce's background provided the broad-based—rather than railroad-inbred—transportation/distribution approach for which the ICG was searching. He had served as trans-

portation research assistant for U.S. Steel Corporation, as vice president-marketing for Spector Freight Systems, and as director of distribution for the Jos. Schlitz Brewing Company. At the time of his election to ICG's top marketing post, Bruce was serving as vice president-marketing for the Western Pacific RR.

Prior to Bruce's arrival, the ICG's marketing efforts were regarded by most industry observers as rather conservative. As Richard L. Rushing, vice president-sales, described the situation:

Except in a few very specific instances, we were not considered leaders. Normally, we would be rather laid back and follow whatever the industry in general was doing. However, we had received a lot of recognition for our efforts in moving grain and we were fairly aggressive in the intermodal area.

The ICG had pioneered the "rent-a-train" concept for grain shipments, which moved in 100-car trains from Illinois and Iowa to ports on the Gulf of Mexico for export. Instead of shippers paying carload rates for grain, ICG had proposed in 1968 that they should rent a train for a year, guaranteeing 52 trips a year. In time, the railroad developed substantial grain export business in this way.

Like many railroads, the ICG had lost market share to truckers. One response was development of trailer-on-flatcar or "piggyback" services, whereby freight could be hauled part way by tractor trailers and the trailers then loaded onto railroad flatcars for consolidation into train-size loads. This approach required good relations with feeder truck lines that lacked interstate operating rights for line-haul movements. By 1979, ICG had developed a number of intermodal hubs at key locations. It was also working to perfect a "Road-Railer" trailer that could run on both steel and rubber wheels, thus eliminating the need for a separate flatcar.

In 1975, ICG inaugurated a fast new intermodal service called "Slingshot," designed to attract traffic from truck to rail on the busy Chicago-St. Louis corridor. Under a special labor-management agreement, it began operating short piggyback trains without cabooses. Soon, three such trains were operating daily in each direction. Trailers were hauled by road to the rail yard, loaded on board flatcars, piggybacked some 300 miles by rail and then either coupled to another train or unloaded and hauled by road to their destinations. By mid-1979, ICG's market share of truckload traffic on this route had risen to 40 percent.

The Slingshot approach contrasted with the historic method of intermodal service based on earthen ramps. ICG had more than 150 of these ramps on its main Chicago-New Orleans line alone. The idea was to offer customers a convenient and simple method of loading trailers on flatcars by pushing them up a ramp at the end of a rail spur. But as Bruce pointed out:

> The costly inefficiency of repeatedly stopping the train to pick up or discharge a few trailers at each ramp slowed service and defeated the real strength of railroads in intermodal service—the line haul. This recognition of the railroad's most suitable and

cost-effective role—the line haul—is the basis for the ICG move to the hub center concept, which is the interface between the rail and truck sections of the distribution systems. The hub center combines the line-haul capabilities of the railroad with the convenience and flexibility of short-haul trucking.

Further product innovations at ICG included a series of new run-through services, operated with interlining railroads and designed to reduce time spent in restructuring trains in ICG yards. For instance, 1977 saw the inauguration of the ICG/ Norfolk & Western "Delta Cannonball" service. This coordinated service provided expedited operation between the Northeast and the South and Southwest, via Tolono, Illinois, by-passing Chicago altogether. Another innovation was the ICG's competitive new daily "truck-rail-truck" service for iron and steel products moving between Chicago and St. Louis/Kansas City. Damage and pilferage were minimized by shrink-wrapping shipments of steel coils, with each flatcar containing up to four separate shipments.

The Sales Effort at ICG

Within two months of joining ICG, Bruce had formed a team of managers to head each of the subdepartments of the Marketing Department. To direct the sales effort, he selected Richard L. Rushing, then a 19-year veteran of the ICG sales force. Rushing was appointed assistant vice president-sales, later being promoted to vice president.

Historically, Rushing noted, the sales function in railroading had been relatively unsophisticated. Salesmen were recruited largely on their ability to make a good impression on the customer and to generate contacts. Appearance was thought to be particularly important and there was an unwritten law that all salesmen had to be at least six feet tall. "The railroad wanted nice big guys in sales," remarked Rushing. He added:

> The emphasis was on *who* you knew, not *what* you knew. Nobody had a handle on what it cost the

railroad to serve each of its customers; the key performance measure was the number of carloads carried. The salesmen made sure that their load count didn't fall, regardless of what was in those loads. But they didn't want to run up the carload numbers too fast for fear of being unable to top these figures the following year.

The salesmen used to be known as solicitors. They'd all line up from the different railroads and wait their turn to see the traffic manager at each company. Half the time they'd just chat about the weather and the manager's golf game or his grandchildren, offer him a cigar and some pads or pencils with the railroad name on them, and then expect their "fair share" of the company's shipments. That's a way of life whose time has come and gone. But it's still hard to get sales reps to back away from regular calls on accounts that are small or, even if they offer lots of loads, have no potential for giving us increased business.

Rushing's career in railroading had begun in 1956 when he joined the Illinois Central's sales department right out of college:

I started as a traffic expert—the only time I've ever been described as an expert—and since then I've held almost every position in the department. I've also moved around quite a bit, being based at nine separate locations in six different states.

The first positions that I held were geared to a customer service orientation where we reacted to customer inquiries. We did very little in the way of initiating calls to customers; in those positions it was simply a matter of responding when a customer called with a particular problem—"Where is the shipment? When is it due?" "I ordered eight cars yesterday and only got six: when do I get the other two?"—those kinds of inquiries that are received daily all over the railroad. These positions enabled the individual to learn the system physically: Where are our major facilities, what trains do we run, why do we run them, what services do we have to offer, and who are the people at the railroad that you need to be communicating with to be able to get solutions to the problems that customers present? No computers at that time—everything was done manually and it was very time consuming to locate a shipment on the railroad.

After that I was given a position called traveling freight agent which was nothing more than a traveling salesman. I had a geographic territory and was responsible for all the accounts there. I was given a callbook and told, "This is the latest we have on customers; we haven't had anyone working that territory for two years, we don't know how dated it is but go to it." Instead of waiting for a customer to call me and reacting to that, I now had to initiate calls on the customers, try to determine what their needs were and then, of course, try to match whatever services we had to offer as a normal salesman would do.

Rushing's next position was in the office of the regional sales manager in Louisville, Kentucky. From here, two years later, he was appointed district traffic agent in Paducah, Kentucky, where he spent four years. In 1967, he moved to Memphis as district sales manager in charge of nine salesmen, subsequently being promoted to regional sales manager in Memphis, a job that entailed sales efforts in a broad geographic territory covering several states. Said Rushing:

In 1973 I made a lateral move to New Orleans. The title remained the same, but it enabled me to gain experience at another location on the railroad. I also got involved in international shipments, since New Orleans is the largest port on our railroad and the second largest, tonnagewise, in the country. I was there just one year and then in 1974 was moved to Chicago as general manager-automotive. That meant specializing in our automotive-related traffic: automobiles and parts. The objective was to establish a profit center for our automotive operations, which I did in one year.

With the arrival of Harry Bruce, Rushing's career at ICG took another turn: he was appointed assistant vice president-sales and given charge of the entire Sales Department.

Market Development and Pricing

Soon after his arrival, Bruce established a market development group responsible for long-range planning and research, tasks for which the sales group was not particularly well-suited. This transfer (and enlargement) of responsibilities in strategic planning freed sales to focus their efforts on what Bruce called the tactical aspects of the marketing task—promptly executing the plans put together by market development specialists.

Prior to establishment of the market development group, work on long-range planning and research was handled in the pricing department. Since the latter's primary responsibility was to maintain competitive prices on existing business and to publish rates that would attract new customers, only a small amount of time and effort was directed toward long-range planning and research.

Harry Bruce described the pricing function prior to 1975 as "a classic example of the mice guarding the cheese." Not enough time, he declared, was spent by qualified people in taking a total systems approach to business opportunities and in making thorough evaluations to determine all the trade-offs available regarding the price quoted versus the service offered. In some instances, subsequent analysis showed that the rates quoted did not cover all the costs associated with providing the service. The functions performed by the market development group provided a sound basis on which to make business decisions, and the interaction between the two departments came to serve as a system of checks and balances.

Bruce argued that a key responsibility of the sales force was to identify what was happening in the marketplace and feed this information to market development and the pricing group, who would then determine what ICG should be doing for its customers. The end result, he anticipated, would be creation and provision of extra services that would differentiate ICG from its competition. Sales personnel would then present the new services to customers and seek a commitment for new or increased levels of business.

Exhibit 3 shows the organization of the Marketing Department in mid-1979 and its rela-

tionship to the other functional departments at ICG.

Organization of the Sales Department

Reporting to the vice president-sales were two general sales managers, each responsible for six sales regions (Exhibit 4). With the exception of the Chicago region where ICG was headquartered, all regions were further subdivided into territories (Exhibit 5). The territories were almost evenly divided between those that were located on an ICG line and those that were off-line.

On-line selling was concerned with traffic originating and/or terminating on ICG tracks. Off-line selling involved shipments that originated or terminated outside the ICG system yet might travel by routes that included segments of ICG. Most ICG lines were paralleled by major highways; additionally its north-south lines ran alongside the key Mississippi-Missouri-Ohio River waterways. Chicago, ICG's headquarters city, was one of the most important railroad intersections in the country and represented an intermediary or starting point for many other railroads' operations. ICG competed for on-line sales with a limited number of other railroads whose lines closely paralleled its own. Competition for off-line sales, by contrast, was much broader.

The nature of the sales task differed somewhat between on-line and off-line territories. In general, there were greater demands on customer service in on-line offices. Customers were much more likely to be calling in to place orders, to inquire about the timing of shipments, or to complain about delays in sending down cars to pick up freight, or about delayed deliveries. "We're just deluged every day," said Rushing. On-line, the railroad controlled more locally originated business and the selling pitch would be made directly to the customer.

Off-line, the sales representative was more of an influencer, seeking to get customers to select

EXHIBIT 3
ICG PARTIAL ORGANIZATION CHART SHOWING STRUCTURE OF MARKETING DEPARTMENT, 1979

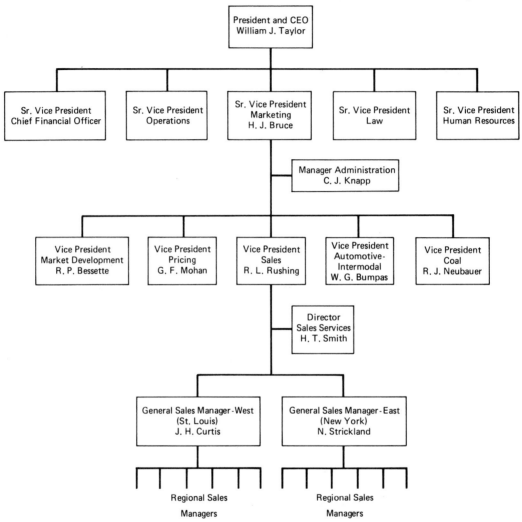

Source: Company records.

routings that would bring business to the ICG. For instance, a shipper planning to send freight by rail from Seattle to Atlanta had a broad array of route permutations available. Many of these would by-pass ICG tracks altogether; others would use ICG for only a short distance, say from Shreveport, Louisiana, to Meridian, Mississippi, a distance of some 300 miles. By contrast, ICG would fare much better if the shipment could be routed from Seattle to ICG's northernmost terminal at Council Bluffs, Iowa, and thence via Chicago to, say, Montgomery, Alabama—a total

EXHIBIT 4
ILLINOIS CENTRAL GULF: SALES REGIONS THROUGHOUT THE UNITED STATES*

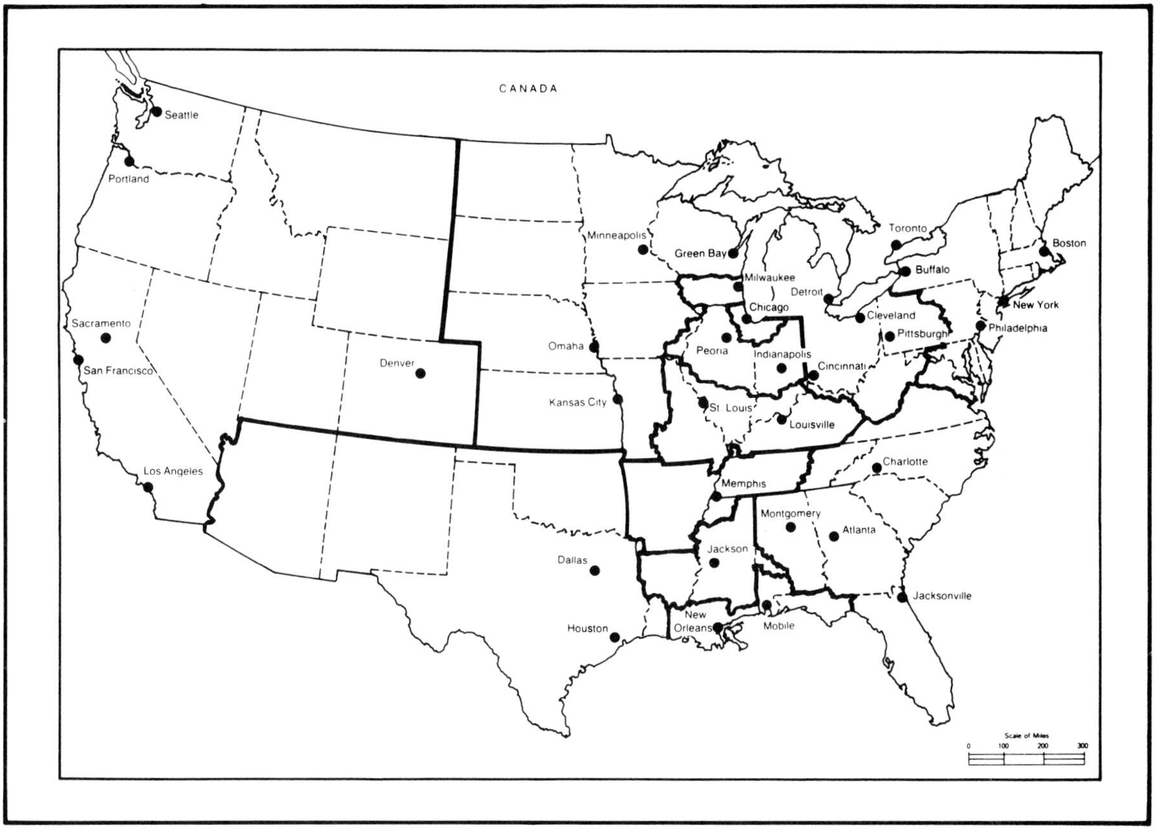

* *Note:* Canadian off-line customers were served by regions contiguous to the Canadian border.
Source: Company records.

distance of 1,318 miles—before continuing on to Atlanta on another carrier's tracks. The sales task was to build a case for the shipper to select the routing that favored ICG. Success in this endeavor required good relationships with interlining carriers and minimal delays at interchange points and switching yards. Creation of coordinated run-through services represented an important competitive tool in winning business that involved interlining.

In Rushing's view more creativity was required of sales representatives working off-line territo-

ries. There were more opportunities (and more time) to initiate calls to customers, identify new leads and develop new accounts. Close contact was maintained with other railroads that interlined with ICG in each territory, especially those with which the ICG worked well. Contact with an off-line customer was most often made by the interlining railroad, whose representative would recommend the ICG; however, there might also be direct interaction between the ICG and the customer.

Sales offices in each territory served as the

EXHIBIT 5

ORGANIZATION OF THE ILLINOIS CENTRAL GULF SALES DEPARTMENT SHOWING GENERAL, REGIONAL, AND DISTRICT OFFICES

R. L. Rushing
Vice President-Sales
Chicago

J. H. Curtis
General Sales Manager-West
St. Louis

N. Strickland
General Sales Manager-East
New York

Regional Sales Manager Chicago*	Regional Sales Manager Minneapolis	Regional Sales Manager Peoria	Regional Sales Manager New York	Regional Sales Manager New Orleans*	Regional Sales Manager Jackson
Chicago*	Minneapolis	Peoria*	New York	New Orleans*	Jackson, MS*
	Kansas City*	Indianapolis*	Boston	Baton Rouge*	Hattiesburg*
	Waterloo*	Decatur*	Buffalo	Mobile*	Tupelo*
	Green Bay	Rockford*	Philadelphia		Monroe*
	Omaha*	Milwaukee			Meridian*

Regional Sales Manager Memphis*	Regional Sales Manager St. Louis*	Regional Sales Manager San Francisco	Regional Sales Manager Atlanta	Regional Sales Manager Cleveland	Regional Sales Manager Dallas
Memphis*	St. Louis*	San Francisco	Atlanta	Cleveland	Dallas
Jackson, TN*	Evansville*	Sacramento	Jacksonville	Detroit	Houston
Little Rock	Louisville*	Seattle	Birmingham*	Toronto	
		Portland	Montgomery*	Cincinnati	
		Los Angeles	Charlotte	Pittsburgh	
		Denver			

Note: * Denotes on-line office.

home base for the account managers who worked in these areas. Under Rushing's direction, the ICG had been gradually reducing the number of sales personnel. By mid-1979, there were 96 account managers, down from 134 in 1975 and 180 in 1970. Most of the offices had a customer service representative (CSR) or clerk to answer the phones, relay messages for the salespeople, take orders, and respond to customer queries; busy offices might have two or more. In the larger offices, there was a customer service manager (CSM) to supervise internal admin-istrative activities as well as respond to customer queries. The ICG had a total of 17 CSMs, 34 CSRs, and 18 clerks.

THE MOVE TO REORGANIZE THE SALES DEPARTMENT

Bruce and Rushing talked regularly about the most appropriate role for the ICG sales force. Were traditional patterns of calling on accounts still realistic or should the frequency of calls be increased or reduced? Who determined the call pattern for each account—was it the account manager or the regional sales manager? Said Rushing:

> We were beginning to think maybe our people were not positioned exactly where they were needed geographically. Did we need more salesmen or could we make do with less? With increasing computerization we had more information on car movements available to us; what were the implications of rapid access to such information for the way our customer service people worked?

The two executives began to feel that it was time to do a full-scale "time and territory analysis" to evaluate current sales-force workloads and account calling frequencies across the country. It was their belief that if they were to take a zero-based approach to sales-force size, geographic positioning, and workload allocation the new sales organization would look very different from ICG's current one.

Several factors stimulated their thinking. Field sales costs were rising rapidly, stimulated in part by sharp increases in gasoline prices. The 1975 recession had led many companies to recognize the high cost of carrying inventories—a cost exacerbated by inflation and rising interest rates. Instead of shipping large volumes by train, many firms opted for shipping smaller volumes on a more frequent basis, using faster modes of transportation to minimize the value of goods in transit. The ICG began to see a significant diversion of traffic from rail to trucks, resulting in more intermodal business as piggybacking began to replace boxcar operations for many product categories. Customers also began to demand faster responses to their requests for information on shipment locations and on pick-up and delivery schedules.

By 1978, railroad deregulation was seen as increasingly likely. Railroad executives recognized that even a partial relaxation of restrictive ICC regulations would be beneficial: facilities could be better utilized and more competitive price and service options developed; abandon-

ment of nonproductive trackage and contracts with shippers would be possible. Such developments would offer important new opportunities for the ICG, but only a revitalized sales force could take full advantage of them.

Bringing the matter to a head was the severe winter of early 1978. The pressure on the railroad to keep customers going, lest they have to shut down for lack of needed supplies or equipment, was enormous. The ICG experienced significant operational difficulties, and there were not enough customer service reps to handle all the inquiries from customers; senior sales personnel grumbled that they seemed to have been converted into trace clerks as they pitched in trying to locate shipments.

Undertaking the Study

By the spring of 1978, Bruce and Rushing were convinced that a full-scale reevaluation of the sales function was needed at ICG. Among the questions which they sought to address were:

1 Is the organizational structure of sales attuned to the changing times within ICG and the railroad industry?

2 Does the organization include an adequate customer service function which permits account managers to spend the major portion of their time selling?

3 Is the time and effort of sales personnel being properly allocated so as to develop and maintain business?

4 Would a realignment of sales functions and territories bring them into a more rational relationship?

In April 1978, Bruce approved Rushing's proposal to conduct a major study that would provide answers to these and other questions. The Sales Department already knew what types of freight were carried and how each contributed to profits (Exhibit 6). What it did not know was how much business was generated by each customer,

EXHIBIT 6
ICG FREIGHT REVENUE CONTRIBUTION BY
PRODUCT CATEGORY, 1978

Chemicals	16%
Paper products	14
Grain	11
Grain mill products	11
Coal	10
Bulk commodities	10
Automotive	7
Piggyback	6
Lumber	5
Metals	5
Other	5
	100%

Source: Annual Report, 1978.

especially when the same corporation shipped freight from multiple locations. Nor did senior sales executives know how account managers were allocating time among their accounts. There were no established standards for calling frequencies and no guidelines for whether calls should be made by phone or in person.

Although recent years had seen more emphasis on sales training and use of proven selling techniques, account managers enjoyed considerable independence and their day-to-day work was not closely supervised. There was little regard for the qualifications needed and many account managers had simply gravitated to a street job from prior office positions as tracing clerks and customer service managers. Getting a handle on what was going on in the field was a key goal of the study.

Responsibility for collecting and analyzing the needed information was assigned to the regional sales managers. Two categories of data were sought: (1) the use of ICG services by each account, and (2) the nature and frequency of interactions between account managers and their customers. The primary burden for collecting the latter data rested with individual account managers, each of whom had to identify all face-to-face and telephone contacts with each account.

Over a period of six months more than 20,000

accounts were analyzed and the results discussed between account managers and regional sales managers. Of particular interest to senior sales executives was to determine how account managers were spending their time: were they busy handling customers' problems or working on sales? Additional inputs were sought from customer service personnel regarding the levels and nature of demand for customer service.

Analysis of customer records was a relatively simpler task than documentation and evaluation of sales force activities, since details of customer shipments and billings were already on the computer. The results of the customer analysis showed that the bulk of ICG's revenues and carloadings came from the 2,871 customers—out of a total of 22,000—that gave the railroad $25,000 or more in business in 1978 (Exhibit 7).

Account managers' sales varied widely in 1978, as did sales volumes between the different regions (Exhibit 8). The findings indicated a lack of consistency between account calling frequency and the volume of business obtained from each account. Questioning of account managers showed that most of them spent between two-thirds and three-fourths of their time engaged in problem-solving—such as tracing missing shipments or trying to expedite service—leaving relatively little time for research, developing new leads, or actively expanding sales. It was rare to find an account manager who spent more than 50 percent of his or her time in selling; some spent as little as 10 percent on this activity.

A Plan Emerges

The final results confirmed the need for major changes in the ICG sales organization. In early 1979, top management authorized development of a formal reorganization plan. A team was put to work in the Marketing Department and quickly set to work.

The team members concluded that the problem-solving and sales components of the account managers' work could be separated. They suggested that problem-solving should be handled

EXHIBIT 7
ANNUAL VOLUME RECEIVED FROM CUSTOMERS GIVING MORE THAN $25,000 IN
BUSINESS TO ICG IN 1978*

Rank	Customer	Industry	No. of Carloads	Revenue ($ thousands)
1	General Motors	Motor vehicles	108,468	$49,007
2	Cargill	Grain	41,150	23,295
3	International Paper	Paper	76,518	21,254
4	Crown Zellerbach	Paper	37,213	14,405
5	Georgia Pacific	Paper	39,226	13,214
6	St. Regis	Paper	33,622	11,787
7	Auto Carrier	Motor vehicles	20,039	11,022
8	Pillsbury Co.	Foods	21,390	10,699
9	Commonwealth Edison	Coal	44,600	10,264
10	Du Pont Co.	Chemicals	18,100	10,004
20	Inland Steel	Steel	22,300	6,229
50	Kraftco	Foods	7,290	3,452
100	Georgia Power	Coal	7,241	1,934
200	Old Ben	Coal	1,488	735
500	Brown Co.	Paper	536	227
1,000	Commercial Feed	Agricultural foodstuffs	407	97
2,000	Simba	Freight—all kinds	91	39

* A total of 2,871 customers had billings of $25,000 or more.
Source: Customer records.

by "inside account managers" (IAMs) located in customer service centers at the regional offices. These individuals would be assigned specific accounts to contact by telephone. Their tasks would include responding to queries on the location of shipments, resolving difficulties with ICG operating divisions or interlining railroads (such as a delay in switching a customer's car at one of the yards), investigating billing errors, and so forth. Assignment of the problem-solving role to IAMs would free "outside account managers" (OAMs) to focus on proactive selling, some of which would be done in person but much of which, Rushing believed, could be handled over the phone. The team concluded that fewer offices would be needed in the future, so that considerable savings could be obtained by closing some of the smaller offices and installing telecommunications equipment in outside account managers' homes. Many cities would lose direct representation altogether.

To maximize the efficiency of the restructured sales organization, the planning team proposed that OAMs and IAMs should work in pairs, handling sales efforts and problem-solving respectively for the same accounts. Although IAMs and OAMs would often be geographically separated, with the former working in regional customer service centers and the latter working out of local offices or their own homes, the team believed that modern communications technology would minimize this distance. However, most of the remaining district offices would still be staffed by customer service representatives, who would be expected to answer calls, take messages for the OAMs, and respond to routine customer queries.[1] The position of clerk would be abolished. This new division of responsibilities would entail withdrawing some existing account managers from field sales and assigning them to inside,

[1] See end-of-case Appendix for the proposed job position descriptions of regional sales manager, inside account manager, outside account manager, and customer service representative.

EXHIBIT 8

ILLINOIS CENTRAL GULF RAILROAD: TOTAL REVENUES AND CARLOADS FOR 1978, SHOWING HIGHEST AND LOWEST PERFORMANCE OF ACCOUNT MANAGERS IN EACH REGION

Regional Office*	Account Manager†	Traffic originating/ terminating in this region		Traffic moving elsewhere on ICG system		Total traffic	
		Revenue (000s)	Loads (000)	Revenue (000s)	Loads (000)	Revenue (000s)	Loads (000)
Chicago*	Highest	$24.6	57.0	$7.0	13.8	$31.6	70.8
	Lowest	0.1	0.3	3.9	11.8	4.0	12.1
	All 10	92.8	246.2	105.0	299.6	197.8	545.6
Minneapolis	Highest	2.6	7.0	33.7	68.6	36.3	75.7
	Lowest	5.0	10.5	0.4	1.2	5.4	11.7
	All 9	85.9	198.0	62.6	137.2	152.5	335.2
Peoria, Ill.	Highest	19.5	43.4	13.3	37.1	32.8	80.5
	Lowest	8.4	20.4	0.4	1.4	8.8	21.8
	All 8	113.4	260.9	44.1	129.9	157.5	390.8
Memphis*	Highest	16.3	50.9	7.7	27.7	24.1	78.6
	Lowest	10.0	31.6	1.7	5.8	11.6	37.4
	All 7	79.6	228.9	42.7	114.4	122.3	343.0
St. Louis*	Highest	31.7	90.3	17.4	75.5	49.2	165.8
	Lowest	5.2	13.2	0.7	1.6	5.9	14.8
	All 8	176.8	566.5	52.4	157.8	229.3	724.3
San Francisco	Highest	17.1	47.5	8.9	22.3	26.0	69.8
	Lowest	1.7	4.6	0.1	0.2	1.8	4.8
	All 8	63.8	179.6	57.7	141.0	121.5	320.6
New York	Highest	0.1	0.2	38.8	102.9	38.9	103.0
	Lowest	4.5	9.5	5.9	14.3	10.4	23.8
	All 10	39.7	100.5	165.3	406.4	205.1	506.9
New Orleans*	Highest	95.6	169.3	18.7	29.3	114.4	198.6
	Lowest	8.3	21.7	1.0	1.8	9.3	23.5
	All 9	194.0	422.8	60.3	180.2	254.2	603.0
Jackson, Miss.*	Highest	22.5	79.7	9.5	36.7	32.1	116.4
	Lowest	15.6	40.8	0.9	2.8	16.5	43.6
	All 7	161.7	542.6	23.3	86.1	185.0	628.7
Cleveland	Highest	26.9	57.1	76.8	163.9	103.8	220.1
	Lowest	7.6	14.9	2.0	4.5	9.6	19.3
	All 8	76.9	159.1	172.7	373.9	249.5	533.0
Atlanta	Highest	15.2	38.8	12.1	26.1	27.3	65.0
	Lowest	6.6	16.4	0.8	2.0	7.4	18.4
	All 9	73.0	195.8	57.7	167.3	130.7	363.2
Dallas	Highest	8.2	17.6	28.7	47.0	36.9	64.7
	Lowest	8.0	16.9	0.6	1.1	8.6	18.1
	All 6	49.1	118.6	58.0	126.3	107.1	245.0
Total all regions	All 99‡	605.3	1,609.7	450.9	1,160.1	1,056.3	2,769.7

Note: Numbers may not add due to rounding.

   * Denotes *on-line* regional office (that is, served by ICG tracks); other offices are *off-line* (served by railroads that connect to ICG tracks).

   † The "highest" account manager in each region is the individual with the highest annual total traffic revenues in 1978; the "lowest" account manager had the lowest 1978 figures (but may have been new to the job or have quit during the year). The third row refers to totals for all account managers in that region.

   ‡ This equals half the column total, since each account manager gets credited for both inbound and outbound loads, thus doubling the actual total. Even then, management indicated that these numbers overstated ICG's total revenues and carloads.

   Source: Company records.

problem-solving jobs. Decisions would have to be made on which account managers should become OAMs and which, IAMs.

Another important conclusion was that pre-defined sales call frequencies—by phone and/or personal contact—should be established for each account, reflecting its current sales volume and potential for growth. Sales managers would be held responsible for ensuring that OAMs observed these guidelines. To determine appropriate calling patterns, detailed discussions were held between sales personnel and regional sales managers. However, the team believed that the resulting estimates tended to overstate the case for frequent contact with customers. Using these data, modified downwards, Rushing and his associates were able to project the total number of OAMs and IAMs needed across the nation, and also to redefine the boundaries of the different sales territories.

As the plan took shape, Bruce and Rushing recognized the magnitude of the changes involved. They concluded that it would be important to obtain as much input as possible from senior sales managers to take account of all opinions and objections. They also debated testing the new sales structure in one or more regions before reorganizing the sales force nationwide. Once the plan was finalized, they intended to hold briefing sessions with all sales and customer service personnel, as well as to explain the changes to customers and interlining railroads.

THE WORD GETS OUT

By the spring of 1979, word was beginning to leak out that the ICG had a major sales reorganization in mind, although the specific plan was still some months from completion. Bruce and Rushing were disturbed, although not entirely surprised, at some of the reactions they heard. Feedback came to them and other staff members in formal meetings with the general and regional sales managers and also in casual conversations with sales personnel, customers, and even competitors.

At a sales department meeting in Chicago in April, senior sales personnel expressed concern about the impact of any reorganization on both customers and their own subordinates. The regional sales manager in New Orleans, who headed the region with the largest sales volume in the ICG system, pointed out that a substantial portion of his traffic came from a large base of small customers who each shipped less than 25 carloads a year:

> We spend a lot of time calling on these folks. The competition down here is something mean. I just can't visualize not making these calls. It would be a catastrophe!

Slapping his hand on the table for emphasis, the regional sales manager in Jackson, Mississippi, declared bluntly:

> It won't work! You just can't go around closing up all these offices. They're small offices in outlying areas, all right, but we need them to be in the middle of our customers. There's no way the customers would approve of such a move. And besides, think of our people. I've got four outlying offices staffed by older men, 55 and up. If we reorganized, I'd have to tell them all to relocate. You just can't do that to men who've been with the railroad 30 years or more.

Before either Bruce or Rushsing could respond, the regional sales manager from Peoria jumped into the fray:

> It's not just the older people we should be worrying about. I'm concerned as to how some of the promising younger fellows are going to react. For instance, under this plan, you'd want to close an office like Rockford, Illinois. That's the nuts and bolts capital of the world. Well, we've got a very ambitious young man in Rockford, Milt Kotler, who's really looking to go places with ICG. Started with us right out of college in Peoria working in customer service. . . .

The regional sales manager from St. Louis cut in:

> I remember Milt from when I worked in Peoria myself. He's a bright, aggressive guy. A fast learner,

too. Wasn't long before he was telling his boss, "Hey look, I've done a good job here and now I want my own office. I want my own territory."

"Right!" responded his colleague from Peoria, jabbing his finger in the air excitedly as he continued:

Well, the opportunity came up. We needed someone in Rockford. Milt had been in Peoria a couple of years. It seemed like he was coming along real well. So we promoted him to Rockford as senior account manager. Now Milt has his own office. He has a chance to sign his own mail for the first time. He has a clerk in the office working for him. He gets the credit if things work out, he gets the blame if they don't. Boy, you could just see him growing in that job! These small offices can be a real proving ground for our up-and-coming young people. Milt's been there, now, for about three years. He's all excited thinking his next step in a few more years could be regional manager.

Now all of a sudden, Milt has got the word from others that we're proposing to close up our small offices like Rockford and consolidate these into large customer service complexes. He figures it out that, because he's still pretty low on the totem pole, he'll end up working on an inside job in Chicago. No more company car, no more expense account, no more independence. Just an 8-to-5 job. That means moving his home and family, too, since the 70 miles from Rockford is too far to commute.

"Fred, has Milt been to see you to talk about this?" asked Rushing, "or is this just hearsay?" Shaking his head, the regional sales manager replied:

No, as a rule people like Milt don't raise those sorts of problems with their boss. Usually they just talk with their peers. As likely as not, first direct contact he'll have with me is to tell me he's quitting and going to one of the other roads.

"So, how did you learn about Milt's concerns?" asked Rushing.

Oh, it was from one of the other salesmen. He told me, "Listen, I don't want to rat on the guy, but you may have a problem in Rockford since Milt's very concerned about what's going to happen with this reorganization plan. You just ought to know about it."

Looking around the table Bruce could see other heads nodding in agreement.

A Visit to the East Coast

In early May, Bruce took a business trip to the East Coast. While in New York, he met with Narvell (Narv) Strickland, the general sales manager-east, who reiterated his concern about the damaging effect that the proposed reorganization was having on employee morale.

"We just lost another man in Cincinnati," Strickland told Bruce somberly. "First the sales rep left last month and now the inside guy quit."

The senior vice president probed for details. The account manager, an aggressive salesman of 27, had been with ICG for six years. He had told the regional manager in Cleveland that he was resigning to take a sales position with a freight consolidating firm. His wife had just had their first child, he said, and he felt that future opportunities at the railroad no longer seemed so promising as they had earlier. The customer service representative, a single man in his early forties, had been with ICG for seven years and had prior railroad experience. Strickland described him as a very cautious individual, nervous about his future in a reorganized sales department. "We lost a good administrative man," remarked Strickland, noting that the individual had joined a piggyback consolidating firm. He continued:

You know, Mr. Bruce, the trouble is that once the word got out that ICG had plans to reorganize, people started to conclude that the railroad would go the whole hog. I know you're thinking of doing a test first, but most folks reckon that any test is just a preliminary. They don't see it as a test of whether or not to go nationwide.

"Do you think there's a risk that we might lose a lot of others before we've even started to test a new organizational structure?" asked Bruce.

"At this point, I just don't know," the general sales manager replied. "A lot of our salespeople will surely hold on till they see how any re-organization affects them specifically. They're still hoping it won't happen and feel they've got some pretty good darn reasons why it should not."

Bruce suspected that the general sales manager had some reservations of his own, even though he recognized the need for change and had been generally supportive. "Narv," he said, "I don't often get to talk to salesmen directly in the course of my job. It would be helpful to me to hear the viewpoint of one or two of our better people. Who would you suggest?"

"Let's see," said Strickland," "you're going up to Boston tomorrow, aren't you?" He thought for a moment then continued: "Try and get together with Bob Olsen; he works the whole of New England and parts of Canada, too. Been with us for 30 years. One of our best. A dyed-in-the-wool New Englander if ever I saw one, but he's sold for the IC in Iowa and other places, too. Ask him what he thinks."

Bruce remembered Olsen, whom he had met before. A quick phone call resulted in a dinner date being set. Two days later Bruce and Olsen dined together. Eventually the conversation got around to the subject of the reorganization. Bob Olsen fingered his dinner fork and looked at Harry Bruce. He spoke slowly, choosing his words with care:

> This change you're proposing, Mr. Bruce, it's going to have a big effect on our image. You're proposing that we close up my office downtown and have me working out of my home. I'm just not going to be able to communicate with my customers as well as I have before. I won't be running into my counterparts from the other roads like I do in Boston and keeping my finger on the pulse of things. With all due respect, Mr. Bruce, I just don't see how it can work out satisfactorily.

Competitive and Customer Reaction

As the word of ICG's possible sales reorganization began to spread, Bruce and Rushing received some interesting feedback about cus-

tomers' and competitors' reactions. A number of customers apparently viewed the prospect of a cutback in the sales force with great dismay. Sales managers reported strong customer resistance to closing down local offices or reducing sales call frequencies; several managers cited this as evidence that ICG could not afford to reduce its presence in the marketplace. On the other hand, Harry Bruce was encouraged by the reaction of a senior distribution executive at International Paper Corporation, who told him that the company had decided to restrict the "relentless volume of calls from carrier salespeople" by instituting a policy of calls by appointment only.

Managers from other railroads reacted with surprise on learning that ICG would probably be cutting its field sales representation; in most instances, their own sales forces were already proportionately larger than the ICG's, so that any reduction by the latter would further widen the gap. The news spread quickly through the railroading fraternity and Rushing and Bruce often found themselves quizzed at conferences and functions about ICG's plans and the rationale behind them. Representatives of roads with which the ICG interlined regularly expressed concern that the reorganization would reduce ICG's traffic volume, including the interlining traffic it fed to them. Rushing suspected that many of the competing roads were secretly delighted at the prospect of a smaller ICG sales force, anticipating an opportunity to take away some of its business. What disturbed him was that some of the rumors circulating about ICG's plans were quite inaccurate. He shared his concerns with Harry Bruce:

> I've got a nasty suspicion that one or two of our own people aren't above putting out an inaccurate picture of what we're trying to do with this reorganization plan because they don't like it and want to head off the change.

Bruce frowned. "Do you have anything specific on this, Dick?" he asked. "I mean, anyone we can point a finger at?" Rushing shook his head:

Not much chance of that. It's usually about third-hand by the time I learn about it. What I tend to hear is a specific customer's reaction, but goodness knows where the leak first started. For instance, I saw the regional sales manager in Jackson last week. He told me he'd had a call from the traffic manager of the St. Regis Paper Company in Ferguson, Mississippi. Seems the salesman from a competing railroad told him that the ICG wouldn't be making any more face-to-face calls in the future, just telephone contact instead. "Don't bother to call us," the St. Regis guy said to Joe, "we'll call you if we ever need you."

A Draft Proposal

By late May, work on the reorganization plan was well advanced. The draft proposal adhered quite closely to Bruce's and Rushing's initial conception of a zero-based sales system, one that reflected the facts of the current market situation and modern technology rather than simply a modification of the existing system.

The proposal called for reducing the number of regions from 12 to 11 and for closing 18 of the 49 district offices (Exhibit 9). In several instances—Boston was one such example—it was suggested that small, off-line offices in the center of town should be closed down and relocated in the outside account manager's suburban home. Although the total number of account managers would only be reduced slightly, from 96 to 91, no fewer than 35 of those who remained would be assigned to inside positions. The number of customer service personnel, including clerks, would be reduced from 69 to 61; most of them would be located in the regional sales offices, which would henceforth function as customer service centers. It was estimated that implementing the new organizational structure nationwide would require a transition period of not less than four months. However, there was strong sentiment for testing the new structure for several months in one or more regions before deciding whether to go national or not. Significant cost savings were projected if the new structure were

to be implemented nationally, amounting to $262,610 in the first year (on a current expense base of $6 million) and $520,661 annually in subsequent years (Exhibit 10).

Bruce was keenly aware of the difficulties inherent in introducing a new order of things. He felt that the time had come to share the draft proposal and its underlying rationale with the president and other senior officers, so he placed this item on the agenda for the group's June meeting.

The day before this meeting, Rushing dropped by Bruce's office with a piece of news from the regional manager in Cleveland. Somehow the Toronto representative of an important competitor of ICG's for interline traffic moving between eastern Canada and the southwestern U.S. had learned of the ICG proposal to eliminate its off-line office in Toronto. "Guess what one of our major competitors has been telling our customers in Toronto," fumed Rushing. "He's saying, 'How much does the ICG *really* care about you? They plan to close their office here and soon you'll have to call Cleveland to deal with them.'"

THE SENIOR STAFF MEETING

Each month the senior staff of the railroad met to review the latest financial figures and to discuss current issues of particular importance to top management. Those attending included the president and the senior vice presidents of finance, law, human resources, marketing, and operations.

Harry Bruce had made a point of periodically briefing the group on the dramatic changes taking place in marketing. Over the previous several years, they had discussed his presentation on why the ICG needed a market development group and how this should interact with the pricing group; they had approved his proposal in 1978 for a major time and territory study of the sales organization; and they had debated the implications of that study's subsequent findings. Now, in June 1979, he was sharing his thinking on the changes that should be made in the sales organization, preparatory to finalizing a formal report and a set of recommendations on the topic.

The senior vice president-law had finished his earnest objections to Bruce's proposals. Now it was the turn of the senior vice president-operations:

> I'm very disturbed about this, too, Harry! Are you sure you're doing the right thing? We've already had a sharp cutback in our sales force in recent years and what I hear from my superintendents is that they no longer see very many salespeople up and down the line. They're really worried that we're losing customer presence. Holy smoke, you put through a reorganization of this magnitude, and we're not going to have any more customers! There's not a competitor out there who wouldn't seize upon this and use it to their advantage.

"Oh, come now," retorted the senior vice president-finance, "you're overstating the case! I can see some important advantages for us here," he added, warming to his theme:

> If we're going to improve the profitability of this railroad, we've got to look at the cost side of the equation as well as the revenues. And our sales costs have been escalating out of sight. This proposal of Harry's could save us millions over the next few years. We'd be getting rid of people, cutting out offices, and eliminating a whole set of expense accounts and automobiles. I'm all for it.

Bruce turned toward the senior vice president-human resources, who had an uncertain look on his face. "I guess I think the basic concept makes sense," the latter began cautiously, then continued:

> It's the implementation that worries me. We're going to have to lay off people or get them to take early retirement. We're going to be totally changing the working environment for those people now out selling in the field who'll be given office jobs under the new system. And we're talking about taking away benefits like cars and expense accounts. Also, I'm worried about the impact on our people's morale of doing an extended test. Turnover among sales and customer service personnel is already up a bit over last year and it's the brighter, younger people who are quitting. Those who are involved in the test are going to feel put upon and those who aren't involved are going to get plain nervous.

Bruce responded in turn to each of his colleague's comments, countering their arguments as best he could and seeking to allay some of their concerns. Then he looked over toward the president. "What do you think, Bill?" he asked.

EXHIBIT 9
ILLINOIS CENTRAL GULF RAILROAD: CURRENT AND PROPOSED SALES AND CUSTOMER SERVICE PERSONNEL DEPLOYMENT

Current

Eastern Region	AM	CSM	CSR	Clerk	Total
New York Area					
New York	5	1	—	1	7
Boston	1		1		2
Philadelphia	2		1		3
Buffalo	1		1		2
Total					14
Atlanta Area					
Atlanta	3	1	1		5
Birmingham	2	1	1		4
Jacksonville	1		1		2
Charlotte	1		1		2
Montgomery	1			1	2
Total					15
Cleveland Area					
Cleveland	2	1			3
Cincinnati	2		1		3
Detroit	1		1		2
Pittsburgh	2		1		3
Toronto	1		1		2
Total					13
Dallas Area					
Houston	3		2		5
Dallas	2	1	1		4
Tulsa	1		1		2
Total					11
Jackson, MS Area					
Jackson	3	1	2		6
Hattiesburg	1		1		2
Meridian	1		1		2
Monroe	1		1		2
Tupelo	1		1		2
Total					14
New Orleans Area					
New Orleans	5	1	1	1	8
Baton Rouge	2	1	1		4
Mobile	2		1		3
Total					15
Grand total	47	8	23	4	82

Proposed

Eastern Region	OAM	IAM	CSM	CSR	Total
New York Area					
New York	3	3	1	2	9
Boston	1			1	2
Philadelphia	2			1	3
Total					14
Atlanta Area					
Atlanta	2	3	1	1	7
Birmingham	2			2	4
Jacksonville	1			1	2
Charlotte	1			1	2
Total					15
Cleveland Area					
Cleveland	2	3	1	2	8
Cincinnati	1				1
Detroit	1				1
Pittsburgh	1			1	2
Total					12
Dallas Area					
Houston	2	2	1	2	7
Dallas	2			1	3
Total					10
Jackson, MS Area					
Jackson	3	3	1	4	11
Mobile	1			1	2
Total					13
New Orleans Area					
New Orleans	2	2	1	2	7
Baton Rouge	1	1		1	3
Total					10
Grand total	28	17	6	23	74

Western Region

Location	AM	CS	CR	OAM	IAM	Total
Chicago Area						
Chicago	8		1	1		10
Markham Yard	2	1				3
Total						13
Minneapolis Area						
Minneapolis	2	1				3
Kansas City	2	1	1	1		5
Omaha	2		1			3
Green Bay	1					1
Waterloo	1		1			2
Total						14
Memphis Area						
Memphis	5	1	1	4		11
Little Rock	1					1
Nashville			1			1
Jackson, TN	1		1			2
Total						15
St. Louis Area						
St. Louis	4	1	1	2		8
Louisville	3		1	1		5
Evansville	1		1			2
Total						15
San Francisco Area						
San Francisco	4	1	1			6
Portland	2	1				3
Los Angeles	1					1
Seattle	1			1		2
Denver	1			1		2
Total						14
Midwest Area						
Peoria	2	1		1		4
Decatur	2	1				3
Rockford	1			1		2
Indianapolis	1			1		2
Milwaukee	1					1
Total						12
Grand total	49	9	11	14		83

Location	AM	CS	CR	OAM	IAM	Total
Chicago Area						
Chicago	5	5	1	5		16
Total						16
Minneapolis Area						
Minneapolis	2	2	1	1		6
Kansas City	2	1		1		4
Omaha	1	1		1		3
Total						13
Memphis Area						
Memphis	3	3	1	4		11
Little Rock	1					1
Louisville	2	1		2		5
Total						17
St. Louis Area						
St. Louis	3	2	1	4		10
Peoria	2	2		3		7
Total						17
San Francisco Area						
San Francisco	2	1	1	2		6
Portland	2			1		3
Los Angeles	1			1		2
Seattle	1			1		2
Denver	1			1		2
Total						15
Midwest Area						
Peoria						—
Decatur						—
Rockford						—
Indianapolis						—
Milwaukee						—
Total						—
Grand total	28	18	5	27		78

Note: AM = Account Mgr.; CS = Customer Service Mgr.; CR = Customer Service Rep.; OAM = Outside Account Mgr.; IAM = Inside Account Mgr.

EXHIBIT 10
ILLINOIS CENTRAL GULF RAILROAD: COST/BENEFIT ANALYSIS OF PROPOSED
REORGANIZATION PROGRAM

	Chicago Area	Mn'pls. Area	Peoria Area	Memphis Area	St. Lou. Area	S. Fran. Area	Total Western Region
Savings:							
Mgt. labor	41,880	47,100	96,000	26,100	22,080	32,200	265,260
Clerical labor	16,159	31,956	32,196	79,776	15,900	—	175,987
Fringe	11,608	19,488	23,904	27,600	10,020	5,328	97,948
Office rent	1,524	—	6,240	2,340	4,800	8,330	23,234
Leased autos	13,840	13,464	13,464	3,366	6,732	—	50,866
Telephone	5,109	17,455	16,905	8,095	20,295	—	67,859
Teletype	5,364	5,364	10,728	5,364	5,364	—	32,184
Total savings	95,484	134,827	199,437	152,641	85,191	45,758	713,338
Expenses:							
Mgt. labor	—	47,100	41,880	26,100	22,080	89,400	226,560
Clerical labor	—	15,696	16,164	33,780	15,900	16,800	98,340
Fringe	—	15,480	9,216	14,484	10,020	26,208	75,408
Leasing reloc.	24,575	3,500	1,000	1,000	6,100	1,100	37,275
Addit'l. rent	—	2,340	—	—	—	—	2,340
'Phone equip.	4,299	—	—	—	17,438	—	21,737
'Phone instal.	480	1,324	948	—	1,681	1,000	5,433
'Phone circuit	1,044	13,032	12,879	—	14,797	6,310	48,062
CRT equipment	17,416	9,764	11,579	18,730	—	9,764	67,253
CRT instal.	1,519	271	240	271	200	271	2,772
CRT circuit	—	4,500	3,096	6,840	456	15,349	30,241
T'type equip.	—	—	—	—	5,280	—	5,280
T'type instal.	160	—	—	—	300	—	460
T'type circuit	2,520	—	—	—	396	—	2,916
Total expenses	52,013	113,007	97,002	101,205	94,648	166,202	624,077
Net savings	43,471	21,820	102,435	51,436	-9,457	-120,444	89,261

EXHIBIT 10 (continued)

N. York Area	N. Orls. Area	Cleve. Area	Jackson Area	Atlanta Area	Dallas Area	Total Eastern Region	Grand Total 1st Yr.	Grand Total Sub. Yrs.
—	15,720	22,500	117,060	23,400	54,120	232,800	498,060	498,060
15,696	18,960	45,180	83,952	17,844	33,024	214,656	390,643	390,643
4,008	9,720	8,627	48,924	9,828	19,488	100,595	198,543	198,543
4,140	—	14,867	10,599	—	3,264	32,870	56,104	60,967
—	6,732	9,870	10,098	6,732	6,732	40,164	91,030	93,520
25,54	—	32,341	19,700	13,250	7,785	98,600	166,459	166,459
—	—	20,580	21,456	—	5,364	47,400	79,584	79,584
49,368	51,132	153,965	311,789	71,054	129,777	767,085	1,480,423	1,487,776
—	—	—	70,740	23,400	54,120	148,260	374,820	374,820
15,696	—	23,712	51,816	—	15,696	106,920	205,260	205,260
4,008	—	—	29,928	5,412	15,276	54,624	130,032	130,032
—	—	8,500	3,250	300	2,500	14,550	51,825	-0-
—	—	6,600	—	—	5,800	12,400	14,740	14,740
—	—	14,780	—	—	—	14,780	36,517	-0-
—	—	3,138	1,250	1,000	1,106	6,494	11,927	-0-
29,164	1,500	15,720	11,904	22,250	26,383	106,921	154,983	154,983
9,764	15,753	15,751	12,075	9,764	9,764	72,871	140,124	-0-
271	278	271	271	271	271	1,633	4,405	-0-
8,780	9,731	5,187	9,240	7,981	10,684	51,603	81,844	81,844
—	—	—	—	—	—	—	5,280	-0-
—	—	160	—	—	—	160	620	-0-
—	—	2,520	—	—	—	2,520	5,436	5,436
67,683	27,262	96,339	190,474	70,378	141,600	593,736	1,217,813	967,115
-18,315	23,870	57,626	121,315	676	-11,823	173,349	262,610	520,661

Source: Company records.

APPENDIX: Position Descriptions for Sales and Customer Service Personnel*

REGIONAL SALES MANAGER

Purpose or Objective

Coordinate area sales efforts to develop profitable business, maintain existing business and fulfill customer service needs. Achieve area portion of company load budget. Operate within limits of expense budget. Select and develop area personnel.

Status and Scope

Reports to General Sales Manager. Plans, organizes and controls total area sales resources and activities.

Specific Responsibilities (see attachment)*

1 Select, develop and train area personnel.
2 Maximize profitable sales within a designated geographic area.
3 Develop and implement short-, medium- and long-range plans to meet area objectives.
4 Monitor sales progress and results.
5 Manage human and budgetary resources.
6 Fulfill administrative requirements.
7 Keep management informed.

Relationships

Reports to General Sales Manager and works as liaison with area personnel and all departments to meet area objectives.

Planning

Assists General Sales Manager in:

1 Establishing regional objectives.
2 Development and implementation of short-, medium- and long-range plans to meet objectives.
3 Planning personnel requirements.

ACCOUNT MANAGER (INSIDE)

Purpose or Objective

Maximize potential with existing accounts and develop profitable business with new accounts. Monitor existing traffic, handle special service requirements and projects as assigned. Provide necessary support for Outside Account Manager.

Status and Scope

Reports to Area Sales Manager. Plans, organizes and controls sales efforts with phone accounts and provides services for Outside Account Manager.

Specific Responsibilities
(see attachment)*

1 Maximize profits by phone sales within a designated territory.
2 Develop and implement marketing strategies.
3 Coordinate implementation of tactical plan with area and company personnel.
4 Maintain updated marketing and sales reports and account profiles.
5 Handle sales territory problem areas excepting traditional customer service.
6 Qualify prospective customers.
7 Submit required reports by due dates.
8 Make face-to-face sales calls when required.
9 Prepare and implement formal Time & Territorial Management Phone Power program.
10 Average eight telephone sales calls per day.
11 Maintain awareness of competitive environment.
12 Keep management informed of relevant changes in territory.

Relationships

Acts as liaison with all departments to meet customer needs and effect maximum profitable market penetration. Serve as conduit for communications flow between field sales personnel and customers and personnel in Service Center, as well as other departments of the company.

Planning

Assists Area Sales Manager in:

1 Establishing objectives based upon system marketing and sales objectives coordinated with the Outside Account manager.
2 Development and implementation of short-, medium- and long-range plans to meet these objectives.

ACCOUNT MANAGER (OUTSIDE)

Purpose or Objective

Maximize potential with existing accounts and develop profitable business with new accounts.

Status and Scope

Reports to Area Sales Manager. Plans, organizes and controls the sales effort within a designated territory.

**Specific Responsibilities
(see attachment)***

1 Maximize profitable sales within a designated territory.
2 Develop and implement marketing strategies.
3 Coordinate implementation of tactical plans with support personnel and other departments.
4 Keep management advised of relevant changes in the territory.
5 Assist in development of sales trainees.
6 Prepare and implement a formal Time & Territorial Management program.
7 Average five sales calls per day.
8 Submit required reports by due dates.
9 Maintain awareness of competitive environment.

Relationships

Works closely with Area Sales Manager as well as Inside Account Managers, Market Development, Pricing, and other department personnel on sales, pricing, equipment and operations to effect favorable solutions to opportunities. Serves as conduit for information flow between customer and the railroad.

Planning

Assist Area Sales Manager in:

1 Establishing goals based on area and system marketing and sales objectives.
2 Development and implementation of short-, medium- and long-range plans to meet sales objectives.

CUSTOMER SERVICE REPRESENTATIVE

Purpose or Objective

To provide timely and accurate responses to customer inquiries related to customer service needs. To relieve the Account Managers of traditional customer service functions and provide necessary support for sales efforts.

Status and Scope

Reports to Area Sales Manager. Utilizes resources to fill customer needs and keep customers informed by initiating calls to them on matters of interest.

**Specific Responsibilities
(see attachment)***

1 Provide car/TOFC location information.
2 Handle reconsignment/diversion and rebilling matters.
3 Support area sales effort.

4 Provide train and switching schedules and industry track location information.
5 Expedite urgent shipments.
6 Coordinate rate requests.
7 Monitor and report current train schedule performance levels.
8 Provide optimum ICG routing information to customers.
9 Establish customer rapport through "phone power" techniques.
10 Perform administrative functions as assigned.

Relationships

Reports to Area Sales Manager, Supervisor Sales & Service or Customer Service Manager. Works as liaison with area personnel and all departments to fill customer needs.

Planning

Assists supervisor in:

1 Monitoring train performance.
2 Planning programs in optimizing customer services.
3 Planning resource requirements.

* Attachments (not reproduced here) described specific job responsibilities in greater detail.
Source: Company records.

GLOSSARY OF SELECTED MARKETING AND MANAGEMENT TERMS

advertising Any paid form of nonpersonal presentation and promotion of a product or organization by an identified sponsor.

agent A business unit that negotiates purchases or sales (or both) of goods and services. Agents are commonly remunerated by payment of a commission or fee.

attitudes Enduring systems of positive or negative evaluations of, or emotional feelings toward, an object.

audit Retail and wholesale audits track the movement of goods through the distribution channel to provide manufacturers with sales and market share data (see also *marketing audit*).

augmented product The core product plus any additional services and benefits that may be supplied.

backward integration Obtaining ownership or increased control of an organization's supply systems (see also *forward integration* and *vertical integration*).

benefit segmentation Dividing the population into different groups on the basis of the benefits they want or require and the costs they wish to avoid.

billings The total charges for advertising space or time, production, and other services provided by an advertising agency to its clients.

bottom-up planning Designing, developing and implementing of programs by middle-level and lower-level managers and other personnel who work out the details and follow through on them (see also *top-down planning*).

brand A name, term, sign, symbol, design, or combination of these that seeks to identify the product of an organization and differentiate it from those of competitors.

branding The process of creating, assigning, and publicizing a brand name, term, sign, symbol, etc., to one or more products.

Copyright © 1985 by Christopher H. Lovelock and Charles B. Weinberg.

breakeven   The volume of sales necessary, at a specific price, for a seller to recover all relevant costs of a product.

broker   See *agent*.

cannibalization   The erosion of sales of an existing product by a new product marketed by the same firm.

car card   An advertisement mounted inside a public transit vehicle.

cash cow   A product in the mature or declining stage of the product life cycle that can be "milked" for as much profit as possible.

catchment area   The geographic region or area from which the bulk of an organization's customers are drawn.

centralized management   The decision-making power concentrated among a relatively small number of managers at the head office (see also *decentralized management*).

chain store   One of a group of centrally owned retail stores of similar type with some degree of centralized control over operations.

channels of distribution   See *distribution or delivery system*.

clutter   See *noise*.

cognitive dissonance   Perceived inconsistency within an individual's own beliefs or attitudes or between these and one's behavior. A person will attempt to reduce the dissonance through changes in either behavior or cognition.

commodity   A generic product category or product that cannot be distinguished by potential customers from similar products offered by competitors.

communication   The transmission of a message from a sender (or source) to a receiver (or recipient).

communication medium   The personal or impersonal channel through which a message is transmitted to an audience or individual (see also *mass media*).

communication mix   The combination of elements (personal selling, media advertising, signage, public relations, publicity, and onsite display) used by an organization to communicate its message(s) to its target market(s).

comparative advertising   Advertising messages that make specific brand comparisons using actual product names (sometimes referred to as "knocking copy" when the comparisons are sharply unfavorable).

competition   See *direct competitor* and *generic competitor*.

concentrated marketing strategy   The efforts, in a segmented market, of an organization that is focusing on one target group and designing its marketing strategy specifically to reach that group, rather than trying to be all things to all people.

consignment sales   Sales not completed until products placed by a supplier with a retailer are resold to customers, at which point payment becomes due from the retailer to the supplier.

consumers   Individuals or households or organizations that are current or prospective purchasers or users of goods and services.

contingency budget   Funds set aside in advance to finance contingency plans and respond to unanticipated events.

contingency plans   Plans, prepared in advance, outlining a course of action to deal with situations that might potentially arise.

contribution (or gross contribution)   The monetary difference between total sales revenues (gross income) and variable expenses (see also *margin*).

convenience products   Products the consumer usually purchases frequently, immediately, and with a minimum effort in comparison and shopping (see also *shopping products* and *specialty products*).

convenience store   A small store, with a limited stock of groceries and household products, that remains open for long hours.

cooperative advertising   Local or regional advertising whose costs are shared jointly by a national advertiser and a retail or wholesale institution.

copy testing   A preliminary test of alternative advertising copy appeals or selling messages to assess their relative effectiveness for specific audiences.

core product   The central elements of a product that serve a basic consumer or societal need (see also *augmented product*).

cost-per-thousand   The cost of advertising for each 1,000 homes reached in TV or radio, or for each 1,000 circulated copies of a publication (often abbreviated CPM).

coupons   Certificates that are mailed, handed out, or incorporated in print advertising and that entitle the bearer to a specified monetary savings on a purchase of a specific product.

crisis management   The result of the occurrence of an unexpected event for which management has not prepared and that requires immediate action (see also *contingency plans*).

cross-sectional data or study   Research information gathered from a whole population (or a representative sample of that population) at a single point in time (see also *longitudinal data*).

cumulative audience ("Cume")·   The net unduplicated radio or TV audience delivered by a specific program in a particular time slot over a measured period of time usually one to four weeks.

customer service   A collective term that describes all the supplementary services provided by an organization to satisfy customers and combat competitors, such as technical aid, information, order taking, complaint handling, refunds, or substitutions.

decentralized management   The result of the dispersion of decision-making power to relevant personnel at lower levels within an organization (see also *centralized management*).

decision-making unit (DMU)   An individual or group of individuals involved in making decisions on the purchase of a specific product.

demographic segmentation   Categorizing or differentiating people based on demographic variables such as age, sex, religion, income, etc.

differentiated marketing strategy   Developing different products and/or marketing programs for each market segment that the organization plans to serve.

direct competitor   An organization offering a product that meets similar consumer needs and is broadly similar in substance or process to one's own product.

direct selling   Selling to the end user by the producer without use of retail or wholesale intermediaries.

discretionary income   Funds remaining to an individual or household after paying for necessities out of disposable income (see *disposable income* below).

disposable income   Personal (or household) income remaining after deduction of income taxes and compulsory payments such as social security.

dissonance   See *cognitive dissonance*.

distribution or delivery system   The combination of internal organizational resources and external intermediaries employed to move a product from production or creation to the final consumer. Goods necessarily move through physical distribution channels, involving transportation, storage, and display. Services may be delivered to the customer directly at the production site or, in certain instances, transmitted electronically.

diversification   The process of entering new markets with one or more products that are new to the organization.

drive time   The weekday commute hours when many motorists are listening to their car radios.

durable goods   Goods such as appliances, furniture, and automobiles that are expected to last several years or more.

elasticity of demand (to price)   The responsiveness of sales volume to a change in price. Demand is said to be *price inelastic* when raising (or lowering) price by a certain percentage has a proportionately smaller impact on sales volume, and *price elastic* when the impact on volume is proportionately greater than the price change.

evoked set   The array of specific brands for a product category to be considered by a consumer in making a purchase decision.

experiment   An attempt to measure cause-and-effect relationships under controlled or natural conditions.

fixed costs   Costs that remain unchanged in total for a given time period despite wide fluctuations in activity, such as property taxes, executive salaries, rent, insurance, and depreciation (see also *variable costs*).

flight of advertising   A part of an advertising campaign that is divided into segments, with periods of time between each segment.

focus-group interviews   A small-group-discussion method of obtaining qualitative information from individuals who are broadly representative of the target market.

forward integration   Obtaining ownership or increased control of the means by which an organization distributes its products to end users (see also *backward integration* and *vertical integration*).

four Ps   See *marketing mix*.

franchise   The licensing of a production and distribution business, dealership, or complete business format where one organization authorizes a number of independent outlets to market a product or service and engage in a business using the franchisor's trade names and methods of operation.

frequency   The number of times an accumulated audience has the opportunity to be exposed to the same advertising message within a measured period of time.

generic competitor   An organization offering a product that, while possibly different in substance or process, is capable of satisfying the same general consumer needs as one's own product (see also *direct competitor*).

geographic segmentation   Segmentation of a market on the basis of region, city/metropolitan area size, population density, climate, or terrain.

gross rating points (GRP)   A measurement of advertising impact derived by multiplying the number of persons exposed to an advertisement by the average number of exposures per person (see also *reach* and *frequency*).

horizontal integration   The process of obtaining ownership or increased control of one's competitors (see also *vertical integration*).

impulse purchase   A purchase decision made on the spur of the moment without prior planning.

industrial/institutional marketing   Selling goods and services to corporate, institutional, or government purchasers as opposed to individuals and households.

intermediary   An organization or individual that serves as a go-between, or facilitator, between producer, marketer, and customer.

knocking copy   See *comparative advertising*.

list price   The price shown on the marketer's sales list and used as the basis for computing discounts.

longitudinal data or study   Research information gathered over time (usually at periodic intervals) from the same population or sample; this allows the researcher to monitor individual changes among members of the study.

loss leaders   A product of known or accepted quality priced at a loss or no profit for the purpose of attracting consumers who may then purchase other regularly priced products.

manufacturer's agent/representative   An intermediary who handles noncompeting but related lines of goods usually on an extended contractual basis within an exclusive territory.

margin   The difference between the selling price of a product and its production cost (for a manufacturer or service provider) or purchase cost (for a wholesaler or retailer). The margin may be expressed in monetary units or as a percentage of the selling price.

markdown   A reduction in the originally established price of a product.

market   The set of all current and potential consumers of a particular product.

market aggregation   See *undifferentiated marketing strategy.*

market definition   An attempt by the organization to determine which segment of the market its operations are or should be serving.

market development   An organization's marketing of its current line of products to new markets or segments.

market niche   A segment of a market where there is demand for a product with specific attributes distinguishing it from competing offerings.

market penetration   An organization's attempt to increase consumption of its current products in its current markets.

market potential   A calculation of maximum possible sales (in units or currency values), or usage opportunities in a defined territorial area for all marketers of a product during a stated period of time.

market segment   A homogeneous subset of the target market that may require a marketing plan tailored to the segment's distinctive characteristics.

market segmentation   The process of identifying distinctive submarkets or segments within the target market.

market share   The ratio of an organization's sales volume for a particular product category to total market volume on either an actual or potential basis.

marketing audit   A systematic, critical, unbiased, and comprehensive review and appraisal of an organization's or subunit's marketing objectives, strategies, policies, and activities.

marketing mix   The four basic ingredients (or elements) in a marketing program that influence consumers' decisions on whether or not to patronize the organization. These four elements are product, price, distribution or delivery systems, and communication. (Note: Some people use the phrase the *four Ps*—product, price, place, and promotion—to describe the elements of the marketing mix, but we regard the terms "place" and "promotion" as too narrow and potentially misleading.)

marketing planning   The tasks of setting up objectives for marketing activity and of determining and scheduling the steps necessary to achieve such objectives.

marketing research   The systematic gathering, recording, and analyzing of data to provide information for marketing decision making.

markup   The amount by which a seller increases the selling price of a product over its original purchase price; markup is generally computed as a percentage of the final selling price rather than of the original price.

mass media   Informational networks, reaching large numbers of people, that carry news, features, editorial opinion, and advertising—specifically newspapers, magazines, radio, and television; the term can also be applied to other communication vehicles, such as billboards, poster sites, and mail service, that can be used to convey marketing messages to large numbers of people.

members   Individuals who join nonprofit organizations and pay dues or support the organization on a periodic basis with funds, services, or their time and efforts.

merchandising   Selecting, displaying, and promoting products in a retail store or other distribution outlet.

national account   A customer operating over extended geographic areas whose service and sales needs are typically coordinated out of a head office.

noise or clutter   Conflicting, counter, or unrelated communications that distract from an advertiser's ability to communicate a specific message to members of a target audience.

nondurable goods   Consumer goods such as food, health and beauty aids, and other items that are consumed or otherwise used up relatively quickly (see also *durable goods*).

opinion leader   An individual who influences other people's purchase and consumption behavior.

opportunity cost   The maximum benefit foregone by using scarce resources (e.g., money, management time, physical facilities) for one purpose instead of the next best alternative.

penetration strategy   An aggressive marketing strategy, based upon low price and heavy advertising and promotional expenditures, that is designed to gain quickly a large share of the market for a specific product.

point-of-sale advertising   Promotional displays used by retailers at in-store locations, such as shelf, window, counter, aisle, or checkout, to promote specific products (also known as point-of-purchase, or P-O-P, advertising).

price   Defined narrowly as the monetary cost to the purchaser of obtaining a product; more broadly it includes other monetary outlays associated with purchasing and using the product, as well as all nonmonetary costs associated with purchase and use of a good or service (or adoption of a social behavior), such as time and physical and psychological effort.

price elasticity   See *elasticity of demand*.

price leader   A firm whose pricing policies are followed by other companies in the same industry.

pricing strategy   The mix of monetary price level charged to the final purchaser, terms and methods of payment (e.g., checks, credit cards, exact change), and discounts offered to both intermediaries and final purchasers.

primary data   Information the researcher collects through observation, experimentation, or survey research (see also *secondary data*).

primary demand   The current level of demand for all sources for the entire product class in question.

prime time   The evening hours of broadcasting (7:30 p.m.–11:00 p.m.) when audience size is usually the largest and advertising rates are highest.

private label brands   Brands owned by retailers or other channel intermediaries, as distinct from manufacturers' brands.

proactive selling   Actively seeking out prospective customers (see also *reactive selling*).

product   What the organization offers to prospective customers for their acquisition, use, consumption, or adoption; the term includes physical goods, services, and social behaviors or causes (such as driving safely, giving blood, etc.).

product class   A group of products that serves the same general function or fulfills the same basic need.

product development   The process of developing or acquiring new or improved products for an organization's current market (see also *diversification*).

product differentiation   Creating and communicating product attributes that cause consumers to perceive the product as being different from the other offerings on the market.

product life cycle   The movement of a product from introduction ("birth") through growth, maturity, and decline to eventual termination; each of these phases requires a distinctive marketing strategy.

product line   All the products marketed by a given organization, sometimes s divided into sets of product lines.

product portfolio   Mix of products offered by an organization, grouped with reference to market share, cash flow, and growth characteristics.

product recall   Retrieval by the manufacturer of products (usually defective) that are already in the hands of customers and/or channel intermediaries.

profit center   An organizational unit whose revenues and costs are clearly identifiable and whose management is held responsible for controlling both sides of the income statement.

promotional activities   Various nonrecurrent selling efforts, usually of a short-term nature, such as contests, discount coupons, special displays, and introductory offers.

psychographic segmentation   Dividing the market into segments using variables such as people's life styles, values, attitudes, personalities, and interests.

public relations   The managing of public perceptions of an organization and its products by making available news about the organization to the media, or by interacting directly with opinion leaders.

publicity   The end result of the staging and publicizing of special events and activities to attract community attention, often via the news media.

pull strategy   A marketing strategy based upon heavy advertising by the manufacturer to potential end users, with the objective of "pulling" the product through the channels of distribution (see also *push strategy*).

push strategy   A marketing strategy in which the channels of distribution take major responsibility for promotional and personal selling efforts to end users, designed to "push" the product out of the store (see also *pull strategy*).

reactive selling   Letting customers take the initiative in seeking out the vendor, who then tries to complete the transaction (see also *proactive selling*).

roll out   The process of extending distribution and advertising/promotion for a new product from a limited geographic area to a wider (or national) area.

secondary data   Existing information in an accessible form that can be used to provide insights for management decision making or serve as inputs to new primary data collection efforts (see also *primary data*).

shopping products   Products that the consumer, in the process of selection and purchase, characteristically compares on such bases as suitability, quality, price, and style (see also *convenience products* and *specialty products*).

specialty products   Products with unique characteristics and/or brand identification for which a significant group of buyers are habitually willing to make a special purchasing effort (see also *convenience products* and *shopping products*).

spot advertising   The purchase of TV or radio time on a station-by-station or market-by-market basis rather than networkwide.

stockkeeping-unit (SKU)   The lowest level of disaggregation at which a product can be ordered; it reflects size, style, color, and other distinctive variations.

strategic business management unit (SBU/SMU)   A unit within a larger organization that is essentially treated as a separate entity and established as an independent profit center, usually with a distinct mission, objective, competitive environment, and managerial requirements (see also *profit center*).

target market   That portion of the total market the organization has selected to serve.

target marketing   Focusing the marketing efforts on specific segments within the total market.

test marketing   Evaluating customer response to a new product by putting it on the market in a limited geographic area.

third-party payers   Persons or organizations that provide the funding for projects, products, or services that benefit the user, or consumer.

time-series data   See *longitudinal data*.

top-down planning   Designing programs to be implemented by top-level management; participation filters down to the lower levels (see also *bottom-up planning*).

trademark   A brand or part of a brand that is given legal protection and whose use is restricted to its owner.

trading up   Encouraging current or prospective customers to purchase a more expensive version of a given product.

undifferentiated marketing strategy   A plan whereby the organization treats the market as an aggregate and designs its products and marketing program to appeal to the greatest number of consumers possible.

usage segmentation   Subdividing the total consumer market on the basis of where, when, why, and in what quantities the product is used.

value pricing   Establishing price levels on the basis of how the buyer perceives the value of the product rather than on the basis of the costs to be recovered by the seller.

variable costs   Costs that change in direct proportion to changes in activity, such as materials and parts, sales commissions, and certain labor and supplies (see also *fixed costs*).

vertical integration   The process of purchasing or acquiring control over one's suppliers (see *backward integration*), or one's distributors (see *forward integration* and *horizontal integration*), or both.

wholesaler   A business unit in the channel of distribution which buys goods or services from producers and resells them to other merchants or to institutional purchasers but not to household consumers.

ECONOMIC ANALYSIS
OF ALTERNATIVES

An economic, or financial, analysis is necessary in evaluating all major marketing courses of action. Whether to introduce a new product, enter a new market, change price, or increase the size of the sales force are all decisions that can have significant financial consequences. Government and nonprofit institutions, while usually less concerned with profits than businesses are, must nevertheless determine how to allocate their own limited financial resources.

In this note, we review some of the basic concepts of economic analysis. We concentrate on simplified situations in order to focus on the key issues.

COSTS, PRICE, AND CONTRIBUTION

Variable costs (VC) vary with the volume of the product produced or sold. For a manufacturer, variable costs typically would include the costs of materials and labor; as more units are manufactured, total variable costs increase. Variable costs are typically expressed as VC per unit. This is often a good representation of the way such costs vary over the relevant range of sales for marketing decision making.

Fixed costs (FC) do not vary with the volume and are those which would still be incurred, at least in the short run, even if no products were manufactured or sold. Fixed costs can include the rent of a building, the cost of display cases, the advertising budget, and other expenses which would not change, once committed, irrespective of the volume sold or produced. See Exhibit 1 for an example of the relationship of variable and fixed costs.

Although in many analyses the two major cost categories are fixed and variable, in some situations a third type of cost, *semi-variable cost* (SVC), is important. Semi-variable costs tend to vary with the capacity to provide volume (often in stepwise fashion) as opposed to directly with volume itself. Such costs are particularly prevalent in service industries. For

EXHIBIT 1
RELATIONSHIP OF VARIÁBLE AND FIXED COSTS

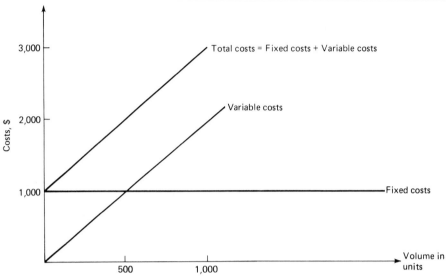

instance an áirline might incur a semi-variable cost of $300 per flight (for fuel, salaries, and landing fees) when adding an extra flight a day on its Atlanta to New Orleans schedule; its variable cost might be only $6 per passenger boarded (for refreshments and ticketing costs). For theater companies the cost of running another performance of a show and for a retail store the cost of opening an additional day are semi-variable costs. For a manufacturer, the decision to add an overtime shift to meet anticipated demand can involve semi-variable costs. Although we will not consider semi-variable costs explicitly in the remainder of this note, they are often quite important and may need to be considered in an economic analysis of alternatives.

Price (P) per unit is the revenue obtained per unit, net of any discount offered to others in the distribution channel. Price per unit times *volume (V)* sold gives the total (or gross) revenue realized by the seller.

Contribution, or margin, per unit is the difference between price per unit and variable cost per unit, i.e.,

$$\text{Unit contribution} = P \text{ per unit} - VC \text{ per unit}$$

Similarly, total (or gross) contribution is the product of unit contribution times volume. Net contribution is equal to unit contribution times volume less fixed cost, i.e.,

$$\text{Net contribution} = [(P - VC) \times (V)] - FC$$

To illustrate these concepts, consider the example of a fruit packer who is thinking of setting up a small factory to produce frozen raspberry juice. Rental costs of the factory and facilities, including such factors as utilities, insurance, and property taxes, are $150,000 annually. Sales force, advertising, marketing, and other management operating costs are

$200,000 per year. The costs of leasing specialized packing and freezing machinery, which has a useful life of five years, is $100,000 annually. The cost of raw materials and labor is $15 per case (12 large cans) of frozen raspberry juice. If the selling price of frozen raspberry juice is $37.50 per case, then we could calculate the following:

Fixed costs   = $150,000 + $200,000 + $100,000 = $450,000
Variable costs per case = $15
Selling price per unit   = $37.50
Unit contribution   = $37.50 − $15.00 = $22.50

If the company expects to sell 24,000 cases in a year, then estimated costs and revenues would be as follows:

Total variable costs = 24,000 × $15.00 = $360,000
Total revenue   = 24,000 × $37.50 = $900,000
Total contribution   = 24,000 × $22.50 = $540,000
Net contribution   = $540,000 − $450,000 = $90,000

Next we shall examine some concepts that can be used to help evaluate the economics of deciding whether to set up the frozen raspberry juice factory.

BREAKEVEN ANALYSIS AND PROFITABILITY

Breakeven analysis allows management to calculate the level of sales required to cover the fixed costs of making any significant marketing change (see Exhibit 2). The breakeven volume is found by dividing the fixed costs by the unit contribution, i.e.,

$$\text{Breakeven volume (in units)} = \frac{\text{fixed costs}}{\text{unit contribution}}$$

In the case of the raspberry juice packer, the breakeven volume is

$$\frac{\$450,000}{\$22.50} = 20,000 \text{ cases}$$

If the alternative being examined involves a change from a current one, then the fixed cost component of the breakeven calculation is replaced by the amount of the change in the fixed costs. The importance of breakeven calculations is that it puts the focus on the profitability of a product, not just its sales volume.

One test of a marketing initiative is the feasibility of attaining the breakeven volume. If the current market size is 50,000 cases, then selling 20,000 cases means getting a 40 percent market share unless the market is expected to grow rapidly. If high market share is necessary for success, then competitive reaction must be carefully considered.

For many marketing alternatives, such as the introduction of a new product, it would be unreasonable to expect the project to achieve breakeven in its first year. In such a case management may look at the feasibility of attaining breakeven within two, three, or more years.

While public and nonprofit organizations may only seek to obtain a breakeven volume,

EXHIBIT 2
ILLUSTRATION OF BREAKEVEN ANALYSIS

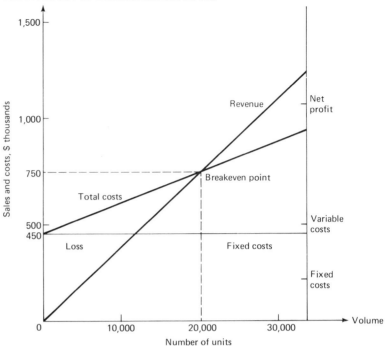

most businesses would not go ahead with a project unless a profit was likely. While the profit required can be set in many ways, one alternative is to specify it as a percentage of the investment required. Target profitability volume, in units, can be calculated as follows:

$$\text{Target profitability volume (in units)} = \frac{\text{fixed costs} + \text{target profit}}{\text{unit contribution}}$$

For example, if the raspberry juice producer had to invest $1,000,000 to establish this business and set a target profit of 18 percent on the investment, then the number of units it would need to sell to achieve target profitability is calculated as follows:

$$\frac{\$450,000 + \$180,000}{\$22.50} = 28,000 \text{ cases}$$

CONDITIONAL SALES FORECASTS AND RESPONSE FUNCTIONS

In many ways, a breakeven analysis evaluates a marketing program from a different perspective than that used in formulating the plan itself. The breakeven analysis produces a target volume and asks how feasible is its accomplishment. In contrast, the development of a marketing plan forecasts that a certain level of sales are expected if the specified plan is implemented. In other words, sales are a function of a specific marketing plan. More succinctly, and in the context of the marketing mix, we can say that the plan represents a *conditional sales forecast* in that the sales are conditional on a particular marketing mix. A response function is the part of the conditional sales forecast that explicitly links a sales response to one or more elements of the marketing mix. Take, for instance, the example of advertising expenditure level for the management of a regional movie chain. In the present marketing plan, a monthly advertising expenditure of $20,000 is expected to result in attendance of 60,000 people. However, increasing the ad budget by 50 percent to $30,000 is expected to increase the number of attenders to 66,000; increasing advertising by another $10,000 is expected, based on tests in other regions of the country, to raise attendance to 68,000 people. On the other hand, reducing advertising by $10,000 from the present budget of $20,000 is expected to reduce admissions to 50,000 people. Given these estimates, then, a forecast of sales conditional on advertising would be as follows:

Advertising Budget	Estimated Attendance
$10,000	50,000
20,000	60,000
30,000	66,000
40,000	68,000

As can be seen in Exhibit 3, attendance is much more sensitive to decreases than increases

EXHIBIT 3
ADVERTISING RESPONSE FUNCTION

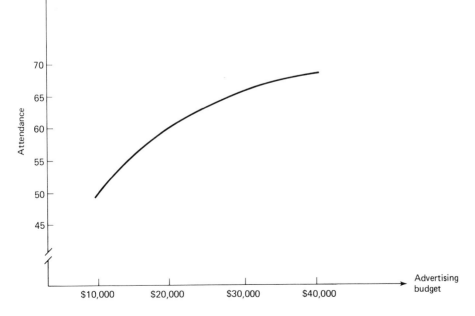

in advertising from its current level. The profitability of changing the advertising level depends upon the contribution per ticket sold. If in this case the contribution is $3 per ticket sold, the following profitability analysis would help management to make a decision about the advertising budget.

(1) = Advertising Budget	(2) = Estimated Attendance	(3) = $3 × (2) = Contribution before Advertising	(4) = (3) − (1) = Contribution after Advertising
$10,000	50,000	$150,000	$140,000
$20,000	60,000	$180,000	$160,000
$30,000	66,000	$198,000	$168,000
$40,000	68,000	$204,000	$164,000

As can be seen, the most profitable level of sales is obtained when advertising spending is $30,000 for a contribution, after allowing for the expense of advertising, of $168,000. As might be expected from looking at the data, the highest level of sales is not the most profitable level in this case.

This section has illustrated one form of profitability analysis. At times more complex techniques may be needed to adjust for the time value of money, to allow for risk and uncertainty, and to account for possible competitive response.

CONCLUSION

Economic analysis is an important part of the evaluation of all significant marketing alternatives. This note has provided an introduction to some of the basic approaches that will be helpful in the cases included in this book. No one form of analysis, however, is sufficient to evaluate a course of action, and the soundness of a plan must be judged against multiple criteria.

EXERCISES

Marilyn Berg is the product manager for the Ball brand of toasters, a nationally recognized brand name. At present, Ball toasters sell for a retail price of $50, but the combined retail and wholesale margin of 40 percent leaves a net sales price to Ball of $30 per toaster. The present market size is 400,000 toasters per year; Ball is the leading brand with a 32 percent market share.

For the forthcoming year, fixed manufacturing costs are $800,000 and variable production costs are $14 per toaster. In addition, there are shipping and transportation costs of $2 per toaster that Ball has to pay. Under the present market plan, salesforce costs are $75,000 per year, the advertising budget is $400,000, and management costs are $160,000 per year.

1 What are Ball's fixed costs, variable costs, and unit contribution at present?
2 What is the breakeven volume for Ball and what market share is needed to achieve this?
3 Is the Ball brand of toasters profitable? To what extent?
4 If establishing the Ball toaster line involved an investment of $1,800,000 and the

company requires a return of 20 percent on its capital, is the toaster line still profitable? To what extent?

5 Ms. Berg is considering changing the advertising budget. If she raises the budget by $100,000 to $500,000 she expects to sell 7 percent more toasters than she now does. If she reduces the advertising buget by $100,000, she expects to sell 10,000 fewer toasters than she now does. Should she raise or lower her advertising budget by $100,000? What would the breakeven level become in each case? What is the profit impact of such a move?

6 As an alternative to a change in the advertising program Ms. Berg is considering running a special sales promotion in which the customer would get a $1.00 rebate for each Ball toaster bought. In addition to the cost of the rebate, it would cost the company an additional $.75 to handle each request for a rebate. If the rebate program is estimated to increase sales by 15,000 toasters, what would its impact on profit be?

THREE

USE OF COMPUTERS FOR
MARKETING DECISION MAKING

An M.B.A. student recently commented to one of us that he couldn't imagine how we studied for our M.B.A. degrees (in the late 1960s) without pocket calculators. The immediate reply was, "Soon, students won't be able to imagine completing their degrees without a personal computer!"

In the early days of computer development, some observers predicted that at most the world market for all computers would be a hundred or less. Others suggested that computers would replace managers and lead to sharp reductions in the number of managers. Neither forecast proved accurate—fortunately for all. Instead, computers and computer-based systems have become important aids to managerial analysis and decision making. Computers, when properly used, can lead to better decisions or decisions made more rapidly or efficiently. Successful computer applications provide help to managers trying to deal with an uncertain, competitive, dynamic environment.

Access to a computer is not necessary for the study of the cases in this book (with the exception of "The Diffusion Game"). However, availability of a personal or other computer will reduce the time in which cases can be analyzed, increase the depth of analysis of alternative courses of action, and allow for an examination of a broader set of options. The course instructor will suggest the appropriate level of computer involvement, depending on the objectives of the course, the availability of computers, and your own computer skills.

COMPUTER AIDS AND MANAGERS

A computer can help in analyzing some, but not all, cases. The optional computer disc that accompanies this book lists the cases for which computer aids are available.

Economic and Profitability Analysis

For most students, the first type of computer aid to be used in a marketing course will be a relatively straightforward program to do breakeven and profitability analyses. This kind of program allows the user to evaluate quickly the financial and economic implications of alternative courses of action from a set of assumptions about future demand, price, cost, and other factors. The program asks the user to input such data in a conversational format and then does the calculations necessary to generate income and other statements. The real challenge lies not in running the analysis but in establishing the appropriate assumptions, as will be seen in cases such as "Southwest Airlines" and the "Fraser Company." These programs are similar to so-called "spread-sheet" programs, but easier to use for the neophyte. They greatly reduce the computational burden in testing assumptions, thereby allowing a more thorough evaluation of the cases.

Marketing Models

Several cases in this book allow the use of specially developed marketing models. These models typically develop some structure that estimates the effect of marketing variables such as price, advertising, and product design on sales. For example, an important issue in "Castle Coffee" is how much money to spend on advertising. A successful analysis requires the manager to estimate the relationship between advertising and sales. While a computer is not necessary for such an analysis, using an appropriately designed computer model will help the manager to specify the nature of that relationship and predict the sales and profit consequences of different advertising levels. Computer models can also help a manager simulate possible market responses to different competitive actions. In "Hinesbury Mills," for instance, a competitor introduces a new type of cake mix. Market research data provides information on market segment structure and how people choose cake mixes. A computer simulation of the behavior of cake-mix-buying households can help the manager predict what share of market the new cake mix will achieve if no action is taken or, alternatively, if the company introduces its own imitative version. This model, in a slightly different form, was used by managers at Hinesbury Mills to help them make a decision. Another model that was implemented by an organization is treated in the "Lively Arts at Hanson" case. In this case, a student can use the product planning computer system employed at Hanson University to forecast attendance at performing arts events and help identify which events should be presented and promoted during the year.

Computer Games

In computer games, as many are aware, the user attempts to develop and implement a strategy to test against a computer model of a real or simulated world. In "The Diffusion Game," the student takes on the role of a change agent seeking to persuade rural villagers to adopt a new agricultural innovation. In doing so, the player develops insights into the nature of communication strategies for new products.

CONCLUSION

In summary, with the exception of "The Diffusion Game," the cases in this book do not require access to a computer. However, the increasing use of personal computers by managers and the potential of computers to help managers suggest that a number of the cases could be analyzed with the aid of "spread-sheet" type programs. Some of the cases in this book can be studied at various levels of sophistication with the aid of specially developed computer programs. Remember, however, that the objective of any computer model—simple or sophisticated—is to help analyze and understand a marketing situation. Responsibility for discovering problems and developing, testing, and implementing sound, creative decisions rests with the manager.

APPENDIX # FOUR

ASSIGNMENTS FOR
WORKING ON
COMPUTER-ASSISTED CASES

CASTLE COFFEE COMPANY, II

William F. Massy
David B. Montgomery
Charles B. Weinberg

Since returning from a one-week management development course a few months before, Adrian Van Tassle had been working with Jack Stillman on the adaptation of a small "marketing planning model" to help him plan Castle Coffee's advertising budget for the coming fiscal year. Stillman, director of research for Castle, was quite experienced in computer models applied to a broad range of management problems. While Stillman had little or no experience in the marketing area, he had welcomed the opportunity to work with Van Tassle.

The model being developed (described in more detail later) was designed to aid a brand manager or advertising manager to determine a reasonable advertising budget for a product. Van Tassle felt that the model might help him to clarify his own thinking, to make sounder decisions, and to communicate better with management.

INPUTS REQUIRED BY THE PLANNING MODEL

After reviewing the marketing planning model with Jack Stillman, Van Tassle asked Stillman to provide a list of the basic inputs required by the model. After much tugging at his red mustache and several conferences with Stillman, Van Tassle arrived at a preliminary set of estimates for the basic inputs. The input list and the preliminary estimates are presented in Exhibit 1. Some of these factors were obvious; only the ones relating to market share and the advertising plan itself required a lot of thought.

Although Adrian Van Tassle had to develop a quarterly plan, he decided that the best first step would be to determine the size of the annual advertising budget. He felt that developing an annual plan would be relatively easier in that seasonal effects could be ignored and questions of how fast sales and market share respond to advertising could be

Reprinted from *Stanford Business Cases 1985* with permission of the publishers, Stanford University Graduate School of Business. Specially revised for inclusion in this book.
Copyright © 1985 by the Board of Trustees of the Leland Stanford Junior University.

EXHIBIT 1
PRELIMINARY VALUES FOR INPUTS TO THE ADVERTISING PLANNING MODEL
(ANNUAL PLAN)

Variable	Preliminary Value
Number of periods	1
Reference market share	.054
Maintenance advertising per year (millions of dollars)	8.0
Market share at end of year if during the year:	
No advertising	.027
Saturation advertising	.10
20% increase in advertising	.060
Market share in long run with no advertising	0
Media efficiency	1.0
Copy effectiveness	1.0
Contribution ($/unit)	4.50
Brand price ($/unit)	17.20
Initial market share (the March-April result)	.054
Annual product sales (industry sales, in millions of cases)	88
Product price ($/unit)	17.20

postponed. In addition, he felt that the experience of developing an annual plan would sharpen his understanding of the model and his ability to use it.

After some thought Van Tassle concluded that if his advertising were reduced to zero for that year, he would lose perhaps half his market share in the first year, cutting it to a mere 2.7 percent. This would result partly from a slackening in consumer demand and partly from an accelerating erosion of Castle's distribution. If a zero rate of advertising were to be continued, he was relatively certain Castle would lose all its distribution, and hence market share. On the other hand, pushing advertising to saturation might nearly double the company's share, to about 10 percent. "Of course," he commented to Stillman, "that figure could as well be 9 percent or even 11 percent or 12 percent. We've never come close to blitzing the ad budget." He also believed that the most likely result on a 20 percent increase in advertising would be a 6 percent market share (up from 5.4 percent) though here again there was considerable uncertainty. Van Tassle still wasn't sure how quickly this increase would be observed, but he felt that this would surely occur by the fourth quarter after the change.

Van Tassle had run the model using data that represented his plans as they had existed at the beginning of the 1982 fiscal year. At that time, the late spring of 1981, he had estimated the previous period's market share at 5.5 percent; however, the market share report he later received estimated market share at 5.4 percent. According to the results of the theater tests, the copy effectiveness for the autumn-winter-spring campaign, he had recently learned, was rated at 0.90. (Curiously, the "old" advertising copy used in the summer of 1981 had been rated at 1.0.) In addition, as compared to last year, Van Tassle now had judgments concerning maximum and minimum shares, a subject he had not thought about last year. In using the advertising planning model, Van Tassle first set the levels of brand advertising at the amounts he had planned for the year, not the amounts actually expended. Given the confusion with the media schedule caused by the abrupt cancellation of 20 percent of Castle's advertising weight during the winter quarter, Van Tassle wondered whether a run of the model with actual expenditures would be meaningful. The inputs and outputs for this run are shown in Exhibit 2.

EXHIBIT 2
RUN OF ADVERTISING PLANNING MODEL
(annual)

```
                            CASTLE COFFEE CASE
                            ===================


    INPUT QUARTERLY DATA AS BASE CASE (Y=YES N=NO)? N
    NUMBER OF PERIODS (MAX 4) IN BUDGET HORIZON? 4

    REFERENCE CASE CONDITIONS
    MARKET SHARE AT START OF PERIOD (IN DECIMAL FORM)? .054
    ADV RATE TO MAINTAIN SHARE (MM $/PERIOD)? 2
    MARKET SHARE AT END OF PERIOD
       IF ADV REDUCED TO ZERO (IN DECIMAL FORM)? .0454
       IF ADV INCREASED TO SATURATION(IN DECIMAL FORM)? .063
       IF ADV INCREASED 20% OVER MAINTENANCE RATE (IN DECIMAL FORM)? .0554
    MARKET SHARE IN LONG RUN IF ADV REDUCED TO ZERO (IN DECIMAL FORM)? 0
    OTHER DATA:
    MARKET SHARE IN PREVIOUS PERIOD (IN DECIMAL FORM)? .054
    PRODUCT SALES RATE AT START OF PERIOD (MM UNIT / PERIOD)? 22

    BUDGET HORIZON CONDITIONS

    PRODUCT HAS A SEASONAL OR OTHER NON ADV TIME EFFECT? Y
    INDEX OF PRODUCT CLASS SALES (REF CASE 1.00) FOR PERIOD:
       1          ? .85
       2          ? 1
       3          ? 1.15
       4          ? 1
    BRAND SHARE HAS A NON ADV TIME EFFECT? N
    MAINTENANCE ADV VARIES? Y
    INDEX OF MAINTENANCE ADV (REF CASE = 1.00) FOR PERIOD:
       1          ? .8
       2          ? 1
       3          ? 1.2
       4          ? 1
    MEDIA EFFICIENCY VARIES (REF CASE = 1.0)? N
    COPY EFFECTIVENESS VARIES (REF CASE = 1.0)? N
    BRAND ADV RATE VARIES? Y
    BRAND ADV (M DOLLARS) IN PERIOD:
       1          ? 1.6
       2          ? 2.4
       3          ? 2.88
       4          ? 2.4


    ACTION [1=CHANGE 2=OUTPUT ON SCREEN 3=OUTPUT TO PRINTER 4=EXIT TO MAIN MENU]? 3


            CASTLE COFFEE

        REFERENCE CASE CONDITIONS

    MKT SHARE AT START OF PERIOD............ = .054
    MAINTENANCE ADV RATE................... = 2
    MKT SHARE AT END OF PERIOD:
        IF ADV EQUALS ZERO.................. = .0454
        IF ADV EQUALS SATURATION........... = .063
        IF ADV EQUALS 20% OVER MAINT....... = .0554
    LONG RUN MKT SHARE IF ADV EQUALS ZERO... = 0
    INDEX OF MEDIA EFFICIENCY.............. = 1
    INDEX OF COPY EFFECTIVENESS............ = 1

    CONTRIBUTION PROFIT.................... = 4.5
    AVG BRAND PRICE....................... = 17.2
    MKT SHARE IN PREVIOUS PERIOD........... = .054
    PRODUCT SALES AT START OF PERIOD....... = 22
    AVG PRICE FOR PRODUCT................. = 17.2


        BUDGET HORIZON CONDITIONS

    PERIOD  SEASONAL  NON-ADV  MAINT  MEDIA  COPY    BRAND
            EFFECT    EFFECT   ADV    EFFIC  EFFECT  ADV
            (PROD)    (BRAND)  INDEX  INDEX  INDEX   RATE
    ======  ========  =======  =====  =====  ======  =====
       1      0.85     1.00    0.80   1.00   1.00    1.60
       2      1.00     1.00    1.00   1.00   1.00    2.40
       3      1.15     1.00    1.20   1.00   1.00    2.88
       4      1.00     1.00    1.00   1.00   1.00    2.40
```

EXHIBIT 2 *(continued)*

```
PERIOD SHARE    PRODUCT      BRAND    CONTR BRAND CONTR CUMUL SLOPE
       PCT       SALES       SALES    BEF   ADV   AFT   CONTR CC$/$
       UNITS UNITS DOLRS UNITS DOLRS  ADV   DOLRS ADV         MARG
             (MM)  (MM)  (000) (000)  (000) (000) (000) (000) PROF
       ===== ===== ===== ===== =====  ===== ===== ===== ===== =====
   1   5.40   19   322  1010 17369  4544  1600  2944  2944  0.44
   2   5.54   22   378  1219 20963  5485  2400  3085  6029 -0.03
   3   5.66   25   435  1431 24620  6441  2880  3561  9590 -0.19
   4   5.76   22   378  1266 21783  5699  2400  3299 12889 -0.05

ACTION [1=CHANGE 2=OUTPUT ON SCREEN 3=OUTPUT TO PRINTER 4=EXIT TO MAIN MENU]? 1

CHANGE [0=NO MORE 1=MAINT.ADV 2=MIN FINAL SHARE 3=MAX FINAL SHARE
        4=FINAL SHARE WITH 20% ADV OVER MAINT 5=LONG RUN MIN
        6=BRAND ADV 7=REFERENCE CASE COND 8=BUDGET HORIZON COND]? 6
BRAND ADV FOR PERIOD (M DOLLARS):
   1            ? 1.6
   2            ? 2.4
   3            ? 2.64
   4            ? 2
CHANGE [0=NO MORE 1=MAINT.ADV 2=MIN FINAL SHARE 3=MAX FINAL SHARE
        4=FINAL SHARE WITH 20% ADV OVER MAINT 5=LONG RUN MIN
        6=BRAND ADV 7=REFERENCE CASE COND 8=BUDGET HORIZON COND]? 0

ACTION [1=CHANGE 2=OUTPUT ON SCREEN 3=OUTPUT TO PRINTER 4=EXIT TO MAIN MENU]? 3


              CASTLE COFFEE

          REFERENCE CASE CONDITIONS

MKT SHARE AT START OF PERIOD............ =  .054
MAINTENANCE ADV RATE.................... =  2
MKT SHARE AT END OF PERIOD:
     IF ADV EQUALS ZERO................. =  .0454
     IF ADV EQUALS SATURATION.......... =  .063
     IF ADV EQUALS 20% OVER MAINT....... =  .0554
LONG RUN MKT SHARE IF ADV EQUALS ZERO... =  0
INDEX OF MEDIA EFFICIENCY.............. =  1
INDEX OF COPY EFFECTIVENESS............ =  1

CONTRIBUTION PROFIT.................... =  4.5
AVG BRAND PRICE....................... = 17.2
MKT SHARE IN PREVIOUS PERIOD........... =  .054
PRODUCT SALES AT START OF PERIOD....... =  22
AVG PRICE FOR PRODUCT................. = 17.2


          BUDGET HORIZON CONDITIONS

PERIOD SEASONAL NON-ADV MAINT MEDIA   COPY   BRAND
       EFFECT   EFFECT  ADV   EFFIC  EFFECT  ADV
       (PROD)  (BRAND) INDEX  INDEX  INDEX   RATE
       ======= ======= ===== ====== ======  =====
   1    0.85    1.00    0.80  1.00   1.00    1.60
   2    1.00    1.00    1.00  1.00   1.00    2.40
   3    1.15    1.00    1.20  1.00   1.00    2.64
   4    1.00    1.00    1.00  1.00   1.00    2.00


PERIOD SHARE    PRODUCT      BRAND    CONTR BRAND CONTR CUMUL SLOPE
       PCT       SALES       SALES    BEF   ADV   AFT   CONTR CC$/$
       UNITS UNITS DOLRS UNITS DOLRS  ADV   DOLRS ADV         MARG
             (MM)  (MM)  (000) (000)  (000) (000) (000) (000) PROF
       ===== ===== ===== ===== =====  ===== ===== ===== ===== =====
   1   5.40   19   322  1010 17369  4544  1600  2944  2944  0.44
   2   5.54   22   378  1219 20963  5485  2400  3085  6029 -0.03
   3   5.59   25   435  1415 24331  6366  2640  3726  9754 -0.10
   4   5.56   22   378  1223 21042  5505  2000  3505 13259  0.16
```

EXHIBIT 3
CHANGES IN PRELIMINARY VALUES OF REFERENCE CASE
CONDITIONS FOR INPUTS TO THE ADVERTISING PLANNING MODEL
(Quarterly plan)

Variable	Preliminary
Number of periods	4
Maintenance advertising per quarter (millions of dollars)	1.0
Market share at end of quarter if during the quarter:	
No advertising	.0454
Saturation advertising	.0686
20% increase in advertising	.0559
Quarterly product sales (industry sales in millions of cases)	22

Quarterly Plan

Van Tassle next decided to test a quarterly plan. Stillman indicated that some changes in the values of the variables would have to be made. Some were obvious: average sales rate per quarter is the annual rate divided by four. Other changes were more difficult. For example, if there were no advertising for a year, market share would drop by 50 percent (i.e., to 0.027) at the end of the year. Stillman suggested that market share fell off by quarter in approximately the same way that a bank compounded interest—in this case at the rate of 16 percent per quarter. Thus, if there were no advertising for four quarters, market share would drop to approximately 84 percent, 71 percent, 60 percent and 50 percent of the initial value. This seemed to be a reasonable approach, so Van Tassle let Stillman make the calculations which led to the data in Exhibit 3. Van Tassle made some trial runs of a quarterly plan, as shown in Exhibit 4.

Next Year's Budget

Van Tassle gave a final pull to his mustache, and turned to the evaluation of the results of running his model on quarterly data. He expected he would want to make a series of additional runs, including tests of alternative plans for fiscal year 1983 before making his advertising budget presentation and recommendation to management. He expected that use of the model would help clarify his thinking and lead to a better recommendation. He also hoped that the model would permit him to develop a better presentation so as to more effectively communicate his objectives and assumptions to management. He was not quite sure how to go about pursuing these goals and recognized he would have to develop his own methods of approach as he went along.

STRUCTURE OF THE MODEL

The advertising planning model available to Van Tassle was designed to help him evaluate the impact of different advertising budget levels primarily on market share. While advertising and other effects on industry sales were also represented in the model, this was not its main focus.

The model was intended to help a manager translate both subjective estimates and data from past events and market research studies about responses to advertising into a systematic framework. The model encompassed enough critical variables to provide acceptable

EXHIBIT 4
RUN OF ADVERTISING PLANNING MODEL
(Quarterly)

```
                          CASTLE COFFEE CASE
                          ==================



    INPUT QUARTERLY DATA AS BASE CASE (Y=YES N=NO)? N
    NUMBER OF PERIODS (MAX 4) IN BUDGET HORIZON? 1

    REFERENCE CASE CONDITIONS
    MARKET SHARE AT START OF PERIOD (IN DECIMAL FORM)? .054
    ADV RATE TO MAINTAIN SHARE (MM $/PERIOD)? 8
    MARKET SHARE AT END OF PERIOD
       IF ADV REDUCED TO ZERO (IN DECIMAL FORM)? .027
       IF ADV INCREASED TO SATURATION(IN DECIMAL FORM)? .1
       IF ADV INCREASED 20% OVER MAINTENANCE RATE (IN DECIMAL FORM)? .06
    MARKET SHARE IN LONG RUN IF ADV REDUCED TO ZERO (IN DECIMAL FORM)? 0
    OTHER DATA:
    MARKET SHARE IN PREVIOUS PERIOD (IN DECIMAL FORM)? .054
    PRODUCT SALES RATE AT START OF PERIOD (MM UNIT / PERIOD)? 88

    BUDGET HORIZON CONDITIONS
    PRODUCT HAS A SEASONAL OR OTHER NON ADV TIME EFFECT? N
    BRAND SHARE HAS A NON ADV TIME EFFECT? N
    MAINTENANCE ADV VARIES? N
    MEDIA EFFICIENCY VARIES (REF CASE = 1.0)? N
    COPY EFFECTIVENESS VARIES (REF CASE = 1.0)? N
    BRAND ADV RATE VARIES? N
    BRAND ADV (MM DOLLARS) ? 9.28


    ACTION [1=CHANGE 2=OUTPUT ON SCREEN 3=OUTPUT TO PRINTER 4=EXIT TO MAIN MENU]? 3



                  CASTLE COFFEE

            REFERENCE CASE CONDITIONS

    MKT SHARE AT START OF PERIOD............ =  .054
    MAINTENANCE ADV RATE................... =  8
    MKT SHARE AT END OF PERIOD:
        IF ADV EQUALS ZERO................. =  .027
        IF ADV EQUALS SATURATION.......... =  .1
        IF ADV EQUALS 20% OVER MAINT....... =  .06
    LONG RUN MKT SHARE IF ADV EQUALS ZERO... =  0
    INDEX OF MEDIA EFFICIENCY.............. =  1
    INDEX OF COPY EFFECTIVENESS............ =  1

    CONTRIBUTION PROFIT.................... =  4.5
    AVG BRAND PRICE....................... =  17.2
    MKT SHARE IN PREVIOUS PERIOD........... = .054
    PRODUCT SALES AT START OF PERIOD....... =  88
    AVG PRICE FOR PRODUCT................. = 17.2

        BUDGET HORIZON CONDITIONS

PERIOD  SEASONAL  NON-ADV  MAINT  MEDIA   COPY   BRAND
        EFFECT    EFFECT   ADV    EFFIC  EFFECT  ADV
        (PROD)    (BRAND)  INDEX  INDEX  INDEX   RATE
======  ========  =======  =====  =====  ======  =====
  1       1.00      1.00    1.00   1.00   1.00    9.28


PERIOD SHARE    PRODUCT      BRAND     CONTR BRAND CONTR CUMUL SLOPE
       PCT       SALES       SALES     BEF    ADV   AFT  CONTR CC$/$
     UNITS UNITS DOLRS UNITS DOLRS  ADV  DOLRS  ADV         MARG
           (MM)  (MM)        (000)  (000) (000) (000) (000) PROF
===== ===== ===== ===== ===== ===== ===== ===== ===== ===== =====
  1    5.89    88  1514  5180 89089 23308  9280 14028 14028  0.41
```

EXHIBIT 4 *(continued)*

```
ACTION [1=CHANGE 2=OUTPUT ON SCREEN 3=OUTPUT TO PRINTER 4=EXIT TO MAIN MENU]? 1

CHANGE [0=NO MORE 1=MAINT.ADV 2=MIN FINAL SHARE 3=MAX FINAL SHARE
        4=FINAL SHARE WITH 20% ADV OVER MAINT 5=LONG RUN MIN
        6=BRAND ADV 7=REFERENCE CASE COND 8=BUDGET HORIZON COND]? 6
BRAND ADV FOR PERIOD (M DOLLARS):
  1         ? 8.64
CHANGE [0=NO MORE 1=MAINT.ADV 2=MIN FINAL SHARE 3=MAX FINAL SHARE
        4=FINAL SHARE WITH 20% ADV OVER MAINT 5=LONG RUN MIN
        6=BRAND ADV 7=REFERENCE CASE COND 8=BUDGET HORIZON COND]? 0

ACTION [1=CHANGE 2=OUTPUT ON SCREEN 3=OUTPUT TO PRINTER 4=EXIT TO MAIN MENU]? 3


            CASTLE COFFEE

        REFERENCE CASE CONDITIONS

MKT SHARE AT START OF PERIOD............ =  .054
MAINTENANCE ADV RATE................... =  8
MKT SHARE AT END OF PERIOD:
        IF ADV EQUALS ZERO................. =  .027
        IF ADV EQUALS SATURATION........... =  .1
        IF ADV EQUALS 20% OVER MAINT....... =  .06
LONG RUN MKT SHARE IF ADV EQUALS ZERO... =  0
INDEX OF MEDIA EFFICIENCY.............. =  1
INDEX OF COPY EFFECTIVENESS............ =  1

CONTRIBUTION PROFIT.................... =  4.5
AVG BRAND PRICE....................... =  17.2
MKT SHARE IN PREVIOUS PERIOD........... =  .054
PRODUCT SALES AT START OF PERIOD....... =  88
AVG PRICE FOR PRODUCT................. =  17.2


        BUDGET HORIZON CONDITIONS

PERIOD  SEASONAL  NON-ADV  MAINT  MEDIA  COPY    BRAND
        EFFECT    EFFECT   ADV    EFFIC  EFFECT  ADV
        (PROD)    (BRAND)  INDEX  INDEX  INDEX   RATE
======  ========  =======  =====  =====  ======  =====
  1       1.00      1.00    1.00   1.00   1.00    8.64


PERIOD  SHARE   PRODUCT    BRAND      CONTR  BRAND  CONTR  CUMUL  SLOPE
        PCT     SALES      SALES      BEF    ADV    AFT    CONTR  CC$/$
        UNITS  UNITS DOLRS UNITS DOLRS ADV   DOLRS  ADV            MARG
               (MM)  (MM)  (000) (000) (000) (000)  (000)  (000)  PROF
=====  =====  ===== ===== ===== ===== ===== =====  =====  =====  =====
  1     5.65     88  1514  4971 85499 22369  8640  13729  13729   0.48
```

outamps—given reasonable judgment in estimating the variables. Yet at the same time it was not so complex and cluttered that it became difficult for the manager to understand and apply.

Using the Model

To use the model, the manager first needs to estimate four quantities (see Exhibit 5):

1 If a brand's advertising is reduced to zero, there is a minimum point (min) to which brand share will fall from its current or initial value by the end of one time period.

2 If a brand's advertising is increased a great deal, to a saturation level, there is

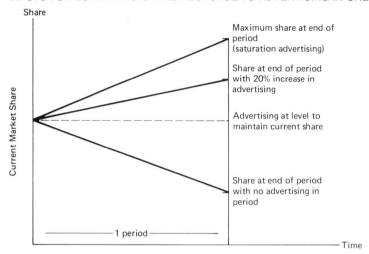

| **EXHIBIT 5**
INPUTS FOR ESTIMATING SHARE RESPONSE TO ADVERTISING IN ONE PERIOD

a maximum point (max) beyond which sales will not rise by the end of one time period.

3 There is some advertising rate that will maintain current market share, called the maintenance level of advertising.

4 If there is a 20 percent increase in a brand's advertising over the maintenance rate, share would increase to a new level by the end of one time period.

The estimates of these four quantities are used to estimate an advertising response function for one period, as shown in Exhibit 6. Algebraically, the relationship can be written as follows:

$$\text{share} = \text{min} + \frac{(\text{max} - \text{min})\,(\text{adv})^b}{a + (\text{adv})^b}$$

The min, max, a and b are implicitly determined by the input data. The diagram in Exhibit 6 shows an S-shaped curve, i.e., at low levels of spending there is very little effect of advertising on share and there are first increasing and then decreasing returns to scale. (This is not required by the equation. If $b > 1$, the curve will be S-shaped, for $0 < b \leq 1$, a concave function. The particular value of b will depend on the estimate provided in response to item 4 above.)

Carryover Effects and Time Delays

To take into account carryover effects and time delays, the model assumes:

1 In the absence of advertising, share would eventually decay to some long run minimum value (long run min). Its value can possibly be zero.

2 The decay in one time period will be a constant fraction of the gap between current share and the long run minimum, i.e., decay is exponential.

EXHIBIT 6
ADVERTISING RESPONSE FUNCTION

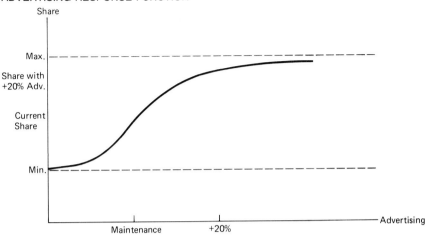

The term "persistence" denotes the fraction of the difference between share and long run minimum that is retained each period after decay. Algebraically,

$$\text{persistence} = \frac{\text{min} - \text{long run min}}{\text{current share} - \text{long run min}}$$

and

$$\text{share } (t - \text{long run min} = (\text{persistence}) [\text{share } (t - 1) - \text{long run min}]$$

$$+ \frac{(\text{max-min}) [\text{adv } (t)]^b}{a + [\text{adv } (t)]^b}$$

For Castle Coffee, where the long run min is estimated as zero, these equations can be written more simply as

$$\text{persistence} = \text{min/current share}$$

$$\text{share}(t) = (\text{persistence}) [\text{share}(t) - 1)] + \frac{(\text{max} - \text{min}) [\text{adv}(t)]^b}{a + [\text{adv}(t)]^b}$$

This is a simple, dynamic model. Share is based on a carryover from last period's share plus the effect of current advertising. It is explainable and it behaves reasonably.

To adjust advertising for media and copy, two time-varying indices are constructed: (1) a media efficiency index and (2) a copy effectiveness index. Both will be assumed to have a reference value of 1.0. The model then hypothesizes that the delivered advertising, i.e., the adv(t) that goes into the response function is given by

$$\text{adv}(t) = [\text{media efficiency}(t)] [\text{copy effectiveness}(t)] [\text{adv dollars}(t)]$$

The media efficiency and copy effectiveness indices can be determined subjectively, but better alternatives exist. Copy testing is helpful; data on media costs and exposures by market segment and relative value of market segments can be used to develop a media index.

Other Factors

Thus far Van Tassle had taken up share responses to advertising, media efficiency, copy effectiveness, and share dynamics. Next he considered product class sales. Two important phenomena here were seasonality and trend. These and any similar effects could be combined into a product class index that varies with time. Thus,

product class sales(t) = [reference product class sales] [product class sales index (t)]

In addition, the model allows for the fact that there may be a product class response to brand advertising and corresponding time lags. The treatment of this is analogous to that for share.

A variety of other factors affect share. Some of these factors are: promotions, competition, distribution, price, product changes, and package changes. These factors are treated, in a simple way, through a composite index of nonadvertising effects. Brand share is modeled as the product of the nonadvertising effect index and the share developed from the advertising response relation. For clarity the latter will be called the unadjusted share:

brand share(t) = [non adv effects index(t)] [unadj share(t)].

Contribution and Slope

Upon looking at the output in Exhibits 2 and 4, Van Tassle was somewhat puzzled by the columns entitled "CONTR AFT ADV" and "SLOPE CC$/$ MARG PROF." Stillman explained that slope (marginal profit) and contribution measured two different elements. Contribution measured the aggregate results in only one period; slope estimated the marginal return (marginal revenue − marginal cost) from advertising. In addition, when used for the quarterly model, slope included an estimate of the revenue impact of the carryover effect of advertising; for example, a fraction of the customers attracted to Castle Coffee in one quarter by advertising might repeat purchase in future quarters, so that advertising in one period might have an impact on future profits. This was a particular concern in planning the quarterly budget. Slope attempted to measure this carryover effect by estimating repeat sales in future periods. In the quarterly model, repeat sales for a full year were included in the estimate of slope.

HINESBURY MILLS, II

Gerald J. Eskin
Christopher H. Lovelock

The marketing research department at Hinesbury Mills, Inc., a leading foods manufacturer, had been assigned the task of developing a simulation model of the cake-mix market. Hinesbury Mills had recently added a premium cake mix, containing real butter, to its existing standard-mix line, only to see the two major competitors, Allied Foods Corporation and Concorn Kitchens, Inc., counter with "add-butter" varieties of mix. These mixes called for consumers to add their own butter, rather than including any shortening in the mix, and retailed at $.79 (the same price as standard mixes) compared to Hinesbury's $1.19 price for its premium cake mix.

Hinesbury's management was concerned about the possible impact of the competition's add-butter lines on its own premium mix. Hinesbury was also undecided as to whether or not it should introduce a line of add-butter mixes of its own; and if so, whether such a line should be allowed to complement or replace the existing premium line.

The objective of the simulation model was to develop a greater understanding of the purchase decision process and to derive predictions of the future market performance of standard, premium and add-butter lines under differing assumptions. Drawing on management's existing knowledge of the cake-mix market, and also on the transcripts of some recently completed interviews with consumers concerning their cake-buying and making habits, the marketing research department began its task of building the model. Duncan Gateau, manager of marketing research, explained how the model was intended to work.

THE DECISION FLOW MODEL

The first step in building the model, Gateau noted, was to develop a simple but explicit depiction of the decision flow involved in the purchase of a cake mix by consumers. The

Reprinted from *Stanford Business Cases 1985* with permission of the publishers, Stanford University, Graduate School of Business, revised. Copyright © 1985 by the Board of Trustees, Leland Stanford Junior University.

resulting flow diagram was based on both managerial experience and information obtained from studying the consumer interview transcripts, and is illustrated in Exhibit 1.

In this flow diagram, consumers are shown coming to the market with a perceived need for a particular type of cake mix. They then form a perception of each product's characteristics concerning factors such as quality, taste and texture, and what is actually involved in transforming the mix into a finished cake, etc.

Consumers try to find a product that matches their perceived needs (these needs being related to particular use occasions). Complications arise whenever there are special deals being offered or when consumers cannot find exactly what they are looking for.

In the case of deals, there are several issues to be considered. First, consumers may or may not be aware that a deal is present in the market. Whenever promotional activity is extensive (for example, displays at 3 for $2) it is assumed that all relevant consumers become aware of this fact. These "Large Deal" promotions in the model contrast "Small Deal" promotions such as "5 cents off" which are sometimes missed. Once consumers are aware of a deal, they will determine if it fits their perceived needs. If it fits exactly they will, of course, purchase the item. If not, they will consider the trade-off between the lower price and the fact that the product is not exactly what they want.

Matches are easier in the deal situation because the consumer will always be willing to accept higher quality than originally desired as long as there is no additional cost to this choice. She or he will also be willing to accept lower prices as long as there is no loss in quality associated with this decision.

If no exact match is found to a deal item, it is still possible that the deal item will be purchased. This will occur when the item is "close enough" to the perceived need to be attractive at the special price. What is "close enough" depends on the use occasion envisioned and the nature of the preference structure. For some special occasions, only an exact match will do, while for snacks, "almost anything" will do at a special price. What is "close enough" is modeled by a set of decision rules specific to each use occasion and initial need structure. These were subjectively assigned by the model building team after listening to the protocol tapes where consumers talked about how they made such decisions.

If no deal item is purchased, non-deal items will be considered and again the consumer will look for a match between needs and perceived product attributes. If a match is found, a purchase results. If no match is found, the consumer considers which component of her or his perceived need is least important and looks for a product that matches needs in all respects except on this one dimension. The way this search is accomplished in the model is to have the consumer change the perceived need in terms of this "least important" dimension and again look for a match. The thing that is "least important" will depend on the intended use for the product. For special occasions "quality" will never be "least important" while for snack use, quality may well play this role. For the snack occasion, the consumer may be unwilling to give up "low price."

Perceived Need

In order to ascertain whether or not a purchase will take place, it was necessary to be able to identify all the perceived needs that a consumer might be expected to have, and to relate these to the perceived characteristics of different brands and types of cake mix. The resulting matching process is illustrated in Exhibit 2, which is a specially prepared excerpt from a model run.

EXHIBIT 1
DECISION FLOW MODEL

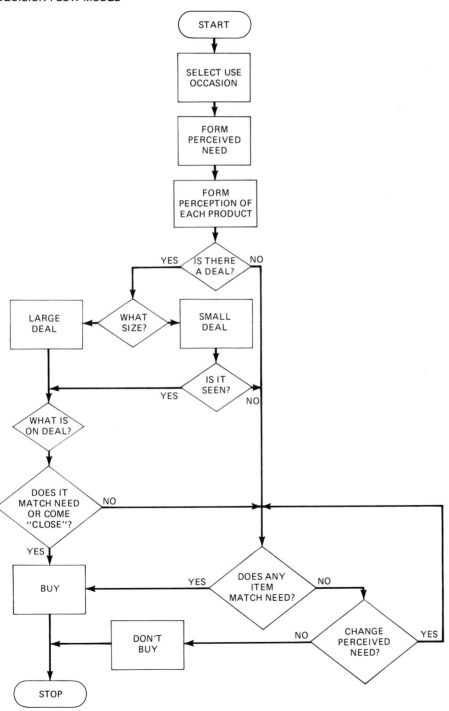

EXHIBIT 2
TRACE OF EXCERPT FROM TYPICAL RUN OF CONSUMERS THROUGH MODEL

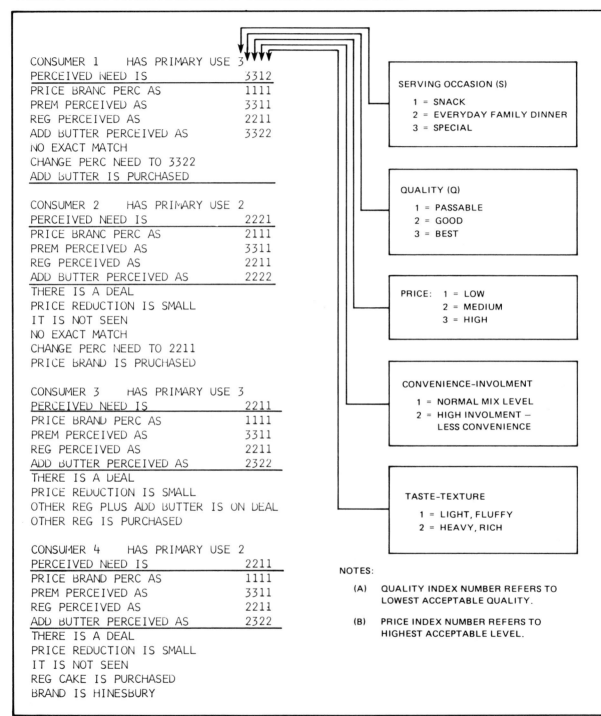

```
CONSUMER 1    HAS PRIMARY USE 3
PERCEIVED NEED IS            3312
PRICE BRANC PERC AS          1111
PREM PERCEIVED AS            3311
REG PERCEIVED AS             2211
ADD BUTTER PERCEIVED AS      3322
NO EXACT MATCH
CHANGE PERC NEED TO 3322
ADD BUTTER IS PURCHASED


CONSUMER 2    HAS PRIMARY USE 2
PERCEIVED NEED IS            2221
PRICE BRANC PERC AS          2111
PREM PERCEIVED AS            3311
REG PERCEIVED AS             2211
ADD BUTTER PERCEIVED AS      2222
THERE IS A DEAL
PRICE REDUCTION IS SMALL
IT IS NOT SEEN
NO EXACT MATCH
CHANGE PERC NEED TO 2211
PRICE BRAND IS PRUCHASED


CONSUMER 3    HAS PRIMARY USE 3
PERCEIVED NEED IS            2211
PRICE BRAND PERC AS          1111
PREM PERCEIVED AS            3311
REG PERCEIVED AS             2211
ADD BUTTER PERCEIVED AS      2322
THERE IS A DEAL
PRICE REDUCTION IS SMALL
OTHER REG PLUS ADD BUTTER IS ON DEAL
OTHER REG IS PURCHASED


CONSUMER 4    HAS PRIMARY USE 2
PERCEIVED NEED IS            2211
PRICE BRAND PERC AS          1111
PREM PERCEIVED AS            3311
REG PERCEIVED AS             2211
ADD BUTTER PERCEIVED AS      2322
THERE IS A DEAL
PRICE REDUCTION IS SMALL
IT IS NOT SEEN
REG CAKE IS PURCHASED
BRAND IS HINESBURY
```

SERVING OCCASION (S)

1 = SNACK
2 = EVERYDAY FAMILY DINNER
3 = SPECIAL

QUALITY (Q)

1 = PASSABLE
2 = GOOD
3 = BEST

PRICE: 1 = LOW
        2 = MEDIUM
        3 = HIGH

CONVENIENCE-INVOLMENT

1 = NORMAL MIX LEVEL
2 = HIGH INVOLMENT –
    LESS CONVENIENCE

TASTE-TEXTURE

1 = LIGHT, FLUFFY
2 = HEAVY, RICH

NOTES:

(A)   QUALITY INDEX NUMBER REFERS TO
      LOWEST ACCEPTABLE QUALITY.

(B)   PRICE INDEX NUMBER REFERS TO
      HIGHEST ACCEPTABLE LEVEL.

EXHIBIT 2 *(continued)*

CONSUMER 5   HAS PRIMARY USE 3

PERCEIVED NEED IS	2211
PRICE BRAND PERC AS	2111
PREM PERCEIVED AS	3311
REG PERCEIVED AS	2211
ADD BUTTER PERCEIVED AS	3222

THERE IS A DEAL
PRICE REDUCTION IS SMALL
IT IS NOT SEEN
PRICE BRAND IS PURCHASED

CONSUMER 6   HAS PRIMARY USE 3

PERCEIVED NEED IS	3321
PRICE BRAND PERC AS	2111
PREM PERCEIVED AS	3311
REG PERCEIVED AS	2211
ADD BUTTER PERCEIVED AS	3222

THERE IS A DEAL
PRICE REDUCTION IS SMALL
IT IS NOT SEEN
NO EXACT MATCH
CHANGE PERC NEED TO 3311
PREM IS PURCHASED

CONSUMER 7   HAS PRIMARY USE 3

PERCEIVED NEED IS	2221
PRICE BRAND PERC AS	2111
PREM PERCEIVED AS	3311
REG PERCEIVED AS	2211
ADD BUTTER PERCEIVED AS	3322

THERE IS A DEAL
PRICE REDUCTION IS LARGE
OTHER REG PLUS ADD BUTTER IS ON DEAL
NO EXACT MATCH
OTHER REG IS PURCHASED

CONSUMER 8   HAS PRIMARY USE 2

PERCEIVED NEED IS	2222
PRICE BRAND PERC AS	2111
PREM PERCEIVED AS	3311
REG PERCEIVED AS	2211
ADD BUTTER PERCEIVED AS	3222

ADD BUTTER IS PURCHASED

CONSUMER 9   HAS PRIMARY USE 3

PERCEIVED NEED IS	3321
PRICE BRAND PERC AS	1111
PREM PERCEIVED AS	3311
REG PERCEIVED AS	2211
ADD BUTTER PERCEIVED AS	3222

NO EXACT MATCH
CHANGE PERC NEED TO 3311
PREM IS PURCHASED

CONSUMER 10   HAS PRIMARY USE 3

PERCEIVED NEED IS	2211
PRICE BRAND PERC AS	1111
PREM PERCEIVED AS	2311
REG PERCEIVED AS	2211
ADD BUTTER PERCEIVED AS	2222

REG CAKE IS PURCHASED
BRAND IS OTHER REG

BRAND SHARES
HINESBURY REG   6.22222E-02
HINESBURY PREM   4.66667E-02
OTHER REG   .186667
ADD BUTTER   9.33333E-02
PRICE BRAND   .124444
TOTAL PURCHASES 10

The Marketing Research staff decided that the basis of the perceived need for a mix was the occasion at which the resulting cake might be served, i.e., the primary use to which the product was to be put. Accordingly, three basic serving occasions were identified:

#1 = Snack
#2 = Everyday family dinner
#3 = Special

Note that each of the consumers in Exhibit 2 is classified first into one of these three primary use categories, and is then assigned a four-digit number describing four other factors which were considered to form part of her or his perceived need. These other factors relate to the quality level desired in the product, the price the consumer is prepared to pay for a product of a given quality, the extent to which she or he desires a convenience product as opposed to one offering a degree of personal involvement, and finally the type of taste and texture desired in the finished product. Various classifications were established for each of these factors, as shown below:

(a) Quality level ("Q")
   1 = Passable
   2 = Good
   3 = Best
(b) Price level ("P")
   1 = Low
   2 = Medium
   3 = High
(c) Convenience-involvement ("C")
   1 = Normal cake-mix level
   2 = Desire for high involvement, less convenience
(d) Taste-texture ("T")
   1 = Light, fluffy
   2 = Heavy, rich

Price and quality are interrelated, in that a consumer wanting a top quality cake would be prepared to pay a high price; alternatively a consumer seeking a low price cake mix would be expected to accept one of passable level of quality. The need for the convenience-involvement index was explained by Gateau as follows: From research findings, it was believed that some consumers were primarily concerned with minimizing the time and effort required to make a cake while others desired the satisfaction obtained from greater personal involvement in the cake-mixing task. The taste-texture classification, while fairly broad, made it possible for the model to reflect varying consumer preferences concerning the consistencies of cakes made from different types of mix.

Interpreting the Trace

With the system outlined above, it was theoretically possible to describe any type of consumer. For example, one who wanted a cake to serve for a special occasion (No. 3) and who had a perceived need (listed in the order QPCT) for a mix of good quality (2), with a normal level of convenience (1) and producing a light, fluffy cake (1) would be designated as having primary use No. 3 and perceived need 2211. Note that the perceived need for good quality (2) implies a willingness to pay a medium price (2) in order to obtain this quality level. However, it is possible that once in the marketplace, the consumer may succeed in finding a cake which is perceived as being medium quality but which also happens to be offered at a low price; in such a case she or he is predicted to purchase a 2111 cake-mix in preference to one perceived as 2211.

On the basis of consumer test results and managerial judgment, Gateau felt it was realistic to try to describe the product in the same kind of terms. Accordingly, the characteristics of each of the four types of regular cake on the market were categorized against their ability to satisfy consumers' perceived needs. *Regular cake* was taken as the norm and always assigned a code of 2211 (see Exhibit 2), namely good quality, medium price, normal convenience-involvement level, and light, fluffy taste-texture.

For other types of cake, there were always some uncertainty components, reflecting varying consumer perceptions. Probabilities were assigned to the occurrence of these components for each type of product. Thus, *private label* mixes might be viewed in the model as being of either passable or good quality, but the other three components were all fixed at level 1. Consequently, they might appear either as 1111 or 2111. *Premium mixes* might be viewed as of either good or best quality, with prices being fixed as high, convenience-involvement as normal, and taste-texture as light and fluffy. Finally, *add-butter* mixes were viewed in the model as high on involvement, and heavy, rich on taste-texture; however, quality perception might be either good or best and price as medium or high.

How the price of *add-butter* was perceived depended on how consumers thought about the extra costs associated with adding their own shortening. The recipe on the box called for adding real *butter* as the shortening agent. If consumers did this and included the cost of butter in their perception of costs, they would view the product as costing about the same as *premium cake*. If butter costs were not included in this perception, the consumer would view the cost of the *add-butter cake* as being the same as *regular cake*. It was possible that some consumers might use margarine in spite of recipe directions. This might result in a cost perception below premium but above regular. This last possibility was not considered in the model.

Based upon the above four factors, it was assumed by the model-builders that every consumer would have an individual perception of each type or brand of cake mix.

To summarize, feasible values for perceived needs for different types of products were as follows:

Regular cake	2211 (always)
Private label	1111 or 2111
Premium cake	2311 or 3311
Add-butter	2222, 2322, 3222 or 3322

Quantifying the Input

Once the design of the model had been formalized, it was necessary to provide the input. Areas requiring quantification were total market profile and presence of a deal or price reduction.

The assignment of consumers into primary use categories was done on a probabilistic basis, reflecting the proportion of total cake mix purchases made for each of the three primary use purposes. Within each of these groups the simulation team then had to quantify perceived needs (e.g., how many of those wanting to serve cake for snacks would require each of the quality/price levels, each convenience level and each texture type).

These data were derived from judgments formed after reviewing the tapes on which consumers discussed their cake-buying and making habits. Previous surveys on cake usage were also used as inputs. A summary of the inputs is shown in Exhibit 3.

Meantime, the presence of deals or price reductions was simulated by estimating the probabilities of an individual consumer's finding a deal of any sort, of such a deal being large rather than small, of the consumer's noticing only a small price reduction, and of the deal being Hinesbury's rather than Allied's or Concorn's.

EXHIBIT 3
SUMMARY OF MARKET RESEARCH DATA AND MANAGERIAL ASSUMPTIONS FOR SIMULATION MODEL

	Occasion		
Use and Preference	**Snack**	**Family Dinner**	**Special Occasion**
Proportion of use for each occasion	.15	.50	.35
Characteristics desired:			
Quality			
Passable	.60	.15	.00
Good	.40	.70	.70
Best	.00	.15	.30
Convenience			
Normal	1.00	.65	.55
High involvement,			
less convenience	.00	.35	.45
Taste-texture			
Light, fluffy	.65	.75	.90
Heavy, rich	.35	.25	.10

	Product		
Perception of Quality	**Price Brand**	**Premium Cake**	**Add Butter**
Proportion of population perceiving product at quality level			
Passable	.50	.00	.00
Good	.50	.40	.50
Best	.00	.60	.50

Other Data	
Proportion perceiving add-butter as high priced	.35
Probability of a deal	.50
Probability price reduction is large	.35
Probability that small deal will be seen	.60
Probability Hinesbury is a deal item	.35
Other regular's share of regular cake sales without deals	.75
Total shortening cake's share of total cake-mix market	.56
Others' share of add-butter sales without deals	.75

EXHIBIT 4

SAMPLE RUN OF SIMULATION MODEL USED TO TEST ALTERNATIVE STRATEGIES

```
              HINESBURY MILLS (HBM) SIMULATION MODEL
              ---------------------------------------

DO YOU WISH TO SEE A DESCRIPTION OF THIS PROGRAM (Y=YES N=NO)? N


       CHOOSE ONE MARKET SCENARIO
       --------------------------
1. HBM REG, OTHER REG & ADD-BUTTER, PRICE BRAND
2. HBM REG & PREM, OTHER REG & ADD-BUTTER, PRICE BRAND
3. HBM REG & ADD-BUTTER, OTHER REG & ADD-BUTTER, PRICE BRAND
4. HBM REG & ADD-BUTTER & PREM, OTHER REG & ADD-BUTTER, PRICE BRAND
? 2
NUMBER OF CONSUMERS TO BE SIMULATED? 1000
DISPLAY BASE CASE CONDITIONS [1=ON SCREEN 2=ON PRINTER 3=NO]? 3

OPTIONS [1=CHANGE 2=OUTPUT TO SCREEN 3=OUTPUT TO PRINTER 4=EXIT TO MAIN MENU]? 2


                    MARKET SCENARIO 2
           HBM REG & PREM, OTHER REG & ADD-BUTTER, PRICE BRAND
           =====================================================
                    CONSUMER CHARACTERISTICS
                    ------------------------
 1) PROPORTION WHO BUY CAKE FOR USE AS A SNACK                     .15
    OF THESE, THE PROP. WHO DESIRE: GOOD QUALITY: .40  BEST QUALITY .00
 2) PROPORTION WHO BUY CAKE FOR THE FAMILY DINNER:                 .50
    OF THESE, THE PROP. WHO DESIRE: GOOD QUALITY: .70  BEST QUALITY .15
 3) OF THOSE WHO BUY CAKE FOR SPECIAL OCCASIONS:
          THE PROP. WHO DESIRE: GOOD QUALITY: .70    BEST QUALITY .30
 4) PROPORTION OF SNACK    USERS PREFERRING HIGH CONVENIENCE      1.00
 5) PROPORTION OF DINNER   USERS PREFERRING HIGH CONVENIENCE      0.65
 6) PROPORTION OF SPECIAL  USERS PREFERRING HIGH CONVENIENCE      0.55
 7) PROPORTION OF SNACK    USERS PREFERRING LIGHT-FLUFFY TEXTURE  0.65
 8) PROPORTION OF DINNER   USERS PREFERRING LIGHT-FLUFFY TEXTURE  0.75
 9) PROPORTION OF SPECIAL  USERS PREFERRING LIGHT-FLUFFY TEXTURE  0.90
10) PROPORTION WHO PERCEIVE THE PRICE BRAND AS NORMAL QUALITY     0.50
11) PROPORTION WHO PERCEIVE THE PREMIUM CAKE AS BEST QUALITY      0.60
12) PROPORTION WHO PERCEIVE THE ADD-BUTTER CAKE AS BEST QUALITY   0.50
13) PROPORTION WHO PERCEIVE ADD-BUTTER CAKES AS HIGH PRICED       0.35

PRESS RETURN TO CONTINUE


                    MARKET CONDITIONS
                    -----------------
14) PROBABILITY OF A DEAL                                         0.50
15) PROBABILITY THAT A PRICE REDUCTION IS LARGE                   0.35
16) PROBABILITY THAT A SMALL DEAL WILL BE SEEN                    0.60
17) PROBABILITY THAT HINESBURY IS THE DEAL ITEM                   0.35
18) OTHER REGULAR'S SHARE OF REGULAR CAKE SALES WITHOUT DEALS     0.75
19) TOTAL SHORTENING CAKE'S SHARE OF TOTAL CAKE MARKET            0.56
20) OTHERS SHARE OF ADD-BUTTER SALES WITHOUT DEALS                0.75

                 CURRENT MODEL CONDITIONS
                 ------------------------
21) CONSUMERS ARE BEING GENERATED IN A CYCLICAL PATTERN
22) MARKET SCENARIO                                                2
23) NUMBER OF CONSUMERS SIMULATED                                 1000

                    MARKET SHARES
                    -------------
HINESBURY REG      .106        OTHER REG          .190
HINESBURY PREM     .033        OTHER ADD BUTTER   .058
HBM ADD-BUTTER     .000        PRICE BRAND        .173
             TOTAL PURCHASES      942

OPTIONS [1=CHANGE 2=OUTPUT TO SCREEN 3=OUTPUT TO PRINTER 4=EXIT TO MAIN MENU]? 1


ENTER THE LINE NUMBER CORRESPONDING TO THE DATA YOU WISH TO CHANGE.
(SEE LISTING OF BASE CASE FOR LINE NUMBERS)
IF ALL CHANGES HAVE BEEN COMPLETED PRESS RETURN? 11

PROPORTION WHO PERCEIVE THE PREMIUM CAKE AS BEST QUALITY? .8

ENTER THE LINE NUMBER CORRESPONDING TO THE DATA YOU WISH TO CHANGE.
(SEE LISTING OF BASE CASE FOR LINE NUMBERS)
IF ALL CHANGES HAVE BEEN COMPLETED PRESS RETURN? 12
```

Note: Consumer-characteristics and market-conditions portion of output not reproduced when no changes are made.

EXHIBIT 4 *(continued)*

```
PROPORTION WHO PERCEIVE THE ADD-BUTTER CAKE AS BEST QUALITY? .3

ENTER THE LINE NUMBER CORRESPONDING TO THE DATA YOU WISH TO CHANGE.
(SEE LISTING OF BASE CASE FOR LINE NUMBERS)
IF ALL CHANGES HAVE BEEN COMPLETED PRESS RETURN?

OPTIONS [ 1=CHANGE 2=OUTPUT TO SCREEN 3=OUTPUT TO PRINTER 4=EXIT TO MAIN MENU]? 2




                              MARKET SCENARIO 2
              HBM REG & PREM, OTHER REG & ADD-BUTTER, PRICE BRAND
              ===================================================
                          CONSUMER CHARACTERISTICS
                          ------------------------
        1) PROPORTION WHO BUY CAKE FOR USE AS A SNACK                     .15
            OF THESE, THE PROP. WHO DESIRE: GOOD QUALITY: .40   BEST QUALITY .00
        2) PROPORTION WHO BUY CAKE FOR THE FAMILY DINNER:                 .50
            OF THESE, THE PROP. WHO DESIRE: GOOD QUALITY: .70   BEST QUALITY .15
        3) OF THOSE WHO BUY CAKE FOR SPECIAL OCCASIONS:
                      THE PROP. WHO DESIRE: GOOD QUALITY: .70   BEST QUALITY .30
        4) PROPORTION OF SNACK    USERS PREFERRING HIGH CONVENIENCE      1.00
        5) PROPORTION OF DINNER   USERS PREFERRING HIGH CONVENIENCE      0.65
        6) PROPORTION OF SPECIAL  USERS PREFERRING HIGH CONVENIENCE      0.55
        7) PROPORTION OF SNACK    USERS PREFERRING LIGHT-FLUFFY TEXTURE  0.65
        8) PROPORTION OF DINNER   USERS PREFERRING LIGHT-FLUFFY TEXTURE  0.75
        9) PROPORTION OF SPECIAL  USERS PREFERRING LIGHT-FLUFFY TEXTURE  0.90
       10) PROPORTION WHO PERCEIVE THE PRICE BRAND AS NORMAL QUALITY     0.50
       11) PROPORTION WHO PERCEIVE THE PREMIUM CAKE AS BEST QUALITY      0.80
       12) PROPORTION WHO PERCEIVE THE ADD-BUTTER CAKE AS BEST QUALITY   0.30
       13) PROPORTION WHO PERCEIVE ADD-BUTTER CAKES AS HIGH PRICED       0.35

    PRESS RETURN TO CONTINUE



                            MARKET CONDITIONS
                            -----------------
       14) PROBABILITY OF A DEAL                                         0.50
       15) PROBABILITY THAT A PRICE REDUCTION IS LARGE                   0.35
       16) PROBABILITY THAT A SMALL DEAL WILL BE SEEN                    0.60
       17) PROBABILITY THAT HINESBURY IS THE DEAL ITEM                   0.35
       18) OTHER REGULAR'S SHARE OF REGULAR CAKE SALES WITHOUT DEALS     0.75
       19) TOTAL SHORTENING CAKE'S SHARE OF TOTAL CAKE MARKET            0.56
       20) OTHERS SHARE OF ADD-BUTTER SALES WITHOUT DEALS                0.75

                          CURRENT MODEL CONDITIONS
                          ------------------------
       21) CONSUMERS ARE BEING GENERATED IN A CYCLICAL PATTERN
       22) MARKET SCENARIO                                               2
       23) NUMBER OF CONSUMERS SIMULATED                                1000

                              MARKET SHARES
                              -------------
    HINESBURY REG      .105        OTHER REG            .187
    HINESBURY PREM     .039        OTHER ADD BUTTER     .055
    HBM ADD-BUTTER     .000        PRICE BRAND          .173
                  TOTAL PURCHASES     952

    OPTIONS [ 1=CHANGE 2=OUTPUT TO SCREEN 3=OUTPUT TO PRINTER 4=EXIT TO MAIN MENU]?
```

Running the Model

Next, an artificial random population of consumers was run through the model. Exhibit 2 shows how ten typical consumers entered the market, what their perceived need was, what their perceptions were of the various brands in the market, whether they were exposed to a deal or not, whether they altered their perceived need based on price, and what each purchase decision was.

A share report based on this trace is then provided. It shows the fraction of purchases by product type and brand. Reported shares total to 56 percent, this being the fraction of the total market accounted for by regular shortening cake produced by major brands.

The remainder (44 percent) is accounted for by foam and specialty cakes and the sale of some minor brands whose purchasing process is not modeled. The shares reported in Exhibit 2 are not reliable since they are based only on a sample of 10 consumers. To evaluate market performance, large samples (1,000 consumers) need to be used, as shown in Exhibit 4. A trace of individual consumers is not produced in this model.

The simulation model can be used to forecast share configurations under a number of product line alternatives,[1] for example (1) Hinesbury with only premium cake (but no add-butter) in its line, (2) Hinesbury replacing premium with add-butter, and (3) Hinesbury also introducing an add-butter product.

MANAGEMENT REQUEST

Marjorie Halstein had asked the market research department for an estimate of the market share impact of the three strategies listed. One concern was whether share gains would come from the Hinesbury brands. She and her colleagues wondered how sensitive the results might be to changes in the estimates listed in Exhibit 3.

---

[1] The computer simulation model uses a random number generator to determine each consumer's needs and preferences. When first experimenting with a number of different scenarios and parameters in the model, it is desirable to generate identical sequences of numbers on successive runs so that the results may be compared on an equal basis. This is done in the base case by generating random numbers in a cyclical pattern. Once the key parameters have been identified, the number sequences may be randomized in order to generate a wider range of results.